HOUSING IN AMERICA

Problems and Perspectives

SECOND EDITION

HOUSING IN AMERICA

Problems and Perspectives

SECOND EDITION

Roger Montgomery
Professor of Urban Design
University of California
Berkeley

Daniel R. Mandelker
Stamper Professor of Law
Washington University

With the assistance of
Leslie Fagadau, Mindy Leiterman & Mary Richardson

THE BOBBS-MERRILL COMPANY, INC.
PUBLISHERS
INDIANAPOLIS • NEW YORK • CHARLOTTESVILLE, VIRGINIA

To the generations of students who have shared
in our struggle through this nebulous field of housing.

Preface

Major changes in housing problems and priorities have occurred since the first edition of this reader. Housing costs increased rapidly as personal incomes stagnated, making the search for adequate housing more than a lower income concern. Changes in the housing economy were accompanied by major shifts in national and local housing policies. Local housing programs turned to an emphasis on neighborhood preservation. After an earlier expansion, federal subsidies were temporarily suspended, then substantially modified in the context of new national legislation. Major federal programs were adopted to maintain the money flow to housing markets. Attention to problems of racial discrimination continued while conflict over environmental controls and exclusionary suburban housing policies sharpened. Direct public intervention in local housing markets and policies such as anti-speculation laws and rent control emerged as new directions.

New ways of thinking about housing have developed over the last decade too. The housing bundle concept has become nearly universal. More sophisticated microeconomics has been directed at the field, most notably the use of hedonic pricing to better understand the relative importance of the indivisible components of the bundle. Among other effects, this new emphasis has given neighborhood factors more importance in analysis. The now universally understood filtering idea has been subjected to searching criticism and at the same time expanded to cover the related phenomenon of neighborhood change. Perhaps most surprising, the past few years have witnessed a broad critical reexamination of urban processes from a structural viewpoint that sees housing in the context of a larger political economy with all its inherent contradiction and conflicts.

While maintaining the structure of the first edition, the second edition of the reader has been modified to reflect these trends. Part I focuses on an analysis of the housing economy. These readings consider its structure, the components of housing supply and demand, and the dynamics of the market. Practically all of the selections in the first edition have been replaced with new readings that amplify and update these themes, and a new chapter has been added reflecting the political dimensions of housing.

Part II focuses on specific problems and the policy responses to them. All of the readings in Part II are new. These chapters consider the policy issues that guide public intervention in housing markets. Topics range from intervention in capital markets to subsidies, neighborhood preservation, and racial and suburban housing problems. Attention is given to new developments, such as the neighborhood housing services program, environmental controls, and housing allowances. The final chapter has been revised to reflect new interventions by governments seeking to reform landlord-tenant and buyer-seller relationships in the private housing sector.

The first edition of the reader made a substantial departure from traditional college texts. Readings were selectively edited, often reducing dozens of pages to but a few. The readings were followed by comments designed to clarify and extend the material. This method of presentation has been continued and augmented in the second edition. The comments have been expanded. They contain references to supplementary material elaborating on the readings. Several short notes written especially for this volume amplify matters on which appropriate readings do not exist. Bibliographies following each chapter provide references to additional sources, for the most part well-known and influential books that should be available in most college libraries.

This book of readings and commentary is intended as a basic text for first-level housing courses at both graduate and advanced undergraduate levels. It should serve undergraduate programs in fields such as urban studies, environmental design, and government. While economic analysis provides much of the material in Part I, previous coursework in economics is not required for understanding. For thoses with background in economics a few passages such as the "Note on Micro-economics and Housing" in Chapter 2 may be passed over. Many of the policies and programs considered in Part II have a legal basis, but their presentation does not require previous study of legal concepts. Some background in American government would be helpful, however, in reading this text.

Much of the material has been specifically chosen to meet the needs of graduate students in urban planning, social welfare, and related areas of public affairs, policy and administration. It is intended as an introduction to the field. As such it might well be supplemented by an additional text covering a specialization such as the methodology of housing market analysis or community development practice. Other related graduate programs in fields such as environmental design, architecture, and urban engineering will find the book useful in a supplementary role to their work in housing technology and design.

The reader is also intended for use in law school courses and seminars in housing and urban problems. Most law students come to law school with a foundation in economics sufficient to take them through Part I. Difficult legal issues are down-played in Part II, but the readings on programs and policies provide a valuable introduction to the more detailed study of housing programs in law school courses. A companion coursebook in housing law is planned as a complementary set of teaching materials to be used together with these readings.

Many people have helped us with various aspects of this new edition. Our own students have provided the necessary feedback that has energized and informed our work. Users of the first edition and colleagues in our own institutions and in many others have given us valuable reactions to it and guidance toward the new edition. They have particularly urged the expansion of the commentary material which is now a central feature of this second edition. Professors Martin Gellen and David Dowall of the Department of City and Regional Planning at the University of California, Berkeley, have been especially helpful. Perhaps the greatest help of all has come from the students who have worked with us as assistants. Leslie Fagadau, Mindy Leiterman, and Mary Richardson have contributed enormously, particularly through their indominable quest for appropriate new readings. Kevin Gilson has expertly prepared our graphics. Our typists, Linda S. Newmark at Washington University and Susan Lund and the typing staff at the University of California patiently typed more than one draft of the manuscript. And finally our editor, Frances Warren, of Michie/Bobbs-Merrill, has provided just the right combination of goad and meticulous colleague to see the project through to conclusion.

Housing continues to be a high priority social issue as the decade of the 1980's approaches. This second edition of *Housing in America* provides an introduction to the study of the field by providing an armature for critical analysis, and by identifying major problems, concepts and issues in public policy on housing.

March 13, 1979

Roger Montgomery
Daniel R. Mandelker

Acknowledgments

We acknowledge with thanks permission to reprint the following materials:

Emily Paradise Achtenberg, The Social Utility of Rent Control (1971). Reprinted by permission of the author.

W. C. Baer, On the Death of Cities, Public Interest, No. 45 (1976). Reprinted by permission of Public Interest and the author.

Baptiste, Attacking the Urban Redlining Problem, 56 Boston University Law Review 989-98 (1976). Reprinted by permission of Boston University Law Review.

Bender & Parman, The Factor Without Walls: Industrialization in Residential Construction. Copyright 1976 by the Regents of the University of California. Reprinted from California Management Review, volume XVIII, number 3, pp. 46-47 and 49-50, by permission of the Regents.

Bois d'Arc Patriots, Organizing in Dallas, Green Mountain Quarterly, No. 5 (Feb. 1977). Reprinted by permission of Green Mountain Editions.

R. Cassidy, Neighborhood Housing Services: Everybody's Getting Something Out of It, Planning (Nov. 1975). Copyright 1975 by, and reprinted by permission of, American Society of Planning Officials.

M. Castells, The Urban Question: A Marxist Approach (1977). Reprinted by permission of Edward Arnold (Publishers) Ltd.

A. Downs [Comments] in H.S. Perloff & L. Wingo, Issues in Urban Economics (1968). Published for Resources for the Future, Inc. by the John Hopkins Press. Reprinted by permission of the Publisher.

M. Edel, Filtering in a Private Housing Market in M. Edel & J. Rothenberg, eds., Readings in Urban Economics (1972). Reprinted with permission.

B. Ellickson, B. Fisherman & P. Morrison, Economic Analysis of Urban Housing Markets (1977). Reprinted by permission of the Rand Corporation.

R. Fishman, ed., Housing for All Under Law (1977). Reprinted with permission from Housing for All Under Law, copyright 1977, Ballinger Publishing Company.

B. Frieden & A. Solomon, The Nation's Housing: 1975 to 1985 (1977). Reprinted by permission of Joint Center for Urban Studies, Massachusetts Institute of Technology and Harvard University.

Herbert J. Gans, The Levittowners: Ways of Life and Politics in a New Suburban Community. Copyright 1967 by Herbert J. Gans. Reprinted by permission of Pantheon Books/A Division of Random House, Inc.

Garrity, Redesigning Landlord-Tenant Law for an Urban Society, 46 (U. Det.) Journal of Urban Law 695 (1969). Reprinted by permission of the Journal.

W. E. Gibson, Protecting Homebuilding from Restrictive Credit Conditions in A.M. Okun and G.L. Perry, eds., Brookings Papers on Economic Activity 3: 1973. Copyright 1973 by the Brookings Institution. Reprinted by permission of the Brookings Institution.

M. Gottdiener, Planned Sprawl (1977). Reprinted by permission of the author.

Graham, The Benign Quota: A Legitimate Weapon to Fight White Flight and Resulting Segregated Communities, 42 Fordham Law Review 898-900 (1974). Reprinted by permission of Fordham Law Review.

W. Grigsby, Housing Markets and Public Policy (1963). Reprinted by permission of the University of Pennsylvania Press and the author.

W. Grigsby & L. Rosenburg, Urban Housing Policy (1975). Reprinted by permission of APS Publications, Inc.

C. Hartman, Housing and Social Policy (1975). Reprinted by permission of Prentice-Hall, Inc.

E. Hoover & R. Vernon, Anatomy of a Metropolis, Harvard University Press for Regional Plan Association, 1962. Reprinted with permission.

Nathanial S. Keith, Politics and the Housing Crisis Since 1930 (1974). Reprinted by permission of Universe Books, New York.

Lachman & Mitchell, New Construction and Abandonment: Musical Chairs in the Housing Stock, Nation's Cities (Oct. 1977). Reprinted with permission.

C. Leven, J. Little, H. Nourse & R. Read, Neighborhood Change: Lessons in the Dynamics of Urban Decay (1976). Reprinted with permission.

S. Lewis, Adams Morgan: Spiffed Up and Speculated Upon, Planning (Mar./Apr. 1976). Reprinted by permission of American Society of Planning Officials.

P. Marcuse, Housing Policy and the Myth of the Benevolent State, Social Policy (Jan./Feb. 1978). Copyright 1978 by Social Policy Corporation. Reprinted by permission of Social Policy, published by Social Policy Corporation, New York, New York 10036.

J. Mollenkopf & J. Pynoos, Boardwalk and Park Place: Property Ownership, Political Structure, and Housing Policy at the Local Level in J. Pynoos, R. Schafer & C. Hartman, eds., Housing Urban America (1973). Reprinted by permission of the authors.

Montgomery & Gellen, Emerging Issues in American Housing Policy in D. Phares, ed., A Decent Home and Environment (1977). Reprinted with permission from A Decent Home and Environment, copyright 1977, Ballinger Publishing Company.

P. Muller, The Outer City: Geographical Consequences of the Urbanization of the Suburbs (1976). Reprinted by permission of Association of American Geographers.

R. F. Muth, Urban Residential and Housing Markets in H. Perloff & L. Wingo, Issues in Urban Economics (1968). Published for Resources for the Future, Inc. by the John Hopkins Press. Reprinted by permission of the publisher.

Oscar Newman, Design Guidelines for Creating Defensible Space (1976). Published by United States Government Printing Office. Reprinted by permission of the author.

L. Ozanne & R. Struyk, Housing from the Existing Stock: Comparative Economic Analysis of Owner-Occupants and Landlords (Washington, D.C.: The Urban Institute, 1976), pp. 2-9, 20, 49. Reprinted by permission of the publisher.

R. Palm, Urban Social Geography from the Perspective of the Real Estate Salesman (1976). Reprinted by permission of the Institute of Business and Economic Research, University of California, Berkeley.

G. E. Peterson, The Property Tax and Low-Income Housing Markets in G. E. Peterson, ed., Property Tax Reform (Washington, D.C.: The Urban Institute, 1973), pp. 112-21. Reprinted by permission of the publisher.

L. Rainwater, Fear and the House-as-Haven in the Lower Class, 32 Journal of the American Institute of Planners 23 (1966). Reprinted by permission of the Journal of the American Institute of Planners.

Lee Rainwater, Behind Ghetto Walls. Copyright 1970 by Lee Rainwater. Reprinted with permission from Behind Ghetto Walls (New York: Aldine Publishing Company).

Richards & Rowe, Restoring a City: Who Pays the Price? Reprinted by permission from Working Papers for a New Society, Winter 1977. Copyright 1977 by the Center for the Study of Public Policy, Inc.

Sands, Housing Turnover: Assessing Its Relevance to Public Policy. Reprinted by permission of the Journal of the American Institute of Planners, volume 42 (1976).

Wallace F. Smith, Filtering and Neighborhood Change (1964). Reprinted by permission of the Center for Real Estate and Urban Economics, Institute of Urban and Regional Development, University of California, Berkeley.

Wallace F. Smith, Housing: The Social and Economic Elements (1970). Reprinted by permission of the University of California Press.

Stegman, The Neighborhood Effects of Filtering, 5 American Real Estate and Urban Economics Association Journal 227 (1977). Reprinted with permission.

Charles J. Stokes & Ernest M. Fisher, Housing Market Performance in the United States. Copyright 1976 by Praeger Publishers, Inc. Reprinted by permission of Holt, Rinehart and Winston.

Michael E. Stone, A House of Cards: Housing, Mortgage Lending, and the Crisis of Capitalism (1977). Reprinted by permission of the author.

K. E. Taeuber, Racial Segregation: The Persisting Dilemma, Vol. 442, Annals of the American Academy of Political and Social Science (1975). Reprinted by permission of the American Academy of Political and Social Science.

Michelle J. White, Self-Interest in the Suburbs: The Trend Toward No-Growth Zoning. Copyright 1978 by the Regents of the University of California. Reprinted from Policy Analysis, Vol. 4, No. 2, by permission of the Regents.

Summary Table of Contents

Table of Contents

PART I. INTRODUCTORY NOTE: HOUSING AS A PROBLEM FOCUS

PART I

INTRODUCTORY NOTE: HOUSING AS A PROBLEM FOCUS

Housing in America has increasingly become a public concern that spreads across all sectors of the society and all levels of government. While Americans once provided their dwellings as part of the land settlement, homesteading, and private town-building process, the provision of housing is now a vast and interdependent enterprise. Today urbanization, industrialization, an enormous increase in social scale, the never-ending further division of labor, and an exponentially increasing interdependence among us make housing a very public affair. This situation is echoed in American learning, where housing has become an important component in new fields like public policy, planning and urban affairs; the more traditional professions such as law, architecture, and social welfare; and the academic social sciences disciplines — economics, politics, and sociology. The readings and commentary contained in this book have been selected to introduce the topic of housing to readers from these many fields and others. Reciprocally, the readings collected here reflect these many points of view. They provide background for critical thinking about housing, for the analysis of housing problems, and for the design of public policy responses to these problems.

Readers will find in the first half of the book a broad introduction to the many dimensions of housing, supported by important quantitative information and an indication of the relevant trends at work today in America. But they will find more. The Part I readings have been selected and edited, and the commentary written, to provide an analytic approach to this multi-sided topic. In large part this approach draws from economics. In the words of one expert, ". . . although the objectives of housing policy may be 'social', its mechanics are always economic." Economics deals with the production, allocation and management of resources, and these are the root matters in any public, societal or governmental concern with housing. Economic analysis is taken to be the foundation on which good thinking is constructed, and forms the foundation of the first half of this text.

Chapter 1 opens with a series of readings selected to define housing in its many dimensions and introduce the closely related concept of the housing bundle. All informed thinking on the subject is grounded on this concept. The next four chapters deal with the housing economy. They treat in turn the overall economy, supply, demand, and the dynamics of the system. The basic perspective in choosing these readings and developing commentary draws on traditional microeconomics and related material in institutional economics. In present American practice this outlook lies behind most analytic thinking, policy design and evaluation. Structuralist and neo-Marxist modes of the analysis are also introduced in Part I as a subsidiary theme to enrich the reader's perception and encourage more critical thinking. Housing is too complex a subject to approach from a single perspective. No matter how widely dominant the microeconomic viewpoint may be, a richer analytical perspective is necessary.

The final chapter in Part I considers housing politics. It explores both federal policy-making and the central role of housing issues in government and politics, especially at the local level. This chapter provides an additional vitally necessary analytic perspective. Because it emphasizes the conflicts that lead us to define housing matters as problematic, it provides a reasonable conclusion to the first part of the text and a transition to the problem focus of Part II.

1

WHAT IS HOUSING?

Housing denotes an enormously complicated idea. It refers to a whole collection of things that come packaged together, not just four walls and a roof, but a specific location in relation to work and services, neighbors and neighborhood, property rights and privacy provisions, income and investment opportunities, and emotional or psychological symbols and supports. These and more come bundled together in what economists have come to call "a heterogeneous set of attributes which must be consumed jointly."

This idea of housing as a bundle of disparate but inseparable elements is perhaps the most important analytical concept for thinking about housing. A recognition of this complexity must underlie action, planning, policy, and practice if they are to be effective and reasonably free of unanticipated side effects. Why is this so? Quite simply, action of any kind directed at any one or more aspects or attributes of the housing bundle will have repercussions on other parts of the bundle. These repercussions may defeat the original objective of the action or involve side effects too costly to be worth achieving that objective however valuable in and of itself. Keeping in mind the bundle concept helps insure that thinking about housing will take this interconnectedness and its implications into account. The first reading, the work of a housing economist, addresses the need to understand more completely what the housing concept means.

W. F. SMITH, HOUSING : THE SOCIAL AND ECONOMIC ELEMENTS 3-4, 7-9, 23-31 (1970)

What Is Housing?

There is probably not a single major city in the world without some form of "housing problem." In Los Angeles and Tokyo, in New York and Moscow, in Hong Kong and Paris, in Stockholm and in Brazilia housing is a serious public issue. Novelists have set pessimistic tales in the slums of Victorian England and Czarist Russia. Architects, planners, social reformers, and ordinary city dwellers have raised protests against housing conditions. Governments in every historical epoch have adopted a bewildering variety of measures to cope with widespread dissatisfaction about housing. The problem is durable and well-nigh universal. But what is the problem? What is housing and how much of it does a community need?

Shelter

Housing is often called "shelter," particularly in textbooks on economics. In some societies that is literally all that housing provides. People in arctic winds and tropical downpours need protection from the elements. Cliff-dwelling Indians in the American southwest sought shelter from their enemies. Shelter itself is certainly a part of what is meant by "housing." Just as certainly it is not all that is meant; and it appears that the simple function of shelter from the elements or from enemies is a relatively minor aspect of housing needs.

. . . .

Privacy

. . . .

Privacy is clearly a social rather than a physical concept. The primitive community with one big roof might conceivably saw the roof into separate pieces. Apart from the effort or expense of providing additional posts on which to set the individual roofs, the housing issue would be one of deciding how many pieces to make out of the one large roof. Here is where social custom enters the picture. Every society has some set of notions about groupings of people who ought to share the same roof. The descriptive term "household" is used to describe such a group, but the normal composition of households varies significantly among cultures. . . . [Smith discusses the household and its various activities which require privacy. He also relates privacy to urban design by suggesting that space between buildings is a substitute for walls in terms of ensuring privacy. — Eds.]

Location

If privacy were the only important attribute which a unit of shelter had to possess, we might solve the problem by dispersing households over the entire landscape. This would be an expensive way to learn another major attribute of housing, which is its relative *location*. Urban households usually derive their incomes from employment which requires daily trips between home and workplace. There is a practical limit to the length of such trips so that the dispersal of households is held in check by the desire to economize on the time and cost of transportation. Urban households must make regular trips to other urban locations as well — for school, shopping, recreation, and general household management. . . .

Environmental Amenities

A major dimension of the housing commodity can be given the long but descriptive name of "environmental amenities." These are the characteristics of the surrounding area which affect the desirability of the residence. Families are concerned not only with the distance to a school for their children, but also with the quality and prestige of that school. Since the quality of schools varies widely in most American cities, American families tend to consider this factor most carefully when searching for a home. To a lesser degree, perhaps, the quality of local fire and police protection are also considered. Other urban services such as parks, playgrounds, and hospitals influence the relative desirability of housing. [Common usage designates these urban services and distinguishes them from aesthetically and psychologically defined environmental amenities. — Eds.] The physical appearance of the neighborhood — trees and grass belonging to prospective neighbors, the view obtained from the house in question, and the peculiarities of the neighborhood's climate (temperature, wind, fog, etc.) are also part of the housing "package."

One very subjective kind of "environmental amenity" which can nevertheless play a most important role in housing is the social character of people in the neighborhood. . . . Sometimes the social desirability of a neighborhood is significantly influenced by the past history of the area; some locations acquire "fashionable" reputations and others suffer from a relatively bad name. For better or worse, the real and the traditional social status of the area will rub off on families moving into it.

Environmental amenity can be influenced to an important degree by community programs of land-use control. If small factories and eating places are mixed in with residential uses, the resulting noise, congestion, and visual appearance may make housing in the area less attractive and enjoyable. . . .

Investment

For a small but influential fraction of the world's urban population housing is an investment as well as a place to live. The fact that a family owns its home gives that family a degree of security in a psychological and financial sense. Psychologically, ownership is an extension of the attribute of privacy, for the home-owning household can be confident that its dwelling will not be entered by others except by invitation and that the family will not be required to surrender the dwelling to others. Financially, ownership is not only a symbol of wealth, but as a practical matter, the most important actual wealth which most families ever manage to accumulate.

. . . .

Housing Status

Both the community and the individual household are interested in the housing status of that household. By "housing status" we mean the whole complex of activities, satisfactions, rights, obligations, conveniences, and expectations surrounding the use of a particular dwelling unit by a particular household. In turn, both the community and the individual household participate in determining what this housing status will be.

The accompanying diagram suggests in broad outline what it is that makes up housing status and what the effects of this status are. From the preceding discussion we can identify at least four major components in the housing status of a household. One of these is the structure itself, which in an earlier epoch might be regarded as "shelter" but which in reality provides far more than mere protection from the elements. In the present context, *Structure* means all the physical attributes of the dwelling itself, including the land upon which that dwelling rests. By inference, it includes the natural environment such as the climate; the threat of earthquakes, landslides, or flooding; and the intangible aspects of the building such as the danger of fire, or the practical necessity of performing certain tasks such as removal of snow in the wintertime and fallen leaves in the autumn.

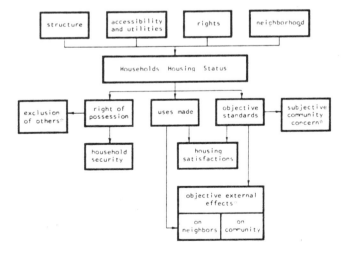

* Effects which are external to individual decision

Figure 1 Components and effects of housing status (Redrawn from Smith)

Accessibility and utilities are tangible services rendered to a particular dwelling by the community or businesses operating within the community. . . .

Accessibility and utilities are usually provided in return for charges of various kinds — taxes for streets and fire protection, prices for gasoline, fares for public transit, rates for water and electricity, premiums for fire insurance, and so on, though the relationship between expense and benefit is often obscured. From the individual's point of view, however, there is often little choice about whether the services are provided or not. They either exist or they do not, and the schedule of charges for them is relatively inflexible. Accessibility and utilities thus constitute a package of services related to housing and tied rather closely to the particular dwelling.

The next bundle of components is labeled *Rights*. The privilege of enjoying a particular segment of real property is established by the laws of the community and transferred from one individual or household to another in a manner prescribed by law. These rights are almost always subject to restrictions of two broad types, public and private. The community itself limits the uses which may be made of a particular dwelling, for example, the number of persons who may inhabit it or the way in which refuse can be disposed of, and usually reserves the right to appropriate the property for a public use. The community offers occupants of dwelling units the enjoyment of certain public facilities such as schools, streets, fire protection, and the right to participate in community government. Taxes are imposed upon occupants, directly or indirectly, which become inescapable parts of housing cost.

Private individuals are free to varying degrees to surrender rights which they have previously enjoyed to others in exchange for money payments or the promise of money payments, or for reciprocal concessions. The seller or landlord may expect a settlement in cash; a mortgage lender awaits future repayment at which time he will relinquish his rights to the property. A neighboring owner may grant an easement or the household in question may itself grant an easement to some other party. Sellers or landlords may place exact restrictions upon the use or disposition of the dwelling place which is given to the household, such as the prohibition of major architectural changes, the keeping of certain types of animals, or the sub-leasing of an apartment unit. Thus, a whole complex of rights and obligations surrounds the enjoyment of a dwelling by a household, matters which do not affect the physical usefulness of the dwelling or its location, but which do constitute real and important attributes of housing.

The fourth block at the top of Figure 1 is labeled *Neighborhood*. It is in the nature of housing, as pointed out in this chapter, that the immediate physical environment and the society about the household qualifies the kind of enjoyment which the household can expect from its dwelling. The appearance of neighboring houses, the activities of neighbors, and the reputation of the neighborhood within the larger community may add to or detract from the ultimate housing satisfactions to be enjoyed by the occupant household. The expectation of change in any of these factors must also be significant for the household's own evaluation of the dwelling.

. . . .

The aggregate of these components is the *Household's housing status*. This status is an assemblage of physical, financial, legal, and social elements of considerable complexity and, therefore, existing in great variety. The whole is called "housing" and it would be a poor housing economist, builder, real estate agent, or city planner who imagined that "housing" is anything simpler. When it becomes known that a community has a "housing problem," we can expect soon to see an entrepreneur or inventor proffering a revolutionary kind of building material, an architect with a tidy sketch, a civil engineer with a new type of public transit vehicle, a city planner with new multicolored maps, a sociologist with a regression equation, a politician with a bill to change property rights, and a housing economist with a financial scheme (probably involving "debentures"). The kind of housing problem which is afflicting a particular city may yield readily to one or the other of these nostrums, but the chances are that by the time that housing has become a problem to the community, it has become a complicated problem. It has to be examined in all its elements and it will probably call for a set of measures subtly integrated and balanced to repair the problem without creating something worse.

Housing status is not inert. The fact that a particular household occupies a certain dwelling does not end the matter, either for that household or for the community. Our diagram shows three first-level effects of housing status, each of which produces a complex of other effects. The first-level effects are the creation of the *Right of possession*, the *Uses* (actually) *made* by the household of the dwelling, and the *Objective* (or largely physical) *standards* of housing enjoyed by the household.

The right of possession is much more than the legal right conferred in the transaction between buyer and seller or between tenant and landlord, for it means that the occupant household comes into a pattern of relationships with its total environment. It enjoys access from that location to other parts of the city, it has the opportunity to call upon community services and to use utilities, and, of course, it becomes a member of a neighborhood. By virtue of the relatively durable nature of housing, this multidimensional privilege can be projected into the future. Indeed, it must be, for it is seldom practical for households to consider themselves completely mobile in their housing arrangements. The trouble and expense of moving again will encourage them to put up with any unforeseen or underestimated disadvantages.

In general, these rights and circumstances create a beneficial sense of permanence or household security. A tenant with an unwritten month-to-month lease has less security in his housing arrangements, obviously, than a family with free and clear ownership of its home, but almost any housing status means some kind of predictability.

The right of possession which accrues to one household creates effects upon other households. Those others are excluded so long as the possession by the occupant continues. The significance of this exclusion is most vivid in a period of severe housing shortage, but it is always present. The fact that household A occupies dwelling X means that household B must occupy some other dwelling, or none at all. Even in a community with an absolute surplus of dwellings, dwelling X might be more suitable for household B, but the normally prevailing concepts of possession would require that household to get some other accommodation. In turn, household B must enter into a competition for other dwellings, perhaps contributing to an increase in value to be enjoyed by sellers of housing and ultimately excluding still another household from the dwelling which B does obtain. In widening circles these external effects of one act in the housing market spread out across the community, perhaps seeming trivial or not susceptible to improvement. Sometimes, however, it may be of real importance to the community that certain households are not able to occupy particular dwellings. For example, if elderly couples continue to reside in large, family-sized houses after their children have grown up and left, then new child-raising households in the community may have to make do with inconvenient apartments or create a demand for the construction of new family-sized homes in excess of the "real" needs of the community.

The basic point is that the effects of exclusion are borne by people other than the household itself. It is of little moment to the household, when deciding whether to accept an offer of a dwelling, that some other household will be discomfited or some other segments of the housing market will be stimulated. The individual household can ignore such external effects, and, indeed, may be quite unaware of them. The community as a whole cannot ignore them, for the agglomeration of individual decisions influences the community's housing welfare.

By *Uses made* of housing, we mean to suggest the activities carried on by the household once in possession. Members of the family will spend certain amounts of time in the dwelling and near it, engaging in certain house-related functions. Ordinary housekeeping, recreational or avocational pursuits, social behavior, and sometimes gainful employment will occur there. Each household has some unique pattern of activities which it brings into its dwelling, depending upon its own membership, their inclinations, and the nature of the dwelling itself. A solitary bachelor may seem to derive little use from a family-sized house, and a family group of cousins and grandparents may seem to make too much use of their dwelling, but some pattern of activities will emerge in every case. One of the more interesting uses of a dwelling appears during periods of absence of the occupants, for it is a safekeeping place for possessions, a proxy for community participation, and a refuge when the journey is done.

These uses combine with the *Objective standards* of the dwelling — its physical dimensions and characteristics — to define the household's current housing satisfaction. This is to be understood in a sense more psychological than material, much as the economist's concept of "utility." . . . Individuals are the judges of what they themselves enjoy, and that is the meaning of our phrase about "housing satisfactions."

The community is wont to make its own judgment, however, about the desirability of a particular dwelling for a particular household. In general, the community conscience aims to evaluate dwelling standards just as occupants themselves do, feeling quite certain that the absence of running water is an inconvenience, for example, or that infestation by rodents is a condition which the family itself would like to see corrected. So the community develops a subjective concern for the housing welfare of its members — to varying degrees — but it does so on the basis of objective standards. The modal concept of what "good" housing should be tends to become the prescription for what all housing should be. The elderly widow who weeps at the thought of leaving a firetrap room in a dismal slum is sometimes thought to be shortsighted. In reality, she may fear losing her friends by being helped to move, or she may simply have an emotional attachment to the room in which her husband died. This is a dilemma in the development of community housing standards, for we let our sympathies become aroused by tangible factors when, in truth, sympathy is of an intangible world.

A family's housing and the uses made of it provide objective effects upon the community and neighborhood in addition to any evocation of sympathy. Let the head of the household neglect his front lawn and he will find that he has offended his neighbors. When a youthful apartment-dweller takes up the drum, or a family accumulates refuse in such a way that pests breed, the neighborhood becomes conscious of these things. It may acquiesce or not, but the fact is that most dwellings are too small and too close together to be regarded as the proverbial "castle." Proximity can be a source of pleasure, as in the case of tasteful gardens facing the streets, but whether comforting or discomforting, it means that housed families are to some extent living with one another. The rules for sharing neighborhoods are never spelled out exactly, and this only adds the further burden of uncertainty to the inhibitions or constraints of being neighbors. "What would the neighbors think?" the family members ask themselves, and part of the problem is that none of us really knows. The timid person may magnify his neighbors' irritability, and the casual person may dismiss it much too lightly.

. . . .

Objective external effects upon the community rather than the neighborhood are illustrated by the problem of commuter traffic. When an apartment complex is created in a suburban area, a new burden is placed upon the roads or transit facilities linking that area to central districts of commerce and employment. Each householder contributes to the inconvenience of every other when these transportation facilities become overloaded. Families also place differential burdens upon the school system of the community and upon the fire, police, and welfare agencies. Many of the latter costs may not be related to housing status, though a number of social scientists have tried to establish the association (of slum housing to crime and delinquency, for example). The household's choice of residential density affects the gross burden of transportation and communication costs for the community and the scale and incidence of location rents.

Housing is as diverse in its effects as in its components. We can suppose that within the range of its information and choices the household tries to select that dwelling which provides the best combination of current housing satisfactions, long-term housing security, and the enjoyment of other goods. Such choice under the most favorable circumstances may not always produce results which the community at large prefers, and the community has always the power, if not the inclination, to enforce some aspects of its own preference.

This multiplicity of effects makes the housing sector something more than just a means to provide jobs and enlarge the gross national product. It is not the only product which influences by its form and use the quality of community life, but it is a principal example of such products.

––––––––

Comments: 1. Smith's diagram and discussion emphasize both the range and the interconnections of the elements in the housing bundle. He helps explain why, for instance, the community's concern with environmental quality, an example of an objective external effect, has repercussions throughout the housing system. The effects the author notes as being external to individual decisions, things economists call externalities, are the source of most of the problems associated with housing to which the second half of this book is devoted.

Among the critical externalities and interconnections of current housing problems are conflicts between objective external effects and subjective community concerns. A community may make a decision to limit or control the growth of households in its jurisdiction in the face of demands and needs of outsiders for the bundle of housing satisfactions that community could provide. The outsiders are external to the decision to limit growth in a community, but they are certainly affected by it. Both environmental (see Chapter 11) and racial issues (see Chapter 10) revolve around this nexus. The elderly widow living in a firetrap room Smith cites in his discussion of the conflict potential between community concerns and objective standards illustrates another externality, an individual decision to minimize rent that goes against community health or safety standards. Such discrepancies between individual and group standards become involved in problems of subsidizing housing (see Chapter 8) and neighborhood revitalization (see Chapter 9). What other current issues can be derived from Smith's portrait of housing?

2. Not every item in the housing status diagram has equal importance in present day housing problems. The structure itself, for instance, has only marginal involvement with the issues upon which this text concentrates. Later this first chapter touches on a very few of the aspects of the physical structure. As crucial as this dimension is to architecture, engineering, and urban planning, the body of these readings deals with other aspects of the housing bundle. Neighborhood, on the other hand, and its tightly related effects on security, satisfactions, and community concerns appears in both parts of this reader. Neighborhood effects play a central role in housing economics and politics at both analytical and policy levels. It is useful to review the various elements diagramed by Smith in terms of their salience to a particular housing issue under discussion.

3. Smith's closing words about the influences of housing on the quality of life provide a transition to another perspective on the question of defining housing. Social studies, sociology in particular, have a long history of concern with housing. In addition to trying to explore and understand better what housing means, sociologists have become involved with housing reform movements. This, in turn, has drawn them and their research to study slums, and the people afflicted by slums, often to the exclusion of other possible housing problems.

Since the first charitable reformers of the mid-nineteenth century, people concerned with the field have perceived the association between bad housing conditions and various types of social and medical problems or "pathologies." This led to viewing housing as somehow the causative agent of all sorts of problems from a high incidence of tuberculosis to the whole behavioral complex we now call the culture of poverty. Some years ago Daniel Seligman quoted a "student of New York's slums" as saying, "Once upon a time we thought that if we could only get our problem families out of those dreadful slums, then papa would stop taking dope, mama would stop chasing around, and Junior would stop carrying a knife. Well, we've got them a nice new apartment with modern kitchens and a recreation center. And they're the same bunch of bastards they always were!" Over the years a great deal of empirically based social reseach has been devoted to exploring the relationships between housing and the social, psychological and physical health of its occupants. The following selection is a brief excerpt from a long review by a well known social researcher and research administrator. In it he draws on many of the hundreds of studies of the interaction between slums and their inhabitants.

A. SCHORR, SLUMS AND SOCIAL INSECURITY 7-12, 31-33 (Research Report No. 1, U.S. Department of Health, Education, and Welfare, 1963)

Housing and Its Effects

Is There a Causal Relationship?

Whether housing affects people and how are old questions. They were examined in Glasgow about 1870, when the city took power to clear land and "reconstitute" neighborhoods. Examining the effects on people who were moved, J. B. Russell found himself perplexed in a way that seems painfully modern. Finding conclusions difficult, he wrote:

A gutter-child from the Bridgegate is a very complicated production. . . . The evil which the Improvement Trust sets itself to remedy was worked in successive generations, and the good which it desires to effect cannot be exhausted in a period short of the life of one generation if not of several.

That we have not come very far beyond this conclusion in a century may be a product of several factors. First, personal experiences testify so dramatically to the effect of housing that one is encouraged to approach research in somewhat patronizing fashion. Second, the motivation to conduct research has been chiefly to produce political action. The ideas that are useful for moving legislatures —

crime, immorality, and ability to pay taxes — are too mixed and, over time, too inconsistent to probe very deeply into human behavior. Third, approached for theoretical purposes, the question of the effect of housing presents difficult problems of definition and method. Does housing mean the house or the neighborhood, and are they separable? Is it at all possible to disentangle the physical facts of housing from the family's image of it, and what is the relative importance of each?

. . . Weighing the net meaning of all the evidence that is available, one must conclude that the placement of houses and apartments in relation to one another and to the total city (downtown, suburban) clearly influences family and social relationships. Though there is no solid evidence, there is at least a hint of the effect of such factors as internal physical arrangement and space per person. In one direction the evidence is overwhelming: *extremely poor* housing conditions perceptibly influence behavior and attitudes.

. . . .

Effects of House and Neighborhood

Housing and Self-Perception. — El Fanguito, in San Juan, P.R., was known, before it was cleared, as the largest slum* in the world. But many residents neglected to mention it when researchers asked them to name a slum. The first redevelopment proposal in the city of Milwaukee, announced in 1947, was defeated by residents. One woman's statement was reported by the *Milwaukee Journal*: "Slums, they call us. Why that's a terrible word — those are our homes, our shrines. We live there." The inertia, not to say intransigence, of those slum residents who resist being moved in one city after another makes it plain that they do not view their surroundings with the same contempt as city planners and municipal officials. Slum neighborhoods may serve other functions that are useful to residents — we shall be discussing these at greater length — but one factor at work is that house and place are regarded as extensions of one's self. In the words of a study in the Chelsea area of New York:

> Housing . . . has represented much more than physical structures, housing is/has become a subject of highly charged emotional content: a matter of strong feeling. It is the symbol of status, of achievement, of social acceptance. It seems to control, in large measure, the way in which the individual, the family, perceives him/itself and is perceived by others.

Thus, one evaluates his surroundings far from objectively, and himself in terms of his surroundings. How indeed call a house a slum if this is to tell the tenant he is a slum dweller!

To the middle-class reader, the social elements that are involved in identifying himself with his housing may be evident. These are the common coinage of deciding where to live: Who is accepted there? Are they my kind of people? Is it a step up or down? What will it do for me and my children? Whom shall I meet? The physical elements of self-evaluation may not be so evident. Indeed, it has been suggested that our culture tends to put out of mind the deep personal significance of what has been called the "nonhuman environment." It is interesting and perhaps also just that psychoanalysts are among the first to bring back to our minds a relationship that more primitive societies understand. Harold F. Searles writes:

---

* The term "slum" has been used to describe houses, neighborhoods and people — and conditions that are physical, moral, and social. Here, slum means a house that is dilapidated, lacking in facilities, or overcrowded to a point that seriously interferes with health, safety, or the reasonable conduct of family life. Housing in an area where slums predominate is considered slum housing, even if otherwise satisfactory.

It seems to me that, in our culture, a conscious ignoring of the psychological importance of the nonhuman environment exists simultaneously with a (largely unconscious) *overdependence upon* that environment. I believe that the actual importance of that environment to the individual is so great that he *dare* not recognize it. Unconsciously it is felt, I believe, to be not only an intensely important conglomeration of things *outside* the self, but also a large and integral *part* of the self.

If physical surroundings are a mirror to us all, they will reflect an especially disturbing image to the people who, lacking the simplest amenities, are made aware of the riches that others quite normally own and consume.

The reciprocal effects of housing and self-evaluation may flow in two directions. On one hand, people who feel they are worth more may avoid slums or low-status neighborhoods, if this is at all possible. Thus Moss Hart, assured of the success of his first play, moved his family within hours, leaving behind apartment, furniture, and clothing. He wrote:

> Each piece of furniture in the cramped dim room seemed mildewed with a thousand double-edged memories. The ghosts of a thousand leaden meals hovered over the dining room table. The dust of countless blackhearted days clung to every crevice of the squalid ugly furniture I had known since childhood.

Who are the people who are eager to improve their housing? Studies show them to be the young, the families who are ambitious for their children, the people who wish to improve their status. (As this listing may suggest, it appears that acceptance of change is a family rather than an individual attribute.) The physical move is a social move, an evidence of aspiration and a functional step in improving one's social or economic situation.

On the other hand, living in poor housing itself influences self-evaluation and motivation. This is the heart of the question we are dealing with, whether causality moves *from* housing *to* attitudes and behavior. A good deal has been written about the pessimism that is common to poor people, the readiness to seize the present satisfaction and let the future care for itself, and the feeling that one is controlled by rather than in control of events. Indeed, so well do we understand these feelings that it has become necessary to be reminded that there is considerable variability, not to say aspiration, among even the very poor. Studies of families living in deteriorated neighborhoods make the same point: pessimism and passivity present the most difficult barriers to rehabilitating neighborhoods or relocating families.

However, where vigorous effort has gone into upgrading neighborhoods — in Chicago, Baltimore, New Orleans, and Miami — observers have seen people "who dropped their old, fatalistic attitudes and embraced new feelings of pride and optimism. . . ." This observation should not be exaggerated; only some people, more in Baltimore and fewer in Miami, responded. Scientifically controlled studies give more ambiguous evidence about the effect of changing housing on self-evaluation. The two or three that have been done do not appear to span an adequate period of time, nor do they have adequate instruments to measure motivation and self-evaluation. It seems clear that families who have improved their housing feel they have improved their situation and status. A substantial, controlled sample of families who moved to improved housing showed higher "general morale" but no change in aspirations.

Certain factors appear to operate selectively to determine who will respond to a change in housing. Apparently, improvement has to go beyond the simplest physical facilities before a change in attitude shows. That is, while sheer physical need continues to occupy the family's attention, attitude is not affected. Even when their parents are not responding at all, children change their feelings about "the whole of life" — a change particularly noticeable in school. There is evidence that children who are rehoused are "considerably more likely to be promoted at a normal pace. . . ." Another factor is that opportunity needs to be genuinely present; otherwise indifference or escapist activities offer equally acceptable retreats. There needs, finally, to be some basic educational and cultural attainment; in a sense, this is another way of saying that opportunity must be genuinely present. . . .

. . . .

[Schorr continues his review, treating in turn the combined effects of house and neighborhood, then the effects of each separately on health, behavior and satisfaction. — Eds.]

Conclusion

Though the evidence is scattered, taken as a whole it is substantial. The type of housing occupied influences health, behavior and attitude, particularly if the housing is desperately inadequate. In the terms that we use today, "desperately inadequate" means that housing is dilapidated or lacks a major facility such as running water. . . .

Those influences on behavior and attitudes that have been established bear a relationship to whether people can move out of or stay out of poverty. The following effects may spring from poor housing: a perception of one's self that leads to pessimism and passivity, stress to which the individual cannot adapt, poor health, and a state of dissatisfaction; pleasure in company but not in solitude, cynicism about people and organizations, a high degree of sexual stimulation without legitimate outlet, and difficulty in household management and child rearing; and relationships that tend to spread out in the neighborhood rather than deeply into the family. Most of these effects, in turn, place obstacles in the path of improving one's financial circumstances. Obstacles such as those presented by poor health or inability to train children are obvious. Those presented by having ties centered in one's neighborhood rather than in one's wife and children are less direct, but significant. Such a family, for example, is less likely to move if a better job requires it.

Reviewing a large number of discussions of the evidence, one may conclude that the impact of physical housing on human behavior is generally understated. Why should this be so? First, because we are only now emerging from a period of absorption in psychological man. Psychological man, being infinitely adaptable, would not be greatly influenced by his physical surroundings. Our growing interest in a sociological understanding of man holds the seed of a comparable misunderstanding. Psychological man, if he was Buddhist in his introspectiveness, was at least dynamic. Seen sociologically, one gets a broader, more eclectic view of man, but may tend to see him so intricately involved in his current relationships as to be unable to change. This is not a sound sociological view, but it is reflected in the conclusions of some studies.

Second, the heavy reliance on technology and material gain that has characterized our progress may require a degree of blindness to its effect on people. In failing to discern the impact of housing on people, we leave ourselves free to think we are meeting their needs through technology. At the same time, we are left free to overlook the possible human costs of material progress.

A final reason that the impact of physical housing may tend currently to be understated has to do with the stage of sophistication of research into housing.

The research that is available, and is cited here, is partial and requires to be pieced together. A conception has yet to be developed that sees man in relation to his physical environment. Until such a scheme is developed, and research adapted to it, we shall not fully perceive the relationship of man to shelter. Meanwhile, we shall build houses.

Comments: The key point that emerges from this reading is the reflexive relationship that it asserts exists between housing and people. In contrast to the perspective of the earlier selection by the economist Smith, sociologist Schorr deals with housing and people in a reciprocal way. One depends upon the other. Put another way this suggests that the question What is housing? is meaningless without specifying whose housing we are talking about and who is doing the talking. Or, in another particularly important case, rather than people's housing preferences being autonomous and internal to the individual psyche as economists are wont to assume, the sociological perspective suggests that people's housing experience and the structure of the housing supply system have much to do with preferences they develop.

From the standpoint of the problems dealt with in this text, the reflexivity between people and their dwellings has special importance. If the problem is bad housing, for instance, it lies as much with the people who define bad housing as it lies in the objective conditions of the housing as such. Without tying down both, the term bad housing is meaningless. The same is true about other problems, be they cost, scarcity, or conflict over occupancy rights. Part I of this book attempts to maintain this duality and give relatively equal weight to both sides, to supply and demand in the usual economic terminology. Later, when the book turns to the problem side, attention necessarily shifts more to housing *per se*. Though people and their housing may be equally implicated in creating housing problems, in responding to them and solving them, action has to focus primarily on the many aspects of the housing bundle.

The next reading, the work of a sociologist, explores in more detail some of the specifics of the relationships between poor people and their housing. In doing so, it emphasizes an important extension of the concept of shelter, the notion of haven from a threatening world, an idea that combines several dimensions of housing status including rights, uses and objective standards.

RAINWATER, FEAR AND THE HOUSE-AS-HAVEN IN THE LOWER CLASS, 32 JOURNAL OF THE AMERICAN INSTITUTE OF PLANNERS 23 (1966)

Men live in a world which presents them with many threats to their security as well as with opportunities for gratification of their needs. The cultures that men create represent ways of adapting to these threats to security as well as maximizing the opportunities for certain kinds of gratifications. Housing as an element of material culture has as its prime purpose the provision of shelter, which is protection from potentially damaging or unpleasant trauma or other stimuli. The most primitive level of evaluation of housing, therefore, has to do with the question of how adequately it shelters the individuals who abide in it from threats in their environment. Because the house is a refuge from noxious elements in the outside world, it serves people as a locale where they can regroup their energies for interaction with that outside world. There is in our culture a long history of the development of the house as a place of safety from both nonhuman and human threats, a history which culminates in guaranteeing the house, a man's castle, against unreasonable search and seizure. The house becomes the place of maximum exercise of individual autonomy, minimum conformity to the formal and complex rules of public demeanor. The house acquires a sacred character from its complex intertwining with the self and from the symbolic character it has as a representation of the family.

These conceptions of the house are readily generalized to the area around it, to the neighborhood. This fact is most readily perceived in the romanticized views people have about suburban living. The suburb, just as the village or the farm homestead, can be conceptualized as one large protecting and gratifying home. But the same can also be said of the city neighborhood, at least as a potentiality and as a wish, tenuously held in some situations, firmly established in others. Indeed, the physical barriers between inside and outside are not maintained when people talk of their attitudes and desires with respect to housing. Rather, they talk of the outside as an inevitable extension of the inside and of the inside as deeply affected by what goes on immediately outside.

When, as in the middle class, the battle to make the home a safe place has long been won, the home then has more central to its definition other functions which have to do with self-expression and self-realization. There is an elaboration of both the material culture within the home and of interpersonal relationships in the form of more complex rituals of behavior and more variegated kinds of interaction. Studies of the relationship between social class status and both numbers of friends and acquaintances as well as kinds of entertaining in the home indicate that as social status increases the home becomes a locale for a wider range of interactions. Whether the ritualized behavior be the informality of the lower middle class family room, or the formality of the upper middle class cocktail party and buffet, the requisite housing standards of the middle class reflect a more complex and varied set of demands on the physical structure and its equipment.

The poverty and cultural milieu of the lower class make the prime concern that of the home as a place of security, and the accomplishment of this goal is generally a very tenuous and incomplete one. (I use the term "lower class" here to refer to the bottom 15 to 20 percent of the population in terms of social status. This is the group characterized by unskilled occupations, a high frequency of unstable work histories, slum dwellings, and the like. I refer to the group of more stable blue-collar workers which in status stands just above this lower class as the "working class" to avoid the awkwardness of terms like "lower-lower" and "upper-lower" class.) In the established working class there is generally a somewhat greater degree of confidence in the house as providing shelter and security, although the hangovers of concern with a threatening lower class environment often are still operating in the ways working class people think about housing.

. . . .

Attitudes Toward Housing

. . . .

In our studies and in those of Herbert Gans and others of Boston's West End, we find one type of working class life style where families are content with much about their housing — even though it is "below standard" in the eyes of housing professionals — if the housing does provide security against the most blatant of threats. This traditional working class is likely to want to economize on housing in order to have money available to pursue other interests and needs. There will be efforts at the maintenance of the house or apartment, but not much interest in improvement of housing level. Instead there is an effort to create a pleasant and cozy home, where housework can be carried out conveniently. Thus, families in this group tend to acquire a good many of the major appliances, to center their social life in the kitchen, to be relatively unconcerned with adding taste in furnishings to comfort. With respect to the immediate outside world the main emphasis is on a concern with the availability of a satisfying peer group life, with having neighbors who are similar, and with maintaining an easy access back and forth among people who are very well known. There is also a concern that the neighborhood be respectable enough — with respectability defined mainly in the negative, by the absence of "crumbs and bums." An emphasis on comfort and contentment ties together meanings having to do with both the inside and the outside.

Out of the increasing prosperity of the working class has grown a different orientation toward housing on the part of the second group which we can characterize as modern instead of traditional. Here there is a great emphasis on owning one's home rather than enriching a landlord. Along with the acquisition of a home and yard goes an elaboration of the inside of the house in such a way as not only to further develop the idea of a pleasant and cozy home, but also to add new elements with emphasis on having a nicely decorated living room or family room, a home which more closely approximates a standard of all-American affluence. Similarly there is a greater emphasis on maintenance of the yard outside and on the use of the yard as a place where both adults and children can relax and enjoy themselves. With this can come also the development of a more intense pattern of neighborhood socializing. In these suburbs the demand grows for good community services as opposed to simply adequate ones, so that there tends to be greater involvement in the schools than is the case with traditional working class men and women. One of the dominant themes of the modern working class life style is that of having arrived in the mainstream of American life, of no longer being simply "poor-but-honest" workers. It is in the service of this goal that we find these elaborations in the meaning of the house and its environs.

In both working class groups, as the interior of the home more closely approximates notions of a decent standard, we find a decline in concerns expressed by inhabitants with sources of threat from within and a shift toward concerns about a threatening outside world — a desire to make the neighborhood secure against the incursions of lower class people who might rob or perpetrate violence of one kind or another.

. . . .

[At this point the author shifts his focus from the stable working class to the poor or lower class. Drawing on three empirical studies, he finds a very different situation. The studies involved intensive conversational interviews with hundreds of lower class residents in Chicago, Cincinnati, and Oklahoma City, and from a five year long participant observer study in the ill-fated Pruitt-Igoe housing project in St. Louis. — Ed.]

In the lower class we find a great many very real threats to security, although these threats often do seem to be somewhat exaggerated by lower class women. The threatening world of the lower class comes to be absorbed into a world view which generalizes the belief that the environment is threatening more than it is rewarding — that rewards reflect the infrequent working of good luck and that danger is endemic. Any close acquaintance with the ongoing life of lower class people impresses one with their anxious alienation from the larger world, from the middle class to be sure, but from the majority of their peers as well. Lower class people often seem isolated and to have but tenuous participation in a community of known and valued peers. They are ever aware of the presence of strangers who tend to be seen as potentially dangerous. While they do seek to create a gratifying peer group society, these groups tend to be unstable and readily fragmented. Even the heavy reliance on relatives as the core of a personal community does not do away with the dangers which others may bring. As Walter Miller has perceptively noted, "trouble" is one of the major focal concerns in the lower class world view. A home to which one could retreat from such an insecure world would be of great value, but our data indicate that for lower class people such a home is not easy to come by. In part, this is due to the fact that one's own family members themselves often make trouble or bring it into the home, but even more important it is because it seems very difficult to create a home and an immediate environment that actually does shut out danger.

Dangers in the Environment

From our data it is possible to abstract a great many dangers that have some relation to housing and its location. The location or the immediate environment is as important as the house itself, since lower class people are aware that life inside is much affected by the life just outside.

In Figure 2, I have summarized the main kinds of danger which seem to be related to housing one way or another. It is apparent that these dangers have two immediate sources, human and non human, and that the consequences that are feared from these sources usually represent a complex amalgam of physical, interpersonal, and mortal damage to the individual and his family. Let us look first at the various sources of danger and then at the overlapping consequences feared from these dangers.

There is nothing unfamiliar about the non-human sources of danger. They represent a sad catalogue of threats apparent in any journalist's account of slum living. That we become used to the catalogue, however, should not obscure the fact that these dangers are very real to many lower class families. Rats and other vermin are ever present companions in most big city slums. From the sense of relief which residents in public housing often experience on this score, it is apparent that slum dwellers are not indifferent to the presence of rats in their homes. . . .

[The author at this point catalogs in some detail the non-human dangers outlined in figure 2. — Eds.]

That lower class people grow up in a world like this and live in it does not mean that they are indifferent to it — nor that its toll is only that of possible physical damage in injury, illness, incapacity, or death. Because these potentialities and events are interpreted and take on symbolic significance, and because lower class people make some efforts to cope with them, inevitably there are also effects on their interpersonal relationships and on their moral conceptions of themselves and their worlds.

The most obvious human source of danger has to do with violence directed by others against oneself and one's possessions. Lower class people are concerned with being assaulted, being damaged, being drawn into fights, being beaten, being raped. In public housing projects in particular, it is always possible for juveniles to throw or drop things from windows which can hurt or kill, and if this pattern takes hold it is a constant source of potential danger. Similarly, people may rob anywhere — apartment, laundry room, corridor.

. . . .

Source of Danger

Non-Human	Human
Rats and other vermin	Violence to self and possessions
Poisons	Assault
Fire and burning	Fighting and beating
Freezing and cold	Rape
Poor plumbing	Objects thrown or dropped
Dangerous electrical wiring	Stealing
Trash (broken glass, cans, etc.)	Verbal Hostility, Shaming, Exploitation
Insufficiently protected heights	Own family
Other aspects of poorly designed	Neighbors
or deteriorated structures (e.g.	Caretakers
thin walls)	Outsiders
Cost of dwelling	Attractive alternatives that wean oneself
	or valued others away from a stable
	life

Figure 2

[The author discusses the many ramifications of human threats and continues to explore the ways people cope with them and use their housing in the process. — Ed.]

It would be asking too much to insist that design per se can solve or even seriously mitigate these threats. On the other hand, it is obvious that almost all the non-human threats can be pretty well done away with where the resources are available to design decent housing for lower class people. No matter what criticisms are made of public housing projects, there is no doubt that the structures themselves are infinitely preferable to slum housing. In our interviews in public housing projects we have found very few people who complain about design aspects of the insides of their apartments. Though they may not see their apartments as perfect, there is a dramatic drop in anxiety about nonhuman threats within. Similarly, reasonable foresight in the design of other elements can eliminate the threat of falling from windows or into elevator shafts, and can provide adequate outside toilet facilities for children at play. Money and a reasonable exercise of architectural skill go a long way toward providing lower class families with the really safe place of retreat from the outside world that they desire.

There is no such straightforward design solution to the potentiality of human threat. However, to the extent that lower class people do have a place they can go that is not so dangerous as the typical slum dwelling, there is at least the gain of a haven. Thus, at the cost perhaps of increased isolation, lower class people in public housing sometimes place a great deal of value on privacy and on living a quiet life behind the locked doors of their apartments. When the apartment itself seems safe it allows the family to begin to elaborate a home to maximize coziness, comfortable enclosure, and lack of exposure. Where, as in St. Louis, the laundry rooms seem unsafe places, tenants tend to prefer to do their laundry in their homes, sacrificing the possibility of neighborly interactions to gain a greater sense of security of person and property.

Once the home can be seen as a relatively safe place, lower class men and women express a desire to push out the boundaries of safety further into the larger world. There is the constantly expressed desire for a little bit of outside space that is one's own or at least semiprivate. Buildings that have galleries are much preferred by their tenants to those that have no such immediate access to the outside. Where, as in the New York public housing project we studied, it was possible to lock the outside doors of the buildings at night, tenants felt more secure.

A measured degree of publicness within buildings can also contribute to a greater sense of security. In buildings where there are several families whose doors open onto a common hallway there is a greater sense of the availability of help should trouble come than there is in buildings where only two or three apartments open onto a small hallway in a stairwell. While tenants do not necessarily develop close neighborly relations when more neighbors are available, they can develop a sense of making common cause in dealing with common problems. And they feel less at the mercy of gangs or individuals intent on doing them harm.

As with the most immediate outside, lower class people express the desire to have their immediate neighborhood or the housing project grounds a more controlled and safe place. In public housing projects, for example, tenants want project police who function efficiently and quickly; they would like some play areas supervised so that children are not allowed to prey on each other; they want to be able to move about freely themselves and at the same time discourage outsiders who might come to exploit.

A real complication is that the very control which these desires imply can seem a threat to the lower class resident. To the extent that caretakers seem to demand and damn more than they help, this cure to the problem of human threat seems worse than the disease. The crux of the caretaking task in connection with lower class people is to provide and encourage security and order within the lower class world without at the same time extracting from it a heavy price in self-esteem, dignity, and autonomy.

Comments: 1. In starting out his discussion, Rainwater mentions the functions of the house in terms of self-expression and self-realization. This suggests that the house can become an extension of the occupant's personality, a concept given a neat name in Clare Cooper's phrase, "the house as the symbol of self." The French philosopher Gaston Bachelard observes that house and non-house divide geographic space very much as self and non-self divide psychic space. This means, again in Cooper's words, "The house, therefore, reflects how man sees himself, with both an intimate interior or self as viewed from within and revealed only to those intimates who are invited inside, and a public exterior or the self that we choose to display to others." Clearly such insights offer a rich field for speculation about the meanings of housing.

2. With respect to the body of Rainwater's essay that concerns the various threats lower class people feel in connection with their housing, most of the non-human sources of danger have rather obvious remedies. Straightforward improvements in design and construction or better levels of service and management can deal with almost all of these problems. With respect to human sources of danger, especially crime and violence, the possibility also exists that physical design and better architecture could make the houses of lower class people into better havens. This possibility has been articulated only recently with the growth of a new interdisciplinary field that joins the social and behavioral sciences with architecture and environmental design. Architect researcher Oscar Newman published a seminal book in 1972, *Defensible Space*, that crystallized efforts to use this new interdisciplinary field to improve the public housing which is home to some millions of lower class Americans. The next selection, by Newman, comes from a recent manual for doing this.

O. NEWMAN, DESIGN GUIDELINES FOR CREATING DEFENSIBLE SPACE 2, 20-25, 29-34 (National Institute of Law Enforcement and Criminal Justice)

The achievement of security in housing has become a critical issue in the past few years because as a nation we have begun to witness the large-scale failure of low- and moderate-income developments — a failure increasingly attributable to rising crime and vandalism rates. The lack of security in housing has produced high vacancy rates and heavy financial losses to management. In some instances it has led to the complete abandonment of housing projects. In the periods before abandonment, residential developments that suffer high crime rates have been found to receive only minimal use by their residents. The areas outside the dwelling units go unused — whether laundry rooms, lounging areas, parking lots, or playgrounds. These areas are also heavily vandalized. Residents living in an insecure housing environment withdraw from each other and from all areas beyond the interior of their homes. They are frightened to make the trip from their homes to neighboring streets, to shopping areas, or to the transportation facilities that will take them to other parts of the city. If they can afford to, they abandon their homes as well. . . .

Effect of Socioeconomic Factors

Early in our analysis it became clear that the social characteristics of the resident population were stronger predictors of crime rate than the physical characteristics of design. Varying aspects of a family's makeup, income, and age of its members affect its adaptability to different environments and its vulnerability to crime.

. . . .

The social variables prominent in predicting crime rate in most categories of crime were, in order of importance:

1. The percentage of resident population receiving welfare (excluding elderly).
2. The percentage of families headed by a female receiving welfare through the Aid to Families with Dependent Children (AFDC) program.
3. The per capita disposable income of the project's residents.

. . . .

In recognizing the socioeconomic factors that are normally designated as critical in predicting crime rate — that is, families with a high, internally generated vulnerability to crime — it is also important to understand the causal mechanisms in operation. These families share many of the following characteristics: they are poor; they are female-headed households; they are black or Puerto Rican; they have a high percentage of teenage children; and they receive welfare in one form or another. The high correlation of each of these characteristics with crime rate, and with one another, has also been established in other studies. Attempts at determining causal explanations for the above correlations have suggested some of the following: that female heads of household are vulnerable to criminal attack and are only minimally able to control their teenage children and/or boyfriends; that the criminal activity of the poor is tolerated, if not condoned, among the poor; that the poor, and particularly the poor of racial minorities, are unable to demand much in the way of police protection; that crime against residents in ghetto areas requires minimal skill and risk; that poor teenagers, who are most of the apprehendees (75% in New York and Boston), are deprived of even minimal recreational facilities and job opportunities; that poor residential neighborhoods are deficient in amenities and opportunities common to middle-income communities.

. . . .

Effect of Physical Factors

Although the strongest predictors of crime rates in residential areas are the socioeconomic characteristics of the resident population, the form of the living environment also strongly affects the vulnerability of housing occupied by all socioeconomic groups. The impact of physical design on security is not restricted to the peculiarities of any one population, income, age group, or urban locale.
. . . [T]hree physical variables are prominent in explaining crime rates. They are, in order of importance:
   1. The height of the buildings in the development (building height correlates very highly with the number of apartments sharing a single entry to a building).
   2. The size of the housing project; that is, the total number of dwelling units making up a project. This factor is important when the project consists of low-income and welfare families because the variable is a measure of the concentration of low-income population in a particular area. Here it is considered a physical variable because it can be controlled through physical planning.
   3. The number of other publicly assisted housing projects in the area; this variable is a further measure of the same phenomenon in (2) but in this case extending beyond the confines of the particular project.

. . . .

The above analysis suggests that there are two classes of physical variables that contribute to crime rates: the first involves physical characteristics that reinforce or counteract social weakness and pathology; the second is a class of specific physical elements that work to prevent or encourage social control of the environment by its inhabitants. The first class of physical variables is a facet of the social variables: if it is known that certain social characteristics produce a crime-prone population, then we can expect that a large concentration of families sharing these characteristics will reinforce criminal opportunities. The significance of this finding is not simply that the presence of more pathology creates proportionally more crime, but that it creates an increase in the rate of crime. Thus the larger the low-income project, or the more the project is surrounded by other low-income projects, the higher will be the number of crimes per thousand population.

. . . .

The most fascinating set of variables to come out of our analyses are of the second group: those physical design features that have been found to assist a resident population, regardless of income level or family structure, to achieve behavior along the lines desired by the noncriminal majority. The central physical variable here is the number of residents who share a defined environment. The smaller the number of families sharing a facility, whether it is a demarcated portion of a project's grounds or the access and circulation space within a multifamily building, the stronger are their feelings of possession, and, ultimately, of concern, control, and responsibility. This explains why, when only two families share a landing in a walk-up building, both will maintain the hallway outside their apartment doors. . . .
In a high-rise building in which more than 100 families with children share an

entry, it is difficult for residents to distinguish neighbor from intruder, or to attempt to enforce an acceptable code of behavior, or even to feel comfortable about questioning the presence or activities of others.

. . . .

In addition to the fact that multifamily buildings experience higher crime rates than walk-ups or single-family buildings, it is important to know that they are also vulnerable to different types of criminal activity. Most of the crime experienced by residents of single-family buildings is burglary. These burglaries are normally committed when members of the family are either away from home or asleep. By contrast, the residents of multifamily dwellings experience both burglaries and robberies (muggings). The higher crime rate in multifamily dwellings (Table 1.8) is, in large part, attributable to such robberies. The interior common circulation spaces (lobbies, hallways) are the areas where most robberies are committed, as well as the areas where criminals wait to follow residents into their apartments for the purpose of burglarizing them.

Table 1.8. Public Housing Crime in Relation to Building Height (Felonies per Thousand Families) * (Redrawn from Newman)

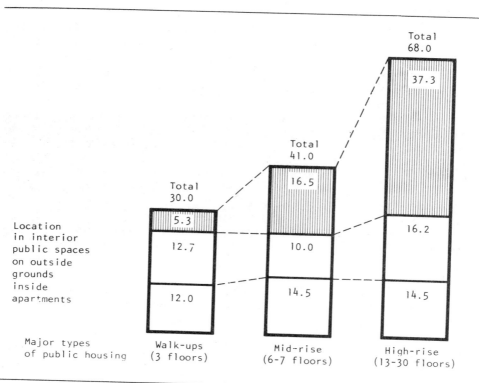

* SOURCE N.Y.C. Housing Authority data. 1967; N = 87.

. . . .

Neighborhood Cohesiveness: Life-Styles

There are social factors other than income, family structure, and ages of residents that predetermine a community's susceptibility to crime. A high degree of recognition among neighbors has been shown to produce comparatively low crime rates. The extent to which recognition occurs among neighbors is in turn a product of the following:

1. The degree of similarity between them as defined by shared ages, life-styles, and backgrounds.
2. The number of years of continued residence in the same building or housing development.
3. The degree of interaction among them resulting from similar life-styles — particularly as expressed in their sharing common needs for and use of facilities in their immediate residential environments.

. . . .

For example, a group of families with young children will need space outside their dwelling units where children can run around and play together. These families may share nothing more than this need, but this fact alone allows designers to define a collective area around the families' dwellings and designate it for this purpose. If it is a genuine and continuing need, the residents will identify with the space, adopt it as their own, and work to ensure that it remains safe, secure, and usable. This collective play space then becomes an extension of the individual dwellings into the outside world. . . .

In contrast, the greater the disparity in life-styles and needs among neighbors — that is, the less they have in common — the smaller is the grouping that can share a spatial collective. . . .

We may therefore have to conclude, albeit reluctantly, that the most desirable way to construct residential environments in today's world is to cluster similar occupants together so that at a certain scale, say 50 to 150 dwelling units, we create groupings that house occupants identified by a similarity in age and family structure, if nothing more. In this way we can begin to create areas outside the dwelling unit for the collective use of neighbors.

. . . .

In designing a housing development for a low-income population, or for a middle-income population that cannot afford doormen, it is important to create an environment in which the design assists residents in their ability to recognize one another. With few residents sharing an entry and fewer still a corridor, it is easy for a common code of behavior to come into being. Pressures can then be easily exerted to restrain resident vandals and criminals from activities affecting the project. . . . With a commonly shared set of values, preventing crime in a development will then depend both on the residents' ability to observe and monitor their neighbors and on their willingness to censure unacceptable conduct. . . .

———

Comments: 1. A word of caution is in order with respect to both Newman's studies and his findings. Some social scientists have been critical of his methods. They have been joined by some designers in questioning his conclusions. His discoveries of small scale territoriality effects, findings such as that certain kinds of high-rise building corridors and stairhalls seem to breed crime as do unfenced, undifferentiated spaces outside buildings, have been widely influential in policy and design despite possible theoretical shortcomings of the research behind them. Other findings, such as the caution about the overall size of projects, have been correctly seen as political issues rather than matters of design (see the Baltimore case study in Chapter 10 for a case in point). Shortcomings or not, Newman's works have proved to be the most powerful example in actual practice of this new interdisciplinary view.

2. This material on defensible space provides a helpful bridge to yet another way to think about and define housing. By focusing on the problems of physical design, Newman calls attention to the saliency of this dimension. Practically all thinking about housing refers in fundamental ways to its physical side. No effort to define what housing means could be complete without giving substantial attention to this aspect.

Many of the professions and disciplines concerned with housing deal primarily with its physical design. Among these fields are architecture, engineering, city planning, urban design, and geography. The following note prepared by the editors deals with the view from these fields.

A NOTE ON HOUSING DESIGN AND ITS IMPLICATIONS

Houses come in characteristic physical forms. Housing design deals with these forms and with their implications, both at the small scale in the details of construction and interior design, and at the large scale in terms of land development patterns and urban form. This way of seeing the physical world as an interconnected system is characteristic of architects and many of their brother professionals such as civil engineers and landscape architects. This view is shared also by some scholars in fields such as geography and art or architectural history.

To give an example familiar to almost everyone, we need only turn to the ubiquitous suburban ranch house of post World War II subdivisions (figure 1). In its simplest terms, this house form consists of a one-story rectangular enclosure standing free of other structures on its own plot of land. The inside of the enclosure usually is divided into several rooms. These may include a more or less formal social space, the living room, a less formal social space, the family room or den, a kitchen, dining spaces in one or more of the foregoing rooms or in a separate space, one or more bedrooms for sleeping with individual or subgroup privacy, one or more bathrooms, and perhaps a utility room or space for storage and mechanical equipment. The interior spaces of the vast majority of all house types are drawn from this same repertoire of rooms, sometimes combined into multifunction spaces as in the case of the studio apartment which combines social space, kitchen, dining, and bedroom in one room.

Figure 1 Typical example of the ubiquitous suburban ranch house of post World War II subdivisions; houses like this one are representative of those occupied by the two-thirds of the American population who own their own homes (Photo by Davis)

To return to the ranch house configuration, it implies or determines many details or possibilities with respect to constructional systems. A simple, relatively inexpensive concrete pad, for instance, usually forms its floor, providing at the same time structural support for the walls and roof in transferring loads to the earth. This system contrasts with the more complicated and expensive structurally supported floors and separate foundations required by most other house types. Entire textbooks are required to deal with all of the ramifications of construction in relation to house type.

The plot of ground on which the ranch house is sited usually contains front and back yards plus vehicular access and storage spaces (figure 2). Automobile access direct to the dwelling unit, usually on the same level, the storage function often being provided within the house structure as such, marks a popular advantage of the ranch house. Yards have advantages. The front yard gives special opportunities for self-expression. The back yard offers supervised, protected, outdoor playspace, storage areas, a place for production and repair of possessions, and the whole plot usually offers opportunities for minimum cost expansion or modification of the dwelling enclosure.

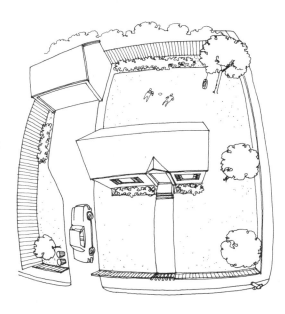

Figure 2 Diagrammatic sketch looking straight down on a typical single family, detached, suburban house and yard The authors of the sketch call it "the domain of the house" because it emphasizes house and yard as a single entity. Note how the space around the dwelling provides for car parking, play, room for expansion and modifying the structure itself, storage, hobbies, and a long list of other activities. From a design standpoint this private space is the special advantage of this type of housing. (Drawing by William and Carol Glass, architects)

A group of ranch houses forms the unit of suburban development, called a subdivision (figure 3). The post World War II suburbs can be defined as the location of these subdivisions. This illustrates a chief point about house design:

each house type is associated with a characteristic land development type and these added together tend to define the characteristic varieties of urban form. The ranch house, for instance, determines a low density* suburban type of urban

Figure 3 Characteristic urban form produced by the type of houses shown in figure 1 above The subdivisions shown in this airview of Long Island, N. Y., form a low density suburban area averaging about 3 dwelling units per acre of land or about 3500 to 4000 persons per square mile. (Photo by Regional Plan Association of New York)

form. The many benefits of the ranch house can very well be offset by some of the disadvantages of the urban pattern it dictates. In a rather polemic attack on low density suburbs, city planner Hans Blumenfeld put these very clearly.

The disadvantages of excessively low density development, of 4.5 houses or less per acre of residential area, can be summarized under three headings: (1) overextension of urbanized area; (2) isolation of daily life; and (3) difficulty in finding labor for industry and commerce.

---

*Density is a measure of the intensity of land development or land occupation. It is usually measured by architects, urban planners, and zoning lawyers by the number of dwelling units per unit area. In the case of ranch house suburbs it usually adds up to between 2 and 5 dwelling units per acre. Geographers tend to measure density in terms of the number of people residing per unit area and use larger areas in their measures. Ranch house suburbs have densities in the range of 2000 to 6000 per square mile (1000-2500 people per square kilometer).

1. Urbanization of a very extensive area has the following inconveniences:

a. Very large investments for roads and utilities to serve this extensive area.

b. Very long travel distances from the inner areas to open areas.

c. Very long travel distances from the outer areas to the commercial, civic, and cultural facilities in the center.

d. An increase of daily vehicle-miles roughly equal to the square of population increase.

2. Even more serious may be the effect on the daily lives of the residents in the newly developed residential areas. Most residents of such areas who work in the city center and practically all who work in other areas travel by car. With growing dispersal of places of work, the percentage of those traveling to work by car will tend to increase.

It must be assumed that the great majority of residents will, in the future, as at present, consist of one-car families. It is therefore important that transit stops and neighborhood facilities such as local shopping and community centers, schools, churches, etc., should be within walking distance of the homes.

Walking distance may be defined as one quarter of a mile as the maximum, or a circular area of less than one fifth of a square mile, which, at a density of 4.5 families per acre, contains not more than 500 to 600 families. This has the following consequences:

a. Bus service at adequate headways of 10 minutes or less can be maintained only during rush hours in the direction to and from the central city. At other hours and in other directions, service can be maintained only at headways of 30 minutes or more. Even such a limited service can be maintained only if heavily subsidized by the taxpayers.

b. A population of 500 to 600 families can just barely maintain a public elementary school of eight classes (or six classes with a three-level system) and kindergarten, if 80 to 90 per cent of all children in this age group attended the public elementary school. If higher percentages of children go to separate schools, public schools have to be more widely spaced. Separate schools as well as junior and senior high schools are beyond the normal walking distance for most of the students.

c. A local shopping center requires a market area of at least 1,000 to 1,200 families. Consequently, at least half of the families in such areas live beyond the normal walking distance from a local shopping center.

d. The same holds true for churches, clubs, and other community facilities. Observations in large communities that have been developed at such low densities confirm that housewives lead isolated lives, restricted to contact only with their immediate neighbors, resulting in lack of participation in civic, school, church, social, and cultural affairs and ultimately in a sense of frustration.

3. Most municipalities designate extensive areas for industry and commerce and want to encourage their development. Practically all industrial and commercial enterprises require a certain percentage of low-wage earners. Many of these workers, notably female labor, do not have cars at their disposal. On the other hand, few workers of this type will be found in detached houses on relatively large lots. The consequences are:

a. At best, many workers have to travel long ways, with adverse effects on morale and productivity; at worst, employers are unable to recruit a full staff.

b. In the long run, the neighboring communities cannot be expected to supply the lower-paid segment of workers but will adopt similar restrictive zoning policies. Carried to its ultimate consequence, this would undermine the economic base of the entire area from which the people occupying the more expensive homes derive their income.

H. Blumenfeld, The Modern Metropolis: Its Origins, Growth, Characteristics and Planning 173-75 (1967).

The costs of sprawl that seem to be inherent in the ranch house variety of housing vividly illustrate the architect's and city planner's point that the choice of residential structure type constitutes a major city shaping force. Each dwelling type determines to a large extent the configuration or plan of an urban district made up of such units, thus the rallying cry of the contemporary architect planners, "The point of departure for all town planning should be the cell represented by a single dwelling, conceived together with similar cells to form the neighborhood . . ." up to the scale of the metropolis.

The ranch house represents but one type of single-family detached dwelling. Other types include the mini-estates of high income suburbs and the exurban fringes and the city house on a small lot often but 25 feet wide by 100 feet deep permitting minimal front and side yards. Figure 4 provides a diagrammatic comparison of a number of house types and their associated type of lot. Moving up the scale of density from the single-family detached house are various types of single-family attached houses. Among these the rowhouse, nowadays frequently called townhouse, is the most prevalent. Townhouses share common walls called party walls with the houses on either side. By eliminating side yards they are more economical in terms of land and can be built to higher densities than can fully detached units. Densities range from 6 to well over 20 units per acre or from five or six thousand to more than 25,000 people per square mile (2000-8000 people per square kilometer). The lower figures are characteristic of recent suburban townhouse areas (figure 5), the higher ones of old Eastern cities like Philadelphia and Baltimore where millions of people live in mile after mile of identical rowhouses (figure 6). In addition to the rowhouse, single-family attached houses include the semi-detached or two-family house, and the zero-lot-line house which omits one or both side yards, and, by judicious placement of interior courtyards, largely eliminates party walls. Densities for these types are the same as for the lower range of rowhouses. The neighborhoods and districts which result from the construction of the various types of single-family attached housing have sufficient density to pass over the urban service and transit thresholds identified by Blumenfeld as disadvantages of ranch house suburbia.

Moving up the density scale from the various types of single units, the next major category has become defined in recent years as high-density, low-rise housing. All of the various types of walk-up apartment units and elevator units of about four stories or below fit in this category. Among the more characteristic types in addition to the garden apartments and converted brownstones shown in Figure 4 are combinations of townhouses and apartments, occasionally two sets of townhouses one on top of the other called maisonettes, four-plexes — a favorite among suburban speculators — and the ubiquitous 3-deckers of Boston, Chicago and St. Louis (figure 7). High density, low-rise units when assembled into neighborhoods and districts exhibit a very wide range of densities from as

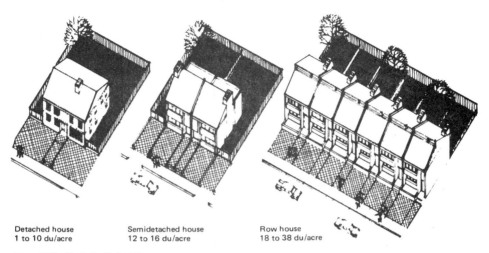

Detached house
1 to 10 du/acre

Semidetached house
12 to 16 du/acre

Row house
18 to 38 du/acre

Figure 2.20: Single-family houses.
· All interior spaces are within the private domain of the family.
· All grounds around the contained unit are for the private use of the family.
· There is a direct abutment between private grounds and the sidewalk.
· The domain of the house encompasses the street.

Private   Semiprivate   Semipublic   Public

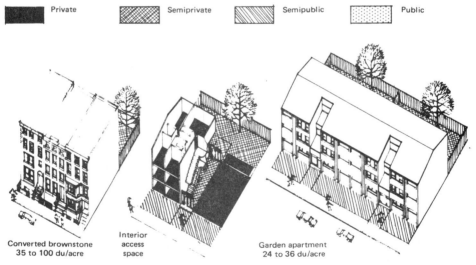

Converted brownstone
35 to 100 du/acre

Interior
access
space

Garden apartment
24 to 36 du/acre

Figure 2.21: Walk-up apartments.
· Private space is within the apartment unit only.
· The interior lobby, stairs, and corridor are semiprivate.
· Grounds can be designated for one family but are commonly shared by all the families in the building.
· Only a small number of families (three to six) are required to share interior space and grounds.
· The street is within the sphere of the dwelling.

Figure 4 Comparative housing design types emphasizing the disposition of public and private space (Reproduced from Newman)

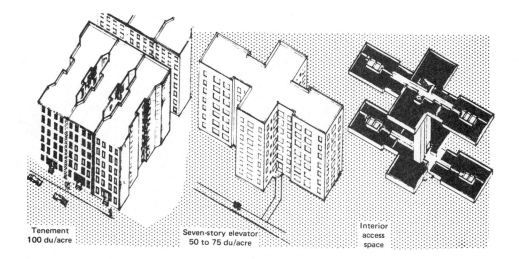

Tenement
100 du/acre

Seven-story elevator
50 to 75 du/acre

Interior
access
space

Figure 2.22: Intermediate high-rise buildings.
· Private space exists only within the apartment units.
· The interior circulation spaces, stairs, lobby, elevators, and corridors are
  shared by many families and so are semipublic in nature.
· The grounds vary in nature from semipublic to public.
· The street is only marginally associated with the domain of the building
  or project.

| ▉ Private | ▨ Semiprivate | ▨ Semipublic | ▢ Public |

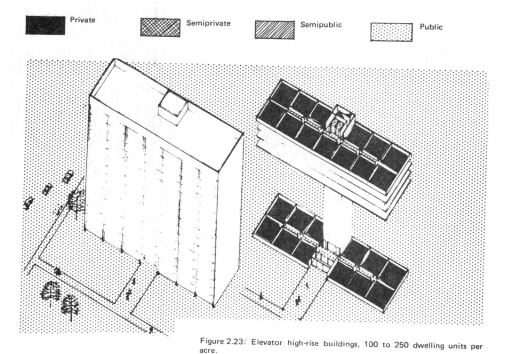

Figure 2.23: Elevator high-rise buildings, 100 to 250 dwelling units per
acre.
· Private space exists only within the apartment units.
· The interior circulation spaces and the grounds are public in nature.
· There is no association between buildings and street.

low as 10 to a top limit of as many as 80 units per acre, from 6,000 to 50,000 persons per square mile. (2,500-20,000 per square kilometer).

Figure 5 Suburban townhouse or rowhouse development in New York State Densities here are about 10 or 12 dwelling units per acre though over large areas openspace and other uses tend to reduce effective density. (Photograph by Davis)

Figure 6 Historic and modern rowhouses in the Georgetown area of Washington, DC, one of the best known rowhouse districts in the country The structure on the left is about 150 years old, the other much newer perhaps only twenty years old. Densities range around 25 units to the acre or perhaps 15,000 persons per square mile. (Photograph by Editors)

Figure 7 Modern three-decker apartments in Madison, Wisconsin This example shows the openness and residential quality possible in medium density, multi-family development. The density in this example is somewhat less than 25 dwelling per acre. Older three-decker development often reached substantially higher densities. Note the raised basement for parking which contributes to the spacious quality. (Photograph by Editors)

Figure 8 A tenement and row house district in Hoboken, New Jersey, a satellite across the Hudson River from New York City The tight row of larger buildings in the upper left are typical tenements, the rest are row houses usually divided internally so that there is one dwelling per floor, a type of unit called flat. Overall this area has a high density, about 100 units per acre or about 50,000 people per square mile. Note the canyon-like street spaces. (Photo by Regional Plan Association of New York)

The many forms of high density, low-rise housing illustrate an important urban design corollary of house type. An urban street lined with 3-deckers (figure 7) presents the appearance and general environmental quality of a residential area complete with shade trees, front yards, ornamental plantings, and sufficient space to somewhat play down the predominance of automobiles. In contrast, high density, low-rise housing built to its maximum intensity, without front and side yards, can present the hard, urban quality associated with New York City's tenement districts (figure 8). Without greenspace or foliage, the street jammed with vehicles, this kind of district seems to many people to be devoid of welcoming residential qualities. Urban designers and planners concerned with the environment, and conscious of these enormous differences, see decisions about house form and density as crucial to the quality of life. What may be a simple legal and commercial transaction, a change in the zoning laws governing development, for instance, may be seen by these professionals as a fundamental change in the quality of life.

One final broad type of housing merits a place in this taxonomy, the elevator apartment building. Like high density, low-rise housing this category also comes in a wide variety of specific types. The diagrams of figure 4 show three that are particularly characteristic of New York, the tenement (originally built as a six-story walk-up), the mid-rise or intermediate high-rise and the true high-rise of more than seven stories. Figure 9 shows the densely clustered high-rise of

Figure 9 The Kips Bay middle-income, highrise apartment project in midtown Manhattan
In the background between the highrise buildings are first, a row of New York "old law" tenements, then mixed apartments and industrial loft buildings with highrise office structures in the extreme background. (Photo by Tsuji)

midtown Manhattan. These contain as many as 400 dwellings per acre and house more than 100,000 people per square mile (nearly 40,000 per square kilometer). In contrast, the infamous Pruitt-Igoe public housing project in St. Louis, often thought to epitomize the evils of high-rise housing, contained 55 apartments per acre (figure 10). This is equivalent to a gross density of about 15,000 people per square mile, less than many low-rise and townhouse neighborhoods.

Figure 10 The Pruitt-Igoe low-rent, public housing project in St. Louis, Missouri shortly after it opened in 1955 It was torn down in 1976. The design of the highrise structures and the lack of site landscaping are typical of such projects in large cities. (Photograph by Mizuki)

As is the case with other house forms, high-rise structures can be designed in a variety of ways which give different qualities to the urban environment. In the central areas of older cities they may line streets solidly up to ten stories or more, creating not only very high gross densities but a very dominant, walled canyon, visual effect (figure 9). In contrast, the individual high-rise structures may be spaced out as they were at Pruitt-Igoe, thus lowering the overall density and providing open space around the buildings.

Open space, the system of streets, sidewalks and other public rights-of-way, various community facilities ranging from schools and churches to playgrounds and athletic fields, local stores and business services, are usually seen by architects and planners as an integral part of house design — together they make up the physical neighborhood. This view is the chief normative contribution of the various urban designers to American housing — to the world, in fact. First clearly articulated by Clarence Perry in the 1920s as the Neighborhood Unit Formula (figure 11), this idea has been incorporated in the city building processes of both governments and private sector housing developers. The modern suburban community perhaps illustrates this most clearly (figure 12). In large developments such as the Levittowns of the 1950s and 1960s, and the large planned unit condominium developments of today, the coordinated and integrated design of housing and the total neighborhood represents a high point in environmental design.

In recent years a much reduced version of the Neighborhood Unit Formula has become a dominant form of housing design. Most often referred to by a name derived from zoning or land use control jargon, the Planned Unit Development or PUD treats a relatively large tract of land and the housing units on it as a single

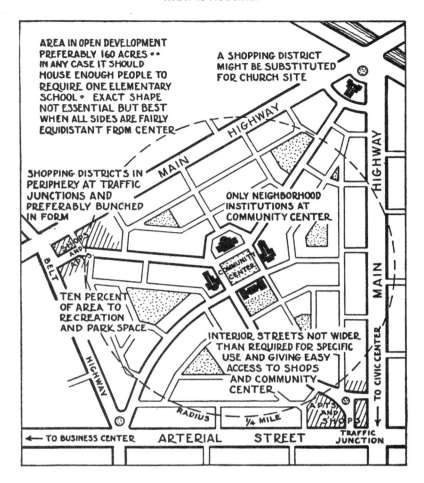

AREA IN OPEN DEVELOPMENT PREFERABLY 160 ACRES •• IN ANY CASE IT SHOULD HOUSE ENOUGH PEOPLE TO REQUIRE ONE ELEMENTARY SCHOOL • EXACT SHAPE NOT ESSENTIAL BUT BEST WHEN ALL SIDES ARE FAIRLY EQUIDISTANT FROM CENTER

A SHOPPING DISTRICT MIGHT BE SUBSTITUTED FOR CHURCH SITE

HIGHWAY

MAIN

HIGHWAY

SHOPPING DISTRICTS IN PERIPHERY AT TRAFFIC JUNCTIONS AND PREFERABLY BUNCHED IN FORM

ONLY NEIGHBORHOOD INSTITUTIONS AT COMMUNITY CENTER

SHOPS AND APTS

BELT

COMMUNITY CENTER

MAIN

TEN PERCENT OF AREA TO RECREATION AND PARK SPACE

INTERIOR STREETS NOT WIDER THAN REQUIRED FOR SPECIFIC USE AND GIVING EASY ACCESS TO SHOPS AND COMMUNITY CENTER

TO CIVIC CENTER

HIGHWAY

RADIUS ¼ MILE

APTS AND SHOPS P

← TO BUSINESS CENTER ARTERIAL STREET TRAFFIC JUNCTION

Figure 11 The Neighborhood Unit Formula, a set of principles put forth by Clarence Perry in the 1920's, and since then widely influential in the design of residential areas (Reproduced from the New York Regional Plan)

entity (figure 13). Rather than assigning individual lots to individual units or structures, in the PUD land is treated as a single indivisible site serving all units and providing for considerable diversity of use. In addition to yards associated with individual units, PUDs borrow from the NUF to provide common open space and recreation facilities and superblock type vehicular-pedestrian separation. Though PUDs are not limited to use with any particular structural type of dwelling, they tend to be used most frequently with various forms of high-density, low-rise housing such as townhouses. PUDs frequently embody condominium-type ownership, that is ownership that uncouples the enclosed unit from a specific plot of ground and provides for joint or common ownership of the site. Together the high-density, low-rise units and the micro-Neighborhood Unit Formula land planning have given rise to a physical design characteristic of the present generation in American housing.

Comments: 1. Though house design and its extensions into neighborhood design

Figure 12 Aerial view of Levittown in Fairless Hills, Pennsylvania This is one of the largest and most successful of the new towns built in accordance with many of the provisions of Perry's Neighborhood Unit Formula. Note the school in the center of the view, the wooded openspace that connects it with the various subareas the school serves, and the outdoor recreation facilities in the openspace below and to the left of the school. No major streets pass through this neighborhood. However, with all of its advanced features it is still practically indistinguishable from the low density suburban area shown in figure 3 above. (Photo by Regional Plan Association of New York)

represent an important and useful way of looking at housing, it is necessary to refer again to the caution expressed by Newman in the selection preceding this note. He calls attention to the dominant importance of social over physical factors. Social research suggests this is as true of the perfectly planned neighborhood as of the slum. For example, a recent study of planned new towns by Shirley Weiss and others showed satisfaction varied with income level. The higher the income the more satisfied people were with their neighborhoods. Speaking metaphorically, general satisfaction with life provides a set of rose-colored glasses through which we see our housing.

2. All of the various perspectives outlined in this chapter reinforce the opening assertion: housing denotes disparate things which must be consumed together. This point is critically important. In reading the chapters that follow, which for analytical purposes dissect housing in a variety of ways, do not forget that in actuality such dissection is impossible. Housing is a complex, indivisible bundle of many, many things, some we only imperfectly understand.

Figure 13 A modern Planned Unit Development that adheres to many of the Neighborhood Unit Formula principles. This project which provides subsidized housing for elderly people is organized around a central open space. No streets pass through the site so that the porches of the cottages face a completely pedestrian environment. (Photo by Hirshen)

BIBLIOGRAPHY

What Is Housing
C. Wedin & L. Nygren, Housing Perspectives: Individuals and Families (1976)
   A collection of introductory readings from a great variety of viewpoints.

The Social Science Perspective
C. Cooper, Easter Hill Village: Some Social Implications of Design (1975)
   An exhaustive case study.

R. Gutman & D. Popenoe, Eds., Neighborhood, City, and Metropolis (1970)
   Collection of introductory readings.

Physical Design
S. Davis, Ed., The Form of Housing (1977)
   An up to date collection of articles dealing mainly with multi-family housing
   and mobile homes.

R. Kennedy, The House and the Art of its Design (1953)
   The classic work on home design.

Chapter 2

THE HOUSING ECONOMY

Because housing is such a complex bundle, thinking about housing demands powerful, simplifying, analytical perspectives. Economics, of the various possible disciplines that might provide such insights, offers those that are most generally useful. Current practice among people concerned with understanding housing problems draws more from economics than any other discipline. Among these perspectives is the idea of a housing economy, an idea that serves as a starting point for the chapter.

An economy is a system of resource allocation, production, distribution, and consumption. The housing economy, then, is such a system directed at the broad bundle of goods and services included in the idea of housing. Of particular interest in thinking about housing are ideas that deal with change and equilibrium among the various aspects of the economy, and with the processes that connect these aspects to one another. Housing economist Frank de Leeuw gives focus to these interests in the following words.

> "Suppose you are revisiting a metropolitan area after ten years' absence. You used to know a great deal about the location and quality of housing within different geographic zones of the area. You know from other sources that population has grown a great deal since you were there and that incomes are generally a good deal higher, although there has been an influx of low-income families as well. You know that employment is less concentrated in the center of the city than it used to be and you know that the cost of new construction has risen a great deal. As you return, you speculate about what types of households will be living where, about what will have happened to the quality and price of the existing stock of housing, and about how much new construction will have occurred and who will occupy new units.
>
> "After some thought you realize that there are basically three kinds of behavior involved in answering the questions in your mind. There is first of all the behavior of households, both individually and through laws and social pressures, in deciding where to live, how much to spend on housing, and how to relate to the stock of dwelling units in other ways. There is in the second place the behavior of owners of the existing housing stock — their decisions to improve their properties, to allow them to deteriorate, or to attempt to remove them from the stock. Finally, there is the behavior of builders of new units — their decisions about the number, quality and price of the units to be added to the stock."
>
> F. de Leeuw, The Distribution of Housing Services: A Mathematical Model (Washington, DC: The Urban Institute 1971).

De Leeuw's brief verbal picture or model of the housing economy raises at least two possible lines of inquiry. It leads to questions about the overall context in which these events take place. Secondly, it calls attention to specific events, especially transactions matching people and housing to each other, and suggests inquiry into these processes. The second set of questions come in the province orthodox economists call microeconomics. The first set belongs to the world of

39

macroeconomics and the national economy. Most of this chapter will deal with the microeconomic category; but, before turning to this, a brief excursion into the larger realm is necessary, with help from the words of the now familiar housing economist, Wallace Smith.

W. SMITH, HOUSING: THE SOCIAL AND ECONOMIC ELEMENTS 10-14, 34-39 (1970)

The Dual Nature of the Housing Sector

In most nations the housing sector — the portion of the economic system which is concerned with the production, management, and distribution of housing — is a blend of private enterprise and government activity. The nature of the mix varies greatly from nation to nation, but the role of government is substantial even in those countries which generally allow the marketplace the greatest freedom in making economic decisions. Public and private components of the housing sector are generally so closely interdependent that the housing sector may be said to have a dual decision-making system. It is important to understand why this is so. The dual nature of the housing sector makes economic analysis of housing both more difficult and more necessary.

Institutions

The private component of the housing sector — that is, the whole range of business activities associated with housing — is heavily dependent for efficient operation upon the existence of a set of laws, institutions, and public agencies. It cannot function effectively unless the community has recognized and clarified the concept of real-property ownership. . . . [Smith next discusses the legal and financial institutions which are critical to the functioning of the housing market. — Eds.]

Public Welfare

Given the best possible set of supporting institutions and well-informed and motivated entrepreneurs, the private component of the housing sector ordinarily does not serve all the housing needs which the public, as a community, may feel should be served. Low-income families are an obvious case in point. The most effective and efficient private housing industry will not meet a housing need which is not backed up with purchasing power. Here, and in similar situations involving public concern about unmet housing needs, the public component of the housing sector acquires an additional function. It must change the nature of demand by means of subsidy or of supply by means of public investment (also involving subsidy) so that these nonmarket needs are satisfied.

Thus, the private component of the housing sector is unable to provide certain legal and financial institutions which are necessary for its own efficient functioning, and it is unable to provide for some housing requirements which communities — because housing is a necessity of physical and social life — feel must be met. The public component of the housing sector has a twofold function; it must act to facilitate the efficient operation of the private component and it must subsidize the housing sector as a whole in some fashion to overcome problems of socially inadequate market demands for housing.

Interactions

It follows that the development of public policy with respect to housing requires a particular type of economic analysis. The establishment of legal and financial institutions will stimulate private housing activity, while public subsidies will change the direction of that activity as well as stimulating it further. In formulating a public program for housing, it is necessary to know not only the current limitations or faults of the private housing-market equilibrium, but also the manner in which that equilibrium would be changed by particular proposals for government activity in connection with housing. The private portion of the sector will respond to changes in institutions or in purchasing power available for housing. The responses may or may not produce the overall changes in the supply and use of housing which is contemplated by the public program. The manner in which a set of institutions is created may freeze a portion of the nation's capital market into a structure which is not best suited to the nation's long-term needs. Housing activities may, at one time or another, be overstimulated or depressed by the very institutions and systems which were intended to make it perform efficiently. The form of a subsidy to needy families or to accomplish other social purposes may produce private housing-market responses which aggravate those needs still further. Public policy does not simply amend what has taken place in the market. It acts as the catalytic agency to alter the very character of that market.

[The Smith reading that deals with housing status in Chapter 1 comes at this point in the original. After this a brief introduction to economics as resource allocation follows, illustrated by Table 1 showing selected dollar values for components of the national housing economy. This table is updated here to include 1977 figures. — Eds.]

Table 1. The Housing Sector in the U.S. Economy, 1968 and 1977 (in billions of dollars)

	1968	1977
Gross National Product	$860.7	$1965.1
Gross Private Domestic Investment	127.5	307.0
Structures	87.1	151.0
New Construction	84.2	178.0
Private	56.6	142.1
Nonfarm residential	28.4	87.9
New housing units	22.4	70.7
Personal Consumption Expenditures	$533.7	$1255.3
Housing services, including imputed value of owner-occupied dwellings	76.2	278.8

SOURCE: *Economic Report of the President* (Washington, D.C., 1969, 1978) (various tables).

A Macroeconomic View

The position of the housing sector in the economy as a whole, and some of the important activities within the housing sector are represented in Figure 2. The starting point is *Total current output,* the aggregate volume of valuable goods and services which the national (or local) economy produces in a period of time such as one year. Gross National Product is another term used to describe the aggregate. A portion of this current output consists of goods and services which are destined for the housing sector, such as the new houses which are constructed

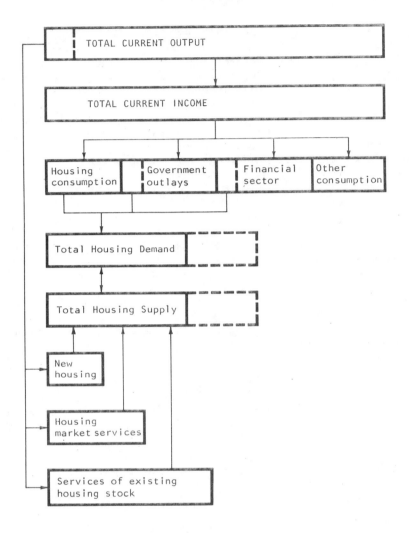

Figure 2 The housing sector — a macroeconomic view (Redrawn from Smith)

during the period; the land which is prepared for housing, renovation or maintenance of older housing units; personal services in managing existing dwellings, and in facilitating transfers of dwellings both new and old (such as brokerage, appraising, and the processing of loan applications). An important part of the housing sector's share in total output consists of housing services performed by previously constructed dwellings ($76.2 billion worth in 1968), although we may question whether this is really a "resource-consuming" activity. The long, branching arrow on the the left side of the diagram shows that these several parts of the community's current economic output become elements of supply in the current housing market.

The production of total current output gives rise to incomes in the form of wages, rents, interest, and profits. These incomes are disposed of for consumption, for saving and investment, and for taxes. A portion of the household consumption expenditure is for housing, but we must be careful to distinguish current expenditures for housing services — that is, for "shelter" enjoyed during the current period — from capital expenditures which reflect changes in ownership of dwellings which will produce services during future periods. *Housing consumption* in the diagram represents only the purchase of current services.

A portion of the income which goes to government is spent on housing. Directly or indirectly government may provide housing for some needy persons in the community or, through tax exemptions, may allow many people in the community to enjoy more housing than their own current incomes would permit. Since the "housing sector" can be thought of as including those community facilities which are important to housing though not part of dwelling structures, we can think of government outlays in the housing sector as including the construction and maintenance of utility systems, streets, and perhaps even schools and firehouses. The concept of the "housing sector" is rather elastic on this point, but whatever we include or exclude in the definition of expenditures on housing, we must reflect in the definition of housing sector output. If we include the expenditure on streets in the total of housing demand, for example, we must include the services provided by streets in the measure of housing sector output.

The block labeled *Financial sector outlays* represents the net investment activities of financial institutions and individuals. Since dwellings are durable goods, a large portion of their value or cost when first produced is investment rather than consumption of current services. Buildings are constructed mostly with funds earmarked as savings rather than with current household budgets for shelter. Thus, the financial sector, which is a pool of the community's current savings, plays a very important role in determining the rate of growth or improvement of the housing stock.

Total housing demand is the sum of housing consumption expenditures, government outlays for housing, and housing investments by the financial sector. *Total housing supply,* as already mentioned, brings together the increment in the housing stock, services related to the functioning of the housing market, and the intangible services derived from the older housing stock by virtue of the fact that it is occupied and enjoyed. Demand and supply meet in an allocation process which we usually think of as a "market." The outcome of the market decisions can be expected to influence the scale and composition of the housing sector's share in total current output of a subsequent period, so that the large process which we are describing is a dynamic one, constantly adjusting itself over time.

The dotted extensions of the *Total housing demand* and *supply* blocks signify that the significant market process in the housing sector is not limited to current output or current income. Exchanges of previously constructed dwellings also occur within any housing sector, and these exchanges may be important to secure the maximum economic advantage from what is, in effect, "sunk capital." These exchanges require the use of current resources (already represented in the diagram) and, in the long run at least, may exert an important influence upon the character and the scale of current housing sector outputs, helping to determine, for example, whether the new houses to be built are for low-income or for high-income families. The housing sector thus deals with the administration of previously accumulated capital as well as with decisions about the creation and use of new capital. It also deals with a variety of current services.

The figure is described as a *Macroeconomic View* of the housing sector. Macroeconomics is concerned primarily with the aggregate size of current production. It is a study of the size of the "forest" rather than the fate of individual "trees." Total current production, or GNP, is made up of output for the housing sector, the nondurable consumption goods sector, the balance of the government sector, the sectors for consumer services and other nondurable goods, and so on, so that macroeconomics is concerned to some extent with the composition of total output as well as its aggregate value. Exactly what types of houses are produced, or what type of bread is baked by bakeries, is a matter beyond the realm of macroeconomics. We may say that macroeconomics is also concerned with the origin of total housing demand, so that it recognizes the divisions among housing consumption expenditures, government outlays for housing, and financial sector outlays for housing which are shown in the diagram. Macroeconomics does not deal with the output of an individual firm, however.

Microeconomics, on the other hand, is concerned with the manner in which equilibrium is reached when total housing demand confronts total housing supply. Each individual in the marketplace must be considered, at least in principle, by microeconomics. In an important sense, microeconomics is likely to involve optimizing concepts such as the maximization of utility by individual consumers or of profit by individual producers, while macroeconomics seeks only to simulate or forecast the overall outcome without attempting to show that what is produced is either rational or optimal. Microeconomics explicitly deals with individual transactions and, in particular, with transactions involving the previously acquired stock of dwellings, while the role of the older stock in macroeconomics is limited, indirect, and obscure.

With this diagram before us, we can list the main types of resource allocation questions which arise in the housing sector, under the two headings of "macro" and "micro."

Macro

What proportion of the *Total current output* (GNP) is for the housing sector?

How much of this housing sector share of total current output is accounted for by new dwellings (or related facilities), by services related to the operation of the housing sector, and by the utilization of the previously accumulated stock of dwellings, respectively?

How much of *Total current income* is to be used for the consumption of current housing services?

How much of total *Government outlay* is to be for housing (or housing-related) facilities?

How much of total net savings and investment activities by the financial sector will be directed to the housing sector?

Micro

Which households will occupy which dwelling units in the enlarged and altered housing stock?

What prices will each of these households pay for current housing services yielded by the dwellings they occupy?

Which households will benefit from government outlays on housing and in what way?

What transactions will occur within the housing sector, between which individuals, involving which kinds of business services and what manner of investment transactions?

What kinds of new dwellings will be created?

What capital values will accrue to each unit of the housing stock?

What alterations or repairs will be made on each unit of the previously existing housing stock?

Comments: 1. Of the substantive points raised by this material from Smith, perhaps the most important is the sharp relative gain shown on Table 1 in personal consumption housing expenditures taken against other national economic indicators. This represents an important recent change. During most of the Twentieth century the housing share has declined as new sectors such as automobiles have emerged. Now that trend seems to be reversing. On the broadest level this trend seems to mean that the importance of housing in the national economy is growing. This raises a nice question. What does this growth imply? In terms of the questions raised by Smith under the heading "Macro," what problems may arise from this change in relative expenditures? What actions of the government and private sectors would provide appropriate responses to these problems? Asking these questions highlights the kinds of issues involved in housing at the macro-level. These questions will reappear later in this book, especially in the problem chapters of Part II, and particularly in Chapter 7.

2. At the end of this excerpt Smith introduces the concept "microeconomic." This concept ties back to the internal processes within specific parts of the housing economy that were noted with respect to de Leeuw's brief word picture, supra, p. 39. Smith offers another useful diagram and some explanatory words that illustrate the housing economy seen from a microeconomic perspective. He emphasizes the roles and transactions on which this view focuses. How do the various actors, institutions and transactions relate to the "Micro" questions he asks in the passage just above?

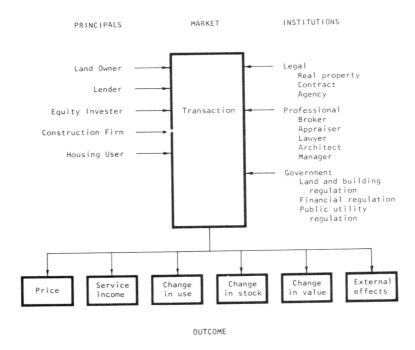

Figure 3 The housing sector—a microeconomic view (Redrawn from Smith)

Figure 3 is a *Microeconomic View* of the housing sector. Its central element is the individual housing-market transaction. This might be the purchase of a home by a family, or the renting of an apartment. It might be the granting of a mortgage loan. or the acquisition of a residential property for investment. It might be the construction of a new residential structure, or the improvement of an existing one. Whatever its nature, it is an individual event involving one item of real property and two principals (at least). These principals "meet" in the market and the conduct of their meeting is affected by a set of institutions such as those mentioned along the right-hand side of the figure. The outcome of the transaction is a set of effects such as those along the bottom of the figure. Much of the subsequent discussion in this book concerns the nature of principals, institutions, and effects in housing sector transactions. . . .

The housing sector is portrayed in this microeconomic view as a process of business decision-making. We might also like to think of microeconomics as a series of more or less physical actions — the arrival of new households in the community, the clearing of land, installation of utility systems, construction and management of dwellings, etc. These tangible aspects of the housing sector's performance may, however, simply be thought of as implied by, or following necessarily from, a business transaction. If a landowner secures financing, and contracts with a home-building firm, houses will be built. The physical aspects do not disclose their origin; we must look into the decision-making process if we are to understand why tangible aspects of the housing sector come into being.

W. Smith, supra p. 40, at 41, 42, 44.

3. Homebuilders, real estate developers, urban planners, other professionals and the economists who work with them have given a great deal of attention to the transaction part of the Smith diagram. In order to make masses of transactions manageable from an analytic standpoint some particular set of transactions is defined as a market. Usually the definition starts with a geographic dimension, most commonly a metropolitan area, or, to facilitate use of U.S. Census data, a Standard Metropolitan Statistical Area or SMSA. Other geographic subdivisions and divisions along lines defined by the various roles, institutions and housing types may be used to further subdivide markets. The market is then articulated in terms of the bundles of housing services or supply on one side, and the various consumers or demand on the other. Professionals and economists dealing with housing markets usually must deal with them dynamically, in terms of change over time. Figure 1 gives a very simplified flow chart representation or model of a housing market according to this perspective. The processes symbolized by the arrows and the quantities by the boxes represent the factors with which experts work. Texts on housing from the standpoint of these professionals and the methods they use in practice incorporate this kind of an armature or model to organize their content (see for instance the Sumichrast and Seldin volume in the bibliography for this chapter).

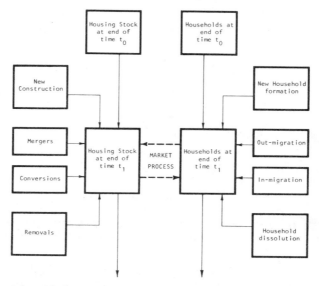

Figure 1 The housing market

The housing market represented in the above flow chart emphasizes changes over time in the numbers of dwelling units and households. It shows schematically how changes in the two sides of the market are functions of such factors as new construction, conversion of units to smaller ones, new household formation, and migration. The symbols t_0 and t_1 refer to any two times in sequence.

4. Subdivisions of the market provide key analytical categories for working with housing. The next short reading discusses them.

W. GRIGSBY, HOUSING MARKETS AND PUBLIC POLICY 33-35, 40 (1963)

Housing Submarkets — Components of Supply

"A housing market area is the physical area within which all dwelling units are linked together in a chain of substitution. . . . In a broad sense, every dwelling unit within a local housing market may be considered a substitute for every other unit. Hence, all dwelling units may be said to form a single market, characterized by interactions of occupancy, prices and rents. However, this view can be maintained only for the most general analysis and even then with great difficulty." In reality, the housing market in a given area consists of groups of submarkets which are related to one another in varying degrees. The test of whether two dwelling units are in the same submarket is "whether substitutability is sufficiently great to produce palpable and observable cross-relationships in respect to occupancy, sales, prices, and rents, or in other words, whether the units compete with one another as alternatives for the demanders of housing space."

The definition of submarkets is, of course, imperfect and somewhat arbitrary. There may, indeed, be closer interrelationships between units of ". . . two classes than between units within the same class." This is because in the real world there are no clean cutoff points between two submarkets, the chain of substitutions being a continuum with sharp breaks or gaps being the exception rather than the rule. Nevertheless, where the distance between two units on the continuum is large, they become weak substitutes and the price or rent behavior of one does not affect the other. Or to put the matter differently, if the distance on the continuum is great, the units will be good substitutes for only a small number of families. The units would be in different submarkets or perhaps even in different total markets.

The linkages between submarkets need not be direct. Bargain house prices in Area A might be completely ignored by potential home buyers in Area C if the latter area were too far distant. These prices might, however, attract a segment of the market from Area B to Area A. This shift might in turn create values in B which would serve to capture a segment of the potential in C. Similarly, although expensive dwelling units may never drop in value far enough to affect prices directly in the lower quality market, they may do so indirectly by initiating a chain reaction on the price continuum. Thus, $20,000 units could move downward to $15,000, causing $15,000 units to decline to $12,000 and so on. It is generally reasoned, and no doubt correctly, that the effect would gradually dissipate as it continued along the chain and that the longer the chain, the less the possibility of a market change at one end appreciably affecting the other end.

The linkages are also not necessarily of equal length in both directions. For example, a price decline of 10 percent among medium-priced single-family homes in Suburb A might reduce the demand for lower-priced homes in Suburb B, but a similar price decline in B might not have any effect on the market in A. A striking example of lack of symmetry is provided by a comparison of the owner-occupancy and rental sectors of the market. Because renters have relatively greater mobility than owners, bargain prices in the single-family home market would generally result in a more significant shift in tenure than would be the case if correspondingly low offerings became available in apartment structures.

[Grigsby's development of the submarket concept turns at this point in his book to several important attributes of the linkages that connect them. Among the attributes he discusses are these: Diffusion: for instance, a price change in one submarket may have effects that are diffused among numerous others. Attenuation: racial barriers, inadequate transit, or other factors can act as barriers among submarkets. Several "continuums" or dimensions of linkage: e.g., "there is a location link, tenure link, type of structure link, value link, etc." Shifting linkages: e.g., relationships among submarkets change continuously, for example, "A new highway or bridge may shorten the location link between A and C and thereby lengthen, relatively, the link between A and B." Linkages among dissimilar units: this is a somewhat subtle but useful point on which it is worth returning directly to Grigsby. — Eds.]

The linkages discussed thus far refer to dwelling units that are on the market for sale or rent. For this group it is almost a tautology to say that similar dwelling units will be close substitutes. But there is, in addition, an extremely close and delicate relationship between the supply of housing on the market and the supply in use. Each home available for sale is a possible alternative accommodation to one currently occupied. This is true, of course, of all consumer durables. New cars must compete not only with used cars on dealers' lots, but also with those in family garages. The crucial point is that for the owner of a home, or a car, or a stove, or refrigerator, goods on the market which are identical to his own are not perfect substitutes; they are extremely poor ones. Nothing is to be gained by a trade, and typically an exchange would involve considerable cost. In the case of housing, the costs, in the form of moving expenses and fees incident to the transfer of title, are quite high; as a result, the good substitutes for a family already ensconced in a home are structures which are entirely different.

Comments: 1. Grigsby then proceeds to construct a matrix of submarkets, using the Philadelphia metropolitan area to illustrate his analysis. His principal point is that "The link distance between two submarkets is determined by the proportion of families in the first market who would react to a given change in the second market or vice versa." Therefore, we not only need an understanding of types of submarkets classified according to attributes of supply, "but also of the types of families that move among these structures and submarkets."

2. In this discussion of submarkets in the Philadelphia housing system, Grigsby places central emphasis on the same three questions raised by de Leeuw at the beginning of this chapter. He makes household behavior with respect to housing, the behavior of the owners and managers of housing, and the behavior of home builders the explanatory variables that dominate the behavior of the housing market as a whole. These factors, as seen by Grigsby, conform to the orthodox economist's concept of "economic man" and his behavior. This idea underlies the field of microeconomics that is discussed in relation to housing in the next note. The economists' man is concerned with maximizing individual satisfaction through the consumption of goods and services. This view of man does not include love, hate, power, dominance, cooperation, or such things as the possibility that satisfaction is not innate but socially constructed. In short, it ignores most of life. The structuralist and Marxist ideas cited later in this chapter draw on a different view of human nature and behavior. The empirical and institutionalist material that forms the bulk of the remainder of this book assumes a broader and more eclectic view than either of these poles.

3. To return to Grigbsy, the concepts of submarket and linkage have proved useful in many realms of theory and practice. They are closely tied to the ideas presented in Chapter 5 that deal with the concepts of filtering and neighborhood change. In dealing with housing problems they prove useful in almost all the contexts covered in Part II.

4. The microeconomic approach to thinking about housing tends to dominate the field. It *is* the mainstream, traditional way of thought in theory and practice, particularly in the academic world and closely related professional fields such as policy analysis and planning. No introductory collection of readings such as this one could do proper justice to the wealth of literature produced by the housing microeconomists. Textbooks, a large number of important monographs, and a flood of academic papers attest to its richness. The bibliography at the end of the chapter offers some suggestions for exploring the material. The following note attempts to briefly characterize some aspects of this set of ideas.

A NOTE ON MICROECONOMICS AND HOUSING

Orthodox microeconomics starts with a set of assumptions about human behavior, individually and in small groups or firms. These assumptions hold that behavior maximizes satisfactions in consumption and profits in production. Microeconomics explores the behavior of consumers, producers and firms under these assumptions, including their behavior with respect to one another. Microeconomics is particularly concerned with the way in which the quantity of things produced, or supply, and the amounts consumed, or demand, come into balance or equilibrium. Prices established in a market act as the equilibrating mechanism. In fact, in times past this field was called price theory.

As noted in Comment 2 above, the behavioral assumptions of microeconomics lead to a view at odds in important ways with the way most people experience life. Most of the time men, women and children simply do not govern their lives in ways that maximize satisfaction through consumption. In the case of housing, the complexity of the bundle defies such rationalizing behavior even if it were the norm. Though microeconomists have indifference curves and other useful tools for dealing with the ways people make tradeoffs among various satisfactions, these tools work only at very high levels of abstraction in dealing with housing. Safety, self-symbolization, property and privacy rights, investment, urban services, and neighbors, just do not fit together so that careful tradeoffs work very well in real life.

Some housing issues, however, can be modeled reasonably well by microeconomists, and the models are often useful in analysis and problem solving. Take, for instance, the effects of the current rising rate of household formation. This is an issue that dominates the housing market today and can be expected to dominate it well into the 1980s. Since housing is so complicated, fixed in space and necessarily expensive, parallel changes in supply occur slowly or not at all. The housing sector of the national economy is both slow to react and susceptible to counter-pressures from other sources. At the individual firm level, production is limited by local factors such as lack of available land because areas are built up or have come under rigid environmental controls. (See Chapter 11.)

Using the familiar supply and demand curves from elementary microeconomics, these relationships can be represented geometrically (figure 1). To start at the beginning before the rise in households occurs, the graph shows supply, S - S, demand, D - D, equilibrium price, P_1, and equilibrium quantity of housing services, Q_1, for either individuals or perhaps for some aggregate in a specific neighborhood. Now, suppose that population pressures on the neighborhood increase. The new people will compete for housing. At the individual and aggregate neighborhood level the available income that can pay for housing will increase. The result is a new demand schedule or curve D'-D'. Assuming no change in the supply schedule, a new equilibrium might be achieved at which a large quantity of housing services, Q_2, for the large population is made available at a higher price, P_2. In a built up neighborhood this might be achieved by conversions of large units to small, replacement of single family dwellings with multiples, or in-fill construction. In a suburban area still containing buildable land, new construction would be the expected response. At an individual level the increase in quantity might mean a move to a larger unit or the construction of an addition.

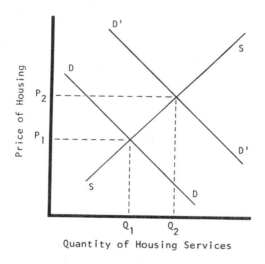

Quantity of Housing Services

Figure 1 Idealized Supply and Demand Curves for Housing The graph can be interpreted as follows. If the quantity demanded at various prices is represented by line (or curve) D, and similarly the quantity that will be supplied by line S, the vertical position of their intersection, P_1, represents the equilibrium or market clearing price. At this price a corresponding equilibrium quantity of housing services, Q_1, is provided. This figure has been constructed to show how a change in demand leads to a new equilibrium price. An increase in solvent demand can be represented by shifting the demand curve to the right, from D to D'. Assuming no change on the supply side of the market, in order for the quantity of housing services to increase to meet the new demand, from Q_1 to Q_2, a new, higher equilibrium price will be required. Thus, given these conditions, an increase in demand from D to D' leads to the housing price rise between P_1 and P_2.

Actually, in the short run the supply of housing cannot increase much no matter what the increase in demand. This is called inelastic supply.* Geometrically, this is represented by a vertical line for the supply curve (figure 2). The whole effect of the change in demand is to increase price and the increase is much steeper than in the ideal case. Compare P_3 with P_2. In the short run quantity remains constant.

---

*Elasticity is a term used to denote the quality of the relationship between two factors, in this case quantity versus price. An elastic relationship denotes a situation in which a change in price would be reflected by a proportionate change in quantity. An inelastic relation is one in which a change in one factor has little or no effect on the other factor.

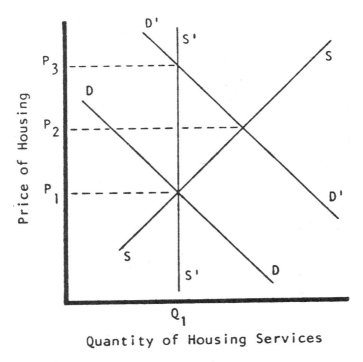

Figure 2 Inelastic Supply of Housing Idealized supply and demand curves for housing modified to approximate what actually seems to happen in the short run when demand increases. Since it takes considerable time to build new units, even an increase in solvent demand that means higher prices will be paid does not generate immediate additions to the supply of housing services. This situation is called an inelastic supply with respect to price. It is depicted graphically by a vertical supply curve. In the case shown in this figure, when demand increases from D to D', instead of reaching a new equilibrium where higher prices lead to larger quantities, the supply curve turns vertical. This means that no matter how much price increases supply remains constant. Thus, instead of the smaller price increase, P_1 to P_2, shown in figure 1, prices will go up much more reaching point P_3 yet not producing any additional housing services. Though idealized, this graph does picture the inflationary pressures experienced in the real world during a crisis housing shortage.

In the somewhat longer run the supply side of the market will respond usually to increases in demand. Since the early 1970s, however, it has responded according to new supply schedules that require constantly higher prices for similar quantities. The reasons for this are complicated. Most inputs to new housing production, especially land and financing costs, have risen more steeply than overall price levels and incomes. Linkages between the new construction submarket and the rest of the housing supply assure that price rises in one will pull up prices in the other. When these forces are coupled with substantial increases in demand the staggering housing inflation of the last few years results. Figure 3 shows this trend in terms of the geometry of microeconomics. The new supply curve requires a higher rate of expenditures from consumers to achieve the higher quantity of housing, Q_2, hence yet another higher demand curve, D"-D". Note the new level of the equilibrium price, P_4. As this process repeats over time, prices continue to spiral upwards. In a vastly oversimplified way this depicts the housing crisis of the late 1970s and early 1980s.

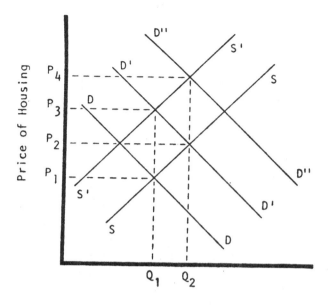

Quantity of Housing Services

Figure 3 Idealized supply and demand curves modified to approximate what actually seems to happen in the longer run when demand increases. Over a period of time, the higher prices resulting from the demand change from D to D' will probably stimulate the construction of some additional new units. But at the same time production cost will probably increase too, in part because the prices of everything tend to rise together. This means that for a given quantity of housing services prices must increase. It is depicted graphically by the leftward movement of the supply curve from S to S'. This in turn means that to achieve an equilibrium price for the increased quantity of housing services originally sought by the demand increase prices will have to increase still further. This can only happen if solvent demand goes still higher. Graphically this is shown by the shift from D to D' to achieve quantity Q_2 being parallelled by a shift in supply from S to S' which then requires the still higher price P_4, and higher demand curve D", in order to achieve equilibrium at Q_2. This sequence of alternating rightward shifts in demand and leftward shifts in supply, and the resultant sequence of ever higher prices, P_1, P_2, P_3, and P_4 depicts the inflationary housing cost spiral characteristic of the 1970s.

Theory and practice in microeconomics have moved far beyond the simple geometry of supply and demand graphs. Nowadays it is a heavily mathematical discipline that speaks in the language of calculus, linear algebra, and statistics. Welfare economics, a branch of microeconomics, has been applied to social justice issues and normative questions about what ought to be. It has become a main foundation for professional and theoretical work in policy. Among the ideas derived from welfare economics that are most widely used in thinking about housing are the concepts "public good" and "merit good." Public good refers to things like air quality from which "each member of society gains satisfaction from the total output," and "no one's satisfaction is diminished by the satisfaction of others." Neighborhood quality is a public good to the inhabitants of the given neighborhood. Rationally allocating resources to produce public goods and distributing the costs of production pose problems not solved by the orthodox microeconomics of the firm.

Merit good refers to something society believes people should have though some people may not be willing and able to pay for it. Like public goods, merit goods pose perplexing problems of resource allocation and cost distribution. Housing of standard quality is a principal case in point. Since the rise of industrialized cities, a succession of social movements have more or less successfully established minimum standards for housing. These standards have been embodied in laws and government programs that either force or encourage specified levels of housing consumption. Housing code laws and public housing subsidies confirm that housing of such standards is a merit good in our society. Many of the problems covered in this book treat this aspect of housing. Much of the microeconomics of housing is concerned with these questions.

Another branch of microeconomics that has proved useful in thinking about housing comes from the marriage between it and the field of economic research methodology called econometrics. Econometrics uses statistics, especially regression analysis, to provide an empirical input into economic thinking. Using econometric techniques, housing analysts seek to test hypotheses about the housing economy and estimate values for the variables in microeconomists' equations.

To cite a case which has been worked over again and again during the last 20 years, experts have sought through econometrics an empirically based understanding of the income elasticity of housing demand. The question refers to whether changes in income lead to equivalent changes in housing demand. In other words, if a household's income doubles, will it seek to double the amount of housing consumed and pay double for it? When the question was first posed the answer seemed to be no. People would increase their expenditures but not proportionately. A short quote from noted housing economists Sherman Maisel and Louis Winnick gives the flavor of this research. They worked with data from a 1950 government survey of consumer expenditures in the U.S.

> The influence of income (without differentiating between permanent and transitory components) appears pervasive. Whatever the principle of classification, housing expenditures are seen to rise with income but at a lesser rate.... [A]verage housing expenditures, including utilities and negligible amounts spent for vacation housing, show a clear tendency to increase for successively higher (measured) income groups. Thus, families with measured income of less than $1,000 before taxes reported $335 annual housing expenditures, families with $4,000 to $5,000, $662, and families with more than $10,000, $1,474. In proportion to measured income, housing expenditures decline from 53 percent for the lowest income group to 7.7 percent for the highest. For all families combined, the housing share was 14.1 percent before income taxes, 15.2 percent of income after taxes, and 15.7 percent of total current consumption expenditures.

S. Maisel and L. Winnick, Housing Expenditures: Elusive Laws and Intrusive Variance 371 (Reprint 25, Real Estate Reseach Program, Univ. of Cal. — Berkeley 1961)

The authors used regression analysis of this data to develop elasticity ratios. They found them to range between .49 and .72 with the average of all households at .6. This contrasts with later studies which have typically estimated elasticities nearer 1.0, meaning that housing demand *is* proportional to income. In Chapter 4 a more extended discussion of this question in a reading by de Leeuw provides a more detailed explanation of these findings.

Because of housing's complexity, microeconomists have had real difficulties dealing with many of its dimensions. In recent years mathematical and statistical analyses have seemed to provide better, more sophisticated tools, more appropriate for unravelling some of these complexities. Among these, one that has achieved rather wide currency is hedonic price theory. It is an approach to the analysis of equilibrium in markets for "heterogeneous, indivisible commodities where price is a function of the various indivisible characteristics." That housing is such a heterogeneous, indivisible commodity makes hedonic theory especially attractive to housing microeconomists. Among the books listed at the end of this chapter, the Kain and Quigley and the Straszheim volumes draw on it. The following excerpts from a Rand Corporation research report give some insight into what these studies are about, and more broadly, into the emerging state of the art in the orthodox microeconomics of housing.

B. ELLICKSON, B. FISHERMAN & P. MORRISON, ECONOMIC ANALYSIS OF URBAN HOUSING MARKETS 3-5, 10-11, 26, 28-29 (1977)

Hedonic Prices and Residential Choice

Housing markets are complex phenomena, not at all well suited to an application of the standard tools of price theory. Housing is not a homogeneous commodity, but rather a label for a collection of commodities that are all distinct to some degree. Houses exhibit substantial variation in structural features, lot size, characteristics of the surrounding neighborhood, and quality of local public services. Indeed, if we simply adopt the usual approach of indexing all commodities by location, it is clear that no two houses can be exactly alike. Housing is also not a divisible commodity. A consumer either chooses to reside in a particular dwelling or he does not. Thus, housing violates two of the most basic requirements for the application of standard price theory, the homogeneity and divisibility of commodities in a given market.

It should come as no surprise, therefore, that the economic theory of urban housing markets developed over the last two decades is not conventional. The essential break with tradition that made this development possible was a shift in focus from the housing commodities themselves, inherently indivisible and distinct, to their underlying characteristics. Consumer choice is assumed to depend solely on these characteristics, and, in this way, an infinite dimensional problem is reduced to one of manageable size and one that is amenable to the use of calculus.

The models that have emerged have reduced the problem still further to one involving only two characteristics, distance to the central business district and lot size. The development of this theory has greatly increased our understanding of the housing market. However, despite the flurry of papers in this area in recent years, there has been almost no progress in extending the theory to the case of multiple characteristics.

Because housing choice is clearly affected by much more than accessibility to the central business district and the amount of housing services, empirical studies have tended to eschew theoretical niceties in favor of the estimation of hedonic price functions. These functions relate the rent or value of a dwelling to a wide variety of characteristics, for example, accessibility of the central business district or other workplace locations, number of rooms, lot size, racial composition of the neighborhood, and the quality of local public services. . . . To most economists, it probably seems to be the most reasonable way to pose the problem. . . . The hedonic approach returns the notion of a housing commodity to its natural definition, the dwelling unit itself, despite the fact that this commodity is inherently indivisible. Housing attributes are not confused with commodities, but rather recognized as a means of capturing interrelations among housing units that reduce an infinite dimensional problem to one of manageable size. A principal advantage of this approach is that there is no barrier to increasing the number of characteristics to be considered in the analysis.

[An exposition of the mathematics of hedonic price theory follows. It concludes with a set of curves and equations that show the relationship between overall consumer utility or satisfaction and the hedonic price function that relates the price of a dwelling to its mutiple characteristics. — Eds.]

This diagrammatic interpretation of the hedonic theory provides a convenient bridge to existing work on residential choice. Much of the literature can be interpreted as arguing that as income increases, the slopes of the bid price curves will increase for desirable characteristics and decrease for undesirable characteristics. This leads to the conclusion that consumer income will be positively correlated with size of house and lot, quality of neighborhood, and of local public services and negatively correlated with structure age and accessibility (assuming that the value attached to commuting time increases with income). Whites are assumed willing to outbid blacks for houses in white neighborhoods, with segregation the result.

However, although these hypotheses about bid price curves seem reasonable, treating characteristics one at a time does not do justice to the complexity of the housing market. In the San Francisco metropolitan area, the setting for the empirical part of this report, simple correlations between household income and housing characteristics are not particularly strong. It is not difficult to see why this should be so. High-income households may opt for less accessible locations where land is inexpensive or for older housing when the neighborhood is well-maintained and the houses are large or otherwise of high quality; attractive housing in the central city may become available to low-income consumers if schools and other public services are poor.

The diagrammatic interpretation of the hedonic theory, by focusing attention on one characteristic at a time, obscures a primary virtue of the hedonic approach — its ability to treat housing characteristics simultaneously. The standard hypotheses of urban economics, translated into statements about bid price curves, seem most reasonable when interpreted *ceteris paribus*. Holding other characteristics fixed, it does seem plausible that willingness to pay for more rooms, a larger lot, a newer house, and so on will increase as income increases. When hedonic theory is used to treat housing attributes simultaneously, as we shall see later, the data support the standard hypotheses about bid price functions. Holding other characteristics fixed, high-income households are willing to pay more for larger houses and lots, better neighborhoods and schools, newer houses, and more accessible locations. When all components of housing bundles are taken into account, the model is able to make considerable sense out of the demographic patterns observed in the housing market.

. . . .

[At this point the authors return to an exposition of the theory in mathematical terms in which among other points they argue that it is better used to estimate probabilities that households of a given type will occupy housing having some specified attribute than to estimate contribution of attributes to bid prices as some authors have chosen to do. Following this analysis they turn to an empirical analysis that applies the model they have developed. They draw upon a data file composed of household and unit data for 5,152 cases in San Francisco and nearby

Alameda County. This data was examined in ways that disaggregated households by owners or renters, white or black, children or not, and income category. Nine dimensions of housing characteristics were included by appropriate indicators. Applying logit analysis, a stochastic model, the authors estimated the change in probability between households of two groups, with respect to whether they would occupy a dwelling having a specific attribute index value. One of the many tables produced is shown below along with an excerpt from the authors' interpretive comments. — Eds.]

Table 3. Logit estimates: white owners

Group	Constant	Z1	Z2	Z3	Z4	Z5	Z6	Z7	Z8	Z9	Z10	
					Parameter Estimates							
Y2,C	−11.1	−.16	−.08	.19	.25	.14	.08	.09	−.28	−.10	.36	
Y3,C	−35.5	−.49	−.37	.35	.71	.41	.34	−.03	−.14	−.05	.73	
Y1,NC	5.0	−.46	.57	.22	−.26	−.43	.43	.23	−.11	−.18	.47	
Y2,NC	−9.4	−.38	.25	.28	−.32	−.08	.38	.09	−.12	−.01	.50	
Y3,NC	−33.5	−.84	−.16	.43	.14	.40	.48	.05	−.07	0	.68	
					t Statistics (Group i Relative to Group j)[a]							
Group i	Constant	Z1	Z2	Z3	Z4	Z5	Z6	Z7	Z8	Z9	Z10	Group j
Y3,C	−6.40**	−4.06**	−3.75**	3.50**	7.93**	2.73**	2.13*	−.22	−1.24	−.43	7.54**	Y1,C
Y3,NC	−6.23**	−3.19**	−4.73**	−2.03*	4.37**	4.55**	.27	−1.38	.42	1.71	2.02*	Y1,NC
Y1,C	−.68	3.23**	−3.45**	−1.82	2.52*	2.11*	−2.12*	−1.59	.88	1.70	−3.90**	Y1,NC
Y2,C	−.31	1.84	−2.90**	−.92	6.52**	1.34	−1.81	0	−1.32	−.89	−1.51	Y2,NC
Y3,C	−.59	4.40**	−2.83**	−1.23	8.58**	.11	−1.37	−.75	−.87	−.48	98	Y3,NC

[a]A single asterisk indicates significance (two-tailed) at the .05 level; a double asterisk, at the .01 level.

[The codes for the various household groups represent the following:

Y2, C   = middle income, with children
Y3, C   = high income, with children
Y1, NC = low income, no children
Y2, NC = middle income, no children
Y3, NC = high income, no children

All are measured against the preferences of Y1, C or low income families with children. The Z values refer to indicators of the following characteristics:

Z1:   travel time to San Francisco
Z2:   age of dwelling unit
Z3:   lot size
Z4:   number of rooms
Z5:   median income of neighborhood
Z6:   median income of elementary school district
Z7:   proportion black students in elementary and high school
Z8:   proportion black students in junior high school
Z9:   proportion black households in neighborhood
Z10: hedonic residual

The hedonic residual "can be regarded as an index of those aspects of housing quality not captured" by the mathematical expression for the listed characteristics. — Eds.]

The results presented in Tables 3 and 4 [Table 4 showed similar statistics for white renters — Eds.] provide strong confirmation of several hypotheses that have appeared in the housing market literature. To interpret these results, we begin with a comparison across income classes, family composition held constant. With only a few minor exceptions, the coefficients of the first six characteristics and Z10 (the hedonic residual) exhibit the pattern one expects. The coefficients of Z1 (commuting time to San Francisco) tend to become increasingly negative as income increases, indicating a stronger relative preference for central locations on the part of higher income households — precisely the result one expects if higher income households attach a higher value to commuting time. Higher income households also prefer newer housing (characteristic Z2), larger lots (Z3), more rooms (Z4), a better neighborhood (as represented by Z5, median census tract income in 1960), and those aspects of housing quality captured by the hedonic residual (Z10). As household income increases, owners and renters with children attach more value to housing within the attendance area of elementary schools drawing from a higher income population (characteristic Z6), while households without children do not. Income differences appear to have no effect on the reaction of white households to racial composition of the schools (Z7 and Z8) or of the census tract (Z9) except for the stronger aversion of low-income renters to junior high schools with a higher proportion of black students. The absence of differences among whites may simply reflect the high degree of segregation in the housing market, a conjecture that receives strong support when we turn to the classification of blacks and whites.

The difference in parameter estimates for households with and without children, income held constant, is also reasonable with one major exception. Owners and renters with children put much more weight on number of rooms and, in the case of owners, newer houses at the expense of accessibility to the center of San Francisco. There is some evidence, particularly with renters, that households with children are more reluctant to live in areas served by schools with a higher proportion of black students, but the effect is not always statistically significant. The most disturbing result, as far as validity of the model is concerned, involves the coefficients on Z6: Owners and renters without children attach a higher value to areas served by elementary schools with higher median income than do their counterparts with school age children, and in half of the cases the difference in coefficients is statistically significant at the 5 percent level or better. It is not difficult to explain this anomaly. Households without children may anticipate their arrival or, in the case of older households, their housing choice may reflect the presence of children earlier in the life cycle. One explanation that apparently will not suffice is that median school income may be a poor proxy for school quality. In discriminant analyses with Berkeley excluded, where it was possible to add elementary third-grade reading scores to the model, both Z6 and the reading score exhibited this anomalous behavior. Rather than trying to explain away the result, we simply note that this is the one significant instance where the model failed to perform as expected.

Comments: The concluding interpretive comments by Ellickson illustrate some of the strengths and weaknesses of microeconomic analysis applied to housing. Working incrementally in a process that deductively proposes hypotheses then tests them empirically, the microeconomists have produced a picture of the housing economy's internal order. For example, the Ellickson study confirms both theory and intuition about changes in preference patterns as income changes. Given the logic of the field, such confirmation is a necessary precondition to legitimate action. Without it, public intervention could not be justified and private activity could be foolhardy.

To take this particular example one step farther, it is necessary to observe first that much public policy in recent years has revolved around whether or not upper income households could be encouraged to return to the central city. Deductive microeconomic theory has been of two minds. Some analysts, William Alonso among them, saw a simple trade-off between space and distance with space the superior good. Thus higher income people opted to gain space at the cost of travelling farther. Others deduced the opposite. Econometricians attempted to empirically verify one or the other theories but the evidence they have provided is mixed. Richard Muth, a leader among researchers in this field, has done studies that seem to confirm the preference for space over distance, though he suggests that age of housing instead of quantity of space may be the other term in the trade-off. (These studies are listed in the bibliography for this chapter.) The Ellickson study, one of the most recent and methodologically sophisticated, and one that is based upon a very promising data set, suggests that Alonso's theory and Muth's empirics are wrong. In several ways this contradiction illustrates the problems with a microeconomic approach. The following comment and the comments following the next reading discuss three of the more important among these problems.

R. MUTH, URBAN RESIDENTIAL LAND AND HOUSING MARKETS, IN H. PERLOFF AND L. WINGO, ISSUES IN URBAN ECONOMICS 305-06, 308-09, 312 (1968)

Most explanations for the growth of slum or poor-quality housing in recent years are based upon factors that influence its supply schedule. In many, the increase in the supply of poor-quality housing results from a decline in the demand for good quality housing. A variety of reasons, such as the development of automobile transportation, physical obsolescence, poor initial planning, and failure of local governments to supply a proper level of municipal services, have been suggested for the initial decline in the demand for good-quality housing. Whatever the reason for it, though, the decline in demand would lead to a fall in housing prices in the affected areas and thus to the returns to investment in residential real estate. For this reason landlords have reduced their expenditures for maintenance and allowed their properties to deteriorate in quality.

. . . .

In my opinion, there is strong evidence that differences in the fraction of the housing stock which is substandard can best be accounted for by variations in the demand for poor-quality housing. . . . [I]n five of the six cities examined there is a strongly negative partial correlation between the proportion of substandard and median-income dwellings. . . . [S]imilar results are found when crowding is compared with income. The income elasticities of the proportion that is substandard and of crowding . . . are quite similar, as would be expected if quality and space per person were inputs into the production of housing. These elasticities average about -2.5. In comparisons made among census tracts in south Chicago for 1950 and 1960, and in comparisons among various U.S. cities in 1950, I likewise find that the proportion that is substandard is strongly and negatively related to income. In these latter comparisons, in which many more variables are include . . ., the elasticity of the proportion of dwellings that are substandard with respect to income was about -3.5. Furthermore, when separate partial regression coefficients of the proportion substandard on income are fitted for the lower and upper halves of the south Chicago tracts by median income, the differences are negligible. If ignorance of housing opportunities operated with greater force among the lowest-income groups, I would expect the response of housing quality to income differences to be greater in the lower half of the income distribution.

. . . .

It is clear, therefore, that the principal reason for slum housing is the low income of its inhabitants. Demolition, as in urban renewal, or programs such as stricter code enforcement, that raise the cost of producing poor-quality as contrasted with good-quality housing, do virtually nothing to attack the basic cause of slums. While these programs reduce the fraction of poor-quality housing, they also raise the price of housing for lower-income households. It appears that not only has the private market not produced too much poor-quality housing relative to the demand for it, but also that the private market has clearly responded to rising incomes by upgrading the average quality of the existing housing stock. Thus, it seems to me that measures taken to raise the incomes of lower-income groups offer the best prospect of solving the problem of poor-quality housing.

Comment: Looking from the outside at the two empirical studies, Muth and Ellickson, one distinction between them stands out sharply. Muth studied Chicago between the 1940s and the 1960s. Ellickson studied San Francisco in the middle of the next decade. Not only had times changed, but, as practically everyone knows, the two places are vastly different. The central area of San Francisco contains grand places to live — though it does have some pretty shabby ones too — and Chicago for the most part does not. This contextual fact alone could account for the divergence between the two results. In other words, the tendency of microeconomics to suppress context compromises its analysis. This constitutes a major problem in applying this type of analysis in housing. Alonso, for instance, assumes that the city in which housing is located has a single workplace at its center in which all employment is concentrated, that it is located on a "featureless plain," that transportation costs are directly proportional to distance, and that all land used to produce housing is identical. Such underlying assumptions completely cancel out variations in context. They are both counterintuitive and at odds with more grounded theory. The issue is sufficiently basic to call into question much of what microeconomics says about housing. For example, the comment on Muth by housing authority Anthony Downs illustrates the context isssue with respect to a somewhat different substantive issue.

A. DOWNS, [COMMENTS] IN H. PERLOFF AND L. WINGO, ISSUES IN URBAN ECONOMICS 423, 425-26 (1968)

In my opinion, Muth's paper also exhibits a breadth of perspective towards housing markets which is too narrow to take account of all of the significant dynamic elements affecting them. To some extent, this criticism is more a matter of taste than of scientific accuracy. Muth has attempted to illustrate in his paper just how much of the activity in housing markets and cities can be explained on the basis of a sophisticated and fully developed model built almost exclusively upon economic factors. Therefore, he pays little attention to social factors, immobilities, market ignorance, and certain insights that might be obtained by using a broader perspective. It is certainly a valid intellectual and scientific procedure to see how much of a given set of empirical phenomena can be explained from [a] relatively narrowly conceived set of premises. . . . Moreover, I think Muth is unusually capable at carrying out such an analysis. He has a remarkable grasp of the analytical tools he employs, and can "push them" farther and with more ingenuity than any other economist I know in this field.

Yet this narrowness of approach necessarily prevents Muth from dealing with some highly significant factors in housing markets. . . .

[Using the non-economics literature as a point of departure, Downs details some of the important aspects of the housing system left out of Muth's analysis. He then turns to Muth's conclusions. He says that Muth is correct in observing that "the principal reason for slum housing is the low incomes of its inhabitants." But Downs asserts that the conclusions drawn from this finding are false. In the just quoted passage, Muth says that "Measures taken to raise the incomes of low-income groups offer the best prospects for solving the problem of poor-quality housing." Downs holds that this conclusion is mistaken. — Eds.]

It is quite true that increasing the incomes of low-income persons would undoubtedly make them better off. But it does not follow that their housing would improve if the actual amount of housing supply made available *to them* did not rise as fast as their incomes. For example, in the past year, high interest rates have "choked off" the increase in the total supply of housing which had been occurring in the previous few years. At the same time, general economic prosperity stimulated the incomes of consumers, including those in the lowest-income groups. But the resulting gains in income by the latter groups did *not* improve the quality of their housing, since the general increase in "tightness" in the housing market caused vacancies to decline, rents to rise, and maintenance levels to fall off. Furthermore, because of tremendous immobilities in the housing market — such as those caused by racial segregation and imperfections in the "trickle-down" process — great increases in income among low-income persons may not be accompanied by commensurate gains in *their access* to good-quality housing. As a result, higher incomes may simply lead to higher rents with no improvement in housing quality. The only cure for this situation is insuring that the amount of standard housing made available to low-income households goes up as fast as their incomes. It is not likely that the free market will produce this result in the short run, though it might in the long run. But housing quality is experienced in the short run and has key effects therein too, as recent slum riots tend to show.

[This problem of the failure of the supply side of the market to respond is the same inelasticity problem diagrammed in figure 2 of the Note on Microeconomics and Housing above. — Eds.]

. . . .

The above reasoning leads me to conclude that narrowly defined analyses of the housing market — though they can be extremely useful in extending our insights into the working of that market — should not be used as the basis for broad conclusions about it. Such conclusions can be accurate only if they are based on a more comprehensive outlook which takes into account some of the social factors, irrationalities, and immobilities that Muth has deliberately left out of his study. Moreover, these supposedly "non-economic" factors are particularly crucial in any analysis of slums and poverty. As more and more studies in many fields are indicating, slum residents are essentially the victims of irrationalities and immobilities in society. They are people who "fall into the cracks" between the neat logical categories dealt with in the disciplines of economics and other social sciences. Precisely the "frictional" factors which tend to be ignored by formal model builders are crucial elements in the lives of these deprived people.

———

Comments: 1. Some critics of housing microeconomics hold that disagreement of the sort voiced by Downs is too gentle and does not deal with the really significant questions.

Rather than mere "irrationalities and immobilities" in society, these critics argue that the basic contextual issues with respect to microeconomics are embedded in the structure of society, in its political and economic power relations, and in the historic processes at work. The existence of poor people and the fact that they typically live in poor housing is not irrational in this view, but rather an inherent characteristic of capitalism and the system of private ownership. This point of view is represented by the Marxists Castells and Stone, the authors of the short selections that follow these comments. With respect to context, perhaps the major contribution of the Marxists is their insistence that economic processes are historical processes and that both theory and practical work must take this into account. The excerpt from Stone especially exhibits this characteristic.

Many less doctrinaire critics also take a structural view and hold that fundamental political, economic, and social class interests not irrationalities lie behind the distribution of housing. A number of the readings in Part II of this book take such positions, the final selection in Chapter 8 by Hartman, for instance. Yet criticism comes not only from the political left. Orthodox *macro*economists see the housing economy in contextual terms. In their eyes, the supply and demand for housing are dependent upon the business cycle, the money supply, and central government fiscal policy. Institutionalists, discussed in the third comment below, also take a contextual and historical view. It is the view dominant in the selections and editing of this text.

2. A second point about the limitations of microeconomics deals with its philosophical starting point in the idea of economic man. This point has already been discussed in the comments on Grigsby, supra p. 48, and the beginning of the Note, supra p. 49, earlier in this Chapter. There are other possible starting points or first principles. The most complete, coherently developed, and outside the United States the most widespread alternative view, is that of the Marxists. Rather than start with the notion of autonomous drives within the individual, Marxism holds that the material world shapes people's consciousness and behavior. It starts not with a *priori* psychological preferences or utilities, but with a particular historic, economic, social, technological, and material order. In more concrete terms, this view holds that the specific material world in which people exist permits certain people to occupy certain dwellings, it teaches them what level of housing services to be satisfied with, and so forth. This book is not an appropriate place in which to debate the pros and cons of economic determinism versus economic man. Suffice it here to note that alternative philosophical first principles exist; and that, in the muddy complexity of dealing with housing, eclectic borrowing from various viewpoints is the norm.

3. Returning to Ellickson and the microeconomists, another weakness in this perspective concerns this very business of complexity. The microeconomists start with radical oversimplications. They focus on decisionmaking at the individual level and attempt to deal with complexity and aggregation by summing individual behavior. Though microeconomists understand that there are limitations in this approach, they are hard pressed to deal with them. In the Ellickson study, for instance, they admit that their analysis "already presses against the limits imposed by computational feasibility," a significant admission coming from one of the leading centers of computerized systems analysis.

Complexity which is the *sine qua non* of housing is the enemy of rigorous microeconomic analysis. For this reason, even its best outputs must be combined with other types of analysis in order to maintain a more rounded and grounded view. For example, in policy planning today, good practice combines historical analysis and in-depth case studies with econometrics.

The general perspective adopted for this book, particularly for the problem focused chapters of Part II, may be characterized as *institutional.* This view searches in all directions for regularities in behavior. It looks for them not only as inhering in the individual, but in social groups as well. While institutional analysis draws on microeconomics, it can transcend it, albeit at the cost of losing the appearance of mathematical certainty. Historical studies, case analyses, perspectives drawn from the other social sciences, and the analytical traditions used by professions such as law and engineering contribute to the institutionalists' world view.

Institutionalists, because they understand relations between housing producers and housing consumers as having in part at least a social structural basis, have affinities with the Marxists' critique of microeconomics. The next reading draws on the recent flowering of Marxist urban studies in Europe and is written by one of its leaders, Manuel Castells. The passage, as is appropriate for one espousing the faith, begins with a quote from the source, Karl Marx and Frederick Engels. The points made in subsequent pages analyze recent experience with the French housing economy, but they do so at a general enough level that they can be applied to the U.S.

M. CASTELLS, THE URBAN QUESTION: A MARXIST APPROACH 145-155, 158 (1977)

"The housing question

It cannot fail to be present in a society in which the great labouring masses are exclusively dependent upon wages, that is to say, upon the quantity of the means of subsistence necessary for their existence and for the propagation of their kind; in which improvements of the machinery, etc., continually throw masses of workers out of employment; in which violent and regularly recurring industrial fluctuations determine on the one hand the existence of a large reserve army of unemployed workers, and on the other hand drive the mass of the workers from time to time on to the streets unemployed; in which the workers are crowded together in masses in the big towns, at a quicker rate than dwellings come into existence for them under the prevailing conditions; in which, therefore, there must always be tenants even for the most infamous pigsties; and in which finally the house-owner in his capacity as capitalist has not only the right but, by reason of competition, to a certain extent also the duty of ruthlessly making as much out of his property in house rent as he possibly can. In such a society the housing shortage is no accident; it is a necessary institution and can be abolished together with all its effects on health, etc., only if the whole social order from which it springs is fundamentally refashioned."

(Karl Marx and Frederick Engels, *Selected Works,* vol. 2, pp. 326-327.)

The housing question is above all that of its crisis. Lack of comfort and amenities, over-crowding (despite the under-occupation of certain kinds of housing), old buildings, unhealthy conditions, make of this question an experience shared by a large section of the population: two French people out of five live in over-crowded housing. . . . What characterizes this crisis is that it affects other social strata than those at the bottom of the incomes scale and that it even reaches large sections of the middle strata better placed in other spheres of consumption, but unable to escape the housing shortage caused by urban concentration. This shortage is not an unavoidable condition of the process of urbanization, but corresponds to a relation between supply and demand, itself determined by the social conditions of production of the market commodity in question, that is to say, housing.

A relation between supply and demand, and therefore a market situation, not a relation of production. Indeed, we know that any assimilation of the tenant-landlord relation to the worker-capitalist relation is meaningless, and that if the crisis is a general one and affects other groups than the working class it is precisely because it does not derive from a relation of exploitation, but from a mechanism of distribution of a particular commodity. . . .

Hence the importance of the theme of speculation and the dependence of the housing question on the economic laws regulating the market. We should not conclude from this that the housing crisis is purely conjunctural and simply a matter of the balance between supply and demand. It is a case of a necessary disparity between the needs, socially defined, of the habitat and the production of housing and residential amenities. It is the structural determination of this disparity and its historical singularities that we wish to establish.

Housing, over and above its general scarcity, is a differentiated commodity, presenting a whole gamut of characteristics, in terms of its *quality* (amenities, comfort, type of construction, life-span etc.), its *form* (individual, collective, as architectural object, integration in the housing context as a whole and in the region) and its *institutional status* (without title-deeds, rented, owned, owned in common, etc.), which determine the *roles,* the *levels* and the *symbolic loyalties* of its occupants.

Too often one considers tastes, preferences, even sensitivity to certain mythical configurations, as determining the choice of housing and, consequently, the diversity of the forms of the habitat, their evolution, their profitability and, therefore, their mode of distribution. Although it is undeniable that the forms have a certain ideological and therefore material influence, they merely reinforce, and do not create, the mercantile organization of the unique commodity that housing is. The sociological problematic of housing must set out from a reversal of the usual psycho-social themes and centre itself on the analysis of the process of production of a certain durable commodity, in the diversity of its qualities, forms, status and in relation to the economic market and, consequently, its social context.

For this, we must set out from the characteristics specific to the commodity (housing), relying, as far as is possible, on the facts of a given historical reality, namely French society.

Housing may be regarded, on the one hand, in relation to its place in the whole of the economic system and, on the other, as a product with specific characteristics.

Concerning the first point, housing is one of the essential elements of the reproduction of labour power. As such, it follows the movements of concentration, dispersal and distribution of the workers and also causes, in times of crisis, a considerable bottleneck in the production process. Historically, the housing crisis appears above all in the great urban areas suddenly taken over by industry. Indeed, where industry colonizes space, the housing of the necessary manpower must be organized for it, if only at the level of camping. On the other hand, by grafting itself on to an already constituted urban tissue, industrialization profits from the potential manpower that is already living on the spot and then causes a strong migratory movement whose dimensions go well beyond the building and amenity capacities of a city inherited from an earlier mode of production. Thus the shortage of housing, the lack of amenities and the unhealthy conditions of the residential space are a result of the sudden increase in urban concentration, in a process dominated by the logic of industrialization. . . .

Thus the higher the rate of industrial (capitalist) growth, the more concentrated it is in the great urban areas and the greater the shortage of housing and the deterioration of existing housing.

Furthermore, one must take into account the multiplicatory mechanisms of the crisis: in a situation of shortage, speculation develops, prices rise, social hardships become greater (and it becomes much more difficult to meet the needs created). The difficulty of the problem slows down any attempt to solve it, thus making it worse and turning a vicious cycle into a spiral.

Although the *production* mechanism of the housing crisis emerges clearly enough, the reasons for its *maintenance* are less immediate. Indeed, housing needs constitute an important demand on the market and, furthermore, the reproduction of labour power is impeded by this, with possible consequences both for labour itself and for social peace. If the response to this demand remains inadequate the reason for it must be sought in the social logic according to which this demand is treated.... In more concrete terms, housing depends, for its realization, on the characteristics and objectives of the construction industry. On a primary level, this means that, in the absence of public intervention, the only demand actually taken into account is solvent demand. Now, from a comparison between the incomes of households and the prices and rents of average apartments, one deduces the difficulty of solving the crisis simply by market mechanisms.

. . . .

[Castells' data shows that 60% of urban families in France could not secure private market housing at prices they could afford. — Eds.]

It is not, therefore, only a question of stratification in consumption, such as exists for all commodities in terms of social stratification, measured by purchase power, but, more directly, of a non-satisfaction of demand. The production of housing is such, in the historical situation studied, that left to itself, it would not be capable of housing most of the population of the cities. The study of the specificity of this process of production will help us to determine the reason for such a situation.

If one sets out from the idea that, on the private property market, housing is a commodity to be sold, that is to say, to produce a profit, one must ask oneself what are the particular characteristics of realizing surplus value that determine a greater inability on the part of private industry to satisfy basic needs in this domain, more than in other sectors of individual consumption. The production of housing results from the articulation of three elements: the land on which one builds, materials and/or elements incorporated into the construction and the actual construction of the building, namely the application of labour power, in a given organization, to the basic materials, to produce housing. The characteristics of the three elements, their forms of articulation and their relation to the market determine a particular form of labour. Let us examine the specificity of the different phases.

In the first place, as is well known, one observes the very high dependence of construction on the availability and price of the land to be built on, and also on the speculation in land values that results....

[Working with data from France, the author shows how the shortage of housing triggers land speculation; and how reciprocally land speculation forces yet higher house prices thus exacerbating the shortage. This phenomenon has been visible in the United States during the last decade. The next chapter of this text touches on it and in Chapter 11 it is a central issue. Having made his point about land, Castells turns to house production. — Eds.]

There is practically no private production of 'social' housing, whereas one finds industries manufacturing consumer goods intended for the whole range of incomes. If this is so, one may suppose that the profitability of capital in this sector is much less than in other industries — so much less, in fact, that investment is discouraged and it requires massive public intervention to limit the damage done. Indeed, the rate of rotation of capital invested in construction is particularly long, owing to the slowness of manufacture, the high price of the product bought, which limits the number of buyers and makes the owners fall back on renting, the length of the delay in obtaining profits from renting and, above all, the sensitivity of housing to social demands that can lead to frequent intervention by the state, with such measures as the rents freeze, which threaten the realization of profits. This fact leads to two others: the limited amount of private investment in this sector, and the search for a high rate of profit in as short a term as possible without the normalization of a moderate, long-term profit, as is the case for the great industrial trusts.

Such a situation, in interaction with the very characteristics of the labour process, which make less easy than elsewhere the mechanization and standardization of operations, gives rise to what is very often an archaic form of industrialization: activity split up between a multitude of small companies . . ., a low rate of technological innovation, a low level of training among the workers and, above all, a low number of workers per company (in relation to other branches of industry), which limits proportionally the sources of surplus value, diminishes profit, increases costs and discourages investment. All these characteristics taken together lead to low productivity which, in turn, perpetuates the shortage, postpones any solution and, at the same time, requires a high immediate profit on each operation, instead of spreading the profit ratio over a future that, under these circumstances, is always uncertain. . . .

. . . .

The situation of scarcity thus created around an indispensable commodity of use which is in a state of permanent imbalance sustained by the acceleration of urban concentration, has made possible the multiplication of intermediaries and the organization of a whole network of services whose sole end is to speculate on the shortages and difficulties in the sector, by creating a solvent demand where it did not exist and seeking to attract hesitant capital into carefully planned operations. . . .

[Castells examines these intermediaries, particularly the large scale developer and marketing firms, and shows how they rationalize production for profit and at the same time snowball new layers of cost burden on housing. "Consultants fees, financial expenses, legal fees, management costs" in 1968 represented 26% of the cost of a new home in France. To illustrate the entire production process more clearly the author developed the flow chart reproduced in the accompanying figure. Finally, he turns to the question of the general validity of this analysis for other nations. On this score he finds differences primarily in the degree of central government intervention in the national housing market. — Eds.]

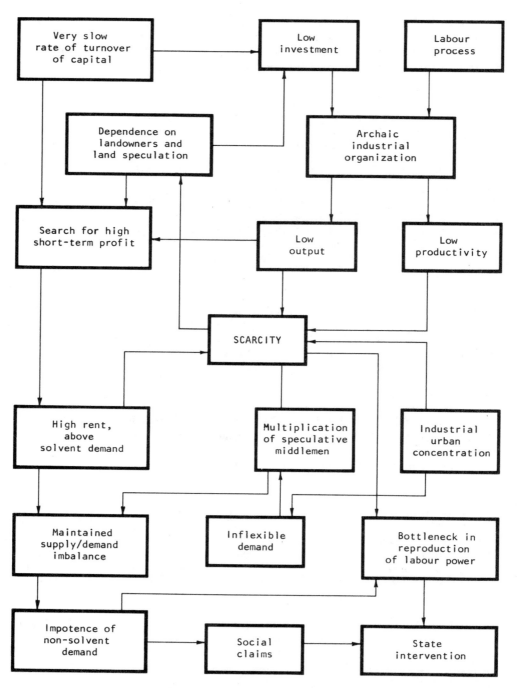

Production process of the housing crisis in the capitalist economy (Redrawn from Castells)

. . . .

The only country in which private enterprise has always provided most of the
residential buildings is the United States. This has well known consequences in

the poor quality of housing and in the discriminatory practices experienced by the 'poor whites', the blacks and other ethnic minorities.

Nevertheless, it is a fact that although public housing is extremely undeveloped in the United States, the housing situation, for the mass of the population, is markedly better than that in Europe. Several factors, quite specific to America, have contributed to this process. . . . Urbanization has scarcely had to graft itself upon pre-industrial cities ill adapted to new spatial forms; the country has not undergone successive destructions in war; industrial growth has made possible a standardization of labour and a high development of prefabrication; the reign of the motor-car and urban dispersal have facilitated the acquisition of land and limited speculation; and, above all, the real high standard of living (due to American power on the world market) has made possible both the creation of a real solvent demand and the extension of the system of individual credit. We should be aware of what all these different factors taken together represent and not forget how difficult it is to transpose into another country the capacity of the American construction industry.

Comments: To make the structural or Marxist perspective more concrete we turn to an analysis by an American housing expert Michael Stone. He examines mortgage lending, perhaps the most important of all housing market institutions. The examination starts from a central conflict or contradiction in Marxist jargon, what Castells called "the problem of solvent demand," and what Stone calls by the more familiar term the "income/housing cost problem." (Microeconomists, curiously, use words very like Castells does; they say "effective demand.")

M. STONE, A HOUSE OF CARDS: HOUSING, MORTGAGE LENDING, AND THE CRISIS OF CAPITALISM 17-18, 20-23 (1977)

The Mortgage System

Although massive state intervention in housing began in the Great Depression of the 1930's, the need for intervention, and its emphasis on homeownership and mortgages, was more than just a response to the general crisis of the Depression. Since the end of the 19th century the housing system had been evolving rapidly in response to the problem of incomes and housing costs, on the one hand, and certain aspects of the development of modern capitalism, on the other. Most significant was the growth of mortgage lending, which in turn became a major contributor to the collapse into the Depression and to the devastation of the housing market.

Since the 1930's, the mortgage system has become even more crucial in the dynamics of both the housing and financial markets. Mortgage loans are now used to finance the construction of most new housing and the purchase of virtually [all] new and used housing in this country. The loans must be repaid — with interest — by the residents. Mortgage payments are generally the biggest single element of occupancy costs, accounting for about 30-70 percent of the cost of housing for both tenants and homeowners. The mortgage system exerts a decisive influence over who lives where and how much new housing gets built. Mortgage lending has been the largest and one of the fastest growing parts of the entire credit system. It has contributed to economic growth, but also to the increasing problems of housing and the economy.

The Rise of Institutional Mortgage Lending

Between the end of the Civil War and the Great Depression of the 1930's, industrial capitalism brought about a tremendous increase in the forces of production. In 1900 the gross national product was two-and-a-half times what it had been thirty years earlier. By 1929 the economy had grown to five-and-a-half times what it had been in 1900. The tremendous amount of surplus value created could not be absorbed entirely through profitable investment in additional productive capacity. New investment outlets had to be found.

Some of the surplus of course went into imperialist expansion in foreign countries. Some went into speculation — buying and selling existing businesses and real estate. New opportunities were also created, though, by the demographic and social changes created by industrial capitalism. Specifically, the growing urban population created the need for and possibility of profitable investment in housing and public works. All that was required were institutions to assemble and channel the available capital.

. . . .

[At this juncture Stone traces the historical evolution of mortgage lending and the institutions to which it gave rise. To the institutionalist and Marxist this historical approach is basic; the present situation unfolds dialectically out of the conflicts of the past. The key immediate events that led to the modern mortgage system occurred during and just before the Great Depression, though many of its roots lie deeply in the rise of industrial capitalism and the urbanization it spawned. Massive mortgage foreclosures, failures of mortgage lending institutions and related events were the proximate causes of the disaster and the changes it wrought in the mortgage system. — Eds.]

The Modern Mortgage System

In order to encourage financial institutions to make loans with low downpayments and long terms, indeed to stimulate almost any lending in the 1930's, the federal government had to provide protection and assistance. This included FHA mortgage insurance so that the banks would not lose money if borrowers could not pay. It also included the FNMA secondary mortgage market, where lenders could sell some of their FHA-insured mortgages and obtain additional investment funds. [See Chapter 7. — Eds.] To undertake any lending at all, though, the financial institutions needed to obtain savings deposits again. The federal government therefore created deposit insurance in the early 1930's to encourage people to put money into savings accounts. Deposit insurance could not generate savings, though, when people did not have sufficient incomes to save. Thus savings and other time deposits in 1940 were more than $3 billion below their 1930 peak of over $35 billion.

It took World War II to restart the economy and generate the savings needed to set the restructured mortgage system in motion. By 1946 savings deposits were nearly twice their 1940 level. These new funds, plus housing needs which had been unmet since the Depression began, provided the impetus for the post-war housing and mortgage boom, facilitated by the low-downpayment, long-term, federally-backed loan.

The modern mortgage loan typically covers 70-100 percent of the price of the house or apartment building and is for a term of 20 to 40 years. Interest rates are usually fixed for the life of the mortgage, ranging from about 4-6 percent for loans made before the late 1960's and 8-10 percent or more during most of the 1970's. Monthly payments are computed so that the loan will be fully paid off by the end of the term and so that payments will be constant from month to month, with a declining proportion of each payment going for interest as the unpaid balance decreases.

The development of high-ratio (i.e., low-downpayment) loans has made it easier to buy residential real estate by reducing the amount of cash needed for a given price house. However, for a given price, higher loan-to-value ratios obviously result in larger monthly mortgage payments unless the repayment term is stretched out. Longer loan terms offset higher loan ratios and substantially increase the sum a borrower's income can support. For example, at the interest rates which prevailed until the late 1960's, a $100 monthly payment would pay for a 10-year loan of only about $9,000-10,000, but would cover a 20-year loan for about $14,000-17,000, or a 30-year loan for about $17,000-21,000.

The long-term, low-downpayment mortgage thus undercut the income/housing cost problem in several ways: economically by both lessening monthly payments for a given size loan and reducing the personal savings needed to buy; politically by promoting the illusion of ownership through the reality of debt. In so doing it of course also stimulated the demand for houses and mortgages, which in the post-war period contributed substantially to overall economic growth as well as benefiting the construction and lending industries.

The fundamental change in mortgage lending led to the rapid growth of residential mortgage debt on the national balance sheet. As shown in the table, between 1946 and 1965 total debt in the economy more than tripled — from about $400 billion to over $1.2 trillion. Residential mortgage debt was by far the biggest single component of the increase — growing by 760 percent. The dollar increase in residential debt during this period was more than double that of federal, state and local, or consumer credit, and nearly twice as great as the total growth of long and short-term corporate debt. In the nine years after 1965, total debt in the economy more than doubled again, and housing continued to be the largest segment of the increase. Over the entire 1946-74 period, housing debt grew two-and-a-half times as fast as the overall economy, while total private debt grew twice as fast as GNP.

Debt outstanding in the U.S. economy 1946-1974 (in billions of dollars)

	1946	1965	1970	1974
TOTAL DEBT	$ 396.6	$1,243.6	$1,868.5	$2,777.3
Federal Government	229.5	266.4	301.1	360.8
State & Local Governments	13.7	98.3	144.8	205.6
TOTAL PRIVATE DEBT	153.4	870.0	1,383.8	2,134.4
Consumer Credit	8.4	89.9	127.2	191.5
Residential Mortgages	29.1	250.1	338.3	503.3
Commercial Mortgages	7.7	54.5	82.3	141.0
Debt of Non-Financial Corporations:				
long-term bonds	24.4	97.8	167.9	226.5
short-term debt	20.4*	71.2	128.9	220.9
GROSS NATIONAL PRODUCT	209.6	688.1	982.4	1,406.9
TOTAL PRIVATE DEBT AS A PERCENT OF GNP	73.2%	126.4%	140.9%	151.7%

* 1950
SOURCES: Federal Reserve Board, *Bulletin;* U.S. Dept. of Commerce, *Survey of Current Business.*

The rapid increase in debt was induced in several ways by the change in mortgage loan ratios and terms. First, higher ratio loans create more debt even if house prices and market activity do not increase. Second, longer loan terms mean lower rates of repayment in the early years of the loans. For example, at the interest rates which were common until the late 60's, after five years of amortization 40-45 percent of a ten-year loan had been repaid, but only 15-20 percent of a twenty-year loan, and only 7-9 percent of a thirty-year loan. Thus more and more reliance has had to be placed on new funds, instead of being able to finance new loans primarily out of repayments on old loans. And as interest rates have risen, the rate of repayment has become even lower, thereby accelerating the need for more mortgage money.

The growth of mortgage debt is also attributable to the rapid increase in the demand for housing following World War II. Rising demand was due to economic growth and the rapid increase in the population of metropolitan areas, but was also the result of the easier availability of mortgage credit. Between 1946 and 1974 nearly 44 million new housing units were started. Over 60 percent of the existing stock of housing has been built since World War II, and nearly all of it has been financed with mortgage loans.

Comments: 1. At the conclusion of his article, some pages after the above excerpt, Stone ties the escalating housing debt to what Marxists perceive as the broader crisis in advanced capitalism. Whether the crisis exists or not is far beyond the scope of this book. The fact of the debt's size is clear. Its size measures the sensitivity of the macroeconomy to housing. The United States has reached a situation in which stability in the housing economy may be crucial to the stability of the nation.

2. Castells and Stone appear here primarily as an antidote to undiluted microeconomics. Their focus is on broad contextual matters such as urban and industrial concentration, and institutional factors such as the proliferation of middlemen. It provides needed balance to the tendency of the orthodox analysts to see the housing economy as an encapsulated system peopled with autonomous, perfectly informed consumers and producers among whom the distribution of power and income is largely irrelevant. Both orthodox and Marxist views have their place in thinking about housing. Both contribute to the institutionalist perspective of this book.

3. Castells, at the end of the passage that appears above, asserts that the American housing economy has performed well. Before concluding this chapter it is appropriate to turn to this matter and examine briefly the output of the housing economy in the United States.

A NOTE ON THE PERFORMANCE OF THE U. S. HOUSING ECONOMY

Whether one takes an orthodox economic perspective or a radical one, the performance of the American housing economy looks very impressive indeed. It has provided increasing numbers of better equipped dwellings for a rapidly growing population. At the same time, the overall quality of the standing stock of housing has improved significantly. On the other side of the market equation, demand has increased relative to the absolute size of the population and new preferences in terms of household composition, location choice, unit type, and neighborhood character have been manifested and accommodated. It is an accomplishment that needs to be outlined quantitatively in order to be better comprehended.

Charles Stokes and Ernest Fisher, a pair of experienced housing analysts, have tried to characterize the performance of American urban housing markets by intensively studying a stratified sample of large- and medium-sized cities. A brief excerpt from their work gives both a sense of the major dimensions of market performance and an idea of the difficulty of working with housing data.

The evidence developed about local urban housing market performance in the century between 1870 and 1970 is scattered. We have been able to establish that population per housing unit was decreasing, while population per housing structure was also decreasing, although at a much slower rate. On the other hand, the number of housing units per residential structure was increasing steadily almost everywhere. The net effect was an impression of increasing density, though, in fact, density by all but the physical measures was declining.

The quality of urban housing was not measured effectively during this period, but what evidence is at hand suggests that quality levels were low in the later 19th century, especially in terms of the gap between the best and the worst neighborhoods. Yet, with increasing incomes and decreasing density per structure and per housing unit, there must have been an increasing quality level in most cities. The special housing census undertaken by the Works Progress Administration in 1934-37 revealed a generally low level of housing quality. After 1934, there was a dramatic improvement in housing quality by all available indicators.

Production was at least adequate in terms of population growth. In fact, in every decade more housing was built than was necessary to meet population increases in each of the key cities examined. The remaining housing was built to replace units lost or to permit density to decrease. Elasticity measures indicate that for every 10 percent increase in population, there generally was on a net basis, at least, a 10 percent increase in housing structures.

What was happening to the equity of housing markets is very hard to establish for measures of this kind of performance are rare and weak in significance. Yet, homeownership did increase, except during the 1930s. Important changes in this indicator have been taking place since World War II.

Integration of the poor and the rich, the middle and working classes, as well as the black and the in-migrants did not proceed at any significant pace, if, indeed, it took place at all. The fact that, for most cities, the word "slum" was consistent with the meaning of the word ghetto suggests that integration was not being attained.

Housing effort appeared to increase. Rodwin's long-range study of Boston's lower and middle classes reveals almost a doubling of the ratio between housing outlays and incomes between the 1840s and the 1950s. The trend appeared to continue at a slower pace through 1970. On the other hand, housing demand elasticity research suggests that income elasticity was generally in the vicinity of 1, at least since World War I. This would imply an overall unchanging housing effort.

Partly because of the underlying Anglo-Saxon dissatisfaction with cities and partly because of effective positive sequent occupance, critics, at least since 1940, have been able to convince most observers that the appearance of the urban housing stock worsened. There is little objective evidence to assess this widely held impression.

C. Stokes and E. Fisher, Housing Market Performance in the U.S. 40-42 (1976).

Turning to aggregate data for the entire country, we find that housing market performance exhibits the same major features. The following tables, develped for this book but based on a format developed by housing economist Frank Kristof, tell the story over the past 40 years. Kristof's comments on this kind of data are worth quoting.

The Thirty-Year Housing Census Record

Given our predilection to be self-critical about the state of the Nation's housing status, it may be useful to place the overall housing picture in historical perspective. The incredible progress achieved by the Nation over the past thirty years is readily summarized by a few comparisons that emerge from the data. . . .

Table 1. Performance of the Supply Side of the Housing Economy, 1940–1975 and 1980

Supply (Stock) In Millions	1940	1950	1960	1970	1975	1980
Total housing inventory at beginning of decade	37.4	46.1	58.5	70.2	—	79.1 (est.)
Units added (new const., conversion, other)	n.a.	16.9	18.6	13.6		
Units lost (demo, merger, other)	n.a.	4.5	6.7	4.7		
Net change at end of period	+8.7	+12.3	+11.9	8.9		
Median value (thousands of dollars)	$3.0	$7.4	$11.9	$17.1	$29.5	
Median gross rent (dollars)	$27.0	$42.0	$71.0	$108.0	$156.0	

	#	%	#	%	#	%	#	%	#	%
All housing units	37.3	100	46.0	100	58.3	100	68.7	100	79.1	100
Occupied units	34.8	93	42.8	93	53.0	91	63.4	92	72.5	92
Vacant units	2.5	7	3.0	7	4.8(e)	8	4.2	6	5.0	6
Overcrowded units	7.0	20	6.6	16	6.1	12	5.2	8	3.6	5
Condition: Sound (or with all plumbing facilities)	17.9	48	29.1	63	47.7(e)	82	59.2	86	74.8	95
Deteriorated or Dilapidated	16.9	45)					n.a.		n.a.	
			) 17.0	37	10.6	18				
One or more facilities absent	15.5	42)					6.9	10	2.7	3

Table 2. Performance of the Demand Side of the Housing Economy, 1940-1975

	1940	1950	1960	1970	1975
					owner
Median HH (household) size	3.3	3.1	3.0	2.7	2.8 2.1
					renter
1-2 persons/HH*	11.3	16.0	21.9	29.9	36.9
2+ persons/HH*	23.5	26.9	31.1	33.5	35.6

* in millions

Table 2. Performance of the Demand Side of the Housing Economy, 1940-1975

	1940	1950	1960	1970	1975
Owners*	15.2	19.0	32.8	40.0	46.9
Renters*	19.7	17.0	20.2	23.6	25.7
					owner
Median Inc.	1231**	3319	5620	9867	13,500 7,800
					renter
Persons below poverty level*				13.7	
Rent income ratio					
Med. gross rent as % of med. income	26.2	15.2	15.2	20.0	23.0
Median value: Median in- come ratio	2.43	2.2	2.1	1.8	2.1

*in millions
**1939 wage or salary income only

1. While the Nation's population increased by half over the thirty-year period, the number of occupied housing units increased by four-fifths.

2. The above reflects an increase of .3 in median number of rooms and a steady decrease in median size of household from 3.3 to 2.7 persons. As a result, a new peak of housing space occupied per person was recorded in 1970 — 1.74 rooms per person compared with 1.30 rooms in 1940.

3. Although the vacant housing supply increased only slightly — from 6.6 to 7.6 percent of all housing units, the latter figure included a five-fold increase in housing units held off the market. A significant portion of these represent second (vacation) homes and reflects one direction of expenditures during the affluent years of the 1950's and 1960's.

4. Crowding (1.01 persons per room or more) decreased from one-fifth (20.2 percent) to less than one-tenth (8.2 percent) of all households.

5. Substandard housing plummeted from slightly less than half (49 percent) of all occupied units in 1940 to less than one-tenth (7 percent) in 1970.

Questions About the Record

The last point will raise serious questions on the part of housing observers:

1. What relationship does this sanguine picture of progress over the past 30 years have to the incessant claims of housing shortages or insufficiency of housing output in the past few years?

2. Again, how does the foregoing picture relate to well documented observations of widespread housing deterioration and abandonment in cities across the Nation?

3. "Condition of housing," an integral component of a measure of substandard housing, was not enumerated in 1970. How can any 1970 comparison be made with previous census records of substandard housing?

F. Kristof, The 1970 Census of Housing 3-4 (1971).

With respect to the questions Kristof raises a few comments are appropriate at this point.

1. The insufficiency of dwelling production may well be a mistaken perception if it is understood in aggregate national terms. If, however, it is understood in terms of submarkets then shortages do exist both in areas of booming growth and for certain subgroups of the population, particularly the poor. The final pages of this chapter and Chapter 4 give more detail on this point.

2. As Kristof notes, housing deterioration and abandonment exist. The reason lies mainly in the uneven growth and decline of various metropolitan areas and regions. The old Northeastern and Midwestern areas have shrinking populations, old deteriorated housing, and continuing abandonment. Other factors are involved, some of which are explored in more detail in Chapters 5 and 9.

3. The short answer to Kristof's third question about the availability of data on housing condition is that dependable comparisons cannot be made. This conundrum illustrates the sensitivity of thought about housing to the existence and quality of measures and indicators. This is a good riddle to keep in mind in reference to all housing questions.

So much for the recent past. What about the future? What can be expected over the next decade with respect to the performance of the American housing economy? Most students of the problem have concluded that basic changes are presently under way in our housing economy. They expect these to continue on through the 1980s. From a turning point in the early 1970s, two trends have dominated the national market. On the demand side the number of households seeking separate dwelling units has grown explosively. On the supply side the relationship between long term trends in household income and housing costs have reversed. No longer do dwelling prices increase more slowly than incomes, but instead go up faster. Excessive costs are now, and will be, for the short-range future at least, the central issue in housing.

The most ambitious and comprehensive recent examination of these trends comes from the MIT-Harvard Joint Center for Urban Studies. Figure 2.4 is from

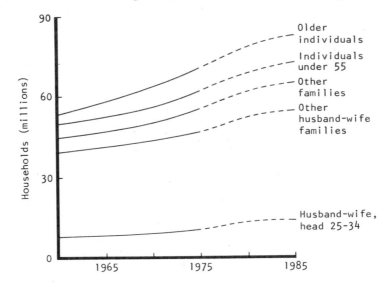

Figure 2.4 Growth and change of the American household, 1960-1985 (Redrawn from Frieden and Solomon)

their report by B. Frieden and A. Solomon, The Nation's Housing: 1975 to 1895. It shows graphically the recent spurt in new household formation. A good deal more detail about this is given in the Alonso reading at the beginning of Chapter 4. Two locational aspects of demand merit note here, though — the relative growth of the South against other regions and of a non-metropolitan areas against the cities. Tables 3.3 and 3.4 from the Joint Center report document and project these trends.

With respect to supply the Joint Center report projects that between 20.2 and 22.6 million new units will be constructed in the 1975-1985 decade. Details of this projection broken down by region and by sector of the market are given in their table 3.5 reproduced here and expanded to show additional aggregate data given elsewhere in the report. Converted to annual production estimates and compared with production in the recent past, the Joint Center projections (updated to 1978) are shown in Figure 3.2.

Table 3.3. The emergence of the South: population increase by region, 1950 to 1985 (in millions of people)

Five-Year Period	North-east	North Central	South	West
1950-1955	2.7	3.9	2.9	3.7
1955-1960	2.5	3.2	5.0	4.2
1960-1965	2.6	2.5	4.4	3.9
1965-1970	1.7	2.4	3.4	2.7
1970-1975	.3	.9	5.1	2.9
TOTAL (1955-1975)	9.8	12.9	20.8	17.4
Projection				
1975-1985	3.3	4.6	15.8	7.2

SOURCE: These statistics were derived from the Social Security Continuous Work History Sample. U.S. Bureau of the Census, Current Population Reports, "Estimates of the Population of the United States with Components of Change: 1970 to 1975," series P-25, no. 640 (1976).

Table 3.4. The back to the country movement, 1975 to 1985 (number of households)

Metropolitan Areas by Region	1975	1985	Absolute Change	Percent Change
Northeast				
Large	12,941,000	13,591,000	650,000	5.02
Medium	1,776,000	1,955,000	178,000	10.02
Small	87,000	90,000	3,000	3.34
Nonmetropolitan	1,422,000	1,655,000	233,000	16.42

Metropolitan Areas by Region	1975	1985	Absolute Change	Percent Change
North Central				
Large	9,572,000	10,204,000	632,000	6.61
Medium	3,512,000	3,932,000	420,000	11.95
Small	1,169,000	1,320,000	151,000	12.93
Nonmetropolitan	4,809,000	5,599,000	790,000	16.43
South				
Large	6,377,000	8,352,000	1,975,000	30.97
Medium	6,757,000	8,695,000	1,938,000	28.68
Small	1,417,000	1,727,000	310,000	21.90
Nonmetropolitan	8,029,000	9,589,000	1,560,000	19.43
West				
Large	8,403,000	9,768,000	1,366,000	16.25
Medium	2,392,000	3,293,000	901,000	37.68
Small	615,000	809,000	194,000	31.61
Nonmetropolitan	1,843,000	2,417,000	574,000	31.17

SOURCE: For 1975 we applied the output of the Joint Center inter-area migration model and of the household formation model to the population data from the U.S. Bureau of the Census, *Current Population Reports,* series P-20, 1976; for 1985 we used a preliminary migration forecast together with the household forecast.

NOTE: The large metropolitan areas are defined as those with 1970 populations of 1 million or more, medium metropolitan areas are those with populations between 250,000 and 1 million, and small metropolitan areas are those with populations of less than 250,000.

Table 3.5. Where will construction be needed? 1975 to 1985 (numbers of housing units and mobile home shipments)

Housing Required *	Northeast	North Central	South	West	Totals
Additional Vacancies	—	—	318,000	122,000	440,000 (590,000)
Replacement of Accidental Losses	493,000	525,000	661,000	434,000	2,100,000
Second Homes	538,000	410,000	418,000	144,000	1,500,000
Upgrading Demand	492,000	793,000	1,059,000	513,000	2,900,000 (3,400,000)
Replacement of Mobile Homes	404,000	319,000	521,000	201,000	1,390,000

Housing Required *	Northeast	North Central	South	West	Totals
Additional Households	1,074,000	1,998,000	5,788,000	3,040,000	11,900,000
	———	———	———	———	(13,600,000)
TOTAL: Low Estimate	3,001,000	4,045,000	8,765,000	4,454,000	20,230,000
TOTAL: High Estimate	3,308,000	4,506,000	9,780,000	5,017,000	22,580,000

* The various categories in the housing required column refer to the following:
Additional vacancies: units required to assure equilibrium in expanding markets.
Replacement of accidental losses: losses from fire, or natural hazard and through demolitions for public programs such as highway construction.
Second homes: seasonally occupied units other than a household's main domicile.
Upgrading demand: new houses for people who want and can afford improved housing.
Replacement of mobile homes: response to the surge of mobile home production in the 1960s and their expected short useful life.

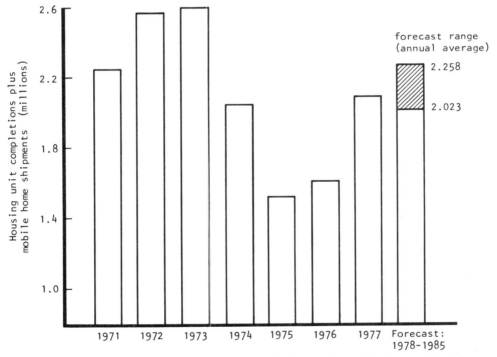

Figure 3.2 Construction trends and forecast (Redrawn from Frieden and Solomon, modified to show 1977)

Frieden and Solomon take pains to make clear that these production estimates do not include particular public or social policy initiatives directed at housing need. These authors refer to need as housing deprivation; it is largely the same thing Castells calls non-solvent demand. The report does not give up to date estimates later than 1973. However, the material for that year and earlier is indicative of a major evolving housing problem — the growth of high cost burden as a form of housing deprivation. Tables 4.1 and 4.2 from the report provide more detail on the nature and extent of housing deprivation.

The last part of the Joint Center report concerns the recent rapid escalation in the cost of home ownership. Presentation of this part of the report and the more detailed discussion of the price of housing is deferred to the next chapter. Suffice it here to note that while the Consumer Price Index rose 46% between 1970 and 1976, and median family income 47%, the price of new houses rose 89% and the monthly costs of ownership rose 102%. Seen against the generally impressive performance of the housing economy in the last generation, these violent relative price increases coupled with the pressure from new household formation promise trouble ahead for a nation that has become used to a very high standard of housing.

Table 4.1. Total housing deprivation, 1973

Type of Deprivation (nonoverlapping categories)	Households (in millions)
Households in physically inadequate units	6.3
Overcrowded households in physically adequate units	0.5
Nonovercrowded households in physically adequate units with high rent burden [a]	6.0
Households in physically adequate units, not overcrowded, without high rent burden, wanting to move because of inadequate public services or objectionable street conditions [b]	4.0
TOTAL households with one or more forms of housing deprivation	16.8
All U.S. households	69.3

a. See note to Figure 4.1.
b. Public services reported were: public transportation, schools, and neighborhood shopping. Street conditions reported were: street noise; airplane noise; heavy traffic; odors, smoke, or gas; trash or litter in the streets, on empty lots, or on properties; abandoned structures; run-down housing; commercial, industrial, or other non-residential activities; streets continually in need of repair; inadequate street lighting; street or neighborhood crime.

SOURCE: Tape of the 1973 Annual Housing Survey, provided by the U.S. Bureau of the Census.
NOTE: Households with annual incomes above $11,400 excluded from table.

Table 4.2. Impact of housing deprivation on low-income groups, 1960 to 1973

	Percent of Households with Housing Deprivation, by Income Level					
	Annual Household Income (1970 dollars):					
	Under $5,000			$5,000-$10,000		
	1960	1970	1973	1960	1970	1973
Households in physically inadequate units	39	24	20	18	13	11

	Percent of Households with Housing Deprivation, by Income Level					
	Annual Household Income (1970 dollars):					
	Under $5,000			$5,000-$10,000		
	1960	1970	1973	1960	1970	1973
Overcrowded households in physically adequate units	2	2	1	2	2	1
Nonovercrowded renter households in physically adequate units with high rent burdens	31	54	49	11	15	19

SOURCES: For 1960 and 1970 charts see David L. Birch, et al. *America's Housing Needs,* pp. 4-6 to 4-8. The 1973 figures are from the tape of the 1973 Annual Housing Survey, supplied by U.S. Bureau of the Census.

NOTE: To correct for inflation, incomes of $5,000 in 1970 are equated with incomes of $3,800 in 1960 and $5,700 in 1973; and incomes of $10,000 in 1970 are equated with incomes of $7,500 in 1960 and $11,400 in 1973. Also see note to Figure 4.1.

BIBLIOGRAPHY

W. Alonso, Location and Land Use: Toward a General Theory of Rent (1964)
Classic microeconomic theory — and heroic oversimplification — concerned mainly with the location of houses with respect to the overall form of the city.

M. Castells, The Urban Question (1977)
The Marxist answer to the microeconomists, though it covers lots besides housing.

J. Kain & J. Quigley, Housing Markets and Racial Discrimination: A Microeconomic Analysis (1975)
State-of-the-art application of mathematical microeconomics.

R. Muth, Cities and Housing (1969)
More heavy duty econometrics dealing mainly with location.

L. Needleman, The Economics of Housing (1965)
Slim little introduction by an English economist.

M. Stegman, Ed., Housing and Economics: The American Dilemma (1970)
A dated, but useful set of introductory readings.

M. Straszheim, An Econometric Analysis of the Urban Housing Market (1975)
Another work in the same vein as Kain and Quigley.

M. Sumichrast & M. Seldin, Housing Markets: The Complete Guide to Analysis and Strategy for Builders, Lenders and Other Investors (1977)
Precisely what its title says it is.

Chapter 3

SUPPLYING HOUSING

Most Americans live in old dwellings, often in structures built many decades ago. This fact highlights one of the most important facets of housing: the stock is composed mostly of existing units, not new production. In a given year only about two or three per cent are newly built for sale or rent for the first time that year. The other 98% are older. At present, of about 80 million units, only about 2 million are new production units never before lived in and each year about a third of a million units are taken out of use. This means the current life expectancy of a dwelling is close to a hundred years. During this time, the chances are remote that the house will be moved from its original location. Permanence in terms of both long life and locational fixity characterizes the stock of structures which are the focal point in providing the bundle of housing services.

This chapter will emphasize the processes involved in supplying housing services, particularly the institutions and actors responsible for making decisions about supply processes. These individuals and groups constitute the suppliers of housing. Referring back to Smith's diagram of the microeconomic view of the housing sector (supra p. 45), this means giving attention to all the listed principals and institutions except the users or consumers. The chapter deals first with those involved primarily with the standing stock, then with entities such as the financial institutions which are involved in both existing dwellings and new ones. Following this, two readings deal with the residential construction industry. The chapter closes with a discussion of price inflation, the most visible and important process at work today on the supply side of the housing economy.

Homeowners make up by far the most numerous and important among the enormous number and variety of suppliers. From an economic perspective, homeowners are people who supply housing to themselves. They are suppliers and consumers at the same time. For decades Americans, both officially and publicly through the federal government, and privately through their shared values, have actively supported, encouraged, and advocated maximum home ownership. This support of homeownership is based on suppositions, preferences, and hard behavioral evidence that suggests people who act as their own landlords supply higher levels of satisfaction to themselves than are available from others who do not combine the two roles. Homeowners are widely believed to be better neighbors, to take better care of their property, to receive important investment benefits, and to be better integrated citizens.

Is this conventional wisdom true? Economists have puzzled over it for a long time. On the left, skepticism is well developed. In the 19th century, Marx's colleague Frederick Engels questioned homeownership. In the 1930s, New Deal social planners actively opposed it for poor people. Some liberals and radicals continue to question it. Among more orthodox students, the skepticism gives way to a general acceptance of widespread homeownership and its facilitation through public policy. Traditionally oriented economists take this stance because it seems to follow the preferences revealed in household behavior. Policy planners support it because dominant expressed values do. As Stone suggested in the reading in Chapter 2, the encouragement of homeownership also conveniently supports the economic system. Despite its general acceptance, some questions need to be answered about homeowners as suppliers. Are they better suppliers of housing services than landlords? Indeed, are there significant differences between homeowners and landlords? The reading below addresses this question. It is excerpted from a rather lengthy microeconomic monograph prepared by two housing economists as part of a study of federal policy in support of homeownership (see Chapters 7 and 8 for more on these policies).

L. OZANNE & R. STRUYK, HOUSING FROM THE EXISTING STOCK: COMPARATIVE ECONOMIC ANALYSES OF OWNER-OCCUPANTS AND LANDLORDS 2-9, 20, 49 (1976)

In light of the critical need for understanding the process of providing services from the existing stock, it is remarkable that little economic analysis of this subject has been completed. This monograph reports on conceptual and empirical analyses of the production of housing services — shelter, heat, and all other aspects of the structure which have economic value — from dwellings in the existing stock of housing. The analysis was undertaken explicitly to help study low-income housing policies, but the work is also relevant for other policy discussions.

The focus is on housing services produced from the stock of housing existing at the beginning of a period. It is this focus that sets this work apart from most prior empirical analysis of housing supply, including analysis of the cyclical variation in new residential construction or of the conversion of structures to different numbers of dwellings. The concentration, then, is on the provision of housing services from structures containing a fixed number of dwelling units, and on how this supply of services changes with variations in the price per unit of housing services, the type of producer, the technology used by the producer, and the prices of factor inputs purchased by the producer.

The importance of the stock of housing present at the start of a decade for the end-of-decade stock is demonstrated through the data in table 1 on the composition of the 1970 metropolitan housing stock by sources of dwelling units present at that time — dwellings present in 1960 and not altered in a major way since then, structures modified during the decade to contain more or fewer dwellings than in 1960, and new units built over the decade. Nationally, about 72 percent of the 1970 stock predated 1960; in Boston, the area we study most closely, the figure is 81 percent. In the decade of the seventies, with the deep cyclical depression of the residential construction industry, the existing stock may be even more important. The dominance of the existing stock over a period as long as a decade is obvious and makes careful analysis of the variation in the amount of housing services provided from this component of the total stock essential to understanding how well urban Americans are housed.

This focus on existing housing brings several central and distinctive characteristics of the housing market dramatically to the fore.

First, housing services are the product of occupant treatment of the dwelling and possibly direct occupant labor, of the maintenance and investment activities of the landlord, and of the initial housing stock.

Second, "housing suppliers" constitute an extremely heterogeneous group ranging from large management firms to homeowners.

Third, an extremely complex mix of housing attributes is lumped together into what is termed housing services.

Finally, every dwelling has a set of neighborhood conditions associated with it, which can have important effects on producer expectations and hence output.

Any meaningful conceptual or quantitative analysis must take these diverse elements into account.

Table 1. Distribution by source of the 1970 housing inventory

Source	All metropolitan areas	Boston metropolitan area
	%	%
All housing units, 1970	100.0	100.0
Same units, 1960 and 1970	71.5	81.3
Units changed by:		
conversion	1.5	3.4
merger	0.9	1.0
Units added through:		
new construction	25.5	14.0
other [a]	0.6	0.3

KEY: [a] Includes units created from nonresidential space such as garages, and units classified as group quarters in 1960 and nongroup quarters in 1970.

SOURCE: U.S. Bureau of the Census, Census of Housing, *1970 Components of Inventory Change*, Final Report HC(4)-1 (Washington, D.C.: Government Printing Office, 1973).

The spectrum of producers includes typical owner-occupied households who own and manage their own dwellings, individual investor-owners with one or two dwellings they may have purchased or inherited but do not presently occupy; individual or partnership investor-owners with a large number of properties but still too few to manage economically on a full-time basis; and large-scale corporate enterprises with professional staff, which frequently own and manage a large number of properties in addition to engaging in other real estate activities.

The most fundamental distinction among suppliers is between the supplier who is an owner-occupant providing services to his own household and the investor-owner who provides services to tenants. Even at an intuitive level one can imagine that owner-occupants can screen themselves as good or poor tenants; they know their own future demand for housing with much greater certainty than do landlords, and they can make their investment and management decisions accordingly. Homeowners may also be able to purchase their own labor at below-market rates. On the other hand, investor-owners have a greater ability to bear risk, they are probably able to purchase some factor inputs at sizable discounts, and they often have the advantage of professional management expertise and the use of skilled workers. For these and a host of other reasons, one expects the two groups to produce housing services differently and possibly to respond differently to direct changes in demand, as reflected in housing prices, and to uncertainty such as that accompanying impending neighborhood racial transition.

Based on this reasoning as well as rather casual empirical observation, a number of commentators have asserted the general superiority of homeowners as providers of housing services. In addition, it has often been argued that one way to improve the housing of poor and lower-middle-income households is through direct subsidization of homeownership. However, the superiority — if any — of owner-occupants in supplying housing services results from the interaction of their demand for housing services with their supply behavior. Hence, careful analysis is required to attribute differences in the level of housing of homeowners versus renters to owner-occupant actions as suppliers.

For these reasons, the differential behavior of owner-occupants and owner-investors ("landlords") as housing suppliers is the main subject of our conceptual analysis, and this distinction is maintained in the empirical work. . . .

The analysis . . . falls into three parts. First, a conceptual analysis of supplier behavior is undertaken. The inputs used by landlords and owner-occupants are enumerated, and the differences between the factor-mixes of the two groups are discussed. Then a supply function of a form general enough to accommodate the actions of both supplier groups is derived using a ten-year time period — the period used in some of the empirical analysis. The underlying production function combines the fixed input of the beginning-of-period stock of capital and the variable inputs of labor and materials used in the production of housing services. The profit function used to derive a supply function from the production function includes the profit of the current period and the expected discounted profits of succeeding periods. Numerical analysis of the supply function, using assumed parameter values for owner-occupants and for landlords, indicates that either supplier might provide more housing services than the other at the same price and point in time, and that either could be more price responsive than the other over time. In short, the issue of whether landlords or owner-occupants provide more housing services is found to be largely empirical.

The second part of the analysis consists of two separate, but related empirical studies. The first . . . looks for differences in the quality of housing achieved by homeowners in comparison to renters. While some attempt is made to determine if the owner-occupant is a more "efficient" producer, the main effort is to test the widely asserted hypothesis that, at any given income level, owner-occupants enjoy a higher level of basic housing services from a structure than renters. Basic services refer to the dependability of various systems and the condition and maintenance of the dwelling.

The second empirical study . . . is of the change over a ten-year period in the quantity of services supplied by owner-occupants and landlords. More specifically, supply functions of the form derived in the conceptual analysis are estimated for each group of producers, and supply elasticities are derived and contrasted. Thus, the first study, which determines the relative quantity of services consumed and supplied by homeowners and tenants at one point in time, is complemented by the second, which determines the changes over time in the quantity of services supplied in response to increases in the price of housing services.

[As noted, the authors find very little to distinguish owners from landlords in their conceptual analysis. In the first of the empirical studies they report their result "strongly suggests that owner-occupants at low-income levels (under $7,500 annually) do have higher levels of housing services than do renters at this income level. At higher income levels much less contrast. . . is seen." The second empirical study, much more complex conceptually and demanding in terms of input data, is rather inconclusive. — Eds.]

To place our results and their policy implications in context, it is important to review recent data on the housing services of owner-occupants and of renters of equivalent incomes and to provide an idea of the dollar value of maintenance and investment activity in the existing housing stock compared to the value of new residential construction. . . .

How important are the expenditures made on maintaining and improving the existing stock of housing? The Bureau of Census estimates that in 1974 about $21 billion, or about 55 percent of the value of new residential construction of the same year, were spent on upkeep of existing units. This amount, though, is very likely a serious underestimation of the full value of maintenance activity, because it does not impute any value to the time spent by owner-occupants in this activity. The data in table 2 show that, even with this downward bias, maintenance and improvement of the existing stock have consistently represented at least one quarter of all residential investment (new construction plus investments in existing units) and about 40 percent of the value of new construction. For 1970, these data imply an expenditure of around $225 for every dwelling in the stock. Assuming alternative average values of $15,000 and $20,000 for all dwellings in the stock, the $225 implies that a minimum of 1.1 to 1.5 percent of the value of the dwelling is expended annually on upkeep and improvement.

. . . .

Table 2. Selected data on new construction and the existing stock, 1968-1974

Item	Year						
	1968	1969	1970	1971	1972	1973	1974
(1) Value of new residential dwellings put into place[a] ($ millions)	24,030	25,941	24,272	35,066	44,879	47,841	36,980
(2) Value of investment in the existing stock[b] ($ millions)	12,703	13,535	14,770	16,299	17,498	18,512	21,114
(3) Ratio of (2) to (1)	.53	.52	.61	.47	.39	.39 .	.57
(4) Number of new units completed[c] (millions)	1,319	1,399	1,418	1,706	1,971	2,013	1,692
(5) Total number of dwelling units in stock[d] (millions)	e	e	65,611	e	e	e	e
(6) Ratio of (5) to (4)	e	e	.02	e	e	e	e

KEY: [a] Includes only private activity; in current dollars.
      [b] Includes maintenance, repairs, and construction improvement for privately owned units, in current dollars.
      [c] Includes only privately built units.
      [d] Includes private and public housing units.
      [e] Data on total stock not available for this year.

SOURCES: (1) U.S. Bureau of the Census, Social and Economic Statistics Administration, *Value of New Construction Put in Place,* Series C30 (Washington, D.C.: Government Printing Office, 1974).
         (2) U.S. Bureau of the Census, *Residential Alterations and Repairs,* Series C50 (Washington, D.C.: U.S. Bureau of the Census, various issues).
         (4) and (5) U.S. Bureau of the Census, *U.S. Census of Housing: 1970,* United States and Regions, HC(2)-1 (Washington, D.C.: Government Printing Office, 1972).

The primary hypothesis of owner-occupant superiority was tested using two specifications of a reduced-form supply and demand model estimated for a combined sample of owner-occupied and rental dwellings in which form of tenure was differentiated by a simple dummy variable. Both specifications were estimated for five income-stratified samples of households. In the first specification, this stratification was the only control for differences in characteristics of the dwellings and occupant households. The results indicate lower-income owner-occupant households — those with 1972 incomes of $7,500 or less — receive more housing services than renters of equivalent incomes; no such pattern for higher-income households is evident. The results of estimating this model under the second specification, in which supply and other demand factors are included as independent variables, show no tenure effects once neighborhood and occupant characteristics (e.g., age of head) have been taken into account. The hypothesis of greater efficiency on the part of owner-occupants was analyzed through the estimation of separate production functions for rental and owner-occupied dwellings. The main finding is that there is very little difference in the efficiency of the two groups of producers as measured here. This analysis was limited, though, by lack of data on some of the productive factors, most notably labor. For this reason, these results are presented with some diffidence.

The overall conclusion, then, is that owner-occupancy per se makes little difference among households in their equilibrium quantity of "basic" housing services — that is, housing services as defined by our four indices. Further . . . those differences for the lower-income households, which are evident where only income differences are controlled, appear to be predominantly demand determined. At the same time, while owner-occupants live in generally "larger" dwellings, these large structures do not necessarily imply better maintenance.
. . . .

Ignoring possible market effects, such as an increase in the price of owner-occupied housing, which might accompany an increase in the overall rate of homeownership, the evidence indicates that low- to middle-income rental households that switch to owner-occupancy will have higher levels of basic and other structural services and will reside in better neighborhoods. These effects assume implicitly that the new owner-occupants will exhibit the same demand for housing services and comparable efficiency as producers as do current owner-occupants. They also assume the presence of a stock of suitable dwellings and neighborhoods to satisfy the economic demands of the marginal homeowners. These are strong assumptions, the validity of which is extremely difficult to assess. Still, the evidence consistently supports the relation between homeownership and improved housing for families in this income range.

The second finding emerging from the elasticity estimates is that the response of owner-occupants and landlords to increases in the price per unit of housing services is quite similar. This implies that programs of direct cash subsidies — either unrestricted grants or grants earmarked in some way for expenditure on housing — may be of the same design regardless of tenure and still achieve the housing quality objectives of the program. This result does not, however, generally apply to capital or operating subsidies. . . . Because of statistical problems underlying the elasticity estimates, the conclusion that landlord and owner-occupants have similar supply elasticities is somewhat tentative, but it is presently the only evidence available on this point.

[The authors next present their conceptual analysis in mathematical terms and their two empirical analyses, the general results of which are summarized above.

Figure 2 was developed as part of their conceptual analysis. — Eds.]

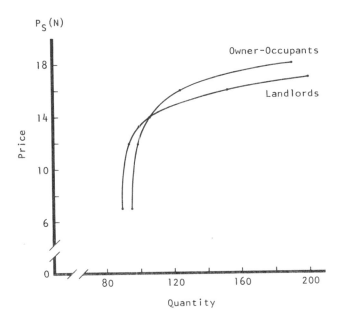

Figure 2. Hypothetical supply curves for owner-occupants and landlords (Redrawn from Ozanne & Struyk)

[Compare the shape of these curves with the straight line curves of the idealized supply graphs illustrating the note on microeconomics in Chapter 2, supra pp. 50-52. What are the implications of the difference in shape? —Eds.]

———

Comments: 1. Note that the Ozanne and Struyk study supports the conventional wisdom about the superiority of homeownership only for poorer households. They find that landlords do about as well for upper income households as they do for themselves as owners. Such a finding has critical implications for public policy on homeownership, especially the long-established policy of homeownership subsidy through tax policy. This topic is dealt with later in this volume in Chapter 8, but the implications are worth thinking about. Does tax policy provide more incentive to low income than high income owners? Should it?

2. The study also makes a provocative contribution to our understanding of the nature of the housing supply curves or functions. Comparing the curves for owners and landlords (figure 2), it appears that at lower prices the former provide more housing services, for a given price, and that both curves are very inelastic. (See also figure 2 in the Note on Microeconomics and Housing in Chapter 2.) As the price increases, both curves become elastic, though landlords reach this point sooner than owners. If, indeed, this hypothesis is correct, it indicates that landlords may respond faster to increased demand than owners, a point that could have useful policy implications in times or places of great need.

However, these curves repeat the central point of this sophisticated, state-of-the-art, economic analysis. That is, they suggest that rather slight differences distinguish landlord and homeowner behavior as measured with the economist's statistical tools. Other ways of looking at housing, particularly ones that use an institutional perspective, may disclose more significant differences. For this reason, the remaining pages of the chapter shift to a more eclectic, institutional view.

3. Popular beliefs characterize the landlords that serve low-income renter households as a special breed. The word "slumlord" typifies these beliefs. If such a special breed exists, it may explain in part the Ozanne-Struyk finding that low-income renters get less for their housing dollar than similar owners. In any case, the notion that the rental market is segmented by the existence of specialization among landlords is a pervasive one in public policy as well as in everyday talk. The following reading is but a fragment from a classic and exhaustive study by housing policy analyst George Sternlieb. It examines the owners of units serving low-income people in Newark, New Jersey.

STERNLIEB, THE TENEMENT LANDLORD 121-22, 124, 128, 131, 137-40 (1966)

Who Owns the Slums? A Profile

The much-publicized popular concept of the "slum lord" relies on the supposition that there are a small number of individuals who own the bulk of slum tenements. While large owners are far from an insignificant proportion of total ownership, as the research presented here indicates, the degree of concentration is much overstated. This is far from unique to Newark. For example, in Grebler's study of ownership in New York's Lower East Side, there is a strong indication that small holdings predominate. He states that, "If concentration is defined as a tendency for identical holders to own large numbers of parcels in the area, the records suggest that there is no wide-spread concentration of private ownership at the present time."

. . . .

. . . [In Newark] [o]f the total sample, 42.8 percent have owners who own no other parcels, 21.6 percent own one or two more, 10.9 percent own more than three and up to six, 7.8 percent own more than six and up through twelve, and 15.8 percent are owned by those who are in possession of more than twelve parcels. In the course of more than three hundred individual interviews undertaken with landlords, there were at least six owners who owned more than forty parcels; two of this group owned approximately two hundred parcels.

The majority of tenements are held in individual form. Just under 20 percent are held by corporations, and a nearly equal number are held by partnerships of two or more individuals. (Notice that holdings by husband and wife are counted as individual.) The comparatively limited use of corporate holdings is undoubtedly largely a function of the fact that borrowing on parcels in the slums of Newark typically requires personal signatures. The corporate indemnity, therefore, is of no value.

The typical slum owner concentrates his holdings in one city. Only 8.3 percent have holdings in Newark and one or more of the other older New Jersey cities, while a trivial proportion own parcels in a wider geographical span. This geographical specialization was paralleled by the types of parcels owned.

. . . [T]he bulk of slum parcels are held by slum specialists. Only 3.7 percent of the sample parcels are in the hands of owners who indicate that the bulk of their holdings are not slums; 6.3 percent indicate that there was a fifty-fifty range; 12 percent own largely slums with some others, while 33.9 percent indicate that all their holdings are of the same order. (Note that the last percentage excludes the 44.1 percent who own no other type of parcel.) *Owning slums, therefore, is a relatively specialized occupation. The investor in this type of property typically is not party to other areas of real estate investment.* Slum ownership is a distinct subset of real estate ownership in general with little crossing over into the broader area. Government programs which might appeal to the latter may have no effect on slum owners and vice versa.

[A study done at about the same time by one of the editors corroborates Sternlieb's specialization finding. It showed that slum landlords in St. Louis who were bought out by an urban renewal project took their sale proceeds and reinvested them in other slum property outside the project area. See Mandelker & Heeter, Investment Activities of Relocated Tenement Landlords — A Pilot Study, 1968 Urban Law Annual 33. This finding raises interesting questions about public policy directed at slum removal. In his study, Sternlieb raises some parallel questions about public efforts to achieve the rehabilitation of slum housing. In the remaining paragraphs of this excerpt these questions are discussed together with the basic study findings. — Eds.]

. . . More than half of the parcels are owned by people to whom real estate represents a trivial supplement to income. Only 19.5 percent are in the possession of people who think of themselves as securing three-quarters or more of their income from real estate holdings. To a considerable degree this reflects the comparatively amateur kind of holder who predominates in the market. The significance of this factor from the viewpoint of securing rehabilitation should not be overlooked. Many of the owners interviewed in the course of this study are owners by default rather than by purpose; are owners by inheritance; or by lack of purchasers to buy unwanted properties; or by a relatively trivial investment which is not too meaningful in terms of over-all capital or income. Shaking these owners loose from their lethargy and making them aware of possible governmental programs for aiding rehabilitation is perhaps much more difficult than doing the equivalent for the full-time real estate owner. The latter may well be a "hard case," but since he derives his living from real estate there may well be less inertia to overcome. *Programs may more easily be explained and more easily sold to the professional than to the amateur.*

There are a significant number of small holders who depend on rental income substantially. Not infrequently these are elderly, retired, or disabled individuals with no capacity for investment either in cash or 'sweat. In the face of a weak market their policy tends to be one of conservatism to the point of immobility.

What are the occupations of slum tenement owners? . . . The largest single occupational classification is nonhouse-oriented craftsmen. . . . Real estate brokers and real estate managers together are second in importance, owning some eighty-two out of the three hundred eighty-nine parcels for which this information was secured. Lawyers, who are often thought of as major investors in slum real estate, are much less important than might have been anticipated. Only twenty of the parcels were owned by this occupational category.

. . . [T]he large-scale owners are largely professional real estate people with lawyers and housecraft-oriented businessmen trailing behind.

There is a wide diversity of occupations among those people who own only a single parcel. The largest proportion are nonhouse-oriented craftsmen, while a substantial number, 16.9 percent, are retired. No other occupational category contains as much as 9 percent of the total group.

There is a little variation in age of owner by area. . . . In the absolute, however, there are a substantial number of elderly owners. More than half of the owners are over fifty; and a quarter of them are more than sixty. (The significance of this age factor, which is in part a function of the ethnic distribution of ownership, will be discussed more fully in a later chapter.) Only 15 percent of all the sample parcels are owned by people under the age of forty. *The typical parcel, therefore, is owned by people of late middle-age.* Certainly one of the inhibitors of investment in the uncertainties of rehabilitation must be accepted as the age of the owner.

As might be surmised by the prevalence of single-parcel owners, 36.6 percent of the parcels in the sample areas are lived in by their owners. An additional 10.2 percent of the parcels are owned by people who live within the study areas, but not within the specific parcel sampled. Fully 35 percent of all parcels are owned by people who live outside of Newark, though within a twenty-mile radius. A relatively trivial proportion live outside this radius. (While this proportion may be somewhat understated by the difficulties of contacting absentee landlords who live at considerable distances from the city ... the understatement is not significant.)

... [T]he same data is analyzed by size of parcel holdings. Few of the major holders live within either the study area or, for that matter, Newark itself. Nearly 90 percent of them live outside Newark. The proportion within this category descends as the size of holdings decreases. The vast bulk of the owners of single parcels live in the house which they own. Typically, those who do not, formerly did.

... [M]ore than a third of the three hundred eighty-six parcels for which data was secured on this point are owned by Negroes. ...

... [T]here are no Negroes in the largest size holding category. Of the one hundred twenty-nine parcels owned by Negroes in the sample that were analyzable in this detail, only one is owned by an individual having six to twelve parcels, nine are owned by holders of three to six parcels, with nearly a quarter in the hands of owners of two or three parcels while the bulk of Negro owners own single parcels.

It will be helpful to examine more closely the various categories of landlords as a function of size of holdings.

The Big-Time Professional

Of the parcels whose owners were interviewed, 15.8 percent were held by owners of more than twelve properties. Who are these people? Typically they are white middle-aged businessmen, representing the earlier immigrant strains in Newark, substantially Jewish and Italian, who now live in the upper middle-class suburbs which surround the city. The major proportion are professional real estate people. Their modular age is in the fifty-to-sixty bracket. With a few exceptions, the bulk of their holdings are in slum properties either in Newark or in other Northern New Jersey cities. They are essentially slum specialists. As such, they can afford an infra-structure which would be too costly for lesser holders. This refers to the fact that typically they employ full-time repair and maintenance people. Their parcels receive at least a minimal degree of maintenance. At the same time, however, they rarely own the best-maintained of parcels. Most of them have been in the rental real estate business for more than fifteen years, and as such they are seasoned operators, wary of doing more than is absolutely required in maintaining parcels.

. . . .

A frequent response to the question of "What source would you turn to if you needed financing?" among this category of owners was "personal resources." By and large, it is, as would be expected, a sophisticated group. Selling a rehabilitation program to owners in this category, assuming that it promised a high enough return, would probably be easiest of all of the landlord categories.

The Part-Time but Still Significant Holder

The owners of six to twelve parcels are a much more diverse group — 13.3 percent of them live within the study area and 23.3 percent live in the balance of Newark. A little less than half of this category of landholders are not real estate brokers or managers by profession. There is a wide diversity of professions with craftsmen, housecraft-oriented businessmen, and, surprisingly enough, unskilled workers being in chief categories. When the question was asked: "Why did you buy the property at [address]?" the answers of this group largely revolved around rental return, though 12.9 percent had inherited their holdings. It is this group ... which shows the greatest degree of disillusionment on the potential profitability of slum holdings. Typically they cannot afford the full-time services of repairmen which larger holders can secure. Only 25.8 percent of this category of holders give full time to rental properties. While a few holders in this category do the bulk of their own repair work and maintain their parcels uncommonly-well, they are exceptions.

How does this category of owners get started? There is no single answer. Perhaps a couple of brief profiles will define the general nature of the ambient. One landlord said:

> My husband was in the installment business and he decided, at the suggestion of a friend, to purchase some rental properties instead of expanding his business. We bought our first parcel about five years ago.

The couple now owns nine parcels with a total of forty-five apartments.

. . . .

The Impersonality of the Larger-Scale Owner

It is obvious that the substantial owner of slum real estate is not in business for altruistic purposes. The really active owner may buy and sell parcels at a considerable rate. As such, the individual parcel may have little meaning for him. It becomes an impersonal element in his business life, having no relationship to the fact that people live in it. For example, one of the major owners interviewed in the course of this study secured a parcel in Area 1 as part of a package deal involving six parcels. He told the interviewer:

> As soon as I bought the parcel; and I bought it as part of a package; I looked around to try to get rid of it. It was in lousy condition, and simply wasn't worthwhile keeping. It took me the better part of four years to sell the parcel in question. . . . It wasn't worth my while to improve the parcel since I planned on selling it.

In this particular case the parcel, for three or four years, just consistently degenerated.

At least on a number of occasions in the course of the interviewing, the phenomenon was found that the owner of record knew very little, if anything, about the parcel to which he held title. . . .

This degree of noninvolvement is often accentuated by the geographical gap between the living place of the owner and the parcel. Perhaps the most poorly-maintained parcel in the sample is in Area 3A. It is a parcel which can best be described in the words of our field surveyor: ". . . surrounded by garbage, stairs rotting, property in terrible shape." The owner, an engineer, inherited the property. He lives in another state; has an income level in the $11,000 to $20,000 bracket; and states his attitude towards the parcel very clearly: "I want to sell it; I'm not afraid of being reassessed because I'm not going to make any improvements." When asked what improvements he would make if he were sure of not getting a boost in taxes, he replied, "None, the parcel isn't worth it." The inheritance factor noted in the above case should not be underestimated as a source of poor maintenance. The recipient frequently has no involvement in the real estate business, no knowledge of proper maintenance procedures, and basically just tries to get out from under the parcel. Given a weak market, however, this may be a very lengthy process. For example:

> Mr. X and his sister inherited a parcel in Area 3A from their father, which at one time had been the family residence. Mr. X has no interest in the building other than to keep it standing until the city buys it for scheduled urban renewal project. He says he makes minor repairs to conform with building and health regulations, but he will not make major improvements. He complained bitterly that someone took out the copper pipes from a vacant apartment and that he had light bulbs taken from the hall. Also, fixtures and electric wires were tapped by the tenants for the tenants' personal use, etc. He finds the whole deal "a pain" and he just wants to get out.

Comments: As noted in the introductory comment, Sternlieb's characterization of tenement landlords offers a plausible institutional explanation for some of the difference in housing services received by low-income tenants in contrast to owners. It also gives an insight into the richness of institutional perspectives on housing questions. The next brief reading offers more along the same line in a somewhat more timely context. While perhaps a majority of low-income urban neighborhoods continue to experience decline, the market in some of these neighborhoods has become hyperactive with strong upward price increases since the mid-1960s when Sternlieb did his research. This change has led to a more complex pattern of landlord behavior. Trading in similar properties, a feature Sternlieb emphasized along with landlord specialization, has become a prime opportunity for profit making through capital gains. The following short excerpt from a work by a team of Boston community development experts illustrates these profit opportunities and provides brief, almost cartoonlike pictures of the various species of landlords and investors at work in inner city neighborhoods.

R. GOETZE, K. COLTON & V. O'DONNELL, STABILIZING NEIGHBORHOODS B-2-5, 7-9 (1977)

The Case of Two Specific Buildings

Let us begin with a hypothetical property in the Fenway section of Boston whose case history is abstracted from Boston Redevelopment Authority research into housing dynamics. Here, within walking distance of Symphony Hall, Northeastern University, and The Boston Museum of Fine Arts, a neighborhood called Seven Streets has experienced traumatic changes in the last fifteen years as students displaced long term family and elderly tenants, only to find in turn that minorities, then hookers and addicts are moving in on their heels. Sensationalizing reporters call it a disaster like the South Bronx.

This illustrative example could be called the Case of Two Buildings in Boston, identical in appearance and on the same street, but one in long-term ownership, the other changing hands several times to take advantage of appreciation and to avoid losses. Ownership turnover correlates inversely with condition and financial stability. Here we will explore this interrelationship more closely, abstracting data from forty building case histories in the area. Data were compiled from the records of the Tax Assessor and Collector-Treasurer, Rent Control, Registry of Deeds, as well as through interviews with owners, tenants, managers, investors, lenders, appraisers, and some newspaper reporters.

The Experience with a Single Owner

The many complex interlinked factors in the multi-family market system can best be understood in a composite case. Figure A reveals the change over the last dozen years in a prototypical thirty unit apartment structure. It shows gross rent, operating expenses and property taxes in 1964 and 1976 as well as some financial indicators used in conventional analysis. Because the analysis offers some startling insights, it is worth following closely.

Figure A. One owner Fenway building financial history (30 Apartments)

		1964	1968	1972	1976
1.	Annual Gross Rent	$ 30,000			$ 68,000
2.	Operating Expenses	10,000			25,000
3.	Property Taxes	7,000			23,000
4.	Owner's Net Income (before financing)	13,000			20,000
5.	Cap Factor	.087			.125
6.	Imputed Market Value	$150,000			$160,000
7.	Outstanding Mortgages	105.000			60,000
8.	Owner's Equity	45,000			100,000
9.	Gross Rent Multiplier (GRM)	5.0			2.3

Figure B. Several owner Fenway building financial history (30 Apartments)

		1964	1968	1972	1976
1.	Gross Annual Rent	$ 30,000	$ 50,000	$ 70,000	$ 68,000
2.	Operating Expenses	10,000	12,000	17,000	25,000
3.	Property Taxes	7,000	8,000	20,000	23,000
4.	Owner's Net Income (before financing)	13,000	30,000	33,000	20,000
5.	Cap Factor	.087	.10	.10	.125
6.	Imputed Market Value	150,000	300,000	330,000	160,000
7.	Outstanding Mortgages	105,000	255,000	285,000	250,000
8.	Owner's Equity	45,000	45,000	45,000	(90,000)
9.	Gross Rent Multiplier (GRM)	5.0	6.0	4.7	2.3

Gross annual rent (line 1) reflects a change in monthly rents from around $83 monthly per apartment to $189, roughly in step with inflation over the period.

Operating expenses (line 2) more than doubled, while city taxes on the property (line 3) more than tripled (primarily due to changes in the tax rate, not reassessment — for years Boston has not regularly reassessed real property). The owner's net income before financing (line 4) increased only a little over 50 per cent because operating expenses and property taxes have claimed more than their share of the increased rents.

This investment in real property has been yielding this one owner a steady and reasonable return on equity, while the value of the structure has actually declined when measured in constant dollars. ($160,000 in 1976 have less purchasing power than $150,000 did in 1964.) This investment resembles a high yield bond in some ways, but is much riskier.

While the market value of the property has risen only marginally (line 6, based on dividing line 4 by line 5, the market rate capitalization factor), the gross rent multiplier or GRM has dropped from 5.0 to 2.3 (line 9, obtain by dividing line 6 by line 1). This is ominous. At a GRM of 5.0 an investor sees a long time horizon. He expects capital improvements to pay back. However, at 2.3 he is discouraged from any further investments that do not bring a quick return.

The Experience with Owner Turnover

Figure B indicates what has happened to the same property when it has changed hands or been refinanced to enable profit taking.

Figure B contains two basic differences from Figure A. Data for intervening years (1968-1972) have been introduced, and the property in 1976 has a much higher outstanding mortgage indebtedness giving the latest owner "negative equity". Gross annual rent (line 1) initially increased sharply due to the influx of student housing demand, but declined after 1972, due to a changing population, rent skip outs, vacancies, and rent control.

Operating expenses (line 2), on the other hand, were slow to increase after the student demand increased, but post-Vietnam and oil inflation have recently forced expenses sharply up.

Property taxes (line 3) were rising with the general tax rate but in 1973 the City assessors used rent control data to revise tax assessments in order to collect *30* per cent of gross rent in taxes, sic.

Net income before financing (line 4), first soared as a result of strong demand, then plunged, because of lags in operating expenses coupled with weakened demand.

Market value rose and fell between 1964 and 1976 (line 6). Translating varying net income through the appropriate capitalization factor reveals that property value has doubled and then dropped back to nearly its former level. The owner who refinanced or traded, saw his $45,000 equity "earn" him $150,000 between 1964 and 1968, and a further $30,000 between '68 and '72. However, from '72 to '76, there was a loss in value of $170,000. If $180,000 was "taken out" between '64 and '72, $170,000 now must be "put back in". Who wants to do that?

The gross rent multiplier (line 9), that conventional rule of thumb for judging value, did not warn of impending reversals, but stayed near 5 until 1976. It was generally accepted that property values were roughly five times annual rents — and even today many Boston real estate actors, including potential buyers, would assume from the financial data that the property is worth around $300,000. Those who have recently seen the area know the current value of the property is uncertain, but insurance is still in force at the higher value. In the event of loss, mortgage holders stand to be reimbursed.

Various Investor-Owner Types Signal Market Changes

New breeds of investors thrive in these rapidly shifting markets. If they do not actually cause the shifts, their presence at least indicates them. . . . [S]even discernible prototypes of owners [were] encountered in the BRA study of multi-family, investor-owned housing in all parts of the City of Boston. . . . [A] few brief words on the types are in order.

Established Owners and *Blue Collar Investors* have traditionally and ably served tenant housing needs in stable markets. . . . [T]hey have a long and steady perspective, acting as trustworthy custodians for their part of the housing inventory. While they easily ride out the ebbs and flows of the market, they have a low tolerance for administrative complexity.

Traders . . . speculate in rising markets and never intend to own or manage their properties for long. Ideally, they just take options, but in fact they outbid [Established Owners and Blue Collar Investors] in rising markets, taking over.

Operators . . . come closest to the stereotypical slumlord and signal a weak or declining housing market. While deterioration proceeds with both *Traders* and *Operators,* they *indicate opposite market tendencies and must not be confused* one with the other. The Operators become or remain owners of properties no one else wants or can handle, "milk the cash flow", and cut all corners they can. While Traders speculate in value, Operators manage what has indeterminate value.

Shareholders . . . dream they can be Zeckendorfs or pursue business school fantasies, but have limited grasp of the actual complexities of housing investment. Frequently Shareholders are the customers of Traders who anticipate a deterioration in market climate.

Rehabbers and Developers . . . have come into being in response to our complex housing programs and are now the primary ones able to make the programs deliver. As an interest group they interact closely (some say manipulate) public administrators and policy makers at the city, state and national level.

Special Forces . . . are so unconventional that they defy categorization, but their wide ranging abilities impress all with whom they interact. Some were formerly Traders and now handle conversions to condominiums and the like. Rehabbers may be another simple subset of this type.

In reality they seldom are as pure as this typology suggests, but once the prototypes are clear and we know what to look for, differentiating actual investors is relatively simple.

Comments: 1. Landlord and investor behavior in both declining and upgrading areas form a central focus among those concerned with housing. Readings in this book will return frequently to this theme, especially in the chapters on dynamics, neighborhood revitalization, race, and landlord tenant relations. The illustrative financial histories by Goetze and his colleagues provide useful background for these forthcoming discussions.

2. The emphasis on real estate professionals in both of the above selections serves to highlight their central role in the housing economy. This is true of nearly all submarkets. In the biggest of them, the market for single, owner-occupied homes priced for the middle to upper income buyer, real estate agents play a key role. The late, great housing authority William L. C. Wheaton called this group of professionals "the prime social engineers of American community life." Geographer Risa Palm deals with this theme in the next selection.

R. PALM, URBAN SOCIAL GEOGRAPHY FROM THE PERSPECTIVE OF THE REAL ESTATE SALESMAN xii, 18-19, 25-28, 72-74, 100-02, 149-51 (1976)

Real estate agents are in an important position as information sources concerning the social geography of a city. They alone possess a breadth of knowledge about comparative prices, qualities of housing, and neighborhood characteristics which place them in a position of being able to provide evaluations as well as facts about probable resale, quality of local schools, and appreciation of the property in price. It is therefore important for those who wish to understand how neighborhoods attract certain types of buyers to recognize the role of the opinions and influences of real estate agents.

   . . . .

[The author then surveys the literature on search procedures of prospective home buyers, linking them to the notion of "neighborhood reputation" as an important determinant in the home purchaser's locational decisions. In the next passage, Palm discusses how brokers match buyers to neighborhoods. — Eds.]

In past years, even the so-called "formal channels" of information were active in directing newcomers to "appropriate" neighborhoods: signs and advertisements indicated those areas which were "restricted," often to white Christians, and real estate agents acted as social filters to maintain the neighborhood character. A 1953-54 study of a New England suburban community characterized the Realtor's role:

> With detailed knowledge of the town and considerable skill in translating the prospective home buyer's outer symbols — occupation, name, behavior — into a "type," the agent steers his client to the "right" house in the "right" neighborhood for him. Houses more attractive to the buyer or locales more in line with his aspirations may never have been shown him if the agent decides the client would not "fit in" there.

In a more recent survey in New Haven, Connecticut, real estate agents were found to exercise a conservative role in maintaining the character of the community. A few agents were known as "block-busters," speculators who purposely placed non-white families in white neighborhoods in an attempt to profit from subsequent panic sales by former residents. However, most indicated a belief that the agent should attempt to "protect" neighborhoods.

Individual realtors were quoted:

> I not only try to sell the house, but I try to sell it to an individual who will pretty much fit into the neighborhood . . .

and

> He [the Realtor] is needed to improve communities by upgrading residents of the neighborhood . . .

and

> You have to ask yourself how they would fit into the neighborhood. You don't want to put a Catholic or Protestant into a Jewish neighborhood because they are generally unhappy there . . . If they're unhappy with their house they blame the Realtor, and they certainly won't go back to him.

Thus, there is substantial evidence that, in the past, real estate agents actually re-directed persons of the "wrong" race, religion, or economic class from certain areas. At present the influence of Realtors is more subtle. . . .

[The author next argues that the influence of the real estate sales person is dependent upon the quality of her or his information. — Eds.]

The most important factor in broadening the stock of information of a real estate salesperson employed by a single company is the company's membership in a Multiple Listing Service. The Multiple Listing Service is defined by the California Department of Real Estate as:

> A cooperative listing service conducted by a group of brokers, usually members of a real estate board. The group provides a standard "multiple listing" form which is used by the members. It is usually an "Exclusive Authorization Right to Sell" listing form, and provides, among other things, that the member of the group who takes the particular listing is to turn it in to a central bureau. From there it is distributed to all participants in the service and all have the right to work on it. Commissions earned on such listings are shared between the cooperating brokers, with the listing broker providing for the division of commission in his listing sent to other participants.

Specific rules detailing procedures, such as how much time can elapse between the time the listing firm lists the property and when it is to turn it over to MLS, and the details on the division of commission vary from one MLS group to another. In the San Francisco Bay Area, many properties are sold by members of the MLS through an "exclusive agency listing," or an "exclusive right to sell listing," in which the listing broker may gain a commission on the property sale if it is consummated within the time limit contracted between the broker and the seller. In this case, properties never reach the Multiple Listing Service. These kinds of properties are typically those in high demand areas, within price ranges which are particularly attractive to buyers. . . .

The general question which was studied here was whether or not real estate salespersons affiliated with the largest realty companies and associated with the Multiple Listing Service, those persons who should have the widest range of knowledge about the nature of vacancies in used housing, had limited knowledge and biased opinions of neighborhoods within the metropolitan area. . . . In other words, an attempt was made to ascertain the limits to the information which may be obtained from even the most knowledgeable of sources.

Two metropolitan areas were selected for study. The San Francisco Bay Area, with its thirteen separate boards of Realtors within a five-county metropolitan area, was selected because it would be expected that with so many independent and possibly competing boards of Realtors, and with a great variety of physical and social environments within the metropolitan area, there would be a highly localized information field. The Minneapolis area was selected as a contrasting study, because of its relatively homogeneous population and less complex physical setting, and the existence of only one board of Realtors with one Multiple Listing Service providing information on the entire area.

The . . . research hypothesis was that overall, the recommendations of real estate salespersons concerning areas which are most "appropriate" for particular family types corresponds with the current patterns of residence. In other words, if one asked a sample of real estate agents throughout the Bay Area where a longshoreman working at the Port of Oakland should live, there would be general agreement, and that this agreement would be accurate in the sense that it would reflect the actual distribution of Oakland longshoremen.

To test this hypothesis, a questionnaire was designed to attempt to obtain real estate salespersons' opinions as to the appropriateness of particular neighborhoods and suburbs. Over 450 agents, at least three and as many as eight from each of the ninety-five largest companies, responded to a mail survey, a response rate of about sixty percent. The questionnaire consisted of a map of the San Francisco Bay Area on which eighty-four neighborhoods or communities were named. . . . Four hypothetical families, each headed by a male working in downtown San Francisco, and whose occupation was selected from one of four positions along a standard occupation rating scale, were to be matched with these districts. In every case the female spouse was a housewife not employed outside the home, and the family included two children aged 8 and 15. . . .

This survey of real estate agent evaluations of the appropriateness of various neighborhoods and suburbs for four family types shows that agents are most familiar with territories in their immediate sales area, and are largely ignorant of other areas. . . . What is perhaps more surprising and even disturbing to those who have had faith in the ameliorating influence of inter-company collaboration, is that the existence of a Multiple Listing Service, and of multi-branched companies with local offices in many if not all the five counties, does little to broaden the perspective of the individual salesman. Whether or not the agent is affiliated with a multi-office company, there is virtually no information exchanged, for example, between Marin and Contra Costa counties.

. . . .

But what if there were only one board of Realtors for companies throughout the five-county Bay Area? Would there be any less specialization in the information available to the buyer if he approached a real estate salesman who, through his company's membership in a wider-ranging Multiple Listing Service, could provide him with information about cities and neighborhoods in any part of the SMSA? Would the agent's information be broader in range if the metropolitan area he worked in were smaller and more homogeneous, as well as being unified under a single system of Multiple Listing Service exchange of information? To try to gain a perspective on these questions, a study was undertaken in such a setting, Minneapolis, Minnesota. The questions which were to be answered were the same as those investigated in the San Francisco area: what is the nature of geographical bias in the information provided by real estate agents to hypothetical families?

In Minneapolis, as in the Bay Area, the three research hypotheses are confirmed. First, realty companies do cover limited portions of the housing market in both price and area. Although a single, unified board of Realtors in some ways mitigates the divisive effects of the many boards in the Bay Area with their seemingly exclusive division of sales territories, areal coverage still varies from companies which list houses in but a single neighborhood to those which cover large portions of the urban area. Similarly, price coverage varies from those companies specializing in high-priced or low-priced houses, to those which list houses in all price brackets.

Second, the overall evaluations of Realtors taken together provide a generally accurate portrayal of the houses listed for sale throughout the metropolitan area. . . .

Third, individual agents show marked differences in their evaluations of those neighborhoods which are most appropriate for certain types of home buyers. . . .

Thus, even in a metropolitan area which is relatively simple in physical structure and composition, in which the complexities of a nearby, competing center have been eliminated for research purposes, and in which real estate companies are organized into a unified Board of Realtors, the information on the housing market is segmented.

Comments: 1. These findings about segmentation make an interesting extension of the concept of submarket developed in the Grigsby reading reproduced in Chapter 2. They show that market imperfections in the form of poor information can define submarkets. Although Palm concentrates on the quality of information possessed by real estate agents, her work gives credence to the idea that this group exerts considerable control over the free market behavior of theoretically perfectly informed and willing buyers and sellers. If true, and it almost certainly is, such control calls into question some of the fundamental assumptions on which microeconomic analysis is based. This in turn substantiates the institutionalist perspective. Through the information they control, though it may be both incomplete and only partially accurate, the real estate professionals exert a powerful, sometimes dominating influence on economic relations by virtue of defining submarkets and steering buyers and sellers.

2. Financial institutions offer another case in which the market power of an institution exerts sufficient control to confound the microeconomists' simplifying assumptions. So powerful is their position that they are thought by many to dominate the housing economy. In discussing the rise of housing debt in Chapter 2, Stone (supra p. 67) has already highlighted this point. His work embodies the Marxist position that the institutions of finance capital create the demand for financing. Stone sees the mortgage system as their self-interested creation, and federal monetary policy as simply another face of finance capitalism. More familiar is the orthodox view that the nature of demand is the prime mover. Economists Keal, Rosen and Swan recently put it this way: "[I]n the long-run stock demand for housing is primarily a function of income, relative prices, the rental rate of housing services and the size and age-structure of the population with monetary policy and the parameters of the mortgage instrument having little, if any, impact on these basic demand factors." So it may be at the macroeconomic level. On the micro level the control exerted by the financial institutions is ever present.

Financial institutions involved in housing finance are also called financial intermediaries, and the essential task they perform is called intermediation. Intermediation refers to the role banks play between savers and spenders in that they act as a conduit of funds between the two. Basically banks, savings and loan associations, and other financial firms borrow money from savers or depositors and lend it to borrowers or, in the case of home loans, to mortgagees. Because of their size, diversity, and the way intermediaries are structured and regulated, the differing time preferences and risk and interest rate requirements of savers and borrowers can be accommodated simultaneously. However, economic conditions and regulatory conditions can strongly influence the ability of banks to intermediate between spenders and savers. These issues are discussed at length in Chapter 7.

The Stone reading in Chapter 2 supra p. 67 describes the mortgage loan system of housing finance.

The following pair of brief readings introduce the major kinds of financial institutions involved in supplying housing capital and give a very brief insight into how they behave in one rather controversial area. Readings on the behavior of such money firms are few. It might have been more reasonable to have an excerpt from a day in the life of a real estate loan officer but that book has not yet been written.

STRATEGY FOR CHANGE: HOUSING FINANCE IN WASHINGTON, D.C. 12, 14 (FINAL REPORT OF THE D.C. COMMISSION ON RESIDENTIAL MORTGAGE INVESTMENT, 1977)

Financial institutions concerned with housing finance fall basically into two categories — deposit and contract. The former receive their funds from depositors through checking and savings accounts, and the latter primarily from life insurance policies and pension funds.

Deposit Institutions

Commercial Banks

By far the largest group of financial institutions are the commerical banks. Their loans primarily are directed to the business community and consumer retail credit (auto loans). The banks generally avoid long-term mortgage loans, but are more active in short-term rehabilitation and construction loan areas.

Savings and Loan Associations

Savings and loans have about one-third of the total assets of commercial banks. However, because 85% of their assets are in residential mortgages, they are the largest single factor in residential mortgage lending; S&Ls held nearly 50% of all mortgage properties of one-to-four-family units by the third quarter of 1974. The growth of the S&Ls is significant: in 1950 they provided only 29% of the total outstanding residential debt.

Of some 5,000 savings and loan associations nationally, about seven out of eight are organized as mutuals, where the depositor members receive the profits of the business and also are presumed to elect the directors and officers. The remaining one in eight is a stock company organized as a commerical enterprise, where control and residual profits are held by shareholders (similar to commercial banks). S&Ls also must be either state or federally chartered.

Mutual Savings Banks

There are no mutual savings banks in Washington, D.C., and only 18 states and Puerto Rico authorize their establishment. They can only be chartered by state governments, although a majority of them have their deposits insured by the federal government. Historically, the mutual savings bank has been a cross between a commercial bank and an S&L. Like the commercial bank, it can make commercial and consumer loans. Like the S&L, it invests heavily in mortgage loans . . . and is controlled by its depositors (conversion to a stock company is prohibited). . . .

Credit Unions

Credit unions generally make a very small number of mortgage loans because of charter restrictions placed on them by state and federal government agencies. Federal chartering requirements place a ten-year limit on all secured loans such as mortgages, and no single loan can exceed 10% of the credit union's total assets (which normally are much smaller than bank or S&L assets). . . . Credit union loans are limited to persons belonging to the membership as defined by the state or federal charter. Each member has one vote for the election of directors. Unlike other depository institutions, credit unions invest a large majority of their funds in consumer loans and, to a lesser extent, in rehabilitation loans.

Contract Institutions

Life Insurance Companies

Life insurance companies are the second largest type of financial institution and have always invested in mortgages, since state law prohibits most of them from investing in common stock. Unlike those of depository institutions, their mortgage holdings on one-to-four-unit residential property have declined sharply during the past eight years. . . . It should be noted, however, that their mortgage holdings on multi-unit residential property have increased steadily, placing the companies second (behind the S&Ls) in this mortgage category. Although the major life insurance companies operate throughout the nation, they are not regulated by the federal government, but are partially regulated by state governments.

Mortgage Bankers

Mortgage bankers actually are intermediaries (middlemen) for financial institutions (particularly life insurance companies) and the federal government. Normally mortgage bankers function in three ways:

1. The mortgage companies originate mortgages, using their own funds or money borrowed from commercial banks.

2. They may service the mortgages they originate, even if a long-term investor has bought the mortgages.

3. They may hold temporarily the mortgages they have originated after making the loan to the borrower, until the long-term investor is ready to make the acquisition.

Unlike depository institutions, mortgage bankers historically have made a substantial number of 100% federally funded, insured loans. Mortgage bankers are *not* regulated by the federal and state governments as are other financial institutions.

Comments: The share of the long-term mortgage market held by each of these financial institutions has remained comparatively stable over the past several years. For example, savings and loan associations provided more than half of the funds for mortgages originated on one to four family homes in 1978. Commercial banks and mortgage companies each provided about one-third of this amount. Savings and loan associations played an appreciably smaller and other financial institutions an appreciably greater role in providing mortgages for multifamily properties.

State and local government retirement funds are one source of mortgage finance not discussed in the above excerpt. Their assets have been growing at a rapid annual rate and they are expected to make substantial increases in their holdings of mortgage loans.

UNITED STATES COMMISSION ON CIVIL RIGHTS, EQUAL OPPORTUNITY IN SUBURBIA 22-23 (1974)

Financial Institutions

For a family to buy a house, or a landlord to provide apartments, a source of credit is necessary. The family, even if it has a substantial income, will require a long term mortgage to be able to purchase a house. The landlord will need a mortgage to obtain the capital necessary for the renovation of his property. It is not surprising, therefore, that the practices and attitudes of financial institutions —savings and loan associations, banks, mortgage brokers, and insurance companies—will have a significant impact on the housing market. If these institutions are unwilling, for example, to give a mortgage loan to a black family that wishes to buy a house in a white neighborhood or if they refuse to make available mortgage loans at reasonable rates in a neighborhood that is predominantly black or substantially integrated, then blacks will not be able to find housing outside of black neighborhoods and housing within black neighborhoods will deteriorate.

. . . .

Institutions which finance the housing market have limited minority access to suburban markets by practices which discourage integrated community development and heighten residential segregation.

A survey conducted by the Federal Home Loan Bank Board revealed a number of discriminatory practices among lending institutions. Some lenders admitted using the race of an applicant as a factor in determining whether he would be given the loan or in determining the terms under which the loan would be made.

Other common practices of mortgage lenders, the survey also found, while perhaps not instituted in order to discriminate, have the effect of discriminating against minority applicants. For example, lenders discount disproportionately a working wife's income and use the existence of an arrest record as a bar to the approval of a mortgage.

"Redlining" is a practice by which certain residential areas, often of substandard ghetto housing, are excluded from eligibility or greatly disfavored for mortgage financing. The justification for this practice generally is presented in terms of the area's "rundown condition." Thirty percent of the responding mortgage lenders admitted to disqualifying neighborhoods for loans because of their residential composition. The predictable result has been to accelerate the area's decline, speeding the exodus of those, usually whites, able to flee to better neighborhoods.

A. J. Wilson, University City's Human Relations Commission director, described the impact of practices such as redlining:

> We in University City have had to face, because of 16 percent of our population being black, many of the same forms of discrimination that black people have experienced for years. We have trouble getting developers to come in, we have trouble getting financing for development, we have trouble getting mortgages, we have some insurance companies starting to say: "We are going to stop insuring."

Another discriminatory practice consists of appraising properties at a lower value in black or mixed areas than in all-white areas, making whites reluctant to sell to nonwhites. Mr. Wilson complained that even FHA appraisers share this bias:

> [T]hese things occur today where FHA appraisers come out and are appraising that property on the basis of the neighborhood . . . on the basis of the fact that there are black people there, when in fact University City is better physically today because of a variety of improvements and code enforcement and in our housing program, better physically today than it was 5 years ago.

Most of the practices described above are specifically prohibited by the latest Federal Home Loan Bank Board guidelines, issued in December 1973.

Comments: 1. The short note by the Civil Rights Commission on financial institutions touches on the same general point made in Palm's study of the real estate business. Both emphasize the critical position of housing institutions and their behavior. In both cases the characteristics of the institutions themselves have perverse effects on the way the market functions. Real estate agents do not provide buyers and sellers with the perfect information on which proper market functioning depends. Financial institutions operate in ways that inhibit open access for certain classes of buyers. Similar effects could be charged to other actors and institutions, not only those concerned with supplying housing services from the existing stock, but also those who supply new units. The last group is collectively referred to as the housing industry. In addition to real estate professionals and financial institutions, the industry involves a vast collection of other participants. Informed observers Meisel and Roulac estimate that the industry is composed of 1.8 million firms. The next reading, a rather long excerpt from an excellent federal government report, familiarly known as the Kaiser Committee Report, describes the housing industry.

2. That an excerpt from a government report appears at this point is significant. Until recently, almost all public policy on housing as such was directed at the new construction industry. Most studies of housing, most textbooks, and most public policy documents exhibit this fixation. The material covered in the next two readings but scratches the

surface of this rich literature. The chapter bibliography offers some supplementary sources.

REPORT OF THE PRESIDENT'S COMMITTEE ON URBAN HOUSING: A DECENT HOME 113-17, 149-58, 161-64, 181-85 (1968)

The Distinct Features of the Housing Industry

The "housing industry"—defined here to include all firms which share in the receipts of expenditures for housing—is one of the most complex in the American economy. The firms which perform the critical function of putting together the finished housing unit make up the heart of the industry. These home assemblers include homebuilders, contractors, home manufacturers (and their dealers) and mobile home producers. These firms procure their materials from an extraordinary range of building products manufacturers, from tiny millwork plants to some of the nation's largest corporations. Distribution of these materials from manufacturer to assembler is carried out primarily by specialized wholesalers and retailers—lumberyards and hardware stores, for example. Acquisition and preparation of land for the ultimate construction of housing commonly involves real estate brokers, lawyers, title insurance companies, surveyors, and civil engineers, and possibly land planners and landscape architects. Engineers and architects are sometimes involved in design. Much on-site construction work is characteristically performed by specialty subcontractors; painting, plumbing, and electrical work, for example. Financing, needed both by the builders to complete construction and development and by buyers to finance purchase of completed units, is available through a battery of lending institutions. Operation of apartments may involve superintendents or management firms. Maintenance of housing adds to the cast of characters—for example, repairmen, janitors, remodeling firms, and domestic workers.

Thus, the housing industry is made up of literally millions of business enterprises. Most are small and specialized, and competition throughout the industry is characteristically fierce. . . .

The housing industry has extremely ill-defined boundaries. Many building and contracting firms are involved not only in housing but in other kinds of light construction. Lenders and real estate brokers who service this industry do much of their business in other areas. Producers and distributors of materials tend to serve the entire construction market, rather than to specialize in residential construction. Craftsmen and laborers may be building houses one week, but working on missile silos the next. Significantly, the Bureau of the Census does not consider home building to be an industry at all. For example, the Census counts contractors as part of the construction industry, and merchant homebuilders as part of the real estate industry.

The housing process can be divided into several phases:

First, the preparation phase: potentially developable land is identified and plans are developed.

Second, the production phase: the site is prepared, financing is arranged, and the housing unit is constructed.

Third, the distribution phase: the house or apartment is marketed. This recurs throughout the useful lifetime of the structure.

Fourth, the servicing phase: the housing unit is repaired and maintained. This continues until the end of its economic or physical life.

The participants and the process and the external influences which affect them are graphically illustrated in Table 4-1.

Table 4-1. The housing process major participants and influences

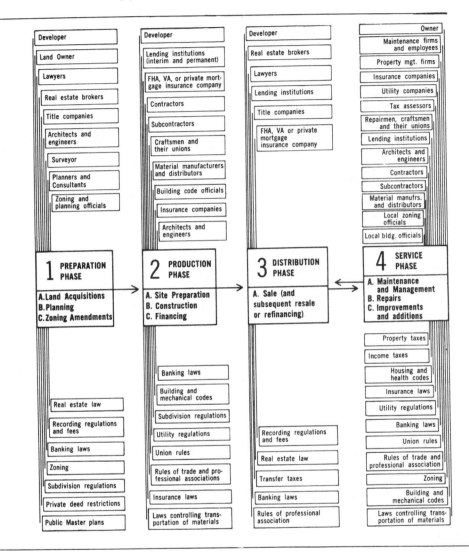

1 PREPARATION PHASE — A. Land Acquisitions, B. Planning, C. Zoning Amendments

Participants:
- Developer
- Land Owner
- Lawyers
- Real estate brokers
- Title companies
- Architects and engineers
- Surveyor
- Planners and Consultants
- Zoning and planning officials

Influences:
- Real estate law
- Recording regulations and fees
- Banking laws
- Zoning
- Subdivision regulations
- Private deed restrictions
- Public Master plans

2 PRODUCTION PHASE — A. Site Preparation, B. Construction, C. Financing

Participants:
- Developer
- Lending institutions (interim and permanent)
- FHA, VA, or private mortgage insurance company
- Contractors
- Subcontractors
- Craftsmen and their unions
- Material manufacturers and distributors
- Building code officials
- Insurance companies
- Architects and engineers

Influences:
- Banking laws
- Building and mechanical codes
- Subdivision regulations
- Utility regulations
- Union rules
- Rules of trade and professional associations
- Insurance laws
- Laws controlling transportation of materials

3 DISTRIBUTION PHASE — A. Sale (and subsequent resale or refinancing)

Participants:
- Developer
- Real estate brokers
- Lawyers
- Lending institutions
- Title companies
- FHA, VA or private mortgage insurance company

Influences:
- Recording regulations and fees
- Real estate law
- Transfer taxes
- Banking laws
- Rules of professional association

4 SERVICE PHASE — A. Maintenance and Management, B. Repairs, C. Improvements and additions

Participants:
- Owner
- Maintenance firms and employees
- Property mgt. firms
- Insurance companies
- Utility companies
- Tax assessors
- Repairmen, craftsmen and their unions
- Lending institutions
- Architects and engineers
- Contractors
- Subcontractors
- Material manufrs. and distributors
- Local zoning officials
- Local bldg. officials

Influences:
- Property taxes
- Income taxes
- Housing and health codes
- Insurance laws
- Utility regulations
- Banking laws
- Union rules
- Rules of trade and professional association
- Zoning
- Building and mechanical codes
- Laws controlling transportation of materials

. . . .

The methods of producing housing have evolved in response to these characteristics of its product.

With the major exception of the mobile home industry (and to a lesser extent the home manufacturing industry) the present characteristics of the housing industry are these:

Localization

The fact that housing is tied to land and locally regulated has meant that most builders, real estate brokers, and mortgage lenders (at least savings and loan associations) restrict their activities to rather small geographical areas. Only a handful of homebuilders look for nationwide market possibilities.

Fragmentation

The variety of the housing product has led to fragmentation of the industry into an elaborate complex of interlocking producing units. Different structures require different combinations of skills. Thus, the industry tends to work through *ad hoc* arrangements for each specific job. The practice of subcontracting, which is prevalent in the industry, is not necessarily irrational, and in fact, is often an efficient response to the need to meet many specialized demands. It is not clear whether greater vertical integration in the industry—that is, permanent alignment of a broader range of skills under the umbrella of a larger organization —would greatly increase efficiency in production. One clearly adverse result of fragmentation, however, has been an inadequate amount of research and development.

Trade associations have evolved to diminish the effect of this fragmentation. For example, in addition to providing technical services to its members, the National Association of Homebuilders has been effectively involved in the councils of government on housing policy, economic issues and other questions affecting the housing industry.

Lack of Size

With the major exception of some building materials manufacturers and a few distributors and lending institutions, most firms involved in the production and distribution of housing are relatively small. Smallness is characteristic not only of most builders, contractors, and subcontractors, but also of architectural and engineering firms, real estate brokers, and real estate management and maintenance firms. The smallness of these firms results primarily from the industry's localized and fragmented nature. There are, however, additional reasons for the smallness and light capitalization of construction firms. The rate of housing production is rather erratic, both on a national basis, and especially in each local market. The main causes of this instability are seasonal fluctuations in production (which now seem to be based mainly on tradition inasmuch as winter protection has been demonstrated to be completely feasible), the sensitivity of the industry to the supply of credit, and the dominance of the existing stock in the market. The erratic rate of output forces construction firms to try to keep their continuing overhead to a minimum, thus discouraging capital investment and assembly of large central staffs.

Dependence on Outsiders

The firms which make up the heart of the industry—primarily homebuilders and contractors—are dependent on larger enterprises not primarily engaged in housing. They are usually too small to bargain on an equal basis with the larger firms on the periphery of the industry. Thus financial institutions probably constitute the single most important locus of power in the industry. Builders and contractors have little influence over the rate of technological development in the industry; most innovations are introduced by building materials manufacturers.

. . . .

The Types and Characteristics of Housing Producers

The various skills needed to produce the final product can be combined in numerous ways. Even if the production process is simplified to consist of only five different steps—supply of land, design of structure, construction financing, construction, and marketing—many variations are possible. . . .

Firms involved in on-site residential building activity, both large and small, tend to specialize in it. Although many occasionally dabble in other kinds of light construction, responding members in the 1964 NAHB survey earned 92 percent of their dollar sales volume through new residential construction. Nonresidential building and remodeling accounted for most of the remaining 8 percent. It is common for residential builders to involve themselves in nonconstruction activities related to housing. The NAHB survey shows that they are most likely to act as land developers for others or as real estate brokers.

In addition, many residential builders specialize solely in single-family or multi-family housing. Slightly less than half of the larger builders (100 units per year or more) built both single and multi-family units. About one-sixth built multi-family only, and three-eighths single-family only. Smaller builders are even more likely to specialize in one type.

Four basic types of builders are grouped into two categories as described below. Countless other combinations are possible. The construction process alone can be subcontracted in almost an infinite number of ways.

On-Site Builders

1. *Merchant builders,* who build housing, usually of their own design, on their own land, for sale or rental to others.

2. *General contractors,* who build on land owned by others, usually according to owners' plans.

Factory Builders

3. *Home manufacturers,* using assembly line techniques to produce sectionalized units or packages of materials for rapid assembly on-site.

4. *Mobile home manufacturers.*

Owner-builders (persons acting as their own general contractors in building housing for their own occupancy) account for almost one-tenth of annual housing starts; they are not discussed because they are not in the housing production business on a commercial basis. . . .

. . . .

There is no dominant firm within any category of housing producer, much less in the entire residential construction market. One of the largest domestic merchant builders, Levitt & Sons, Inc., produced 5,100 units in 1967; the largest home manufacturer, National Homes, produced 11,500 units in that year; and the largest mobile home manufacturer, the Skyline Corporation, produced 18,000 units.

When compared to the size of the market even these very largest producers control only a tiny fraction of the output. Even the 50 largest housing producers (ranked irrespective of type) account for less than 15 percent of annual production. The contrast between this industry, and others, like automobile, steel, and aircraft, which are highly concentrated in the hands of a few large firms, is striking.

Small firms survive because the market tends to be local and these firms are familiar with local demand. The local building markets are not only diverse; they are also unstable, and this, too, discourages large firms. The instability deters capital investment and encourages building and contracting firms to avoid large fixed overhead costs. Homebuilding has a high rate of entry and exit by firms— a big turnover.

Table 4-20. Approximate shares of annual housing starts, by type of producer, in the United States for the middle 1960's

Type of producer	Approximate number of units annually	Percent of total annual production
Merchant builders:		
One-family (not including factory-built)	450,000	26
Multi-family	*260,000	*15
General contractors:		
One-family units for private owners (not including factory-built)	170,000	10
Multi-family construction for private owners	*260,000	*15
For public agencies	30,000	2
Factory built:		
Home manufacturers	180,000	11
Mobile homes	200,000	12
Owner built one-family homes intended for ultimate occupancy of the owner and built with the owner acting as general contractor and often doing some or all of the work	150,000	9
Total	1,700,000	100

*There is no data on the split in multi-family starts between merchant builders and general contractors. These units were split evenly between the two simply to minimize the maximum possible error; the numbers do not represent an estimate of how these units are actually divided between the two kinds of producers.

SOURCES: Bureau of the Census and Trade Associations.

On-Site Residential Building Firms

In 1968, at least 50,000 firms were assembling finished residential units on specific sites. This figure includes both merchant builders and general contractors (or contract builders). The majority of on-site residential building firms are small contract builders who do custom jobs. A 1964 survey by the National Association of Homebuilders (NAHB), found that roughly 50 percent of its members were primarily contract builders.

At present, the best evidence indicates that roughly 50 percent of all site-assembled housing is started by building firms producing more than 100 units per year. A 1949 survey found that firms of this size were responsible for only about one-quarter of production. Thus, the over-all trend toward greater concentration in the industry may now be leveling out. The biggest surge in concentration appears to have come in the late 1940's and early 1950's as the industry expanded rapidly to meet the demand pent up during the Depression and World War II.

Regardless of these trends, a large share of on-site building firms still put up no more than 10 residential units per year. The smaller builder is well entrenched in the custom home market, and dominates the field outside the larger metropolitan centers. A 1964 NAHB membership survey revealed that 60 percent of NAHB members had less than four full-time employees, and that only 1.4 percent had 50 employees.

The Prevalence of Subcontracting

As in most construction firms merchant builders and general contractors subcontract a substantial portion of the construction. The 1964 NAHB survey found that almost two-thirds of responding builders subcontracted over 50 percent of their construction dollar; some three-fifths had subcontracted half of their work in 1959. A survey by the Bureau of Labor Statistics in 1962 indicated that on average, 14 subcontractors are hired during construction of a private one-family house. A similar survey found that an average of 20 subcontractors were used in public housing construction projects. The incidence of subcontracting does not seem to vary significantly with the builder's volume.

Operations most likely to be performed by the builder's own employees are building layout, rough and finished carpentry, and final cleanup. Operations most likely to be subcontracted are heating, electrical work, plumbing and finished flooring.

The subcontracting system is flexible. It permits rapid mobilization and dispersal at scattered sites of workers and supervisors with specialized skills and equipment. Unless a merchant builder has a continuing and steady need in a rather small geographical area for specialists such as electricians or plumbers, he simply cannot afford to have them as his permanent employees. The amount of subcontracting varies with the type of construction. If more assembly operations can be regularized, the practice of subcontracting can be expected to decline. Recent trends, however, seem to be toward an increasing number and variety of specialty subcontractors, partly because of the greater intricacy of structures.

Special trade subcontractors are small, commonly one-man operations. Only 8 percent were incorporated in 1963. Of the 200,000 special trade contractors who made social security contributions on behalf of their employees in 1966, 56 percent had less than 4 employees. The number of special trade contractor firms has increased slightly in the last decade, indicating that their economic position is apparently more viable than, say, that of the Mom and Pop grocery stores or small farmers.

Merchant Builders

A merchant builder's involvement in actual construction activity can cover a broad range. Some merchant builders are primarily managers who subcontract out most construction on a work-in-place basis with subcontractors providing both materials and labor. At the other end of the spectrum are builders who perform a substantial portion of construction work within their own organizations. Between are a variety of types who undertake some functions and contract out others. For example, the largest merchant builder—Levitt & Sons Inc.—purchases all required materials and subcontracts all labor.

Merchant builders often extend their subcontracting activity to steps outside the construction process itself. Land development activities such as grading, surveying, and landscaping, are likely to be subcontracted to specialists. Architects, engineers, and land planners may be hired to assist in design. Only the largest builders can afford to have such professionals on their permanent staffs. The 1964 NAHB member survey indicates that while a large majority of builders have their own sales force to market their housing, most salesmen are paid by commissions only; in addition, over one-quarter of NAHB members hire other real estate firms to market their houses.

The merchant builder, who builds on speculation, is largely a post-war phenomenon. Merchant builders, as they first emerged after World War II, were engaged primarily in building single-family homes. The rising importance of multi-family housing in the market in the 1960's has attracted some merchant builders into building rental dwellings on their own land. The evolution of merchant builders has led to a somewhat greater degree of integration in the highly fragmented housing industry. Today, merchant builders account for a greater volume of housing production than any of the other three kinds of major housing producers.

. . . .

General Contractors

General contracting firms, as defined here, are those that manage the assembly of completed structures on land they do not own. In most cases, a general contractor has limited influence over the design of the structure he is to build, and plays no part in land acquisition, construction finance, and marketing operations. General contractors are the servants of the land owners. They may be hired through a number of methods, including private negotiation and public bidding. Some act only as managers, receiving a flat management fee for supervising subcontractors hired and paid by the property owner. More commonly, the general contractor will have a fixed-price contract with the owner covering the entire job, and will himself hire the subcontractors he needs. Like merchant builders, most general contractors have only a small nucleus of workers on their staff and are likely to subcontract the bulk of the construction work.

. . . .

The number of general contractors has been increasing steadily. The 1939 Census of Construction identified 35,000 general contractors. Internal Revenue Service data derived from business tax returns indicated 140,000 such firms in 1957 and close to 200,000 in 1965. Like most construction firms, general contractors show some tendency to specialize, the major break being between those who concentrate on buildings (residential and nonresidential) and those who specialize in highway and heavy construction. Most general contractors fall in the former category. Like the merchant builders, most general contracting firms are small. Today, perhaps 30 percent of them are incorporated, although this percentage has been rising slowly over the years.

. . . .

Factory Builders

The past decades, and even centuries, have witnessed a steady shifting of construction operations to off-site locations. On-site builders are making ever greater use of pre-assembled and pre-finished components. Two major types of housing producers—home manufacturers and mobile home producers carry out a major portion, if not all, of their assembly operations in factories.

The Home Manufacturer

Home manufacturers market rather complete packages of the materials needed for construction of housing units. They preassemble major components and precut other pieces, and typically distribute these packages through a network of franchised builder-dealers. These dealers often have exclusive rights to distribute the product line in a given territory.

. . . .

Trends in the home manufacturer's share of the market are difficult to trace. Private statistics collected by those most familiar with the industry show an increase in shipments of manufacturer homes from 132,000 in 1959 to some 230,000 units in 1967. Only units with pre-assembled exterior and interior walls, and the bulk of material necessary to finish the unit were included in this estimate. On the other hand, Census figures show a drop in the shipment of prefabricated wood buildings from 68,000 in 1958 to 60,000 in 1963. In addition, the largest producer in the industry now turns out only slightly more than half the number of units it produced a decade ago. Recent NAHB surveys show a small increase in the fraction of their members using "factory built" homes — from 4.6 percent in 1959 to 5.1 percent in 1964. Despite the weakness of the data, it is generally agreed that the home manufacturing industry accounts for somewhat more than 10 percent of total housing production and that its output in units has not increased dramatically in the last six years.

. . . .

Mobile Homes

The mobile home industry is the fastest growing subsector within the larger housing industry. In recent years, it has accounted for over 15 percent of total housing production (counting the mobile home production itself).

[This is the most volatile subsector. Since publication of the Kaiser report the mobile home industry experienced a traumatic decline in sales and production during the early 1970s recession. Since then it has been unable to reach the levels attained in the late 1960s. — Eds.]

Production and marketing of mobile homes involves, in most cases, the combined efforts of three kinds of firms. The mobile home manufacturer produces a completely finished and furnished unit in its factory. Like automobiles, the units are normally sold through local dealerships who often accept older mobile homes as trade-ins. These dealers may also help service the units after purchase. Operators of mobile home parks, where almost 90 percent of mobile home units are located, provide sites and utility connections in return for rental payments. Densities in new parks run 10-12 units per acre. At present, there are close to 300 mobile home manufacturers, 7,000 dealers, and 20,000 mobile home parks.

Although the mobile home industry accounts for over 15 percent of housing starts, less than 3 percent of all occupied housing units are mobile homes. The basic reasons for this discrepancy are that mobile homes have much shorter expected lives than conventionally built housing, and that this industry has only come into prominence in recent years. In 1968, some 4.5 million people occupied approximately 1.7 million mobile home units. The 1960 Census of Housing found that 88 percent of occupied mobile units are owner-occupied, and that 9 out of 10 are located outside central cities or metropolitan areas. There are significant regional variations in the popularity of mobile homes. In some southwestern states, they may exceed 10 percent of the total housing stock.

. . . .

Although designed for mobility, mobile homes once positioned are rarely moved. They depreciate much more rapidly than conventionally built homes because of their lighter construction, and the obsolescence of nonreplaceable built-in elements. There is no firm data on the average life expectancy of mobile homes. However, lenders are becoming somewhat more generous in the terms for financing the purchase of mobile homes. The length of the loan may now run up to 10 years or more, still much shorter than the 30-year (or longer) mortgage loans available for purchase of conventional single-family homes. In addition, a 1964 survey of commercial banks and finance companies involved in new mobile home financing indicated that only about 25 percent of all purchase contracts had maturity periods exceeding five years.

Although scale efficiencies are more apparent in mobile home production than in any other kind of housing production, most companies in this industry are surprisingly small. According to Census data, the average production establishment for mobile homes had 45 employees in 1947 and 60 employees in 1963. Surprisingly little capital investment is needed to enter this business. It has been estimated that only $100,000 to $125,000 is needed to purchase the equipment for producing 1 to 6 mobile homes a day. On the other hand, production in this industry is more highly concentrated in a few companies than it is in on-site assembly operations or home manufacturing. This indicates the presence of some scale economies. Perhaps as many as five different companies now manufacture over 10,000 mobile home units per year. The top 20 companies account for somewhat over half the total industry production.

. . . .

The Jobs and the Work Force in Homebuilding

In manpower, as in other regards, the housing industry is unusual— fragmented, transitory, localized, varying, and—as is especially important for the work force—seasonal in its operations. It is important to understand that even with a very full supply of manpower and construction skills in the economy in general, there still might not be an adequate number in the particular field of homebuilding. That field competes for skilled labor with other kinds of construction, and all of the construction industry in turn is in competition with other industries for skilled and able men. In this doubly competitive situation homebuilding is not in a strong position, for reasons we will indicate. With respect to manpower, as elsewhere, housing may too often be last and least among the nation's priorities.

Perhaps the most helpful way of looking at the work force in construction and homebuilding is to think of it as a pool of persons possessing the needed skills. People within this pool are constantly moving in and out of construction and homebuilding in response to the level of demand in the industry and alternatives available elsewhere. In their study for the [Kaiser] Committee, John T. Dunlop and D. Quinn Mills report that it takes 1.8 workmen to fill each average annual job, a higher ratio than prevails in any other industry. Of workmen who report earnings in construction, only slightly more than half received the major portion of their earnings from this industry. Even among those who received earnings from construction in all four quarters of the year, only 7 in 10, according to social security data, received the major portion of their earnings from construction. We do not have similar data for homebuilding, which is not enumerated as a separate industry by the Census Bureau or the Social Security Administration, but there is reason to believe that these patterns are even more pronounced in homebuilding. The homebuilding industry has been subject to greater peaks and valleys of activity, has smaller-scale individual operations, and relies less upon labor unions that rationalize the supply of manpower, than other construction subdivisions. Moreover, homebuilding has traditionally been least flexible in price among consumers of construction manpower. Therefore, it has been the last to draw construction workers in times of labor shortages.

. . . .

[The Kaiser Report presents some interesting detail about the labor force in the housing industry. In addition to the points touched on above, they include the following: Homebuilders as a group employ few people, about half have three or fewer employees. Wages though high in hourly terms tend to be lower than factory wages when figured on an annual basis. Employment is very seasonal; in much of the country the industry shuts down for the winter. Unions cover only a minority of the housing industry workers. And the work force tends to be surprisingly aged. Journeymen tend to be at least in their forties, and in some trades the average is more than sixty. — Eds.]

Building Materials Manufacturers

Although housing construction requires inputs from most major industrial groups, four are particularly significant. The lumber and wood products industry is by far the most important single supplier to the residential construction industry. The stone and clay products industry; the heating, plumbing and structural metal products industry; and the primary iron and steel manufacturing industry are the next three in importance. The manufacturers of building products, such as sawmills, often depend heavily on other firms, like loggers, to supply them with raw materials.

Although there are several giant corporations which are primarily concerned with building materials—for example, Johns-Manville, U.S. Gypsum, and Weyerhauser—no single company comes close to dominating overall production. Concentration of production in most product lines is less pronounced than in many major American industries. The degree of concentration varies substantially from product to product; production of some products, like window glass, is especially concentrated. The easy substitutability of building materials adds significantly to the sharpness of competition. Wood siding competes with aluminum. If the price of steel rises, more concrete will be used. This fact helps keep manufacturers on their toes.

The lumber and wood products industry, the most important supplier, is the least concentrated of all major manufacturing industries in the United States. The Census of Manufacturers indicates that sawmills and planing mills shipped $3.2 billion of lumber in 1963. The four largest companies accounted for about 10 percent of these shipments. The average mill employed only 17 workers. Production of veneer and plywood is somewhat more concentrated, with the four largest companies accounting for somewhat less than a quarter of total production. The average plant producing veneer or plywood has about 100 employees.

. . . .

Building Materials Distributors

The Census of Business for 1963 indicates that some 80,000 establishments were engaged in retail selling of building materials. Although large housing producers often buy directly from manufacturers, smaller builders and contractors rely heavily on retail distributors to perform inventory and delivery functions for them . . . lumberyards dominate the retail trade of building materials.

Home manufacturers, mobile home producers, and larger builders and contractors are more likely to "eliminate the middleman" by buying building materials directly from manufacturers. This practice is not without its costs, because the housing producer must then do his own warehousing, sorting, and delivery. According to the Producers' Council survey, a majority of builders starting over 100 units per year in 1960 had their own distribution yards. In many cases, these yards were set up primarily to carry out cutting or fabricating operations, not because builders were anxious to perform sorting and storage operations for themselves. The percentage of larger builders operating distribution yards appears to be fairly stable. Smaller builders, on the other hand, apparently have not found them profitable as they show a clear trend toward discontinuing operations of their own distribution yards.

Comments: The housing industry described so carefully by the Kaiser Committee has frustrated any efforts at industrial reform for years. It appears to be amazingly resistant to modernization, rationalization, and the introduction of factory methods. But this resistance may be mainly in the way one looks at it. The following short passage comes from an analysis of these longtime efforts by a somewhat revisionist-minded pair of architect-engineers.

BENDER & PARMAN, THE FACTORY WITHOUT WALLS: INDUSTRIALIZATION IN RESIDENTIAL CONSTRUCTION, 18 CALIFORNIA MANAGEMENT REVIEW 3, 46-47, 49-50 (1976)

Since the 1930s there has been a call for the industrialization of the housing industry in the U.S. This effort has had a very specific image — the image of the auto industry and of the gradual domination of the housing industry by larger and larger firms involved in factory production of housing units. This image reflected the belief that the methods of the auto industry—the assembly lines and mass production, as well as the industry's financing and marketing methods—could be brought to bear on the problems of housing.

But the experience of the last forty-five years seems to show that industrialization in the housing industry has occurred at another level, and in another form. This has involved mass production as well, of building materials, products, and tools, but in a more significant way it has involved creation of an industry that serves builders and that has provided new methods, tools, materials, and products that greatly expand the number of persons who can so describe themselves. In this way the entire industry has been transformed.

. . . .

The Dream of Mass Production

The failure to realize this dream has not been for lack of effort. This can be illustrated by a capsule history of such attempts. Several firms with names like "General Houses" or "American Houses" were started in the early 1930's to make and market steel-based prefab housing. These firms had backers such as Inland Steel and General Electric, but despite in one case a direct connection with an existing retail chain, Sears Roebuck, and despite apparently favorable initial publicity, they were unable to set up adequate dealer networks or reach volume production of any magnitude. . . .

[The authors provide a capsule history of the efforts to prefabricate dwellings since the 1930s. The high points are the success of the federal government program of war housing in the early Forties and the failure of efforts to stimulate prefabrication in the private sector to house returning veterans later in that decade. They conclude with a brief account of the abortive Operation Breakthrough, an effort by the Nixon administration to provide a technological fix that would increase new unit production at prices moderate income households could afford. —Eds.]

This lack of success brings us back to a central question: how is it that factory-built housing, which enjoys reasonable success elsewhere in the world, has remained only a negligible factor in American housing, despite periodic efforts to stimulate its growth?

The answer is two-fold. First, the aggregated market for standardized, factory-built housing that exists in Europe, Japan, and the Soviet Union does not exist here. Aggregation can really only occur where the government takes a role in creating projects or allocating production, so that an acceptable volume of steady production can be maintained. Second, the nature of conventional residential construction in the U.S. has become increasingly streamlined and amenable to the use of prefabricated components and semiskilled or unskilled workers. It has also grown increasingly productive, as was evidenced by its ability earlier in this decade to surpass 2 million units per year in construction volume. . . .

The dream of factory mass-produced housing was based on the view of conventional construction as static and backward. This view has historical validity but is no longer tenable: conventional construction may continue to harbor counterproductive practices, but its central tendency since World War II has been toward greater productivity through the use of new tools, methods, building products, and organizational patterns. This tendency is one form of industrialization, but one that requires a different outlook, and has different implications, than the one that has dominated our thinking since the 1930s.

Residential Construction Today

Residential construction today combines the use of prefabricated components with on-site assembly and finishing of the housing unit. This process continues to use on-site labor, the function of which has changed from one of handcrafting such building parts as the windows, doors, walls and floors, roofs, and molding to one of assembling these parts as prefinished components. The last decade has seen these prefinished components become larger and more complex.

The general simplification of residential construction processes has been reinforced by simplifying the means by which the various building components are combined in the assembly process. This later simplification is best described in terms of its objectives, which apply not only to components, but also to construction methods and tools.

The first objective of such simplification is to decrease the time needed for a worker to master the skills needed to use a building product or tool. Ideally the product or tool should be so straightforward that any worker can use it after a few minutes of practice. The implication of this objective is that the level of skill required in residential construction will decline steadily, and the number of workers available for residential construction will increase correspondingly.

The second objective is to increase the productivity of the worker. In general, this has meant that new building products and tools have sought to accomplish more with fewer steps. Thus, wall panels have come to replace hand-tiled bathroom walls, and automatic nailers have replaced conventional hammers. A synergistic effect between tools and products has sometimes occurred, allowing even greater productivity than envisioned by the original designers of one or the other.

The changes that have occurred in the organization, methods, tools, and products of residential construction have turned today's residential building site into a place of final assembly—almost a factory without walls, to which are brought a host of prefinished building parts, to be assembled by workers whose tasks increasingly resemble those of other industrial workers.

There are other resemblances between the residential building site and the modern industrial assembly line and its working conditions. Suburban tract sites, for example, have come to resemble assembly lines in configuration. Their site plans are designed to accommodate special equipment for putting in foundations, utility lines, streets, and sidewalks. The site-development and housing-assembly processes have been coordinated to allow them to occur concurrently. Assembly of the housing units tends to be carried out by workers moving from house to house, as opposed to the industrial assembly line, where workers tend to remain in one place while the work moves by them.

———

Comments: Behind the dream of mass production lay a concern with the cost of housing and the possibilities of reducing it relative to personal incomes. The revisionist view of Bender and Parman highlights an important fact that has been masked by the general tendency of dwelling prices to rise over time. Productivity with respect to building materials and site labor has risen dramatically. Over the last few decades these factors have become less significant in terms of their effects on final prices. Figure 1 shows this change graphically. It shows something else too: the very steep escalation in new house sale prices.

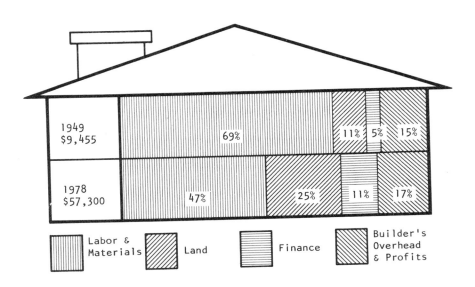

Figure 1. Cost components of a typical, new, single-family house (Redrawn from National Association of Homebuilders)

This increase has been paralleled by an increase in the prices of existing units and in the costs of operating and maintaining housing. The next two readings deal with this sharp inflation.

U.S. DEPARTMENT OF HOUSING AND COMMUNITY DEVELOPMENT, FINAL REPORT OF THE TASK FORCE ON HOUSING COSTS 2-4 (1978)

Scope of the Housing Cost Crisis

During the past 25 years housing costs have been of continual concern to the American people. They have been the focus of many Congressional actions and the subject of Presidential commissions. In very recent years, the cost of building, buying, and operating a decent home has increased faster than family income. This is true for new, existing and rehabilitated housing, and for renters and owners alike. The rising cost of shelter is a nationwide problem which affects all of us. It is exacting a heavy toll which must be measured not just in statistics but in human costs.

Housing costs to the consumer have been increasing faster than prices generally (as measured by the Consumer Price Index) during both the 1960s and the 1970s. During the 1960s this was not a serious problem for most families, because their income kept pace with housing prices, the overall costs of homeownership (which include loan amortization and operating costs), and rents. The accompanying table shows that median family income increased at an average annual rate of 6.60 percent between 1963 and 1972, while the price index of the median new single-family house of constant size and quality rose at an average rate of only 4.23 percent per year. The index of homeownership costs increased at 5.17 percent per year. Rents rose at only 2.55 percent during the same period.

During the 1970s, however, the picture changed dramatically. Between 1972 and 1976, family income lagged well behind housing inflation and did not even keep up with the Consumer Price Index. Income rose annually at an average annual rate of 7.05 percent, compared to a rate of 9.94 percent for the price of new single-family homes of constant quality and 12.49 percent for the median price of homes unadjusted for quality. During the same period, the costs of homeownership rose at an average annual rate of 8.15 percent. Trends in resale prices of existing homes followed a similar pattern.

Trends in income, prices and housing costs, 1963—1976 (Data indexed to 1967 base year, where appropriate)

Item	Year				Average Annual Rate of Increase	
	1963	1967	1972	1976	1963-1972	1972-1976
Median Family Income	78.8	100.0	140.0	184.0	6.60%	7.05%
Consumer Price Index	91.7	100.0	125.3	170.5	3.53%	8.00%
Median Sales Price, New One-Family Homes [1]	79.3	100.0	121.6	194.7	4.86%	12.49%
Price Index, New One-Family Homes of Constant Quality [1]	90.2	100.0	131.0	191.4	4.23%	9.94%
Median Sales Price, Existing One-Family Homes [1]	NA	100.0	138.4	197.5	NA	9.30%
Cost of Homeownership (CPI series)	89.0	100.0	140.1	191.7	5.17%	8.15%

Trends in income, prices and housing costs, 1963—1976 (Data indexed to 1967 base year, where appropriate)

Item	Year				Average Annual Rate of Increase	
	1963	1967	1972	1976	1963-1972	1972-1976
Rent (CPI series)	95.0	100.0	119.2	144.2	2.55%	4.97%
Boeckh Residential Construction Cost Index	85.1	100.0	145.8	198.6	6.16%	8.03%
Site Value, New One-Family Homes[1]	NA	NA	$5500	$8900	NA	12.79%
Effective Mortgage Interest Rate, New Homes (FHLBB)	5.89%	6.46%	7.60%	9.00%	2.87%	4.32%
Operating Expenses, Median Priced New Home[2]	74.7	100.0	140.0	218.7	7.23%	11.80%

(1) Data from the Bureau of the Census.
(2) Operating expenses are based on actual experience under the HUD/FHA Section 203(b) program and include insurance, property taxes, maintenance and repairs, and fuel and utilities.

While rents have not increased as fast as incomes, nonetheless they have risen twice as fast since 1972 as in the preceding decade. The human dimension of increasing rents appears especially urgent to the millions of poor people who pay what for them are excessive rents. According to recent testimony by the Ad Hoc Low-Income Housing Coalition before the Senate Budget Committee, 25 percent of all renter households—concentrated at the bottom of the income scale—paid more than 35 percent of their incomes for rent in 1975, when payment of 25 percent of income is the accepted norm. As all housing costs rise, existing Federal subsidies do not stretch as far to help these citizens most in need. In many areas both new and rehabilitated rental rent housing are becoming commercially infeasible without subsidies.

The underlying costs of producing, financing, and operating housing have all risen more rapidly in recent years than in the 1960s. As the accompanying table shows, residential construction costs grew at a rate of 8 percent per year between 1972 and 1976, compared to slightly more than 6 percent between 1963 and 1972. The cost of improved lots increased at almost 13 percent per year during the most recent period. Higher mortgage interest rates, when applied to higher sales prices, have increased the typical monthly loan amortization costs for the buyer of a median priced single-family home by 80 percent between 1972 and 1976, or an average annual increase of 15.9 percent. Operating expenses increased almost 12 percent during the same period.

The statistics cited above are nationwide figures and the housing cost experience will vary, sometimes sharply, depending on the particular market area studied. Housing markets are local rather than national. Nevertheless, there is growing evidence that rising housing costs are a problem in the vast majority of markets in the United States and pose an urgent situation in those high growth regions where more Americans increasingly are choosing to live. In some areas, developed lots are not available at any price, while in others, site availability is not as crucial an issue as access to financing or to skilled labor and needed materials.

There is abundant evidence that the housing cost problem has accelerated in recent years. Some observers have concluded that this means that rising housing costs are but a short-term problem. We have determined otherwise. Certain structural problems, most notably the cyclical nature of the housing industry, have contributed to rising housing costs in both the long and the short term. Since the early 1970's however, the problem of rising housing costs has been greatly exacerbated by two other factors—growing environmental and land-use regulation and the fiscal difficulties of many American communities. Communities have slowed their growth and new housing development has been restricted. These new factors that have quickened the pace of rising housing costs portend a long-term problem for the future unless major steps are taken.

Comments: 1. A more detailed picture of cost inflation of overall housing costs is provided by the following table by housing authority Anthony Downs. (From Public Policy and the Rising Cost of Housing, 8 Real Estate Review 29 (1978).

Table 1. Estimated changes in cost of occupying the median-priced new single-family home, 1970-1976

Item (1)	Percentage of 1976 total monthly housing occupancy cost (2)	Estimated percentage increase, 1970-1976 (3)	Percentage contribution to total dollar increase, 1970-1976 (4)
Total monthly occupancy costs [a]	100.0%	+ 102.3%	
Interest rate		+8.3%	+ 5.2%
House price		+88.9%	+56.2%
Mortgage payment	63.0%	+97.2%	61.4%
Materials	19.6% ⎱		23.1%
On-site labor	10.4% ⎰ +68.1%		
Land	15.5% ⎰	+113.1%	15.6%
Construction financing	6.5%	+159.4%	7.6%
Other building costs [b]	11.0%	+92.2%	9.9%
Operating costs	37.0%	+111.6%	38.6%
Property taxes	13.5%	+102.6%	14.9%
Hazard insurance	6.1%	+122.1%	3.2%
Repair and maintenance	6.0%	+135.6%	7.5%
Heat and utilities	11.4%	+109.3%	13.0%

a) Median total monthly occupancy costs in 1976 were $441, an increase of $223 from 1970.
b) Includes overhead and builder's profit.

NOTE: For comparison purposes, median family income rose 47.0% from 1970 to 1976, and the Consumer Price Index rose 46.6%.

SOURCES: Joint Center for Urban Studies of MIT and Harvard. *The Nation's Housing: 1975-1985*, pp. 119, 123; FHA Section 203 Homes, *Recurring Report #250*; Michael Sumichrast, "Housing Costs," Washington Star, March 4-April 15, 1977.

Note particularly the steep climb in land and money prices. They have powered housing inflation. Money plays the most critical role because it compounds the inflation experienced by all other factors. Since money prices are exogenous to the housing economy, they pose an especially intractable problem. It forms a main focus of Chapter 7. Land price escalation is at least partly related to the prevalence of enviromental controls on development. Chapter 11 treats this issue.

2. Price inflation is but one-half of the matter. It can interact with demand to further accelerate prices. This is just what is happening today. The interaction between dwelling cost increases and rising demand is discussed in the following brief passage from the paper on future housing trends cited at the end of the last chapter.

B. FRIEDEN & A. SOLOMON, THE NATION'S HOUSING: 1975 TO 1985, at 112-116, 130 (1977)

Production and Price Levels for Single-Family Houses: Single-family housing starts in 1976 reached near-record levels, comparable to those of the boom years of the 1950s and 1971-1973. Although the total starts of 1.16 million single-family houses represent an impressive upturn from the slump of 1974-1975 and an exceptionally high volume by historic standards, neither the slump nor the historic record is a suitable benchmark for judging how well housing production is meeting the needs of the American people. As Table 5.8 shows, single-family production is no longer reaching the mass market that it did in the 1960s. Rather than serving a broad spectrum of the public, including families with average income and below, it has moved far toward providing primarily for the top fourth of the population. In contrast to the situation in the 1960s, the volume of new single-family housing is high, not because sales are going to a broad market, but because homebuilders are reaching a narrow segment of an exceptionally large number of young families.

Table 5.8. Homebuilding: from mass market to luxury market in 10 years

| | Share of All New Homes Bought (percent) | |
Income Group	1965-1966	1975-1976
Top Quarter	31	58
Middle Income	53	38
Lower Third	17	4
TOTAL	100 [a]	100

a. Due to rounding, total does not sum to 100 percent.

SOURCES: Tables 5.6 and 5.7, this chapter.
NOTE: In current dollars, the top quarter had family incomes of $10,000 or more in 1965-1966 and $20,000 or more in 1975-1976; the middle-income group had family incomes of $5,000-9,999 in 1965-1966 and $10,000-19,999 in 1975-1976; and the lower third had family incomes below $5,000 in 1965-1966 and below $10,000 in 1975-1976.

One reason for the narrowness of the 1965-1976 market was that it offered very limited options for families who wanted to buy homes for the first time. Although young families dominated the market (median age of heads of homebuying households was only 33), those buying homes for the first time accounted for only 35 percent of total purchases. And first-time buyers were able to afford only the lower-priced homes that were available. Of the small volume of houses priced below $30,000 (9 percent of the total), first-time homeowners bought 54 percent.

At higher price levels, their share declined sharply — from 51 percent of homes priced between $30,000 and $40,000, to 31 percent between $40,000 and $50,000, and 24 percent between $50,000 and $60,000.

Looked at another way, this pattern means that most families buying new homes were able to do so by trading up from the home they already owned. If they were fortunate — or farsighted — enough to have bought another home a few years earlier, they were likely to benefit from the rising prices of existing houses, and their gains on resale helped them pay the cost of the even more expensive new housing.

How well a housing market such as that of 1975-1976 will serve the needs of families with average or below-average incomes in the future is an open question. In the mid-sixties, middle-income families bought new houses and moved out of older houses which then became available to lower-income groups. In 1975-1976, families with high incomes bought new houses and moved out of existing homes that they owned, which became available to middle-income families. The poor, as well as newly formed families, had to depend on whatever vacancies the middle-income groups, in turn, left behind them. It is possible that we still will be able to depend upon this process of housing turnover to accommodate the needs of many middle- and lower-income families during the next several years. However, the turnover process will work for families with average and below-average incomes only if a very large number of upper-income families buy new homes every year.

Whether the 1975-1976 market really represented a typical year is, of course, another open question, as noted earlier. Home sales for that year may have had a special character resulting from the slump of 1974-1975. During the slump, when production was low and personal income uncertain, many people deferred buying homes. As the recovery started, the first people to buy may well have been those in high income brackets, who were most confident of their future earnings and who could shape housing quality standards to suit their own tastes and pocketbooks. If this explanation is accurate, then cyclical factors as well as longer-term trends led to an emphasis on homes for high-income families in 1975-1976. As the economy recovers in the next few years, more middle-income families may return to the new home market and they may create greater demand for the "basic" house built to more modest standards.

In any event, the high-volume and high-priced market for new single-family housing in 1975-1976 resulted from an unusual combination of circumstances. Homebuilders faced increased costs even to provide houses that were of no better quality than those built in earlier years. However, they chose to respond to the shift from a middle-income to an upper-income market and compounded the price increase by building houses of higher quality. Meanwhile, the huge growth of young families swelled the size of the potential market. This meant that there was a larger number of families able to manage the high cost of new houses by stretching their resources, pooling husband-and-wife incomes, and trading up from existing homes whose values were also climbing fast. But entry into the new home market was very difficult for families wanting to buy their first homes as well as for families of near-average income and below.

Despite big cost increases and a continuing production shortfall relative to the increase in household numbers and the other pressures . . . consumers are finding ways of coping with the situation. However, the adjustments they have made are, so far, no more than short-term reactions. And because the cost squeeze is recent, it has not yet had much effect on the overall trend toward increasing homeownership. At least through 1974, when the latest information is available for the nation at large, the proportion of all households owning their own homes continued to increase and so, too, did the proportion of homeowners among young households with heads from 25 to 34 years old. The shrinking purchasing power available to new homebuyers, then, is more an emerging problem than one whose full dimensions or long-range consequences are yet understood. It is far from a current crisis, but it is a warning signal, especially in view of the strong drive of the blue-collar and middle-income groups who are now renters to become owners. Moreover, the unprecedented number of young households coming of typical homebuying age (the baby-boom children grown up) will surely focus more and more public attention on the increasingly restricted market for new housing.

If the trends from 1971 to 1976 were to continue for another five years — and, given the extremely unusual circumstances over the last few years, we do not predict they will — typical new homes in 1981 would sell for $78,000, and only the most affluent groups would be able to afford them. Should this exceptional inflation of house prices continue, however, the United States would become less and less a nation of homeowners and, despite decades of federal encouragement and massive tax subsidies, the new single-family house would become a luxury item.

Comments: The dire trend in house cost inflation gives every sign of continuing despite the earnest hopes of authors Frieden and Solomon. By the end of 1978 preliminary government reports indicated that nationally the median selling price for a new dwelling had risen to more than $60,000, and in California to nearly the $78,000 level Frieden and Solomon predicted for 1981. Whether or not the general economy prospers, it seems safe to predict that further inflation will continue well on into the 1980s, and continue to dominate thinking about housing. Keep this probability in mind in reading the chapters to come.

BIBLIOGRAPHY

A. Dietz & L. Cutler, Industrialized Building Systems (1971)
    An engineering perspective on housing technology, accessible to non-engineers.

E. Eichler & M. Kaplan, The Community Builders (1966)
    Wide-ranging study of the largest homebuilders, the ones who develop entire suburban communities or new towns.

J. Herzog, The Dynamics of Large Scale Housebuilding (1966)
    Overall survey of the industry concentrating on the larger firms.

M. Mayer, The Builders (1978)
    A popular account of the whole housing field, this book includes a fine, properly critical analysis of the problems of introducing high technology along with its coverage of nearly all facets of the housing supply system.

Chapter 4

HOUSING NEED AND HOUSING DEMAND

People and the household groups they form give housing its reason for existence. Without the human need for dwelling places there would be no housing problems. Most housing problems reflect the inability of some people or groups to gain or maintain the levels of housing satisfactions they can afford, they desire, or that society believes they should receive. Such problems emphasize a key distinction necessary to thinking about housing, the distinction between need and demand.

British housing economist Lionel Needleman puts it this way:

> The social concept of housing "need" has to be distinguished from the economic concept of housing demand. The effective demand for housing relates to the accommodation for which people are able and willing to pay. It takes no account of social desiderata, of a personal aspiration that cannot be fulfilled because of lack of money. Housing need, on the other hand, is the extent to which the quantity and quality of existing accommodation falls short of that required to provide each household or person, with accommodation of a specific standard or above.

L. Needleman, The Economics of Housing 18 (1965).

Needleman continues by making the important observation that in practice the distinction between predicting need or demand tends to fuzz together. The minimum standards on which need estimates are based derive in large part from the prevailing income and price levels. In the aggregate, both need and demand are derived from the general characteristics and main trends in population factors. A current estimate of such factors provides a good starting point to look at the demand side of the housing economy. The following paper by planner-urban economist-population expert William Alonso provides an acute and timely estimate of these matters.

Following the Alonso reading the chapter will return to the need and demand dichotomy. After readings and discussion on aspects of aggregate demand, several readings are presented that deal in a more behavioral way with households. These treat such questions as why people select the houses they choose, how they go about making a selection, and how behavior varies across social groups. In thinking about these themes a sense of the big picture and a main focus on population change is necessary background, hence the next paper.

W. ALONSO, THE POPULATION FACTOR AND URBAN STRUCTURE 4-15, 19-25 (1977)

By the 'population factor' I mean the number of people as a whole and its age composition, the ways these people arrange themselves into families and households, and how and how often they rearrange themselves; the 'population factor' also involves their participation in the labor force, how they run their households, and how they raise their children if they have them. And the 'population factor' must include consideration of the social, economic, cultural, and attitudinal components and shifts that accompany behavioral changes.

The recent and prospective changes in the population factor are remarkable and will mold the evolution of urban areas in years to come. These effects are already being felt and the popular press begins to report on singles in the suburbs, and 'gentrification' of parts of central cities, the pains of school consolidation in the suburbs, the absolute decline in population in whole metropolitan areas (not just their central cities), and most recently on the rapid increase in the cost of single-family homes and the fact that a diminishing proportion of American "families" can afford them. The quotation marks in the last sentence are meant to alert the reader to the ambiguousness of what a family is.

The recent and impending changes in the population factor are so strong that their influence has not gone unperceived in urban matters. Some extrapolations have been made of the coming patterns of age composition and the formation of households, but these are highly aggregated and try to estimate future housing demand or need, without distinguishing between these two very different matters. Moreover, whatever their accuracy, they do not tell us enough about the changing social and economic characteristics of the units which go to make up the aggregate. These changes in the units not only affect the total number of households, they importantly shape the internal structure of the housing market and its manifestation in urban geography.

The three most visible changes in the population factor in the mid-1970's are (1) the increasing prevalence of population decline in entire metropolitan areas, (2) the seismic waves passing through the age composition of the population as a result of the baby boom which followed World War II and the more recent drop in fertility, and (3) the radical changes in lifestyles which are reflected in the shifting composition of households and their economics. In this paper I will try to show that these three changes in the population factor are interrelated, and that they hold important consequences for the evolution of urban structure.

The Increasing Prevalence of Metropolitan Population Decline

In the past almost all metropolitan areas grew in population except for some of the smaller ones (and very rarely a large one, such as Pittsburgh in the 1960's) which encountered severe economic deterioration. But in recent years it has become commonplace for metropolitan areas to decline in population. In the early 1970's ten out of the largest twenty-five metropolitan areas were losing population in absolute terms. In the period from 1970 to 1974 one sixth of all metropolitan areas were losing population; in the last year of that period more than one fourth of all areas were doing it, so that the trend is accelerating. Because the phenomenon of decline is stronger among the larger metropolitan areas, the proportion of the metropolitan population living in declining areas is even larger, and stands now at about one half of all metropolitan residents.

Much has been made of another startling change in the population factor in relation to this decline. Ever since the Industrial Revolution in the XVIII century people have migrated in the net from rural to urban areas; but since 1970 net migration has proceeded from metropolitan to nonmetropolitan areas. A reversal in a trend with more than two centuries standing is indeed important and interesting. The net flow out of metropolitan areas amounted to nearly 400,000 people in the single year 1975-76, and this is a large number indeed, and a strong contributor to the decline of metropolitan populations. But it is not the principal factor.

The factors behind the prevalence of metropolitan population decline are three: changes in the rate of natural increase, changes in the net migration of metropolitan areas, and migratory exchanges among metropolitan areas. Of these, the strongest is the decline in the rate of natural increase which has resulted from the drop in the birthrate. Whereas in the 1960's the natural increase of metropolitan areas stood at 1.1% per year, in the 1970-74 period it amounted to 0.7% and under 0.6% in recent years. This amounts to a drop of 0.5% in the rate of population growth from the last decade to the present. The net migration rate from metropolitan to nonmetropolitan areas was under 0.3% in 1975-76; it had been between 0.1 and 0.2% in the other direction in the 1960's, for a change of about 0.4% per year. While these numbers are comparable, the drop of the natural increase is larger and more important than the reversal in metropolitan migration. At the same time, net migration from abroad has continued at a substantial rate (about 0.2% for net legal migration, and perhaps at least as much for illegal immigration), so that metropolitan areas have had a net immigration in spite of their losses to nonmetropolitan areas.

About one half of the non-metropolitan growth results from the overspill of metropolitan functions beyond censal definitions. These are not people who have gone back to the land, but people who work in the suburban ring or in economic activities which can thrive at a modest distance from metropolitan centers, with access to major airports, business services, and other facilities. The remainder of nonmetropolitan growth is attributable to shifts in the location of labor-intensive industry to small cities and rural areas, to the growth of the recreation industry, to the increased number of retired people whose income is not tied down geographically, to increased rates of investment in energy, resources, and environmental projects, and, in the recession of the past few years, to the return of earlier migrants to metropolitan areas for whom it is easier to endure the hard times back home. A number of these factors, but not all, may be expected to continue to operate in the coming years and a net migration toward nonmetropolitan areas will probably be a frequent, if not a continuing condition.

The decline in the birthrate together with outmigration will result in very low but still positive rates (about 0.6% per year) of population growth for the set of metropolitan areas for the foreseeable future. But because many metropolitan areas will be net winners in their population exchanges with other metropolitan and with nonmetropolitan areas, the simple arithmetic of differences in the rates of growth means that many metropolitan areas will have declining populations.

While I know of no reason why slight rates of decline need to be especially problematic, the fact remains that up to now our experience has been one of population growth in our metropolitan areas. We are therefore ill prepared for the phenomenon of decline. We have neither well-developed theories of how it works nor practical experience for how to deal with it.

Consider for instance two conceptual work horses of our perception of how urban areas are put together. One is our concentric view of the geography of metropolitan areas which has evolved in many variants from Ernest Burgess's original formulation in the 1920's. The other is the conception of housing markets that work by the filtering process. Both of these, which are really two forms of the same idea, are premised on continued growth. As new housing is added at the geographic margin of the urban area, the older housing nearer to the center is taken up by those of lesser income. But note that unless there were a high rate of demolition, this requires that there be an expanding population to inhabit the expanding housing stock. Or, perhaps more accurately, it presumes that there is a certain interplay in the rates of population growth, of increases in income for various groups, of physical obsolescence, of additions to stock, and so forth.

How then does the geography of the urban area evolve and the housing market function if there is a decline in the total population? Will the rate of new construction be reduced sharply? Will there result a growing hole in the center in the form of abandonment? What will happen to the linked chains of prices, quality, and location?

Our existing models, both formal and informal, have been based on an arrow of time which has always pointed upward for population. It is unlikely that these models will serve without major modifications in situations of population decline. They cannot merely be run backward because growing and shrinking are not symmetric. Disinvestment is not the mirror image of investment, and cutting down the size of an operation is not the same as expanding it, only in reverse. This can already be seen vividly in many areas where school enrolments are sharply down.

The Effects of Population Composition

It will be seen, however, that the decline in population is no simple matter of the arithmetic of total numbers. It is strongly influenced in its effects by changes in the composition of the population. Note, for instance, that the average size of households has been declining steadily and rapidly. Average household size was 3.67 persons in 1940, 3.33 in 1960, 3.14 in 1970, and 2.89 in 1976. The drop from 1970 and 1976 alone amounted to 8%, and no metropolitan area has approached this rate of population decline. Therefore decline is accompanied by increased numbers of households.

And since even households consisting of one or two people require a bathroom, cooking facilities, corridors, and the like, the amount of space per capita is higher for smaller households. Thus, the total amount of space in terms of square meters of housing increases faster than the number of households, and total demand for housing space can increase quite briskly in a metropolitan area of declining population.

One might then say that, thank goodness, as luck would have it, smaller household sizes come along just at the time of population decline and we need not worry about reversals in the filtering process and other complications. Things are to go on as usual. But it is the thesis of this paper that neither is it coincidence that the decline in household size accompanies population decline, nor is it possible for things to go on as usual.

The decline of household size stems from changes in our society that encourage more adults to set up their own households, so that for every sex and age category of the population the proportion of people heading their own households (headship rate) has been increasing. At the same time, these same social changes have resulted in lower birthrates, and hence in even smaller households. And it is, of course, the same drop in the birthrate which is the principal factor in the phenomenon of metropolitan population decline.

Neither can things go on as before. The decline in household size must end sooner or later. Moreover, smaller households are not shrunken versions of larger ones. As we shall see, they represent changes in attitudes, behavior, and economics. And most clearly, we will continue to be buffeted by the waves of changing age composition.

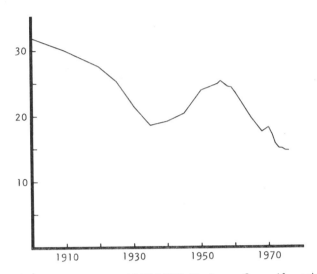

Figure 1 United States birth rate, 1900-1976 (Redrawn from Alonso)

The Waves in the Age Composition

Everyone knows that the birthrate was quite low during the Great Depression, that it rose dramatically during the 'baby boom' which followed World War II, and that it has been plummeting in recent years in what has been termed the 'baby bust'.

But there is a simpler way of looking at this. The birthrate has been declining steadily from the turn of the century in this country as in the rest of the developed nations. The baby boom, whatever its cause, was a very large and unusual departure from this long term trend (see Figure 1). It produced very large cohorts of people at a particular time, far larger than those who preceded them or those who followed them. Much of our recent and future history consists of this giant generation passing through infancy into youth, the middle years and, eventually, old age. This has been likened to a watermelon's passing through a boa constrictor.

The effects of this giant generation are part of our common experience. As children in the late 1950's they produced, not unnaturally, a high degree of child-orientation, and it was not uncommon for half of the population of a suburb to be enrolled in its public schools. In the late 1960's, when this giant arrived on college campuses, its very size contributed significantly to unrest and to youth culture. And now the peak of the wave is coming to young adulthood, joining the labor force, making in its diversity their choices of housing and way of life. It is because this giant is so large that the choices it makes will be decisive to our urban future in the coming years.

The magnitudes of these changes in the age composition may be seen in Table 1. Note the increase in the population aged 25 to 35 years old through 1985. It amounts to 14,553,000 people from 1970 to 1985 (a 58% increase), and to 9,539,000 from 1975 to 1985. Thereafter the increase in this age group will slow down markedly, and after 1990 it will begin to decline in absolute numbers.

The 25 to 35 year-old group is of particular importance because that is the age at which most people have in the past settled down to family life and moved to single family housing in the suburbs. After 1980, when their increase is combined with the decline in the numbers of under 25 years of age, who tend to live in apartments, and with the sharp growth in the 35 to 45 year old group, the following picture emerges as a possible one:

> A large demand for multifamily units and mobile homes will continue into the early 1980's. . . . overcapacity in apartments may occur by the late 1980's as the number of households under 25 greatly declines.

> By the late 1970's and 1980's a great increase in demand for one-unit structures should occur. This demand will at first be greatest for some type of moderately priced housing unit. Later, the demand for more expensive homes should build up as the households begin to update their housing units. In the 1990's a new era of individually styled and custom-built homes may develop as an affluent, middle-aged society seeks to improve the quality of its housing.

In spatial terms this picture amounts to a tremendous wave of suburbanization, for this is what single family housing amounts to. In areas of declining population the phenomenon may be even stronger in relative terms because it is the young who migrate, and thereby increase the proportion of older people.

Table 1. Five-year changes in the U.S. population by age class, for population 20 years and older, 1970-1990, in thousands.

Period	Age class					
	20-25	25-35	35-45	45-55	55-65	65+
1970-75	2,208	5,902	−375	334	1,131	1,433
1975-80	1,640	5,720	2,706	−1,153	1,284	2,114
1980-85	−751	3,819	5,807	−319	328	1,814
1985-90	−2,514	885	5,624	2,638	−990	1,993

SOURCE: computed from Bureau of the Census, *Statistical Abstract* projections.

One may wonder what this picture implies for energy and transportation, for central cities, and for metropolitan governance as a wave of suburbanization (which has been quiescent recently because of the age composition of the population and the economic recession) meets the rising dams of local growth-control in the suburbs. But even if this scenario of massive suburbanization comes true, one must consider that the suburbs would be very different from those of the 1950's in at least one respect: the relative scarcity of children. With all that this means for their fiscal situation and the manner of their daily life, one must conclude that these suburbs would be different.

Changes in Lives

The picture just presented must be considerably modified if we consider that the last years have seen strong changes in the ways Americans live their lives. If these changes are not transitory fashions, as I believe they are not, then coming waves of changes in age composition may result in different outcomes. This is because the picture just presented rests on the children of the baby boom behaving as their parents did in matters of housing and residential location. If substantial portions of them behave differently, that picture changes.

We have noted the steady decline in the size of households, and the rise in the proportion of individuals who head their own households, together with the drop in the birthrate. These are, to my mind, signals of a deep and abiding social change which is mirrored in statistics but which is rooted in the evolution of a modern society. Since talk about ongoing social change often sounds excitable and utopian, in the next pages I will present a statistical picture of some aspects of this change to nail down that something is indeed going on, whatever interpretation one may place upon it.

From 1970 to 1976 the U.S. population grew by slightly over 5%. Total households grew by 15%. The number of households consisting of primary families grew by 9%, and of these, husband-wife families grew only by 6%, while single-parent families headed by a male grew by 16% and those headed by a female grew by 33%. Meanwhile, the number of households consisting of primary individuals increased by 41%; the number of individuals living alone increased by 38%, and the number of households consisting of nonrelatives by 67%. The number of two person households consisting of unrelated persons of the opposite sex more than doubled, and increased more than five-fold for younger people. Obviously the population is distributing itself more finely into households, and the traditional husband-wife mode is growing least.

Consider child-bearing. The current fertility rate of 14.7 births per thousand population is at a historic low, at less than three-fifths the rate of the late 1950's. Moreover this rate is in a sense inflated, because at this time we have such a large proportion of young women in their prime childbearing ages. The total fertility rate is the lifetime number of births which a young woman would have if she followed during the course of her life the current fertility patterns of women of various ages today. A rate of 2.1 births per woman represents the replacement level of the population in the long run. While the fertility rate was as high as 3.7 in the late 1950's, it is now below 1.8.

. . . .

One may go on citing statistics that relate to this basic change in the family and household composition of our society. It is not only that there has been a diminution of the proportion of the population in the traditional family of husband-wife-children; there has been a marked increase in the fluidity of family and household arrangements, so that individuals change their circumstances far more often. Indeed, since the current number of divorces is half as large as the number of marriages and the median duration of marriages has been dropping steadily (it is now 6.5 years) while remarriages have recently decreased, the image of marriage for life at an early age as the dominant mode must now come into question.

In the light of these changes, it is difficult to believe that the choice of housing type and location can remain unaffected. It is unlikely that the same mix of housing units can accommodate this bubbling social soup that held the calmer broth of some years ago, although no one to my knowledge is in a position to make firm predictions. Yet as the vast numbers of the children of the baby boom set on their life paths, their changing mix of housing and location choices will play a determining role in the evolution of urban form.

Working Women

I have to this point avoided giving my interpretation of the causes and meanings of these rapid social changes and have limited myself to trying to show from data that they are real and strong, not mere rhetorical fashion. But I will now suggest that they are manifestations of a long-run social and economic evolution.

The principal causes for these changes seem to me to be the result of the greater emphasis placed upon the individual and the greater legitimacy accorded to a variety of life choices, including that of changing choices. This is in contrast to the earlier emphasis on the nuclear family and its stability as the dominant mode. The reasons for the change in emphasis lie in the increasing education of the population, which has revealed the variety of choices open to individuals and broadened the range of choices acceptable under evolving social norms.

But rather than essaying an extended discussion of overall social change, I will focus on the changes which have been occurring in female employment because this seems to me one of the root causes, because decent statistics are available, and because of its importance for the evolution of urban structure.

Anyone living in this country is aware of the increasing labor force participation of women, but the numbers are so startling that they bear some recapitulation. The rate of labor force participation for women has risen steadily from 33.9% in 1950 to 46.7% in 1976. But it is among married women that the increase has been strongest. In 1900 less than 6% of wives worked outside the home. The share had risen to 9% by 1920 and to 24% by 1950. The growth has continued steadily to 30% in 1960, 41% in 1970, and 44% in 1976.

. . . .

[Alonso provides considerable detail about the sharply increasing labor force participation of women. It increased most strongly among mothers of young children and married women living with their spouses. He then turns to the question "Are these enduring changes?" Despite disagreements from some other population experts, and the fact "social forecasting is a chancy thing. . ." he believes "the ongoing changes will be of long standing." — Eds.]

The Effects of the Population Factor on Urban Form

In the light of these societal changes, the view that the coming of age of the giant generation will result in a suburban explosion requires considerable modification. As in any other guess at the future, there must be a mixture of extrapolation and of intuition. In this case the task is all the more difficult because we do not even have a good statistical basis as to current patterns. Our statistics on employment, on households and families, on housing type, and on urban location are not coordinated, and the essential cross-tabulations are not available. But I will make some suggestions nonetheless.

Since many will continue to live more or less in the traditional patterns and the giant generation is so large, there will be continued growth in the suburbs. But since many will behave in different ways, there will not be the suburban explosion which would be implied if there were no change in behavior. At the same time, many millions will lead lives substantially different from those of their parents and my speculations will focus on these.

It seems reasonable that there will be a shift away from the free-standing, owner-occupied single family house. . . . This is because, first, smaller households require less space. Second, because the fluidity of households and the looser legal links among their members is contrary to the rigidity of tenure associated with ownership. Third, because the maintenance of such a house and its grounds is time consuming and with most people working, time for domestic work becomes scarce and costly. One may therefore expect a greater prevalence of apartments, row or town houses, and innovative forms of design. Similarly one may expect some experimentation in forms of tenure, such as condominiums and cooperatives, which preserve some of the tax advantages of ownership but which provide greater liquidity. One may also expect increases and new forms of contracting arrangements for the operation and maintenance of housing. Since many of these features are already available when renting or leasing, it would be reasonable to expect that these traditional forms of tenure will prosper.

The fact that most adults will be working points to other consequences. First *available jobs ?* and simplest, to there being more money per member of the household. A household in which the husband is the sole earner, making $25,000, living with his wife and three children has a per capita income of $5,000. A household of two where one makes $11,000 and the other $9,000, has a per capita income of $10,000. The second effect, as mentioned above, is that time for domestic work is scarce and therefore valuable. Especially if there is more money available, the economic response is to substitute money for time. This can be done by investing in capital goods such as household equipment, by purchasing food that embodies more prior preparation (including eating out), by shopping less often and buying larger quantities (in effect transferring inventories from the retailer to the household), by contracting for services in the house or sending work to be done outside. All of these carry fairly obvious implications for the geographic relation between households and services and for the design of dwellings.

Travel to work may also have important consequences when there are several commuters rather than only one per household, and when non-working time is more valuable. It suggests to me that locational factors may play a stronger role, and that this factor may result in more concentrated development to reduce travel time. The most convenient point to two distant suburban work places may in many cases be a location more near the center. Nonetheless, the geometry of the relations between houses and work places may hold surprises, especially since the location of services and industry will in turn respond to the location of workers and customers.

This is reinforced by an interesting consideration raised in the sociological literature on women. They point out that in most households the role of the woman, even if she works, retains responsibility for such tasks as shopping, dropping the children off to school or to the doctor, stopping at the laundry, and many other errands. Therefore the woman's travel is more complex than the man's, who takes a straightforward route from home to work. Since the working women typically retains in addition much of the domestic work in the home, as shown in time-budget studies, her time is particularly at a premium. Therefore working wives place great stress on access to work jointly with access to services. They also place high value on flexible working hours. It must be remembered, too, that when women work they gain in economic power and independence and that their wishes gain weight in family decisions.

These factors of housing type, journey to work, and access to services seem to point quite clearly to more clustered development than that which has prevailed in the expansion of urban areas for the past quarter century. This would apply whether the development is central or suburban.

Further, these various factors also point to the possibility of increasing locational attractiveness of more central locations, in the core city and the older suburbs, where there is an appropriate stock of housing and access to services and probably in many cases locational convenience for the journey to work. Moreover, since many of these households have no children, the racial factors of school integration would not act as they have in the white flight to the suburbs. In addition, surveys of residential preferences over the years have indicated that people thought the suburbs were good places in which to raise children. Obviously this plays no part in the location preferences of those without children.

It seems to me that this phenomenon is already taking place at a considerable rate, from the Mission District in San Francisco to the South End in Boston, but no statistics are available as to its rate. Yet it remains an important one to watch and one which is easy to misunderstand. For instance, some are interpreting it as a return of the upper classes and the term "gentrification" has been coined for it. Georgetown in Washington, D. C. is a well-known older instance. Undoubtedly some of this has happened and may continue to happen, but the numbers can never be large. The large numbers would come from households of few dependents if any and multiple workers, none of whom necessarily has a large income or a high social status. Such households may have very considerable income and they are increasingly numerous.

Some may view this as a very good development, the often proclaimed and long-delayed "rebirth of the cities". It would indeed have many virtues, such as strengthening the fiscal base, increasing the life and animation of many districts and supporting city businesses, reversing the disinvestment in many urban properties and, not least, increasing the amount of racial and social integration among adults on a reasonably voluntary basis. But there is a strong danger that it may be regressive in certain consequences and that these may be aggravated by the increasing anti-redlining legislation.

Much of this process appears to be taking place in neighborhoods which are poor and run down but not desperate. These are typically inhabited by lower working class blacks or white ethnics who rent rather than own. Because of rising taxes, fuel costs, and sometimes rent control, these properties have become poor investments for their owners, as is amply attested by the prevalence of abandonment. The owners are very happy to sell. The new laws regulating the issuance of mortgages in these areas in effect give greater weight to the earning capacity of the household over the consideration of the credit-worthiness of the property as security. Therefore they make it possible for the new households to borrow, buy the property, and displace the former occupants.

Over the past twenty years the housing of the poor and the working poor has improved primarily because they have fallen heir to what used to be called "the grey areas". The softening of middle class demand for this housing stock lowered its relative price and permitted a sharp decline in overcrowding for low income people. Whatever the troubles of the cities, this has been a fortunate outcome. But the danger appears imminent that the housing stock available to working and welfare poor will now be sharply diminished, squeezed between abandonment at one end and the childless multiworker household at the other. The consequence would be higher prices and more crowding for those of lower incomes. Yet another reform may benefit the middle class rather than those to whom it was ostensibly aimed.

In Conclusion

Earlier in this paper I said that, whatever happens, the population factor insures that things cannot stay the same. In a nutshell, if people behave as they always have, we will have an explosive suburbanization. If behavior changes, we will have clustering and re-urbanization, or perhaps some other effect that has not occurred to me. But over the next ten years things will not stay the same and it becomes important that we act intelligently and with foresight about these changes.

I am quite aware that there are many changes occurring concurrently with those in the population factor. Some reinforce my inferences. For instance, the higher costs of energy would pull toward clustered development for savings both in space-heating and in transportation. No doubt others pull in other directions. And perhaps, since the world is full of surprises, women will return to domesticity, and birthrate will rise, economic activity will return to the production of goods rather than services, and energy will become cheap.

Comments: 1. Before moving to more consequential matters one probable correction needs to be made in Alonso's predictions. He sees a decline in single unit houses and a rise in various kinds of multiple dwellings. So far the actual record of the late 1970's shows the opposite trend, a relative increase in single dwellings over multiples, and a rather striking growth in home buyers for such units from among the increasing numbers of non-nuclear family households. More about this appears later in this Chapter in the Savings and Loan League survey data. Why this counter-intuitive trend has emerged is not clear. In part at least it reflects the greater relative value of home owner tax breaks as price and income levels increase (see Chapter 8). And in part it probably reflects a shift away from rental housing among investors (see Chapter 12).

2. Alonso in broadly sketching out the population factors has not dealt directly with the need-demand distinction. Nor has he dealt much with the disadvantaged sectors of the population from whom many of the most pressing housing questions arise. At the end of Chapter 2 in the Note on Performance of the Housing Economy Table 3.5 drawn from the Frieden-Solomon study offers a summary of housing need and demand in America between 1975 and 1985. Among other factors it considered were the population issues Alonso discusses. In doing so it fuzzes the distinction between need and demand just as Needleman predicted. Over the decade it gives a figure of 11.9 to 13.6 million units *needed* to house newly formed households to which it added a *demand* for 2.9 to 3.4 million new units for people who can upgrade their present housing and 1.5 million units to satisfy second home *demand.*

Given the unpredictability of the complex of causal factors that include personal income, the state of the national economy, and the future trajectory of new house prices, no attempt in this prediction is made to really separate need and demand. This analysis contrasts with some earlier efforts at making such predictions. During the 1960's when public discussion focused more on social issues, need forecasts were in fashion. The first edition of this text, for instance, included the U.S. President's Committee on Urban Housing forecast that proposed a 1965-1975 need for 26 million units. Interestingly this is a higher total than the 1975-1985 Frieden-Solomon forecast even though the rate of new household formation was substantially lower in the earlier period. Why the difference? Primarily it is because the second case is partly a demand forecast based on what people will be able and willing to pay. The difference highlights the need and demand distinction.

In much of the economics literature need is referred to as non-effective, or ineffective demand, a Keynesian word. This is the same concept Castells called non-solvent demand (supra p. 62). This terminology offers a clue to the widespread fixation of housing policy on questions of subsidy. The housing problem is seen as a problem of transforming non-effective demand or need into effective demand. Either certain incomes are supplemented or the prices of certain units are subsidized. Chapter 8 deals at some length with this problem and possible solutions to it. As further background for thinking about such problems the next reading discusses the various dimensions of housing need. This discussion should clarify additional distinctions between need and demand. The senior author is the housing economist whose work has already appeared briefly in Chapter 2.

W. GRIGSBY & L. ROSENBURG, URBAN HOUSING POLICY 31-32, 37-42, 45-49, 53, 56-58 (1975)

Solvent Housing Needs and Objectives: A Conceptual View

Low-income families are deprived with respect to housing in a number of different ways. Their homes are frequently in disrepair, as well as lacking in: space, privacy, and ventilation; cooking, bathing and heating facilities; basic furnishings; and protection from weather, fires, accidents, and vermin. Their neighborhoods are often crowded, strewn with trash, unsafe at night, interlarded with obnoxious uses, devoid of green space, and underserved by community and commercial facilities. To obtain even unsatisfactory living quarters, they are forced to pay such a high proportion of their income for housing that they have insufficient funds remaining for other necessities of life. Having secured a place to reside, not a few of them live in the knowledge that an interruption in income may suddenly force them to move. Were all this not enough, the poor find themselves discriminated against in the home ownership market by onerous financing terms, and prevented, by zoning restrictions and poor public transit facilities, from having access to housing, job, educational opportunities at the urban fringe. Special groups among the poor suffer even further. Those with physical handicaps cannot find housing services to meet their special needs; blacks are daily reminded of their second-class status in the real estate market, and are frequently forced to pay more than whites for comparable dwellings. Finally, recipients of various forms of housing assistance may find that although their shelter problems are solved, they are stigmatized for accepting public aid. A similar fate befalls many of those who are forced to depend upon the benignity of private landlords for their survival.

These then are the 12 dimensions of the housing problem of the poor: lack of adequate housing space, quality, and furnishings; poor neighborhood environment; excessive housing costs relative to family income; lack of security of occupancy; restrictions upon choice of tenure; restricted locational choice; lack of special housing services for the physically handicapped; racial discrimination; excessive housing cost relative to quality and quantity of space received; and the stigma attached to receiving housing assistance.

. . . .

[The 12 dimensions the authors identify rather closely parallel items in the housing bundle discussed at length by Smith in Chapter 1. For instance, Grigsby and Rosenburg's "security of occupancy" and "choice of tenure" tie back to Smith's "rights of possession," "household security," and "exclusion of others." The dimensions of need also tie in directly to the way many housing problems are defined, and thus to the issues covered in Part II of this text. "Excessive cost relative to income" refers to the issues that give rise to subsidies, for example, and racial discrimination to the related issues of eliminating discrimination in housing and opening up the suburbs. After discussing the relationship of these objectives to larger categories of deprivation, Grigsby and Rosenburg turn to the problem of establishing measurable goals for performance on each of these dimensions. The exposition is lengthy but some fragments of it will give an insight into problems of defining housing need. — Eds.]

Housing Quality, Including Equipment and Services
Although the goal of a decent home for every American family was adopted in federal housing legislation over 25 years ago and has been an objective of social reformers since the turn of the century, it is still surrounded by controversy. In various quarters it is held to be undesirable and unachievable. And there is a sharp division of opinion as to what standards are implied in the term "decent."

Reservations about the desirability of the goal are largely academic. It is argued simply that if an individual is able to exercise an informed choice in the matter and yet selects to live in a (legally defined) substandard dwelling, he or she should be allowed to do so, if this decision would not adversely affect innocent persons such as neighbors or children. Practically speaking, the universe of such situations is probably so limited as to make the point meaningless. There is a related argument, however, which is not meaningless. It might be described as analogous to the doctrine that enforced segregation of schools yields inherently inferior education to those against whom the practice is designed. In essence, the proposition as it applies to housing is that if discriminatory practices prevent certain groups in the population from having access to the more desirable sectors of the stock, their housing is inherently unsatisfactory even though it meets accepted standards of health and safety. Regardless of its physical quality, it cannot meet the minimum needs that a home should provide in a free society. In Stockholm, to illustrate the point in reverse, a considerable portion of the residential stock would fail to meet the plumbing and heating codes in many U.S. cities, yet it is regarded as perfectly acceptable, not because the Swedes have a lower standard of living than do Americans, but because much of the housing in question is occupied voluntarily by families who can afford better quarters.

The question of whether the goal of a decent home is achievable also sounds academic, and also raises some substantive issues. It is argued by a few analysts that standards of decency will keep rising with the increasing affluence of the country. As a consequence, there will always be a segment of the inventory that is regarded as below acceptable norms, and the demand for more public attention to the nation's housing dilemma will never recede. There is some support in the record for this point of view. Standards have indeed risen over time, and it has usually taken a period of years to bring the inventory up to the new levels of acceptability. Eventually, however, outdoor plumbing does disappear, lead paint is removed, and electrical wiring is made safe. If, in the meantime, standards have risen again to include new community concerns, this fact should not deny the value of setting goals in the first place.

The most serious difficulty with elastic quality goals occurs not because achievement is impossible, but rather because rising standards permeate society gradually. Hence at any point in time there may be serious differences regarding what constitutes acceptable quality. This is currently the dilemma in most communities. The standards embodied in local housing codes, which are confined primarily to matters of physical health and safety, do not reflect, in the view of many policy-makers, the much higher aspirational levels of the average American family. If all the dwelling units in the United States were brought into compliance with any one of the good local codes, the unmet housing need as reflected in the goal statements of various advocates of better housing would still be enormous.

A gap between what is legally enforceable and what is regarded as minimally acceptable is not new either in housing or in other sectors of the economy. There is something new in the current relationship, however. For the first time in history, the better local housing codes do not seriously lag behind scientific knowledge in matters of health and safety, and even incorporate a few purely aesthetic items. It would be surprising, therefore, if these codes were upgraded significantly in the next decade or so. As a result, the gap between enforceable standards and generally accepted norms of housing consumers may become pronounced.

Because of the diversity and intensity of opinions about appropriate standards of housing quality and condition, a single set of standards, even if advanced only as a benchmark, runs the risk of being widely rejected as either too high or too low or both. Moreover, obtaining agreement on standards is only half the problem. In order to calculate the extent of need with respect to whatever quality objectives are deemed appropriate, the large number of disparate elements in each dwelling must be rated and the ratings somehow combined into a composite score. This is a problem that has engaged the attention of analysts for years, yet no completely satisfactory solution has been found. The most obvious common denominator is market value, or rent, but prices are influenced by a number of variables besides quality, including amount of indoor and outdoor space, landscaping, modernity, location, and racial discrimination. In the case of substandard units, a single index of quality can be created by weighting housing code violations either according to their presumed seriousness or by the amount of money required to abate them. This approach, while basically sound, excludes most dwellings of good quality. Moreover, it would give a lower ranking to expensive homes having a few violations than to accommodations that were far more modest but were in full compliance with the code.

. . . .

[Here the authors describe the three ways they measured housing quality in their study of Baltimore. These were: (1) the rough measures reported in the 1960 U.S. Census which classified units as sound, deteriorating, or dilapidated; (2) detailed building inspections by professionals who estimated the cost of upgrading to a standard level; (3) the perceptions of households themselves about the quality of the units they lived in. Each of these measures has been regularly used in practice by housing policy workers. — Eds.]

The subjective and objective measures just described leave one important aspect of the problem virtually untouched. The occupant of a residential structure, whether owner or renter, purchases in essence a stream of services, the quality of which is a function of the way in which the structure is managed as well as of the structure itself. For low-income families, the quality of management is increasingly being perceived as more critical than the quality of structure. The flow of heat is frequently interrupted; repairs are not made in a timely fashion; and so on. Some of these problems are covered by housing codes, but they cannot be measured by inspections, and records of complaints to public agencies probably grossly understate their prevalence.

Although what the measurable objective should be with respect to quality of services requires more thought, reliance would probably have to be placed on opinion surveys to identify the problem. Since a certain amount of dissatisfaction with management should be expected throughout the market, the proper objective would be a random distribution of discontent among income and ethnic groups, or perhaps a greater expression of discontent among the more advantaged sectors of the population. Given the possibility of systematic differences in levels of expectations, even this standard is not entirely satisfactory without an underlying base of objective measures.

One final note. Even if all dwelling units complied with the housing code and all residents were reasonably satisfied with their home or apartment, it could not necessarily be presumed that the residential inventory was of acceptable quality. Analysis of data on fires, accidents in the homes, and sickness and disease might reveal that portions of the stock were deficient in ways that had not previously been recognized. Such indicators do not, of course, necessarily measure housing deficiencies, so they cannot be used as measurable objectives, but they can serve as valuable signals of a possible need to adjust existing objectives.

. . . .

Indoor Space

Overcrowding is one of the oldest concerns of housing policy in the United States. It has been viewed as a factor in physical and mental illness and moral degradation. Although few could quarrel with the proposition that at some level overcrowding might indeed have these effects, what that level may be is far from certain. Much depends on whether the dwelling unit both can be and actually is adequately ventilated by the occupants; the amount of time spent in the dwelling;

population density in the neighborhood as well as in the structure; the social mores of the culture; and resistance of the subject population to disease. In America, efforts to establish a relationship between overcrowding and various health and disorganization indicators have met with little success. And populations in other countries somehow manage to live at much higher densities than do most Americans, with apparently no adverse physical, mental, or moral effects.

The case for various U.S. standards of overcrowding must, therefore, be made largely on grounds of comfort and equity, not health and safety. Stated as a goal, each low-income family should be able to acquire an amount of housing space that prevailing norms have established as sufficient for pleasant living.

. . . .

Locational Choice

The fact that inexpensive housing accommodations are not widely dispersed throughout urbanized areas, but instead tend to be geographically concentrated, creates several problems for low-income families and may aggravate others. Many analysts feel that these problems are of greater importance than those which are alleged to be created by substandard housing.

. . . .

Although the problem can be defined as one of transportation and not housing, if the location of low-cost housing, employment opportunities, and community facilities were planned in a more coordinated fashion, the transportation requirements of many low-income persons would be reduced. Expressed differently, for part of the population there may be a housing approach to a transportation problem which to a limited degree has nontransportation origins.

A broader range of locational choices is important for reasons other than mobility. Low-income families, even those who own automobiles, lack access to good schools. If the findings of the Coleman report are correct, intermixing children from various income groups in the classroom would reduce inequality of educational attainment, thereby weakening one of the supports of rigid social strata. Although the Coleman study has been challenged on various grounds there does seem to be general agreement that social-class mixing in the schools increases educational equality to a modest degree. This mixing often cannot be achieved very effectively by busing, at least at the primary school level. [The Coleman report is a study of school integration. — Eds.]

. . . .

Housing Expense Relative to Income

The fact that the high cost of shelter is a serious problem for low-income families is so widely accepted that it scarcely needs elaboration. Or does it? Almost by definition, the cost of everything which a poor family must purchase is excessively high in relation to total income. In this sense, the problem is not one of high housing expense but of low income. Housing, however, is frequently singled out for special attention for several reasons. First, it absorbs a very large proportion of the family budget, so on a percentage basis, progress in reducing housing costs could relieve pressure on other parts of the budget quite substantially. Second, with minor exceptions, housing costs cannot be deferred or reduced by low-income families, whereas other expenditures can be and are. As a result, households suffer from inadequate diet, clothing, and medical care, just to keep a roof over their heads. Third, low-income families do not get much housing for what they pay in rent, a matter to be discussed separately . . . below.

If it is accepted that the problem is one of housing cost as well as income, a measurable objective with respect to what is an excessive expenditure relative to income must be established. A widely accepted objective in the U.S. is for no family to pay more than 20% to 25% of its income for housing, with a small adjustment for family size. However, both the figures themselves and the way in which they are derived seem open to question. The adjustments for family size have universally been inadequate, favoring small households over large ones by a substantial margin. More serious, the basic percentages are much too high for low-income families. Middle-income families, on the average, spend less than 20% of their earnings for housing. Using the reasoning that is implicit in any percentage standard, namely that housing expenses above a certain proportion of earnings will create serious hardship, poor families should be expected to allocate a *lower* proportion of their income to housing than do other families. Some poverty-stricken families should receive their living accommodations for only a nominal fee. The fact that they do not and are expected instead to spend up to one-fourth of their income for shelter, even in subsidized projects, is due to the limited amount of subsidies for housing, not the limited depth of the need.

One possible measurable objective, then, could be derived by matching family income against the total cost of an acceptable living standard, as reflected, for example, in one of the family budgets of the Bureau of Labor Statistics. The family's housing expenses should not be so great as to leave it with insufficient money to acquire the nonhousing necessities in any budget that is deemed appropriate. If housing expenses are found to be excessive in this respect, the problem still may not necessarily be one of low income. The excess could be due to discrimination or to the fact that the family is overhoused. The latter situation is not uncommon among the elderly.

Objection could be raised to the above standard on the grounds that it converts a housing problem entirely into one of income. Families in poverty automatically have the problem; others normally do not. The entire income deficiency may seem to stem from excessive housing expenditures when in fact it could just as logically be assigned to food, clothing, transportation, health care, or some other large item in the family budget. Moreover, if families were provided with funds sufficient to bring their housing expenses in line with their incomes, it seems probable that many of them, even some who were adequately housed, would move to more expensive accommodations and continue to appear to be in need.

To avoid these objections, one is forced back to using one or another rent-income ratio as a standard. The question then becomes whether any particular ratio, adjusted for family size and other relevant variables, is in some sense most reasonable and appropriate. Within limits the answer would seem to be no. Simply as an indication of the general dimension of the problem however, it might be acceptable to use as a standard the median rent-income ratio of non-low-income families of the same household size. This benchmark would produce a substantially lower estimate of need than would the one described above. It would say, in effect, that low-income families should not be obliged to allocate a larger proportion of their incomes to housing than do other families, particularly when they do not obtain shelter of equal size and quality. Unfortunately, this standard implies that one-half of non-low-income families are also spending an unacceptable proportion of their income for housing.

In the absence of any adequate standard, this study accepted both of the two inadequate ones in order to produce a high and low estimate of need and thereby minimize later controversy. Regardless of which of the two is preferred, the information for the calculation of excess housing expense would have to come from field surveys. Without considerable probing by interviewers, the validity of such data may be questionable. Income is likely to be underreported and rent payments overreported, thus considerably exaggerating the extent of the problem. The reasons for the income bias are commonly known and need not be described. The bias in the typical rent figures stems from the widespread practice of rent forgiveness among landlords in the low-rent market.

In addition, rent-income ratios derived from annual income data hide the fact that the earnings of many families fluctuate widely from year to year with shifts in business and personal conditions. If ratios were based on a longer time span, the problem might be revealed to be much smaller, or larger, or different from what is suggested by conventional data.

Housing Expense Relative to Quality and Size of Dwelling

Through the years what has probably disturbed housing reformers most is not simply the condition of slum structures, bad as they are, nor the rents of slum quarters, high as they are, but the two in combination. Measured in terms of square feet per occupant, the cost of substandard housing is frequently found to be more expensive than much better residential accommodations. This phenomenon is not simply a function of overcrowding, for even ignoring the question of occupancy, low-quality units often do not command the cheapest rents. And even where rents for poor-quality housing are not as high as rents in dwellings which offer more amenities, they frequently are not appreciably lower. As a consequence, an apparently wide range of quality can be found at low rent levels.

. . . .

[Persuasive evidence exists for concluding that a poor or minority person's dollar buys less housing than the dollar of a person in a higher socio-economic class. In terms of policy planning there is substantial overlap possible particularly with the housing-quality and housing-expense issues. The authors point out that, "In fact, if these other two goals were reached, low-income families would receive more quality and space for their dollar than would upper-income families." — Eds.]

Racial Equality in the Ownership, Rental, and Home-Financing Markets

Although the objectives here seem clear enough on the surface, when attempts are made to translate them into measurable terms various difficulties arise. This is due both to the numerous ways in which discrimination can manifest itself in real estate markets and to the complex nature of the concept of discrimination itself.

Taking the conceptual aspects first, for analytical purposes, discrimination can be described as either "direct" or "indirect" and as either "benign" or "nonbenign." Indirect discrimination occurs when an individual or group seeks to avoid another, but not in such a way as to consciously deny anyone else's rights. The most common example of this is the flight of whites from racially changing neighborhoods. Direct discrimination, by contrast, does infringe on the legitimate freedoms of others, and hardly needs illustrating. The terms benign and nonbenign attempt to reflect the thought behind the act. If a homebuyer chooses a particular house because it is near a synagogue or a Catholic church, this discrimination against gentile or Protestant areas bears no unpleasant connotations. If, however, he has no special preferences except to avoid neighborhoods where certain ethnic groups reside, his feelings could not be regarded so charitably.

These distinctions among types of discrimination are not unimportant. As recently as four or five years ago, the predominant concern was to eradicate all categories of discrimination, implying a racially homogenized residential environment and a color-blind community. It was felt that every neighborhood should have a mixture of blacks and whites (where there were enough blacks to go around). More immediate importance was attached, however, to eliminating all-white neighborhoods than to integrating all-black ones. All-white neighborhoods, the argument went, forced white children to mature in a sterile environment — a predicament faced in earlier times by most white children, since prior to World War I there were too few blacks in most American communities to achieve the white liberal goal. Arguments to the effect that perhaps not all blacks desired this pattern of living were dismissed as ill-disguised bigotry, as they sometimes were.

Recently, positions have undergone drastic change. Emphasis has shifted to eliminating only direct, nonbenign discrimination, with ethnic clustering being viewed as a societal strength, so long as it is not preserved at the expense of freedom of choice. And the goal of uniform mixing is now seen to be benignly racist. It assumes blacks would be happy to be in the minority in white neighborhoods, but not the reverse; and its espousal of color-blindness is really an appeal for whites to be blind to the color black.

When mixing was the goal, the problem of establishing measurable objectives with respect to discriminatory practices was rather simple. As black families actually moved into more and more neighborhoods, it could be presumed that the reasons for landlords, brokers, and others to make racial distinctions would correspondingly diminish. Thus increasing intermixture in the spatial distribution of whites and blacks could be used as a proxy for progress in all facets of the market.

Now that freedom to choose, not a particular choice, is the goal, the measurable objective cannot be easily defined. The residential intermixture of blacks and whites is not relevant, unless the proportion of blacks who are desirous of various degrees of intermixture is known. In the absence of such knowledge, it is necessary to retreat to several individual measures of discrimination. Landlords, home sellers, home builders, mortgage lenders, real estate brokers, and even municipal governments all engage in subtle and blatant discriminatory acts. They either may deny blacks access to a particular sector of the market entirely or may exact an extra price of admission. Although it is relatively simple to define the objective as elimination of these practices, so many different actors are involved and the practices themselves are often so difficult to detect that measurement is both difficult and expensive.

. . . .

Housing Services for Persons Who are Ill or in Poor Health

An increasing number of individuals, particularly the aging, find themselves in a position of being too healthy to require hospital care, but not well enough to cook their meals or get up and down stairs or use normal bath facilities. Well-to-do individuals can cope with the problem by purchasing special equipment, hiring practical nurses, or moving to quarters more suited to their special needs. Many persons are assisted by relatives or friends. A large number are also serviced by volunteer agencies. A growing proportion are moving to homes for the aged. It is probably still true, however, that adequate care for most partially disabled persons does not exist, and they suffer silently.

The objective of eliminating this situation can fairly easily be put in measurable terms, even though agreement as to means probably could not be as readily obtained. The measure of need would have to be obtained from a sample survey of the disabled themselves and those who care for them. Some judgment would have to be exercised in interpreting the seriousness of the expressed needs, but this is the case with all of the objectives.

Some Summary Observations

Now that we have expanded the traditional list of low-income housing objectives, placed them within a larger hierarchy of societal goals, and expressed a number of them in measurable terms, the question again arises . . . . as to what this approach to housing issues contributes to policy formation. . . .

[T]he multiplicity of housing objectives, the difficulties which surround efforts to cast them in measurable terms, and the maze of possible links among objectives in any hierarchy of community goals provide a partial explanation of why conflicts concerning housing policies and programs are so widespread. Differences of opinion arise not only over which strategies are likely to be most efficient in achieving particular objectives but also over which objectives should be sought. For example, "fair-share" plans differ sharply from proposed housing allowance programs with respect to both the housing objectives which they favor and the relationships which they assume to exist between housing and other societal goals. Ultimately, therefore, the decision as to which of these two strategies should receive greater public support is likely to be made not on the basis of which one is most cost effective, but rather according to which set of intended outcomes is preferred.

Comments: 1. Even in the truncated form presented here, this discussion of housing needs and the objectives to be sought in developing policies and programs suggests the complexity of trying to determine need. This complexity has been one of the main theoretical arguments in favor of a market housing economy. To the extent the market really functions, and people have sufficient income to make effective their preferences, it can allocate housing in a manner both efficient and, within limits, equitable. The complexities introduced by the housing bundle's heterogeneous attributes and peoples' inchoate preferences among the various attribute bundles are incorporated in equilibrium prices. To take but one simple dimension, by shifting from a social concern with need to a market perspective on demand we ask no longer how much people *should spend* but merely how much they *do spend* on housing. The question is the subject of the next reading.

2. The Note at the end of Chapter 2 which considers the performance of the American housing economy again makes this last point more concrete. The Frieden-Solomon estimates included considerable information on the relative size of various types of housing deprivation during the 1960s and early 1970s. Table 4.2 (supra p. 78) presented a summary of this information. It showed that the only form of deprivation that grew in absolute terms was high rent burden. This is the issue Grigsby and Rosenburg call excessive cost relative to income. Their discussion of this matter touches on the arbitrary nature of the standards employed in making these judgments. Almost all analysis and policy draws on the arbitrary thresholds such as 20, 25 or 35 percent of income. Against these arguable standards for determining housing need the comparative simplicity of discovering what people actually do spend on their housing in a market economy suggests that estimating demand is conceptually easier.

A great deal of information on people's housing expenditures is available from such ubiquitous sources as the U.S. Census. A bit of it is sampled in Table 2 in the just cited Note in Chapter 2. From the standpoint of analysis and policy, related but somewhat different aspects of what people spend are more important — and more difficult to answer. Among these is the degree to which changes in income are reflected in changes in the amount people spend on rent or housing expenses. This is the income elasticity of housing question that was introduced in the Note on Microeconomics and Housing in Chapter 2 (supra p. 49). A well-worn question, no less a person than economics founding father Marshall pronounced on it: "Where the condition of society is healthy, and there is no check to general prosperity, there seems always to be an elastic demand for houseroom, on account both of the real convenience and the social distinction which it affords." The next reading provides support for Marshall from recent empirical studies.

F. de LEEUW ASSISTED BY N. EKANEM, THE DEMAND FOR HOUSING: A REVIEW OF CROSS-SECTION EVIDENCE 1-3, 23-26, 39-40 (1970)

Past studies of the demand for housing leave a very wide margin of uncertainty about the response of housing expenditures to a change in income. Estimates of the percentage change in housing expense accompanying a one percent change in income — that is, the income elasticity of the demand for housing — range from .4 to 2.1. A range as wide as that makes it very difficult to draw quantitative conclusions about many housing developments or policies.

One reason for the wide range of estimates is that different investigators have made use of different concepts of income. Much of the discussion of the income-housing relation has focused on the difference between "normal" or "permanent" income in relation to housing and measured income of a single year in relation to housing. As a result of the discussion, there is by now widespread acceptance of the proposition that the elasticity of housing with respect to normal income is higher than the elasticity of housing with respect to measured income of a single year. If it is the elasticity with respect to normal income in which we are interested, then the range of elasticity estimates facing us is not quite so wide as .4 to 2.1.

The range of estimates is nearly that wide, however, even with respect to normal income. On the low end, Lee's study based on incomes of a sample of households for more than one year yields elasticities of about .6 for renters and .8 for households. On the high end, Reid's study based on groups of households stratified by census tract and housing quality yields elasticities of 1.2 for tenants and 2.1 for owners. Other cross-section studies — those of Muth and Winger and Reid's study based on city or metropolitan area averages — yield estimates in between these extremes. Thus, the clarifying of income concepts has not helped very much in reducing our uncertainty about the income elasticity of housing.

The present paper is an attempt to make our understanding more precise by setting forth some basic hypotheses, examining past cross-section studies (that is, studies of many households at one point in time) for relevance to the hypotheses, and then analyzing an additional body of cross-section data which is closely related to the hypotheses and provides some detail about housing demands of different household size groups and of nonwhite households. The data refer to median housing expense and median income per household for metropolitan areas and to price differences among metropolitan areas, all as of 1959-60. Adjustment of the results of these studies so that they refer as nearly as possible to the same population and hypotheses does appear to reduce greatly the range of uncertainty.

One conclusion supported by the paper is that the overall income elasticity of rental housing is probably in the range of .8 to 1.0. A second conclusion is that the income elasticity for owner-occupied housing is probably higher than that for rental housing, though there remains more uncertainty about owners-occupants than about renters. A third conclusion is that for nonwhite households, the income elasticity is probably lower than for all households. Finally, income elasticity appears to increase with household size. If these conclusions are confirmed by future studies, they will provide a more reliable basis than has been available in the past for analyzing housing markets. . . .

[In Section IIa] . . . careful review of the relation of these five cross-section studies to our underlying hypothesis suggests that the range of uncertainty is appreciably narrower than the range of elasticity estimates of .6 to 2.1 actually reported in the studies. For renter families, the adjusted estimates are .8 to 1.0 based on Reid's inter-area comparisons and .85 based on Lee's reinterview study. For reasons discussed above, we disregard Reid's estimate based on stratification by housing quality but the possibility that her estimates based on 1950 data are biased because of the persisting effects of rent controls remains to be investigated in the next section.

For homeowner families, the adjusted estimates are 1.35 based on Muth's study, 1.35 to 1.46 based on Reid's inter-area comparisons, 1.25 based on Winger's study, and .7 based on Lee's study. Instead of the reported range of elasticities of .6 to 2.1, then, the range of adjusted estimates for both renters and owners is .7 to 1.46. This narrower range is a more accurate reflection of the degree of uncertainty we presently face with respect to the income elasticity of annual housing expense.

[Section III] contains some additional evidence on the demand for housing based on median income and housing expense in 19 metropolitan areas as reported in the 1960 Census of Housing. The 19 areas are those (excluding New York) for which the BLS estimated city-worker budget costs in 1959. There are separate regressions for renters in several household size categories, nonwhite renters in several size categories and homeowners in several size categories.

The results presented in this section are useful for a number of reasons. At a minimum they bring an additional, important body of data to bear on the question of housing demands. The use of the city-worker budget data permits a more accurate representation of price differences than has been possible in any other cross-section study. Reid's conjecture that results based on 1950 evidence were seriously biased because of the persisting influence of rent control is testable through repeating her procedures using 1960 data. Finally, separate examination of different household size groups and different racial groups may enrich our understanding of housing market behavior.

We begin with a graphic presentation, shown in Chart 1, of median housing expense and median income for 19 metropolitan areas in 1960. Households are not separated by size in the chart, but medians for households with nonwhite heads are shown separately. The chart clearly indicates the positive relation of rents and income, with observations for all households clustered around the line representing a 20 percent rent-income ratio and observations for nonwhite households tending to center nearer the line representing a 25 percent rent-income ratio. . . .

Chart 1. Annual rent and annual income, metropolitan area medians, 1960 census

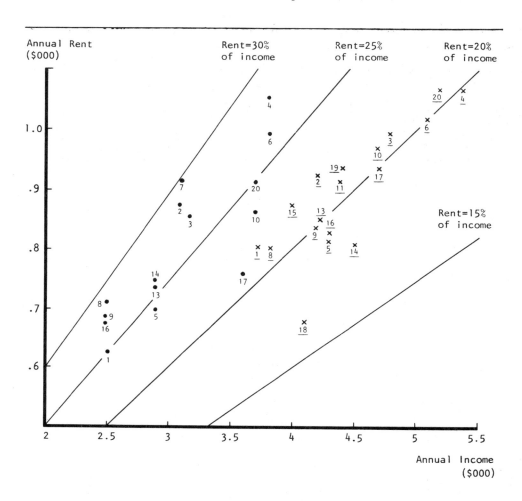

Annual Rent ($000)

Rent=30% of income

Rent=25% of income

Rent=20% of income

Rent=15% of income

Annual Income ($000)

*   all households
x   nonwhite households
City Key

1. Atlanta	10. Los Angeles
2. Baltimore	11. Minneapolis
3. Boston	(author omits 12.)
4. Chicago	13. Philadelphia
5. Cincinnati	14. Pittsburgh
6. Cleveland	15. Portland, Oregon
7. Detroit	16. St. Louis
8. Houston	17. San Francisco
9. Kansas City	18. Scranton
	19. Seattle
	20. Washington, D.C.

NOTE: Separate data for nonwhites were not published for Minneapolis, Portland, Scranton and Seattle; consequently medians for nonwhite households are not shown for these areas.

The additional evidence in Section III is generally consistent with the findings reviewed and adjusted in Section II. For renter households the view is clearest; based on a variety of cross-section sources, the overall elasticity of rental expenditure with respect to normal income appears to be in the range of .8 to 1.0. For owner-occupants there remains more uncertainty; corrected estimates in Section II range from .7 to 1.5, and those in Section III range from .75 to 1.25. The assumptions underlying the .75 estimate in Section III are fairly speculative, however; if we disregard that estimate, then all of the corrected estimates in Sections II and III except one (namely, Lee's) are in the range of 1.1 to 1.5. Thus, the preponderance of cross-section evidence supports an income elasticity for homeowners moderately above 1.0, or slightly higher than the elasticity for renters.

For a deeper understanding of how housing markets behave, some of the other findings of Section III may prove to be of value. A price elasticity for renters somewhere in the neighborhood of -1.0 implies that forces which change the price of housing, such as rising operating costs of technological advances, will have a substantial effect on the demand for housing services. The rise in income elasticity with increasing household size has implications for the elusive concepts of "equivalent" treatment of families differing in size (for example, in public housing or in income maintenance programs). The generally lower income elasticities for nonwhite households may be a consequence of restricted choices due to housing discrimination. The diversity of results for different groups of households — renter and owner, small and large, white and nonwhite — suggests that while we may be reducing our uncertainty to a tolerable range as far as the behavior of housing demands in the aggregate is concerned, we are still far from a unified view of how households in different circumstances make the choice between housing and other goods and services.

Comments: 1. Since de Leeuw's survey other research has produced discrepant findings. Kain and Quigley (see bibliography Chapter 2) in their St. Louis data discover substantially lower income elasticity values. Their findings are consistent with others based on individual household rather than aggregate data. In part at least they ascribe the differences to variations in research design. In housing as in all other fields, the way the question is asked in part seems to determine the answer. The debate on elasticities continues though on one point considerable agreement does exist — homeowners have higher elasticities than renters.

2. A different cut at housing demand emerges from a U.S. Savings and Loan study of recent home purchasers. During 1977 they collected data on 8,500 new mortgages written by 200 different savings and loan institutions in a sample stratified by region and size of metropolitan area. Obviously, this group represents a sample skewed to include no renters and only people who could qualify to buy houses at today's high prices. Still, the results as summarized below are revealing:

Most house buyers are young, with a median age of 32.

Most purchasers are married, 83% in all. The rest are singles and non-married couples or groups (note the conflict with the Alonso findings about the population as a whole).

Buyer household size breaks down as follows: 13% contain one person, 32% two people, 40% three or four, and 14% five or more.

With respect to income the sample is distributed as follows: 15% have less than $15,000 per year, 23% have $15,000 to $20,000, 22% have $20,000 to $25,000, and 40% have $25,000 and above.

The study bears out the conventional view that there is a close relationship between income and price paid for housing, and that the dwelling represents the major wealth possessed by most homeowner households.

Significant regional differences exist, particularly between the West, where houses cost more and buyers were older and richer, and the rest of the country. Only 10% of Western houses cost less than $30,000 in contrast to 16% in the Northeast, 20% in the South, and 25% in the North Central region. In the West 17% of home buyers had incomes less than $17,000, their median net worth was $49,000 and 28% were under 30 years old. In the Northeast the comparable numbers were 27%, $28,000 and 37%; in the South 29%, $29,100 and 32%; while in the North Central area 30%, $22,400 and 46%.

House prices and income of purchasers varied positively with city size. Household composition data indicated more buyers at the extremes in smaller localities, and the incomes of buyers increased rapidly with increasing city size.

U.S. League of Savings and Loan Association, Homeownership: Realizing the American Dream (1978).

Given the tremendous numerical dominance of households continuing to live in the same place they inhabited the year before, the Savings and Loan League survey gives only a partial picture of demand. Many other studies have looked at occupants in the standing stock. Kain and Quigley, looking at household expenditure patterns in their empirical study of the St. Louis market, drew conclusions generally representative of these other studies. They found that owners pay higher total housing expenses than renters of the same socio-economic class. Job duration and age prove to have a positive effect on expenditures among owners but not among renters. People long in their current job were more likely to own their own homes.

The Savings and Loan League data highlight the degree to which effective demand misses major categories of housing need. The total absence of disaggregation along racial and ethnic dimensions gives away the near certainty that black, Hispanic-Americans and other minorities are vastly underrepresented. The median income of surveyed home buyers, $22,700, contrasts with current estimates of the national median income of households as of 1975, which average about $16,000. Further comparisons would reveal other aspects of the skewed character of effective demand in today's American housing economy.

3. In practice, studies of housing demand and need in local markets disaggregate the totals along such dimensions as income, household size, a putative measure of tenure preference, and possibly separate categories for elderly and minority households. The Housing Assistance Plans mandated by the federal Community Development Block Grant Program, and the housing allocation planning undertaken by some metropolitan regional planning agencies typify such studies (see Chapter 11).

A NOTE ON HOUSING CLASS

Another potentially very powerful way of disaggregating the demand side of the housing economy has been used in recent years by European analysts. The concept is called housing class. British sociologist John Rex first used it in studying an area of Birmingham, England, into which immigrant populations of West and East Indians had been moving. He found that they and the preceding inhabitants of the district broke down into "classes produced by the system of house-ownership and allocation." Based on this work he developed a seven-level system of "groups differently placed with respect to the means of housing," among whom struggles may take place "which at the local level may be as acute as the class struggle in industry." The classes defined for his study city

1. The outright owners of large houses in desirable areas.
2. Mortgage payers who "own" whole houses in desirable areas.
3. Council tenants in Council built houses.

4. Council tenants in slum houses awaiting demolition.
5. Tenants of private house-owners, usually in the inner ring.
6. House owners who must take lodgers to meet loan repayments.
7. Lodgers in rooms.

In the class struggle over housing, qualification either for a mortgage or a council tenancy are crucial. They are, of course, awarded on the basis of different criteria. In the first case size and security of income are vital. In the second "housing need", length of residence and degree of affiliation to politically powerful groups are the crucial criteria. But neither mortgages nor council tenancies are available to all so that either position is a privileged one as compared with that of the disqualified. It is likely, moreover, that those who have council houses or may get them soon will seek to defend the system of allocation which secures their privileges against all categories of potential competitors. Thus local politics usually involves a conflict between two kinds of vested interest and between those who have these interests and outsiders.

J. Rex, The Sociology of a Zone of Transition, in Readings in Urban Sociology 215 (R. Pahl ed. 1968).

A fascinating application of the housing class concept comes from another European, Hungarian sociologist Ivan Szelenyi. He found six, quite different classes in his country.

They are: 1. Those who rent new state owned housing. 2. Those who rent old state owned housing. 3. Owners of 'home-unit' flats. 4. Owners of new one-family cottages. 5. Owners of old one-family cottages, and finally 6. Those who have no self-contained dwelling. The difference between housing classes 1. and 2. is that the rent of the first category is subsidised by the state to a much larger degree, in other words those who rent them are in receipt of much greater subsidies. The essential difference between classes 4. and 5. is also not exhausted by the adjectives 'old' and 'new'. What is far more important is that the bulk of the older type largely fulfilled agricultural productive functions in Hungarian villages, and even in provincial towns. They have, therefore, largely lost their function and are obsolete, and a large proportion are beyond restoration.

Szelenyi, Housing System and Social Structure in Hungarian Sociological Studies, The Sociological Review Monograph No. 17, at 281 (P. Halmos ed. 1972).

One of the editors of this volume has suggested that at least six distinct housing classes exist in the United States. The first two are essentially the same as the first two in Rex's taxonomy, but the rest are different.

1. Outright owners of large houses in desirable areas.
2. Mortgage payers who "own" houses in desirable areas.
3. Tenants of houses and apartments in desirable areas.
4. Owners of houses in less desirable areas with or without mortgages.
5. Tenants of houses and apartments in less desirable areas.
6. Tenants and lodgers in public housing, urban slum housing, and rural shanty towns.

Perhaps the most interesting point in looking at comparative housing class in America concerns the radically different position of occupants of subsidized housing. In this country they are in the lowest class, in England in the middle of the class structure, and in Hungary they are at the very top. Perhaps the comparative evidence indicates once again the relativism of housing preferences and the dependence of demand on the structure of the housing political-economy.

Comments: Another fruitful approach to analysis on the demand side has concentrated attention on the decision to move and the concomitant decision about where to live, what kind of a unit to live in, etc. On this question the work of many social scientists and housing experts converges. It has not always been so, however. Traditional microeconomic analysis such as the work of Muth and Alonso cited in Chapter 2 (supra p. 79) has tended to make residential location decisions a function of employment location and the rather simple notion of space or quality preference. Lowden Wingo, a planner-economist, gives the following brief but more ramified idea of the housing choice issue, and he puts it in fine economese.

'In addition to the journey-to-work, the choice is influenced by the distribution of the stock and quality of housing, prestige and culture group associations, variations in the quality of highly valued local services, such as schools, and many other considerations. Complex substitution effects are certain to take place among these if rational behaviour asserts itself at all. Some of the advantages of nearness to employment may be given up for a neighbourhood of greater prestige, or a household may pay a higher rent in order to enjoy access to an unusually good school. The importance of such considerations in the locational decisions of individual households is not to be depreciated'.

L. Wingo, Transportation and Land Use 92 (1961).

Sociologists studying the same issue have found evidence that the attributes of house and immediate neighborhood far outweigh employment location determinants of residential preference. Recently some microeconomists, armed with the necessary statistical and data processing hardware, have begun to shift to a position closer to the sociologists on this question. Kain and Quigley found that about three quarters of the price difference among rental units in St. Louis was tied to unit quality, size, age, neighborhood quality and services. In contrast, within the confines of a metropolitan area "accessibility to employment has little or no effect on housing values and rents."

The mainstream sociology position is illustrated in the following brief excerpt from a well-known study by Herbert Gans of the first settlers in the new community of Levittown, Pennsylvania.

H. GANS, THE LEVITTOWNERS: WAYS OF LIFE AND POLITICS IN A NEW SUBURBAN COMMUNITY 32-35 (1967)

People's reasons for moving *to* Levittown were primarily the need for more spacious housing and the desire to own a free-standing house — "to own our own home," as many put it. Table 1 shows that these reasons, together with transfers to the Philadelphia area by the purchasers' employers were volunteered most frequently as the principal reason for moving *out of* the previous residence. More important, the vast majority were moving because of the inadequacy of the housing. Only 9 percent volunteered the inadequacy of the neighborhood or community as the most important reason, mostly city dwellers.

Table 1. Principal reason for moving from previous residence, by type of community

Principal Reason	Percent of Purchasers Previous Community		
	Urban	Suburban	All[1]
House-related Reasons	60	58	58
	—	—	—
Need for more space	24	27	26
Want homeownership and free-standing house ..	17	21	18
Dwelling too hard to maintain, or want new and modern house	9	4	7
Moving out of parents' home	4	2	4
Evicted, need less space, etc.	6	4	3
Community-related Reasons	19	6	9
	—	—	—
Inadequacy of schools, other facilities for children	2	1	1
Dirt, noise, other physical inadequacies	2	1	1
Racial change in neighborhood	4	0	1
Other dissatisfactions with social aspects of neighborhood or community	1	1	1
General dissatisfaction with neighborhood or community	10	3	5
Job-related Reasons	19	34	29
	—	—	—
Transfer by employer	11	17	15
Change of job	7	11	9
Want shorter journey to work	1	6	5
Other	2	2	4
	—	—	—
N	(170)	(238)	(520)

[1] Also includes people from small towns, farms, army camps

The purchasers could have moved to Levittown either because they needed to leave their prior residence or because they were attracted by suburbia and by Levittown — because they were *pushed or pulled.* An analysis of how they worded their volunteered reasons for leaving their previous residence indicated that more were pushed than pulled, 55 percent indicating the former, 34 percent the latter. The people with the most urgent space needs, large families and blue collar workers, were pushed most often, but only among childless couples did those pulled outnumber those pushed. Even apartment dwellers and tenants, who might have been expected to want home ownership, were pushed more often than they were pulled, indicating again that the need for space was more urgent than all the possible attractions of suburbia in explaining why people moved to Levittown.

The major reason for choosing Levittown specifically, people explained, was that it offered "the best house for the money": that is, a new single-family house which was the best value within their price range. Many had shopped around, 52 percent having inspected ten or more other developments, and 38 percent having looked at houses for from one to five years before buying in Levittown. Table 2 describes in more detail their reasons for choosing Levittown.

Table 2. Principal reason for buying in Levittown, by type of previous community

Principal Reason	Percent of Purchasers Previous Community		
	Urban	Suburban	All[1]
House-related Reasons	85	84	84
Value: "Best house for the money"	48	48	48
Low price	16	21	16
Low down payment	6	7	7
Amount of space	2	1	2
Modernity, other qualities of house	13	7	11
Community-related Reasons	5	2	3
Provision of schools	*	*	*
Playgrounds, pools, other facilities for children ..	2	0	1
Shopping, other facilities for adults	2	1	1
Neighbors, other social aspects of community ...	1	1	1
Job-related Reasons	5	8	8
Journey to work	4	6	6
Business and professional opportunity in Levittown	1	2	2
Other	5	6	5
N	(159)	(222)	(484)

*Less than 0.5 per cent
[1] Also includes people from small towns, farms, army camps

Comments: A slightly different cut at the question Gans asked comes from the results of a monumental research campaign carried out by sociologist William Michelson. He studied selected households during and after a change of dwelling over a five year period during which he tracked the same 750 households. The site of the study, Toronto, Canada, is often said to be more like a U.S. city than any major Canadian city, so the findings are strongly indicative for the U.S. housing market.

Michelson limited his view to middle and upper-middle income families whose demand in economic terms was definitely effective, and who were contemplating a move at the beginning of the five year period. He partitioned his sample into four residence type-location combinations combining high-rise apartments or single unit houses in either central city or suburban locations. As one reviewer observed, his "answers to the questions 'who moved where?' and 'why?' were not very surprising." The general assumption that families who have children and who are concerned with their neighborhood and interested in access to open space will move to suburban single-family homes, and that childless couples who are interested in access to amenities such as theaters, museums, and restaurants will move to downtown apartments, was clearly supported.

Regardless of which house-location situation people moved into, and which they came from, nearly all were quite satisfied with their new dwellings. Expectations about the satisfactions to be provided by the moves were generally felt to have been met. A particular interest of Michelson concerned the longstanding debate over whether people selected their residential environment to facilitate preferred behavior patterns, or whether life style was a product of the new environment. His findings seem to support the first hypothesis. People self-select the house and location that suits their life style. The alternative, environmental determinist hypothesis got little support.

The study is very wide-ranging, many other interesting findings and insights emerged. Among the more interesting and unusual was an examination of the process through which households search the market to find their new home. The following excerpt gives some of these findings. They should be seen in the context of the Palm study of real estate salespeople included in Chapter 3 supra p. 96).

W. MICHELSON, ENVIRONMENTAL CHOICE, HUMAN BEHAVIOR, AND RESIDENTIAL SATISFACTION, 97-101, 106-109 (1977)*

The Search for Housing

People spend longer, on the average, in *deciding* to look for new housing than they do in actually inspecting and choosing it. The median length of thought before starting an active search in our whole sample is over two months, while the search itself is typically less than one month. While those who took longer to decide to look for housing also tended to take somewhat longer in the active search process, the lengths of the two processes are not highly related.

The critical question under investigation here, however, is whether the length of these processes differs according to the type of housing or location chosen. The first way to assess this kind of question is to view the factor thought related to housing and location choice, in this case length of thought process, with each of the categories of housing and location. Reference to these same factors, aggregated according to the type of *change* in housing and/or the type of change in location, may then be necessary, to understand whether the relation observed is one which reflects the specific kind of housing or location chosen or the nature of change undertaken.

For example, the first section of Table 4.1 shows the relation between combinations of housing type and location and the amount of time families took to decide to look for new housing. It shows that although families buying single-family houses in the downtown zone took slightly longer to decide to move, the overall differences between those moving to homes and those moving to apartments are relatively minor. Furthermore, virtually no difference is indicated between those moving to downtown as opposed to those moving to suburban locations.

* From *Environmental Choice, Human Behavior, and Residential Satisfaction* by William Michelson. Copyright © 1977 by Oxford University Press, Inc. Reprinted by permission.

Table 4.1. Time taken for decision to move, by mobility

	Time Taken for Decision to Move		
Type of Mobility	Two months or less (%)	More than two months (%)	(N)
Destination Environment			
Apartment downtown	45.8	51.5	(105)
House downtown	39.1	60.9	(92)
Apartment in suburbs	44.1	55.9	(279)
House in suburbs	44.6	55.4	(258)
Total Respondents			(734)
Missing Information			(27)
Change in Housing Type			
House to house	48.0	52.0	(198)
House to apartment	50.7	49.3	(67)
Low-rise to house	33.7	66.3	(83)
Low-rise to apartment	43.8	56.2	(89)
Apartment to house	37.1	62.9	(62)
Apartment to apartment	44.9	55.1	(214)
Total Respondents			(713)
Missing Information			(48)
Change in Location			
Downtown to downtown	38.4	61.6	(104)
Other Toronto to downtown	49.2	50.8	(63)
Other city to downtown	53.3	46.7	(30)
Suburbs to suburbs	48.1	51.9	(177)
Other Toronto to suburbs	41.5	58.5	(270)
Other city to suburbs	54.0	46.0	(89)
Total Respondents			(733)
Missing Information			(28)

Nonetheless, one might ask whether those *changing* housing types or locations took longer to make such a decision to move, something perhaps hidden since these persons are only part of the total sample. For changes in housing type and location, respectively, one must refer to the second and third parts of Table 4.1.

With respect to housing type, this material shows that families making the change from apartments (high or low rise) to single-family detached houses do in fact take somewhat longer to decide to move than those moving from one detached house to another. While only 52 percent of those moving from one home to another take over two months to decide to move, 66.3 percent of those moving from a low-rise apartment to a house and 62.9 percent of those moving from a high-rise to a house take over two months to decide to move. On the other hand, there appear to be no consistent differences of this kind among those moving to apartments. A small but consistent difference throughout this second part of the table is that those moving to apartments from any given type of housing take less time in deciding to move than those moving to houses.

With respect to changes in location, the data indicate that those remaining within their respective locational zones take longer to decide to move than those whose move represents a significant change in location. This no doubt reflects that job changes are commonly a factor in locational change, especially among those making intercity moves; in such cases, decisions about residential mobility follow job change decisions without much delay.

The length of time necessary to initiate the mobility process is in no way related, however, to the mechanics of the subsequent search process. There are no differences on this basis in how many dwelling units were inspected or what sources of information were consulted.

Length of Active Search Process

The same logic of analysis as in the last section, when applied to Table 4.2, leads to clear differences separating those moving to new houses from those moving to apartments in the length of the active search process. Hence, there is a need to concentrate on the upper two sections of Table 4.2, although not ignoring the third.

Table 4.2. Search period, by mobility

Type of Mobility	Length of Search Period		
	One month or less (%)	Over one month (%)	(N)
Destination Environment			
Apartment downtown	75.9	24.1	(108)
House downtown	47.8	52.2	(92)
Apartment suburbs	67.6	32.4	(284)
House suburbs	45.5	54.5	(266)
Total Respondents			(750)
Missing Information			(11)
Change in Housing Type			
House to house	53.4	46.6	(202)
House to apartment	73.1	26.9	(67)
Low-rise to house	31.0	69.0	(87)
Low-rise to apartment	68.5	31.5	(89)
Apartment to house	40.3	59.7	(62)
Apartment to apartment	69.8	30.2	(222)
Total Respondents			(729)
Missing Information			(32)
Change in Location			
Downtown to downtown	58.6	41.4	(104)
Other Toronto to downtown	62.5	37.5	(64)
Other city to downtown	78.1	21.9	(32)
Suburbs to suburbs	58.0	42.0	(181)
Other Toronto to suburbs	50.2	49.8	(279)
Other city to suburbs	75.2	24.8	(89)
Total Respondents			(749)
Missing Information			(12)

The first part of the table shows that those moving to houses take considerably longer to look for their new housing than those choosing apartments. Over 50 percent of those who move to houses took over one month to search for their new homes, while about 30 percent of those moving to apartments took that long.

The next part of the table indicates that although this difference is present regardless of the amount of change in housing represented by the choice of new home, those moving to detached houses from some other kind of housing took longer in their search. There was no such differentiation among the different types of movers to apartments. The family buying its first home may well be more hesitant and less certain when in the search process, while the established homeowner may be more certain in 'snapping up' just the home desired when it appears on the market.

Reference to the section of the table on location change indicates only the not surprising finding that those moving to Toronto from other cities typically spend much less time in the search process than those already resident in the local area. The alternative may be a park bench!

Number of Dwelling Units Inspected

As one might expect from the length of the active search process, there is a tremendous difference among those who chose apartments and those who chose houses in the number of units they inspected before the choice was finalized. Home buyers looked at very many places during the search process. . . . [A]bout three-quarters of the home buyers looked at seven or more housing units, compared to only about one-third of those who eventually chose apartments. The slight differences indicating greater shopping on the part of suburbanites, regardless of housing type are not large enough to demand further investigation or elaboration.

. . . .

Sources of Information

We asked respondents where they received the information that led them to their final choice of housing. We also used a checklist to assess all the sources of information they consulted during the search process. Answers to both questions show heavy reliance on several sources of information: newspapers, real estate agents, and 'driving around' [a phenomenon Clark referred to in his work on Toronto suburbs]. Information from friends and relatives did not appear to be either widespread or important. The reputations of developers and builders (despite advertising) turned out to be the least important of the elements involved in the search. As one might expect, however, sources of information consulted proved differentially effective according to the housing type and location people chose.

As Table 4.7 indicates, newspapers are consulted much more frequently by people moving to apartment houses than by those moving to single-family homes. Furthermore, although the differences are not so great, people retaining the same type of housing consult newspapers less than those changing housing type.

While people searching for apartments may thus *look* at newspaper advertising more than those searching for houses, the former are even more likely to find their new housing this way. As reported in Table 4.8, newspapers are much more effective as sources of productive information about apartments than they are as sources about houses. This may, however, reflect the practice of going directly from a newspaper advertisement to a rental agent, when looking for an apartment, while the search for a home may go from a newspaper to a real estate agent, and only indirectly to the vendor of a particular house, leaving the real estate agent as the effective party. Just as with respect to their role as an initial source of information, newspapers are more helpful for families *changing* from one form of housing type or location to another than they are to those not changing.

Real estate agents are consulted mainly about houses, and their effectiveness is considerably greater than their rate of consultation indicates. Our respondents used real estate agents more for downtown moves than for suburban moves, and the effectiveness of real estate agents seems greatest with downtown housing, even including downtown apartments.

'Driving around,' on the other hand, is more a suburban method for finding a home. Its effectiveness seems to be mainly limited to the suburbs, as the data in Tables 4.7 and 4.8 show it to be a very ineffective way of looking for downtown housing.

Table 4.7. All sources consulted, by mobility (Percentage)

Type of Mobility			All Sources Consulted*				
	Newspapers	Friends	Real estate agents	Relatives	Driving around	Builder's reputation	(N)
Destination Environment							
Apartment downtown	69.4	27.8	21.3	4.6	51.9	5.6	(108)
House downtown	69.6	33.7	94.6	9.8	54.3	1.1	(92)
Apartment suburbs	71.1	22.9	12.7	9.5	55.6	5.3	(284)
House suburbs	57.9	27.4	61.7	14.7	77.1	12.4	(266)
Total Respondents							(750)
Missing Information							(11)
Change in Housing Type							
House to house	53.5	28.7	67.8	11.9	70.3	12.9	(202)
House to apartment	67.2	20.9	9.0	9.0	58.2	1.5	(67)
Low-rise to house	64.4	25.3	67.8	9.2	67.8	4.6	(87)
Low-rise to apartment	79.8	24.7	19.1	8.9	49.4	6.7	(89)
Apartment to house	79.0	33.9	79.0	24.2	80.6	6.5	(62)
Apartment to apartment	68.5	25.2	14.4	6.8	55.4	6.3	(222)
Total Respondents							(729)
Missing Information							(32)
Change in Location							
Downtown to downtown	63.5	28.8	54.8	8.7	49.0	2.9	(104)
Other Toronto to downtown	75.0	29.7	54.7	4.7	57.8	3.1	(64)
Other city to downtown	78.1	37.5	56.3	6.3	59.4	6.3	(32)
Suburbs to suburbs	56.4	19.9	35.4	9.9	70.2	6.1	(181)
Other Toronto to suburbs	67.7	26.5	33.3	12.5	62.7	10.0	(279)
Other city to suburbs	73.0	31.4	48.3	14.6	67.4	10.1	(89)
Total Respondents							(749)
Missing Information							(12)

* More than one answer permitted.

Table 4.8. Most Effective Sources Consulted, by Mobility (Percentage)

Type of Mobility	Most Effective Sources Consulted*						
	Newspapers	Friends	Real estate agents	Relatives	Driving around	Builder's reputation	(N)
Destination Environment							
Apartment downtown†	38.9	10.2	16.7	0.9	24.1	4.6	(108)
House downtown	20.7	8.7	79.3	5.4	14.1	1.1	(92)
Apartment suburbs	44.0	15.1	10.2	5.9	32.4	4.9	(284)
House suburbs	18.7	11.2	39.4	4.5	44.7	12.0	(266)
Total Respondents							(750)
Missing Information							(11)
Change in Housing Type							
House to house	14.4	12.4	48.0	4.5	39.1	12.9	(202)
House to apartment	46.3	11.9	6.0	4.5	37.3	1.5	(67)
Low-rise to house	24.1	5.7	49.4	4.6	34.5	3.4	(87)
Low-rise to apartment	52.8	12.3	13.5	5.6	24.7	5.6	(89)
Apartment to house	29.0	9.7	53.2	4.8	33.9	6.5	(62)
Apartment to apartment	38.2	14.9	12.6	3.6	30.6	5.9	(222)
Total Respondents							(729)
Missing Information							(32)
Change in Location							
Downtown to downtown	25.0	8.7	49.0	3.8	18.3	1.9	(104)
Other Toronto to downtown	34.4	9.4	42.2	1.6	18.8	3.1	(64)
Other city to downtown	40.6	12.5	40.6	3.1	28.1	6.3	(32)
Suburbs to suburbs	23.2	9.4	22.7	4.4	45.3	6.1	(181)
Other Toronto to suburbs	35.1	16.5	22.9	5.4	34.8	9.3	(279)
Other city to suburbs	39.3	11.2	32.6	6.7	34.8	10.1	(89)
Total Respondents							(749)
Missing Information							(12)

* More than one answer permitted.

† Miscellaneous sources not quoted in this table, keeping this category under the expected minimum of 100%.

Comments: 1. Michelson's findings on house search behavior may well hold true for most upper middle class North Americans. However, recent research among potential recipients of housing assistance indicates strikingly different patterns among lower class households. Here word of mouth appears to be the major source of information, word of mouth information from kinship and friendship networks proves to play a critical role among such less well-off housing consumers.

2. All of the materials assembled in this Chapter have dealt with housing need and housing demand in a rather impersonal way. They provide little sense of the everyday reality of dwelling in a place. In this they contrast somewhat with the material presented in the first Chapter by sociologist Rainwater who wrote of the house as haven from the threats and blows of daily life (supra p. 14). Even the most squalid house, the dreariest slum, can shelter the richest moments of human experience. Rainwater's studies in the infamous Pruitt-Igoe housing project (supra p. 16 and fig. 10) share with much ethnography of slum dwellers a sense of the everydayness and humanness of dwelling.

L. RAINWATER, BEHIND GHETTO WALLS: BLACK FAMILIES IN A FEDERAL SLUM, 12, 17-18 (1970)

Ordinary Lives

Despite the world of troubles that Pruitt-Igoe and the ghetto generally present to their inhabitants, systematic observation of family life in the community impresses the observer also with its ordinariness. The basic pattern of life is simply the ordinary American way of family living. The Pruitt-Igoeans get up in the morning like everyone else, the men put their pants on one leg at a time, the women cook meals, someone shops for groceries, brothers and sisters bicker with each other, children go off to school and straggle home at the end of the day, mothers worry about their children's behavior as they try to live up to their responsibilities for socializing them — all like everyone else. There are variations sometimes slight, sometimes major, on the basic themes of American life that are distinctive to this place and time and to these people, and these variations will be treated problematically in the analysis that follows because we must understand them if we are to understand the particular suffering that ghetto life represents and thereby help to eliminate this special suffering. But we cannot appreciate daily life, family life, child-growing-up life in Pruitt-Igoe without realizing that it mixes in complex and ineffable ways the ordinariness of all American life (indeed of all human life) with the special qualities of the ghetto, and the even more special qualities of the Pruitt-Igoe community.

. . . .

In the fall of 1963 Boone Hammond climbed to the fifth floor of one of the Pruitt buildings to knock on the door of a two-bedroom apartment which opened to the tiny stairwell landing. Mrs. Coolidge invited him into the living room after he explained that he was a student from Washington University interested in knowing how she felt about living in Pruitt-Igoe. As they sat down at the kitchen table in the combined living-dining room, he observed that the apartment was clean but bare, without any other furniture, floor covering or curtains on the windows. Hammond learned later from the Housing Authority records that the Coolidges had been married about a year and a half and that they had a 15-month-old son. Mr. Coolidge was 21 years old, and Mrs. Coolidge, 19. Mrs. Coolidge explained that they had lived in their apartment for only three months, having lived in the West End of St. Louis for the first few months of their marriage. Both, however, had grown up in Pruitt-Igoe, and he learned later that both their parents still lived in the project.

Hammond asked Mrs. Coolidge why they moved to the project.

> Cause we could save on rent. When we lived on Waterman, the rent was $13 a week, which was $52 a month. But we just had a kitchenette — one room with an icebox, stove, and bed all combined. So we thought we could save money here because it's only $43 a month for the apartment.
>
> Is there anything else you like here?
>
> We have enough heat and we have a private bath. It's more convenient. We don't have to run out and catch the trash man; all we have to do is just take the garbage downstairs and dump it into the incinerator. When you move in here, there aren't any insects, rats, and so on, like the other place. In these apartments, after every tenant moves they clean up the apartment and repaint it.
>
> Do you have some other likes and dislikes about the project?
>
> What I dislike is when people mess up the hallways, when they don't cooperate, and when the elevator is broken I have to carry the baby upstairs. What I do like is that I have the type of kitchen and bath that I can keep clean. It's easier to keep these apartments clean except the dust that comes in from having so many windows. They also just put these new locks on which are sturdier than the old ones, and you can't lock yourself out as easy as you could with the others. You know when I lived over on Waterman Street, the apartments used to get so cold in the winter time that you had to put the baby's blankets into the oven to warm them up so he wouldn't be too cold. You could talk to the landlady all of the time and complain about there not

being enough heat, but she never turned it up. That is one thing you don't have to worry about here in the project, because in winter time it's always warm in these apartments.

At this point Mr. Coolidge came into the living room from one of the bedrooms. Hammond, after explaining his interests, asked how he felt about the project.

As far as I'm concerned, if the rent wasn't as reasonable as it is I'm sure that many of the people wouldn't be here. The environment is definitely bad. The conditions here are fair. *This is a city within a city, and the people make their own laws.* To a person who cannot afford the luxuries that a person can have, Pruitt-Igoe is what you might say was forced upon them. This is the last resort. It could be better than what it is. But then again the people help destroy it.

Just before its final demolition, Mrs. Lillian Towns, a resident of Pruitt-Igoe since it opened, was interviewed by the St. Louis Post-Dispatch in the apartment she occupied until the very end:

The tenants who are left live in three buildings. The surrounding deserted buildings' plumbing has been ripped out, windows smashed and walls torn down as thieves continue their relentless pursuit of valuable copper pipes. There are authority maintenance and security personnel at the project.

"The quiet sometimes is unsettling," Mrs. Lillian Towns said looking down at the empty streets from the eighth floor apartment she moved into 18 years ago. She is looking forward to moving into a house with a son, one of 10 children reared in the five-room apartment.

"It was beautiful, just beautiful when it opened," she said. "I really did like it then."

"Right now, it is so empty. It was nice, but it went wrong, people all stacked up on one another in these tall buildings. I guess they should tear it down," she said.

"It's been home to a lot of people and leaving hurts some real bad," Mrs. Towns said.

St. Louis Post-Dispatch, April 22, 1974.

[These words remind us of the infinite human variety that lies beneath the impersonal concepts used in thinking about the housing economy and its problems. — Eds.]

BIBLIOGRAPHY

N. Foote, J. Abu-Lughod & M. Foley, eds., Housing Choices and Housing Constraints (1960)
Somewhat out-of-date but very informative collection of monographs on housing demand.

C. Rapkin & W. Grigsby, The Demand for Housing in Racially Mixed Areas (1962)
Housing market analysis of racism.

M. Reid, Housing and Income (1962)
Econometrics on the demand elasticity questions.

D. Rossi, Why Families Move (1955)
Classic sociological study of a well-honed question.

U.S. President's Committee on Urban Housing, A Decent Home (1968)
Contains ambitious, and quasi-official estimates of housing need during the late 1960s and 1970s.

Note: Several of the works cited in the Chapter 2 bibliography contain useful material on demand. See Kain and Quigley for instance.

Chapter 5

HOUSING MARKET DYNAMICS

Households and houses change constantly. On the demand side of the economy, household composition, income, preferences, racial makeup and life cycle patterns are in continuous flux. On the supply side, dwellings, their quality and age, price and the operating practices of their owners also vary. The two preceding chapters have separately dealt with important dimensions of these changes. This chapter will treat the two together in terms of some major dynamic features of housing markets.

Housing problems almost invariably occur in the context of these dynamic relationships. Shortages of capital, non-effective demand or needs, neighborhood decline, and most of the other shelter related problems experienced by our society come about because of changes or failures to change. Increasing supply prices, incomes that do not rise as steeply, and increasing numbers of households combine to create today's crunch between supply and demand. These factors also escalate requirements for capital funds and create a pool of deprivation or need from people forced either to pay more than they can afford or go without adequate housing. Shifts in preferences and the aging of structures and their supporting facilities together produce blighted neighborhoods and housing. Suburbanization with its associated environmental problems and issues of racial and income class exclusion are consequences in part at least of many housing supply and demand factors. The problems addressed in Part II of this text can all be seen as results of changes in the housing market.

In order to deal effectively with these dynamic features, strong organizing ideas are needed. Again the most important concept comes from the economists. It is called "filtering." Filtering refers to the apparently systematic tendency of both houses and households to sequentially exist in or occupy different submarkets. In the most common version, it refers to the situation in which households of successively lower incomes will sequentially occupy or filter through a dwelling or neighborhood from the relatively well-to-do original owners to the welfare recipients who last occupy the units before final abandonment. Seen the other way around the dwelling in question has filtered down into ever lower price and lower quality submarkets until it drops from the market entirely.

Actually filtering often denotes both trickle-down and trickle-up processes. It is an omnibus concept applied to several distinct processes. Housing filters down in quality, and, as it does, so it filters down through the spectrum of household incomes moving from the richer to the poorer. Paralleling this there is a filtering of prices and values, the process of depreciation with advancing age. Filtering implies the constant flow of people through the housing stock. When a person buys a new house it usually means he moves out of an older one. One move leads to another. A species of musical chairs game ensues as people circulate or filter through housing. The rules of this game are among the imputed laws of housing market dynamics. The following brief comment by housing economist Michael Stegman explains why filtering has been and continues to be a central area of concern for housing analysts and problem solvers.

[F]iltering has played a prominent role in the economic theory of housing markets, and continues to provide the framework for analytic attempts to gauge the strength of, and linkages among, various market sectors and the effects of

161

turnover on the housing circumstances of the population. Filtering has been considered the principal dynamic feature of the housing market because it encompasses the entire range of price, quality, and occupancy implications of shifts in supply, demand, and excess vacancies. Continued interest in this phenomenon can probably be attributed to the view that it is an indirect process for meeting the housing demands of lower income populations. Indeed, it is largely because of its social welfare connotation that both the otherwise academic issue of whether filtering actually works and the results of empirical research on turnover and vacancy chains continue to command the interest and attention of housing program and policy officials. If, as has been commonly presumed, filtering produces the important linkage between the scale of new housing construction on the suburban fringe and the level of housing market opportunities and the price structure in older inner city neighborhoods, then there is a clear low-income policy interest in achieved levels of unsubsidized as well as subsidized housing starts. If, as has been demonstrated by Lansing, White, and Sands, the construction of different kinds of new housing tends to initiate vacancy or turnover chains that vary in their respective lengths, in the populations they directly affect, and in the market sectors through which they pass and eventually terminate, then a policy which attempts to maximize the number of lower income housing opportunities generated from any given level of housing starts may legitimately seek to stimulate new construction in selected market sectors as part of a turnover or filtering strategy.

Stegman, The Neighborhood Effects of Filtering, 5 Journal of the American Real Estate and Urban Economics Association, 227-28 (1977).

Smith, in the following reading, attempts to uncover the economic rationale underlying the distribution of housing units of varying quality among income groups. The model of the filtering process he presents discusses the flow of people through housing units as market conditions change. It is important to remember that such models are intended to simplify the universe for the purposes of analysis. For example, the following discussion assumes the households will and can move freely without friction or transaction costs. Smith's notion of optimality — when things are best in the economic sense — does not account for external costs and benefits either. In the hypothetical community he devises, residents do not think of their neighbors or their neighborhood, but respond to market conditions solely by their ability to pay.

W. SMITH, FILTERING AND NEIGHBORHOOD CHANGE 17-33 (1964)

A Theory of Filtering

... [T]he concept of filtering as a "well recognized phenomenon" ... represent[s] efforts to read either logic or predictability into the observed pattern of occupancy of an urban area's housing stock. The pattern can be studied in terms of household characteristics (especially income) vis-a-vis housing characteristics (such as quality or age of the structure, or location). Low-income households seem usually to inhabit older, less adequate, centrally located dwellings. New residential construction, by implication, is concentrated at higher price or income levels and at the fringes of the urban area. From what underlying economic circumstances do these patterns arise? How might the pattern be affected by some change in those circumstances? The filtering discussion has succeeded in raising these questions, but not in providing satisfactory answers.

. . . [W]e offer a very simplified but operational model of the matrix type which suggests that such questions do have determinate answers. This model is in terms of the "assignment problem," of recent operations research literature. It involves a hypothetical community consisting initially of an equal number of households and housing units; the households differ with respect to income (or ability to pay for housing in general), while the housing units differ with respect to desirability. We ask of this model several questions which have real world counterparts, and for which the model is able to provide at least partial and qualified answers. These are the questions:

1. Given the two-sided differentiation of households and housing units, what pattern of occupancy — of assignment or matching of families with houses — will a free market tend to produce?
2. How will this pattern change if there is a change in the income distribution of the community?
3. If the community remains unchanged in size (number of households), what will be the quality of new houses when depreciation of the stock requires some replacement building?
4. When such replacement building occurs, what pattern of changes in occupancy of the housing stock will accompany it?
5. If the community increases in size, what price level of housing will be constructed?

The model is dependent upon several assumptions which must be borne in mind in conjunction with the effort to find answers to these questions. These assumptions imply important qualifications to the conclusions reached, and indicate the imperfect state to which the assignment model technique for housing market analysis is as yet developed.

The Assumptions

The hypothetical community consists of five families, differing as to income but not otherwise, and five houses differing as to quality. Adopting a yardstick of value, which might be the monthly rent or rental equivalent, we need to make assumptions regarding the amount each family would be willing to offer for each of the houses, since each family is a potential occupant of any dwelling. That is, for purposes of simplification we do not consider independent submarkets (apartments vs. one-family homes, for example).

The first step in deciding how these rent offers would differ for different families and for the several houses is illustrated by Figure I. In this table the vertical columns represent the houses, A, B, C, D, and E. A is the lowest quality dwelling, B the second lowest, etc., and we assume all families rank these houses in the same order. The horizontal rows represent families 1, 2, 3, 4, and 5, with family 1 being the one with least income, family 2 having the second lowest income, etc.

Figure I. Effects of income change and house quality on lowest rent offer

Families	Houses				
	A [Lowest quality]	B	C	D	E [Highest quality]
1 [Poorest]	L	+5	+10	+15	+20
2	+10				
3	+20				
4	+30				
5 [Richest]	+40				

There is some lowest amount of rent that would be offered for any house by any family, and this amount can be designated L. It is the differences from L which will determine the pattern of occupancy rather than the value of L itself, so this value does not need to be specified.

The first figure shows that family 1 would offer $5 more for B than for A, $10 more for C than for A, and so on. Thus, rent offers increase with house *quality*. Figure I also shows that for a given house, such as A, rent offers rise with *income*. Family 2 would offer $10 more for A than family 1 would offer. Family 3 would offer $20 more than family 1 for house A, etc.

If we were to complete the table of rent offers with only this information we would enter in each cell the sum of the amounts at the top of its column and at the left of its row. For example, this would make family 2's offer for house B equal to L+15, family 3's offer for house B equal to L+25, etc. This, however, would imply an assumption which seems unrealistic. It would say that family 2, with a higher income than family 1, would pay no greater premium to have house B rather than house A. The income elasticity of demand for quality would be zero.

One might expect, however, that one step up in quality, from house A to house B, would be worth more to the higher income family. This accords with the notion that housing space itself is a necessity but extra housing quality is a luxury, the consumption of which increases with income.

To represent this income elasticity of demand for quality, Figure II shows some assumed increments for each of the cells outside row 1 and column A. Each step up the *income* ladder brings an increase of $1 in the rent offer; each step up the *quality* ladder also brings a $1 increase. There is no necessary reason for these $1 amounts to be the same; the argument is unchanged so long as the effects of both income and quality are always positive.

Figure II. Effects of income elasticity of demand for quality

Families	Houses				
	A	B	C	D	E
1					
2		+1	+2	+3	+4
3		+2	+4	+6	+8
4		+3	+6	+9	+12
5		+4	+8	+12	+16

Figure III then adds these several assumptions together. The *market demand matrix* consists of amounts of L plus some increment for income and/or quality. The amount offered by family 2 for house B is L+10+5+1 or L+16. The amount offered for house C by family 3 is L+20+10+4 or L+34, etc.

Figure III. Market demand matrix

Families	Houses				
	A	B	C	D	E
1	L	+5	+10	+15	+20
2	+10	+16	+22	+28	+34
3	+20	+27	+34	+41	+48
4	+30	+38	+46	+54	+62
5	+40	+49	+58	+67	+76

The Optimal Assignment

We may now answer the question, which pattern of occupancy will produce the maximum aggregate of rent offers? This maximum sum should be realized by a well-organized competitive market of mobile families, and is optimal in this restricted sense.

It can be proved that any assignment — i.e., pattern of occupancy — not lying on the main diagonal of this matrix is non-optimal; the aggregate of rent offers could be increased by rearranging the pattern in a specific way. Figure IV illustrates one such nonoptimal assignment. The circles indicate the pattern of occupancy; family 1 lives in house C, family 2 in A, family 3 in E, family 4 in B and family 5 in D. Referring to the market demand matrix (Figure III) it can be seen that the aggregate of rents offered for units actually occupied under this arrangement comes to $L+173$.

Figure IV. Non-optional assignment

	Houses				
Families	A [Lowest quality]	B	C	D	E [Highest quality]
1 [Poorest]	←		0		
2	0 →				
3					0
4		0			
5 [Richest]				0	

We note, however, that by switching family 1 to house A, and the family initially occupying A to the house initially occupied by family 1, we decrease the aggregate of rent offers by $10 and increase it by $12, for a net gain of $2. We could then switch families 2 and 4 for a further gain of $2. So long as any pair of families is not "located" along the main diagonal of this matrix a profitable switch is possible. When they are all on the diagonal any switch means a greater loss than gain. The optimal assignment, represented by Figure V, has an aggregate rent offer of $L+180$. No other assignment of these families to this supply of houses can add to a greater sum.

Figure V. Optimal assignment

	Houses				
Families	A	B	C	D	E
1	0				
2		0			
3			0		
4				0	
5					0

Response to a Change in Market Conditions

Our simulation model has now produced a not-too-surprising result. The less desirable houses are occupied by the lower-income families. It is important to point out that this result has nothing to do with the *cost* of building such houses, for at the outset of the problem the five houses were assumed to be already in existence. Their cost, in an economic sense, was nil. In the short run, any commodity which is fixed in supply will be priced and utilized without regard to its cost of production, which by that time is a "sunk" cost.

The real usefulness of the model is yet to be demonstrated. The diagonal assignment is only a starting point from which patterns of *response to changes* in market conditions can be derived. Suppose, for example, that the income composition of the five-family community is changed, so that there is no longer a family 5 with its high income, but there are two families at level 1. If we substitute in the market demand matrix a row 1 for 5 (and rearrange the rows so that the higher income families are in lower rows) we know that once again the optimal assignment will be along the diagonal. This will require some shifting about of the families, however, with the exception of family 1, who can remain undisturbed. Figure VI shows the outcome of this "filtering" response to the change in income composition.

Figure VI. Effect of change in income distribution

Families	A	B	C	D	E
1	0				
1		0			
2			→ 0		
3				→ 0	
4					→ 0

The response consists of having family 1 ' occupy house B, after family 2 moves from B to C, family 3 moves from C to D, and family 4 moves from D to E. The new aggregate rent offer, L+130, is less than before, reflecting the loss of a high-income family. Note that the decrease of $50 in this value is less than would have been realized if the new family, 1 ', had moved into the house vacated by family 5. That loss would have been $76 – $20, or $56. The filtering process has improved by $6 the resale value, in a sense, of house E. It is interesting to note that while the aggregate situation is improved by this filtering activity, the rent offers for houses B, C, and D, as well as E, are now lower than before; they have "filtered down." Yet families 2, 3 and 4 now occupy better quality houses; they have "filtered up." The net result is, in this hypothetical situation, a gain of $6 through filtering; if actions within the community successfully fend off value decline for houses B, C, and D, this net gain will not be realized.

The Implied Values of Houses

The *"assignment" model, despite its hypothetical nature, may thus assist in forecasting neighborhood changes.* If the assumptions made in developing this model correspond to real market conditions in a specific community, the model will not only point to patterns of change which specific new circumstances are likely to produce, it will also "explain" why those changes in the use of the housing inventory take place. This helps to avoid the common mistake of thinking that the housing market is irrational, or imperfect, and therefore in need of public control simply because the logic underlying its performance is difficult to see. On the other hand, if we are fairly sure what the pattern of rent-offers in the community for its housing stock looks like, and we observe a pattern of movement or occupancy not in accord with the simulation model, we can with greater justice criticize the operation of the market and perhaps discover realistic remedies.

The usefulness of the assignment model approach goes beyond forecasts of changes within the existing inventory of houses. The model provides a means whereby the type of new construction which the market requires, as the community grows or as the original stock of houses depreciates, can be predicted. The essential tool for this purpose is an indication from the model of the "economic value" of a specific type of new house, which value can then be compared with its construction cost.

"Economic value" in this context refers to the effect of an additional house on the aggregate of rent offers. (Of course, if the rent offers are thought of as monthly amounts they would have to be capitalized in some way to obtain present value.) Thus, going back to our original market demand matrix, with five families occupying a total of five houses, what would be the effect on aggregate rent offers if an additional house were added? For example, suppose that another house exactly like D were added to the supply. After all profitable shifting about of families among the enlarged housing supply had been completed, how much would the aggregate of rent offers have increased? This situation is illustrated in Figure VII.

Figure VII. Effect of adding house D'

	Houses					
Families	A [Lowest quality]	B	C	D'	D	E [Highest quality]
1 [Poorest	⟶ 0					
2		⟶ 0				
3			⟶ 0			
4					0	
5 [Richest]						0

We note that family 3 would move into house D', family 2 into C, and family 1 into B; house A would be left vacant. By referring to Figure III, the market demand matrix, all the plus and minus effects on the aggregate rent offer can be determined. The net result is an increase of $18.

If the added house were like C rather than D the aggregate rent offer would increase by $11 rather than $18. Completing this process for all of the original types of houses yields Table 1. The values rise from $0 for A' to $26 for E'; all these values are depending on the many assumptions made concerning the pattern of rent offers embodied in the market demand matrix and the mobility of the several families.

Table 1. Change in aggregate value when one house is added

House Added	
A'	+0
B'	+5
C'	+11
D'	+18
E'	+26

Table 1, then, provides indicators of the economic value of the various types of new houses which may be added to the supply. The fact that value rises with quality stems from the assumptions about market conditions. Cost of construction has not yet been brought into the picture.

The "normal market" assumptions are also responsible for the most significant feature of the list of values in Table 1. In such a market higher-income households offer greater premiums for housing quality than lower-income households offer. The function relating value to quality is *convex:* that is, it increases by increasing amounts. A *cost* function, relating the cost of construction to the quality of the dwelling which is built may be linear, convex or concave. Unless it has more convexity than the value function, efficient new construction will never occur in the middle quality range.

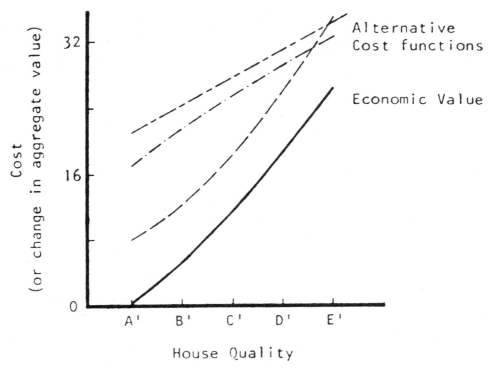

Figure VIII Selecting quality level for new construction — replacement case (Redrawn from Smith)

This is illustrated in Figure VIII. Here the economic value figures from Table 1 are plotted: the convexity of the curve can be noted. Three different types of cost functions are also shown; X is a linear relation between cost and quality, Y is a convex relation in which cost rises faster than quality, and Z is a concave relation with costs rising less rapidly than quality. All three cost curves are shown lying well above the value curve; if such is the case no new construction will be justified. The cost curve, whichever shape it has, must for some reason fall until it touches the value curve; the quality level at which the curves first touch is then the quality level for new construction which the market requires.

If the community in question does not increase in population, new housing demand will be of the replacement variety, a response to the gradual deterioration or obsolescence of the stock of houses. This loss of desirability will encourage households to offer premiums for newly constructed houses; the premiums being offered will increase as time goes by. For example, more would be offered for a new unit E' than for E, if the latter unit has depreciated. In other terms, there is a *latent* matrix of demand for *new* units of the several qualities. These premiums, due to the wearing out of the original stock, can be represented in relation to values derived from the initial matrix for existing units by a downward shift of the cost function for new construction. Part of the cost of the new construction will be covered by this premium.

As the cost curve shifts downward, the quality level at which it first touches the value curve depends on the shape of the cost curve. If the latter is linear or concave (as X or Z in Figure VIII) replacement construction will usually take the form of the highest quality of dwellings. If the cost function is sharply concave (as Y in Figure VIII) construction may occur at a middle quality level.

We have no information from which to draw the cost function linear, concave or convex; in fact its shape may well vary among communities and over time. The important observation is that for most of the range of *possible* shapes of the cost curve, new construction would be economically warranted for replacement only when it is at the upper end of the quality spectrum *in our model,* given the assumptions regarding a "normal market" and in the absence of any submarkets.

This says something about the quality level of new construction in a static community, in which the only demand pressure for new houses is a result of deterioration or obsolescence of the old units. What of a community which is growing in population? The same technique allows comments as to the quality level of new construction in this case, too. Under this condition, however, the economic value of an additional house will differ from the value derived in the previous case. Instead of there being a surplus of houses when one unit is created, there will be a positive deficiency of houses until another is supplied, in the community which expands by one family.

The economic value of a house under conditions of scarcity can be determined from our market demand matrix by *removing* one house at a time from the five-house stock, and computing the effect on aggregate rent offers. Again, the filtering process is assumed to operate sufficiently so as to make optimum use of the now inadequate housing stock, as is illustrated in Figure IX. When house D is removed, family 4 moves into house C, family 3 into house B, family 2 into house A, and family 1 is left, initially, without a dwelling. Thus, wherever the scarcity arises, whether by the immigration of a well-to-do family, a poor family or a middle-income family, the tendency in this model is to force out the lowest rent-payer, whoever that may be.

Figure IX. Effect of removing house D

Families		A	Houses B	C		E
1	←					
2		0 ←				
3			0 ←			
4				0 ←		
5						0

New economic values may now be derived for each of the original types of houses under the condition of absolute scarcity. If house D is removed the aggregate rent offer will diminish by L + \$21. If it is A that is removed, the loss will be just L dollars. In Table 2 all the economic values under conditions of scarcity are presented.

Table 2. Change in aggregate value when one house is removed

House Removed	
A	$-L$
B	$-(L+6)$
C	$-(L+13)$
D	$-(L+21)$
E	$-(L+30)$

Figure X compares the new function relating value and quality to a single illustrative cost function. It is to be noted that in this case the value function does not start from zero for a house of type A, but from the value L. Initially we let the cost function lie entirely above the value function, with no new construction being warranted.

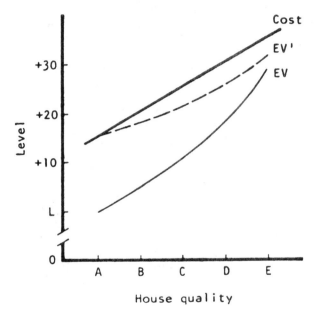

Figure X Selecting quality control for new construction — growth case (Redrawn from Smith)

Family 1, however, requires housing of some sort. Its minimum demand is for simple housing space — the bare necessities for which it previously offered L. Now that there is an absolute shortage of housing space this family — and all the others as well — must offer more than L. The value curve must shift upward until it touches the cost curve, permitting some type of new dwelling to be constructed.

The value curve may simply move vertically upward, but there is reason to believe this will not be the case. As higher-income families find the price of housing space rising, their real incomes are reduced; they cannot afford to be quite so choosy now about housing quality. As a result, quality premiums associated with higher incomes, such as were assumed in Figure II, will very likely diminish. The value curve will thus not simply move upward; it will tilt towards a flatter position as it does so. This is shown by the EV and EV' lines in Figure XI.

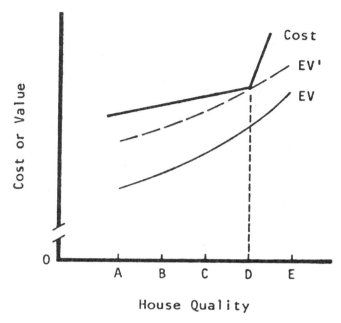

Figure XI Replacement demand — excluding luxury dwellings (Redrawn from Smith)

[The case illustrated here is not mentioned in the reproduced Smith text; however, because it seems to correspond better with the behavior of actual housing markets than the case shown in figure X, we include it. A footnote in the original described this case as follows, "If house E represents a very luxurious dwelling outside the ordinary market range, a kink in the cost curve could induce the construction of house D to meet this demand . . . — Eds.]

With the type of cost function shown in Figure X the first contact of the value and cost curves occurs at the lowest quality level; the new house which is needed to meet the demands of an enlarged community will thus be of minimum permissible cost.

It is of course possible that the value curve will move upward more rapidly than it flattens, in which case high quality new construction would be the answer. The chances for middle-quality construction appear slim, however.

One interesting point about this new construction response is that the quality level of the home which is constructed bears no necessary relation to the income level of the family which migrates into this community. So long as the filtering effect takes place the increase in demand operates, in this model, to produce any new dwelling so that the enlarged community may be housed. But the income level of the added family is not significant in determining which kind of new dwelling will be built.

Locational Significance

If it is possible to anticipate the quality level of new housing construction within a community, it follows that the location of new residential building activity can also be forecast more readily. High-quality dwellings may reclaim areas in the central area of the community, particularly if they stem from replacement demand which will leave the lowest quality part of the housing supply vacant. Alternatively, high-quality building may take place in the suburban fringe, in which case it would be directed toward sites which contribute to the appeal of expensive homes — view locations or areas with special amenities such as parks, pleasant atmosphere, or country clubs nearby.

If the economic need is for relatively low-quality new homes, however, central sites will probably be unavailable, as this type of home-building is likely to occur when residential facilities are scarce. Then the construction will occur in suburban tracts large enough to provide economies of scale by which costs may be reduced as much as technology allows, but situated in districts which do not command premiums for amenities. The amenity areas would be on reserve for later high-quality replacement demand.

The assignment model, hypothetical though it is, thus offers interesting suggestions for the rationale behind neighborhood filtering, the quality and price level of newly constructed homes, and the location of residential building activities.

Comments: 1. Smith's finding that houses are rationed by ability to pay squares with common sense knowledge. But like all findings derived from over-simplified models, it needs to be critically examined in practice. Smith's model neighborhood is composed of five houses of sharply distinct and increasing quality, and five households having a range of incomes large enough to put them in different consumption, and by inference, different social classes. In reality such variety is uncommon within a single neighborhood. Instead, neighborhoods or geographic submarkets within a city or metropolitan area often tend to be fairly homogenous with respect to the quality of the housing stock and the socioeconomic status of residents. This characteristic means that changes in market conditions occasioned by changes in population, incomes, or number of units can have a rather astounding effect on any given community. Since the dwelling and the household can form a single cohort resembling but one of Smith's types, the entire neighborhood may filter almost simultaneously. The article on abandonment by Lachman and Mitchell which appears later in this chapter testifies to the severity of problems which can result, and the materials on neighborhood change following it explore conceptual models of such neighborhood scale processes.

2. Refer to Smith's description of housing as a bundle of indivisible elements (Chapter 1) including neighborhood, public services, and schools, and note that changes in the housing status of individuals may be accompanied by commensurate changes in neighborhood quality and other effects external to individual decisions. In the case of filtering, it may be that the externalities are far more costly than the net gains resulting from the optimal matching of households to houses Smith describes. In the following selection, Matthew Edel, an urban economist, discusses and critiques these and several other aspects of Smith's model of filtering. Edel's essay concentrates on the effects of the American institution of decentralized home ownership as it relates to new construction and to the social and often external effects of the filtering process. In so doing, Edel raises serious questions about the definition and measurement of social welfare, rejecting Smith's criterion of maximizing aggregate rent bids.

M. EDEL, FILTERING IN A PRIVATE HOUSING MARKET, IN READINGS IN URBAN ECONOMICS 204-15 (M. Edel & J. Rothenberg eds. 1972)

When two institutions are as closely linked in practice as decentralized home ownership and filtering are in the United States, it is surprising that models of the effects of one often ignore the other. Yet models of a competitive housing market, based on the interaction of supply and demand, often assume supply consists of new construction and old buildings of given qualities, ignoring conversions that form part of the filtering process. Models of filtering, on the other hand, may neglect decentralization of ownership. This is the case with Wallace F. Smith's theory of filtering, which implicitly assumes all housing is owned by one firm. A slight variation on the model's assumptions, however, allows examination of the effect of decentralized ownership on housing markets. The effect of decentralization on the quantity of new housing constructed will be examined first, and then several implications of the combination of filtering and private decentralized ownership of housing upon economic and social welfare will be examined. In particular, problems will be considered which result because one owner's construction of a new house may result in a decline in prices of other owners' houses.

II

Smith's model of filtering is based on a simple matrix of prices bid by different families for houses of different qualities. For each house a higher-income family would be willing to bid more than a lower-income family, assuming that it could not obtain a higher-quality house at its bid price. For each increase of house quality, Smith assumes each family would be willing to pay a specified higher price than that it offers for lower-quality housing. Smith then shows that an allocation of housing results, such that houses of increasing desirability end up occupied by families in increasing order of ability to pay. This "not too surprising result" will be sustained by a private market for houses, in which a family that bids more for a house than another will receive it if it is for sale or rent. If the house is already occupied by a lower-income family, the higher bidder can pay the family enough to allow it to move to a lesser house, and keep a profit over the maximum price it is willing to pay for the lesser dwelling. Smith argues the assignment also maximizes "economic value," which he defines as the aggregate of rent offers. Smith appears to take this aggregate as a measure of economic welfare. The validity of this measure is discussed below.

. . . .

[At this point Edel develops hypothetical cost data consistent with Smith's model. By combining it with Smith's Market Demand Matrix (Fig. 3) and Change in Aggregate Value (Table 1) he derives the prices the various income levels of households would offer for new units of the various quality levels, and the overall effects on aggregate rent (Smith's Aggregate Value) from adding additional units to the supply. Analyzing these results, Edel shows that "the separation of construction decisions from rental of older units may serve. . .to increase the incentive for new construction," and that this incentive increases at the high end of the market. — Eds.]

There will thus be more luxurious housing (and perhaps more houses) built in a decentralized housing market than would be built by a housing trust. A similar situation arises if population growth imposes a need for new construction. So long as the new inhabitants enter the housing market at lower-income or quality-demand brackets, construction for higher brackets will free housing units to filter down. But these units' prices will fall, so that the total change in aggregate rents will be less than the price received by the producer of the new house.

In effect, each homeowner at a level of housing quality below that at which new houses are being constructed will find himself the owner of an asset which is declining in value. If he and his family should rent a higher-quality dwelling and lease the old home they own to others, not only will they be paying more for the new home than they would have considered their old dwelling to be worth but they will also be receiving less for their old home than they would have been willing to pay for it.

. . . .

III

The decline in house values implicit in filtering contributes to some social problems, as will be argued below. But does the accentuation of the filtering process which decentralized home ownership brings about itself reduce economic welfare? If Smith's equation of the aggregate of rents with "economic value" is followed, this might appear to be the case. The imputed or actual annual rent on dwellings is the value of housing services which enters into the gross national product; if all rents are capitalized in a market with a going interest rate, maximizing property values should be equivalent to maximizing this annual contribution. . . . [A] housing trust which centralized all construction and ownership of housing would achieve the greatest possible excess of this value over cost of construction. If, however, housing ownership were decentralized, a builder would not consider as a cost the losses in value occasioned to the property of others by filtering. In the aggregate, the excess of property values over construction costs would be lower.

At first glance this might appear an example of an external diseconomy imposed by the builder on other homeowners. As in other cases of external diseconomies, an excessive level of production would then be engaged in by the party who did not take into account the costs he imposed on others. This interpretation is debatable, however, because the decline in prices imposed on old buildings by new ones is not distinguishable from the loss of profits that any producer imposes on his competitors in a market economy. This competition, by driving out all excess profits, is in most markets presumed to equate the minimum average cost with which a product can be produced with its marginal value to consumers (as expressed by their demand curves) and to maximize welfare. In the case of a housing market it might be better said that a housing trust of the sort implicit in Smith's example is a monopoly. Like any monopoly it will restrict supply or produce less than would be produced under perfect competition, because this restricted supply will increase prices and total profits. This interpretation would indicate that economic welfare (measured at least by the excess of aggregate consumers and producers surplus over costs, rather than by the aggregate of price over cost) would be maximal under decentralized ownership of housing.

. . . .

[Edel suggests aggregate consumer housing satisfaction is a better performance measure than Smith's notion of aggregate rent. The technical term consumer surplus refers to an approximation of aggregate satisfactions. This idea accounts for the possibility that households who sustain losses upon the sale of one unit may receive offsetting benefits from improved satisfactions provided by the new unit. — Eds.]

This model does indicate, however, that filtering might lead to a decline in over-all welfare if there are externalities in the relationship between one family's housing choice and that of other families. Suppose one family sells its dwelling at a loss and moves to a better dwelling in another neighborhood, obtaining a more-than-compensating rise in consumers' surplus in the process. If the departure of the family reduces the value of their homes to other families in the neighborhood, by allowing the decay of social relationships, a cost may be imposed by filtering on those who do not accept it voluntarily. These neighborhood effects are, however, not encompassed in Smith's model. The failure of a family leaving a neighborhood to consider the costs this will impose on those remaining is not, in economic terms, the same as the failure of a builder to consider losses imposed on other buildings. In one case the victims are market competitors; in the other case they are not.

The welfare effect of either a centralized or a competitive filtering process may also be affected by its effect on the maintenance of dwellings. Ira S. Lowry has argued that if owners of buildings know that the building will decline in value because of the availability of a surplus of better dwellings, they will have an incentive to undermaintain their property. Less will be spent on repair and on preventive care of buildings, and capital will be wasted. "The effect of a general policy of undermaintenance would be an accelerated decline in the quality of the housing inventory." The decline will not be unlimited, because if buildings are deteriorated too far, they will not find users even after filtering to the next lowest level of demand. On the average, though, it will reduce the quality of the housing stock. He concludes, "it is evident that a policy which implements price decline within the standard stock of housing cannot also nourish the hope of using this stock to raise housing standards."

Undermaintenance from a technological viewpoint could occur in the case of ownership of all buildings by one landlord. If a landlord were to plan reassigning a building to lower-income users, he might let it run down somewhat. However, because the landlord would eventually bear any costs in terms of lower rents brought about by excessive undermaintenance, economic incentives would limit his neglect. However, with decentralized housing ownership, this is not the case. Because houses are such differentiated products it may be possible for a seller to hide some defects. An owner who plans to sell at a loss need not undertake all repairs that affect the longevity of his property. Undermaintenance may be reduced in a decentralized market in which owners live in their properties. It is well known that owner occupiers have more of a stake in maintenance than do landlords. Decentralized ownership by large numbers of nonresident landlords, however, is compatible with undermaintenance, and is indeed often found in slums.

Neighborhood effects and undermaintenance can, conceivably, lead a filtering process to impose social costs that exceed its benefits, and either influence might be more severe if decentralized ownership prevents long-range planning for neighborhoods. In general, however, these effects do not invalidate two general conclusions. First, voluntary filtering will only take place if for each family the implicit value of the new home exceeds the added cost of that home plus the capital loss on sale of the old home. Second, the aggregate of these excesses of consumers' surplus over capital losses and costs will be greater under decentralized ownership than under a housing trust. The "economic value" maximized by a centralized owner in Smith's model is a monopolist's profit. From the viewpoint of increasing aggregate producers' and consumers' surplus the acceleration of new construction and filtering implied by wide-spread housing ownership would seem to be optimal.

Of course, the maximization of aggregate surplus is not necessarily the criterion for social welfare that all observers would choose. If, for example, the provision of housing of some specified standard to all citizens is the goal (and improvements for higher-income groups already above this standard are not to be taken into account), filtering may not be an efficient means for its attainment. Increasing the quality construction of a house does not necessarily increase the number of residents who can use it proportionately. Building a house at twice the cost of a minimum-standard house may increase the availability of acceptable housing by only one dwelling unit. Twice as many standard units could be built for the same cost if less expensive homes were built. Because a decentralized housing ownership will encourage more opulent construction, even though it will encourage more total construction, its advantages from the viewpoint of improving minimum housing standards may be limited. From this viewpoint filtering in either a centralized or a decentralized market may be less desirable than direct (public or subsidized) construction of low-cost housing at the minimum acceptable level.

If incomes are unequally distributed, it may not make any difference for the quality of housing available to lower-income groups whether filtering occurs in a monopolized or decentralized housing market. From the viewpoint of maximizing total consumers' and producers' surplus over cost, decentralization of ownership will be advantageous. From a social viewpoint, however, one additional problem of decentralized home ownership must be considered. The decline in values that filtering can impose on owners of homes may at times obscure income inequality and contribute to intergroup tension. . . .

There are, of course, cases in which a filtering model will show houses increasing in value. If, for example, families rise in income, with no change in the total number of families, old houses may rise in value. If there is insufficient construction compared to an increase in the number of families, the value of houses may rise and the low bidders be left unable to do better than share lowest-quality homes. Or if population growth is concentrated in upper-income brackets or the gap between costs of high- and low-quality housing is great enough, housing may be built at the level demanded by new families, without filtering occurring. Rising demand resulting from increasing urban population and growing incomes placed general upward pressure on real estate prices in cities during the postwar period, as is reflected in the 7.4 per cent annual growth rate of the total value of urban land. Studies of specific chains of moves initiated by the construction of new homes during this period have shown that in many cases each participant in a filtering process did in fact receive more for the home sold than had been paid for it initially. Home prices did rise more rapidly (3.2 per cent per year) than the cost of living (1.8 per cent per year). However, the tendency of filtering to lower prices, all other things being equal, is not removed by the over-all expansion of demand: housing prices did not increase as rapidly as the prices of competing assets held in greater concentration by the very rich.

Among homeowners also the filtering process may distribute value changes unequally. The lower the house quality, in Smith's model, the greater the chance that new housing built will be at a higher-quality level. Thus filtering will be more pronounced at lower wealth levels. Neighborhood effects and deterioration may also be more severe in these lower wealth-holder categories. Differential effects of housing price changes are most easily visible where ethnic groups are unevenly distributed among different income groups and neighborhoods. . . .

. . . Laurenti has investigated changes in property values in the San Francisco Bay area and in Philadelphia, in neighborhoods where black population increased after World War II. He found that neighborhoods which became integrated or black ghettos did not decline in property values compared with comparable white neighborhoods. However, in several of the cases he considered, both neighborhoods in the comparison were areas of declining values before one neighborhood's ethnic composition began to change. In such cases, filtering apparently made homes available to the low-income black population, but did so only after imposing capital losses on the previous owners. The former owners, in such cases, often blamed the new residents for the decline in values. Laurenti shows this was not correct attribution, but the filtering process, when it leads to this understandable misperception, must stand accused of contributing to intergroup tensions as well as of imposing capital losses on the old residents.

Both filtering and dispersed ownership of housing are often presented as American institutions worthy of admiration. . . . [H]istorians and economists have supported the conventional wisdom that individual home ownership has both housed people adequately and given them a stake in society. If the decentralized nature of the private home-building industry has been faulted, it is for inefficiency in adopting new technological innovation. But housing has also been the scene of widespread complaint, and homeowners' feelings of being threatened have been linked with social conflict between the lower middle class and the poor. The analysis presented above indicates some reasons why a decentralized housing market with filtering may maximize aggregate benefits from housing while at the same time leaving inadequate housing for the poor and presenting middle-income groups with an ambiguous mixture of quality improvement and value decline.

To criticize American housing institutions, it is necessary both to reject aggregate surplus alone as a measure of benefit and to posit some alternative to the filtering system as it has evolved. In practice, it is impossible to envision any sort of private housing market without some filtering, as long as incomes are not perfectly equally distributed or mobility not perfectly nonexistent. Some builders will always gear their construction to upper-income groups, who in turn will abandon older homes to filtering. Unless housing is a monopoly, new construction will compete with and cause value declines to middle-income owners' houses, except during periods of rapid over-all urban expansion. Nonetheless, public policy may either accentuate or offset the filtering process. Public policies might be envisioned which give some subsidy and institutional support to efforts of middle-income homeowners to improve their consumption of housing by upgrading and maintaining their homes and neighborhoods. These policies would require also the provision of new homes for the poor, by means of subsidies or public housing. They would reduce the ability of the wealthy to sell off old homes to middle-income groups, giving them more incentive to improve old dwellings instead of building anew. More maintenance of buildings and more stable neighborhood structures would result from these policies. Because they would require subsidy, their welfare effect from an aggregate surplus viewpoint is hard to compare with that of a decentralized market. They would involve some aggregate cost, which would be compared with the benefits of better housing for the poor and with community stability. . . . To allow filtering to operate without any government intervention might have meant the maximization of aggregate consumers' and producers' surplus in housing (although given the presence of monopoly elsewhere in the economy this cannot be certain). Even then upper-income groups would have benefited somewhat more than proportionally. Government action to reinforce filtering by the subsidization of new housing, further reinforces the inequality of benefits. The moderate- to low-income homeowner is left subject to capital losses; the lowest-income renter is left ill housed; and the two groups are pitted against each other when neighborhoods change hands in the filtering process.

Comments: 1. The chief contribution of Edel's critique is to inject some sense of the real institutional setting into the otherwise ideally abstract concept of filtering. He starts right out with the most obvious and consequential institutional aspects, the fragmentation of supply among millions of homeowners and thousands of other producers, chiefly landlords and builders. He argues correctly, for instance, that producers of new housing will not consider the effects of their actions in terms of the sum of rent offers or bids in a community, nor will they consider negative externalities or spillovers. Instead, builders base their decisions on the profits they hope to realize over the cost of production. They do not worry about the declines in value of existing houses new production may cause. Public policy which encourages new construction can therefore strongly affect the economic, physical, and social status of older neighborhoods. The following excerpt from the previously quoted article by Stegman highlights the relationship between new construction on the suburban fringe and abandonment in the core of St. Louis:

> Though St. Louis' recent experience is not unique, no better illustration exists of how a central city housing market and household and supplier interdependencies can combine to reduce to rubble neighborhood housing stocks which, under normal conditions of demand, would have years of remaining social and economic value. The context is one of racial and class differences between the present neighborhood population and the pool of potential demand for what was an older but generally physically sound housing stock. . . . [Stegman refers here to the findings of the research by Leven et al. reported in part in the excerpt later in this chapter. — Eds.]
>
> In short, rather than there having been an insufficient supply of new dwellings to trigger the filtering mechanism over the most recent fifteen year period, it is likely that, in St. Louis at least, a substantial portion of the excess new stock that became available to satisfy upgrading demands triggered mobility processes which were eventually to contribute to the deterioration of the core city housing market. . . . [T]echnical reference to the surplus new supply as inventory available for upgrading or for the retirement of the older stock lacks the sufficiently rich connotation necessary to depict "the shocking and demoralizing effect of wide-scale abandonment. Yet, since filtering implies abandonment and devaluation of the existing stock, and devaluation implies lower maintenance levels, as long as the turnover process is stochastic and vacancy accumulation remains beyond policy control, more core city families may suffer from the spillover effects of filtering than will directly benefit from the chain of moves the process initiates.

Stegman, supra at 231, 233.

Undermaintenance, as Edel notes and Stegman makes more pointed, can be an unintended consequence of the filtering process. As income levels of successive waves of residents decline, landlords caught in a squeeze between operating costs and declining rent rolls will seek to reduce their operating costs in order to maintain their cash flow. This means that many units which are basically sound and livable may deteriorate rapidly as landlords attempt to cut their expenses. The analysis of the financial statements of two buildings in Chapter 3 suggests how this cost-income squeeze works. At the end of the process it is the low income core city households who, as Stegman shows, live with these burdens.

2. Edel shows how the filtering process can trigger a species of class conflict. He gives the example of tension between white lower or middle class owners who blame the filtering caused depreciation of their housing assets on in-migrant blacks. In his closing sentence Edel speaks of moderate income owners and low income occupants "pitted against each other when neighborhoods change hands in the filtering process." This aspect of filtering ties in directly with the concept of housing class introduced in the previous chapter. Filtering can be seen as the specific conflict process among housing classes in America.

3. Filtering can occur in an upwards rather than downwards direction. This point is clearly implied in Smith's matrix. Because it has seldom happened in reality until recently, little attention has been given it. Over time, richer rather than poorer households may

enter a neighborhood or occupy a unit. In a corresponding fashion, house prices and implied values may increase relative to area-wide norms. This special case has only recently become the subject of study. Nowadays such upgrading is sometimes referred to as gentrification, a term of British origin describing a process in which the gentry moved into historic working class districts of London. The process is briefly considered in this text in Chapter 9 on Neighborhood Revitalization.

4. Thus far, the discussion of filtering and neighborhood change has centered upon the results of filtering in a hypothetical housing market. The pivotal question whether the process improves housing opportunities for low income households needs empirical examination and it has received considerable attention from researchers. The next selection by Sands is one such empirical study. In it, the author, an urban planning professor, attempts to measure the effects of new construction upon housing opportunities by counting the number of vacancies generated by each unit added. His research calls into question the theoretical filtering precept that building new houses for upper income groups will ultimately improve the housing opportunities for lower income groups.

SANDS, HOUSING TURNOVER: ASSESSING ITS RELEVANCE TO PUBLIC POLICY, 42 JOURNAL OF THE AMERICAN INSTITUTE OF PLANNERS 419-25 (1976)

In general, vacancy chain studies are concerned with the identification of all households that change their residences as a result of the construction of a new housing unit. When an existing household moves into a new house or apartment, a vacancy is created in a previously existing housing unit. This vacancy in an older unit provides an opportunity for a second household. That household moving into the vacated older unit in turn leaves behind a housing opportunity (vacancy) for a third household. The housing units, both new and existing, for which there is a change in occupancy (turnover) constitute the links of the vacancy chain.

Although in theory a vacancy chain may extend indefinitely, the majority terminate fairly quickly. A vacancy chain ends when a change in either the supply of or demand for housing makes the next dwelling unit in the chain unavailable. When a new household enters the housing market, the move does not create a vacancy available to another household. Similarly, when a household moves from a dwelling which is then demolished or converted to nonresidential use, no available vacancy is created and the vacancy chain is terminated.

The length of the vacancy chain resulting from new construction may be relevant to public policy consideration in either of two ways. First, it may be considered as a *multiplier,* providing an indication of the total number of households who benefit (by having the opportunity to move) from the new construction. Second, if the vacancy chain is long enough and if the successive households differ sufficiently in their attributes, housing policy objectives may be achieved by indirect means. For example, if households in a vacancy chain have successively lower incomes, the construction of high-cost new housing may (indirectly) result in improved housing for low-income households. In this respect, the turnover process corresponds to one conceptualization of the filtering process.

Empirical data

This article describes a study of the vacancy chains generated by the construction of new rental housing in three New York State metropolitan areas: Rochester, Buffalo, and New York City. The original samples of new units were selected from categories structured to represent meaningful alternatives with respect to public policy. New housing was classified according to its subsidy status (subsidized, nonsubsidized) and its location (central city, suburban). These two characteristics were used to identify four mutually exclusive categories: nonsubsidized suburban, subsidized suburban, nonsubsidized city, and subsidized city. . . .

Creation of housing opportunities

Table 1 indicates the relative effectiveness of the different types of new housing in the creation of housing opportunities. The average vacancy chain length includes the new unit and all the housing opportunities subsequently created through turnover.

Table 1. Average vacancy chain length

Location and type	Number of new units	Median monthly cost	Average vacancy chain length
Rochester			
Nonsubsidized suburban	47	$302	2.09
Subsidized suburban	77	205	2.06
Nonsubsidized city	48	215	2.18
Subsidized city	75	50	2.35
Total	247		2.18
Buffalo			
Nonsubsidized suburban	51	$194	1.55
Subsidized city-family	62	129	2.43
Subsidized city-aged	35	37	2.29
Total	148		2.09
Bronx			
Subsidized city	135	$170	2.23

Rochester

In the Rochester metropolitan area, there is little difference in the number of housing opportunities resulting from the four categories of new housing. All four generated a total of between 2 and 2.5 vacancies for each new unit. There is a statistically significant difference (at the 90 percent confidence level) in average chain length between the two nonsubsidized categories and the subsidized city housing. However, the absolute difference amounts to less than .3 of a unit. There are no significant differences in average chain length between the two subsidized categories or between the two nonsubsidized housing types.

Buffalo

In the Buffalo metropolitan area, a clear difference can be observed between the two broad categories of housing. The two samples of subsidized city housing produced vacancy chains comparable to the longer chains from the Rochester area (2.43 for the subsidized family units, 2.29 for the aged units). However, the suburban nonsubsidized units provided only about one-half of a turnover vacancy for each new unit, for a total vacancy chain length of 1.55. This figure is significantly lower than the average for the subsidized chains in the Buffalo area.

Bronx

The single category of new housing sampled in the Bronx generated an average of 2.23 housing opportunities for each new unit. The average vacancy chain length in the Bronx was similar to the averages for the other categories of subsidized city housing in Rochester and Buffalo.

The findings for these three metropolitan areas can be compared with the hypothesis and data derived from other studies. Lansing . . . hypothesized that more expensive new housing would generate a larger number of housing opportunities through turnover than less expensive units, since the higher cost housing provides more opportunities for filtering down (incremental decreases in housing cost or household income).

These data from New York State generally do not show a positive correlation between housing cost and vacancy chain length. The greatest amount of turnover results from what is generally the lowest cost housing in each metropolitan area — the subsidized city sample. However, it is evidently not the subsidy alone which accounts for the longer vacancy chains. In the Rochester area, there is virtually no difference in vacancy chain length between the two nonsubsidized housing categories despite the fact that the suburban new units were substantially more expensive than those in the city. Similarly, in both Rochester and Buffalo, the samples drawn from more expensive (to the tenant) subsidized units do not generate significantly more housing opportunities than do the less expensive subsidized units in the same metropolitan area.

The fact that the construction of more expensive new housing does not ensure a longer vacancy chain (that there is actually not much difference in the amount of turnover, no matter in which category the chain originated) may in itself be relevant to housing policy development. If the primary objective of government housing policy is conceived to be the maximization of housing opportunities (that is, an output oriented strategy), then there is little reason to favor one of these types of new construction over the others. These data indicate no clear advantage to either direct (subsidized) or indirect (high cost) construction strategies. Both approaches were about equally effective in the creation of turnover vacancies.

Table 2. Reasons for terminating vacancy chains (percentage of completed chains)

| Location and type | New Family | | Stock change | |
	Local	Inmigrant	Demolition	Other
Rochester				
Nonsubsidized suburban	22	68	7	2
Subsidized suburban	45	39	8	8
Nonsubsidized city	36	44	8	11
Subsidized city	52	24	13	11
Buffalo				
Nonsubsidized suburban	29	71	0	0
Subsidized city-family	35	23	29	13
Subsidized city-aged	70	17	0	13
Bronx				
Subsidized city	33	10	52	4

Reasons for ending chains

Table 2 indicates that there were distinct differences in the reasons why vacancy chains ended. For most categories of new housing, the majority of the vacancy chains ended because a new household had been introduced into the local housing market. Over two-thirds of the chains of moves generated by the nonsubsidized suburban new units in Rochester and Buffalo were terminated by a family moving from a different metropolitan area. These in-migrant households probably initiated vacancy chains in the housing market of their origin. However, within the market where the new unit was constructed, the high proportion of intermetropolitan migrants limited the creation of indirect housing opportunities.

The majority of vacancy chains initiated by the two senior-citizen public housing projects also ended because new families entered the local housing market. However, in these instances *local* new families predominate, accounting for half of all chain terminations in Rochester and 70 percent in Buffalo. Frequently, the *new* family which ended the sequence was the senior citizen moving into the new subsidized units. Many of the senior citizens had been living with friends or relatives for a short period of time, evidently while waiting for the new public housing to become available.

In contrast, the chains from the subsidized family housing in Buffalo and the Bronx were frequently terminated because of changes to the previous unit. Over half of the Bronx chains ended because the respondent's previous dwelling had been demolished. In Buffalo, many of the chains ended because the former unit had been demolished (29 percent) or abandoned (13 percent).

In sum, although they were located in different metropolitan areas, similar types of new units tended to produce similar patterns of vacancy chain terminations. The vacancy chains of the nonsubsidized suburban units can be characterized as ending because a family moved into the local housing market from another metropolitan area.

On the other hand, the subsidized units for the elderly produced vacancy chains which were ended because a new household had been formed within the local market. The vacancy chains from the subsidized units for families in Buffalo and the Bronx tended to be terminated by a decrease in the supply of housing (removal of a dwelling) rather than an increase in demand (addition of a household).

Housing assistance for disadvantaged families

The primary objective of public policy may not be to promote a greater number of housing opportunities for all households, but rather to provide aid to particular categories of households considered to be disadvantaged relative to the population at large. When specific types of needy households are considered, the effectiveness of the different types of new housing in creating housing opportunities is found to vary considerably.

. . . .

[The author disaggregates his data to determine which type of housing in which location best creates housing opportunities for specific income groups. For low income families he found that central city subsidized housing was most effective, followed by housing for the aged, while the addition of new units in suburban locations, subsidized or not, was relatively ineffective. For moderate income families, Sands found that all housing types and locations are about equally effective if only turnover vacancies are considered. If the occupants of the new units are included, subsidized suburban housing created more housing opportunities for moderate income households than all other categories. In general, Sands found that the indirect housing opportunities generated through turnover vacancies were relatively ineffective in dealing with the housing needs of the elderly, large families, and minorities. For minorities, the prospects were particularly small in suburban areas. He notes, as other readings in Chapter 10 of this text suggest, that minority participation in vacancy chains is related to the presence of minorities in new units. — Eds.]

Quality of Turnover Vacancies

. . . .

[The quality of units in vacancy chains created by newly constructed units is a significant variable for evaluating the effectiveness of filtering in improving housing status. After describing the quality measures used in the study, Sands concludes that the majority of turnover vacancies appeared to be adequate. About 50% of participating households felt their new dwelling was better than their former unit, one quarter thought the two were about the same, and the remainder preferred their former unit. In the next section, the author examines the relationship between new construction and abandonment. — Eds.]

Substandard housing

Vacancy chains may trace the linkage between new housing and the abandonment of substandard units. Theoretically, each new housing unit could eventually lead to the abandonment of one substandard dwelling. . . . Actual reduction in occupied substandard housing was much less for the units sampled. In the Rochester area, all of the samples of new housing had some effect on dilapidated housing, with 4 to 10 percent of all chains ending with the elimination of a substandard unit.

One of every six subsidized family units in Buffalo produced a vacancy chain which ended with an abandoned substandard unit. The other two Buffalo area samples were not effective in reducing substandard occupancy in the Buffalo area. About 28 percent of the new units in the Bronx eventually caused a substandard unit to be vacated permanently.

Matrix model of turnover

. . . .

[At this point, Sands uses the empirical data he has developed to construct matrices of vacancy chains not unlike the matrices Smith constructs to exhibit the filtering idea. Sands' first matrix is a table of transitional probabilities expressing the likelihood that a vacancy in one price category of dwellings will lead to another vacancy in the same price category, or in a different category, or will disappear from the local market entirely. (A vacancy disappears when a new household forms or when a household enters the local market from elsewhere outside.) This type of probabilistic portrayal of housing dynamics has been used fairly extensively by housing planners in recent years. — Eds.]

In several respects, the data . . . are compatible with common conceptions of housing market behavior. Most transitions within the local market . . . are between similar units. Transitions between extremes (high to low) are rare. Generally, more vacancies move to lower cost units than to higher cost units. Since the household is moving in the opposite direction, a tendency toward increased housing expenditure is indicated.

Vacancy transition can be directly related to the concept of vacancy chain length. . . . Table 9 shows the results of this. . . . The matrix model not only provides an indication of the total number of housing opportunities generated by new construction, but also the sectors of the housing market in which these vacancies may be expected to appear. This additional information is particularly helpful when the housing sectors represent different levels of cost or quality. For example, the creation of high-cost turnover vacancies may be considered of little relevance to the housing needs of low-income households. The matrix model permits identification of those turnover housing opportunities which are suitable for a particular client group.

Table 9. Rochester multiplier matrix number of vacancies produced at each cost level

	New construction level				
	High	Middle	Moderate	Low	Total vacancy chain length
High	1.24	0.52	0.25	0.10	2.11
Middle	0.04	1.41	0.57	0.25	2.27
Moderate	0.03	0.33	1.83	0.31	2.50
Low	0.01	0.11	0.63	1.36	2.11

Conclusions

. . . .

The relatively narrow differences in vacancy chain length conceal substantial differences in regard to opportunities for housing-disadvantaged families. It is true, that, in most cases, the construction of expensive new units does eventually affect poor households. But the empirical data indicate two things. First, most vacancy chains were short, including only one or two existing units. Second, the difference in income (and other variables) between the family moving in and the family moving out of a unit was usually small. As a result, the vacancy chains generated by the most expensive of new housing had little effect on the housing needs of low-income families.

There are hardly enough empirical data on turnover to permit definitive policy conclusions. Additional data, perhaps employing the matrix model described here, are necessary. Nevertheless, it seems clear that chains of vacancies or *filtering* effects should not be relied upon exclusively to meet the needs of housing-disadvantaged families. The data from this study indicate that, although indirect opportunities from some types of new units may be substantial, some form of direct assistance is still required. Paradoxically it is the subsidized new construction which seems to be the most effective in generating indirect opportunities. Thus, subsidized housing should be an important component of both direct and indirect strategies.

———

Comments: 1. Several other empirical studies of filtering have produced findings generally paralleling those of Sands. The very large, earlier study by Lansing and others followed the vacancy chains in a national sample independent of local housing markets. Understandably, since it did not arbitrarily cut off data when the vacancy moved outside a given submarket, longer chains were uncovered, averaging 3.5 against Sands' 2.09-2.23. As the title suggests, Lansing's study focused on the possible benefits of filtering for poor people and it uncovered more positive evidence than did Sands. On the matter of race, the earlier study offered considerably richer information and concluded:

First, it may be asked, do Negroes move into new homes in the same proportion that one would expect on the basis of their incomes? The finding is that they do not. In fact, Negroes comprise about six-tenths of the number of occupants of new dwellings which one would predict on the basis of their incomes.

Second, Negroes in the low income group can benefit from new construction if they are able to move into a home which has been left vacant by a white family. "Trickle-down" can work if property changes from Negro to white occupancy. Such transitions do occur, but they are infrequent.

The result of these two factors is that Negroes do not benefit from new construction to the extent that their incomes would lead one to expect. We estimate that the proportion which Negroes represent of families in the sequences of moves begun by new construction is about .70 of what would be predicted on the basis of the incomes of all families in the sequences and the proportion which Negroes form of each income group in the metropolitan areas being studied.

We cannot attribute to racial discrimination the difference between .70 and 1.00. Negroes are at an economic disadvantage because of their low assets as well as their low incomes. The extent of their disadvantage in assets is indicated by the fact that their average net worth is less than a fifth of that for the population as a whole. Young Negro families are likely to be unable to obtain gifts or loans from their parents to finance the down payment on a home as well as limited in their own resources. We have not attempted to separate this factor from direct racial discrimination in housing. J. Lansing, C. Clifton, & J. Morgan, New Homes and Poor People 67 (1969).

In summary, the empirical studies corroborate the idea that the filtering model does indeed seem to describe an important aspect of housing market dynamics. At the same time, the studies call into question the efficacy of relying on filtering for social policy objectives like improving housing for poor people or racial minorities by constructing expensive new units for occupancy by relatively well-off, white households.

2. Sands' concluding comment about the policy implications of his analysis needs a bit of qualification. Subsidizing new construction is not the only approach to improving opportunities through filtering. Demand subsidies such as direct housing allowances to households in theory should work equally well or better. This theme is treated in more detail in Chapter 8. Another approach to achieving the same ends involves intervention into the household-house assignment function of filtering. For example, tax incentives might be used to discourage small households from occupying units with more than a specified number of rooms, or to encourage the construction or rehabilitation of units targeted for residents on the lower end of the income spectrum. Localities might also require the construction of relatively low cost units in new housing developments, which might determine allocation patterns different than those of an unregulated market.

3. Abandonment is the final stage of the filtering process. Smith makes this point clear in his treatment of the effects of adding a new unit to his hypothetical neighborhood when no corresponding new household exists. Sands notes in his empirical study that some vacancy chains ended with abandonment, or retirement of a unit from the housing stock. The following reading, from a team of consulting housing analysts, deals with this phenomenon and the closely related problems of its traumatic neighborhood effects. This reading ties nicely into Sands since it also deals with Rochester.

LACHMAN & MITCHELL, NEW CONSTRUCTION AND ABANDONMENT: MUSICAL CHAIRS IN THE HOUSING STOCK, NATION'S CITIES, OCTOBER, 1977, Vol. 15, No. 10, at 14-15

Who would think of housing abandonment being a significant problem in Rochester, New York? In Dayton, Ohio? In Kansas City, Missouri? In Richmond, Virginia? These and many other "livable" cities are now boarding up and demolishing habitable housing — not because the neighborhoods are crime-ridden slums, but because there are too many housing units in the metropolitan area. Construction volumes have been so high that households have moved upward into newer units and outward into younger neighborhoods. When the band finally stops in this game of musical chairs, the empty units are the oldest and cheapest ones in the central city. And there they sit, blighting the properties around them.

The necessary balance between housing supply and demand seems to have been forgotten in a large number of urban markets. The real impacts of population stability or nongrowth have not been fully recognized: if there isn't net migration into a metropolitan area, you can't add housing units faster than new households are being formed. You can't, that is, unless you want abandonment. Several metropolitan areas with slow population growth experienced high new housing construction in the early 70s. Abandonment showed up in the central cities of these metropolitan areas in the mid-70s, and the now troubled cities are facing the prospect of record new construction again this year.

Dysfunctional Cause & Effect

Because new units are generally built in suburbs and abandonment shows up in central cities, cause and effect occur in different jurisdictions. The cities can do little to control abandonment, but they are the ones left to deal with it. They bear the demolition costs, the subsequent vacant lot maintenance, the neighborhood instability created by vacancy and declining property values, and the tax delinquency that accompanies weakening real estate markets.

This new form of housing abandonment, the result of excess new housing construction in a metropolitan area with a stable population, can be seen in Rochester, New York. Real Estate Research Corporation's analysis showed that between 1970 and 1975, population growth in the Rochester metropolitan area was minimal — about 8,300 persons. Nonetheless, the level of housing production was extremely high — 39,500 units in the same 1970-75 period. Assuming that 25 percent of these units replaced homes and apartments lost from the inventory through fire, conversion, and demolition, the net housing addition was about 29,500 units. Using an average size of three persons per household, the new housing would have accommodated 88,500 people, or more than 10 times the actual population increase.

The result of that excessive construction was abandonment in Rochester's core area. The first manifestation of the unrealistic housing volumes was high vacancy in new projects. In a happy economic coincidence, construction financing dried up just when absorption was becoming difficult, providing time for gradual marketing of the inventory. Households moved into the brand-new homes and apartments from older housing in the metropolitan area, making units in the existing stock available for other households in older housing and older neighborhoods. Through chains of moves, households filtered upward into newer buildings. Over time, the excess housing was shifted from the new inventory to the oldest areas of the city. The end result was abandonment.

Developed & Abandoned

Rochester's situation is not unique. It is duplicated in a number of nongrowth or slow-growth areas in all regions of the country. When housing supply exceeds demand, the traditional U.S. urban development process inevitably leads to abandonment.

This filtering or "trickle-down" process of urban development has worked relatively well for most people. However, it has led to concentration of the poorest people in the oldest and cheapest housing, most of which is in central cities. When there was a housing shortage in the 1950s and a steady flow of poor immigrants to the cities, there was a great deal of overcrowding in physically substandard buildings. As migration into cities slowed down in the 1960s, new construction continued on the edges of metropolitan areas; population densities fell in the oldest neighborhoods, and the worst housing was removed. In the early 1970s, birth rates were down; the move to the cities, especially to northern cities, had essentially stopped; and people were moving out of many metropolitan areas. Thus, the total number of households was stable or beginning to fall. Yet new residential construction continued, and in areas like Rochester, the supply exceeded demand.

New suburban housing in these areas no longer has the social and economic benefit of relieving overcrowded, substandard conditions. Instead, construction of the middle- or upper-income suburban dream house indirectly causes an inner-city house to be discarded. Nearly 400 structures and vacant lots had been abandoned in Rochester by June 1976, the bulk of them in core neighborhoods adjacent to the downtown. In addition, tax delinquency, often a precursor to abandonment, had escalated. About 5,000 properties had unpaid real estate taxes by early 1977, and well over 1,200 of them were eligible for immediate foreclosure. Most of the latter properties were also located in the core neighborhoods.

Housing Market Weakened

Despite heavy abandonment and high tax delinquency, the housing market in Rochester's core neighborhoods is still functioning, albeit weakly. This is not the case in the heavily abandoned areas of such cities as Newark, Detroit, and Cleveland. There are at least two reasons for market activity continuing in Rochester's core areas. The first is the fact that these areas are not plagued with the problems, such as serious crime, that are common in most heavily abandoned areas elsewhere. The second reason is the speed with which housing abandonment emerged. What were yesterday relatively stable lower- to moderate-income areas suddenly became end-state neighborhoods with large amounts of castoff housing. Because these neighborhoods are not viewed negatively and because the phenomenon of gross oversupply is so new, market values have not fallen as sharply as one would expect.

Many of Rochester's long-term inner-city residents continue to view their neighborhoods as places to be improved, not deserted. Yet vacant, boarded structures stand beside occupied, well-maintained homes, and the problem is spreading. The city, with its existing demolition program, simply has not been able to keep up with the volume of abandonment. In transitional areas adjacent to the core neighborhoods, vacancy rates are rising, housing turnover is increasing, and residents' confidence in their neighborhoods is waning. The deterioration caused by abandonment in the oldest housing is leading to instability in adjacent neighborhoods. This ripple effect accelerates neighborhood change and weakens more and more of the inner-city housing market. The geographic pattern of tax delinquency, rapidly expanding outward, reflects the contagiousness of real estate market decline.

Rochester is by no means alone in falling victim to this new form of abandonment. The majority of the metropolitan areas with stable or declining populations are experiencing some housing abandonment. Also, a large number of urban areas with modest population growth but high new construction volumes are saddled with excess housing. In most cases, neither the problem nor its cause has yet been acknowledged. Thus, abandonment is appearing across the country — in the sunbelt as well as the northern tier, and in the East, Midwest, and West.

Comments: The Rochester case discussed above makes very concrete the general trend towards metropolitan population decline set forth in the Alonso reading at the beginning of Chapter 4. Most metropolitan central cities seem to be following this type of trajectory. But, as Alonso points out, some cities, particularly those in the South and West, exhibit counter trends in population growth that more than offset high rates of new construction. In these places the addition of new units often has not kept up with in-migration and increased rates of household formation. This means that, instead of abandonment, Rochester-style old neighborhoods have risen sharply in value and show very low vacancy rates. These two conflicting trends seem destined to continue over the next five or ten years though the upward filtering pattern may become more dominant. The account of inner city housing abandonment in Rochester not only illustrates abandonment as the final stage in the filtering process, but it emphasizes the externalities or neighborhood effects of this process. These follow a pattern all too familiar in mass society in which, to paraphrase Thomas Schelling, micro-motives of individuals aggregate into perverse macro-behavior.

A NOTE ON NEIGHBORHOOD THEORY AND HOUSING EXTERNALITIES

Students of housing have repeatedly focused attention on the neighborhood effects, spillover or external effects of individual housing preferences and decisions, or micro-motives in Schelling's language. The Wallace Smith reading that opened Chapter 1 discussed the phenomenon as the objective external effects and subjective community concerns. Perhaps the most powerful treatment of the matter comes from economists Otto Davis and Andrew Whinston. They use the game theory prisoners' dilemma model to provide a persuasive representation of this phenomenon applied to the neighborhood effects of individual optimizing motives. The following passage presents an easily grasped example of the model:

[L]et us assume for the moment that the primary determinant of a house's market price is the quality of the neighborhood in which it is located. If so, the rehabilitation of one or two houses in a rundown neighborhood will have only a minor impact on the neighborhood's overall condition and a correspondingly minor impact on the rehabilitated houses' market price, *unless* the other houses in the neighborhood are also rehabilitated. As an example, consider the owners or prospective purchasers of houses in a rundown neighborhood where house prices currently average $8,000. Unknown to each other, each owner or purchaser contemplates rehabilitating a house at a cost of $10,000. They face the following outcomes: If all the owners rehabilitate, the market prices of all houses will rise to $22,000, giving each a gain of $4,000. If no one rehabilitates, prices remain the same. But if one owner rehabilitates while the other owners fail to do so, his house's price will increase by only $4,000 (to $12,000) and he will suffer a loss. Conversely, if he does nothing while *other* owners rehabilitate, the value of his house will rise to $9,000 and he will enjoy an "unearned" gain of $1,000.

Given the accuracy of this "model," success in the "rehabilitation gamble" would appear to depend heavily on the actions of neighboring owners, who in turn have a strong incentive not to rehabilitate.

Barnes, A Strategy for Residential Rehabilitation, Real Estate Review, Vol. 6, No. 3, at 40, 41 (1976).

IF OWNER A

		rehabs	does not rehab
WHILE OTHER	rehab	$ 22,000 value −18,000 cost ────── + 4,000 gain	$ 9,000 value −8,000 cost ────── 1,000 gain
OWNERS	do not rehab	$ 12,000 value −18,000 cost ────── − 6,000 loss	$ 8,000 value −8,000 cost ────── 0

Owner A's hypothetical net profit or loss (new price of house less initial house value and rehab costs) depending on the actions of other owners.

The critical neighborhood effects and externalities from filtering direct attention to parallel neighborhood change processes. The most recent systematic approaches to neighborhood dynamics are in fact drawn directly from the filtering model. Before turning to these, however, some work in the older, more widely used neighborhood stage theory merits attention. It has its roots in the concentric ring sociological model of city growth. In this model, new growth occurs on the perimeter and as the housing ages in the older, more central rings. Each ring tends to be inhabited by a succession of occupants. Versions of this idea have dominated thinking about neighborhoods. They form a stage theory of development in which neighborhoods have a "natural" life cycle corresponding to the ages of a living being. The following brief excerpt from the New York metropolitan area study by urban economists Edgar Hoover and Raymond Vernon exemplifies the idea.

The shifting pattern of metropolitan residence areas has often been schematically described in terms of gradually widening concentric zones pushing out in all directions from a growing central business core like ripples from a splash. Nonresidential "downtown" land uses, pre-empting the very center of the metropolitan area almost exclusively, expand into the immediately surrounding old residential areas, and also extend an aura of blight far beyond the range of their actual land-taking. Housing nearest the center is mainly slum — because it is the oldest, because it is cramped, because the street traffic and other aspects of downtown development make it undesirable for residence, and because it comes to house a concentration of disadvantaged people who are shunned as neighbors by those more fortunate or longer in residence. These slum characteristics are persistent, even cumulative, since the economics of slum property deters extensive replacement, modernization, or even maintenance of the antiquated housing.

The near-central slum area, eroded from the inside and along its main streets by competing land uses, and having to accommodate an influx of bottom-income people, expands outward into the next nearest and next oldest zone, mainly by the down-grading and conversion of old apartments and houses to higher densities. This pressure, as well as over-all population growth, forces the population of the next zone to push outward in turn, and so it goes till we reach the out-crawling fringe of urban development where new houses replace farms, woodland, or golf courses. . . .

What then are the stages of evolution we can identify and where in the Region are they found?

Stage 1 is residential development in single-family houses. This stage, the earliest of all, is just beginning to appear in some outlying parts of the Region, is currently in full swing in the outer parts of the Inner Ring, and was passed long ago in most of the Core and in the central parts of the large Inner Ring cities . . . .

Stage 2 is a transition stage in which there is substantial new construction and population growth in the area, but in which a high and increasing proportion of the new housing is in apartments, so that average density is increasing. Much of the apartment construction replaces older single-family houses . . . .

Stage 3 is a down-grading stage, in which old housing (both multifamily and single) is being adapted to greater-density use than it was originally designed for. In this stage there is usually little actual new construction, but there is some population and density growth through conversion and crowding of existing structures . . . .

All of which brings us to *Stage 4,* the thinning-out stage. This is the phase in which density and dwelling occupancy are gradually reduced. Most of the shrinkage comes about through a decline in household size in these neighborhoods. But the shrinkage may also reflect merging of dwelling units, vacancy, abandonment, and demolition. This stage is characterized by little or no residential construction and by a decline in population . . . .

We come at last to *Stage 5.* This is the renewal stage, in which obsolete areas of housing, after arriving at Stage 4, are being replaced by new multifamily housing. Quality and the effective use of space are improved, but the overall population density of the area affected may not change much. By and large, such redevelopment in recent years has tended to increase over-all densities somewhat in Manhattan projects and to reduce them a little in projects elsewhere in the City . . . .

E. Hoover & R. Vernon, Anatomy of a Metropolis 183-86, 188, 191, 194, 198 (1962).

The notion of stages as natural and inevitable is open to question. The specific pattern of urban development from which it is derived is highly unique to the American urban political economy. In Latin America the oldest, centrally located, residential areas tend to be occupied by high income, high status groups, while new housing frequently tends to be shanty town slums built on the farthest suburban perimeter. In France, a similar pattern occurs except that a higher income working class occupies the subsidized housing projects which predominate in the suburbs. Perhaps the errors implicit in blind acceptance of stage theory appear most clearly in current public policy planning documents, such as the following published by the U.S. Department of Housing and Urban Development.

The Stages of Neighborhood Change: The stage a neighborhood is in affects what must be done to change it, and how likely that is to be successful.

Therefore, a more detailed description of each of the stages is necessary. The five stages are:

1. Healthy
2. Incipient Decline
3. Clearly Declining
4. Accelerating Decline
5. Abandoned

The Healthy Neighborhood: In a Healthy neighborhood the values of the houses and the social status and incomes of the residents rise gradually, and in a reasonable relationship to one another. The value of the houses does not outstrip the purchasing power of the residents or owners, otherwise renters would have to move out and owners would find taxes and upkeep prohibitive and be forced to seek cheaper housing.

The Incipient Decline Neighborhood: When those who leave are replaced by less affluent people, and, over a period of time, the less affluent are replaced by people with even lower incomes, a neighborhood is in the "Incipient Decline" stage. A neighborhood moves into the "Incipient Decline" stage from the "healthy" stage because of several different circumstances.... Its competitive position relative to other similar neighborhoods has slipped. Both house prices and the range of rentals that can be charged begin to decline. Owners and landlords both may begin to wonder a little about their investments. It may be just a little harder to get a mortgage or a home improvement loan on as favorable terms as in a "healthy" area.

The Clearly Declining Neighborhood: The change in neighborhood status from "incipient decline" to "clearly declining" can be gradual or in certain circumstances, abrupt and turbulent. In general, a neighborhood is in the "incipient decline" stage as long as it provides a decent economic return for people who own property and a standard of housing that is, by reasonable definition, adequate. A neighborhood starts clearly declining when owners can't make enough money to keep their property up, much less make a profit. This is because the people who want to live there cannot afford to pay so-called "economic" rents and if they own their home cannot afford adequate maintenance or major repairs.

The Accelerating Decline Neighborhood and the Abandoned Neighborhood: After the declining stage, things start to go downhill much more rapidly. The last two stages — accelerating decline and abandonment — occur quickly (and sometimes even simultaneously). Anyone living in the area with any options at all will get out and go elsewhere. Residents and tenants are by now very poor; many are welfare families, female-headed households and unemployed people. Crime rates begin to rise and vandalism increases. Owners of buildings decide not to keep them up at all; they'll accept *any* tenant they can get. As their income from the building decreases, they stop putting money into it; then they decide to stop paying taxes. Banks won't even think of lending. Efforts to "save" the area grow — code enforcement programs, rehabilitation projects, building new low-income housing — but often they make things worse rather than better. Speculators start buying buildings for next to nothing, jamming in whatever tenants they can get; providing no maintenance, sometimes no heat; paying no taxes. Then when they've milked the building for all it will take, they dump it — leave it, abandon it. Vandals rip the building apart, set it on fire.

Public Affairs Counseling, The Dynamics of Neighborhood Change 11-13
(Prepared for the Office of Policy Development and Research, U.S. Department
of Housing and Urban Development, 1975).

The neighborhood change process outlined in these two standard works ties
back neatly into the filtering concept. As Alonso writes (supra p. 123), these are
but two ways of looking at the same underlying process. This implies a reciprocity
between actions taken at the two poles of the house-neighborhood dichotomy.
Just as housing decisions taken by individuals have neighborhood effects, so
neighborhood decisions have effects on individuals and the housing units they
occupy. This explains the sensitivity of housing satisfaction to areal decisions by
governments, powerful private corporations and financial institutions, informal
citizen action by groups, and the behavioral regularities of social classes. It
explains why a consideration of housing issues must deal as well with phenomena
at this larger scale.

What about a spectrum of neighborhood stages in which four out of five are
pejoratively labelled declining or worse? What about the use of words like
"health" which imply an analogy to biological systems and medicine? What are
the causal factors behind these inexorable steps toward abandonment?

Comments: 1. Despite the fact that the characterization of neighborhood stages
prepared by public Affairs Counseling for HUD closely follows the ideas outline in
mainstream thinking like that of Hoover and Vernon it has a disturbing tone.

2. Recent analytical and empirical work on the dynamics of neighborhood change has
begun to set forth a more complete and causally refined model. The following excerpt
from a book by a team of St. Louis based urban economists manifests this new clarity and
rigor.

C. LEVEN, J. LITTLE, H. NOURSE & R. READ, NEIGHBORHOOD CHANGE: LESSONS IN THE DYNAMICS OF URBAN DECAY 37-47 (1976)

The Arbitrage Process

[Arbitrage refers to a situation in which a single commodity has different prices
in different markets. It is used here to denote the idea that a specific unit or
housing bundle has a price determined by the submarket it is in — a high price
if in a high income submarket, a low price if in a low income area. — Eds.]

In a competitive housing market, the assignment of households to units and
market prices are determined by households' tastes and incomes and the
characteristics of housing supply. However, rather than being a single market,
housing is divided into a series of interrelated submarkets that are defined by
types of units and patterns of neighborhood occupancy. The arbitrage process
is the mechanism by which supply shifts from one submarket to another;
sometimes this occurs by households moving from one neighborhood to another,
sometimes by a change in the housing bundle in particular ways so that the
neighborhood can serve a new clientele.

The basic components of the arbitrage model are hypotheses as to the nature
of preferences. The most important feature of the model is its emphasis on the

fact that neighborhood socioeconomic and racial change alters the housing bundle characteristics of all units in the neighborhood, bringing about a change in the preference rank of these units and a consequent change in occupancy and prices. Furthermore, since households make decisions on the basis of their expectations as to the future nature of housing bundles, expected change will have similar consequences.

Let us begin our discussion in a very simple world with two kinds of households — high-income and low-income. Further, suppose that only high-income families can purchase new housing: the economics of the construction industry push the price of new housing too high for low-income families. The poor, whose incomes also exhibit a range from low to high, feel most at home among others of their approximate income level, but at the same time their desire to improve their situation makes them prefer to live as close as possible to the exclusive neighborhoods of the rich. The situation produces four prices for property as indicated in our discussion of the Bailey model . . . .

[The Bailey model holds that if blacks or other ghetto dwellers and whites or other non-ghetto dwellers both have an aversion to living in the center of the ghetto, and as a result of population pressure or otherwise the price of housing at the ghetto boundary is higher on the ghetto side, the location of the boundary will move until the prices are equalized across it. Concurrently, prices will tend to fall at the center of the ghetto and rise at places remote from it. During the equilibrating process houses at the boundary may have either of two prices depending upon which side of the boundary they are on. Therefore, as the process takes place essentially similar houses can have any of four different prices depending upon location. — Eds.]

In descending value, there is the price for the rich deep within the exclusive neighborhood; next, one for the rich in neighborhoods adjoining the poor; next, one for the poor in the adjoining boundary neighborhoods; and finally one for the poor deep within the poor neighborhood.

The double boundary between the two basic markets moves one way or the other depending on whether it is profitable to change boundary property from high-income to low-income occupancy or vice versa. Prices, in turn, depend upon the available stock of housing relative to growth in the number of households in each group.

Thus, we need to account for changing demand through new households, changes in family size and composition and movement of new families into (out of) the metro area, relative to changing supply that occurs via demolition and construction for each group.

As the boundary moves into the erstwhile rich neighborhood, housing formerly commanding a premium for its location near the high-income families no longer elicits that extra value; the income associated with the property declines, placing downward pressure on property values in the immediate area. Although it is true that there is no necessity for property to deteriorate with age, if income falls there will be fewer resources available for normal repairs. Maintenance is reduced because other property costs, such as taxes and mortgage payments, remain fixed. In a period of inflation, the decrease in property value may not be absolute, but in any case value declines relative to the cost of new housing. Declining maintenance inexorably leads to deterioration in the housing quality.

The end of this cycle is abandoned housing. The boundary is pushed too far, driving the price of housing within the exclusively poor neighborhood so low that it is no longer feasible to meet building code standards or such fixed costs as taxes and mortgage payments. The least expensive solution is then abandonment of the property.

If we incorporate racial factors into this market process, we have an extended version of the Bailey model. Prices on the white (high-income) side of the transition boundary, after an initial rise, eventually fall to a point equal or below those in exclusively black (low-income) neighborhoods. If the boundary impinges too deeply or too rapidly within the white neighborhood, then at some point behind it there would no longer exist any demand for the exclusively black housing, even by blacks.

Let us now consider the arbitrage process as the way in which household preferences are manifest as housing market prices. We return to our adjoining neighborhoods grouped into high-income, low-income, and boundary areas; and we define high-income families as those who can afford newly constructed housing, low-income families as those who cannot. As before, we note that the highest prices will obtain deep within the upper-income neighborhood, the lowest prices deep within the low-income neighborhood. We also note that the high-income families will insist on a discount for living on the boundary, while the low-income families will be willing to pay a premium for a boundary unit.

Figure 3.1 diagrams the general configuration of the disposition of housing between the high-income and low-income populations. In the boundary area, it will be noted that the two kinds of occupancy are fairly randomly dispersed, and it may be inferred that the larger, better houses will be occupied by the somewhat less-rich who still can outbid the better-off poor. (This ability of the rich to outbid the poor explains, of course, why no poor live in the exclusively rich neighborhood.) The scheme thus accords with the four levels of housing price we noted previously and we have, in effect, four submarkets.

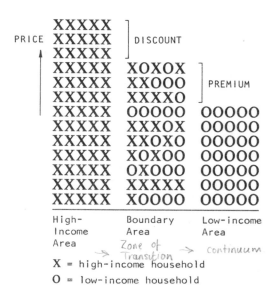

Figure 3.1 Equilibrium price and occupancy patters (Redrawn from Leven)

So long as the housing supply remains a reasonably close match to the demand of each of these submarkets, the market may be said to be in equilibrium, a condition under which arbitrage remains inoperative. But anything that disturbs the supply/demand balance in any of the submarkets will initiate price changes that cause the boundary to shift, affecting all the related submarkets. Population increase on the high-income side, for example, will inspire new construction. Population increase on the low-income side will have a different effect: since there is no recourse to new construction, families must double up; increased demand pushes prices upward within the low-income neighborhood and the premium paid for boundary units increases. This widening gap in boundary prices makes it profitable to shift occupancy from high-income to low-income households, and at this point arbitrage comes into play.

Supply factors also can disturb the balance. Demolition of low-income housing in order to build highways or high-income housing, as in urban renewal, will generate a shortage of housing for low-income families. With the price of housing for the poor rising as a consequence, it would become profitable to shift housing from high-income to low-income occupancy. This movement, in turn, would reduce the stock of upper-income housing, but only temporarily, since new construction would respond to the increased high-income demand. Another factor affecting the supply side of the balance is rising absolute income: here the shift is initiated on the upper-income side as the increased income inspires moves to new housing, reducing demand within the rich neighborhood and lowering prices of the better homes within the boundary area. It would then be profitable to arbitrage these boundary units to low-income use.

It is understood, of course, that the distribution of housing and incomes in the argument presented above is as oversimplified as the diagram in Figure 3.1. In reality, income groups do not neatly divide themselves into four categories but rather cluster at points along a continuum from lowest to highest. This dispersal creates additional submarkets, so that several boundary areas may exist, some so finely graded as to be unidentifiable.

Here we are describing the ways in which housing-price changes are initiated, causing boundaries to shift and bringing arbitrage into play; upon a little reflection it will be seen that to inject the racial factor into the situation alters the process very little at this point. That is, given the general socioeconomic characteristics of the white and black populations in the inner city, it is almost possible to repeat the analysis given above, merely substituting "white" for "high-income" and "black" for "low-income."

The slight additional factor, of course, is the already noted fact that families commonly prefer to live among families of their own racial and ethnic identity, and its major impact would be the creation of additional submarkets, additional boundary areas. These are not hypothetical, but very real: that is, there indeed exist income-level boundaries in both all-white and all-black areas; and there exist white slums as well as black.

Race has another kind of impact, however, in its effect via expectations. We have noted that the value households put on their housing includes the expected future stream of value. Based on the perception that "black" often is associated with "low-income," a shifting boundary between white and black neighborhoods that results in black entry into a formerly all-white area can have an impact on the expectation component of the area's housing bundles and their perceived value. Exploring this development in more detail, we discover some unexpected results.

Expectation plays an important role in the householder's assessment of his property's value because it represents his estimate of the likelihood or unlikelihood that his bundle of housing may change in his or others' preference rankings. Because this estimate is made in a highly uncertain environment, the householder is particularly sensitive to signs and portents — to "changes in the wind."

His housing bundle may be upranked, the kind of windfall gain that would be associated with commercial development in a suburb that provided a large tax base, thus enhancing the public-sector element of the associated housing bundles. Other external events might as easily downrank his bundle — capricious zoning changes, for example, or construction of an airport nearby.

For householders in some situations, the sum of perceptible probabilities could suggest that his housing bundle would be subject to upranking — those so situated as to take seriously the canon of conventional optimism. But for the inner-city householder of the postwar decades, the most likely prospect was that, through no action of his own, his housing unit might experience downranking.

All of the elements of the housing bundle exert some measure of effect on the expectation component. Most easily calculable is the future value of the structural characteristics — soundness, modernity, and so on — whereas all the locational attributes are subject to uncertainty. Among these latter, however, it is observable that in the normal course, the factors of access and local government change slowly. On the other hand, it is equally apparent that neighborhood characteristics — income-level and racial composition — can alter very swiftly. It is, then, to trends and developments — "changes in the wind" — that may alter the neighborhood characteristics of his housing bundle that the householder reacts with the greatest sensitivity.

. . . .

We have been tracing here the role of expectation as a motivating force in householder decisions, but this is only half the story. To lenders whose business is the financing of housing purchases, expectation is the very substance of daily operation; their calculations of probability have immediate and overt effect on the market.

Since housing transfers rarely proceed on a cash basis, lenders heavily influence the market and their assessment of future values is of direct importance. Thus, although lenders do not set values or prices, their control of the money required to effectuate the value householders place on their property becomes another market factor — like shifts in supply and demand — influencing prices. In this way, a householder's first realization that the market value of his property is declining often comes when the purchaser he has found at his asking price is unable to obtain financing at that price-level: the householder must then decide whether to become the lender himself, assuming the mortgage risk, or lower his asking price.

Lenders' perceptions of probability are from the outset areal in nature: they too give heavy weight to the future neighborhood characteristics of the housing bundle. If they see a high probability that a neighborhood's income-level will fall or that its racial composition will increasingly shift to black occupancy, their projections of property values will fall. Their response to lowered estimates of future market values (in the absence of mortgage insurance) would then be more restrictive terms — larger down payments, shorter-term loans, and stronger assurances as to the financial soundness of the borrower. Not to tighten the loan in these ways would be to increase their risk of loss, since their possible return in the event of foreclosure would be less. When lenders perceive a probability of continually falling values in a neighborhood, they will refuse further lending in the area, for this is the only way in which they can be certain of avoiding loss. This withdrawal of financing results, of course, in the inability to sell houses in the neighborhood, so that vacant units stand idle and subject to vandalism for long periods, producing yet steeper declines in values, sometimes virtually to zero. *+ve feedback*

Centrally involved in this sequence, and directly associated with lowering income levels, is the deterioration of maintenance we have noted earlier: it contributes both to the fall in values and to loss of lender confidence. New owner-occupants of lower income have less reserves for upkeep . . . . Typically, the same result ensues when owners opt to rent out their property in order to avoid selling at a loss: they lack experience in tenant selection or in maintenance procedures for renters, and they have no access to cost-saving maintenance techniques. Renting the unit soon becomes a losing operation and in desperation the owner finally sells to a real estate operator at a loss simply in order to be out from under the investment burden.

We have been considering the maintenance problems of down-ranked middle-income housing, but it is clear that for the low-income units that the in-migrants have vacated the identical problems of insufficient funds apply, but in more critical degree. For these units, then, the decline in value becomes precipitous, the chute to abandonment swift.

When the syndrome of falling income, falling prices, and structural neglect becomes manifest in a neighborhood, such institutional lenders as banks and savings and loan associations will no longer invest in the area. At this point, the individual investor becomes the sole source of financing for sales to owner-occupants; but in actuality most sales are to speculators whose typical operation is to extract a quick return in undermaintained rentals.

The heavy weight of neighborhood characteristics on the perceived value of the housing bundle is made particularly clear by the 1960s practice of the Federal Home Loan Bank. Although fiscal prudence may admittedly have dictated such action, its examiners, up to 1970, implicitly "red-lined" those postal zip code areas in which the syndrome of falling values described above had been observed. The device employed was a requirement of higher reserves for mortgages in these areas. The stipulated higher reserves resulted in few if any loans being made there. In St. Louis it happened that in several cases "private streets" of fine old mansions in good repair existed within these postal zones (surrounded, however, by rapidly decaying blocks). The prices of these fine homes became hugely devalued: 20-room residences with marble-floored ballrooms could be had for $25,000. And stably employed, low-risk purchasers were available. Despite these high loan qualifications, however, neither the candidate buyer nor the complaisant seller could prevail against the areal blanket-effect of the red-lining. The transfer could be accomplished only with very large cash equity and on short terms with payment of discounts, or with a loan using collateral other than the housing unit itself.

The clear inference of these observations is that when the dynamic of arbitrage is set in motion and the housing market becomes disordered, the market exhibits disfunction in all its sectors, and all operate not to arrest or delay the process, but to speed it up and intensify its effect.

An Extension of the Filtering Concept

. . . .

[At this point the authors tie their neighborhood change model back into the more general filtering concept and offer some extensions derived from their study. — Eds.]

... The obvious extension of the Grigsby-Smith approach is to switch completely from considerations of supply to those of demand, to define filtering in terms of households' preferences. We begin by viewing households rather than dwelling units as the active participants in the filtering process. That is, households filter through the housing stock, rather than vice versa. We then define filtering as follows: Filtering takes place when a household, without change in its income or tastes, experiences a change in its housing bundle to a different rank on its scale of preferences. "Filtering up" — or upranking —occurs when the change is to a more preferred bundle; "filtering down" — or downranking — when it is to a less preferred bundle.

An important implication of this definition is that filtering can occur even if the household does not experience a locational change in its dwelling unit. This consideration elicits two significant corollary definitions — for active and passive filtering: Active filtering occurs when a household experiences a change in the ranking of its housing bundle by moving to a different unit. Passive filtering occurs when the household does not move but experiences a change in the ranking of its housing bundle nonetheless.

The concept of passive filtering introduces a significant new dimension to the formulation of housing policy and to the filtering process itself as an analytic tool. For example, a program of subsidized upgrading could be expected to achieve passive upward filtering without any movement of households. In general terms, the notion of passive filtering implies that change in housing utility does not necessarily involve relocation.

The most important analytic applications of passive filtering are to neighborhood change. Since changes in neighborhood are beyond the control of the individual household, such changes can bring about passive filtering. The concept of neighborhood filtering provides a means of identifying situations in which passive filtering occurs in individual areas.

Neighborhood filtering is defined as follows: neighborhood A filters down relative to neighborhood B if, over time, the differential price of A over B, standardized for differences in the physical characteristics of the units involved, changes from a premium to a discount. Intuitively, then, A filters relative to B if the same house that once sold for more in neighborhood A now sells for more in neighborhood B. The symmetry of this definition is important: if A has filtered down relative to B, then B has filtered up relative to A. Nonetheless, it must be the case that households that resided in A both before and after the change in differential have experienced filtering down or their counterparts in B have experienced filtering up.

Thus, one cannot infer directly from the occurrence of neighborhood filtering that either group has experienced a utility change. However, if the characteristics of B have remained unchanged while A has experienced considerable change in its social and physical characteristics, then it is reasonable to assume that those households remaining in A have experienced downward filtering.

Passive filtering has largely been ignored in the literature; implicit in all definition is the presumption that households must be moving in order to be involved in the filtering process. The disregard of the potential for filtering down inherent in the dynamics of urban housing markets has in large part been responsible for overestimating the benign effects of the relocation process. While housing market analysis has overlooked the potential for the filtering down of occupants in existing locations, it is clear from the empirical results that we present later that participants in the market consider it highly important and react strongly to indicators of a neighborhood's potential for downward filtering. The empirical finding of considerable discounting of neighborhoods with a high proportion of renters and high nonwhite populations in adjacent neighborhoods suggests that in a market characterized by frequent and rapid downward filtering of neighborhoods, a large proportion of moves are in response to changes in the expected utility of given locations. The fact that these expectations are in the end responsible for the filtering down in no way affects the conclusion that the possibility of filtering down is a real and important aspect of the dynamic process.

To sum up, the analytic framework within which the filtering theory has been developed has simply been too narrow. The result is a widely held belief that the relocation process leads, in general, to an improvement in the welfare of urban households. Yet, considered in the broad context of household decision making, this conclusion is clearly unwarranted on a priori grounds and other portions of our research suggest it is unwarranted on the basis of existing evidence. This is not to deny that many households have improved their housing situation over time; clearly, technological change in transportation, rising levels of income, and government intervention in mortgage markets have made the purchase of preferred housing possible for many households. At the same time, these events may have produced costs that have not been taken into account. These costs include not only the welfare losses to households that experienced downward filtering but also the resources devoted to relocation and the substantial opportunity cost of underutilization of the existing housing stock resulting from premature abandonment and removal of housing units.

Comments: 1. The obvious conceptual closure between Leven's neighborhood dynamics and Smith's local housing market dynamics represents an important advance in our capacity to think about housing. Analysis drawing on this complicated, but powerful model, a model now rather well tested empirically, will help in thinking about housing problems as varied as the basic shelter needs of poor people and the negative impacts of stringent environmental control. Keep this useful model firmly in mind during a reading of subsequent parts of this text.

2. Leven's arbitrage model shares with microeconomics a common starting point in the assumption of autonomous individual preferences. This tendency to psychologize social phenomena is characteristic of much American thought. Common sense, empirical observation showing the contingency of preferences with respect to social and political-economic contexts, and alternate theories that posit starting points in economic relations and social structure all call into question the "naturalness" of the psychology of preference approach. The major institutions in housing may possess keen interest in neighborhood turnover since they are ever needful of expanding markets for new and rebuilt neighborhoods. The Marxist picture of the housing economy referenced in Chapter 2 and in the Harvey reading in Chapter 7 implies such a critical view. A less extreme attack on the notion of psychological primacy comes from the critical analysis of media and corporate-consumer relations. This perspective questions the source of racial and class prejudices or preferences that power the arbitrage model. It suggests that preferences are learned, not innate.

3. Perhaps the most telling criticism of the neighborhood change models deals with the macroeconomic context of housing and neighborhood dynamics. Seldom in thinking about neighborhood change do analysts seem able to back away sufficiently to view it from the perspective of the national economy. Yet even the most cursory analysis will suggest the power and pervasiveness of conditions at large in neighborhood happenings. Historic evidence abounds at a fairly general level. The Great Depression of the 1930s abruptly cut off new construction, stimulated massive numbers of foreclosures, dried up capital flows, halted turnovers in the standing stock, and forced people, unemployed or underemployed

to double up. The Second World War had equally powerful local effects on housing. Curiously, with few exceptions, most talk and writing about housing markets and neighborhoods takes them to be self-sufficient entities, largely unaffected by outside events, and understandable as isolated systems.

In one area, however, there is a long tradition of connecting local and national events by tying housing market activity to the macroeconomy by relating new housing construction rates to the cost and availability of mortgage credit. In the short run at least, most economic analysts believe that fluctuations in the housing economy are closely correlated to the rate of interest required on new mortgages and even more strongly to the degree of rationing of mortgage funds. In a careful review of recent research, housing economists J. Kearl, K. Rosen, and C. Swan found that "there was relatively unanimous agreement that increases in mortgage rates reduce demand for mortgages and the number of starts." Other factors seem to have a powerful mitigating influence, however. The predominant influence of the supply of funds, for instance, can be clearly observed in the late 1970s, when interest rates peaked at twentieth century highs yet new construction surged on at near record levels. It was a period when ample funds were available as a result of various macroeconomic factors such as high gross income and relatively favorable savings interest rates from the main home finance institutions. A recent piece by a national economic policy analyst elaborates upon this connection.

W. GIBSON, PROTECTING HOME BUILDING FROM RESTRICTIVE CONDITIONS, BROOKINGS PAPER ON ECONOMIC ACTIVITY 3: 1973, AT 661-63, 675-76

The experiences of 1966 and 1969-70 provide a rough indication of the response of homebuilding to restrictive credit conditions. These periods are not particularly helpful by themselves in determining the interest elasticity of demand for housing to the extent that curtailment of cash flows to thrift institutions at the time caused nonprice rationing of funds. Furthermore, income growth slowed, likely curtailing the demand for new homes. But the experience gives some overall idea of the impact of restrictive government policies on housing production. As Figure 2 indicates, residential construction was roughly stable in 1965 and dropped sharply in 1966. In the fourth quarter of 1965 residential construction in 1958 dollars was at a $23.8 billion seasonally adjusted rate. By the fourth quarter of 1966 it was $18.6 and the trough of $18.0 billion came in the first quarter of 1967, an overall decline of $5.8 billion. By the end of 1967 it had rebounded to early 1966 levels, and it stayed at or above these levels until 1969.

Market interest rates rose throughout most of 1966. The AAA corporate bond rate was 4.74 percent in January and 5.39 percent in December. The greatest pressure on market interest rates came later in 1966, however. The sharpest run-up occurred in the third quarter, which included the famous "credit crunch" in August. By June 1966 the AAA corporate rate had risen to 5.07 percent, but in September it peaked at 5.49 percent, then fell to a low of 5.03 percent in February. The Federal Home Loan Bank Board (FHLBB) rate on conventional mortgages on new homes was 5.81 percent in January 1966 — only 5 basis points above its 1965 average (which was 2 basis points below the 1964 average). It rose to 6.07 percent in June and 6.49 percent in December 1966.

Inflows of funds into thrift institutions slowed at the same time that construction slowed. From a $13.8 billion annual rate in the fourth quarter of 1965, inflows fell to a $9.5 billion rate in 1966:1, to $4.4 billion in 1966:2, and to $5.1 billion in 1966:3. By 1967:1 they had surged to $17.2 billion.

Figure 2 Real expenditures for U.S. residential construction, quarterly, 1953-73; quantities on vertical axis are billions of 1958 dollars, seasonally adjusted annual rate (Redrawn from Gibson)

The weakness in homebuilding early in 1967 can be plausibly related to high interest rates, but the slowing early in 1966 is difficult to explain solely on the basis of an increase in interest rates of about 30 basis points, particularly relative to the sharper increases later. The large impact on construction for these two quarters seems in considerable part due to the slowing of inflows of funds into thrift institutions. Homebuilding apparently was depressed by lessened availability of funds before, and probably during, the time it was falling in response to interest rate increases.

Residential construction in real terms again fell in 1969 and 1970 at and after a shift to a restrictive monetary policy stance. From a peak of $24.6 billion (1958 prices) in 1969:2 it fell to $20.8 billion in 1970:2, paralleling an upward movement in interest rates:

Date	AAA corporate bonds	FHLBB conventional mortgages
November 1968	6.19	7.07
June 1969	6.98	7.62
December 1969	7.72	8.07
May 1970	8.11	8.28

Flows of funds into savings institutions showed the same pattern as residential construction. From a $13.5 billion seasonally adjusted annual rate in 1969:1, inflows fell to $8.8 billion the next quarter and to $4.5 billion in 1969:4. They inched up to $5.2 billion in 1970:1, but jumped to $15.8 billion and $21.9 billion in the following quarters. It is difficult to know what residential construction would have done in the absence of the credit tightness of 1969 and 1970, but after experiencing such a sharp drop in 1966 and 1967, one might guess, it would not have declined. The $3.8 billion drop in residential construction thus can be taken as a rough measure of the impact of restrictive economic policies on housing production. It is interesting to note that a larger rise in market rates produced a smaller decline in homebuilding in 1969-70. This may be because part of the 1966 decline would have taken place anyway. It is also true that in 1969 and 1970 thrift institutions were aided by friendlier supervision and more federal programs of mortgage support than in 1966. Mortgage acquisitions by federal credit agencies rose from a $2.06 billion rate to a $6.35 billion rate, compared with a decline in 1966 (see Figure 1).

. . . .

[In fact, this author argues that housing, or at least new residential construction is especially susceptible to the dynamics of national economic policy. — Eds.]

The first part of the argument that high volatility raises the required rate of return in housing is that homebuilding activity experiences more fluctuation than other industries do. Table 5 tends to support this assertion. It reports coefficients of variation around logarithmic trend lines of major GNP spending components. They demonstrate that investment in residential structure is the most variable of these components in both current and constant dollars. Nonresidential construction, both nominal and real, displays much less variability, less in fact than investment in producers' durables.

Table 5. Coefficients of Variation around Logarithmic Trends of Major Spending Components of Gross National Product, Constant and Current Dollars

	Coefficient of variation	
	1958 dollars	*Current dollars*
Spending component	*(1947:1-1973:2[a])*	*(1946:1-1973:2)*
Investment in residential structures	0.0417	0.0598
Durable goods consumption	0.0233	0.0259
Nondurable goods consumption	0.0037	0.0093
Services consumption	0.0249	0.0298
Investment in nonresidential structures	0.0249	0.0298
Producer's durable equipment	0.0358	0.0347
Government purchases	0.0317	0.0337

a. Period of fit.

Comments: Gibson's next to last sentence deserves underlining. Of all major parts of the national economy, housing is the most volatile. Given this fact, the consideration of housing dynamics might properly have started as a treatise on the American macroeconomy. This is beyond the realm of this book. However imperfect an oversimplification it may be this text perforce must treat housing primarily as an isolated system and concentrate on the internal workings of that system. To do so it relies heavily on the concept of market and submarket to describe the system. The reader should keep firmly in mind, though, that housing markets have a dominating dependency on the state of the national economy.

A CONCLUDING NOTE ON FILTERING

The bulk of this chapter has dealt with models that have been developed to provide a better understanding of the dynamics of housing markets. Filtering is by far the most important of these models. It has proved serviceable as an analytic device. Despite its utility, though, it shares with all models certain inescapable limitations. It cannot reflect the obdurate complexity of the real world. Nothing really behaves just like the tidy matrices of the filtering formulations. The real housing problems that bring people to study this field, and that form the focus of attention in Part II of this text never fit into the neat compartments of the idealized representations. Even so, the models have greatly aided thinking about housing dynamics in America. Keep in mind that the contradiction between the analytical idealizations and the real world exists; we cannot think without one and there is nothing to think about without the other.

An equally fundamental caveat concerns the tendency to confuse models of what seems to exist with ideas about what ought to exist. In the case of filtering there has been a tendency to take the possibility that poorer people may get adequately housed by the hand-me-down process to mean that they *should* be housed this way. This conclusion, of course, is nonsense. In a specific situation, given the constraints of time and place, it may be the best thing we can do. But that is a long way from saying it is what we should do. Yet this error is rampant. Public policy seems almost to be founded on it. To the degree that is so, our thinking is the poorer for it and so are the housing satisfactions of many real people.

Issues of this sort that emphasize the distinction between what is and what ought to be end up in the political arena. In large measure that is what politics is about. Appropriately the next chapter moves on to treat the politics of housing.

BIBLIOGRAPHY

B. Boyer, Cities Destroyed for Cash (1973)
   A lurid, conspiracy theory account of neighborhood and housing decline.

W. Grigsby, Housing Markets and Public Policy (1963)
   Landmark exposition of filtering theory which ties it into the Philadelphia housing market and the problems of inner city renewal.

S. Maisel, Managing the Dollar, ch. 5 (1973)
   This revealing analysis of government monetary policy in action by a former U.S. Federal Reserve Board Governor contains a powerful account of its impact on housing in Chapter 5.

M. Martin, The Builders (1978)
   Among its other virtues this book includes an accessible exposition of some of the paths connecting housing to the macro-economy.

H. Nourse, The Effect of Public Policy on Housing Markets (1973)
   A collection of short, sometimes difficult papers by a leading housing microeconomist.

R. Ratcliff, Urban Land Economics (1949)
   Contains the classic first exposition of the filtering model.

G. Sternlieb & R. Burchell, Residential Abandonment: The Tenement Landlord Revisited (1973)
   This sequel to the work excerpted in Chapter 3 deals in detail with the final stage of the filtering and neighborhood change processes.

K. Taeuber & A. Taeuber, Negroes in Cities: Residential Succession and Neighborhood Change (1966)
   A careful statistical analysis of neighborhood change as a racially motivated phenomenon seen from a sociological rather than economics viewpoint.

Chapter 6

THE POLITICS OF HOUSING

Up to this point this book of readings and comments has taken a largely economic view of housing. It is time to turn to housing politics. Politics touches almost every aspect of housing. Neighborhood change, filtering, problems of need and non-effective demand, the various housing supply institutions, the field's dependence upon the general state of the political economy, the dynamics of matching people and dwelling, and the complex, multi-dimensional character of housing itself, make housing politically salient. Even this list is not exhaustive. Over the last two generations housing has become more and more centrally enmeshed in national politics. A national housing policy has arrived as an accepted feature of American politics.

At the other end of the political scale, housing issues have become among the most ubiquitous and bitterly contested aspects of local politics. Suburban governments rise and fall on tract house development policy, neighborhoods at the grassroots level organize around housing conflicts, older central cities are dragged down by political struggles over an aging housing stock. Because housing has become so enmeshed with politics, a serviceable analytic approach to thinking about housing must include an approach to political questions. This chapter deals with these issues.

To introduce this theme, short excerpts from a book by the late Nathaniel Keith, a liberal housing lobbyist, first give a very brief overview of the politics of national housing policy. From Keith's extensive historical presentation, a brief episode is then reprinted to illustrate Congressional housing politics. It discusses one of the lesser known pieces of Great Society era housing legislation, the Rent Supplement Program. The author's opening reference to the urban social strife of the late 1960s reflects on the temper of those times.

N. KEITH, POLITICS AND THE HOUSING CRISIS SINCE 1930, 11-15, 160-65, 177-79 (1973)

The housing problem, its role in the crisis of the cities, and its relations to riots and urban unrest represent a central issue in the contemporary American scene of turmoil, tension, and pressures for change.

This current focus on the housing problem reflects an intensification and crystallization of pressures which have been evolving since the great depression of the early Thirties. Since 1933, there has scarcely been a session of Congress without controversy and debate on the housing problem. And, in the communities, there has been continuing conflict on what housing to build for whom — and where. In the background increasingly is the race issue.

Out of this controversy, there has developed over the years a substantial national housing policy and national housing program. Yet the absolute accomplishment of these efforts in meeting the housing crisis are amazingly small when measured against the dimensions of the need, aggravated by massive population growth and massive migration of poor whites and poor Negroes from rural areas to the cities. In the depression era of the mid-Thirties, Franklin D. Roosevelt raised the slogan: "One-third of a nation ill-housed." Today, in a national economy surpassing the trillion-dollar a year level, the best that can be said is that only one-fifth of the nation is ill-housed. And that one-fifth is in the ghettoes, the urban blighted areas, and the rural pockets of poverty.

. . . .

What are the political forces which, on the one hand, have forged the nation's housing policy as far as it has evolved and, on the other hand, have opposed and inhibited the carrying out of that policy? For it is a basic premise . . . that it is the alignment of political forces, not the availability of material and financial resources, which has primarily determined the rate of progress over the past 40 years, or lack of progress, in housing in the United States as in other essential human enterprises in the modern era.

Since shelter involves the largest immediate capital cost of any personal commodity except for the very rich, the potential supporters of effective government housing programs might seem to comprise all households. But events have shown that there are likely to be political differences between those households which can readily afford that capital cost and those which cannot. Similarly, there is likely to be political division between those households which have relative freedom of choice as to the location and character of their home and those which do not, for economic or racial reasons. There also are relics of American folklore which can still evoke positive or negative political responses in relation to housing — the tradition of making your own way and the Puritan ethic that the poor deserve only poor housing are examples. These have also been translated at times into political slogans that Federal intervention in housing is "socialistic," a threat to "the American way of life," and also a threat to "the American free enterprise system."

In the time-span of four decades . . . progress in housing legislation has generally been a response to crisis conditions. Until the catastrophic depression of the Thirties, housing was considered a matter of total Federal unconcern. Private enterprise built the tenements and workers' housing in industrial centers to shelter the successive waves of immigrants required for the nation's industrial expansion. (Today, much of this housing is still in use but now occupied predominantly by Negroes and Puerto Ricans.) There was some concern about the sanitary conditions in the tenements, some corrective state legislation, and few eleemosynary attempts by the wealthy to develop better housing for the poor. During the boom of the Twenties, the burgeoning middle class built homes in the suburbs, financing them with first, second, and third mortgages for short terms. But these were not matters which were considered to demand Federal involvement.

All this was changed by the collapse of the early Thirties. By the time that the first Roosevelt Administration took office in March, 1933, homes were being foreclosed at a rate over one thousand per day, the foreclosing financial institutions (banks, building and loan associations, insurance companies) were closing their own doors or were threatened with insolvency, building construction was at a standstill, and the unemployment rate of one-third combined with underemployment of most of the balance of the population had paralyzed purchasing power. President Hoover had stubbornly and calamitously refused to intervene in this or other sectors of the private economy.

Franklin D. Roosevelt did intervene and on a massive scale. However, it is important to distinguish that this intervention was primarily an emergency action rather than the assumption by the Federal Government of responsibility for the housing welfare of the American people. The acute emergency thus was the rationale for refinancing with Federal funds home mortgages facing foreclosure, thereby rescuing both the homeowners and the mortgage holders. While the establishment of the FHA mortgage insurance program had some reform aspects from the standpoint of correcting the mortgage abuses of the Twenties, it was primarily sold politically as a program to unfreeze the home-building industry and thereby stimulate employment and the economy. Even the first venture into direct Federal financing of housing in 1934 was presented more as a public works program to provide jobs and consume materials than as a program to improve the housing conditions of the poor. FDR later was to embrace public housing as part of the New Deal crusade but this also was accompanied by a bow to the impact of public housing on increased construction employment.

The onset of World War II brought a halt to almost all construction except for war purposes. However, the resulting postwar housing shortage, intensified by the housing demands of returning veterans, provided much of the political pressure that ultimately resulted in the passage of the Housing Act of 1949 in which for the first time Congress and the Executive Branch formally established a national goal of decent housing for all Americans.

After the lull during the Eisenhower years in the White House, the pressure for housing received impetus from the mounting urban tensions and the increasing demands from the cities for Federal aid. This was reflected in the significant housing legislation enacted in 1961, 1965, 1966, 1968, 1969, and 1970. The serious riots in 1966 and 1967 played a significant role; in part by penetrating the calm of the big corporations and by frightening the top power structure. Previously, the big corporations had generally ignored these tensions as no affair of theirs and had not participated in the production or financing of housing aside from manufacturing the materials and equipment used in construction.

Throughout this period since the early Thirties, the political alignment on housing issues has followed what have become familiar lines. The Northern Democrats in Congress have generally supported strong housing legislation; most Republicans and most Southern Democrats have generally opposed. There have been exceptions, of course: the late Senator Robert Taft of Ohio, the epitome of Republican conservatism on most issues, was, as a sincere gesture of capitalist *noblesse oblige,* a strong advocate of Federal aid for public housing, urban development, education, and health. Other outstanding exceptions are the two Alabama Democrats — Senator John Sparkman and former Representative Albert Rains — who have been consistent, imaginative, and progressive legislative leaders in the field of housing. However, the liberals of both parties have tended to cluster in the legislative committees and have been largely responsible for the major housing and community development legislation which has been enacted. On the other hand, the conservatives have tended to cluster in the Appropriations Committees of the two Houses where control over the purse-strings has largely determined what can actually be accomplished under the legislative mandates.

Thus far, notwithstanding the mounting pressures for decisive Federal action to relieve the physical and financial crisis of the cities, there has not yet developed the political power consensus essential for achieving this decisive action. I refer to the political power consensus responsible for the massive appropriations achieved by the military-industrial complex, by the interstate highway program, by the space program, by the farm lobby, and by the health and education movements.

. . . .

[The next passage appears some hundred pages later at the point Keith discusses the so-called Great Society programs initiated in the 1960's by President Johnson. — Eds.]

Housing and community development ranked high on President Johnson's legislative agenda for 1965. On March 2, 1965, he presented his program in this area in an eloquent special message to Congress. . . .

The substance of the President's message was a renewed request for the establishment of a Department of Housing and Urban Development and a wide range of substantive program proposals. In addition to a four-year funding of urban renewal for a total of $2.9 billion and a four-year public housing authorization at the rate of 60,000 dwellings per year, the President recommended a comprehensive package of new urban development programs, including: matching grants for sewer and water facilities on a basis consistent with area-wide plans for future growth; financial assistance for advance acquisition of land for new public buildings and other facilities; Federal insurance of loans for acquisition and development of land for privately-sponsored new communities and planned subdivisions; financial assistance to State land development agencies for land acquisition development; matching grants for building multipurpose neighborhood facilities for health, recreation, and community activity; and an expansion of the open-space grant program to include small parks and playgrounds in cities, landscaping, tree planting, and improvement of existing city parks.

Within this comprehensive package, what turned out to be the most controversial recommendation was the President's proposal for the establishment of a rent-supplement housing program. Under this plan, Federal rent subsidies would be paid to the private developers and owners of rental or cooperative housing to cover the difference between 25 percent of a tenant's income and the amount necessary to support his dwelling, including mortgage debt service, real estate taxes, operating expenses, and profit. The mortgages would be insured by FHA, would pay a so-called market rate of interest, and would be made by private lending institutions.

The motives of the Administration in advancing this proposal were mixed. On the one hand, the proposed housing was intended to accommodate families with a range of income from low to moderate to middle-income, with the rental subsidy to the individual family being geared to its income. This would break away from the pattern of economic segregation which characterized the existing Federal-aid housing programs for low- and moderate-income families. Furthermore, the proposal would have waived for this program the usual Federal requirement that any Federally-aided housing in effect be sanctioned by the local governing body of the locality. The intent here was to help penetrate the wall of exclusion erected by many suburban communities against the introduction of housing for low and moderate-income families. These both were principles which were supported by the progressive forces in the housing field.

On the other hand, the financing mechanism in the rent-supplement proposal in essence represented Bureau of the Budget gimmickry intended to phase out eventually the existing programs for low-interest direct Federal loans for housing for moderate-income families and for the elderly. This gambit stemmed from the intrinsically absurd Federal Budgetary policy of treating an expenditure for the purchase of a guaranteed, repayable housing mortgage, which eventually would be recouped in its entirety and with interest, in precisely the same way as an expenditure to meet a Federal payroll or to pay interest on a Federal bond. Since the mortgages financing rent-supplement projects would be made by private lending institutions, the capital cost of the housing would not enter into Federal budget expenditures and the annual charge to the Federal budget would be limited to the amount of the rent supplement subsidy. Of course, over the long run the cost to the Federal Government of borrowing is almost always less than the interest cost of private mortgages even when insured by FHA.

During this same period, there developed a curious lapse in liaison between the President and the big-city mayors. Notwithstanding the political importance of the urban vote, the President persistently declined repeated requests for direct meetings with the U.S. Conference of Mayors or the National League of Cities. While he reportedly conferred individually on occasion with mayors like Richard Daley of Chicago and Robert F. Wagner, Jr. of New York, he declined formal sessions with the municipal organizations, perhaps because he wished to avoid public identification with the big cities. Finally, this impasse was partially broken when the President designated Vice President Hubert H. Humphrey to be his personal liaison in dealing with the problems and complaints of city governments.

In the committee hearings and in the Congressional debate on the President's program, the rent-supplement proposal proved to be the lightning rod for controversy. This had the indirect effect of smoothing the way for the rest of the legislation, including urban renewal and public housing and also including most of President Johnson's other new proposals. The alignment of political forces, pro and con, on rent supplements was interesting. Since the projects would be sponsored, financed, owned, and operated largely by private building and lending institutions, the proposal gained support from the National Association of Home Builders, the Mortgage Bankers Association of America, and the American Bankers Association. On the other hand, the proposal drew opposition from some of the old-line local public housing authorities who saw it as competitive to their predominant position in developing and managing housing for low-income families and as a program which would draw away scarce financial resources which might better go into additional low-rent public housing. Also, a number of them sincerely believed that private developers lacked the experience and motivation to do a satisfactory job in the management of housing for low-income families.

The strongest political opposition to rent supplements stemmed from the provision which would authorize projects to be undertaken without specific authorization by the local governing body of the community. While never specifically so stated on the public record, this was considered to be a device to bring about the development of housing for low- and moderate-income families in the suburbs and, more precisely for Negro families. It was therefore anathema to most suburban communities. This generated strong political pressures on Congressmen from suburban districts who, in the North, were predominantly Republicans. While normally these Republican Representatives would have gone along with legislation supported by the home building and mortgage financing interests, in this case most of them responded to the opposition from home.

The liberal lobby on housing, headed by the National Housing Conference, the AFL-CIO, and cooperating organizations, supported the rent-supplement proposal. However, the lobby strongly opposed the phase-out of the low-interest direct-loan programs for housing for moderate-income families and for elderly households. Instead, it proposed that the interest rate on these loans, which had risen to 4 percent, be reduced to 3 percent and that substantial additional funds be provided. The legislative committees accepted these recommendations, increased the funds available for Federal purchase of 3-percent mortgages on housing for moderate-income families by more than $1.6 billion over a four-year period, and authorized an increase of $150 million in direct 3-percent loans, for housing for the elderly. In response to pressures from the cities, the committees also seized on President Johnson's recommendation for a one-year appropriation of $100 million for 50-percent grants for water and sewer facilities and expanded it to a four-year program at the rate of $200 million a year.

When the time came for final legislative action, the rent-supplement program was the center of opposition, for the reasons previously cited. In the House Banking and Currency Committee, the revised bill was approved by the Housing Subcommittee 10 to 1 and was reported out by the full committee by a vote of 26 to 7. However, the seven Republicans in opposition issued a strong minority report attacking the rent supplement program as "foreign to American concepts" and claiming that it "kills the incentive of the American family" and "is the way of the socialistic state." It was significant that the report made no mention of the real underlying reason for opposition to the program.

It was clear that the key vote on the floor of the House would be on a motion to recommit the bill to the committee with instructions to strike out the provisions establishing the rent-supplement program. The White House mobilized its lobbying forces, still under the direction of Lawrence O'Brien on crucial issues even though he was now the Postmaster General. President Johnson himself was reported to have made personal intercessions with individual members of Congress. The liberal lobby was brought into play, especially the AFL-CIO with its extensive lobbying force on Capitol Hill. I participated in some of the planning sessions in which the doubtful or uncommitted members of the House were identified, arrangements were made to exert maximum pressure on them either directly or from their districts, or failing results from that route to attempt to arrange "live pairs" in which the opposing Representatives agreed not to vote in return for abstention by a favoring Representative, or to encourage absenteeism on "official business." As was traditionally the case in House votes on critical housing issues, the vote on recommital was extremely close, but the motion was defeated 208 to 202. The Republican Representatives voted overwhelmingly — 128 to 5 — for recommital. The Democrats provided the narrow margin against the motion by a vote of 203 to 74. Even on the vote for final passage of the bill, when opponents frequently shift their vote in order to work both sides of a controversial issue, only 26 Republican Representatives voted for the bill while 109 were in opposition. The Democrats divided 219 for to 60 against on the final vote, with the opposition being entirely from the South.

In the Senate the key vote likewise was on a motion to strike the rent-supplement provisions, which was defeated by a vote of 47 to 40. Only 5 Republican Senators voted against the motion to strike rent supplements; the Democrats divided 42 against the motion and 17 for. The Senate vote for final passage was 54 to 30. The Democrats voted 47 in favor to 11 against, with all the opposing votes except for Senator Frank J. Lausche of Ohio being from the Deep South. Only 7 Republican Senators voted for the bill, with 19 opposed.

The passage of the Housing and Urban Development Act of 1965, which was signed by President Johnson on August 10 of that year with considerable fanfare, was a major addition to the Federal programs for housing and community development. The only important setback was an amendment setting the income limits for families eligible to receive rent supplements on a level comparable to the income ceilings for low-rent public housing in the same locality, thereby eliminating any benefits for moderate-income families just above the public housing level. This amendment was pressed by long-time liberals like Senator Paul Douglas of Illinois and Senator William Proxmire of Wisconsin on the grounds that the rent-supplement funds should be concentrated on families at the poverty level. Others who were equally on the progressive side of the housing effort felt that this was a short-sighted position in view of the increasing disenchantment of lower-middle-income white families, and especially blue-collar workers, with the concentration of Federal aid programs on the poor, and in view of the social and political desirability of achieving greater economic integration within Federally-aided housing programs.

. . . .

[At this juncture Keith reviews the jockeying for position among various factions following passage of the legislation establishing the new cabinet level Department of Housing and Urban Development and the so-called Model Cities Program. He then turns to the intensifying Vietnam War and its growing dominance over budgetary priorities. After some pages he returns to rent supplements. — Eds.]

These disparate priorities in Federal expenditures for housing and related urban programs, on the one hand, and the other programs cited above were augmented by Congressional prejudices. In general, the legislative committees of Congress — in this field principally the Banking and Currency Committees of the two Houses— had majorities which supported progressive substantive legislation for housing and community development. But the Appropriations Committees, which control the purse strings and which are largely dominated by conservatives (especially in the House of Representatives), frequently display a cavalier attitude toward funding the substantive programs authorized by Congress.

This attitude was vividly illustrated by the appropriations actions on the rent supplement program. Enacted in August, 1965, the program received no appropriation in that calendar year and thus was inoperative. In May, 1966, annual rent supplement contracts of $12 million were finally approved by the Appropriations Committees, out of $30 million authorized by Congress. In September, 1966, $20 million was approved out of an authorization of $35 million for that fiscal year. Thus, out of $65 million in annual rent supplement contracts authorized by Congress for the first two years of this new program, the Appropriations Committees allowed only $32 million, or slightly less than half, to become operative, notwithstanding strong lobbying support from realtors, builders, and mortgage bankers in addition to liberal organizations. This represented the difference between about 72,000 and 35,000 homes for poverty families. The explanation of how the Appropriations Committees were able in this fashion to ride roughshod over the intent of Congress as a whole as expressed in enacted laws rests primarily on the Committees' power of financial life or death over myriads of projects of great political importance to individual members of Congress. Hence, members are usually reluctant to risk antagonizing the Appropriations Committees by sponsoring amendments on the floor to override the Committees' recommendations. This is particularly true in the House of Representatives.

In this case, while the Appropriations Committee reports made a bow to the overall Federal Budgetary situation in justification of their drastic cuts in the rent supplement program, the underlying motivation appeared to be primarily racial and especially a desire to protect white suburban communities from incursions by housing projects to be occupied predominantly by low-income Negro families. The rent supplement law waives the usual requirement that any Federally-subsidized housing projects must be approved by the governing body of the locality in which it will be built. The intent of this provision, which survived despite extensive controversy, was to facilitate the development of housing for low-income families in suburban communities which officially would debar them. Notwithstanding this provision of Federal law, the House of Appropriations Subcommittee handling HUD appropriations inserted language in the appropriations bill prohibiting the execution of a rent supplement contract for any project which had not been approved by the governing body of the locality involved. This clearly was legislation in an appropriations bill which, in theory, was prohibited under the rules of the House of Representatives. However, with the cooperation of the House Rules Committee, the House Appropriations Committee generally secured a rule for the consideration of its bills on the floor of the House which waived all points of order. So the subcommittee's gambit prevailed.

The bias of the subcommittee against the rent supplement program was further illustrated by restrictive language which it incorporated in its report. Evidently proceeding on the Calvinistic premise that the poor deserve only inadequate housing, the subcommittee declared that no dwelling covered by rent supplements could have more than one bathroom (regardless of the number of bedrooms), and that no project covered by rent supplements could have a swimming pool. In short, the subcommittee required that a housing development involving rent supplements be obsolete upon completion, in terms of contemporary housing standards. While these restrictions were not included in the appropriations bill itself, HUD interpreted them as legislative history which was equally binding as the statute itself.

Incidents such as these prompted the National Commission on Urban Problems to make the following observation, in its final report in December, 1968:

> In State legislatures and in the Congress itself there are strong indications that the old rural-city rivalry is being replaced by a rural/suburban-city rivalry. This new suburban and rural coalition until now has significantly limited the ability of urban legislators to change the nature of statutes and programs which affect the central city, and it also reinforces suburban exclusiveness, and the power blocs behind it. This reinforcement, in effect, exacts a subsidy from the central city and sharply limits the dispersion of low-income families to the suburbs.

Comments: 1. Several basic points emerge from this very brief sampling of Keith's informative book.

First, it gives an indication of how central the national government and national politics have become in the American housing system.

Second, note that Keith introduces the concept of housing class, supra p. —, though he does not use the phrase to explain differences in interest among the rich, those in the middle who can afford market rate housing prices, and the poor.

Third, Keith cites one of the chief concepts to have emerged recently in the analysis of American domestic politics. This is the central city-suburban conflict. Many of the problems discussed in the remainder of this text exhibit effects of this split. Chapter 11 is essentially devoted to it.

Fourth, in the account of the Rent Supplement Program Keith refers to the opposition of the local public housing authorities. Later after passage of the act and reduction in its appropriations he asserts that the national housing bureaucracy followed not the law but their own interpretation of the Appropriation Committee's intent. These actions show the bureaucracy acting politically to try to make or modify policy. This is a general characteristic of the federal system. It has developed to the point that the federal bureaucracy, in this case HUD, and its clients in the counties and cities form a mutually supporting political interest. Community development scholar Roland Warren has called such mutual interests input-output constituencies. The dollars outputted by the HUD bureaucracy form the inputs for their local counterparts. In turn, local outputs in programs and services to people generate the political support inputs necessary to maintain the federal bureaucracy and its programs.

Fifth, Keith's whole presentation suggests that just as major features of the macroeconomy dominate the housing economy so the main currents in the national political life govern housing politics and housing policy. War and peace, conservative or liberal ascendency, and the existence or absence of domestic political crises tend to carry housing policies in their wake.

2. In this short excerpt Keith gives only a hint of the enormous variety and the sheer quantity of specific components of national housing policy. The next reading from a Nixon era federal review of the subject provides a more complete chronological catalog of policies and programs. In reading this catalog, however, be aware that it is an official publication of a specific political administration. It gives no critical background on the political interests and alignments behind the various policies and programs. And it is in itself a species of political document as the comments following it make clear. Another caveat should be made to call attention to the fact much of the text that deals with program details and programs of lesser importance has been eliminated in the interest of brevity.

U.S. DEPARTMENT OF HOUSING AND URBAN DEVELOPMENT, HOUSING IN THE SEVENTIES: A REPORT OF THE NATIONAL POLICY REVIEW 7-21 (1974)

The Role of the Federal Government in Housing

Response to the Great Depression
President Hoover's Conference on Home Building and Homeownership provided, in December 1931, the first impetus for the basic home financing legislation that evolved during the 1930's.

. . . .

The Conference highlighted for the Nation the existing inadequacies of home construction and rehabilitation, the need for further research and distribution of information on the subject, the crucial problems of building and loan associations and other lenders arising from the Great Depression, and the flaws in foreclosure, zoning, and other State and local laws. . . .

In response to this crisis, Congress acted in broad and sweeping ways that permanently changed the nature of housing credit markets. It created three emergency and four permanent institutions, most of which continue to this day to exercise vast influence over the housing industry. In 1932, 1933, and 1934, these agencies were established in rapid succession: the Reconstruction Finance Corporation, the Federal Home Loan Bank Board and Federal Home Loan Bank System; the Federal Deposit Insurance Corporation; the Home Owner's Loan Corporation; the Public Works Administration, the Federal Savings and Loan Insurance Corporation, and the Federal Housing Administration (FHA). Since 1934, new FHA mortgage programs have been enacted as amendments to the 1934 act and are commonly known by their section number in that act.

[In fact, none of these responses to the depression crisis in housing was the work of the Hoover administration except for the conference itself. The Reconstruction Finance Agency was a holdover from the post World War I period, the others were accomplished under President Roosevelt who took office in 1933. — Eds.]

. . . .

Encouragement was given to the formation of institutions to provide long term mortgages from the regular and long-term savings of individuals under the Federal Home Loan Bank System. The Federal Deposit Insurance Corporation and the Federal Savings and Loan Insurance Corporation provided new protections for the small depositor to dispel fears of financial collapse and to renew a steady stream of deposits and savings from which credit might once again begin to flow.

Under the Home Owner's Loan Corporation program, new emergency loans were made on a long-term, self-amortizing basis to refinance defaulted and foreclosed home loans, in an attempt to end the panic of homeowners and lenders alike. The Public Works Administration initiated a program of public works to provide jobs, clear slums, and construct or repair low cost housing projects. And finally, a new agency, the FHA, was created to insure the type of long-term home mortgage loans for new construction, resale, and rehabilitation that had first been offered under the Home Owner's Loan Corporation for defaulted home loans.
. . . .

There were two other consequences of the Depression of enduring significance: one, to provide further means to assure an adequate and balanced flow of housing credit; the other, to serve the housing needs of the poor.

In enacting the National Housing Act of 1934, the Congress sought to encourage the liquidity of mortgage credit by authorizing the formation of private secondary mortgage markets, particularly for the new, long-term mortgages it had fostered. In contrast to other investments there had been no ready market for the purchase and sale of these mortgages. Even FHA insurance backed by the full faith and credit of the United States behind the loan had been insufficient to arouse adequate investor interest. A mortgage holder, having less opportunity to shift freely from one investment to another, did not have "liquid" assets. In 1938, the Federal National Mortgage Association (familiarly known as "Fannie Mae") was created to fill this gap in the housing credit market. Its primary functions were to provide a conduit between pools of savings and borrowers in need of funds for new construction and repair, and to encourage the flow of capital across the Nation from areas of surplus to areas of short supply.
. . . .

The United States Housing Act of 1937 made permanent, on a modest scale, the goals of slum clearance and low cost housing set forth earlier in the emergency public works program under the National Industrial Recovery Act. Demonstrating its Depression-era heritage, the 1937 act gave as its first aim ". . . to alleviate present and recurring unemployment . . . ." In addition, it was intended to "remedy" the unsafe and insanitary housing conditions and the acute shortage of decent, safe, and sanitary housing for families of low income that are ". . . injurious to health, safety, and morals of the citizens of the Nation."

A basic feature of the new low rent public housing program authorized by the 1937 act was a Federal contract to pay the annual principal and interest on long-term, tax-exempt bonds, which financed construction by the local public body. With the payment of the costs of permanent financing and construction thus assured and the State and local tax exemption of the property authorized by the act, rents by the local agency could be set at low levels, since rents had to cover only operation and maintenance costs in order for the project to break even. . . .

In the 36-year history of the public housing program, it has provided only a modest part of the Nation's annual housing production, averaging about 30,000 completed units per year. [Since 1972, construction of public housing has continued at the same and sometimes slightly higher levels. — Eds.] As of December 31, 1972, the program had under contract a total of more than 1,260,000 units, of which 1,055,000 were under management, thus providing approximately 1.5 percent of the Nation's total housing stock.
. . . .

Impact of World War II

President Franklin D. Roosevelt, using his emergency war powers, created the National Housing Agency in 1942. The new agency centralized all Federal housing authorities under a single administrator for war needs. Through the auspices of the National Housing Agency, nearly 853,000 units of defense and war housing were provided by direct Federal construction under the Lanham Act of 1940 and related acts of the early 1940's. Subsequently, lacking the stimulus of the war effort, the Federal Government abandoned its role of directly supplying housing; it demolished two-thirds of the wartime-constructed units and sold the remainder.

. . . .

The wartime shortage of housing, due to shutdown of nearly all residential construction except in defense areas, and the low level of production in the 1930's, was compounded by the number of returning veterans in 1945. As part of a broad package of benefits in the G.I. Bill of Rights (Servicemen's Readjustment Act of 1944), a new homeownership program was enacted for veterans. To date, it constitutes the largest program ever enacted for a single target group. All other programs for the poor, the elderly, the handicapped, minority groups, and college housing, are dwarfed by the scale of the Veterans Administration (VA) housing program.

By 1973, 8.7 million veterans' loans had been placed, totaling close to $100 billion. Of these, about 3.9 million loans with a balance of $45.5 billion, are still outstanding. Only the cumulative outstanding balance of FHA mortgages insured under its basic Section 203 single-family home mortgage insurance program of $5.1 billion exceeds the total loans guaranteed by the VA.

. . . .

Postwar Enactment of National Housing Policy

. . . .

The Housing Act of 1949, which was enacted with broad support from both political parties, contained the clearest statement to that time of a national commitment to housing and reaffirmed the use of private resources, local governmental initiatives, the Federal financial assistance in achieving housing goals. Section 2 of the act states:

The Congress hereby declares that the general welfare and security of the Nation and the health and living standards of its people require housing production and related community development sufficient to remedy the serious housing shortage, through the clearance of slums and blighted areas, and the realization as soon as feasible of the *goal of a decent home and a suitable living environment for every American family,* thus contributing to the development and redevelopment of communities and to the advancement of the growth, wealth and security of the Nation. (Emphasis added.)

It was a commitment to provide decent housing for all citizens and to remove slum conditions, but it was a commitment without a timetable and without adequate means for accomplishment.

Beyond the statement of policy, the act created the Urban Redevelopment Program (Title I), which later became the urban renewal program; greatly increased the funds available for public housing (Title III); and established new programs for rural housing (Title V).

Urban redevelopment was seen as an expansion of the related programs of low income housing and slum clearance established by the Housing Act of 1937. Basically, Title I provided Federal assistance to local public agencies for projects consisting of the assembly, clearance, site-preparation, and sale or lease of land at its fair value for uses described in a redevelopment plan for project costs. The

Federal grants generally could not exceed two-thirds of net project costs, and the local agency was required to furnish the remaining one-third, which could be in the form of cash, donation of land, or public facilities such as schools to support or serve the new uses of land in the project area. The Housing Act of 1949 also required that the redevelopment plan be approved by the governing body of the locality.

In Title II, the act of 1949 authorized 135,000 new public housing units for each of the next 5 years — a number far in excess of the previous low rent housing efforts and far in excess also of the amounts Congress subsequently voted to fund each year.

Under the provisions of Title V, the Farmers Home Administration (FmHA), established by the Farmers Home Administration Act of 1946, was authorized to establish a program of grants and loans for the construction or reconstruction of farm dwellings. . . .

Refining and Broadening Housing Laws for Special Groups

. . . .

President Dwight D. Eisenhower's Committee on Government Housing Policies and Programs was established in 1953 to review broadly the housing and urban development programs and make recommendations for changing and eliminating programs or establishing new ones. . . .

[A] major problem [arose] under the 1949 Housing Act: the difficulty of initiating housing construction on a cleared site. To qualify under the program, a redevelopment project site either had to be "predominantly residential" before clearance, or to be redeveloped for predominantly residential purposes after clearance. The existing FHA insurance programs were wholly inadequate to attract credit and sponsors.

Accordingly, Congress included in the 1954 act a new mortgage insurance program, known as Section 220, to generate housing credit and production in urban renewal areas. Traditional insurance terms were liberalized in several respects and purchase of the mortgages by the Federal National Mortgage Association was authorized. The program has been one of the major special purpose programs of FHA. Criticism of it in later years stemmed from the fact that it produced housing for high income families and not for those displaced from the area. . . .

[T]he Eisenhower Committee recommended a special liberalized mortgage insurance program for housing displaced families; it was enacted in the 1954 act as Section 221. This new authority required that the housing involved be "programed" for each area on the basis of the number and income of families displaced by Federal, State, or local governmental action, and that these families receive priority of opportunity to purchase or rent the completed dwellings.

. . . .

Another important recommendation by the Eisenhower Committee that was enacted by the Congress in the 1954 act was a complete reform of the Government's secondary market structure, both as to the role of the Federal Government and that of the private financial community. It conformed with a basic element of the Eisenhower Committee's approach, which involved an effort to design a secondary market facility that would derive capital from participating lending institutions and would eventually finance itself in the private capital markets, rather than relying upon the Federal Treasury as had been done in the past.

The Federal National Mortgage Association statutory authority was rewritten completely in a new Federal National Mortgage Charter Act, which was part of

THE POLITICS OF HOUSING

the 1954 act. It divided Federal National Mortgage Association operations into three parts: "secondary market operations," "special assistance functions," and "management and liquidation functions." The chief result of this division was to isolate the special assistance functions (which need Government financial aid) from other Federal National Mortgage Association operations. The special assistance functions continued primarily for special FHA mortgage insurance or the VA guaranty loan program requiring Government purchase of mortgages.

. . . .

The growth of the scope of FHA mortgage insurance programs through the years has resulted primarily from the gradual liberalization of mortgage terms under FHA's regular insurance operations and the enactment of special insurance programs — especially during the 1950's — to meet the emerging housing needs of specific groups or in response to the new forms of cooperative and condominium ownership. It was in this way that the overall character of FHA was changed from an agency concerned almost entirely with increasing the supply of adequate housing to an agency widely concerned with serving special public purposes in the housing field.

. . . .

The trend established under the 1954 act expanded from liberalized lower cost insurance to indirect subsidy without insurance with enactment of Section 202 in the 1959 Housing Act. Under this new and separate program, direct loans were to be made through the device of Government-subsidized low interest rates to provide housing for the elderly. Under the program a loan could cover 98 percent of development cost and have an interest rate as low as 3 percent.

The Subsidy Initiatives of the 1960's

Housing legislation in the 1960's took an evolutionary approach toward meeting the Nation's housing needs. New emphasis was placed on providing housing to groups such as the poor. Instead of relying upon revising the financial mechanisms, as in the 1950's, the Government embarked on direct and indirect subsidies. It also added new emphasis to the goal spelled out in the 1949 Housing Act of providing a "decent home and a suitable living environment" for all Americans.

. . . .

The principal feature of the Housing Act of 1961 was the subsidized, below-market interest rate mortgage insurance program to assist rental housing for moderate income families, known as Section 221(d)(3). Not only was the new program an interest subsidy program, it also was a direct loan program. Since private lenders would not make mortgage loans at below-market interest rates, the funds were provided through the purchase of the originator's mortgage by the Federal National Mortgage Association under its special assistance functions. The chief beneficiaries of this program were those families whose incomes were above public housing limits set by local housing authorities but were below the amounts necessary to meet rental requirements in decent, new, unsubsidized private housing.

. . . .

In the Housing Act of 1964, . . . Section 312 was amended to authorize a new program of 20 year, 3 percent loans to property owners or tenants in urban renewal areas to finance rehabilitation required to make the property conform to the local housing code or to carry out the objectives of the urban renewal plan.

Two additional subsidy programs were enacted by the Housing Act of 1965 to provide housing for families eligible for regular public housing through the utilization of privately owned housing. These programs also served to avoid a growing stigma communities had begun to attach to the concentrations of public housing. Both programs permitted broader dispersal of the very poor among varied income groups.

One of these programs was the rent supplement program. . . . [Discussed in the previous Keith reading. — Eds.]

The other new subsidy program enacted in 1965 was the Section 23 leasing operation, which became one of the major public housing programs. Under this program, local housing authorities are authorized to lease units in privately owned existing structures and make them available to low income families eligible for regular public housing. The usual public housing assistance is made available by HUD so that the local authority can pay the economic rent to the owner without charging the tenant more than the usual public housing rental.

In 1967, HUD initiated, as an administrative procedure, the "Turnkey Method." Under this variation of the regular public housing program, a private developer enters into a contract with a local housing authority to sell the project to the local authority upon completion. . . .

The Creation of the Department of Housing and Urban Development

The Department of Housing and Urban Development Act, passed September 9, 1965, created HUD, although it was not actually organized until February 1966.

The act was a watershed in housing legislation. Most importantly, it raised the functions of the Housing and Home Finance Agency to Cabinet level and simplified the administration of all its functions by consolidating most statutory authority in the Secretary of the new Department. It did not, however, consolidate housing and urban development functions existing in other parts of the Federal Government. . . .

Douglas and Kaiser Commissions

The urban disturbance of the late 1960's led to the creation of two Presidential Commissions that were to have a profound impact upon the redirection and expansion of Federal housing policies. In 1967, President Lyndon B. Johnson directed the creation of the National Commission on Urban Problems, known as the Douglas Commission after its chairman, Paul H. Douglas, Senator from Illinois from 1948-1966. The Commission's mandate was to recommend ". . . solutions, particularly those ways in which the efforts of the Federal Government, private industry, and local communities can be marshaled to increase the supply of low cost decent housing." The Douglas Commission's prime recommendation was to direct the Nation's housing assistance toward the poor, a group the Commission found had been neglected in national housing endeavors to that time.

Also in 1967 the President's Committee on Urban Housing, known as the Kaiser Commission after its chairman, industrialist Edgar F. Kaiser, was appointed with a charge to "find a way to harness the productive power of America . . . to the most pressing unfulfilled need of our society — that need is to provide the basic necessities of a decent home and healthy surroundings for every American family now imprisoned in the squalor of the slums." Among its many recommendations, the Committee called for the establishment of a 10-year goal of 26 million new and rehabilitated housing units, including at least 6 million for lower income families. That recommendation was to shape future congressional action and Federal policy.

National Housing Goals

The Johnson Administration recommended, and the Congress enacted, in the Housing and Urban Development Act of 1968, the housing goal proposed by the Kaiser Commission. . . .

In that provision, the Congress declared for the first time a national housing goal in terms of housing units to be produced, and established a time frame for production.

. . . .

An extremely significant expansion of the subsidy concept was contained in the Housing and Urban Development Act of 1968, which adopted the principle of subsidizing interest rates, thus resulting in a rapid increase in all appropriations for housing subsidies.

One of these programs was the Section 235 homeownership assistance program. . . . As enacted, Section 235 established a homeownership program providing special mortgage insurance and cash payments to help low and moderate income home purchasers meet mortgage payments by subsidizing debt service costs in excess of an amortization at 1 percent interest. Under this program, an eligible buyer may purchase a private home with an FHA-insured mortgage, bearing the prevailing rate of interest, and the Federal Government makes a monthly assistance payment to the lender on his behalf. Provided the purchaser is applying at least 20 percent of his monthly income to the mortgage payments, he could pay each month as much as the same amount he would pay if the mortgage loan provided for only 1 percent interest. The Federal Government pays the rest.

Another significant addition to subsidy programs was the Section 236 multifamily rental housing program also enacted in the 1968 act. This program provides a subsidy formula similar to that under Section 235, although the mechanics of the Section 236 subsidy payment are geared to rental housing.

An accompanying provision of the 1968 act contained a subsidy feature, Section 238, which established a special risk pool for which appropriations were authorized. This fund was authorized to be used for carrying out insurance obligations under the subsidized and certain other mortgage insurance programs. They included a new Section 223(e), which authorized insurance in "older, declining urban areas," where not all of the usual mortgage insurance requirements could be met.

. . . .

[The authors then go on to describe FmHA rural housing programs which parallel FHA programs structurally, although interest subsidies and eligibility limitations vary. — Eds.]

Partition of Federal National Mortgage Association

. . . .

[T]he Housing and Urban Development Act of 1968 partitioned the Federal National Mortgage Association, as it then existed, changing it into two new corporations. One was a Federally chartered private corporation that, after a brief transition period, was to be privately owned, operated, and financed. This corporation was to retain its name — Federal National Mortgage Association. The second, a new wholly owned Federal Corporation to be known as the Government National Mortgage Association, was to assume the functions of the former Federal National Mortgage Association with respect to special assistance and the management and liquidating operations.

. . . .

An administrative procedure called "Tandem Plan" was developed under the Federal National Mortgage Association partition. Under this procedure the Government National Mortgage Association issues a commitment to purchase a mortgage qualifying for special assistance at a predetermined price more favorable than that available in the market (special assistance being unnecessary otherwise). This commitment is transferred to the Federal National Mortgage Association; when the mortgage is ready for delivery, the Government National Mortgage Association pays the Federal National Mortgage Association the difference between the committed price and the price the Federal National Mortgage Association would have paid in its regular market purchase program. Thus the immediate budget expenditure is reduced from the full amount of the purchase commitment to this difference. In this manner, by paying above-market prices and selling at market prices, the Government National Mortgage Association provides indirect subsidies to borrowers and lenders. . . .

Modification of Low Rent Public Housing Program

An important change in the low rent public housing program was made by Section 213(a) of the Housing and Urban Development Act of 1969, known as the Brooke amendment. The amendment limited rents charged by local housing authorities to 25 percent of the tenant's income. Subsequently, the Congress authorized Federal public housing subsidies for operating expenses, where necessary, to assure the low rent character of the public housing project. . . .

[In 1974 this subsidy was converted into an explicit operating subsidy. It does not guarantee to make up in full the deficits caused by the Brooke amendment rent limitation. — Eds.]

Aid to Displaced Persons

Subsidies for the relocation of displaced families in connection with all Federal programs were placed on a uniform basis by legislation that was debated during much of the 1960's but finally enacted as the Uniform Relocation Assistance and Real Property Acquisitions Policies Act of 1970. This legislation . . . gave both owners and tenants who were displaced the right to substantial payments under Federal or federally assisted development programs. . . .

Model Cities

During the 1960's, support developed for a new and broader approach to the housing undersupply and other problems of urban areas. A program which became known as "Model Cities" was authorized as the principal provision of the Demonstration Cities and Metropolitan Development Act of 1966. . . .

Under the 1966 act, the Federal Government was authorized to make grants and provide technical assistance to city demonstration agencies to enable the agencies to plan, develop, and conduct programs to improve their physical environment, increase their supply of housing for low and moderate income people, and to provide educational and social services vital to health and welfare.

That enactment was significant in giving cities the broadest discretion in developing proposed programs, subject only to general criteria prescribed in the statute. Discretion remained in HUD, however, to select and fund those undertakings it considered best for demonstrating to other cities the potential benefits of such initatives.

New Communities

    . . . .

Recognizing that mortgage insurance alone was inadequate to stimulate sufficient volume of credit for new community development, HUD recommended in 1968 an entirely new additional assistance program based on the Federal Guarantee of bonds and other obligations issued by the private developer of the new community. . . .

[The new communities program ran into financial difficulties and most of the new communities have now been closed out. — Eds.]

———————

Comments: 1. This account ends by covering policy only through the early 1970s. As the editors stated in the comment introducing it, the report from which it is taken is in itself a political document. In 1973 the Nixon administration used the arguments set forth in this report as part of the justification for placing a moratorium on all housing subsidy programs. The moratorium had two overt and immediate motives. First, the explosive growth of the Section 235 and 236 subsidy programs had begun to concern federal budget watchers who anticipated that the modest yearly interest subsidies would snowball into billions of dollars in long term commitments. Second, the programs, particularly Section 235, had been wracked with scandals and were believed in many cases to be hastening the decline of central cities.

2. More important than the moratorium, Housing in the Seventies signalled a major shift in the direction of thinking. For some time, social policy experts and leading Republican political figures had advocated shifting subsidies to directly support housing demand. In other words they believed the dollars should flow more directly to the poor consumers rather than the construction firms and landlords on the supply side of the market. Additionally, such a change could have the great budgetary advantage of subsidizing cheaper old units instead of more expensive new ones. The Nixon administration favored this change. In 1974 Congress passed new basic housing legislation within days after Nixon resigned. In part it realized the shift from supply- to demand-site subsidies. It made other fundamental changes too. The following note provides additional information on this important legislation.

A NOTE ON THE HOUSING AND COMMUNITY DEVELOPMENT ACT OF 1974

The 1974 Act joins those of 1934, 1937, 1949, 1954, and 1968 as the pivotal federal legislation in the housing field. The Housing and Community Development Act of 1974 embodies a major political realignment between federal and local governments with respect to urban development assistance as well as a realignment of the housing subsidy system. To take the urban development component first, it changed the structure of federal aid from a system of purpose earmarked federal grants-in-aid to local governments to a system of broad entitlements for a formula-determined level of federal aid. Initially the formula was an index of overcrowding, population, and size of poverty population. Later 1977 legislation modified it to include age of housing stock and population change. The 1974 Act phased out urban renewal, Model Cities and other programs, and consolidated all HUD funds for community betterment into a single program, hence the term Block Grants. Unlike earlier programs, once eligible cities and counties receive their community development block grant they may budget it largely as they see fit. Allocation between housing rehabilitation and central area refurbishing, for instance, is basically left to the discretion of the cities and counties. This arrangement was explicitly intended to simplify the arduous application and approval procedures characteristic of urban renewal and Model Cities. It also had political connotations as part of Nixon's New Federalism strategy aimed at shifting somewhat the power balance from federal to local levels of government and politics. Because the grants are distributed by formula, HUD is taken out of local land development politics. Mayors and city councils control the allocation of federal funds.

The formula allocation concept embodied a redistribution of federal urban development funds from central cities, largely Democratic in political allegiance, to suburban communities which were traditional Republican Party strongholds. Critics of the political strategy inherent in the Act contend that it reallocated scarce funds for housing and other social purposes from relatively needy populations to more affluent ones. Several studies have substantiated these regressive redistributional consequences. It is largely for this reason that the 1977 legislation introduced formula changes. This struggle over the distributional impact of the Block Grant program provides a prime example of the city-suburban conflict noted by Keith.

The second main thrust of the 1974 Act concerned housing subsidy policy. A provision called Section 8 was intended to supplement public housing and replace the Section 235 and 236 interest rate subsidy programs for the rehabilitation and new construction of single and multi-family housing. Section 8 subsidies are rental subsidies; no contributions are made directly to the capital or financing costs of buildings. One subsection of Section 8 deals directly with the demand problems of low income families by subsidizing their rental payments for existing units. Other subsections have a more mixed incidence. Developers are given up to 40-year commitments from HUD for rental subsidies to encourage them to build new units or to substantially rehabilitate, modernize and maintain older ones.

In spite of the fact that Section 8 was designed by the Republicans to supercede earlier programs, the fact is that the federal government continues to make some funds available for some of them. Congress, ever sensitive to politically effective input-output constituencies, has continued to appropriate limited funds for the construction of new public housing, for instance, and has invented a new version of urban renewal called Urban Development Action Grants. This tendency demonstrates a practical truism in American federal policy: it is far easier to start a new program than to terminate an old one. Nevertheless, though some retrenching has occurred the main thrusts of the 1974 Housing and Community Development Act remain. Block grants have largely replaced the so-called categorical grant-in-aid programs. Housing subsidies based on need have begun to supplant those designed to produce lower cost new units.

Comments: This short review of the 1974 Act concludes the brief historic catalog of federal housing policies. These policies are formed in the national political arena. To understand housing problems it is necessary to think critically about this policy formation process and the nature of the interests it serves.

The very idea of housing policy presupposes a view of government and politics as beneficient and concerned with achieving the best for everyone. Most careful students disagree with this view. They see housing politics and the policies that result as favoring narrow interests, producers, accumulators of wealth and capital, or simply the great, reasonably well off, middle that dominates American markets and electoral politics. In a marvelously acute legal history of housing policy listed in this Chapter's bibliography, Lawrence Friedman observes that laws designed to help house poor people "are unlikely to be generated unless (a) the poor are a majority and have fair and adequate political representation, or (b) on balance, proposed legislation serves the interests of some class larger and broader than the poor." The first alternative has not obtained in America since the Depression or before, though the house price-income squeeze could make the mass of Americans housing poor by the late 1980s. The second alternative has clearly obtained over the period since the 1930s during which housing policy has blossomed. This skeptical, critical view holds that policies claimed as benefiting poor people are really working for powerful interests. In the following brief selection, housing lawyer, planner and educator Peter Marcuse offers a vigorous exposition of this view.

P. MARCUSE, HOUSING POLICY AND THE MYTH OF THE BENEVOLENT STATE, IN SOCIAL POLICY, Vol. 8, No. 4, at 21, 23-26 (Jan.-Feb., 1978)

Much intellectual analysis of government policies is premised on the myth of the benevolent state. In brief the myth is that government acts out of a primary concern for the welfare of all its citizens, that its policies represent an effort to find solutions to recognized social problems, and that government efforts fall short of complete success only because of lack of knowledge, countervailing selfish interests, incompetence, or lack of courage.

In the field of housing the view that government policies are addressed to meeting real housing needs or solving housing problems has pervaded the mainstream of the professional literature for the past 30 years. On this basis efforts are made to determine the nature and scope of housing needs, their origins, the mechanisms by which they may be met, the context in which they must be dealt with. Evaluations gauge the results of housing programs against the goal of providing adequate housing for all, and recommendations proposed to better achieve that goal are thought to contribute to improved housing policy.

The analyses informed by this view are not necessarily useless, and some, like Henry Aaron's are perceptive enough in their criticisms of policy outcomes. But the weakness of most such analyses arises from the assumption that decision makers' mere exposure to the irrationalities in housing policy will be a major factor leading to their improvement. Even those politically sophisticated analyses which attend to interest group pressures, popular prejudices, economic laws, regional conflicts, and the rigidities of bureaucracies still are premised on the belief that, underneath it all, there is a movement toward social amelioration. It is the contention of this paper that the view of the benevolent state in general, and particularly in regard to housing, is radically and demonstrably false.

The very phrase "housing policy" is witness to this underlying myth. What is housing policy? It is the set of government actions (and inactions, in the sophisticated view) that is intended to deal with housing problems. Housing policy may indeed be criticized as illogical, incoherent, ineffective; a set of policies, rather than a single policy; a set of policies that is internally contradictory and even self-defeating in particulars; a policy lacking in focus, philosophy, clarity of goals, certainty as to priorities. Yet the underlying existence of a governmental thrust toward the solution of the social problems of housing — of a benevolent state — is implicit in the use of the phrase. The task of analysis is to make clear the goals of housing policy and the means of their achievement, so that the benevolent state may act more rationally to solve housing problems.

Yet an historical analysis of government actions and inactions affecting housing reveals no such housing policy or any common thrust toward one. Housing policy is an ideological artifact — in Manuel Castells's phrase, not a real category. Hypotheses may be formulated as to what state actions one would expect to find if there were, in fact, a housing policy evolving from the efforts of a benevolent state to solve existing problems. These hypotheses may be tested and verified or invalidated. A good starting point may be the benevolent-state account of housing policy as moving from a restrictive approach, i.e., the enactment and enforcement of housing regulations required by mid-nineteenth-century health problems, to the more positive contemporary approach of government provision of improved housing facilities.

. . . .

[The author synopsizes the history of 19th Century tenement house regulation to show it was not undertaken out of benevolence toward the slum dwellers but out of upper class fear of public health menace from insanitary conditions and public disturbance of the tranquility of the urban scene. He then turns to the direct public provision of housing. — Eds.]

There is nothing obscure about motivations for the public provision of housing in the United States. Rather than arising out of a benevolent concern for the poor, housing efforts were more closely related to the manufacture of war supplies to support American efforts in the First World War than with concern to appease the discontent of returning veterans of that war . . . and finally with the provision of employment for the vast army of the unemployed following the Great Depression. . . .

The public housing program finally adopted in 1937 stemmed from concerns about social unrest among unemployed city workers; it hoped to deal with that unrest, not so much through the provision of better housing, but through the provision of jobs. The expansion of the supply of housing was not its goal; indeed, the demolition of an equivalent number of units (of substandard housing) was mandated in the U.S. Housing Act of 1937. . . .

If benevolence was the guiding principle behind state policies affecting housing, one would expect successive major housing acts — after 1937, these would include 1949, 1954, administrative and funding changes in 1964-66, 1968, and 1974 — to show an evolution of sophistication and effectiveness in dealing with the problems of bad housing. History shows no such pattern.

The Housing Act of 1949 did two things: it reinstituted the New Deal public housing program, dormant since World War II, and it laid the groundwork for slum clearance in the United States. . . .

If benevolence was a major factor in the evolution of housing policies, one would expect to find the quantitative levels of production of public housing to be increasing as housing needs increased, and declining as needs declined. Such figures as are available indicate a steadily growing need from 1930 through about 1949, and a rather steady decline in absolute numbers needed since 1949. The figures for publicly subsidized units, however, show an altogether different and almost opposite pattern.

The explanation is not hard to find. The U.S. Housing Act of 1937 was adopted to provide jobs, not housing; its construction standards were such that twice as many units might have been provided for the same cost had the provision of housing been its purpose. The private sector saw to it that no such result ensued. After World War II, in a period of major absolute housing shortage, assistance went to private builders and mortgage-lending institutions in the form of financing aids and guarantees, and vast expenditures were made on infrastructure, highways, and related facilities. The suburban boom thus massively encouraged did not aid the poor; it led inexorably to the further decline of central-city housing, neighborhood deterioration, and reductions in public services available to the poor residents left behind by the governmentally encouraged outward movement. Public housing, on the other hand, the only housing program directly providing shelter for the poor, was starved for funds throughout the postwar period.

Accelerated state support of housing construction for families below the level of economically effective demand was not forthcoming until a way was finally found to make it serve private profit. The process is a perfect example of, in Castells's words "the constant tendency ... to make the sectors of public subsidization profitable in order to bring them into line with the criteria of private capital so as to be able to transfer them gradually over to it." The first step was the turnkey construction process, which permitted private builders to do all of the construction on their own land and then sell the completed development to the public authorities. The second step was the perfection of the limited dividend tax benefit approach, which permitted private interests not only to build privately on public land, but to continue to own and manage the resultant publicly subsidized housing. They thus enjoyed the tax benefits of depreciation, with special acceleration provisions, agreeing in return only to limit cash profits. The tax benefits vastly exceeded in value the immediate cash benefit.

The final step, being explored today through the Section 8 program of the Housing Act of 1974 and housing allowance experiments will permit private interests to build, own, and manage housing intended for the poor with no limits on profit whatsoever besides those nominally imposed by a requirement that rents be based on an administratively determined competitive level. The state will nevertheless support the payment of rent to the private owner through a subsidy based on the occupant's income. Any claim to benevolent intervention in the housing situation to bring about more rationally organized and improved housing for the poor is now abandoned altogether in favor of a restricted income support to throw into the private market those whose own resources would make their participation in it otherwise profitless. Formal housing policy thus turns parallel to what has always been the largest public program providing housing for the poor: direct welfare payments. The difference between outright welfare and the newer programs is simply its restriction to certain forms of housing and its organization in such a way as to provide more direct benefits to the private providers of the housing.

. . . .

Comments: 1. Most mainstream housing policy people would disagree with Marcuse. They would either take the opposing view, that a program such as Section 8 is aimed primarily at helping poor people, or more likely, they would agree with Lawrence Friedman and accept a mixed view. This more widely held position sees social policy aimed at poor people to have mixed objectives that include benefiting elites or majority interests at the same time. However, Marcuse looks critically behind the official line and thus provides a valuable counterweight.

2. At the other end of the scale from the national scene, as the introductory paragraphs of this chapter asserted, housing in America constitutes a chief focus for local politics and local government. This focus derives, in large part, from the constitutional system of separation of powers between the national government and the states. The states in turn have bestowed on local government most of the authority to regulate and control housing, land development, and land use. Local general purpose governments such as counties, towns and cities wield most of the direct power over housing. They do this through local laws, building codes, housing codes, occupancy regulations and the like. Local government regulates new dwelling construction through zoning which controls the use of land and its development, and controls such as subdivision regulations, preservation and grading ordinances. The daily business of managing these controls, and open and behind the scenes politics that decide who regulates whom and to what degree, constitute

a major part of local politics and government activity, some would say the major part. This is especially true of suburban areas, where new dwelling construction is a chief industry. The next reading explores this situation and exhibits the central place of housing in the politics of developing suburbs. The author is a sociologist-economist-planner long involved in the events he reports about.

M. GOTTDIENER, PLANNED SPRAWL: PRIVATE AND PUBLIC INTERESTS IN SUBURBIA 73-79, 82-86 (1977)

The Town Board

The locally elected government in Privatown consists of a seven-member town board including a supervisor and six councilmen. The members of the board are elected on an at-large basis with three councilmen standing for election every two years. At each of its bi-monthly meetings, the local government makes a variety of decisions and holds discussions on matters related to township business. The board has at its disposal only residual powers of decision-making not covered by the higher levels of government. Its political power arises from its control over zoning, its small supply of patronage positions, and its ability to award contracts for township services, such as sanitation, construction and maintenance of roads, public buildings, and recreational areas. Roughly 70 percent of Privatown's operating budget is raised through real estate taxes which had an assessed valuation in 1969 of 4.2 percent. In that same year, Privatown's total budget was $12,976,527 with 17.7 percent supplied to the township by outside aid from New York State.

At its bi-monthly meeting, the board receives petitions and proposals from local residents and businessmen as well as schedules township meetings to air important issues. Field observations revealed that such meetings were sparsely attended with from thirty to sixty people. Only a cadre of regulars holding diverse perspectives on local government appeared at each meeting. These included representatives from opposition Conservative and Democratic parties, an observer from the League of Women Voters, members of several civic associations, and an occasional observer from the Privatown Housing Coalition. When important issues were discussed, however, especially in connection with land-use, attendance increased greatly and, at times, numbered well over one hundred people. At all meetings public discussion was encouraged by the board and, occasionally, spirited exchanges between councilmen and local residents were observed. In appearance then, Privatown government seems quite democratic as it operates in the light of the open forum of bi-monthly meetings.

The Local Republication Party

In spite of this observation, the local government has been overshadowed by the presence of the Republican party leader, Carl Middleton. For the past fourteen years, his organization has exercised control, at times only weakly, over political patronage and the selection of slates for local elections. Except for the recently elected Democratic town board, virtually all the councilmen sitting on the board during Middleton's tenure as township leader have been loyal party functionaries, and they have given his political organization control over at least the board's land-use decisions. The open appearance of town board meetings cannot always mask the operation of this political organization. This was particularly the case whenever controversial land-use decisions were discussed, and open challenges to the political leadership were made by housing coalition groups and local civic associations.

Lacking much patronage and support from local citizens or the larger business community, the party has limited financial resources. The task of making local government work, which falls to the township political organization, means making the best of the political resources that are available. In the case of Privatown, control over the decision-making apparatus of local government and, especially, its zoning and land-use regulatory powers has become the major revenue source for the party. The political process is highly dependent upon the construction industry, which needs local government cooperation for permits, inspections, and public decisions on zoning in order to commence work. Town boss Middleton and his party exploit this need in a business-like way to generate money for party support and personal gain.

. . . .

The Problems of Political Control

The zoning process in Privatown has the appearance of being an open and democratic one. Every land-use decision involves businessmen, who make most of the proposals, and the participation of local civic associations and private citizens, who are allowed to air their views regarding the project's impact. In addition, the town board also receives an evaluation of a petition from the township's planning board and, in some cases, an analysis from the professional planners of the regional planning board as well. Each decision, therefore, involves political, economic, social and technical planning considerations. It is left up to the town board to weigh such factors and make the decision. Although professional planners may be called upon to explain their visions of the future, it is left up to the town board to *implement* land-use decisions and to respond to the many kinds of influence in the township. It might be argued that this separation of function between planners, citizens, and political implementors is as it should be, because most of the affairs of government are conducted precisely in this manner. As we shall see, however, this exercise of local power through representative democracy results in unforeseen and often unpopular consequences.

I have examined 372 zoning cases covering the years 1968-1971, a period with rapid suburban growth. With the aid of local informants, interviews of residents and local newspaper reporters in a two year field study, information was obtained on the community interest groups participating in these decisions and the benefits they received. In considering the re-zoning record for the four year period, the initial research question was to what influences was the board most responsive. In the majority of the 372 cases (over 60 percent) the board acted in agreement with the recommendation of its own planning board and with the desires of the local residents. Whenever these desires were the same as the interest of the petitioner, there was also complete concordance in the decision-making process. This often happened. In approximately 30 percent of the cases, however, the town board rejected the recommendation of its own planning board. . . .

In appearance, then, a pluralist pattern is suggested by the bulk of land-use decision-making. Often, however, personal interests are served at the same time as the public trust is fulfilled. In order to identify other factors of influence which might be at work, the cases of disagreement were examined in detail, while cases of complete concordance were temporarily ignored.

. . . .

Cases in which public officials ignored the wishes of civic associations and planners were the most promising for obtaining a picture of the patterns of influence. As it turns out, these thirty-two cases are essential to the township for planning purposes, as well as critical to its ability to control submetropolitan development, and they are the most controversial ones arising during the period studied.

Out of the thirty-two discordant zoning cases only three did not represent a change of land-use category, i.e., twenty-nine of them altered the zoning pattern. Of the thirty-two discordant cases, nineteen were changes in classification for parcels to recipients who were identified through fieldwork investigations as either being party supporters or direct business associates of town boss Middleton. The largest category represented changes of parcels located in residential single-family or limited commercial zones to multiple-family dwelling classification. This is the most lucrative re-zoning of land because the township has a severe shortage of apartments brought about by the widespread opposition to such housing in the region. Eight of the cases, or 25 percent, were changes to the multiple-family category. Of these eight, seven were received by active business partners of Middleton.

Eight other cases involved changes from residential to limited commercial categories along main residential roads. Commercial re-zonings in residential areas create strip zoning of residential roads and often pave the way for wholesale changes of zone to commercial purposes. Of these eight re-zonings, three were received by business associates of Middleton and by the township boss himself. The remainder were all obtained by Republican party supporters. Although thirteen of the re-zonings, or 40 percent, went to corporations or individuals with *no* known connections to the local political organization, this does not necessarily imply that the party did not receive compensation for the town board decision. As we shall see, payment to the party can take a number of forms.

The business associations of the political leadership and the patterns of influence identified in the analysis of the discordant cases were then used as a basis for the analysis of all the re-zoning cases which occurred during the four year period. This work was supplemented by field investigations. Local informants indicated the names behind most of the development corporations operating in Privatown and their connections with the political organization. Interviews with newspaper reporters, lawyers, builders and real estate agents helped to complete our view of the patterns of association. This investigation indicates that the town boss Middleton and a select group of associates utilize political control as a business resource to benefit directly from rapid suburban development. For example, in 1968 *Newsday,* the Long Island newspaper revealed that Middleton, working closely with his friends, obtained over $1,000,000 in a series of township re-zonings. His connections worked through partnership in at least twelve different corporations active in real estate development. In addition to this personal gain, political control of the zoning power is also utilized to generate revenue for the party from grateful businessmen who have obtained favorable decisions. This holds for many cases in which the planning board and residents agreed with the town board decision. There is, then, a network of connections between party officials and private businessmen, creating many opportunities and conduits for financial transactions which enable the local political organization to appropriate value in land-use decisions for personal and party gain. It is not simply corruption, but also a way for the relatively weak local party and its political leadership to support themselves financially.

. . . .

Local Government as Corporate Business

Due to the weakness of political control and to the opportunities afforded by rapid suburban growth, local government is highly receptive to the interests of the real estate and construction industry. The Privatown Republican party has adopted a strategy of decision-making which uses zoning powers for financial support, while recognizing the limitations of local government control. These limitations arise from public awareness of corruption, minority factions within the party, growing electoral competition from the opposition, and the broader activities of national corporations and banks. The opportunities for gain are carefully weighed against the political risks in the private caucuses of loyal Republican councilmen held prior to town board meetings at the direction of boss Middleton. Such occasions give the political leadership the opportunity to discuss how votes should be cast in re-zonings so that political costs and benefits can be assessed. Like other features of community political control, this procedure is quite legitimate and can be defended under our system as a party caucus of the political leadership. These meetings, however, have enabled the councilmen who are loyal to the local political organization to act in the best interests of the party as well as the polity, and to plan a decision-making strategy which would not jeopardize their political future. Because Middleton's "cronies" have often enjoyed a voting majority on the town board, such meetings also enabled them to decide how each particular vote should be cast. In this way, specific councilmen up for reelection might dissent from an unpopular decision and give the appearance of independent voting without endangering party control and with the blessing of the political leadership.

Party control of the town board has been exploited for two distinct purposes. On the one hand, the granting of favorable zoning decisions and construction permits can be reciprocated by businessmen in the form of payment to the local leadership and the party. This has most often been accomplished through political contributions. Large-scale developers of housing, national corporations and banks, as well as commercial interests in shopping center malls generally have used this method of compensation for favorable political decisions. Often payment has been effected through the purchase of blocks of tickets to local party functions in addition to giving campaign contributions. This impersonal type of payment has been utilized because of the relative lack of direct connection the large corporations have to the local area. A personal appearance by the representative of one of these national enterprises at a local party function would be an extreme rarity. Furthermore, the ability to exercise this power needs only to be demonstrated occasionally to the business community for them to become regular supporters of the local political organization. The latter is less in the business of selling specific votes to national enterprises than in offering an attitude of cooperation and sensitivity to profit-making interests in exchange for financial support to the party. Consequently, yearly political contributions have been made to insure the continuance of such sensitivity over the tenure of office with the implication that town board receptiveness could always be withdrawn or cooperation made more difficult in the event that business ceased its support. Just as is the case with the operation of social control through other bureaucratic and legal regulations, local political control can operate effectively by structuring activities through its *implied* powers, even when they are directly used. In these dealings, the zoning power of the town board and the political regulation of the construction industry have been exploited to enrich the party's campaign fund. This enhanced its competitive position at the polls and helped it to remain in power.

Control over the decision-making apparatus of local government enabled the holders of office to perform a second function. A persistent fraction of all town board decisions directly benefited the economic position of a select group of local political leaders and their business associates. The people involved in the use of public office for personal gain did not represent the business elite in the township. They were a small number of speculators, lawyers, politicians, investors of capital, and local housing developers. The close relationship between Middleton and this group was not a "conspiracy" of the social elite, but, rather a collection of entrepreneurs who used local government control to make money the way businessmen use economic organizations. Other political and economic interests operating in the township and region bargained with this select group whenever the necessity arose. Economic and political exchange characterized the interaction between these individuals and not a confluence of interests.

Personal gain from political control of land-use and the presence of rapid suburban development could be realized in many ways through numerous financial avenues. At times, money was made by direct re-zonings involving enterprises in which some of the members of the select group were partners. A controversial re-zoning for multiple-family housing, for example, went to several of Middleton's business associates. The value of the land could also be manipulated through local tax assessment procedures or the proposal of township government developments so as to directly benefit the holdings of this group. In one instance, a parcel of land owned by the leadership's associates was purchased by the township for recreational use at many times its market value. Finally, contracts for construction and other services, such as legal representation, were often given to this select group by corporations in return for favorable consideration of re-zoning proposals. . . .

The use of political decision-making for financial benefit in Privatown has several other characteristics: (1) Unlike the traditional political machine, local suburban government was little involved in electoral politics on a mass basis. Because political life in Privatown was a dead end, the leadership was more concerned with using public decision-making to support the party. (2) The township boss and his associates did *not* attempt to squeeze out every cent possible from their control of land-use because the political risks were much too high. There was also a limit on the tolerance of national businesses. If the price of cooperation was set too high by local leaders, the corporations could always locate elsewhere in the county. Due to the critical nature of land-use decisions, however, it was necessary to exploit control in only a small fraction of decisions in order to realize significant monetary gain. One reason for this is, as we have already indicated, that the implied use of such powers can be as effective a fund raiser as their actual application. Strict control over decision-making, therefore, was *not* necessary in order to make money for the local political leadership. This is a major reason why the overwhelming majority of town board decisions had the appearance of siding with public opinion. (3) The operations of the local political organization are as diverse as the activities of any corporation in the pursuit of gain. The web of connections characterizing the activities of Middleton and the select group of lawyers, speculators, and developers surrounding him made use of both public and private resources. That is, businessmen used local government to create favorable opportunities, to supply them with benefits from public works, such as highways, and to supply them with information on the housing and land-use needs of the community, such as the patterns of township growth. At the very same time, the political organization used the capital and activities of private business. There appears, then, to be little difference between the actions of public and private individuals at the local level. The relationships between the various groups involved and the exchanges which characterized their interaction can be illustrated by Figure 3.

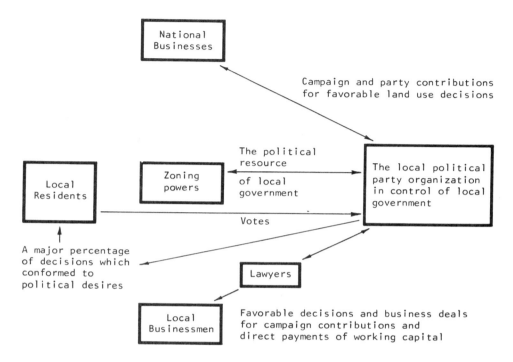

Figure 3 Political relationships in Privatown (Redrawn from Gottdiener)

Comments: If housing provides the money for local politics in the suburbs, it is hardly less important to politics in older central areas. Here, where the development process is largely complete, other powers of local government are more salient than development and land use controls. Chief among these is the regulation of relations and conflicts among the various actors in the housing economy, especially landlord-tenant relations. Local governments and the politics that direct them have a range of concerns from the simple police intervention in violent conflicts between landlords and tenants to the blanket adoption of rent controls and the like. These matters in a problem context are dealt with extensively in the final chapter of this text. As background, however, the next reading gives a vivid picture of inner city housing politics.

J. MOLLENKOPF & J. PYNOOS, BOARDWALK AND PARK PLACE: PROPERTY OWNERSHIP, POLITICAL STRUCTURE, AND HOUSING POLICY AT THE LOCAL LEVEL, IN HOUSING URBAN AMERICA 55-73 (J. Pynoos, R. Schafter & C. Hartman eds. 1973)

Public policies related to the housing market, no matter what the goals or intent of those who draft them, frequently run head-on into entrenched, powerful local interests. Analysis of the structure of these interests, the power that they wield, and how that power shapes the local housing market goes far toward accounting for the failure of public policy to provide adequate housing for all.

. . . .

Our method of analysis may prove useful in gathering further information about this relationship in other cities. In brief, the method is as follows.

1. Examine recent trends in the city's development, such as migration of population and industry, and determine how the costs and benefits of this process are distributed.
2. Ascertain how property is held, who mans the institutions (such as savings banks) which determine investment in housing and urban development, and how these individuals are related to local government officials who make urban development policy.
3. Determine whether this set of relationships is stable and whether it exercises and consolidates control over development policies.
4. Examine how the benefits and costs of public and private policies are distributed.
5. Trace the successes or failures of opposition groups which seek to alter this distribution.

Trends in City Development

Cambridge is a mature industrial city of 100,000 adjacent to Boston. It contains a large but old manufacturing district, many ethnic blue-collar neighborhoods, and two large universities — M.I.T. and Harvard. The postwar boom set the scene for major alterations in Cambridge's economic structure.

. . . .

These trends — university growth and the shift from manufacturing to research and development — have had severe effects on Cambridge's poor and working-class ethnic population. Students and young professionals have steadily invaded ethnic neighborhoods, causing rents and land values to skyrocket. The poor and elderly, in turn, have been forced out.

According to one source, "The relocation department of the Cambridge Redevelopment Authority estimates that . . . some 500 persons and families are evicted every year in Cambridge by actions of private landlords in the process of assembling private development sites, raising rents, or converting structures into higher-income producing uses." This figure is of the same magnitude as the annual net population decrease (700) for the city.

Are these trends simply the result of freely operating economic forces? The answer, of course, is that behind all such forces stand institutions whose needs and interests create and shape them. For example, the 17 major defense contractors in Cambridge would hardly have located there were it not for M.I.T.'s presence. To discover the nature of these interests we will examine the concentration of property ownership and the relationship between owners and the political system. Keeping these relationships in mind we will then turn to their consequences.

The Nexus Between Property and Politics

Land tenure patterns, the obvious place to begin this analysis, are difficult to document. Since the federal government will not release individual tax returns and city governments do not require owners to divulge their aggregate property holdings (which owners often have reason to conceal), the evidence presented here is necessarily somewhat circumstantial.

One way of estimating inequality is by examining the makeup of the housing stock. In 1960, according to the U.S. Census, approximately 77.5 percent, or 26,500 of the city's housing units were tenant occupied. It is safe to assume that these tenants owned very few of the city's 34,000 units. Single-family and two-family owner-occupied structures contained a total of 5,600 units. Given the large number of university personnel, professionals, and other homeowners whose source of income is not the housing market, it is reasonable to estimate that the 5,600 households in these units owned at most 5,000 additional units. Thus 5,600 (or 16.5 percent) of the city's households owned roughly 10,600 units. The remaining 23,400 units (in large, nonowner-occupied structures) are owned by the remaining 6 percent of the city's households and an unknown but probably small number of outsiders. . . .

[At this point the authors use two different means to ascertain a measure of ownership concentration, one based on the landlord organization's data, the other on the findings of a Cambridge Tenants Union study. Both indicate substantial concentration with some 20 largest owners holding at least 13,600 and possibly as many as 18,000 or 20,000 units. — Eds.]

As imperfect as this information is, it is strong enough to show that a relatively small number of landowners own a very large proportion of Cambridge's housing stock. While this concentration does not correspond directly to the economist's concepts of monopoly or oligopoly, tacit or explicit combinations among landowners, banks, and politicians can give it the same extensive economic and political power. It is by exploring these interlocking networks that we begin to see the enormous implications land tenure patterns have for housing market performance and urban development.

In Cambridge, as we shall demonstrate, concentrated property ownership is at the heart of a political nexus that wields power vastly out of proportion to the number of Cambridge citizens it represents. The extent of this nexus is indicated in . . . Figure 4.2. The 9 savings banks which finance more than 75 percent of Cambridge housing acquisitions have a total of 237 directorships (including 19 direct and at least 25 indirect overlaps).

These directors include: key officers of M.I.T. and Harvard; 4 of the 9 city councilors (several of whom sit on more than one board); 2 of the 3 district court judges (who have jurisdiction over landlord-tenant relations); 2 superior court judges; the county clerk of court; many board members of such agencies as the Cambridge Housing Authority (CHA), Cambridge Redevelopment Authority (CRA), and the Planning Board; the city's tax collector; 2 of 3 city assessors; and at least 30 of the city's large rental property owners and developers. In addition, the savings bank boards contain 50 lawyers, insurance brokers, realtors, and contractors who derive their primary income by serving the housing market. The remainder represent various commercial, industrial, and financial interests. . . .

The government agencies involved in this nexus play crucial roles in shaping local policies bearing on the operation of the Cambridge housing market. The city council appoints the city manager, and together they set the tax rate. The manager, in turn, appoints the members of the governing boards of the other agencies and the city solicitor. . . .

The Board of Assessors (three men, all of whom are real estate owners and two of whom are bank directors) not only determines the value of real estate for property tax purposes but also has the power to grant tax abatements. It thus determines the relative incidence of taxation. The courts (including three bank directors and a real estate owner) act as a collection agency for landlords, determine whether city agencies are behaving lawfully, and secure landlord

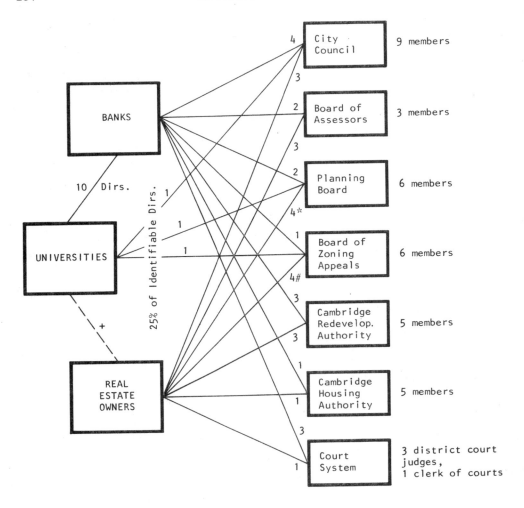

* Through three contractors and a lawyer.
+ Both universities are large landholders.
# Through four lawyers.

Figure 4.2 Cambridge real estate, banking, and political interlocks, 1970
(Redrawn from Mollenkopf and Pynoos)

property rights when necessary. Thus, the institutions which oversee the housing market and determine the relative incidence of taxation are dominated by those with banking and property interests.

. . . .

This three-cornered set of relationships — between politicians, bankers, and property owners and developers — is based on a solid coincidence of interest. Bankers and politicians get along well because, for the banker, the politician attracts depositors, provides important contacts, and ensures that no policies which are likely to hurt land values are adopted. For the politician, the banker represents a source of inside deals on development, a way of influencing mortgage decisions and thus a way of influencing constitutents, and a source of status. Hence there are many politicians on bank boards. Owners and bankers have an even closer identity of interest. Banks provide the crucial credit source for large-scale owners, and thus owners seek to become directors. For banks, large owners provide sound investments and additionally provide detailed information on land value trends. Finally, politicians and owners find mutual interest in the influence which owners can extend in behalf of candidates (money, votes of relatives, endorsements) and the favorable government decisions which politicians can render (both collective, such as against rent control, and individual, such as zoning changes and tax abatements).

In Cambridge such interests are meshed in a very old-fashioned way: personally, in key figures and the patronage-based machine government they have created. Although these same interests exist in other cities, they may not be integrated in the same fashion: bank boards, businessmen's committees, or even "good government" organizations based on a prodevelopment platform may serve this purpose instead.

It might be held that this is a desirable state of affairs — those most knowledgeable about real estate make city policy concerning it. Yet, as we shall see, the actions of this interlocking network have not been benign. One city councilor (who is a lawyer associated with a large developer, a director of two local banks, and who was for many years the city's mayor) defended his opposition to rent control by stating "the property owners are the city's backbone — we should be grateful to them." This attitude has been echoed repeatedly by other councilors in debates on rent control, urban renewal, and other housing-related matters.

How Power Is Maintained and Consolidated

. . . .

While the specific makeup of this coalition has changed slightly from time to time, each administration has had a consistent stance on basic property-related issues. Ethnic electoral organizations which have competed against each other for such offices as county sheriff, for example, joined together to vote against rent control in 1969 and joined once again in 1971 to prevent the removal of a rent control administrator who favored landlords. These property-oriented council elements also joined on important zoning decisions. The unity on these issues is so clear that such elements might be called the property-politics coalition.

Aside from the council's indirect control over appointments, it has two main property-related functions: setting the tax rate and approving or vetoing federal projects such as urban renewal. In both areas the property-politics coalition has struck a deal between the interests of large rental property owners and those of homeowners. It has also relied heavily on retaining support in ethnic working-class neighborhoods by granting personal favors and attention.

There seem to be two reasons why voters support these politicians. First, in advancing the interests of developers and rental property owners, the city government has been constrained to give some concessions to small property owners and homeowners. In exchange for support, the government, according to one study, employs assessment practices which give a tax break to owner-occupied residences. Thus tenants, a larger but politically less cohesive group than owners, bear the burden of the regressive property tax, which is passed on to them in the form of higher rents.

. . . .

The second major source of support for property-related politicians lies in the fact that most of them control rewards and sanctions within their neighborhoods. Those who sit on bank boards influence who gets mortgages; others owning small businesses have neighbors as clients and have extended them credit, or have political associates who are in this position. Through their partonage control over bureaucracies, they may grant or threaten to withhold scarce resources such as public housing. They can and do give their friends city jobs. Residents, if they know and support a city councilor in the property-politics faction, may have a large hospital bill forgiven or gain a place in public housing without undue worry about the waiting list. Tales of such happenings abound in city hall gossip. More important, political associates are appointed to boards where they have an excellent chance to do favors for friends in return for monetary and campaign support. In other words, by constraining policies so as to minimize antagonism with small property owners, exercising considerable influence over their neighborhoods, and offering rewards where necessary, the dominant property-politics faction is able to manage the electorate. The Cambridge Election Commission's recent refusal to enfranchise 18- to 20-year-old college students is but another example of this policy.

The Distribution of Economic Benefits

Concentration has the potential for squeezing surplus from the consumer while providing a shoddy product. The average citizen relies for protection on government regulation of concentration and economic performance. Because of interlocking interests among owners, bankers, and politicians, however, the Cambridge city government has failed to protect the interests of the majority of its citizens (the tenants in this case). It has promoted development of commercial facilities and luxury apartments. It has failed to enforce housing codes, build low-rent housing, or regulate rent increases.

. . . .

The benefits of public and private actions taken by the owner-banker-politician network seem rather clearly to accrue to the members of that network. The costs have been of several kinds and have been borne by housing consumers, especially by working-class and elderly tenants. These costs include direct monetary costs and uncompensated losses, such as loss of neighborhood. Concentration by itself probably leads to relatively higher prices and a relatively poorer housing stock, although we presently lack adequate time series and comparative data to demonstrate this relationship.

. . . .

The demand for housing has led to a "filtering up" of housing from less well-off working-class tenants to more well-to-do professionals and students. The role of the universities, whether they consciously plan it or not, is crucial in attracting new tenants from outside Cambridge who will bid up housing prices. In addition to increasing profits for landlords, this situation diminishes any incentive to improve the housing stock.

Rent increases for Cambridge housing have been spectacular. They have also been disastrous for low-income residents. Median rents, according to census figures, rose from 63 dollars per month in 1960 to 119 dollars in 1970. . . .

Furthermore, these increases were concentrated among the poor and elderly — those least able to bear them. Not only have they incurred the largest percentage increases (a possible statistical artifact of moderate increases on a low rent as compared to moderate increases on a luxury rent), but poorer tenants are (a) more likely to have received increases at all and (b) have received on the average a higher dollar amount.

One response to increased rents has been to move out of Cambridge. . . .

Another response to increased rents has been for tenants, especially low-income and elderly tenants, to pay an increased portion of their income for housing. . . .

A third response of low-income residents faced with rising rents is to overcrowd units. . . .

It might be argued that much of this increase would have occurred whether or not ownership is concentrated. Given a scarcity of land, the difficulty and price of new construction, and growing student demand, rents will inevitably skyrocket. Even if the city council so desired, this argument goes, it could do little one way or the other about the rent increases.

There are three problems with the claim that concentration is irrelevant, however. First, given a market-generated base, rates will vary additionally according to such factors as how effective well-organized owners are in pressing increases and how well-informed they are about the profitability of different uses and rent levels. Bigger owners tend to evaluate and act on these factors more effectively. Smaller landowners (particularly owner-occupants) are constrained by having relatives, friends, or long-term residents as tenants, and because housing investment is usually a long-term income supplement. Such tenants would greatly resent increases over and above rising costs.

Secondly, this argument ignores the way in which demand comes to pass. Large property owners are particularly sensitive to land value trends (exploiting them is their main source of income) and are in a unique credit position to capitalize on them. They thus push for policies and developments which will enhance values — something numerous small owners would not do.

Finally, this argument ignores the ability of a small number of large producers to "administer" the prices when they control the bulk of the supply. While consumer choice to consume less housing or to leave the area involves a small constraint, large owners still have great latitude in raising rents. Nor is this situation threatened by the entry of small, inefficient owners into the market. We must conclude, then, that the structure of ownership probably has a great deal to do with the way rents increase. Ownership structure has not only a direct impact but a very important indirect impact on rents through its influence on demand-generating public policy decisions.

. . . .

Attempts to Rectify Maldistribution of Benefits

Working-class, poor, and student tenants have responded to city policies on three fronts: agitation for low-rent housing construction, rent control, and opposition to specific developments. Students are part of the problem because they are both displacers of working-class residents and sufferers from it because of the high rents they must pay. This produces the potential organizing problem of overcoming student versus working-class antagonism. At some points the tenant movement has two components, one student and one long-time resident. At other times this tension has been masked by common efforts. In each instance, however, the city government has tried to coopt, obstruct, or defeat tenant efforts.

In order to protect themselves from being forced to move from Cambridge, community groups have attempted to pressure the city and the universities into sponsoring federally assisted low-to-moderate-rent housing. Except for a small amount of housing for the elderly, homeowners have opposed low-rent housing in their neighborhoods. Besides arguing that low-income housing poses a threat to property values, some individuals have used implicitly racist appeals to mobilize their neighborhoods. Second, because the poor lack technical resources, they must pressure other institutions to produce housing, and these institutions generally treat such pressure as an obnoxious distraction from their main goals. These institutions are the very same ones (banks, large landowners and developers, city officials, and the universities) which have exacerbated the housing crisis for their own benefit and whose long-term interests are best served by transforming Cambridge into a white professionals' community.

. . . .

The inability of working-class Cambridge residents to get low-rent housing built has led them to seek redress through ad hoc and formal regulation. These piecemeal attempts have usually taken the form of rent-withholding actions (rent paid into escrow account) or rent strikes (rent not paid). Massachusetts law provides for the former where there are serious housing code violations. With the assistance of OEO lawyers, a small number of tenants (on the order of 200) have succeeded in forcing their landlords to make repairs. Deficiencies in administering the law have, however, made the tenants' experience with rent-withholding less than satisfying. When landlords indicate to the court that repairs are under way, judges frequently release escrow funds. Tenants thus find it difficult to retain their bargaining power. The biased laws and the property-oriented judges are key elements in weakening tenant attempts to enforce minimum housing standards.

. . . .

The failure of ad hoc efforts to resist rent increases and low-rent housing depletion has led to appeals for rent control. While the same cry has been raised in other cities, Cambridge is one of the few cities where rent control legislation has been recently passed. Its promulgation has been a superficial concession by the dominant property-politics coalition; its history demonstrates this coalition's resilience and strength.

. . . .

This victory, however, proved to be illusory. The dominant faction, through their city manager, at first appointed the city solicitor temporary administrator, and then appointed a lawyer with landlord ties as permanent administrator of rent control. The solicitor unilaterally "exempted" many large landowners from the law, and the permanent administrator promulgated definitions of "fair return" which converted the law into a device for rationalizing and in some cases *increasing* rates of return to landlords.

. . . .

The third area of popular attempts to influence the housing power structure concerns development trends. Property interests (including the universities) have directed this policy through their influence on bodies such as the CRA, Zoning Appeals Board, and city council, and through their own activities. Community efforts to influence development have as a result manifested themselves as more or less backward-looking attempts to halt official projects because of the difficulty of proposing a socially progressive alternative plan.

. . . .

Conclusion

It is clear on the basis of this evidence that the city government has, at the behest of property interests, successfully opposed all political action aimed at altering power relationships within the housing market. The city government has failed to use its influence to construct low-rent housing. The legal machinery has been used to attack tenant unions and rent strikers. The city council has turned rent control inside out so that tenants now feel compelled to attack the law. The bodies officially concerned with directing urban development have failed to take steps to assist Cambridge's working-class, poor, and student tenants who are by far its majority of citizens.

These actions have taken place during a period of rapid increase in land values, rents, and real estate profits. It has been a period of steady transformation. The city's government and universities have chosen to do little about the social costs of this transformation. Instead, they have responded to the loss of manufacturing plants by searching for alternative contributors to the tax base — such as office buildings, luxury housing, and highly technical light industry. A very small number of individuals have profited from these changes. As we have seen, the bulk of land ownership is in a few hands; these same people dominate the city's lending institutions and are closely associated with those who man planning-related agencies. Those who have paid the costs are the elderly pensioners, working-class families forced to locate elsewhere, and students paying exorbitant rents.

In this process local government and federal programs have played a crucial role. Local government actions can be explained by analyzing the network of shared interests among owners, bankers, and politicians, and matching these interests against the differential impact of official policies. Any program aimed at "community control" of housing or a "decent home and a suitable living environment" must address itself to these structural relationships. Unless these relationships are broken down, any new housing policies are destined to provide simply another means of entrenching and enriching those who are already in control.

Comments: 1. Mollenkopf and Pynoos have documented for one older city the close interconnection between local government and politics on one hand, and, on the other hand, powerful institutions and individuals on the supply side of the housing economy. Gottdiener has built a similar case for a developing suburban area. Though these are but two isolated cases, considerable evidence suggests that they are representative. Because local government plays the central role with respect to the public interest dimensions of housing, it is subject to powerful interests. This local interweaving of housing and politics shows signs of intensifying with the passage of time.

2. Local governments and their politics impinge in another way on housing. These governments typically provide the urban services that comprise an integral part of the housing bundle. As noted by Smith in the first reading in Chapter 1, such services typically include police and fire protection, parks and recreation, schools, and utilities. Because of this it is possible to say that local government actually constitutes a part of the heterogeneous, but indivisible, housing bundle. This fact needs special emphasis. A consumer's choice of housing is a choice as well of a package of public services and the governments that provide them. This fact was recognized some years ago by the late Charles Tiebout, an urban economist. He formulated a theory of residential location based on such service choices. Empirical evidence has tended to argue against Tiebout's theory (see the Gans reading supra p. 148), but certainly the public services offered by local government count for a lot in a household's housing status.

3. This is the place for a brief parenthetical comment on local public housing authorities. Mollenkopf and Pynoos mention the Cambridge Housing Authority. It represents the type of local agency that manages federally subsidized low-rent public housing. Such governmental units were established in response to the U.S. Housing Act of 1937 and subsequent acts dealing with public housing. Typically each such agency, called a Local Housing Authority or LPA in federal jargon, is governed by a local citizen commission appointed by the mayor or council and managed by a professional staff. In size LHAs range from single employee units that operate a few dozen units to the New York City Authority that employs thousands to develop and manage some 180,000 apartments. The original legislation viewed the independent citizen commission organization as a way of keeping public housing outside of politics. Perhaps so, but it also has the effect of making LHAs unresponsive to their client publics and developing a caretaker mentality among commission members. Planners Chester Hartman and Gregg Carr studied the attitudes of LHA board members. They found that the great majority of commissioners were "white male, in the middle or upper-middle income ranges, well

educated, in either business or a profession, middle-aged or elderly." This profile could not be more socially distant from that of public housing tenants most of whom are non-white and female. By law all are low-income, most have relatively little education, and most are either unemployed or hold low status jobs. LHA commissioners tend to take a very *status quo,* non-entrepreneurial view of their agency's role. To the question "how much public housing would you like to have in your community?" most answered Hartman and Carr that "the present number of units is about right." The commissioners felt little pressure to develop more although many LHAs had long waiting lists for units. In recent years the picture has changed somewhat. The federal government has actively pressed for representation of tenants on commissions. In a few cities tenant management has been tried and works well. However, concurrently the changes in federal housing policy under the 1974 Act have further eroded the entrepreneurial spirit among the local housing authorities and offered little but occasional rehabilitation funds for tenant managers to entrepreneur with.

4. The end of the Mollenkopf and Pynoos article deals with efforts of citizen groups to redress through politics the imbalance in effects and outputs of local housing policy. In recent years grassroots political mobilization around housing issues has become one of the characteristics of inner city politics. The next reading provides a powerful case study of such grassroots politics in which local housing problems function as effective issues for political agitation.

BOIS D'ARC PATRIOTS, ORGANIZING IN DALLAS, IN GREEN MOUNTAIN QUARTERLY, No. 5, at 9, 13-16, 19-20, 81-84 (Feb. 1977)

The Bois d'Arc Patriots were founded in late 1972 in Deep East Dallas, as a response to rapidly deteriorating living conditions. The neighborhood is primarily a low-income inner-city community and most of the residents are White and Chicano. The majority of people, approximately 80%, are tenants, and the majority of owners are absentee slumlords. As the neighborhood is located close to downtown, Dallas City Hall has begun making plans to replace its residents, via various redevelopment schemes, with upper income residents, who would provide a stronger tax and political base for the downtown establishment.

. . . .

Organizing

The Patriots began organizing upon an understanding of two basic principles: 1) the cause of "political backwardness" ascribed to low income Whites by everyone from political hacks to movement leaders had been incorrectly analyzed, generally. No ingrained reactionary philosophy dominated the political or social views of low income Whites. Poor people who live in a system where property worth defines human worth tend to see themselves as worthless. Then, when they are ignored and even blamed for various social ills, the doors that get slammed in their faces make a very provocative noise. As a result, people tend to lack confidence in themselves and, in addition, tend to lack hope that they can do anything themselves to bring their circumstances under control. One of the results is cynical, reactionary political and social views. One of the best cures is meaningful involvement in political self-determination on a neighborhood basis. Politics, as defined by the Patriots is "the process of people organizing on the basis of common needs." 2) The great majority of needs of the people in East Dallas were then and are still, in immediate proportions. It is impossible to gear people up for tomorrow when they are unsure of whether they will get through today. The Patriots knew that in order to provide a foundation for on-going organizing, they would have to get a handle on meeting immediate needs of people in the community. Then, once this had been accomplished, people would have the slack to dig into root problems. Politically speaking, organizing around immediate needs (which in many instances were extreme and involved confrontation and violence) would be a way of demonstrating to people in a concrete way that people are the priority. The process itself was inevitably a people first exercise. Low income people could establish the people priority only by pulling together, only by collectively struggling to project themselves and the needs shared by others of their class.

. . . .

On the Streets

In early 1973 the Patriots implemented their first program: Free Pest Extermination. The neighborhood was infested with roaches and rats due to the degree of absentee ownership.

The program was designed not only to help meet an immediate need, but to demonstrate the Patriots' practical problem-solving commitment and to do so right in people's homes. Once the doors opened, contact was instantly established and communication and participation could and did follow. Residents were asked, 1) "What is the biggest problem in the community," and 2) "Would you join in to help solve it?" The answer to the first question was: "Something has got to be done about these slum landlords — they're killing us." The answer to the second question was an overwhelming "yes."

The Patriots had a core of four people then, and all worked, full or part time, at workaday jobs, ranging from construction and warehouse work to temporary labor. Core Patriots pooled resources to offset living expenses, cost of pest control chemicals, etc.

By the time a hundred or more units had been exterminated, the Patriots had enough support to start their next program: the East Dallas Tenants' Alliance.

Slumlords, historically, have never been receptive to the concept of tenants' (or homeowners') rights in the community where they have investments. Texas statutes and case law provide so few rights for residential tenants that slumlords did not even bother to familiarize themselves with the law. Basically, they did not have to: it was whatever they wanted it to be, if not in the way it was written, then in the way it was enforced.

Evictions were the critical problem. State law requires that no one can be evicted without the landlord filing an eviction suit. However, on the landlord's signature an "immediate possession bond" went into effect, and this bond could legally remove a tenant from the premises before a court date. Appeals were prohibitive, averaging around $1000 cash to file. (Eventually two lawsuits filed by the Alliance have succeeded in changing these laws to a more suitable form.)

More often than not, however, the law, such as it was, never entered into the eviction process. Landlords regularly intimidated tenants into moving immediately. Many times they used goons, and simply threw the tenants' belongings into the street, stole the tenants' possessions, removed the doors, cut the utilities, or physically intimidated the tenants.

Causes of eviction usually fell into two categories: 1) the tenant had no money; or 2) the tenant refused to pay until the landlord made good on a promise to repair. In the first type of case, the landlord was often lenient for a while, figuring to get the money (or other compensation) at a later time. In the second category, landlords showed no leniency. (Texas has no "warranty of habitability" law as do over 30 states.)

The Patriots understood that the first priority was to stop slumlords from abusing tenants' legal rights. Once landlords began, in practice, to acknowledge legal rights of tenants, the issues of tenant organizing could be directed to expanding those rights. Until that time, day to day survival was the priority.

Intimidation would have to be met with intimidation. Once landlords saw that the use of muscle could be effectively countered in such a way as to cause chaos for them, they would begin to withdraw to the plane where the law offered better protection.

Although this stage took over a year and a half, the incident that marked the turning point occurred in late spring of 1973. Two tenants had called Patriot co-ordinator Charlie Young at work (in a warehouse) and asked him to come by after hours to explain to their landlord that he would not be allowed to evict them by removing the door of their apartment. When Charlie arrived, the landlord grabbed a 12-gauge shotgun and declared "I'll show you what the law is." He fired, winging Charlie in the left arm. (Later, he would maintain that Charlie had not been shot, because "he didn't run." In fact, after promising the tenants he would be back, before going to the hospital, Charlie got a pistol himself and came back, but the landlord had run.) Tenants who witnessed the scene called the police who, after hearing the story, threatened to give the landlord a ticket for discharging a weapon in the city limits — but did not.

Subsequently, the landlord agreed to give the tenants proper notice, find them a new place, pay the first week's rent, plus move them himself. The Patriots knew it would be futile to take such a case to the D.A., as he would probably welcome the opportunity to turn the tables on these uppity tenants. So a suit for damages was filed in small claims court, which had an informal format. The Patriots decided to make the suit into a political case.

. . . .

The Patriots' strategy was 1) to have a jury trial (in Texas j.p. courts the jury is empowered to interpret the law *without* the judge's instruction); 2) to get all the witnesses on and get the story told in context; and 3) to anger the landlord so the jury could get a good look at a slumlord in form. Charlie was to be his own counsel.

The trial lasted five and a half hours. By the time it was over the judge had virtually thrown up his hands and the jury had been politicized. The landlord stated that the Patriots, in the eyes of East Dallas landlords, were "troublemakers", "rabblerousers" and "subversives". Charlie told the jury that if they ruled in the landlord's favor, then the tenant community would take the landlord's statement ("I'll show you what the law is") as a mandate. Charlie informed the jury that if this was the case, he would not spend any money on further legal action, but would buy a shotgun, as this would be the proper avenue of appeal. The jury, in less than 15 minutes, returned a unanimous verdict against the landlord, and the word spread rapidly among slumlords.

Groups of tenants regularly began to band together to repel slumlord goon tactics and tenant consciousness began to develop spontaneously. Before it was over, however, one East Dallas landlord had been killed and several others had gone to the hospital. In the case where the landlord was killed (stabbed through the heart with a butcher knife), the tenant, on the basis of testimony by neighboring tenants and homeowners, was no-billed: "Self-defense."

It was during the "fight fire with fire" stage of the tenant struggle in East Dallas that the news media began to get interested. Newspapers, TV news and special programming, radio news and talk shows — all jumped onto the bandwagon. (The fact that 52% of the residents of Dallas are tenants guaranteed tenants' rights as a popular cause.) It seemed that after the ice was broken, there was something in the media daily concerning the East Dallas Tenants' Alliance. This lasted for about six months.

The Patriots utilized this new avenue of awareness to focus public attention on several critical aspects of the growing tenants' struggle. 1) Tenants were now the majority in Dallas, and as such constituted a force to be reckoned with; 2) Concepts of neighborhood stability now had to take tenants into account; 3) Absentee and slum landlords were the enemy of every decent citizen; and 4) Warranty of Habitability with rent withholding provisions was needed, now. [Warranty of Habitability refers to a modification of the traditional common law holding that a rent or lease agreement implies no warranty by the landlord as to the habitability of the dwelling in question. — Eds.]

The media were very responsive. Landlords (even those who projected themselves as being responsible) and government officials were not. This only heightened tenant consciousness. With Patriots focusing now on substantive issues of law, middle-income tenants began to join the struggle. . . .

Once the issues of tenants' rights became focused on reform rather than survival in the face of intimidation, the Patriots calculated that the middle income community would begin to dominate the struggle. This had to be dealt with carefully, because of the middle income community's tendency to transform such issues into an anti-poor people brand of consumerism.

The Patriots knew that they needed middle class support, as this is where the biggest reservoir of political and economic power is located, at least as it concerns those who dominate the rental housing industry. And East Dallas, as well as other inner city communities, desperately needs a warranty of habitability law for purposes of organizing a meaningful, ongoing offensive against slumlords and those who follow, viz., developers.

After the Patriots had forced the warranty of habitability issue on the City Council in mid 1975, and after the Council had made sympathetic noises, held hearings and then dropped the matter in the face of opposition by the housing industry, the media coverage peaked and began to decline.

At this point the struggle was so time consuming, both in terms of organizing and litigation (mainly through the Dallas Legal Services Foundation), it was clear that a new strategy was needed. Many middle-income tenants were willing to get involved, but had hesitations and fears about doing so from the East Dallas vantage point. They needed a structure of their own. Here, Patriot administrative co-ordinator, Lisbeth Stewart, conceived a new, city-wide organization, the Dallas Tenants' Union. The DTU was to address itself to substantive housing issues, be separate from the Patriots and East Dallas Tenants' Alliance, and develop the tenant struggle, city wide, from a case by case consciousness-raising effort, into a movement.

The DTU was founded in January, 1976. Since that time, it has become self-supporting, through donations, and has proceeded to organize tenants in mass. Though it is still illegal, formally, to withhold rent in Texas, the DTU experience has shown that if enough people get together, they can do anything they want. The landlord is not so concerned about the law as he is his pocketbook. This struggle reached fruition in the summer of 1976, when DTU organized 31 groups of tenants, negotiated out 25 cases of organized tenant groups and led 6 rent strikes, all of which were won. The tenants' movement in Dallas is rapidly growing to steamroller proportions, and by the end of the summer, members of the housing industry, who largely determine the industry's statewide directions, asked to set up peace talks with DTU. They understood, now, they said, the need for warranty of habitability. Dallas Tenants' Union organizers fees assured that there will be such a law in Texas in the near future.

The Bois D'Arc Patriots Analysis of Class Relations Among Neighborhood and Out-of-Neighborhood Elements

[The following section reprints the publicly articulated political analysis used by the Patriots in their organizing activities. — Eds.]

I. Tenants, Small Homeowners and Resident Landlords

Most all residents — small homeowners, resident landlords, and tenants — of older neighborhoods are more interested in seeing their neighborhood fixed up rather than run, torn or burned down. This is especially true in low/middle income working class neighborhoods.

A. Tenants in neighborhoods such as ours have a daily struggle with housing which is run down, because it causes them inconvenience and many times hazardous living conditions. Also, because it is hard for most people to move, and most tenants feel it is not right for them to have to move because of a landlord's irresponsibility.

B. Homeowners, many of whom are retired and living on fixed incomes, also have no place to go. And if they wanted to move, they couldn't sell their property for enough money to move because slumlords have run property values down so low. Also, many homeowners have lived in this neighborhood for many years and have roots here. However, many homeowners hesitate to spend what little money they have on repairs because they're afraid the city or developers will come in and take their property away from them, and pay them only what the land is worth. Some of the homeowners see that the neighborhood has changed — has gotten "rougher" — and they sometimes blame tenants instead of landlords for running the neighborhood down.

C. Resident Landlords, that is, landlords who *live in* the neighborhood and don't own much property, suffer when an area runs down as they oftentimes have the same kind of roots as homeowners, and like the homeowners don't have and can't get the money to maintain or repair their property. Usually they don't like absentee slumlords and blame them for running the neighborhood down. Oftentimes, they blame tenants, too. They suffer, as do homeowners, or would-be homeowners, from redlining. Redlining is where banks decide an area is run down and can't be saved — or is too risky to try and save — and as a result, the banks refuse to lend money in the area. As a result, the small resident landlords may own property which is "slum" property, not because they want to, but because they are "the little guy" and have no choice. Many of these people would fix up their property if they had the chance.

II. Slum Landlords

These are the landlords who buy up property in older neighborhoods, for the purpose of draining it of rent, and not putting their money back into the property for repairs or maintenance. They are strictly interested in a fast buck, in easy money. Most of them live in other areas of town, or even outside Dallas. Many of them are a little crazy; they have come to enjoy watching people suffer, as this is how they make their money.

They figure on running property values down, so they can buy more. Then when the neighborhood has been run down, so far that it *can't* be repaired, they know the real estate companies and developers will come in to "re-develop" the neighborhood and build new housing, mainly for the rich people. Then the property values will go up again. Slumlords who have blocked up enough property, once values start to go up, will be able to almost ask their own price and they will make lots of easy money again. Slumlords are more interested in the lots their housing sits on than the housing itself, because it is the lots that the developers want to build on. Many times a slumlord will burn his property as it runs down to collect insurance — then he has the lot, plus insurance money. The Dallas Fire Department estimates that one out of every five fires is set for insurance money.

III. Developers

The developers count on slumlords to do mainly two things: (1) to run property values down and (2) to clear the land by tearing or burning down housing. This makes an area a better bargain for them to buy into for the purpose of building new housing. *Under our present economic system, it is not profitable for developers to build housing for low income people. They make their highest profits by building and selling expensive housing to the rich.*

IV. City Hall

The city government is controlled by the wealthy people — developers, realtors, landlords, bankers. Because of this, they will act in ways which will benefit the rich.

In the Spring of 1975, the city manager, George Schrader, proposed a plan, passed by the City Council, where the City would "subsidize" the risks of developers building in the inner city. Under this plan, the city will pay developers up to $2.25 per square foot for inner city land the developers buy — if the developers decide, after a period of five years, that they don't want to build on it. Much land in East Dallas now sells for $1.00 per square foot.

At the same time, the City refused to make low interest, long term loans available to low income residents for the purpose of repair or home purchase. They refused to do this, even though the Federal Government is giving the city $73 million over the next six years in Community Development funds — which by law are *supposed* to be used to benefit people of "low and moderate incomes."

The only money the city is making available is for upper income homeowners with good credit.

The city has drawn up a land-use plan. This is a zoning plan, which will force upper income people — especially upper income tenants and town house owners — into the inner city. This will *guarantee* developers a market in East Dallas for upper income housing — and will help *force* low income people out.

The City is worried that too many low income people are living in the city of Dallas, so they want to force us out. One reason for this is because we can't pay high enough taxes to support their bureaucracy. Another reason is that if enough people get together, we will start to vote poor people into office and the rich people would sooner die than see this. The city government will fight tooth and nail to protect slumlords, because slumlords are paving the way for the big developers. This is why so many City Council members oppose a Warranty of Habitability. Not just because they don't like tenants — but because they don't like poor people — tenants, homeowners and resident landlords.

V. Banks

Banks are part of the power structure: they hold and control much of the money supply. Redlining exists because bankers don't want to spend money to help poor people stabilize their neighborhoods; banks want to see developers come in and re-develop older neighborhoods so that rich people can move in.

Many local banks, however, get much of their money from East Dallas residents, but yet refuse to spend it to help East Dallas residents. One way of fighting this is called "greenlining." Greenlining is where residents band together and threaten to withdraw their money from a bank unless it starts investing in the neighborhood. Neighborhood organizations in Chicago, Indianapolis, and Boston have used greenlining with a good deal of success.

Comment: This short account of grassroots organizing shows analytical thinking about housing at a simple, paradigmatic and practical level. The struggle of the Bois d'Arc Patriots to mobilize the tenants in East Dallas, and as a spinoff to mobilize a city-wide coalition strong enough to change local housing law, depended upon clear analysis. The main concept they used is a version of the housing class idea introduced in Chapter 4 of this text (supra p.146). Additional discussion of landlord-tenant problems can be found in Chapter 12.

This down-to-earth example provides an indication of the importance of systematic thinking in dealing with housing problems. It provides an appropriate conclusion to the first half of these collected readings and comments. Equally well it serves as a transition to the remainder of the book which is devoted to a series of critical contemporary housing problems.

BIBLIOGRAPHY

C. Abrams, The City in the Frontier (1965)
  A politically savvy account of housing and urban renewal policy.

M. Derthick, New Towns In-town: Why a Federal Program Failed (1972)
  Study of successful local resistance to an aggressive program initiative by President Johnson.

L. Friedman, Government and Slum Housing (1968)
  A superb history of housing policy, full of flashing insights, the work of a legal historian.

A. Jackson, A Place Called Home: A History of Low-Cost Housing in Manhattan (1976)
  Precisely what the title says with plenty of supporting political detail and interpretation.

C. Hartman, Housing and Social Policy (1975)
  A slim volume that proves good things come in small packages. Hartman has a keen critical insight and a worthy set of motives with which to examine housing politics and policy.

J. Pressman, Federal Programs and City Politics (1975)
  Just as the title indicates, this book discusses the ways in which local politics and priorities interface with federal programs.

J. Pynoos, R. Schafer & C. Hartman (eds.), Housing Urban America (1973)
  The first section of this edited collection concentrates on housing politics. It contains the complete text of the Mollenkopf and Pynoos article excerpted in this Chapter.

U.S. National Commission on Urban Problems, Building the American City (1969)
  Commonly known as the Douglas Commission Report after its chairman it shares honors with the President's Committee on Urban Housing report excerpted in Chapter 3 as the official 1960s era housing policy document.

J. Wolman, Politics of Federal Housing (1971)
  How federal housing policy is developed and who influences it during idea formation, legislation, appropriation, and administrative regulation making. Draws heavily on the law establishing the U.S. Department of Housing and Urban Development.

PART II

INTRODUCTORY NOTE: GOALS AND OBJECTIVES IN HOUSING PROGRAMS

American housing programs and policies are in a state of transition. Historically, the federal government initiated extensive public efforts to increase housing production and eleminate slums and blight. These efforts were considered the appropriate response to the set of housing problems that kept us from achieving the goal stated in the national Housing Act of 1949: "a decent home and a suitable living environment for every American family."

This historic orientation has increasingly been questioned. Substantial improvement in the quality of the housing stock and new perceptions of the federal government's role in housing have led to major changes in the structure of housing programs. Equally important, changes in the demand for housing and the impact of housing inflation on housing costs have altered the economic and political climate in which housing policy must be considered. These changes in the character of the housing problem will have profound effects on housing programs in the decades that follow.

Changes have also occurred at the local level. Historically, local governments played a rather passive role through regulatory controls enacted to maintain housing safety and quality. In recent years, two broad trends have emerged. Local governments have intervened more directly at the neighborhood level. Perhaps more significantly, local regulatory controls over housing have been scrutinized for their equity and distributional effects.

The nature of these changes and their impact on housing policy is indicated in the article that follows. The authors also highlight a series of problem areas in the housing sector which will be examined in more detail in the chapters in this Part.

MONTGOMERY & GELLEN, EMERGING ISSUES IN AMERICAN HOUSING POLICY, FROM A DECENT HOME AND ENVIRONMENT 157-79 (D. Phares ed. 1977)

Forces Affecting Housing Policy

In some sense every era is an age of transition. This is especially so in public policy because of the long lags that separate the appearance of new social forces and economic trends from their emergence as issues of policy. We are in the midst today of a transition between old policies shaped by past conditions and a new set of housing policies arising out of current forces in U.S. society. . . . The shape of the transition is somewhat clear, and what follows examines some of its demensions.

The Politics of Housing

In American academic circles housing policy typically denotes a style of rational, microeconomic analysis of alternative courses of government action. This tendency should not obscure the fact that in most areas of public policy, ideology and interest politics often have a far greater impact on specific policy moves. Legislators holding critical positions in the distribution of power, the bureaucracy, and the regulatory agencies have become more or less the captives of the giant corporate suppliers. Housing, in this regard, offers a somewhat curious picture because the key lobbies do not represent highly concentrated industries. Rather, the fragmentation among housing suppliers supports a continuous debate over policy directions which in other sectors have already largely been determined. Housing policy often gives the appearance of an ongoing social dialogue. For example, production policy assumes a continuing contest between those who favor an active role for government in setting targets, rationalizing supply factors (especially money), and using broad subsidies to bring the product within reach of mass demand, and those on the other side who favor a hands-off, minimum public intervention stance. The first group seeks to achieve high levels of production and believes the trickle-down and multiplier effects will take care of equity. The latter wants the best possible approximation of the classical marketplace; they tend to accept as inevitable certain market failures and seek to aid the unfortunate victims through a direct income strategy. . . .

Our two major political parties tend to reflect these positions. The Democrats generally advocate an activist role for government, while the Republicans seek to minimize regulation and omit direct financial aid. As the two parties alternate control of the presidency, the thrust of national housing policy fluctuates accordingly. Johnson's Great Society program set staggeringly high production targets and enacted a broad set of supply-side subsidies in order to attain them. The program was a brief success after a lag of several years. Ironically, success came only toward the end of Nixon's first term and lasted into the first year of his second term. That year marked a traumatic policy shift as Nixon extinguished overnight all the Great Society production subsidy programs in the "moratorium" of January 1973. Thereafter, the Republicans experimented with income supplements. In a small way, the Housing Act of 1974 contains the first steps toward this market approach to housing demand subsidies. Recent scholarly analyses have supported this shift in the orientation of national housing policy. Academics have argued that welfare economics generally confirms the demand-subsidy perspective and raises serious questions about the spillovers and unanticipated effects of the Keynesian Great Society production strategies.

In the next decade, however, housing policy will face a quite different range of difficulties. Primary among these are changes in the demographic structure of demand and housing price inflation. . . . In general, if inflation and this unique decade of housing-demand problems absorb the attention of policy-makers, we shall in all likelihood see the emergence of much broader ranging policies targeted at a much larger number of American households.

Demographic Changes Affecting Demand

. . . .

[The article reviews the material covered in more detail in Alonso, supra p. Chief among the demographic factors are the one-time-only population bulge caused by the post-World War II baby boom and the astonishing increase in the relative rate of household formation. — Eds.]

The Impact of Housing Inflation

The era of the suburban housing bargain has passed. Gone is the decent, affordable, single-family, detached, suburban villa for the stably employed working and middle class. Beginning in the middle 1960s, housing prices relative to income began a steady rise. Nothing suggests that this trend has yet run its course. In fact, prices can be expected to continue to rise faster than income. . . .

This price escalation has many sources. Direct construction costs have increased somewhat faster than the consumer price index since 1968, partly because of the rising cost of lumber and oil. Financing costs have escalated because of higher interest rates. Maintenance, energy, and other utility prices, as well as property taxes, have all climbed sharply as well. Of all the cost factors, however, land has exhibited the most meteoric rise. The most recent Federal Housing Administration (FHA) data show that land prices doubled between 1969 and 1972, a period when the consumer price index increased by about 25 percent.

While the mid-1970s slowdown in construction may have tempered the inflation of housing cost, three convergent institutional forces have pushed hard on urban-fringe land prices: First, for almost fifty years officials in suburban communities have been forcing developers to internalize in the sale price some of the social costs of urbanization such as streets, utilities, parks, schools, etc. The recent fiscal problems of cities is lending added momentum to this trend. Municipal cost-revenue studies have shown that many of the conventional forms of residential development aggravate the fiscal crisis. Local governments have used such studies to coerce developers into absorbing even more infrastructure costs, especially school construction. Second, the environmental movement in its desperate quest for amenity rights has succeeded in halting development in many suburban communities, notably in Florida and California. This trend also shows no sign of abating. The third of these convergent pressures — exclusionary zoning — may, however, weaken substantially as a result of legal action by civil-rights groups and developers and requirements for community development funding set by Congress. Yet even if suburban zoning barriers are lowered, increases in permitted development densities will not necessarily result in lower land prices; rising demand and tightness in the land market would probably keep land prices up and shift to landowners much of the productivity benefits of increased density.

The Demand-Price Crunch

Taken together, these broad currents on the supply and demand sides of the American housing market promise to trap middle-class consumers and the industry in a terrific crunch. With potential demand at unprecedented high levels, income rising only modestly, additions to supply constrained and costly, these ripple effects will intensify inflationary pressures, reduce vacancy rates to minimal levels, contribute to instability in financial markets, and lead to new low dwelling production rates. Barring improbable changes in exogenous factors such as startling increases in productivity or GNP and thereby real income, millions of people, particularly the old and the young, will experience great difficulty in obtaining housing. Either they will be forced to pay a burdensome price or to cut back in their expectations. These people will not be poor in terms of their access to other consumer goods. Rather, they will be in the mainstream of society and thus quite different from ghetto residents whose unfulfilled demand represented such a serious social problem in the 1950s and 1960s. These newcomers to the ranks of the housing-deprived will better fit the mold of the "submerged middle class" of the Great Depression and the immediate post World War II period.

Over the next decade, the problem of ensuring adequate housing for middle-income Americans suffering from the demand-price crunch will loom as the central issue of U.S. housing policy. The government will undoubtedly attempt to subsidize demand and production, reduce housing costs through regulation, or some combination of these. Unfortunately, years of effort at cost reduction have offered little promise. The Kaiser Committee study of production efficiency in housing concluded that, at most, monthly costs of a single family house could be reduced by 12 percent through a variety of reforms, including the introduction of more efficient methods and technology. However, the authors added the reservation that for each 1 percent increase in interest rates, monthly costs would go up by 5.3 percent; so that if interest rates rose from 6 to 9 percent (as they have since 1968), most of the cost savings due to these efficiency measures would be eaten up by higher financing charges.

Inflation in combination with the demand factors mentioned earlier will, however, lead U.S. housing policy in three directions. First, both financial institutions and the government will attempt to restructure the mortgage contract and to alter the institutional arrangements in mortgage markets. Second, consumers and government will adopt a more positive attitude toward the existing housing stock as the demand-price crunch continues; for as the reproduction cost of housing increases, the stock of existing dwellings will become a more highly valued resource. Finally, at the local level, the mismatch between demand and supply promises to release strong drives for broader regulatory power such as rent control and institutional changes in landlord-tenant relations.

The Elements of Housing Policy

The four most important variables in our national housing policy are the demand for housing, the supply of housing (in terms of both services and stock), the supply of credit (purchasing power), and taxation. The first two are largely exogenous variables. The U.S. government does not produce much housing nor does it directly generate much demand aside from the military. It does, however, regulate money and collect taxes, and these have been the key variables for national housing policy ever since the 1930s. Through monetary policy, credit regulation, and tax deductions the federal government attempts to manage aggregate housing demand and supply. It is unlikely that this general framework of policy will change in the near future.

Housing Finance

The supply-demand problem in housing credit policy has traditionally been viewed as a problem of stabilization, that is, managing interest rates and expansion of the money supply so as to provide adequate finance for housing purchase and construction. Since 1966 the federal government has relied on restrictive monetary policies to reduce the rate of inflation in the economy as a whole. This approach to controlling inflation has destabilized the housing sector. Housing has borne the brunt of anti-inflation policies not simply because credit plays such a large role in housing purchase and construction, but also because the bulk of funds used to finance housing have come from short-term, highly liquid deposits of savings associations and banks. During periods of monetary restraint, upward swings in short-term rates interact with interest-rate ceilings (Regulation Q) to induce depositors to withdraw savings deposits for the purpose of investing directly in treasury notes, treasury bills, commercial paper, etc. Twice in the past seven years these wild fluctuations in the supply of credit have forced mortgage-lenders to ration credit, thereby reducing both the level of housing purchases and construction starts.

At the same time, lenders tied into fixed interest rates and expecting the purchasing power of their money to decline in the future because of inflation have added sizable inflation premiums to the interest rates they attach to new mortgages. These premiums interact with the rising sale price of both new and existing houses to generate extraordinarily large increases in monthly mortgage payments. This practice has produced distortions in the payment stream of the traditional fixed-level payment, fully amortizing mortgage. Inflation premiums tilt the time profile of monthly payments expressed in constant dollars upward in the early years and downward in the later years. Borrowers are thus forced to make considerably higher monthly payments in relation to income in the early years of the mortgage. The most severe impact falls first on owners, particularly young families who because of their growing numbers in the adult population constitute a growing proportion of today's mortgage demand. Unable to meet high monthly costs, these borrowers have reduced their demand for housing in terms of quantity and quality or have simply foregone purchase until they accumulate enough savings to cover a larger down payment and thereby achieve a lower monthly payment. Both consumers and lenders believe some type of structural reform of the mortgage credit system is necessary in order to ensure an adequate supply of credit at suitable prices and to stabilize the supply of and the demand for housing at a level commensurate with the current rate of household formation.

One avenue of reform lies in the direction of altering the structure and regulatory environment of financial markets themselves. . . .

Taxation Subsidies

Despite criticism that reformers have directed at "loopholes" in the federal income tax system during the past few years, the tax expenditure approach to subsidizing housing will probably endure and perhaps be expanded in several directions. . . .

The future will probably bring expanded income tax benefits for homeowners. . . . Proposed deductions will cover rehabilitation, improvements contributing to energy conservation, and special tax credits for first homeowners. State governments have themselves been moving in this direction through programs of property tax relief for the elderly and tax abatement for rehabilitation. . . . Today all fifty states have established some form of relief, and twenty-six provide special abatement programs.

Generally speaking, property tax subsidy and relief schemes are designed to aid the middle class more than lower-income groups. In addition, the strong emphasis by state governments on relief for homeowners means that only a small proportion of these subsidies will find their way to renters. The use of the property tax system for subsidizing homeowner operating costs and rehabilitation will increase significantly over the next five or six years. Many states, especially in the Midwest, Far West, and South, periodically accumulate large surpluses in their treasuries, much of which can be used to finance tax relief. Because state governments cannot run deficits without engendering a legal and political crisis, this type of subsidy approach has distinct and relatively fixed limits as an escape valve for the high pressure of inflation unless property tax relief is federally financed.

Neighborhood Preservation

The contradiction between strong demand among middle-income households and the spiraling inflation that afflicts new construction has turned popular attention to preserving the existing stock of housing. Ever since the Eisenhower administration began to aim some of its housing efforts in that direction some twenty years ago, rehabilitation, code enforcement, and neighborhood betterment have played a minor but noticeable role in housing policy. Recently, under Nixon and Ford, a new rhetorical emphasis and locally determined portions of block-grant revenue sharing programs have added to these efforts. Now the market has joined in. Led by adventurous and youthful sectors of the middle class, buyers have begun searching in older areas for the housing bargains of the 1970s and 1980s. As a result, prices have risen swiftly in these areas. This illustrates the tight linkage between new construction and existing dwellings. The high price of new construction has rippled through the entire stock. Even in some of the most depressed inner city markets, islands of old houses located in defended neighborhoods have experienced substantial appreciation in value.

As middle-income demand shifts to housing bargains in older areas, a process begins for which the British have coined the word "gentrification," units filter up from lower to higher income occupants. Price increases reinforce the upward filtering of the stock. . . . From the standpoint of the physical condition of the stock, the shift produces a highly beneficial result. Increased income triggers a sequence that includes catching up on deferred maintenance, investment for rehabilitation and modernization, and upgrading of neighborhood facilities and services. Conversions occur, not to maintain rents in the face of poorer classes of tenants, but to respond to the demand of small middle-income households. Gentrification makes it possible to preserve neighborhoods that a few years ago would have been "urban renewed" or abandoned. The irony of this is underscored in strong inner city markets like San Francisco, where a massively destructive urban renewal program limps along in the face of a buoyant market for old houses, particularly the "Victorians" that renewal action targeted.

Associated with gentrification is a powerful demand for antiredlining policies. Blessed for years by the FHA and regulatory authorities, banks, savings and loan associations, and other mortgage-lenders practiced redlining as a systematic way to avoid the high risk associated with low-income and changing neighborhoods. Attacks on this practice have become a popular cause in the mid-1970s. As the market picks up in older areas, these traditional discrimination practices come under fire. At the state and federal level disclosure legislation has forced certain classes of lenders to reveal the geographic patterns of their activities. This applies moral suasion directly to the lender and arms consumer activists with hard data on their practices. As more middle-income people join this consumer movement, pressure for change will build. Antiredlining activity will have the effect of bringing to the older standing stock and its new owners more of the package of housing finance aids that traditionally have supported middle-class demand in suburbia. This nicely illustrates another of the ironies of the present and near future: as trickle-down becomes trickle-up, downward filtration — the cornerstone of America's traditional low-income housing policy — comes to a halt.

Federal aid seems certain to flow toward neighborhood preservation in increasing amounts. . . . [H]undreds of cities and counties have gone into the housing finance business. Many more will follow, for the movement has just begun. . . .

Perhaps the most interesting aspect of all this activity, and the one that holds the greatest meaning for the future, is the degree to which it puts local government firmly in the business of housing and housing finance. General purpose governments and special districts have traditionally held entrepreneurial responsibility for important pieces of community development and neighborhood preservation, but not for housing. Basic services and facilities, parks and schools, main streets and trunk drainage, recreation, education, and public safety typically came from local government in neighborhood-sized chunks. What is new, and what promises to burgeon in the years to come, is direct intervention in housing finance and in relations among owners, tenants, landlords, and financial institutions.

. . . .

Local Housing Institutions

The recent growth of neighborhood preservation programs suggests that much of consequence in future housing policy will emerge in government and regulatory law at the local level. Traditionally speaking, most regulation in housing markets comes from state and local law. With the exception of zoning, local regulation has by and large remained passive. In the future, however, local and state governments are going to intervene more actively in housing markets through special finance agencies, strong efforts to preserve the standing stock, rent control, and eventually perhaps a restructuring of landlord-tenant relations. The design of such intervention raises critical policy issues.

. . . .

[The authors then review state housing finance and allocation programs and the movement for local rent control. — Eds.]

These [rent control] developments on both coasts illustrate the remarkable degree to which the current crunch in housing costs has opened the possibility of local public regulation of the rental market on a scale never before seen in peacetime United States outside of New York City. Especially as middle-income tenants experience sizable annual rent increases, this type of market regulation gains enormously in political appeal. Unlike the rent controls of the World War II era, this "second generation" of rent control has received little federal encouragement. In fact, the Department of Housing and Urban Development has overridden local regulations covering federally subsidized projects and projects financed with federally guaranteed mortgages.

Other more daring forms of local regulation may also be in the offing. Tenant unions, for instance, have appeared only fitfully in the past. Now they may become more prevalent as the crunch deepens. If they proliferate, local or state governments may seek to establish and supervise — either formally or informally — collective bargaining relations between tenant and landlord. In the past, tenant unions were commonly found among lower-class renters, particularly where effective community organizers had been at work. In the years ahead, we may see instead the growth of coalitions of lower-class and middle-class tenants. Already intimations of this have appeared in the amazing neighborhood-based, multiclass tenant movement in Dallas, Texas. In a city with 60 percent of its population renters, the Dallas Tenants' Union has as its goal the establishment of a collective bargaining system for the Dallas rental housing market. The flowering of a large tenant movement may prove to be a long and slow process because of enormous political resistance to the idea on the part of landlords and banks; but the objective basis for it may develop swiftly if rents continue to rise faster than income and community organizing continues to spread throughout big cities in the United States.

These various trends in local housing market regulation will undoubtedly reinforce one another and may eventually lead to an elaboration of large organizations by the different factors in the market. We may, in fact, be witnessing the "cartelization" of the housing market as tenants, landlords, and lenders operate more and more through organized interest groups and associations.

. . . .

Strategies to Meet Housing Needs

The overriding importance of the conflict between rising middle-income demand and price inflation has begun to redirect attention away from several other housing policy issues that were of much concern in the recent past. These issues, many of them key components of Great Society programs, include production targets, deep subsidies to the poor (as distinguished from shallower subsidies to middle-income households), technological solutions to high unit costs, new towns and the related idea of new towns in-town, and the concept of geographic dispersion of racial and lower-class minorities in order to achieve the ideal of a balanced community. Discussion continues to revolve around these issues, but with less sense of national urgency.

Production Policy

Since the 1930s Americans have shown enthusiasm for housing policies that emphasize high rates of new unit construction. Behind this lies the firm conviction that trickle-down is good and works. This means that new homes and new urban or suburban environments are, in Downs' word, "inserted" at the top of the income spectrum. This, in turn, opens up a chain of vacancies permitting the rest of us to march through the housing stock, or "filter," in carefully ordered class and income-defined cohorts. Great Society housing policy adhered to this tradition. A series of well-known studies has defined the policy problem as a shortage of standard quality units and, secondarily, as the inability of a poor minority to afford such standard units. Put another way, the problem was a supply that was inadequate to keep filtering going at a rate sufficiently high to satisfy all of the *needs* for shelter. Once quantified, the need figures became production targets: 26 million new or substantially rehabilitated units in ten years, 6 million of which would be subsidized so that they could be inserted at lower levels in the income spectrum.

. . . .

[The authors next note that Congress embodied these production targets in the Housing Act of 1968, which also enacted a new set of production subsidies. Production rose dramatically over the next five years, due in large part to these new subsidy programs, and fell only one million units short of the 13 million unit target for this period. The Nixon Administration suspended the 1968 subsidy programs in 1973. — Eds.]

Democrats and Great Society supporters have interpreted the target shortfalls as an exacerbation of the housing problem. Not so, in fact. High production policies had worked so well that even before these programs had begun to take effect, substandardness and overcrowding had ceased to be the dominant housing problems they once were. Perversely, instead of solving a no longer critical old problem, the high production policy helped create new problems of neighborhood decline and price inflation. By stimulating new home production at a rate substantially above the rate of household formation, the policy intensified filtering and suburbanization, thus destabilizing old neighborhoods and hastening their abandonment. By adding to the stock at the high end of the price continuum, and destroying units at the low end, it tended to shift upward prices of the standing stock. By maintaining market pressure on land and money resources the Great Society programs helped power inflation.

. . . .

[The authors note that new production is an inefficient way of providing housing for poor people. Leasing standard quality housing from the existing housing stock would house nearly 60 percent more households. — Eds.]

Despite these counterarguments, the building industry and its allies will continue to advocate high production. Now, however, formal targets have all but disappeared in the split between the pro- and anti-federal interventionists. The new national policy emphasis on supporting middle-income demand will place an effective floor under production and thus deflect the conflict. In the years to come, demand changes coupled with the revived interest in old houses, a strengthening market in many metropolitan areas, and the two decades or more of heavy demolition behind us suggest that high production will have less destabilizing, abandonment-provoking effects than it has had in the recent past. In a perfect demonstration of the lag phenomenon so characteristic of public policy, now discredited production targets as such may reappear later in this decade. If that happens they will be resurrected ironically in close synchrony with a precipitous drop in household formation that can be predicted for the late 1980s from present declining birthrates.

Subsidies to House the Poor

Almost as a by-product of policies directed at maintaining high levels of economic activity and employment, the federal government has since the 1930s provided a small quantity of deep and expensive subsidies aimed at housing the urban poor. The great bulk of this effort has gone into constructing low-rent public housing projects. After more than forty years of program activity, these units sheltered about 4 percent of the population with 1970 and 1972 incomes below $6000. Little has changed since. This program has been under almost continuous attack since its birth in the New Deal. During the intervening years it has been closed down repeatedly due to Supreme Court action, lapsed enabling legislation, congressional failure to appropriate authorized funds, and hostile policies like the Article 34 referendum requirement in the California State Constitution. Only a die-hard public housing management lobby with occasional help from big labor and big city mayors has kept it alive at all. Now even they seem to have failed the cause of low-rent public housing. In recent years the final blows have come from the same scholarly program evaluations that questioned production policy, the moratorium of 1973, and the dynamiting of the infamous Pruitt-Igoe project in St. Louis which provided the coup de grâce.

With low-rent public housing thoroughly discredited, and with the overshadowing policy issues generated by the effects of inflation on middle-income demand, perhaps the less said the better about the future of deep subsidies....

Out of this disenchantment a strong thrust has emerged to shift deep subsidies to the demand side of the market. Among the early advocates of this shift, sociologist Rainwater, who studied daily life in Pruitt-Igoe, came to believe that only an income redistribution strategy could cope with the defects of the projects. Soon economists joined in.... HUD undertook a number of social experiments designed to reveal the efficacy of the approach. So far, reported results are inconclusive. While people do use earmarked aid to improve their housing and to reduce its economic burden, the experiments indicate a substantial fraction of the aid can end up as inflated rent. As markets get tighter, it is safe to predict that rents will increase faster. Demand subsidies may not look as promising from the vantage point of the late 1970s as they did five or ten years ago. Also, from a political point of view, it is unlikely that an expensive, new program of income supplements or housing allowances for the poor will be enacted in a period when the middle class is experiencing such a crunch. Perhaps the decade to come will not see major efforts directed at housing the poor.

. . . .

Dispersion

Housing policy, the balanced-community concept, and a concern with racism have had a long-standing association. Among the earliest federal policies related to these themes were FHA regulations designed to insure homogeneous neighborhoods in race and class terms. Only recently have these objectives changed, at least in terms of official action. The principal thrust of these newer policies has been directed at dispersing housing opportunities for low-income and nonwhite people on a metropolitan-wide "fair-share" basis. Beginning with the Dayton Plan in 1970, recent successes of dispersion in the Minneapolis-St. Paul metropolitan area and in a few other places support modest hopes. However weak the federal administration of the dispersion provisions of the 1974 Housing and Community Development Act, the cumulative effect of it, the A-95 review, and the subsidization of metropolitan planning have generated quite a bit of momentum behind this thrust.

Much policy in this area is now being made in the court system as legislatures have evidently found race too tough a question for open action. This trend is likely to continue. It will grind painfully slow, especially since the U.S. Supreme Court has taken a hard line, acting only against overt racial discrimination and not admitting litigation on class and income discrimination. State courts, however, show much variation in outlook, and one, New Jersey, stands out for its activist position on class and race dispersion policy. Other state courts are likely to follow New Jersey's lead in mandating fair share allocations of low- and moderate-income housing to all comers. . . .

Conclusion

In the decade to come, more and more Americans, especially those just starting households, will find themselves unable to afford what they have come to define as a decent home and a suitable living environment. To some extent they will react individually and psychologically by redefining downward their own subjectively ordered housing standards. They will also modify their preferences in the opposite direction in terms of their ideas about what is affordable. . . . Some people will find traditional housing standards inappropriate as they opt for single, nonfamily life-styles or adopt resource-conserving ethics. For most people, however, the decade will witness a real contradiction between rising costs and restricted supply on one hand, and less swiftly rising incomes and competition for housing because of high household formation rates on the other.

To a great extent, the central questions for policy-makers will revolve around maintaining the effective demand of the great middle-class mass. These problems may prove to be so intractable that the traditional policy issues — substandard housing and provision for the poor — will fade into relative insignificance. From this vantage point, it looks as though the response of public policy to these new conditions will lead to a changed housing economy which looks less and less like the classical market and more and more like the state-managed housing economies of Western Europe.

While such a shift in policy orientation may emerge simply through drift, it is more likely that political clashes over extending government intervention in our housing market system may become almost as heated as those of the 1930s and the immediate postwar years. During the previous decade we have witnessed a continuing debate over the rationale for, and the forms of intervention in, housing, health care, and other services. In the housing policy area these debates are bound to intensify as the costs of housing market disequilibrium grow at a compound rate and the demands for intervention multiply. Ideological differences will also intensify, especially if property relations are altered by interventions such as rent control. Indeed, as local governments become more active in regulating housing markets, we may find that debates over policy which to date have been confined to small groups of academics, bureaucrats, and politicians that cluster around federal and state agencies will be extended to countless citizens who have an enduring stake in these issues.

Comments: The six chapters which constitute Part II of these readings and comments take up most of the problems and policy issues raised by Montgomery and Gellen. Money, and more particularly the problem of housing capital formation are treated in Chapter 7. Chapter 8 deals with subsidy policy, perhaps the most widely debated of the housing policy areas in which the national government is involved. In contrast to the federal level focus of these chapters, the next four turn to largely local problems in policy formation. Chapter 9 considers neighborhood programs, principally programs combating blight and housing deterioration on an area basis. Chapter 10 treats race and discrimination in housing, problems which are among the most difficult to solve. The next chapter covers the somewhat related problem associated with suburbanization — the exclusionary zoning and environmental protection policies that tend to thwart housing need, inflate the price of housing, and generally build walls around suburbs. The final chapter ranges over considerable terrain having to do with the relationships, both legal and economic, between landlords and tenants and between buyers and sellers.

The set of problems and policies covered in these six chapters by no means exhausts the universe of housing issues, but it does touch on most of the main ones. Critical matters such as dwelling price inflation are not treated in a separate chapter but figure centrally in several of the problem areas covered by the array of chapter topics. Price inflation, for example, in addition to figuring importantly in Part I, is a principal aspect of the capital formation problem covered in Chapter 7. The inflationary effects of environmental protection and exclusionary zoning on land as a factor in house pricing and production are treated in Chapter 11. The same comment can be made of housing need, a problem which underlies the subsidy, race and suburban issues of Chapters 8, 10 and 11. Nevertheless, space has necessarily required a process of selection in what is included in the second half of the book. The topics chosen reflect a careful assessment that winnowed out all but those issues most salient to housing in America during the decade to come.

Chapter 7

CAPITAL RESOURCES FOR HOUSING MARKETS

The American housing economy has an enormous appetite for money. As the background material presented in Part I indicates, in monetary terms the housing sector has been growing faster than the economy as a whole. This means equivalent escalation in the housing sector's capital requirements in order to provide money to finance house construction and purchase. At the beginning of Chapter 2, Table 1 (supra p. 41) shows new house construction investment increased 216% from 1968 to 1977 while total domestic private investment increased only 141%. Over the same period, housing services consumption expenditures increased 266% and it is believed that the relative share of those expenditures attributable to capital costs increased even more steeply. Housing capital has burgeoned both absolutely and relatively. The trend seems destined to continue.

The vast flow of capital funds required to finance construction and purchase of new and existing housing are financed through long term debt, usually in the form of mortgages. As Stone showed in Chapter 2 (supra p. 67), housing debt has expanded at a pace that parallels the overall expansion of the housing sector. His figures showed also that the relative increase of housing debt to all public and private debt was equally spectacular, from 7% in 1946 to 18% in 1974 when it reached about one half trillion dollars. As noted in Chapter 3, capital funds for housing are channelled through financial intermediaries, mainly the banks and comparable institutions that collect or create deposits and make loans available to the housing market.

Maintaining this enormous flow of funds into housing has become the most important public policy problem in housing. This is so even though as later readings in this chapter suggest, skeptics from both left and right question the true effects of such policies. Before turning to the readings that amplify the problem of capital resources and discuss related policy responses, it seems useful to ask why housing requires ever increasing funds beyond what simply inflation might suggest. The accepted mainstream answer is that a combination of interlocking and mutually reinforcing factors have produced enormous demand which the economy, behaving rather automatically, struggles to satisfy. The enormous bulge in household formation and the migration and lifestyle trends listed by Alonso (supra p. 123) create the primary demand. Factor price increases and scarcity in relation to demand stimulate price increases on the supply side. As a result of primitive supply and demand factors, more money for housing is needed. The relatively higher increases in housing capital needs reflect changes in taste that lead people to spend proportionately more money on housing; time lag effects that make supply respond slowly to increases in demand; and technical factors such as the nature of the conventional mortgage contract, or housing debt instrument, which has the effect of multiplying inflation rates in order to compensate for long-term level interest rates.

Stone in Chapter 2 provided in part at least an alternative basis for understanding the growth of residential mortgage debt and the aggregate needs of the housing sector for funds. In a nutshell, he ascribed it to the discovery that "the growing urban population created the need for and possibility of profitable investment in housing. . ." (supra p. 67). From a left wing perspective, this expansion of the mortgage credit market is seen as dovetailing with the capitalist system's ever-expanding need to produce new wealth through capital gain and profits, a process the Marxists call capitalist accumulation.

In between these two views lies the position that most often guides housing policy in America. In this view the overall level of the economy and major sectors such as housing are seen as highly sensitive to public expenditures and taxation, and to the government's capacity to control, even create, supplies of money. This view has an opposite side which argues that government can to a lesser extent control the economy through fiscal policy, or expenditures and taxation, and through monetary policy, or the control over money and banking. This view in turn leads to heavy federal government involvement in such activities as trying to stabilize the tendency of the private economy to experience more or less violent booms and recessions, inflations and deflations.

Swings in the private economy and government responses to them affect the housing sector in two ways. First, as the Gibson reading in Chapter 5 (supra p. 200) made clear, of the various spending components of the Gross National Product, "investment in residential structures is the most variable." This fact means that housing is terribly sensitive to fiscal and monetary policy. Second, because the housing sector is so sensitive, macroeconomic policy tends to impact it very heavily. The U.S. Federal Reserve Board, the agency with the most responsibility for monetary policy, has routinely singled out housing as vulnerable and therefore an effective sector to control. Secondarily, even efforts to control other sectors tend to have magnified ripple effects in housing. This means, according to the mainstream viewpoint, that much of the present cost imbalance in housing funds and therefore a major component of inflation — increased demand crunch — can be laid at the door of public policy.

Assuring an adequate flow of funds into the housing sector creates complex problems for monetary policy. On the macroeconomic level, housing must compete with other sectors, such as the stock market, for investment funds. In order to compete effectively, the housing sector must provide investors with similar returns or profits, similar risks, and liquidity, which means convertibility into cash. The readings in this chapter discuss governmental efforts to facilitate the flow of capital into housing by making it more competitive to investors in terms of earnings, risk and liquidity. The first article, by a former Governor of the Federal Reserve Board, deals broadly with housing capital in a macro-economic and monetary policy context. In it, he emphasizes the problems caused by the widely fluctuating flow of capital into housing and by Federal Reserve efforts to smooth out these swings. The second article evaluates the performance of institutions designed to encourage the flow of capital into housing by providing liquidity, and the remaining selections discuss risk reduction and the development of new ways of raising capital for housing. The chapter ends with a critical examination of the complex array of institutions which exist to deal with the money aspects of housing, and relates them in a fine-grained fashion to a case study of the Baltimore housing market. Throughout this chapter it may be helpful to keep in mind Smith's outline diagram of the macroeconomy of housing (supra p. 42), and his set of related macroeconomic questions (supra p. 44).

S. MAISEL, STABILIZATION AND INCOME DISTRIBUTION POLICIES AND HOUSING PRODUCTION, FROM RESOURCES FOR HOUSING, PROCEEDINGS OF THE FIRST ANNUAL CONFERENCE 139, 142-49 (Federal Home Loan Bank of San Francisco, 1975)

[As noted in Chapter 3 (supra p. 81), most debt passes through private financial institutions called intermediaries. The five major types are deposit or thrift institutions, — savings and loan associations (S&Ls), mutual savings banks, and commercial banks, — and the contract institutions — life insurance companies and mortgage companies. Two federal regulatory agencies govern many of these financial institutions. The Federal Home Loan Bank Board (FLBB) regulates savings and loan associations, while the Federal Reserve Board (FRB) regulates commercial banks. — Eds.]

The Stabilization Problem

The cyclical relationship of housing to the economy seems to grow directly out of the manner in which we have tried to achieve national economic stability. Almost our entire emphasis has been placed on monetary policy to slow expansions. The use of other policies has been rare.

How do the deflationary pressures of monetary policy work in the housing sphere? Whether money and credit are contracted as a matter of policy or they are simply not allowed to expand with demand, the effect is the same. Because the demand for credit exceeds its supply, short-term interest rates rise. Climbing prices and expectations of further price increases also lead to higher interest rates. In effect, nominal (market) rates exceed the real interest rate by sizable amounts. [Nominal or market rates include premiums for inflation, risk, and administration, whereas the real rate of interest reflects the rental price of money, or the profit which the lender actually expects to realize. The real interest rate, however, is never stated and must be inferred from market rates. — Eds.]

When short-term rates rise:

1. Flows to financial institutions, particularly to the deposit-thrift institutions, contract. Both because of the regulations under which they operate and because an imbalance with respect to maturities exists between their assets and liabilities, these institutions cannot offer rates matching the increase in the market. [Here Maisel notes an especially problematic issue for the primary mortgage lenders, S&Ls. Their profits depend upon the spread between interest payments they receive on mortgages and other investments and the rates they pay to depositors. Most mortgages carry a fixed rate of interest for the entire term, usually 20 to 30 years. On the other hand, interest rates on deposits must rise comparably with rates for other investments if banks are to make new loans, thus sqeezing the profits of intermediaries having older mortgages in their portfolios bearing considerably lower rates of interest. — Eds.]

2. Shifts occur in the percentage of assets that institutions place in mortgages. Mortgage loans may reach usury or Federal rate ceilings. Risks increase. The relative marketability of mortgages falls. For many lenders, home mortgages appear to be marginal investments. When other preferred loans are available, they withdraw from the mortgage market. Such withdrawals are especially likely if the lender has established relationships with other borrowers whose demand is rising. For some or all of these reasons, when credit tightens, most lenders with portfolio flexibility decrease the share of mortgages in their lending. . . .

3. Higher interest rates are accompanied by a drop in the demand for housing. Again, several forces are at work. Higher interest rates mean higher costs. Particularly for developers of rental property, higher costs may cut so far into profitability of new ventures that construction comes to a halt. Another group — owner-occupiers — may also reduce their demand. They cannot buy and borrow because a gap develops between what they can afford to pay and the payments required with higher interest rates. Because the financing gap due to inflation is so significant, I discuss it in detail later.

All of these forces arising from higher interest rates and less available credit cause the demand for housing and its production to fall. While other factors play a minor role, literally hundreds of studies agree that the forces dominant in housing fluctuations are changes in the availability of mortgage funds and movements in their interest rates. . . .

The Costs of Housing Cycles

Fluctuations in housing production lead to significant economic and social costs. Most important are the unemployment of resources, a resulting maldistribution of income and of sacrifices, a decrease in the efficiency with which resources are used, and a price structure with serious inflationary tendencies. The direct effect on housing availability is less clear.

. . . .

[Maisel notes that employment in the construction industry falls at a much faster rate than employment generally during downswings in the housing cycle. Similar wide fluctuations occur in the production of materials for housing and related services. The costs of these unstable market conditions must be borne by the housing consumer. Unemployment for construction workers and in the materials industry fails to exert a downward pressure on housing prices, which continue to rise. — Eds.]

Overall Costs

The economic and social costs in the housing sector caused by efforts to stabilize the overall economy must be measured against gains which these policies make possible for the economy as a whole. They also, of course, must be measured against possibilities of equalizing the burden throughout the economy. In such an analysis, agreement is not easy to achieve. Evaluations of the existing system of attempted stabilization depend on an analyst's theory as to what causes the movements, as well as upon value judgments.

Some believe that housing declines result from unwarranted credit expansion in other parts of the economy, bidding money — and therefore resources — away from housing. To them, methods of guaranteeing housing more credit in crunches and holding back expansion elsewhere promote the general good. It would both remove the problems now afflicting housing and reduce inflationary pressures elsewhere.

Similarly, some believe that the fight against inflation must both take cognizance of differences in demand in specific sectors and deal with individual sector prices. Special policies aimed at stabilizing housing would be worthwhile, even if they placed more pressure on the rest of the economy.

Those who attribute a great deal of the overall inflationary problem to the failure of housing demand to remain moderate in major upturns disagree. They point out that the 1972 level of housing was bad both for the industry and for the economy as a whole. [Here Maisel means that the events of 1972 were bad for the industry in the sense that production far outstripped demand, and were bad for the economy as a whole because they fueled interest rate inflation and unbalanced economic growth. — Eds.]

Others argue against special housing policies, because it is the total of demand that matters in fighting inflation. No matter who must pay, any decrease in demand is good. Clearly, they are less concerned with the inequities which arise when some sectors' incomes react with greater sensitivity to overall policies than do others. They believe that efforts to change the system of impacts will not work, and would be harmful if they did.

There has been a fair amount of empirical and theoretical work on the question of whether selective attempts to stabilize housing production would help or hinder efforts to achieve the general goals of greater economic and social stability, more economic efficiency, and increased equality of opportunity. . . .

Some believe that all allocational decisions should be left to market forces. Others point out that the choice of macro tools determines the market impact on specific sectors. Which policies are chosen alters the costs to particular groups. The choice of policy determines who pays the cost. Both overall effectiveness and sectoral costs must be considered in making this choice.

Additional economic policy tools, including those specific to the housing area, can increase efficiency and equity by dealing directly with those sectors where demand is either rising too rapidly or is too low. They also are needed to reduce the overuse of monetary policy. Monetary policy entails significant costs, which probably rise exponentially as its use increases. Tight money causes sharp cuts in housing and in loans to small businesses, to new businesses, and to local governments. Many of these appear to have high social priorities, in contrast to speculative uses of credit, which may continue to be funded even at high rates.

Rapid changes in interest rates have large-scale, and unfortunate, impacts on balance sheets, monetary wealth, and well-being. When interest rates move up, the effect on income distribution also seems unsatisfactory. Those with wealth to lend get more, while incomes of those who have less are further reduced. Wide interest-rate swings increase uncertainties and, therefore, the risks and costs of doing business.

Financial crises have played an important role in our history, and their recurrence appears possible. The extent of pressure which monetary policy can bring to bear on the economy is limited by the probability of the collapse of financial institutions or other firms. We seem to have approached this limit in each recent period of tight money. Therefore, if other policies are not developed, a stable economy will be more difficult, if not impossible, to achieve, especially in the inflation sphere.

A general economic rule states that one should want as many policy tools as there are goals. In applying stabilization policies, the degree of uncertainty and the number of variables involved are large. If the number of policy tools can be increased, each can be more effective. This is especially true since dependence on a few tools increases their costs, which rise the more often they are employed and the more extreme the pressure they bear. Equity will also be enhanced because the more tools there are, the easier it is to consider their sectoral costs in deciding whether and to what degree to adopt them.

While such reasoning and the empirical studies leave some analysts unconvinced, I believe that the predominant weight of the evidence, both empirical and theoretical, indicates that more attention ought to be paid to the problems of housing in devising and utilizing policies for stabilizing the general economy. Successful reduction of the massive swings which occur in housing production would improve the battle against both recession and inflation. Current policies lead to a waste of resources, inefficiency, and a higher price level.

Thus, those concerned with the instability of housing are on the right track when they argue for more flexible policies. Much of the overuse of monetary policy is due simply to the fact that it is available. Its use entails fewer administrative and political problems than other policies. The failure of overall policy resulting in an even more rapid inflation would threaten the housing market still more than recent events, so some substitutes for the extreme use of monetary policy must be found if the use of resources in housing is to be stabilized and rationalized.

The Increase in Instability

Some urgency is injected into the need to reexamine policies because the basic situation appears to be deteriorating. The steady use of monetary policy in the anti-inflation battle results in less "bang" for every buck lost. In any market situation, there is a learning experience. Those who can protect themselves against being cut off from credit take the necessary steps to do so. To achieve any given degree of restraint through monetary policy, a greater movement in interest rates is required than the last time around.

Each recent cycle has witnessed higher short-term rates. This tendency will probably continue. If so, it will exacerbate one of the basic institutional problems of the mortgage market and of thrift institutions. The movements of short-term rates about long-term rates will increase in amplitude. With time, savers become aware of alternatives. We should expect that the next time short-term rates rise, disintermediation will be more rapid.

Similar problems plague the mortgage market. The shocks that long-term lenders sustained as a result of capital losses from increases in long-term interest rates make them wary of committing funds to this market. Inflation has been driving rates up, while the number of investors who have lost money on long-term issues grows. The size of fluctuations in rates, and therefore their risk, rises. People will put their money in mortgages only if these risks are offset by higher interest rates.

. . . .

The Inflationary Gap in Mortgage Financing

A second critical housing problem is the technical gap which inflation has created between what families can currently afford in monthly payments and the actual amounts the market requires them to pay. Families cannot buy the house they would be able to afford if inflationary expectations affected equally interest rates and the ability to borrow. . . . The gap is called "technical" because it would not exist if all markets adjusted properly; but it is very real to the family that cannot buy the house it desires.

To understand the gap, we must recall the reasons why rates of interest are high in an inflation. A saver or lender tries to include in his interest rate a return sufficient to compensate for the fall in purchasing power. If prices and incomes are expected to rise 5 percent a year and real interest rates are 4 percent a year, the actual market interest rate (the nominal rate) will be 9 percent. If prices rise 5 percent a year, the lender will still be able to buy as many goods as he could have purchased with the money he loaned, and in addition he will receive 4 percent real interest.

A general inflation means that the price of a house with a 9 percent mortgage is also expected to rise 5 percent a year. Similarly, the wages of the purchaser are expected to increase at this same 5 percent rate. However, in this situation a borrower will find that while a lender would be willing to make a loan to him at the real rate of interest, he will not make the loan when nominal rates are high. Lenders will take expected future income into account only to a small degree. They base a maximum mortgage loan on current, not expected, income.

This can be illustrated by a specific example. Assume that in a non-inflationary economy, 30-year mortgages are available at 4 percent interest. A family with an annual income of $6,880 (4 x mortgage payments) could buy a house with a $30,000 mortgage and meet the annual payments of $1,720. Now, however, interest rates rise to 9 percent because of inflation. The required annual payments are $2,900. The family no longer can meet the payments on this house.

In fact, under our assumptions, its income would have to rise by about 70 percent to $11,600 before it could qualify.

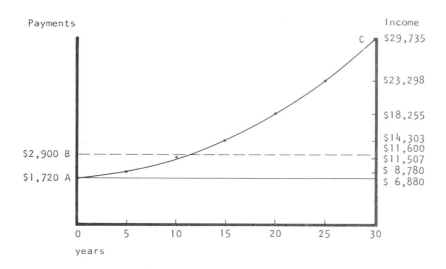

Chart showing the inflationary financing gap that arises because the mortgage payment immediately takes into account the expected inflationary increases while family income adjusts only with time; income levels at 5 percent annual rate of increase (Redrawn from Maisel)

Examine the chart, which illustrates this situation. In the first year, the family income and annual payments at 4 percent are shown at A. The annual payment is shown on the left-hand axis, while expected income is on the right-hand axis. The family can make the purchase.

Because of inflation, interest rates rise to 9 percent. Necessary payments for the same mortgage are shown by the dotted line at B. The family is now priced out of the market. Line AC shows how the family's income is expected to develop with an inflation rate of 5 percent. While too low initially to meet the inflationary mortgage payment, it will eventually be more than adequate. The family will be able to meet the full payment of amortization and interest based on the 9 percent rate in the twelfth year. By the end of 30 years, it will be able to afford payments more than four times the initial 9 percent rate. The inflationary financing gap arises because the mortgage payment immediately takes into account, through the nominal interest rate, the expected inflationary increases in future prices and wages. However, the family income adjusts only with time.

The effect of the gap is to reduce the amount of housing services a family can buy from its current income. The total demand for housing production is reduced. A clamor arises to increase subsidies, both in order to aid housing producers and to allow families to buy houses more in line with their demand before nominal interest rates went up (the type of houses that they could afford on the basis of their expected incomes and the anticipated changes in the value of the houses, assuming both move with prices). To solve this problem, either the rate of inflation must decline or some means of bridging the gap must be found.

Comments: 1. Short though it is, Maisel's essay raises a rich set of critical issues. Before tackling these issues, a few clarifications are in order. Since Maisel wrote this article, many economic analysts have noted that tax shelter benefits rather than rents are increasingly becoming the largest component of developers' profits. As a consequence, developers have the incentive to increase those costs which are tax deductible. Since interest payments fall into this category, the availability of credit instead of the interest rate per se may be most influential in determining the rate of new construction. This factor primarily affects multi-family housing because investors in this housing are especially sensitive to tax shelter opportunities. While tax shelter benefits also increase for owner-occupiers as the interest rate increases, the basic issue of housing costs relative to income as elaborated in Chapter 4 remains problematic.

Maisel continues to emphasize the presumed effects of the costs of borrowing housing funds or, alternatively, the mortgage interest rate on the level of demand. This traditional position suggests that high mortgage interest rates choke off demand. In pre-inflation days it tended to work this way. More recently, in the late 1970s, demand has remained strong while interest rates have matched all-time highs. The reason for this change can be deduced from the final part of Maisel's exposition, where he demonstrates that most of the market interest rate today represents a compensation for inflation. Since housing values seem to inflate faster than the general price level and other comparable investments, an investment in houses has become an inflation hedge of such convincing quality that buyers willingly pay the inflated interest rates. Only in the absence of rapid inflation does the traditional concept work. Only then does high interest seem to decrease housing demand.

2. Before continuing it might be useful to review the major specific housing policy actions surveyed in the U.S. Department of Housing and Urban Development account reproduced in Chapter 6 (supra p. 213). This history, which began so traumatically with the vigorous federal response to the Great Depression of the 1930s, contains most importantly a long record of direct involvement in money markets. Initially, most of this action was depression-related. The FHA, for instance, was created to insure lenders against loss should borrowers be unable or unwilling to repay money borrowed to finance single family home ownership. (The agency was later greatly diversified.) But most important, the federal government took the lead in restructuring the mortgage instrument, that is, in revising the contractual details of the loan agreement. The result was the high-ratio, long-term, level payment, fully amortizing mortgage (or deed of trust, a similar instrument used in some states such as California). This development is discussed by Stone (supra p. 67). For a generation this type of mortgage instrument has been the norm. An important federal innovation has diffused completely throughout the private market.

Today the situation is far different. Rather than depression, when foreclosure and risk of loss were the key issues, both fiscal and housing policy are concerned predominately with inflation. As Maisel observes, the level payment mortgage is a poor instrument for dealing with inflation. Of necessity the lender must incorporate all of the expected price increase, or inflation, into the interest rate charged at the beginning of the term. Thus, rates and payments are increased at just the time that most buyers will find their ability to pay at the lowest point. This last fact is true because the cost of money and payments decrease with time as inflation continues, and because most borrowers expect that their real incomes will increase with time. This problem is often referred to as the "tilt" problem of borrowers. That is, when inflationary expectations are built into the current long-term interest rate, the standard mortgage generates a declining payment burden for borrowers. The heavy burden of the early years constrains demand. Thus the present standard mortgage is poorly adapted to inflation. Redesign of the mortgage instrument has become a chief thrust of public policy.

Changing the structure of the residential mortgage instrument could not only deal with the inflationary pressures placed on borrowers, but might also remedy the profit squeeze experienced by lenders and thus improve their competitive position in capital markets. One innovation is the variable rate mortgage or VRM. It carries a flexible interest rate that changes as the market interest rate changes. Upward adjustments in the mortgage interest rate during periods of high interest could match upward movement of interest rates on deposits. Variable rate mortgages have been available for some time in Canada, and are becoming available in some areas of the United States. Because the VRM shifts the risk of inflation to the borrower, financial institutions favor it. From a theoretical standpoint, by reducing risk it should reduce the inflation premium. This has not happened to a significant degree in practice. From the borrower's perspective not only has it failed to reduce premium rates, but it looks risky unless the borrower expects income to keep pace with inflation. For this reason, VRMs have not caught on well. Political resistance to upward adjustments in interest rates should inflation continue may also make the VRM vulnerable over time from the lender's viewpoint.

Another innovation in mortgage finance, the Graduated Payment Mortgage (GPM), gradually increases payments over the life of the mortgage. This innovation directly addresses the tilt problem. If a steady rate of inflation continues, the GPM may be designed so that its payments increase over time at an equal rate, thus eliminating tilt. Should an even steeper graduation be used, the GPM could be designed to enable borrowers to budget for housing on the basis of their income as averaged over their earning cycle rather than on the basis of their income at the time of purchase.

Unlike the VRM, the GPM tilts most of the mortgage payment to the end rather than the beginning of the payment period, and to this extent shifts the risk of loss to the lender should housing prices turn downward. For this reason, lenders have been wary of these mortgage instruments. The GPM can also create an equity problem for the homebuyer as equity in the home increases more slowly under this form of mortgage instrument. In the early years of the mortgage, the homebuyer must be able to count on continuing increases in housing price levels should he move and need the proceeds from a first home to help finance the purchase of another dwelling. Nevertheless, the obvious demand side benefits have led to considerable acceptance of this alternative to the standard, level payment mortgage.

In an effort to capture the advantages of these two types of alternative mortgage instruments, and at the same time avoid their disadvantages, many other designs have been put forward. These generally combine some features of the variable interest rate mechanism with a device for levelling out the tilt effect. They seek simultaneously to ease pain to the borrower and ease risk to the lender. While some of these schemes look very attractive on paper, the financial community has been reluctant to institute such complex instruments because of presumed marketing and management problems. In the present climate there is an open field for new ideas for the appropriate alternative mortgage instrument for a continuing inflationary economy. In what other ways could housing policy address this problem?

A NOTE ON INTERMEDIATION

Another critical issue raised only indirectly by Maisel concerns the problems inherent in the nature of intermediation, or the processes by which financial institutions form the link between savers and borrowers. A whole series of problems tend to make this process work imperfectly. Chief among them are these:

1) *Individualization of risk:* Because loans of relatively large size compared with incomes are characteristic of mortgages, because an individual or household or but a few individuals are the borrowers, and because a single, discrete, immovable, unpredictably vulnerable structure is the collateral, mortgages and housing credit generally suffer from a rather high degree of risk. A perfectly routine event such as a single person's death or a fire in a single structure can catastrophically wipe out a substantial investment. In this fact lies a very basic problem in attracting capital investment in housing.

2) *Geographic distribution:* Savers may be located some distance away from potential borrowers, yet the financial intermediaries tend to be very localized — in general state banking laws place severe limits on their locational freedom. This limitation means that one region of the county may have a surplus of savings while another has a surplus of borrower demand.

3) *Liquidity:* Because mortgages are not readily bought and sold on an open market like stocks, bonds, and currency, they are not liquid assets and pose problems of adjustment for the financial intermediaries. Should there be a sudden increase in demand for mortgages on a particular institution, they might ideally sell part of their present investment portfolio if it were composed of liquid assets and use the proceeds to meet the new demand. Reciprocally, an institution with a sudden influx of savings but no current demand for loans might buy loans originated elsewhere. Obviously, the market would work better if mortgages could be made more liquid, or more readily marketable. If this is done capital could flow smoothly from the savings rich East to the West, where demand is great but the pool of deposits small.

4) *Maturities mismatch:* While the deposits of savers may be withdrawn relatively freely, mortgage loans are recouped or mature only gradually over long periods of time. This forms another obvious barrier to a smoothly functioning market. It means that financial institutions cannot react swiftly to changing conditions in the local market or the national economy.

5) *Interest rate mismatch:* A similar problem looms very large in an inflationary period because of the spread between the interest rates charged on the mortgage portfolio of an institution and the interest paid to depositors or investors. Financial intermediaries find themselves in the socially questionable position of having to charge current borrowers interest rates high enough to offset the negative balance between relatively low rates on their portfolio of old mortgages and higher current rates paid on deposits. In other words, current borrowers in an inflationary period tend to subsidize earlier borrowers.

6) *Disintermediation:* This splendid neologism refers to the process tied to the business cycle in which there may occur massive withdrawals of deposits from the financial institutions or intermediaries — thus they can no longer do their work of intermediation. Such withdrawals are usually substantial in periods in which interest rates on alternative investments are higher. This happens often because of conscious governmental policy regulating money flows by stimulating higher interest levels. A complex interacting set of factors are involved in disintermediation. Federal monetary policy and returns on alternative investments, lag effects, the often contradictory regulatory structure around banking, demand pressures from other sectors of the economy, and the various technical problems listed above compound each other. But nothing compounds it more than inflation. While the thrift institutions serve the intermediation function quite well in a stable economy, in an inflationary one they do poorly. Depositors become increasingly volatile and choose interest rate advantage with single-minded zeal. Disintermediation becomes an ever-present spector.

Comments: Public policy has addressed these problems in a variety of ways. In response to the maturities matching issue, for instance, suggestions have been put forward for coordinating deposit term regulations with a redesigned mortgage instrument.

In terms of reforming financial markets, the most logical approach might be the development of a mortgage system based on the matching of the maturities of a lender's assets and liabilities. Under this approach, the vast bulk of housing credit would come from long-term liabilities such as mortgage bonds and pension funds. The Canadian mortgage system, for example, operates with such a matched maturities system and maximizes the supply of credit by utilizing roll-over mortgages. The latter have been widely used in Canada since the 1930s. In 1973 virtually all single-family residential mortgages were of the roll-over type. They were written with a twenty-, thirty-, or forty-year amortization rate but with a fixed interest rate for only a five-year term. When the term is reviewed the interest and amortization rates can be renegotiated. The bulk of savings deposits in Canadian institutions are five-year certificates. Although inflation has affected housing costs in Canada over the past decade, the Canadian mortgage market, because of its matched maturity system, did not suffer the effects of credit rationing in 1970 and during 1973-74 which were so widespread in the U.S. Since it would require a vast institutional restructuring of financial markets with all sorts of unanticipated distributive effects, this approach has received little attention in the United States except as a means for expanding the financial base of the secondary mortgage markets.

Montgomery & Gellen, supra, at 164.

2. An additional set of strategies aimed at increasing the flow of capital funds to the housing market attempts to improve the position of banks and savings and loan associations in the competition for investors. Montgomery & Gellen (supra p. 247) noted, for example, that interest rate ceilings imposed on these institutions by federal Regulation Q encourage disintermediation as depositors withdraw funds during periods of upward swings in interest rates outside the housing market:

One avenue of reform lies in the direction of altering the structure and regulatory environment of financial markets themselves. Conservatives, for example, believe that the removal of . . . interest rate ceilings on time deposits and savings accounts would solve the supply problem. In their opinion, . . . [w]ere interest rates allowed to find their "natural" level, adequate supplies of credit for housing would be forthcoming. The saving and loan associations, however, have opposed this type of measure for fear that in an unregulated savings market commercial banks would easily outcompete them and reduce their market share. In order not to run the risk of further disrupting mortgage markets, Congress has supported the savings and loans and refused to remove Regulation Q.

Montgomery & Gellen, supra, at 163-64.

While Regulation Q has not been withdrawn, the ability of financial institutions to attract and hold depositors has been strengthened by changes made to governmental regulations in 1978. Commercial banks, savings and loan associations and mutual savings banks were given the authority to issue two new types of savings certificates. One is a six-month certificate with interest tied to the U.S. Treasury rate for short-term borrowing, and the other is an eight-year savings certificate with interest set at a slightly higher rate than for shorter term certificates (the eight-year certificates are also aimed at the maturities matching issue, supra p. 275). The interest rates allowed on these certificates are established with numerous monetary policy objectives in mind. They may not always be set at a rate advantageous for housing. The problems discussed by Maisel early in this chapter regarding cyclical stabilization and inflation policies continue to impinge on the housing sector's access to capital. Disintermediation is a constant threat to housing.

More dramatic changes affecting thrift institutions, some of them recommended by a federal study commission, the Hunt Commission, in 1971 but not enacted by Congress, would further ease federal regulatory controls and broaden their powers. These and other proposed changes would blur the distinctions among lending institutions and substantially alter their competitive advantage. Some changes have already occurred. For example, a Federal Reserve Board order has authorized commercial banks to make automatic transfers between savings and checking accounts. This order represents a step on the road toward permitting banks to pay interest on checking accounts. (The order was invalidated by a federal court and now requires congressional approval.) Further steps in this direction seem likely, thus eliminating one competitive advantage of the S&Ls as depository institutions. Reciprocally, savings and loan associations in some states have also been authorized to establish checking accounts in order to improve their position vis-a-vis the commercial banks.

A NOTE ON SECONDARY MARKETS

Policy makers at the federal level and experts in both public and private sectors conceived that these problems could be met by the creation of a secondary mortgage market to provide another level of intermediation. Such a market could improve the flows of funds across geographic barriers and improve liquidity by providing an assured market in which to sell mortgages. By stabilizing flows and improving the competitive position of the housing sector in the capital funds market, it could perhaps overcome some of the mismatch and disintermediation problems which periodically afflict the housing economy. Much of this improved competitive position is seen as the outgrowth of technical improvements in the intermediation process that come from establishing a second level of market activity. First, the additional level de-individualizes the transaction from a highly local affair involving an individual borrower to a national pool. By doing this it spreads or reduces risk to the individual investor. Second, in the event of loss due to inflation and the resulting interest rate mismatch, financial institutions and investors know they can contain their loss in a one-shot loss sale on the secondary market and maintain liquidity.

There has been a long history of policy dealing with secondary markets. Again it is useful to refer back to the Chapter 6 reading from the U.S. Department of Housing and Urban Development (supra p. 213) to review the evolution of government efforts to establish a secondary mortgage market. It began in the 1930s after several years of simply hoping risk insurance and a new mortgage instrument would lead automatically to establishment of a viable secondary market by the private sector. In 1938 the U.S. Government established the Federal National Mortgage Association, known familiarly as FNMA or Fannie Mae. As outlined in Chapter 6, its functions broadened over the years and recently these and related functions have been divided among Fannie Mae and two newer agencies, the Government National Mortgage Association, called GNMA or Ginny Mae, and the Federal Home Loan Mortgage Corporation, FHLMC or Freddie Mac.

Initially, Fannie Mae was authorized to develop a secondary market for residential mortgages. It was also given a special function, the financing of mortgages the private market would not assume, such as mortgages for subsidized housing. FNMA became a federally chartered but privately financed and managed corporation in 1970, freed from federal budgetary constraints and thus enabling it to carry out its market support function without congressional appropriations during times of disintermediation. Fannie Mae purchases mortgages from thrift institutions and other lenders with money borrowed in regular private capital markets. In addition, Fannie Mae also issues commitments for purchase under which it commits to buy a stated dollar amount of mortgages during a specified period. Even if money is tight or disintermediation underway, these commitments provide an incentive to lenders to extend credit because they have the assurance that Fannie Mae financing will be available if necessary.

Ginnie Mae was chartered through an amendment to the FNMA Charter Act of 1968 primarily to assume Fannie Mae's special assistance function. Through this function GNMA plays a primary role in housing subsidy programs under the control of the Secretary of HUD. It obtains its funds for mortgage purchases by borrowing from the U.S. Treasury, from proceeds from its own sales, and from related sources.

GNMA is also authorized to issue mortgage-backed securities. Under this program, GNMA guarantees the payment of principal and interest on long-term securities issued by private lenders and backed by a self-liquidating pool of conventional or governmentally insured mortgages. GNMA guarantees are intended to encourage long-term investors to enter the housing market who ordinarily would not do so. This objective is accomplished by issuing the mortgage-backed security as a liquid, fully transferable investment instrument.

When Freddie Mac was created in 1970, it was intended to support thrift institutions by providing a secondary market for conventional or non-FHA residential mortgages. By standardizing mortgage contracts and underwriting procedures which previously had varied from state to state, Freddie Mac facilitated the sale of mortgages across state lines so that regional capital surpluses and deficits could be accommodated. While FHLMC was originally organized to provide a market for conventional mortgages, in recent years the distinctions between it and FNMA have blurred and both trade in conventional and government-insured mortgages.

The secondary agencies, GNMA, FNMA, FHLMC, gain access to private capital in a number of ways. As mentioned earlier, FNMA sells stocks to finance its operations and GNMA funds its activities with public funds from the treasury and by issuing pass-through securities in a joint venture with financial institutions. Freddie Mac also issues securities which are very similar to those issued by GNMA, except that the mortgage pool which these issues represent are comprised of conventional mortgages. Freddie Mac issues two types of mortgage-backed securities structured to meet the needs of different types of investors. Participation certificates (PCs) are called pass-through securities. They provide for a monthly return of both principal and interest and are sold primarily to thrift or savings institutions. Guaranteed mortgage certificates (GMCs), which provide for an annual specified payment to investors, are sold to institutional investors such as pension funds and bank trusts. While the details of the securities issued by secondary market organizations vary, their common purpose is to convert individual mortgages into investments marketable on the private capital market in order to bring more funds into the intermediation market.

A principal target of these changes are the pension funds. These funds constitute the fastest growing pool of capital in the private sector. To the extent secondary market securities can be made into attractive basic investment instruments, pension funds may be available to the housing economy. Today this potential on the part of the government established secondary market has found an echo among the conventional private sector intermediaries. Thrift institutions have issued mortgage-backed bonds which have found some favorable attention among institutional investors.

Whether federal programs of intervention in the secondary market add to supply of capital for housing or simply divert capital from one source of supply to another is an important question that demands analysis. An evaluation of federal secondary market intermediaries that considers this question is presented in the next reading. The author, Leo Grebler, is an elder stateman among housing economists and policy experts.

GREBLER, THE ROLE OF THE PUBLIC SECTOR IN RESIDENTIAL FINANCING, FROM RESOURCES FOR HOUSING, PROCEEDINGS OF THE FIRST ANNUAL CONFERENCE 77-80, 83-84, 89 (Federal Home Loan Bank of San Francisco, 1975)

Some Aspects of the Public Sector's Performance

. . . .

An evaluation requires in the first place some measure of the public sector's *net* contribution to residential financing. . . . [S]tatistical magnitudes are reduced or may be wholly offset by secondary effects. Security issues of public agencies at yields substantially exceeding the rates on savings accounts aggravate disintermediation and thus constrict the mortgate lending potential of private institutions. Stepped-up loan purchases by public intermediaries may keep mortgage interest rates below levels that would induce primary lenders to expand their mortgage investment. If mortgage interest rates are held down relative to other rates, people may be encouraged to use mortgage loans for non-housing purposes, diluting whatever benefits accrue to the housing sector. Apart from such offsets within the mortgage and housing markets, support of the housing sector may entail costs to other sectors of the economy. The securities offered by housing credit agencies may crowd out other demanders for funds and/or raise yields on debt instruments generally, including Treasury obligations. This adverse effect may or may not be balanced by housing-induced gains in total output. And there is the awesome question whether the net funds provided by the public sector have contributed to disproportionate increases of factor costs in residential construction and of existing house prices during certain periods or even in the long run.

. . . .

Moderating Market Imperfections

Granting that the long-term benefits of Federal agency intermediation are negligible or may be negative with regard to the total volume of mortgage loans, some of the agencies were created to reduce or compensate for market imperfections which interfere with optimal resource allocation. True, many of these imperfections result from regulation of primary institutional lenders as well as their market structure, but the rationale for Federal intervention took the system "as is" rather than as "what it might be." The agencies have helped overcome the traditional localism of much of the mortgage lending industry. Localism in the sources of funds, mainly savings deposits, resulted in large geographic variations of monies available for lending; it has been modified as Federal intermediaries obtained access to the national securities market. Localism in mortgage investment has been reduced as the standardized FHA and VA mortgage instruments replaced the variety of instruments under state mortgage and foreclosure laws, at least for the Government-underwritten sector. Hence, the marketability of residential loans and the inter-regional flow of funds have greatly improved. Since 1970, FNMA and FHLMC have also developed more nearly uniform mortgage documents and lending standards for conventional loans, and these are now adopted in non-agency transactions as well. The Federal Home Loan Bank System has perfected the market by providing an organized and dependable facility for meeting secondary liquidity needs of S&L associations. Federal intermediaries have reduced imperfections by adding much needed market information. Whether agencies acting solely as regulators would have provided data of similar scope is questionable.

The Federal intermediaries have contributed to market efficiency by easing the effects of short-run credit rationing in the private sector. For reasons not fully understood, rising mortgage interest rates in periods of credit stringency do not clear the market, and private lenders resort to non-price rationing by rejecting borrowers willing to pay the going rate ("we are loaned up") or by requiring larger downpayments. To the extent that the Federal agencies increase the *net* supply of funds — a matter to be discussed shortly — they improve the availability of loans for borrowers who otherwise could not obtain them.

To be sure, all this is "old hat" and much of it eludes measurement, but no benefit-cost analysis can ignore qualitative improvements in market organization. It must come to grips with such questions as how the S&L capacity to make commitments and loans would be affected should the FHLB System be abolished, or how much the marketability of mortgages would be impaired if FNMA ceased to exist. And the analyst would bear the burden of demonstrating that private-sector arrangements could take the place of current Federal agency impacts on market efficiency. It is not enough to assert that deregulation of financial institutions will produce the perfect or near-perfect market.

Access to the Securities Market

That the public intermediaries have provided the residential mortgage market with funds raised by security issues remains a good thing, in principle. They were the logical pioneers in this type of financing; American investors, unfamiliar with market obligations secured by mortgages or, worse, remembering the debacle of mortgage bonds sold in the 1920s, would have been unresponsive without the prestige of Governmental agencies as issuers or guarantors. The conversion of securities into mortgages is desirable because it can produce permanent additions to funds for residential loans, traditionally dependent mainly on savings deposits and life insurance reserves. Further, the terms to maturity for the assets and liabilities can be more nearly synchronized than in the conversion of basically short-term deposits into long-term mortgage loans. Also, savings institutions must raise deposit rates across the board for old as well as new accounts (with some time lag for fixed-maturity deposits) if they seek additional funds to meet greater demands for mortgages. This is true for a free savings market as well as for rate adjustments in a regulated market. The issuer of securities needs only to make the yields on new obligations sufficiently attractive for this purpose.

A financial analyst in 1970 labeled the instrumentalities tapping the securities market a "new system of housing finance" that promises some lasting improvements in the ways of funding the residential sector. This may be a valid long-run projection, but the massive foray into the securities market in recent years turned out to be ill-timed. For the most part, capital obtained through security issues was high-cost money compared to the average cost of rate-controlled deposits, causing incremental disintermediation. So long as this condition persists or to the extent it recurs, security offerings by Federal housing agencies need to be constrained more effectively. Further, a good case can be made for a gradual shift of securities financing from the public sector to private intermediaries which are subject to strict market discipline. Investors are now sufficiently familiar with mortgage-backed obligations to remove the crutches of Federal support in successive steps.

As for the timing of security issues, both public and private intermediaries find themselves in a dilemma. The best time for low-cost issues is a period of credit ease, but additional funds for mortgage lending are hardly needed in such periods. Under conditions of credit stringency when the demand for supplemental funds is greatest, security yields are high and induce a rechanneling of savings deposits. In these circumstances, security offerings of depositary or other private institutions have at least the advantage that the cost of incremental disintermediation is balanced within the private sector by the benefits of more continuous mortgage lending from the proceeds of security issues. When public intermediaries are the sole issuers, *they* augment their mortgage portfolios while private institutions suffer from drains on their deposits and must reduce their mortgage investment.

. . . .

What would be the implications of bolder counter-cyclical action? If FNMA had shifted to net sales in the periods of relative credit ease, the sales would have sopped up private-sector funds potentially available for new loans. This would be a desirable policy to moderate peaks in the mortgage supply and the usual consequence of overbuilding. However, there would be formidable resistance by builders, trade unions, and civic groups interested in new construction. Further, massive loans sales by FNMA or similar agencies might be associated with large capital losses, and discontinuity in purchase operations would affect adversely their earnings. These complications are compounded by the huge amounts of public-sector mortgage holdings and become even more acute for an agency with private capital stock traded on the exchanges, as has been true for FNMA since 1968. It seems that we have maneuvered ourselves into a real dilemma. We are damned if the agencies attempt to sell parts of their portfolio, and we are condemned to inexorable growth of the public sector if they don't.

Summary and Conclusions

. . . .

While the public sector's gross participation in mortgage lending can be readily quantified, an appraisal of its performance rests on its net contribution, and this is far more difficult to assess. Large-scale substitutions and displacements of funds reduce substantially the effectiveness of Federal agency market support in tight-money periods — the time when support actions are at their peak. Massive issues of securities by Federal agencies to finance their stepped-up operations result in incremental disintermediation. ... By raising yields generally, the security offerings by the agencies also involve costs to other sectors of the economy.

Net benefits of mortgage market support seem limited to short-run increases in the supply of loans and short-run restraints on the rise in mortgage interest rates. Short-term benefits are important, however, even if long-run quantitative impacts are zero. The Federal intermediaries can also be credited with long-run benefits of a qualitative type by moderating or compensating for market imperfections. They have pioneered in tapping the securities market for residential financing. Under the adverse circumstances of recent years, this device was probably used to excess. Nevertheless, the housing sector stands to gain from organized access to the securities market in the long run. The gain would be enhanced if private issuers could gradually replace governmental borrowers.

. . . .

The cyclical performance of Federal agencies, quite dubious in the pre-1965 period, has improved. The agencies have consistently taken expansionary action in periods of credit stringency and falling housing starts. They have consistently curtailed their market support under opposite conditions.

———

Comments: Grebler's analysis suggests the complexities that must be unraveled in order to understand the effects of public policy aimed on the macroeconomic level at rationalizing the housing capital formation process. For example, several studies by Allan Meltzner, a conservative economist, indicate one dimension of this complexity. In these studies Meltzner developed the argument that over the long run policies designed to increase the flow of funds into housing are translated simply into more inflation. They do not really generate new money, but simply power upward price effects. While few experts agree with Meltzner's position many economists feel that the macro issues are so complex as to defeat complete understanding.

At the end of this chapter the final reading treats housing money market policies in terms of local effects, particularly their distributional dimensions. It introduces the problem of complexity and contradictory effects on another level. Before turning to that realm, however, several other policy directions addressed to the money problem merit discussion.

In addition to the various market restructuring and institutional approaches, housing policy occasionally has attempted direct intervention with public dollars. These direct approaches are discussed in the following report by a research arm of the U.S. Congress:

CONGRESSIONAL BUDGET OFFICE, HOUSING FINANCE: FEDERAL PROGRAMS AND ISSUES 11-17 (1976)

1. Interest Rate Subsidies

Government National Mortgage Association (GNMA) Tandem Plans [the Tandem Plans were described in more detail in Chapter 6, supra p. 205 — Eds.], the Farmers' Home Administration (FmHA) Interest Credit, and HUD's Section 235 Homeownership Programs provide below-market-interest rate loans. Basically three methods apply: the government either pays part of the interest on private loans, makes the direct loans bearing interest rate subsidies, or (under the so-called "Tandem Plan") commits to purchase private lenders' below market interest mortgages at prices providing a slightly higher than market return. When the government buys them, it ultimately intends to sell at a price that usually represents a loss, because the *selling price* on the mortgages purchased at below market interest rates must reflect the current market rate of interest. Interest rate subsidies on GNMA programs are typically 1 1/2 percentage points (below market rates) for single-family units, and are expected to average 2 percentage points for multifamily housing. FmHA interest credit loans typically carry a subsidy of 6 percentage points. Section 235 subsidies vary with the market interest rate, currently subsidizing the difference between market rates and an income-related rate as low as 5 percent on single-family home mortgages.

The major objective of the GNMA programs is to mitigate cycles in housing construction. When interest rates are cyclically high and housing construction is declining, GNMA makes commitments to provide funds at below- market-interest rates in order to induce additional construction. According to cyclical patterns in the housing industry, GNMA-financed construction should have some effect on housing during tight money periods.

. . . .

The FmHA programs, in contrast to GNMA and the 235 program, are basically aimed at providing adequate housing in rural areas — not in countering construction cycles. The program does appear to expand rural credit provision although the number of beneficiaries is limited.

2. Direct Loans

The federal government makes loans directly to those specific kinds of borrowers who are unable to find mortgage credit elsewhere. Direct lending was a preferred approach during the 1950s, a period of frequent budget surpluses. The shift away from direct loans to "tandem plans" (discussed earlier) occurred primarily to avoid increases in the budget deficit. Existing direct loan programs include:

(a) *Section 502 Homeownership Loans* made from the Rural Housing Insurance Fund under the Farmers' Home Administration to low-and-moderate homebuyers in rural areas. Loans are financed by the sales of guaranteed FmHA notes (e.g., Certificates of Beneficial Ownership) to the public or to the Federal Financing Bank (FFB), an off-budget agency. Recently the FFB has been the only purchaser. The FFB charges one-eighth to one-half percent higher than the interest rate charged by FmHA on the direct loans, depending on FFB costs of borrowing from Treasury.

. . . .

(b) *VA Direct Loans* are made to veterans from the Direct Loan Revolving Fund for new purchases, construction and improvement and for farm purchases. Proportionately, the number and value of annually approved loans have decreased substantially in the last decade; only 2,665 loans were closed in fiscal year 1975. The average loan was $18,344, bearing a 9 percent interest rate on a 25-year life. Generally, net income is realized by VA, since their borrowing costs from Treasury are lower than their direct loan interest rates.

(c) *Section 312 Rehabilitation Loans* are available through HUD for substantially rehabilitated properties in areas specifically defined "uninsurable, high-risk, and in serious decline." . . . Loan priority is given to low- and moderate-income families subject to discretionary approval by HUD field offices. Private lending institutions service the loans for which HUD pays the fees. The interest rate is also subsidized, HUD paying the difference between the market rate and 3 percent. . . .

3. Insurance and Guarantees

Currently, the government provides numerous insurance and guarantee programs. The primary objective is to increase the availability of mortgage credit, possibly on more liberal terms. An insurance or guarantee eliminates almost all risk of default, generally covering up to 90 percent of any losses. The insurance or guarantee may come at two different points in the lending process: mortgage payments by the homeowner to the lender may be insured or guaranteed by a federal agency (as is done by FHA), or the agency may guarantee privately-issued securities backed by home mortgages (as in the GNMA mortgage-backed securities program). Federally insured lending has declined as a share of all mortgage lending, giving way to private insurance, but remains important in at least three specific submarkets: (1) a portion of the conventional market not privately insured, including lower-income families; (2) the multifamily market in which FHA remains the major insurance force; and (3) primary market lenders that originate loans for their own portfolios and require insurance in order to market or improve the "sales-value" of mortgage backed securities issued by them and guaranteed principally by the Government National Mortgage Association or the Federal Home Loan Mortgage Corporation. Federal insurance programs are numerous and only the major ones are described here.

(a) The Federal Housing Administration (FHA) has 40 major insurance programs administered through four subaccounts under the Federal Housing Insurance Fund. Paid-in premium fees are the principal income source and until recently, FHA insurance operations yielded net income. Sizeable budget . . . outlays have resulted from increasing defaults. In general, the traditional FHA insurance programs . . . still yield net incomes. But the high default rates, particularly in subsidized . . . programs, have caused net losses in General and Special Risk Funds. . . .

(b) The Veteran Administration (VA) guarantees mortgage loans taken out by eligible veterans. No charge is made to the borrower for the guarantee. Premiums paid by lenders provide revenues to cover the operating expenses of the VA Loan Guaranty Revolving Fund. Unlike the FHA fund, no appropriations have been required.

(c) Under the GNMA mortgage-backed securities program, GNMA guarantees securities issued by private lending institutions and backed by mortgages insured or guaranteed by FHA, VA, or FmHA. . . . [T]he long-run future of the program is limited by the decline in the number of new mortgages now being insured or guaranteed by FHA, VA, or FmHA. The program has been somewhat successful in attracting additional funds into the mortgage market — for example, roughly one-third of the securities are purchased by pension funds, which would probably not otherwise invest as much in mortgages. However, a large number of securities are held by primary mortgage lenders themselves; to this extent the program does not increase funds available for housing but merely adds the GNMA guarantee to the FHA, VA, or FmHA insurance or guarantee on mortgages held by mortgage lending institutions.

. . . .

(d) The Federal Home Loan Mortgage Corporation (FHLMC; called "Freddy Mac") guarantees securities issued by S&Ls that are members of the Federal Home Loan Bank System. The securities are backed principally by government insured or guaranteed mortgages (i.e., FHA/VA).

Comments: 1. This congressional report omits mention of two, long-standing federal programs that use U.S. Treasury money directly to pay the capital costs of housing. The public housing program in one form or another has been operating since 1934 (see HUD Housing in the Seventies, supra p. 213). The great bulk of public housing in existence today is financed with the proceeds from the sale of bonds paid off with federal budget dollars. The military establishment in some periods has also spent large capital sums on housing. These two programs, public housing and the military, do not figure in the readings in this chapter because they are direct and bypass the financial sector of the private market. Since the vast majority of housing capital flows from this sector it is the focus of attention for housing policy. Direct investment in housing would also show up in the annual federal budget at the total capital cost in one lump sum. This is true even when the investment is in the form of loans to be paid off with interest over a term of years and therefore productive of a net profit to the government. Such budgetary impacts of direct government capital investment are widely viewed as politically too costly to contemplate.

2. One other form of direct federal provision of housing capital funds was embodied in the Housing Act of 1974 Community Development Block Grant program. Under this legislation, localities may use Block Grant funds directly for housing rehabilitation loans and grants. Alternatively, the funds may be used in a variety of ways to leverage or provide

incentives to private capital to invest in rehabilitation. At present rates of appropriation, this source provides only a few hundred million dollars a year and is small compared to the multi-billion dollar mainstream activities of the private financial sector.

3. State and local levels of government have increasingly become involved in providing capital for housing. While a few states, notably Massachusetts and New York, have had operating programs over a considerable span of years, in general state efforts at housing finance are rather new. The last decade has seen establishment in practically all states of housing finance agencies that have the authority to engage in a series of market support and subsidy programs. How state housing finance agencies operate is indicated in the following reading:

R. FISHMAN, ED., THE STATE ROLE IN HOUSING FINANCE AND DEVELOPMENT, IN HOUSING FOR ALL UNDER LAW 492-98, 503-05, 510-11, Report of the American Bar Association's Advisory Commission on Housing and Urban Growth (1977)

The Advent of State Housing Finance and Development

The emergence of the states as a force in housing finance and development is a relatively recent phenomenon. While there have been a few significant state housing initiatives dating back to the early 1920s — notably the veterans home loan program in California and the limited dividend housing law in New York — the basic pattern of public-sector involvement in housing finance has been largely defined by the federal government. Since the Great Depression of the 1930s, Congress, through a variety of federal housing programs, has channeled resources to various private and public beneficiaries. Aid to private beneficiaries has come either through direct subsidies or through indirect mortgage loan guarantees and preferential tax treatment. Aid to local public housing authorities has come in the form of annual contributions that service and secure the principal and interest on tax-exempt bonds issued by the authorities to finance the construction of publicly owned and managed low-income housing.

The pattern of state housing involvement began to change in 1960, when New York established the nation's first state HFA. The New York State Housing Finance Agency was created to finance moderate- and middle-income housing primarily in urban areas so as to stem the rapid out-migration of the middle class to the suburbs — a trend that was attributed in large part to the Federal Housing Administration's favored treatment of single-family suburban homes. The New York State HFA was structured as a statewide public corporation that could raise capital in the tax-exempt bond market and lend the proceeds, at below-market interest rates and at favorable loan-to-value ratios and mortgage terms, for privately owned and constructed housing. ... [Practically all states now have housing finance agencies.—Eds.]

. . . .

Mortgage Financing Role

State HFAs are generally constituted as public-benefit corporations independent of state executive departments. Their primary function is to borrow capital in the tax-exempt bond market and to lend the proceeds in the form of below-market rate construction and permanent mortgage loans for the private development of low-, moderate-, and middle-income housing. These loans are made directly to qualified housing sponsors or indirectly to them through loans to private lending institutions; both in turn are partially regulated by the agencies. Legislation creating the state HFAs typically requires a finding that loans such as the agency would make are otherwise unavailable in sufficient volume from private lending sources.

Source of Mortgage Capital — The Tax-Exempt Bond Market. Mortgage capital is raised by HFAs through the issuance of negotiable bonds and notes in amounts usually limited by statute. It is well established that as independent public corporations — political instrumentalities of their states — HFAs may issue their own tax-exempt revenue obligations without affecting the credit of the state or running afoul of state constitutional debt limitations. The bonds of those agencies which in the past were most active have been secured by a pledge of project mortgages and revenues, reserve funds, federal subsidies (when available), and commonly the non-binding moral obligation of the state to make up any deficiencies in debt service payments. Those agencies which have been authorized to issue revenue bonds but which lack either a moral obligation or debt service makeup provision (such as Colorado, Idaho, Missouri, and South Carolina) have been able to market their bonds largely by restricting their lending operations to federal, state, or privately insured mortgages, and have thus been more limited in their lending volume and flexibility.

HFA bonds — with or without a state's moral obligation pledge — are designed to be completely self-liquidating from pledged project revenues. As a result HFA bonds have generally received high investment grade ratings and the agencies have thus obtained favorable yields, often only slightly lower than those on the state's general obligation bonds, which are supported by the full faith and credit of the state's taxing power. . . .

Direct Financing for Multifamily Housing. The proceeds of HFA securities are used primarily to make direct construction loans (through the sale of short-term notes) and permanent mortgage loans to qualified housing sponsors — principally to limited dividend, nonprofit, and cooperative entities, and to individuals — who own, build, and finance the housing. About 98 percent of the units financed by direct loans from HFAs have been in multifamily residential developments.

The HFAs have low borrowing costs because the interest on their obligations is exempt from federal and many state taxes. These lower costs are in turn reflected in interest rates to borrowers that have averaged 1.5 to 2 percent below private market rates, and in more favorable loan-to-value ratios and mortgage terms than are available from private lenders (90 percent vs. 75-80 percent, and 40 years vs. 25-30 years). The saving is passed along to the developer and reflected in moderate reductions in the monthly cost of housing for the consumer. In exchange for these favorable financial considerations, the agencies retain the power to limit the developer's rental and other charges, its profits and fees, and to control the sponsor's disposition of the property.

In addition the agencies charge a one-time fee from developers on each project to meet their processing costs, and they receive annual fees in the form of a markup on the interest rate that they charge borrowers to meet their mortgage servicing costs and to provide for reserves. In this way, and often only after a small initial start-up loan or grant to provide funds for administration, the agencies eventually become self-sufficient. The Virginia Housing Development Authority, for example, returned its $300,000 start-up appropriation within the first two years of operation.

While the private sector constructs, owns, and manages HFA financed housing, the agencies actively participate in site selection and design review, and in the determination of size and number of units in a given project. Standards for equal employment opportunity and marketing for the housing are also established by the agencies.

Linkage with Federal and State Subsidy Programs to Meet Low and Moderate-Income Housing Needs. Since FHA tax-exempt bond financing provides at best only a shallow capital subsidy, additional federal or state assistance is essential for state HFAs to effectively serve families and individuals in the low- and moderate-income range; that is, those earning less than $9-11,000 a year. In the seven year period from 1968 to 1974, well over half the more than 200,000 units completed have received federal interest-reduction subsidies under the Section 236 (multifamily) and Section 235 (home ownership) programs, and have thus been available for moderate-income families. More than 25,000 units were additionally made available to low-income families through assistance from the federal rent supplement and leased public housing programs.

. . . .

Indirect Financing — Mortgage Purchase and Loans-to-Lenders Programs. A large number of HFAs are using their tax-exempt borrowing power to carry out indirect financing programs in the secondary mortgage market. Designed to increase the amount of capital available for credit, the two major programs in use — mortgage purchase and loans-to-lenders — are in large part a direct outgrowth of the national credit crunches experienced in the 1970s and the lack of significant federal subsidy funds subsequent to the 1973 housing moratorium. Virtually all HFAs established in this period have been authorized to undertake these indirect lending activities.

[These secondary market activities are similar in their broad outlines to the federal FNMA and GNMA operations discussed earlier in this chapter, but on a much smaller scale. State-to-state variations in operational details, however, introduce some measure of variety in these HFA programs. The author discusses several of these. The flavor of their differences can be gained from the following paragraph. — Eds.]

While not oriented to the lower income home purchaser, several of the indirect lending programs are designed to assist in meeting particularly serious housing needs. The New Jersey Mortgage Finance Agency, which established the prototype loans-to-lenders programs, provides incentives to lending institutions, in the form of higher permissible interest charges, for loans made in high need areas of the state as designated by the agency, particularly in high-risk inner-city neighborhoods. Massachusetts, like New Jersey, has established a separate state agency — the Massachusetts Home Mortgage Finance Agency — to operate a loans-to-lenders program aimed at making mortgage credit available in older neighborhoods. The Illinois Housing Development Authority has established a loans-to-lenders program aimed at combating mortgage redlining of older communities in Chicago. The program makes funds available to community banks and savings and loans institutions at tax-exempt rates, provided that these are matched in equal amount by mortgage loans by the local lending institutions within their communities.

State Insurance Programs. Another indirect method of housing finance likely to be used increasingly by the states in the future is the provision of mortgage insurance. These programs, generally funded with legislative appropriations from general funds or through the issuance of the state's general obligation bonds, permit housing to be financed under riskier circumstances for inner-city neighborhoods, for older homes, or for purchasers who are considered credit risks by private conventional lenders.

Among the most innovative and successful state mortgage insurance programs is the one operated by the Maryland Housing Fund, a division of the Maryland Department of Economic and Community Development. Funded with a $20 million insurance reserve from the state's general obligation borrowing, the Housing Fund is authorized: (1) to insure the top 20-25 percent of the loan amount of conventional single family first mortgage loans on 80-100 percent of the loan-to-value ratio; (2) to provide 100 percent single family mortgage insurance coverage on 80-100 percent of the loan-to-value ratio in high risk inner-city areas of Baltimore in which conventional lenders are not active; and (3) to provide construction loans and permanent mortgage insurance for multifamily projects financed by approved public and private lenders. The fund is capable of leveraging its $20 million insurance reserve to insure mortgages at a total face value amount of $190 million.

. . . .

The Future of HFAs — Regaining Easy Access to the Bond Markets

Because of several major events having widespread influence in the national bond markets during 1975 and 1976, many HFAs found it exceedingly difficult to borrow at the favorable rates they could obtain in the past. Among the developments that adversely affected the marketability of HFA bonds and notes were the financial difficulties of the New York State UDC [Urban Development Corporation] and of other New York State finance agencies. These agencies relied heavily on moral-obligation bond financing and their troubles caused a reassessment of this method of financing. Other factors which have had an impact on HFA borrowing include the fiscal crises in New York City and State; increasing investor wariness of long-term real estate investment in the aftermath of widespread failures of real estate investment trusts; and declining institutional interest in tax-exempt bond investment.

. . . .

The difficulties experienced by HFAs over the past two years illustrate well both their vulnerability to exogenous forces and their durability (and commitment to survive) as efficient mechanisms for housing delivery. During the darkest periods in the financial crunch, pressure was brought to bear on the federal government to implement several programs authorized by the Housing and Community Development Act of 1974 which could have greatly helped the HFAs to more easily and quickly regain access to the bond markets. The federal response was excruciatingly slow; by the time the programs were made operational by HUD they were either no longer immediately needed by the HFAs or were deemed to be so overburdened with federal red tape and restrictions as to seriously limit the HFAs' highly valued flexibility.

Comments: 1. In addition to the state level housing finance agencies, a few states have authorized similarly financed local government programs. The Marks-Foran bill in California is representative of these. It enables local jurisdictions to sell revenue bonds that provide loan funds to finance the rehabilitation of housing units by their owners. A very few localities have seized the initiative for such needs and provided direct rehabilitation loans to homeowners from general revenue funds. Seattle, Washington, operates such a program. It is very small in total dollar volume but it is a conceptually significant realm of direct local government support.

2. Up to this point in this chapter the examination of housing capital problems and policies has remained largely descriptive or tied to the most rudimentary ideas of market mechanics and macroeconomic efficiency. In the main it has dealt with the sometimes contradictory actions of the federal government taken to improve or perfect the operation

of private money markets, or financial sector, in terms of service to the housing economy. The next reading, the final article in this chapter, provides a broader, more critical perspective. It emphasizes especially the distributional impacts on local markets of such macroeconomic policies. Among the possibilities it suggests is the perverse implication that the rationalization of the money market, and its transformation into a national market, may be a principal causal factor in the deterioration of inner city housing. The article presents a penetrating empirical study of the inner city Baltimore Housing Market by a left-oriented geographer.

HARVEY, THE POLITICAL ECONOMY OF URBANIZATION IN ADVANCED CAPITALIST SOCIETIES: THE CASE OF THE UNITED STATES, FROM THE SOCIAL ECONOMY OF CITIES 119, 140-56 (G. Gappert & H. Rose eds., 1975) Vol. 9, Urban Affairs Annual Reviews)

The Financial Structure and Local Markets: The Case of Baltimore

There is abundant evidence that the financial superstructure [or financial sector — Eds.] plays an important role in the organization of local housing markets and that many of the "urban problems" with which we are familiar — racial and class segregation, housing abandonment, neighborhood decay, speculative change, fiscal inequalities between cities and suburbs, inequality of access to services (such as education and health care) — are in some way tied to residential differentiation in cities which is, in turn, tied to the way in which investment is channeled into local housing markets. There are numerous studies which document certain aspects of this process in detail while it is a familiar topic for Congressional hearings. Rather than attempt a summary of this material, Baltimore will be used as an example to show how the financial superstructure relates to a local housing market and through this to all aspects of community life and politics.

The financial superstructure is so organized that it can resolve a social aggregation problem. It links local activities to national aggregative needs by creating local "decision environments" as contexts within which individuals exercise choice. Relations between the total social structure and individual activities are in part established through the financial superstructure. I have elsewhere sought to show in some detail how and why this social aggregation process necessitates the creation of distinctive housing characteristics. The central proposition of that argument, which will be treated as an assumption here, is that the financial superstructure serves to coordinate the urbanization process in a particular locale with the overall aggregative push toward stimulating effective demand and facilitating capital accumulation. This proposition requires qualification, for the coordinations are not perfect nor are they established by way of a conscious conspiracy. The coordinating process has, in fact, been arrived at in much the same ad hoc adaptive way that has characterized the setting up of the financial superstructure in general.

An analysis of the activities of the various kinds of financial intermediary in the housing mortgage market in Baltimore City shows two things. First, different intermediaries are responsible for originating mortgages over different price ranges (see Table 8). Small-scale state chartered S&Ls were the only institutions willing to originate mortgages on housing in the below-$7,000 category, where savings banks and commercial banks confined themselves to the upper price ranges. Second, different intermediaries serve different geographical areas and act to form distinctive housing submarkets as far as housing finance is concerned (see Figure 4 and Tables 9 and 10). A "snapshot" of activity in 1970 shows, for example, that small-scale, community-based S&Ls dominated housing finance in the traditional ethnic areas of South and East Baltimore, that the middle-income white areas of northeast and southeast Baltimore were largely served by the federal S&Ls, that the affluent areas drew upon the financial resources of savings banks and commercial banks, while areas of high turnover were strongly associated with mortgage company finance in association with FHA insurance.

Table 8. Distribution of mortgage activity in different price categories by type of institution, Baltimore city, 1972

	Under $7,000	$7,000-$9,999	$10,000-$11,999	$12,000-$14,999	Over $15,000
Private	39	16	13	7	7
State S&Ls	42	33	21	21	20
Federal S&Ls	10	22	30	31	35
Mortgage banks	7	24	29	23	12
Savings banks	–	3	5	15	19
Commercial banks	1	1	2	3	7
Percent of city's transactions in category	21	19	15	20	24

SOURCE: "Homeownership and the Baltimore Mortgage Market," Draft Report of the Home Ownership Development Program, Department of Housing and Community Development, Baltimore City, 1973.

Table 9. Housing submarkets — Baltimore city, 1970

	Total Houses Sold	Sales Per 100 Properties	Cash	Pvt	Fed S&L	State S&L	Mtge Bank	Comm Bank	Savings Bank	Others	FHA	VA	Average Sale Price (3)b
Inner City	1,189	1.85	65.7	15.0	3.0	12.0	2.2	0.5	0.2	1.7	2.9	1.1	3,498
1. East	646	2.33	64.7	15.0	2.2	14.3	2.2	0.5	0.1	1.2	3.4	1.4	3,437
2. West	553	1.51	67.0	15.1	4.0	9.2	2.3	0.4	0.4	2.2	2.3	0.6	3,568
Ethnic	760	3.34	39.9	5.5	6.1	43.2	2.0	0.8	0.9	2.2	2.6	0.7	6,372
1. E. Baltimore	579	3.40	39.7	4.8	5.5	43.7	2.4	1.0	1.2	2.2	3.2	0.7	6,700
2. S. Baltimore	181	3.20	40.3	7.7	7.7	41.4	0.6			2.2	0.6	0.5	5,102
Hampden	99	2.40	40.4	8.1	18.2	29.3	4.0		3.0		14.1	2.0	7,059
West Baltimore	497	2.32	30.8	12.5	12.1	11.7	22.3	1.6	3.1	6.0	25.8	4.2	8,684
South Baltimore	322	3.16	28.3	7.4	22.7	13.4	13.4	1.9	4.0	9.0	22.7	10.6	8,751
High Turnover	2,072	5.28	19.1	6.1	13.6	14.9	32.9	1.2	5.7	6.2	33.2	9.5	9,902
1. Northwest	1,071	5.42	20.0	7.2	9.7	13.8	40.0	1.1	2.9	4.5	48.8	7.4	9,312
2. Northeast	693	5.07	20.6	6.4	14.4	16.5	29.0	1.4	5.6	5.9	34.5	10.2	9,779
3. North	308	5.35	12.7	1.4	25.3	18.1	13.3	0.7	15.9	12.7	31.5	15.5	12,330
Middle Income	1,077	3.15	29.8	4.4	29.8	17.0	8.6	1.9	8.7	9.0	17.7	11.1	12,760
1. Southwest	212	3.46	17.0	6.6	29.2	8.6	15.1	1.0	10.8	11.7	30.2	17.0	12,848
2. Northeast	865	3.09	21.7	3.8	30.0	19.2	7.0	2.0	8.2	8.2	14.7	9.7	12,751
Upper Income	361	3.84	19.4	6.9	23.5	10.6	8.6	7.2	21.1	2.8	11.9	3.6	27,413

a. Assumed mortgages and subject to mortgage.
b. Ground rent is sometimes included in the sales price and this distorts the averages in certain respects. The relative differentials between the submarkets are of the right order however.
SOURCE: City Planning Department Tabulations from Lusk Reports.

Table 10. Housing submarkets — Baltimore city, 1970 (Census Data)

	Median Income[a]	% Black Occupied D.U.'s	% Units Owner Occupied	Mean $ Value of Own. Occ.	% Renter Occupied	Mean Monthly Rent
Inner City	6,259	72.2	28.5	6,259	71.5	77.5
1. East	6,201	65.1	29.3	6,380	70.7	75.2
2. West	6,297	76.9	27.9	6,963	72.1	78.9
Ethnic	8,822	1.0	66.0	8,005	34.0	76.8
1. E. Baltimore	8,836	1.2	65.3	8,368	33.7	78.7
2. S. Baltimore	8,785	0.2	64.7	6,504	35.3	69.6
Hampden	8,730	0.3	58.8	7,960	41.2	76.8
W. Baltimore	9,566	84.1	50.0	13,842	50.0	103.7
S. Baltimore	8,941	0.1	56.9	9,741	43.1	82.0
High Turnover	10,413	34.3	53.5	11,886	46.5	113.8
1. Northwest	9,483	55.4	49.3	11,867	50.7	110.6
2. Northeast	10,753	30.4	58.5	11,533	41.5	111.5
3. North	11,510	1.3	49.0	12,726	51.0	125.1
Middle Income	10,639	2.8	62.6	13,221	37.5	104.1
1. Southwest	10,655	4.4	48.8	13,470	51.2	108.1
2. Northwest	10,634	2.3	66.2	13,174	33.8	103.0
Upper Income	17,577	1.7	50.8	27,097	49.2	141.4

a. **Weighted average of median incomes for census tracts in submarket.**
SOURCE: 1970 Census.

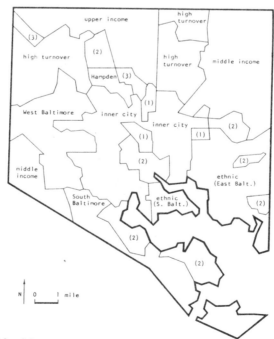

KEY: (1) Special residential areas
      (2) Census tracts with little or no private housing or subject to urban renewal
      (3) Unallocated census tracts (mixed housing stock and mixed financing)

Figure 4 Housing submarkets in Baltimore city, 1970 (Redrawn from Harvey)

The structure of financing across the various housing submarkets, and the residential differentiation which this implies, has a history and is constantly in the course of evolution. Changes occurring within submarkets promote boundary shifts. On occasion, too, whole new submarkets can be dramatically created. Such changes are a response to a variety of forces which stem from changing relative wage rates, changing job opportunities within a changing structure of the division of labor, migratory movements, and so on. But all of these forces are marshalled and given coherence in the urban context through the mediating power of the financial superstructure. The contemporary history of residential differentiation in Baltimore can be used to illustrate this point.

A. West Baltimore and the Land-Installment Contract

The snapshot of activity in 1970 (Figure 4 and Tables 9 and 10) shows West Baltimore as a quiet, almost stagnant, housing market populated largely by blacks, many of whom had achieved the status of moderate income homeowners. This submarket was not always this way. Throughout much of the 1960s it had been the scene of turmoil, rapid social and racial change, community conflict and outrage. At issue during this time was how could blacks, many of whom were experiencing modest gains in income and rising expectations, gain access to reasonable quality housing. In the early 1960s financial institutions were not prepared to provide mortgage finance to this social group. The grounds for such denial varied from scarcely concealed racial prejudice to rationalizations based on creditworthiness or the expected future value of the properties being bought. Government institutions seldom intervened and when they did so, as was the case with the FHA prior to 1964, they frequently acted to formalize discrimination.

Into this vacuum created by rising effective demand and the failure of financial intermediaries to provide credit crept the landlord-speculator. And the tool which the landlord-speculator used was known as the land-installment contract. [Land installment contracts are loans in which ownership remains with the seller until the buyer has paid off the purchase price and interest in its entirety. — Eds.] The submarket of West Baltimore was dramatically carved out during the 1960s by the use of this device. A community group, the Activists, documented over 4,000 land-installment contract transactions in Baltimore City in the early 1960s and the majority of these were in West Baltimore. One organization bought 1,768 houses for $10.8 million and sold 742 of them on the land-installment contract for $9.4 million (the rest going into the rental inventory). The average purchase price for the speculator on the houses finally sold was $6,868 compared to final average sales price of $12,706. The net mark-up, called the "black tax," became the center of controversy in Baltimore during the 1960s, as did the very high rate of induced turnover in the housing stock. The latter had all the marks of a well-organized block-busting operation. As the Activists sought to track down the origin of this problem, they quickly became aware that it was to be attributed in large part to the unwillingness of financial institutions to provide the black home-seeker with mortgage credit except through the intermediary of the speculator. They learned, for example, that several small S&Ls, and not a few not-so-small ones, were using most of their financial resources (80% or more in several cases) to finance land-installment contract activity, i.e., to finance the speculator rather than the prospective homeowner directly.

The speculators' use of the land-installment contract required additional capital to that which could legally be provided by the S&Ls. The commercial banks provided short-term loans (at prime interest rates) to finance the initial purchase of the house and also lent to the speculator for longer periods to help cover the difference between the appraised value of the property and the final purchase price to the buyer. For the commercial banks this was sound business. It yielded them prime rates of return on short-term loans to fairly secure speculative operations which were successfully pooling risks. This kind of business was obviously to be preferred to making illiquid and usually small homeownership loans at an interest rate held down by state usury laws.

By 1969 the use of the land-installment contract and the speculative activity associated with it were much diminished. The urban riots (in which discontent over housing exploitation played an important role), public presssure on the S&Ls not to finance this kind of activity (backed up by tightening Federal Home Loan Bank Board regulation of federal S&Ls), and the public pillorying of landlord-speculators who used the land-installment contract were, perhaps, the most important factors. But by 1969 the new submarket of West Baltimore had been created and the land-installment contract had served its purpose. The immediate purpose, of course, was to generate profits (and in some cases excess profits) for the speculator-landlords and to yield relatively high rates of return to the financial institutions. But we can identify a deeper purpose by relating the events in West Baltimore to the interpretation of the urbanization process in general set out in the preceding section.

The financial institutions, by denying funds to certain groups in particular areas and channeling investment to preferred speculative borrowers, created a decision context in which speculative activity was almost bound to succeed. In the process, a new submarket was created by displacing a middle-income white population which was forced, as a consequence, to look elsewhere for new housing opportunities. Most of these new opportunities were being created on the suburban fringe where land-speculators, developers, construction interests, and the like were actively investing with the resources channeled to them through the financial superstructure. There was, consequently, a multiplier effect to investment in inner-city speculation in the form of a new effective demand for housing largely registered on the suburban periphery. Such a multiplier effect does not have to be consciously or explicitly manipulated, although some institutions (and even individual speculators) operate at both ends of this geographically segmented process and are clearly aware of the connections. The market mechanism and the structure of fiscal and monetary policies on the part of the government along with the specific objectives of the private elements in the financial superstructure and of other intermediaries in the housing market are sufficient in themselves broadly to guarantee this outcome. The creation of the submarket of West Baltimore has to be interpreted, therefore, as an example of the operation of those processes, coordinated through the financial superstructure, which give sufficient dynamism to the urbanization process to match the dynamism of capital accumulation in general.

B. Northeast Baltimore and the FHA

The history of West Baltimore and the land-installment contract during the 1960s was being repeated in many cities in the United States during that period. The processes described and the resentments they aroused contributed to the urban discontents which culminated in the urban riots. During the 1960s, responses were in the process of being fashioned to allow the growth of effective demand and capital accumulation to proceed more smoothly. Regulatory action — over the S&Ls, over the discriminatory red-lining practices of the FHA, over open housing — began to change the emphasis of urban development while leaving the overall goals of economic growth, price stability, and reasonably full employment intact. But something more was needed, as both the Kerner and Douglas Commissions pointed out, and this "something" was provided by the 1968 Housing Act. Among the provisions of this Act were a whole series of measures designed to bring the social and economic "benefits" of homeownership to low- and moderate-income people. One of the programs for doing this was the 221(d)(2) program which permitted the purchase of a house without a down payment.

The 221(d)(2) program basically replaced the land-installment contract in Baltimore as the means whereby relatively low-income groups could obtain access to housing. It therefore held out the prospect of continuing the process of neighborhood change accomplished by means of the land-installment contract prior to 1968, but doing so via a very different set of financial intermediaries. It brought together mortgage companies and FHA insurance. The connection between these two institutions had been strongly developed post-1945. Mortgage bankers do not hold mortgages. They originate them and then sell them in the secondary market mainly to life insurance companies and mutual savings banks. Risk-free mortgages are generally easier to sell in the secondary market and for this reason mortgage companies deal extensively in FHA-insured mortgages. With a tradition of dealing with the FHA, mortgage companies played a vital role in promoting the use of the 221(d)(2) program.

The effects in Baltimore were quite dramatic. First, there was a marked decline in the use of the land-installment contract in the city. Klugman collected data for two transects in northeast and northwest Baltimore; Table 11, taken from his work, illustrates the substitution process. The rise of the 221(d)(2) program was rapid and became highly concentrated in the areas designated High Turnover in Figure 4 (see also Table 9). Figure 5 demonstrates the rapid rise and fall of the FHA-mortgage company combination over the period 1970-1973 in these high turnover areas, while Figure 6 portrays the geographical distribution of FHA-insured mortgage finance in 1970. Most of this was of the 221(d)(2) variety (at least three-quarters) and in the areas of great FHA concentration it was almost exclusively so. Plainly, the FHA programs, with mortgage company finance, were functioning on a geographical basis consistent with long-run processes of changing residential differentiation within the city.

Table 11. Numbers of land-installment contracts and 221(d)(2) insured mortgages in northeast and northwest Baltimore, 1965-1972

Area	1965	1966	1967	1968	1969	1970	1971	1972
Northeast Baltimore								
Land-installment contracts	36	100	73	45	35	19	29	19
221(d)(2)	—	—	—	149	204	191	364	238
Northwest Baltimore								
Land-installment contracts	33	64	79	71	34	19	23	15
221(d)(2)	—	—	—	131	129	244	364	234

SOURCE: Klugman, 1974: Tables VI-2 and VI-3.

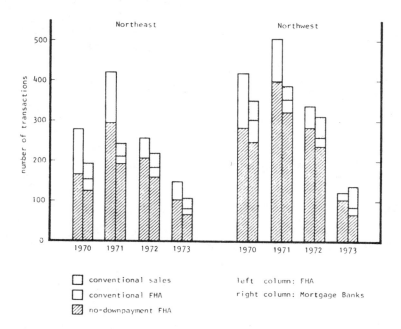

Figure 5 FHA-insured sales and mortgage originations by mortgage bankers in Northeast and Northwest high turnover submarkets, Baltimore, annually, 1970-1973, distinguishing between conventional sales, conventional FHA-insurance and no-down-payment programs (Redrawn from Harvey)

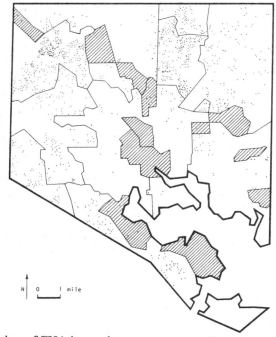

Figure 6 Distribution of FHA-insured mortgages across housing submarkets, Baltimore city, 1970 [Hatched areas are those labelled (1), (2) and (3) on figure 4. — Eds.] (Redrawn from Harvey)

The FHA's powers are basically powers of denial. The Agency cannot initiate the use of programs although it does have ways of signaling to various housing intermediaries what it will or will not do. The FHA plays a vital role, therefore, in creating a "decision context" within which housing intermediaries operate. Figure 6 demonstrates, for example, that the FHA was not insuring in the untouchable zone of the inner city, but Klugman shows that during the period 1969-1972, at least, the FHA was receiving no requests for insurance in that area. The obvious "red-line" in mortgage finance is an excellent example of how something very firmly etched into the geographical landscape of the city can arise by the complex of interactions and expectations which exist in the housing market. The FHA received no requests for insurance because realtors anticipated that requests would be denied; and financial intermediaries would not undertake the risk in areas which were decaying — in part, because mortgage finance was not available. Nobody in particular is at fault, but the red-line nevertheless exists.

The 221(d)(2) program was viewed by all parties as mortgage finance of last resort. It was, in addition, a program which could be used to continue the processes of neighborhood change. Speculators, for example, could pick up a house for, say, $8,000, make some improvements and add all the usual expenses and the profit margin, and then sell it under a 221(d)(2) program for, say, $13,000. This was certainly happening in Baltimore. Landlords (often the same persons as the speculators) could also benefit. For a variety of reasons, largely to do with leveraging practices and taxation arrangements, landlords find it advantageous to purchase a house with the assistance of a mortgage and then to sell it to recover their own part of the equity after seven years or so. The market for such housing was not particularly good, and in effect the 221(d)(2) program created a market into which landlords could sell frequently to the sitting tenant who was then faced with the option of buying or moving. There had been a large volume of landlord purchases in northwest Baltimore during the early and mid-1960s as the area was transformed from owner-occupancy to absentee-landlord ownership and by 1970 many of these houses were ripe for selling. Again, there is evidence that landlords used the 221(d)(2) program to bail out the equity from a housing stock that was rapidly depreciating in some areas — how extensive this was is difficult to judge.

But perhaps the most important agent for change, particularly in the northeast high turnover submarket, was the realtor. Under the 221(d)(2) program it was possible to move low-income black families into middle-income white neighborhoods and thereby to mount a block-busting operation. In the northeastern area, which was largely owner-occupied, the prospects for stimulating turnover by such techniques were favorable, particularly as conventional lenders were beginning to show signs of nervousness and to withdraw financing. Realtor activity, some of it quite unscrupulous, grew remarkably in the northeastern high turnover submarket after 1968, and the 221(d)(2) program and mortgage company finance provided the wherewithal. Community reaction was fast and direct. One group in particular, organized on Saul Alinsky lines, adopted confrontation tactics initially against realtors and subsequently against the FHA which, they claimed, was forcing neighborhood change and artificially depressing house prices. Community activism reached a peak in 1971-1972. But thereafter FHA and mortgage banker involvement in this submarket declined (Figure 5), and with it community activism declined also.

The reason for the gradual disengagement of the FHA-mortgage banker combination from this market had little to do with the level of community activism. By 1972, the 221(d)(2) and 235 program scandals had erupted in Detroit and in other cities, and the FHA was required to adopt stringent new consumer protection measures and to adjust its appraisal practices. Consumer protectionism meant more red tape and delays in mortgage commitments and generally made FHA insurance less attractive. At the same time, mortgage companies were finding FHA mortgages less profitable because of relative movements in interest rates. Mortgage companies began to withdraw from the less profitable small-price range market (in Baltimore, as a matter of policy, they did not finance transactions much below $7,000; but by 1973 this has moved up to $12,000) as well as from participating in the origination of FHA mortgages. Instead, they began to move into the conventional mortgage market on higher valued homes. In addition, S&Ls, which had suffered a heavy savings outflow in 1969 (a process called "disintermediation") were flush with funds in 1971 and 1972 and were willing to service more loans in areas such as the northeast where there was still a substantial demand for conventional mortgage finance. The credit crunch in housing finance, which set in by the summer of 1973, quieted the turnover in the northeastern submarkets and with it died the final remnants of confrontation tactics and activism.

It may sound odd to suggest that community activism is interest rate-sensitive, but in effect this proved to be in part the case in the northeast high turnover submarket. The general point, of course, is that events of national import were being transmitted via the financial superstructure into the decision environments of local housing submarkets. The land-installment contract successfully fashioned a new submarket in West Baltimore and in the process spawned community opposition in the form of the Activists. When the land-installment contract diminished in use, so the Activists became a rump organization without an issue to confront. The rise of the 221(d)(2)-mortgage banker combination continued the processes of neighborhood change in a different manner and in a different area; and this, too, spawned an opposition group. When the mortgage bankers began to withdraw from servicing FHA mortgages and the FHA became much more consumer protection-minded, the problem diminished and the community group was left with nothing to fight over. But, again, by then substantial changes had already been wrought by the FHA programs, and a mixed and somewhat volatile situation had been created — particularly in the northeastern part of the city. All was quiet in 1974 because the housing market was extremely depressed. What will happen in the next boom is, however, problematic.

C. The Ethnic Submarkets and the Evolution of National Financial Policy.

The submarkets designated "ethnic" in Figure 4 are dominated by relatively small-scale state-chartered S&Ls as far as mortgage finance is concerned (see Table 9). These institutions, many of which are quite old, are rather special intermediaries; they take in savings from the community and then, making use of detailed local knowledge about both housing and people, apply these savings to foster homeownership within the community. Many of these S&Ls are ethnic in origin (as names like Golden, Prague, Kopernik, Kosciuszko, and Slavie suggest) and some continue to serve identifiable ethnic groups within the population. This helps to stabilize communities and to provide mortgage finance for not very affluent blue-collar workers who thereby gain access to reasonable quality housing at a relatively low cost compared to their incomes. The mode of operation of these S&Ls means, however, that they are often exclusionary towards other ethnic and racial groups. It also means that savings, far from entering into the mainstream of capital markets, remain locked into the community from which they originate.

Over the years these community-based S&Ls have weakened somewhat under a number of pressures. Some of them, easy prey to the penetration of unscrupulous interests, fell to financing speculative activity. Increasing geographical mobility and rising incomes forced some to expand their operations to finance migration, and in the process they lost their strong neighborhood identity. Others became expansionary-minded and profit-oriented and in businesslike fashion began to put funds where the rate of return was highest and to chase savings aggressively by offering attractive deposit terms. These last, in particular, would typically attract savings from wherever they could and lend where it was most profitable; they typically performed the savings-investment function in a fashion that fostered suburban growth while starving the inner city of financial support. These last practices were critically viewed in the Baltimore City Homeownership Program Report because they involved the export of savings from the city to enhance development (and the tax base) in the surrounding counties. The Report recommended legislative action which would put pressure on the S&Ls to do more business in the area from which savings originated, thus segmenting the market for homeownership finance even further. In 1970 there were still a substantial number of S&Ls which continued to operate either on a neighborhood basis or to serve the needs of distinctive classes of people, thereby contributing to the social stability of the city. From the standpoint of the City, these S&Ls were invaluable and action was advocated to preserve and, if possible, to promote them.

Unfortunately, this logic flies in the face of that explicitly developed in the Hunt Commission Report. . . . The Hunt proposals were arrived at through a consideration of serious problems in the national flows of credit and savings in a period of inflation dominated by an apparently serious capital shortage. The Commission did not attempt to recommend monetary and fiscal policies which would channel savings into mortgage markets on a stable basis even though it admitted that "past failure to meet national housing goals was largely a result of the effects of these policies on housing demand and the supply of mortgage funds." Nevertheless, the Commission was greatly concerned to eliminate barriers to the flow of credit in general and to make capital markets much more competitive. The Commission proposed a reorganization of the ways in which financial institutions would operate which, if carried out, would have far-reaching implications for mortgage finance and housing markets.

The recommendation which is of particular interest here is that which would transform S&Ls into "mini-banks" by permitting them to offer a wide range of customer services (consumer credit, for example). At the same time S&Ls would lose their privileged position with respect to interest rates and be forced to compete in the open market for savings with all the other intermediaries. Such a reorganization would, as Lane Kirkland notes in his dissenting opinion, probably increase the profitability of the S&Ls without necessarily generating any additional funds for the mortgage market — "in fact, in periods of tight money, the mortgage market would be hard hit."

It is difficult to predict what the effects of the Hunt proposals would be. But we can venture a scenario of the following sort. Almost certainly, S&Ls would be forced by competition to become more businesslike and in general to increase in size and sophistication if they are successfully to compete with large commercial banks. Under these conditions it is doubtful if the small-scale, community-based S&L would survive. The S&Ls which could compete successfully would probably be those which, in the name of business rationality, are currently fostering the flow of funds into areas of greatest profit (the suburbs for the most part) at the expense of the inner city. In competition with the banks, the S&Ls would presumably become more bank-like in their behavior and chase the more lucrative business in the more affluent submarkets or lend to speculators, developers, landlords, and the like (unless compensating arrangements, such as tax credits for servicing low-value mortgages, were forthcoming).

If we project these changes into the Baltimore situation, then the effects upon the ethnic submarkets would likely be quite devastating. Financing for low-value mortgages would be hard to obtain — at best it would be "residual" finance after the more lucrative upper-income market had been served. The community-based S&Ls would disappear as would be localized structure of savings and investment in housing. Savings, which usually get channeled into housing finance, would not be protected from the depradations of corporations hungry for external sources of funds. The flow of funds to meet the needs of the not-so-affluent white ethnic and blue-collar worker would be seriously curtailed particularly in times of general credit shortage. A major mechanism for ensuring neighborhood social stability would be destroyed and the disruption of communities by external forces made that much easier.

The Hunt Commission proposals, if accepted in raw form, would in fact perpetuate and accentuate certain of the urbanization processes which we have examined in this article. The land-installment contract devastated existing communities and created new ones in their place. The 221(d)(2) program took over where the land-installment contract left off. Now before the Congress, as the FHA and all of its programs lie in disrepute, are a set of proposals for the reform of the financial superstructure which, if they pass uncompensated for, will perpetuate the processes of neighborhood change and displacement merely by encouraging the flow of investment funds to wherever the rate of return is highest (the more affluent areas and areas of new development and redevelopment) at the expense of less-well-off groups in older areas. Under the Hunt Commission proposals, the pace of urban development and redevelopment will almost certainly quicken, effective demand will thereby be artificially stimulated, and sustained capital accumulation, from this standpoint at least, will be facilitated. The proposals seem almost tailor-made to perpetuate and enhance the dynamics of an urbanization process which, since the 1930s, has been strongly directed to stimulating consumption. The irony is, of course, that these connections lie largely unnoticed, for we still live in a world where it is presumed that the urbanization process can be left to look after itself and that major reforms of the financial superstructure can be contemplated in relationship to extremely limited goals.

BIBLIOGRAPHY

N. Betnun, Housing Finance Agencies: A Comparison Between States and HUD (1976)
    Reviews state housing finance agency programs.

R. Buckley, J. Tuccillo & K. Villani, eds., Capital Markets and the Housing Sector: Perspectives on Financial Reform (1977)

Papers from HUD study assessing proposed financial reforms in mortgage markets and the role of federal intermediaries.

Federal Home Loan Bank of San Francisco, Change in the Savings and Loan Industry (Proceedings of the Second Annual Conference, 1977)
Papers on institutional changes and capital needs of savings and loan associations.

Federal Home Loan Bank of San Francisco, Resources for Housing (Proceedings of the First Annual Conference, 1976)
Papers on private sector and public sector role in housing finance.

R. Starr, Housing and the Money Market (1975)
Basic text on housing finance.

Chapter 8

HOUSING SUBSIDIES

The disparity between the price and quantity of housing on one hand, and the numbers of households and the money available to them to pay these prices on the other hand, constitutes the central problem of housing. Earlier in this text, Castells put the problem succinctly: In the private housing economy, "in the absence of public intervention, the only demand actually taken into account is solvent demand. Now, from a comparison between the incomes of households and the prices and rents of average apartments, one deduces the difficulty of solving the crisis by market mechanisms."

The chapter that follows treats public policy directed at this problem through subsidizing the price of housing and its production, through subsidizing demand, or both. Among the panoply of public measures that bolster the housing economy and improve housing conditions, subsidies stand as the major thrust of American housing policy. Although the various interventions in capital markets including the reconstruction of the mortgage instrument have undoubtedly had a greater aggregate effect on housing and on national life, subsidy policy has usually occupied the spotlight of public attention such as it is. A governmental subsidy is generally defined as a transfer payment from government to private sector. A housing subsidy is a governmental payment designed to increase housing consumption in terms of quality, amount, or both, or to increase production at established price levels. Speaking generally, housing subsidies are designed to transform need into effective demand at socially approved quality levels.

American housing subsidy programs had no clear and carefully articulated beginning, and the role and function of these subsidies continue to be controversial. As related in the Keith, USDHUD, and Marcuse readings in Chapter 6, housing subsidies arose in the Great Depression of the 1930s to support employment and the construction industry. Support for housing consumption was a secondary objective, and one that changed incrementally over the years in response to new priorities and new demands. These policies are predominantly federal government initiatives although they may involve local public and private agencies in the delivery process. Historically, housing subsidies have been used to augment the housing supply, and for a long period were available solely to fund the construction of new housing projects explicitly designated for eligible lower income families. Equity and efficiency problems in these programs, their tendency to subsidize a welfare bureaucracy and the construction industry, and the inhumanity of many subsidized housing projects have stimulated a reorientation in the design of housing subsidy programs. Today, greater consideration is being given to demand subsidies, which are usually proposed in the form of cash allowances that leave the subsidy recipient a freedom of choice in the selection of housing accommodation.

Viewed from a market perspective, some of the various opportunities available for supply and demand subsidies are indicated in the chart in figure 1. Different sectors of the housing supply can be subsidized; subsidies may be directed to new, rehabilitated or existing housing; and different components of the cost of housing may be covered. Historically, subsidies have covered land, construction and financing costs, and publicly owned housing has also enjoyed a property tax

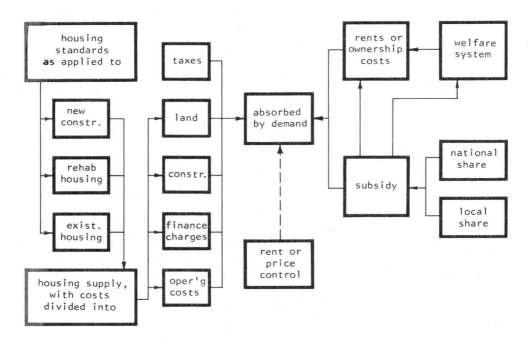

Figure 1 An outline of the housing subsidy system (Redrawn from D. Mandelker, Housing Subsidies in the United States and England)

abatement. The housing subsidy also affects the share of housing costs carried by the tenant or owner. For example, a construction subsidy for rental housing lowers rents by reducing that portion of the housing cost borne by the tenant. Alternatively, there may be no construction subsidy and rents may be subsidized directly. Such subsidies are referred to as demand-side subsidies, the most common of which is the housing allowance.

Many of these types of subsidy are discussed in the pages that follow. This chapter covers three main sub-topics: first, policy alternatives in the design of housing subsidy systems, second, indirect subsidies through the federal income tax, and third, direct subsidy programs for the poor considered under two main themes — the nature and experience with recent programs, and the on-going debate over supply-side versus demand-side subsidies. The first sub-topic is considered in the following reading authored by an eminent housing scholar and former undersecretary of the United States Department of Housing and Urban Development.

SCHUSSHEIM, SUBSIDIZED HOUSING—WHERE DO WE GO FROM HERE, from Hearings Before a Subcommittee of the Committee on Appropriations, House of Representatives, 95th Congress, 1st Session 12-20 (1977)

Policy designers do not start with a clean slate. In weighing an appropriate national housing policy for the future we need to consider previous commitments, experience with earlier programs, and budgetary and institutional means available. It would be foolish, for example, to set a production target for housing so high that prices or rents would rise by 25 percent a year; it would be futile to lay out a set of programs that require a level of managerial or administrative competence far beyond what Federal agencies or local governments have been able to achieve. Ends must be adapted to means just as means must be shaped to carry out realistic goals. Some of the issues involved in this meshing of means and ends are set forth below.

1. *What is the main objective?* Is it to save older neighborhoods? To widen the range of housing choice of lower-income families? To stabilize the homebuilding industry by guaranteeing a steady level of support for new assisted housing? To assure that households with insufficient income are able to afford adequate houses? If the last of these is taken to be the major purpose of Federal housing policy, another set of questions suggest themselves.

2. *How many households need help?* The Urban Institute says that 17 to 18 million households would qualify for assistance. The estimate excludes nonelderly single person households and those with substantial assets. Low-income homeowners — many of whom are elderly — as well as renters would be eligible. . . .

3. *What standards will be applied?* It is generally agreed that housing for which subsidies may be paid should be modest but structurally sound and adequate in terms of basic facilities such as kitchens and bathrooms and with sufficient space for the size of family. Localities participating in the section 8 housing assistance program utilizing existing housing have apparently not had great difficulty in setting standards, although complaints that HUD has not permitted sufficiently high fair market rents may cloak disagreements about acceptable quality of housing. In fact, there may be serious difficulties if one looks at the whole bundle of residential services made available to the family rather than the house alone. Should minimum standards be set for the quality of community facilities and services? The caliber of the schools? Access to recreation and open space? Adequacy of public transportation? These problems are not insuperable if the test of reasonableness is used. But there may be genuine differences of opinion between local officials and representatives of the low-income community both as to standards initially established and adequacy of enforcement. This suggests the need for systematic monitoring by Federal personnel to make sure that Federal assistance is not simply being siphoned off by landlords of substandard rental properties.

If the main objective of Federal assistance is as stated above, the housing occupied by subsidized families need not be new. But if new construction is deemed necessary due to real shortages of adequate housing in the community, standards for new units will probably be set in terms of location, concentration, amenities, and costs. A guiding principle is to recognize that the newly built structures have to yield acceptable housing services over a long period of years. Maintenance and operating costs over time have to be considered, not just initial construction costs. And while the construction need not be luxury quality, it may be false economy to omit facilities deemed essential in market-level developments, such as central air-conditioning in areas with long hot and humid seasons.

4. *Existing versus new housing or both?* From a cost standpoint, existing housing has an advantage over new construction. Families assisted in existing housing under section 8 in fiscal year 1976 required average subsidies of $2,200, compared with $3,600 in new or substantially rehabilitated units. Estimated

subsidy payments in fiscal year 1978 will be $2,200 for existing units and $4,000 in new units. . . .

In addition to lower unit costs in existing housing, the contract commitment can be of far shorter duration than in new construction. And with such assurances as are necessary to induce private owners to rent to assisted families, such as reimbursement for a limited period as a result of the tenant leaving before the lease has expired, the benefits can be tied to the family, not to the unit.

There is, of course, the possibility that rents will be driven up as a result of a leased-house program involving existing housing. Not only would program participants (and therefore the Federal Government) have to pay more, but other families ineligible for subsidies or unwilling to take them would also be adversely affected. . . .

When there are serious housing shortages for particular segments of the population, new construction for subsidized households may be the appropriate response. If new construction is undertaken, the lessons of the recent past with subsidized rental developments must not be forgotten. Are the proposed sites suitably located and serviced and potentially attractive for market-level housing as well as for subsidized families? Have allowances been made for the probability of rising operating expenses? Do the interested sponsors and builders have a record of long-term commitment to stay with their developments? Or do they appear primarily interested in immediate profits on land and construction and the sale of portions of the equity as tax shelters to high-income investors with nonrelated income? Do the sponsors have experience in the management of rental housing occupied by subsidized families? If not, what arrangements have been made to retain competent management? These are some of the questions that prudent program administrators will ask.

5. *Is there a rationale for shallow subsidies?* [Shallow subsidy is jargon for a relatively small subsidy to each unit or household; the contrasting term, deep subsidy, refers to large amounts. Obviously the same total expenditures can be spread more widely with shallow subsidies. Public housing is considered a deep subsidy program. Sections 235 and 236 are shallow. — Eds.] This type of assistance is aimed at lower middle income and working families who presently cannot afford better housing at current market prices. Programs of this sort generally provide interest subsidies or reduced mortgage payments for a period of time to enable certain families to buy homes. If such assistance is to be provided, it may be wise to limit it to relatively strong families with good credit patterns and good prospects of raising their incomes. Home ownership for very low income families with no prior experience with this form of tenure is risky not only for the Federal Government but for the family itself. Earlier program experience suggests that the very poor do not have the resources to cope with home ownership expenses. The upward trend in operating expenses will make it even more difficult for the poor. . . .

6. *What is the role of rehabilitation?* Rehabilitation of housing can range from moderate fixup to gutting and complete reconstruction. The appropriate level of rehabilitation will depend upon incomes and types of families to be served, location and age of properties, and costs compared with new construction (including streets, utilities and other supporting facilities). What we are mainly concerned with here is the potential of rehabilitation for lower income families in their present neighborhoods or areas to which they might gain access. Rehabilitation is important in its own right as a means of extending the economic life of the supply of existing housing. It may also be helpful in improving the housing conditions of lower income families but it is not the only vehicle for this purpose.

For several decades housing officials have seen in rehabilitation an approach of considerable potential but accomplishments have fallen far short of the promise. In laying out the national housing targets, for example, the first goals report of 1969 projected 2 million assisted rehabilitations over the next 10 years. The second goals reports reduced the target to 1 million units and said that even this level would be difficult to achieve because of limited entrepreneurial capacity for rehabilitation. The ninth goals report issued in January 1977 estimates that 274,000 units of subsidized housing were actually begun between 1969 and September 1976 with the possibility of another 100,000 by the end of fiscal year 1978. . . .

The volume of activity is not the sole measure of a program's success or shortfall. One must also consider how long the improvements last, the consequent living conditions of the residents, and the effects on other properties in the vicinity of the rehabilitation. While rehabilitation holds promise, past experience must make us cautious about expecting too much or settling on one particular approach or level of rehabilitation. A check of rehabilitation efforts conducted in four cities with HUD support 7- to 10-years-ago presents a sobering picture. In all four cities — New York, Boston, Pittsburgh, and Detroit — the rehabilitation outlays were substantial, ranging from $8,000 to $18,000 per unit on top of acquisition costs of $2,000 to $5,000 per unit. (Rehab costs for comparable work would be much higher today.) In none of these cities was the rehabilitation a financial success. In all of these cases the mortgages on practically all of the rehabilitated structures have been foreclosed or assigned to FHA. . . .

By and large, rehabilitation of owner-occupied houses has been more successful than of rental properties. This probably reflects the higher incomes and social patterns required for home ownership. It may also work better in neighborhoods or communities that are relatively cohesive and where people are concerned about each other. Thus, neighborhood rehabilitation may tend to reinforce ethnic or racial boundaries. Since fair housing is a matter of national concern and law, local officials must be prepared to reconcile this social objective with neighborhood preservation efforts.

In selecting neighborhoods for rehabilitation, the dominant view today is to give priority to areas that are in early stages of disrepair rather then deep decline. Caught in time and with the proper infusions of public improvements, private credit, and resident participation, many older neighborhoods can probably be stabilized and kept livable for the next 10 to 20 years or longer.

The toughest problems in rehabilitation have to do with low-income renter families in the inner city. In such districts, rehabilitation may have to include not only repairs to houses but improvements in municipal services, efforts to find jobs for the employables, and social services to families. Grigsby's studies in Baltimore suggest that inner city tenants are realists: they ask for better police protection, more frequent garbage pickups, and more play space for children rather than sumptuous improvements to their houses. Rehabilitation of the houses in such areas probably should be limited in type and moderate in cost.

7. *Block grants for housing.* Is this an idea whose time has come? . . .

Under a block grant approach, Federal funds would be distributed by formula to local governments to enable them to carry out a broadly stated Federal purpose. Local recipients would decide how to spend the money in accordance with local priorities as spelled out in some sort of plan. They would not have to obtain Federal approval for individual projects or activities. The Federal department in charge of the program would confine its role to such oversight as necessary to assure financial integrity and program conformance to the local plan and to keeping Congress advised as to progress, problems, and costs of the program. There would also be Federal enforcement of relevant laws such as fair housing and nondiscrimination in employment. The essence of a block grant concept is that local officials and technicians set priorities, choose strategies, and determine specific projects and undertakings with minimal Federal participation.

There are many considerations in the formulation of a block grant for housing such as the scale of the program, the range of permissible activities, and the Federal programs it would or would not replace. . . . A congressional decision to adopt such an approach would seem to turn on at least three crucial questions:

1. Would national purposes and priorities be properly served under a housing block grant system?

2. Can assisted housing be adequately funded through block grants?

3. Do local governments have the competence to develop strategies and implement a broad-gauged program of this type in the complex field of housing?

It is in the nature of local politics that funds for community improvements and housing will be spread widely. Every district and every ward will want some of the Federal money. Funds may be spread too thinly and without particular attention to the needs of the most deprived sectors of the population. This is a finding of several studies with respect to the community development block grant program. There is no reason to think it would not be the same with a housing block grant program.

Second, there is the question of funding. Relatively large numbers of families are now assisted under annual contracts between a sponsor and the Federal Government. Would the Congress be prepared to convey to 2,000 or more localities the power to commit the Federal Government to make payments for assisted housing over 30 or 40 years? If not, the alternative is full funding of all projects. That is, the locality could only make agreements to the extent of funds in hand. This would seem to limit activities to one-time payments or relatively short-term assistance or to needs that can be met with comparatively thin subsidies.

Third, there is the question of local administrative competence. This matter requires more information than is available. Some observers who are familiar with local efforts to administer such programs as Model Cities, urban renewal, and local economic development, among various federally assisted local enterprises, have expressed doubts that local governments as a group currently have the institutions and personnel to carry out effectively and efficiently a housing block grant program. . . .

8. *Should localities be required to share in housing subsidies?* [Schussheim notes three arguments for a local contribution: 1) it demonstrates the locality's commitment; 2) it places some of the costs of expensive programs on local taxpayers; and 3) it makes for closer supervision and better management. — Eds.]

9. *Can housing programs be administered more effectively?* There is widespread dissatisfaction with the administration of housing programs in the United States. Carping about inefficiency and waste in government is a cherished tradition in democratic societies, but it has a special shrillness in this country when directed to programs that are supposed to help the poor. Certainly this is true in connection with subsidized housing. Residents will invariably oppose location of a public housing "project" in a pleasant neighborhood; later, when it has been sited in a ghetto or near the city dump, people will point to the ill-starred development as another example of government bungling.

How do we get an administrative agency to implement effectively a policy or program? "Three conditions must obtain. First, the agency must identify with the goals of the policy. Second, there must be clear communication of what the top officials really want. Third, a penalty and reward system must be available to back up the official policy. Outside the administrative apparatus, the intended beneficiaries of a program must be convinced that real benefits will be forthcoming, and the community at large has to be persuaded that the policy or program is needed and is worth the cost."

Comments: 1. Schussheim's perspective in discussing housing subsidies follows the standard viewpoint taken by policy planners. It is not politically oriented, nor does it look critically at motives. Rather, it accepts the stated, manifest purposes of policy as the actual purposes. Contrast this analysis with the viewpoint of Marcuse in Chapter 6 (supra p. 223).

Nor does Schussheim deal with subsidies in the ways economists typically do. For instance, in writing about housing subsidies the traditionally oriented economist Henry Aaron concentrates on income distribution, inefficiencies of the free market, adjustment lags, and cyclical problems which are built in by the nature of housing itself. Other economists, working from a more radical position, emphasize the problem of high price versus low income and view subsidies as a necessity to keep the housing economy running, and therefore a necessity to a modern industrial national economy. The quote from Castells in the introduction to this chapter takes this view. Is it possible to deduce implicit, ideological views of the housing economy behind Schussheim's perspective?

2. Housing subsidies are in the manifest sense a public response to need as defined by Needleman (supra p. 123) and Grigsby and Rosenberg (supra p. 133) in Chapter 4. How do the fourteen dimensions of housing needs identified in the latter article fit with the nine subsidy policy questions set forth by Schussheim? The endless permutations possible in such a comparison may serve to explain the extraordinary interest among academics in the housing subsidy issue. It also explains some of the intractibleness of the issue, for any policy design that can be tried, there are many others that remain to be tested. Thus the questions about housing subsidy policy seem to remain perpetually open. Some of the later readings in this chapter will make this point more concrete.

3. Schussheim's article deals largely with housing subsidies made available through direct government expenditure programs. Another, and quantitatively more significant, set of subsidies in America comes from the income tax and provides tax advantages for home ownership and rental housing. Table 1 exhibits the scope of these subsidies for a recent year.

Table 1. Direct and indirect federal expenditure for housing (in millions)

I. REVENUE LOSSES FROM INCOME TAX (FISCAL 1977)[a]

Deductibility of Mortgage Interest for Homeowners	4,490
Deductibility of Real Estate Taxes for Homeowners	4,205
Deferral of Capital Gains on Home Sales	890
Exclusion of Capital Gains on Sales by Elderly Homeowners	40
Accelerated Depreciation for Rental Housing	320
Favorable Treatment for Construction-Period Interest and Taxes	150[b]

TOTAL	10,095

[a] Table does not include subsidy from fact homeowners imputed rent not taxed.
[b] A substantial portion of this amount is attributable to nonresident construction.

Table 1. Direct and indirect federal expenditure for housing (in millions)

II. HOUSING ASSISTANCE EXPENDITURES (FISCAL 1978 OUTLAYS)[c]

Direct Housing Subsidy Programs	4,007
Community Development Block Grants and Urban Development Action Grants (estimated share devoted to housing)	662
Section 312 Rehabilitation Loans	43
Urban Homesteading	10
FmHA Direct Loans	414
VA Direct Loans	-75[d]
FHA Insured Loans	650
GNMA Tandem Financing	-225
TOTAL	5,530[e]

[c] Outlays are based on current policy projections.

[d] The negative outlay is attributable to an anticipated sale of loans.

[e] Note that outlays are expected to increase to 11,567 billion by fiscal 1983.

SOURCE: Congressional Budget Office, Congress of the United States, Federal Housing Policy: Current Programs and Recurring Issues 44, 55-59 (1978)

These tax subsidies need to be considered in any appraisal of housing subsidy programs; they constitute a subsidy expenditure in the form of governmental revenue foregone. Federal income tax subsidies for housing are considered in the next section. In reading this material note that the wide use of income taxes by the various states tends to further enlarge these subsidies because state tax laws are modeled on the federal law.

Housing subsidies provided by tax policy have objectives that range far beyond the simple aspects of non-solvent demand. Foremost among these has been the commitment to home ownership that has been an important feature of national housing policy since the 1930s. The Keith and USDHUD national housing readings in Chapter 6, the Stone reading in Chapter 2 and the discussions of secondary markets and the mortgage instrument have all dealt with dimensions of this policy. This commitment to home ownership has been reinforced by the favorable tax treatment homeowners receive under the federal income tax. In total effect tax policy constitutes perhaps the most important single component of housing policy.

A neutral tax system would levy the same tax on the owner and renter. In fact, . . . the United States collects a larger personal income tax from the renter than from the homeowner. Three aspects of the . . . [tax] explain this differential. If the homeowner were taxed like other investors, he would have to report as gross income the rent he could have obtained on his house. He would be allowed deductions for maintenance, depreciation, mortgage interest, and property taxes as expenses incurred in earning income. The difference, or net rent, would be his taxable income. In fact, rather than paying a tax on his imputed net rent he is allowed to deduct mortgage interest and property taxes from his gross income. The taxable income of a homeowner is thus below that of other investors by the sum of net rent, mortgage interest, and property taxes.

H. Aaron, Shelter and Subsidies 54-55 (1972).

In fiscal 1978 it was estimated that mortgage interest and property tax deductions to homeowners provided a tax saving or subsidy of 12.4 billion dollars. Aaron has estimated that the tax saving from the failure to tax imputed rent exceeds the saving from these deductions by 25 percent. The importance of these tax subsidies is likely to be augmented as mortgage interest rates and property taxes continue to increase.

Whether any tax subsidy, such as the tax subsidy for home ownership, is an acceptable means of providing governmental assistance to housing raises important public policy issues. These issues are reviewed in the next selection written by a leading housing economist and research worker.

R. STRUYK, SHOULD GOVERNMENT ENCOURAGE HOME-OWNERSHIP? 28-36 (URBAN INSTITUTE 1977)

Tax Costs

Their Size and Distribution. It is well known that homeowners save substantial taxes because of the provisions of the Internal Revenue Code which allow the inclusion of property tax and mortgage interest payments as personal deductions and the exclusion of the imputed rent from the dwelling as taxable income. Further, these tax savings largely represent net tax advantages to owner occupants compared to renter households even though the Internal Revenue Service allows landlords to use an accelerated depreciation schedule.

. . . .

Of equal importance to the overall value of the tax advantages is the distribution of these benefits by income class. Table 5 displays the distribution of tax benefits based on actual income tax returns. The table shows the taxes paid (before application of tax credits) as a percentage of adjusted gross income for nonaged households filing joint tax returns in 1966. Three tax-filing categories of these households are included: owner occupants filing itemized returns, itemizing renters, and renters using the standard deduction. The households included in these tabulations were deliberately restricted to nonaged families, filing jointly, to make the nonhousing situations of owner occupants and renters more comparable. Also note that the real difference in tax treatment between owners and renters is understated because the imputed net rent for owner-occupied units is not included in owners' taxable income.

Table 5. Total taxes before credit as a percentage of adjusted gross income in 1966*

Adjusted gross income class	Itemizing owner occupants	Renters	
		Standard deduction	Itemizing
Under $5,000	3.5%	3.8%	3.0%
$5,000-$6,999	5.8	7.9	6.8
$7,000-$9,999	8.5	10.6	9.3
$10,000-$14,999	10.9	13.4	11.6
$15,000-$19,999	13.5	16.3	13.9
$20,000-$30,000	15.5	19.4	16.5

*Data apply to jointly filed tax returns for nonaged families. Source of figures: Special tabulation using the 1966 Brookings MERGE tax file. For a description of this file see B. Okner, "Constructing a New Data Base from Existing Microdata Sets: The 1966 MERGE File," *Annals of Economic and Social Measurement* 1 (July 1973) 5: 325-42.

With the exception of the lowest-income households, the actual tax rates of owner occupants are consistently lower than renters at the same income level. The difference in tax rates is on average about 2 percentage points lower for owners than for renters using the standard deduction and 0.6 percentage points lower for owners than for itemizing renters. The dollar value of the homeownership deductions clearly rises with income, because the same percentage differences are applied to increasingly greater incomes.... Clearly, most tax savings are accruing to higher-income households.

Matching Costs with Benefits. Is this pattern of tax savings justified? There are three criteria that any tax expenditure should meet: (1) that the tax provision serves a valid public purpose, (2) that the benefits exceed the costs, and (3) that a tax subsidy be the most efficient means of reaching the public objective. It will be assumed here that these tax provisions serve a valid public purpose. But, in terms of special benefits, it is hard to argue on behalf of the present income-progressive structure of tax benefits; if anything, the greatest benefits to society are derived from moderate-to-low income homeowners. Thus, while we cannot demonstrate the benefits and costs at each income level, it is fairly clear that the largest positive difference between benefits and costs is for lower-income households. Among higher-income households, costs could easily exceed benefits.

At the same time, it is not clear how great an incentive may be required to induce households of different income levels to buy a home. The key information is the extent to which households respond to changes in their after tax income by shifting from renter to homeowner status. It is this information which will demonstrate the difficulty of achieving tenure shifts for different income groups. If the shift is relatively difficult (or expensive) to achieve for low-income households, the emphasis on higher-income households in the present tax structure may be defensible.

There are few quantitative estimates of this responsiveness and none based on econometric analysis of data for individual households. The one study which has yielded plausible, internally consistent estimates was recently completed by Franklin James. It links together aggregate data for the United States in one estimate and, in a second, evaluates Canadian homeownership rates in view of the differences between Canadian and U.S. tax structures, incomes, demographic mixes, and urban-rural household location. Overall, both analyses indicate that a 1 percent increase in tax subsidy will produce about a 1 percent increase in the homeownership rate. James' work shows that tax subsidies indeed influence the homeownership decision, but it does not provide much guidance on differences in the response among income groups.

The use of cash grants, either directly or indirectly through cash refunds administered as part of the federal income tax system, is an alternate governmental mechanism for encouraging homeownership.... [Struyk then discusses income elasticities for housing and notes that elasticity declines as income increases. See Chapter 4 supra. — Eds.]

The evidence, then, indicates that the government may be able to induce households to switch to owner occupancy tenure status more efficiently when the households have low-to-moderate incomes. If this is indeed the case, there are clearly less costly methods of achieving the benefits of homeownership than the present income tax regulations.

. . . .

[Struyk then discusses proposals for limiting the income tax deduction for mortgage interest and property taxes and indicates two caveats to these changes. — Eds.]

Two Caveats. There are two important qualifications to the analysis presented above. One is that the net amount of additional revenue realized by the Treasury from major reform of homeownership tax provisions will be substantially less than the $11 billion cited earlier. The reason is that most households will search out alternative ways of sheltering their incomes from taxes. So, to some degree, reducing homeownership-associated tax savings will serve merely to increase other forms of such savings.

The second qualification has to do with the reforms themselves. It is often argued that the homeowner deductions of mortgage interest payments and property taxes are perfectly parallel to interest and tax deductions from owning other goods. It follows, then, that "reforming" the tax treatment of homeowners is to discriminate against them. In some regards, though, housing is not like other goods. In particular, the very cost of houses (as an asset) is sufficient to preclude homeownership — and the deduction therefor — for a major segment of society. This clearly sets this deduction apart from those for consumer credit loans or payments of personal property taxes on automobiles. Housing is not as sharply distinguished, however, from other major durables. This last point leads naturally into a final comment: Any major reform of the tax treatment of homeownership expenses should be part of a more comprehensive tax reform, if further serious inequities are to be avoided.

Comments: 1. Some people see this system for subsidizing homeownership through tax policy as a perverse and unjust support for high income people at the expense of poorer people. Struyk raises this issue in a dispassionately technical way. In doing so he draws on the work of other housing economists including his former colleague Ozanne whose contribution appeared in excerpted form at the beginning of Chapter 3. Put simply, Ozanne's empirical evidence suggests that only homeowners below median income levels secure markedly better housing services for their money than do renters. Hence on efficiency criteria the tax subsidy is as perverse as it is regressive on equity criteria. Why then this enormous public support of homeownership among the relatively richer households? Perhaps the explanation in part lies in Friedman's concept of social policy rationales cited in a comment in Chapter 6 (supra p. 222) and Stone's view of the economy's drive to continuously expand housing credit (supra p. 67).

2. Table 1 in the comments introducing the Struyk reading showed a second variety of tax subsidy targeted for owners and developers of rental housing. This subsidy provides owners with accelerated depreciation of capital costs and developers with favorable treatment for construction period interest and tax expenses. The congressional study that follows details the nature of the federal tax subsidies for rental housing, including subsidized rental housing.

An understanding of some accounting concepts is necessary to an appreciation of this analysis. Depreciation is one of the important tax advantages available to owners of rental housing, since it is a tax deduction that owners may take against gross rental income, and is a non-expense deduction, meaning that no outlay of income is required. This deduction represents an assumed annual depreciation in the value of the building, which is deducted from gross rental income as an imputed expense. It is a tax shelter because the deduction shelters from income taxation, a portion of the income that otherwise would be subject to federal tax. As the congressional study explains, depreciation also reduces the capital gains tax payable on sale profits when a housing project is sold.

CONGRESSIONAL BUDGET OFFICE, REAL ESTATE TAX SHELTER SUBSIDIES AND DIRECT SUBSIDY ALTERNATIVES 15-18, 25 (1977)
The Components of Real Estate Tax Shelters

Real estate tax shelters have two main goals: to defer the payment of taxes for as long as possible, and to "convert" ordinary income — which is taxed at rates as high as 70 percent — into capital gain income which is taxed at substantially lower rates. Deferral or postponement of tax payments can be quite valuable, because it in effect provides the taxpayer with an interest-free loan from the government. If payment can be deferred for nine years, and if the taxpayer can invest his money at 8 percent, deferral will permit the taxpayer to double his money over that period. Looked at in another way, an investor could break even if he paid $50 today for the right to postpone a $100 tax bill for nine years. This is a measure of the present value of the nine-year deferral.

Accelerated Depreciation and Expensing of Construction Period Interest and Taxes

two main features of real estate tax shelters which permit deferral of tax payments are:

- depreciation deductions in the early years of a building's life which substantially exceed real economic depreciation; and
- immediate deduction of the interest and property tax costs incurred during the construction period, rather than writing these costs off over the life of the building.

Because of the special rules governing limited partnerships, the value of these deductions is substantially enhanced when a large share of the total development cost is financed with borrowed money.

[As the congressional study points out, a limited partnership is a form of business organization that "permits the outside investors to share fully in the partnership's tax deductions, while limiting their personal liability for any actual partnership losses only to the amount of their cash contribution." Id. at 25-26. The deduction of construction period interest and taxes is explained as follows:

[The other main feature of real estate tax shelters — the opportunity to deduct construction period interest and taxes right away rather than over the life of the building — was never designed by the Congress to be a real estate construction subsidy. Interest and property taxes incurred as part of the cost of doing business have always been deductible. The issue in the case of building construction is when they should be deducted. If they are viewed as a current cost of doing business, it is appropriate to deduct them right away; if they are viewed as part of the cost of the building, they should be added to that cost ("capitalized") and written off over the life of the building. During earlier periods, when interest costs were relatively low and only a relatively small part of the cost of construction was borrowed, the issue of how construction period interest and taxes should be treated was not too significant. Now, however, construction period interest and tax deductions can amount to as much as 10 to 15 percent of the total cost of the building and 50 percent or more of the total deductions taken over the first three years. These deductions have therefore become a very substantial "front-end" subsidy for real estate construction, even though they were not originally intended to serve that purpose. — Eds.]

Special Limited Partnership Rules

Special tax rules permit outside investors in a limited partnership to take deductions for tax purposes which may substantially exceed the amount of money they have invested in the partnership. The outside investors' deductions are limited only by their "basis," which in a limited partnership can include not only the amount the outside investors have contributed to the partnership, but also the money the partnership has borrowed, but which no one is personally liable to repay. Take for example the $1,000,000 project discussed earlier, in which $900,000 was borrowed and $140,000 was received from outside investors or limited partners. A limited partner who contributed 10 percent of the equity capital ($14,000) would be able to add 10 percent of the borrowed money ($90,000) to his $14,000 equity share, thereby greatly increasing the ceiling on his tax deductions. In this sample project, the total accumulated tax losses or deductions by the end of the fifth year for the project as a whole come to about $270,000. The 10 percent limited partner is able to deduct a full 10 percent share of that ($27,000), which is nearly twice as much as his $14,000 investment in the project. If the outside investor is in a 60 percent tax bracket, he will save $16,200 in taxes as a result of these deductions (60% x $27,000), thereby getting more than his total cash investment back in only five years.

Converting Ordinary Income into Capital Gains and Provisions for Recapture

Real estate tax shelters also provide investors an opportunity to convert ordinary income into more favorably taxed capital gain income. The high early-year depreciation deductions which permit deferral of taxation are also an important ingredient in the alchemy which converts ordinary income into capital gains. It works like this. As the depreciation deductions are taken each year, they reduce the taxes due on ordinary income, which is taxed at rates up to 70 percent. These depreciation deductions are also subtracted from the initial cost of the property (its "basis" in tax terms), so that when the property is sold its "adjusted basis" (initial cost minus accumulated depreciation deductions) is likely to be lower than the sale price. The difference between the sale price and the adjusted basis is the gain on the sale, and it is subject to tax. But should it be taxed at the ordinary income rates, or at only half those rates as a capital gain? If the gain on the sale is taxed as a capital gain, it would mean that the deductions which earlier reduced the taxes on ordinary income have now produced more favorably treated capital gain income, in effect converting ordinary income into capital gains.

In the case of machinery and equipment, this result is avoided by requiring that the entire difference between the adjusted basis and the sale price be taxed as ordinary income, up to the amount of the depreciation deductions previously taken. This "recaptures" the earlier tax break. In the case of buildings, however, the only part of the earlier accelerated depreciation tax break that is recaptured (taxed as ordinary income) is the amount which exceeds straight-line depreciation. The difference between the sale price and the adjusted basis using straight-line depreciation is taxed at the lower capital gains rates. Only the extra difference due to accelerated depreciation — the "excess" depreciation — is recaptured by being taxed as ordinary income.

Comments: 1. Limited partnerships became a factor in the financing of subsidized rental housing when the federal housing acts of 1964 were changed to permit partnerships to own and operate FHA-sponsored rental housing. Since then, changes in the federal tax laws have enhanced the tax advantages of rental housing as an investment. The Tax Reform Act of 1969 substantially reduced the accelerated depreciation allowed for used buildings and newly constructed commercial buildings, but this change did not apply to newly constructed rental housing. Recapture rules were also tightened, and the more favorable recapture rules previously applicable were retained only for low- and moderate-income, government-assisted housing. Other rental housing enjoys continuing but less favorable recapture advantages.

Additional restrictions were imposed by the Tax Reform Act of 1976. No changes were made in the accelerated depreciation rules, but a new rule was adopted requiring construction period interest and taxes to be added to the cost of the building and written off over a period of time. Low-income, government-assisted rental housing was again favored, as the application of the new rule for construction period interest and taxes was delayed. Changes made in the federal minimum tax, however, will reduce the advantage of accelerated depreciation for investors with substantial tax-sheltered income, and for most investors will increase the capital gains tax on the sale of real property.

Federal real estate tax shelters provided an estimated 1.3 billion in subsidies for past and current real estate construction in fiscal 1978. Only 11 percent of this amount assisted low-income housing. The use of tax shelters for low-income housing has been limited by the availability of governmental housing subsidies, under which most low-income housing is built. A greater portion of tax shelter subsidy may go to low-income housing now that this housing has received substantial tax shelter advantages under the federal income tax law.

2. Tax shelter subsidies are usually viewed as incentives designed to encourage private entrepreneurs to make socially valued investments. This way of viewing tax shelters tends to mask the fact that the financial benefits of such policies accrue directly to entrepreneurs and investors. The ostensible beneficiary, the possible low income tenant, only gains indirectly if at all. Here again the Friedman concept of social welfare as the by-product of satisfying the interests of powerful groups seems to be appropriate.

And again there is an efficiency argument to stand beside this equity one. Critics of the use of income tax benefits to attract investors to low-income housing argue that they create the wrong set of incentives for low-income housing investment. Tax benefits deteriorate rapidly after the initial years, so that investors lose interest and management suffers. This problem has been addressed to some extent by efforts in the United States Department of Housing and Urban Development to improve project management, but the tax disincentive will continue as long as the income tax structure remains unchanged.

3. The final section of this chapter consists of readings that deal with recent experience and current thinking about federal subsidies directed at the problem of housing need among poor people. The general evolution of these policies was presented in the readings in the first half of Chapter 6. The next selection drawn from a report by an arm of the United States Congress brings a more detailed focus on those programs now operating. It includes information on operating experience some of which is quite candid. This critical tone indicates the problematic nature of housing subsidies directed at poor people and serves well to introduce this last main theme of the chapter.

CONGRESSIONAL BUDGET OFFICE, HOUSING POLICY AND RECURRING ISSUES 26-34 (1978)

Housing Assistance Programs

The Department of Housing and Urban Development (HUD) administers several programs designed to reduce the housing costs of lower-income persons and to provide them with physically standard housing. The principal federal housing assistance programs are: (1) low-rent public housing, (2) Section 8 new construction/substantial rehabilitation, (3) Section 8 existing housing, (4) Section 235 homeownership assistance, (5) Section 236 rental assistance and (6) rent supplements. For thirty years following its authorization in 1937, the public housing program served as the federal government's primary housing assistance mechanism. The Section 235, Section 236, and rent supplement programs were authorized during the late 1960s and were the most heavily utilized programs for several years thereafter. In 1973, activity under all of these programs was halted under a national moratorium imposed by the Nixon Administration. Housing assistance activity resumed with the passage of the 1974 Housing and Community Development Act, which authorized the Section 8 programs. Since then, Section 8, public housing, and a revised Section 235 program have been the most heavily used housing assistance devices. During fiscal year 1978, federal outlays for assisted housing are expected to total about $4 billion. . . .

Although all assisted housing programs serve limited-income persons, each program assists a somewhat different group of families and individuals. Section 8, public housing, and rent supplements serve the poorest households, those with an average annual income between $3,500 and $4,500; Section 236 serves somewhat higher-income persons; the Section 235 program serves the highest-income persons among those receiving housing assistance. . . .

Low-Rent Public Housing

The low-rent public housing program funds the construction or the purchase and rehabilitation costs (including financing expenses), and a portion of the operating expenses, of rental projects that are owned and managed by state or local government agencies and made available to lower-income tenants at reduced charges. Public housing is generally limited to low- and moderate-income families and to elderly, handicapped, or displaced individuals. Tenant rental and utility charges are limited to a total of not more than 25 percent of adjusted family income. As of the end of fiscal year 1977, nearly 1.2 million public housing units were available for occupancy, with more than 40 percent designated for elderly or handicapped persons.

In addition to being designed as a mechanism for providing lower-income persons with physically standard low-cost housing, public housing is also viewed as a means of increasing housing production. Nevertheless, during the last 20 years, public housing construction and rehabilitation starts have averaged only about 36,000 units annually and that figure has exceeded 50,000 only four times during that period. Further, there is no way of determining the extent to which public housing construction may be merely substituting for private development. By building units specifically designed for the elderly or handicapped or for large families, public housing may, however, serve special housing needs inadequately met by the private market.

During the years of large-scale urban redevelopment, in the 1950s and 1960s, public housing was viewed as a tool for dealing with displaced households and encouraging the creation of heterogeneous neighborhoods in redeveloped areas. The program has been used more recently as a means of expanding the housing opportunities of lower-income families and minorities in areas previously closed to them. The overall record of the public housing program in promoting either redevelopment or residential integration has, however, not been good; in fact, some critics have argued that public housing has actually contributed to segregation and urban decay by accelerating the flight of whites and higher-income families from racially mixed and declining areas.

Section 8 New Construction/Substantial Rehabilitation

The Section 8 new construction/substantial rehabilitation programs provide assistance on behalf of lower-income households occupying newly built or significantly rehabilitated units that meet certain criteria as to cost, physical adequacy, and location. Under these programs, public agencies or private sponsors develop housing projects in which a portion of the units are made available to low- and moderate-income renters at reduced costs. The difference between the HUD-established allowable rent for each unit and the household contribution — limited to 15-25 percent of family income — is made up by regular payments from HUD to the project owner/manager. Assistance contracts between HUD and project sponsors cover five-year periods and are renewable at the owner's discretion for 20 to 40 years, depending on the type of sponsor and the kind of financing used. Income limits for Section 8 assistance recipients are set at approximately 80 percent of the area median. Only about 30,000 new construction/substantial rehabilitation units were occupied as of December 1977, but more than 500,000 units were in the processing pipeline.

The brief time these programs have been underway precludes firm conclusions concerning their effects. Although they are intended to encourage the production of additional housing by guaranteeing an income stream to potential developers, interest among private developers has not been strong during the initial implementation period. Further, concerns have been raised that the interest the developers have shown may merely reflect a desire to have a federal guarantee of rental income for units that will be made available to lower-income persons only if unassisted tenants cannot be found.

The effect of the Section 8 new construction and substantial rehabilitation programs on racial and economic integration will depend largely on the location of Section 8 projects and the ability of project managers to maintain a demographic mix among tenants. Anecdotal evidence suggests that the new construction program may be somewhat more successful in locating projects in desirable neighborhoods than earlier subsidy programs have been. The designation of nearly all Section 8 new construction/substantial rehabilitation projects as 100-percent subsidized suggests, however, that the program may be less successful in maintaining economically mixed projects than had been expected. The substantial rehabilitation program may be especially useful in promoting neighborhood revitalization; it may also encourage economic integration, if the projects enable lower-income persons to remain in previously depressed areas undergoing housing cost increases.

Section 8 Existing Housing

The existing housing component of the Section 8 program provides assistance on behalf of lower-income households occupying physically adequate, moderate-cost rental housing of their own choosing in the private market. Public housing agencies under contract to HUD subsidize the housing costs of lower-income families by paying their landlords the difference between the tenants' rental fee and the tenants' contribution of 15 to 25 percent of their monthly income. All housing units must meet standards of physical adequacy, must be located within the jurisdiction served by the local agency, and must rent for an amount equal to or less than a HUD-established maximum. Beyond these restrictions, assisted households are free to select the location and type of housing, so long as the landlord is willing to enter into a lease with the tenant and a participation agreement with the administering agency. The reliance on the initiative of the household and the latter's freedom to choose from among existing rental units in the private market distinguish this program from all other federal housing assistance efforts. After some initial delays, implementation of this program has been quite smooth and much more rapid than has been the case with the new construction and substantial rehabilitation programs. As of December 1977, more than 300,000 households were receiving assistance under the Section 8 existing housing program.

The most obvious effect of the Section 8 existing housing program has been on recipients' housing costs. Of households receiving assistance in October 1976, the average share of their income going towards housing before joining the program was in excess of 40 percent; after enrollment, that figure dropped to between 20 and 25 percent. The effect of the program on recipients' housing conditions has been less striking. About half of all households receiving assistance remained in their original units, only a minority of which had to be upgraded in order to enter the program. But studies of similar programs indicate that, in the absence of a requirement that households live in physically adequate units, many families living in standard housing would either move to substandard housing or allow their units to deteriorate.

There is no evidence that the demand generated by an existing housing program is sufficient to induce the construction of new units. On the other hand, this type of program does not appear to inflate housing costs — a commonly expressed fear — even when assisted households constitute a substantially greater proportion of a local market than is now the case with Section 8 households.

One of the arguments in support of this kind of program is that it can both promote racial and economic deconcentration and revitalize neighborhoods. Available evidence indicates that although it does not induce mobility, when minority-headed households receiving this type of assistance do move, they are indeed more likely to relocate in areas of lower concentrations of minority households. Its effects on neighborhood revitalization, on the other hand, appear to be minimal.

Section 235 Homeownership Assistance

The Section 235 program provides mortgage assistance to lower-income households purchasing new or substantially-rehabilitated homes. Families with an income of up to 95 percent of the area median may buy modest homes at a reduced rate of interest on the mortgage, with HUD making up the difference between the family's payment and the amount due the mortgagee.

The Section 235 program was first authorized in 1968 and was suspended in 1973 as part of the national moratorium on housing assistance programs. Because program rules permitted minimal downpayments and effective interest rates as low as 1 percent many families unable to handle the financial burden became homeowners under this program. In addition, many only marginally adequate or completely inadequate units were certified as eligible for the program. As a result, more than 15 percent of all the homes purchased under the original Section 235 program have already been acquired by HUD, often in barely salvageable condition. Section 235 was reinstated in 1975, with the minimum effective rate of interest to the buyer raised to 4 percent and the minimum downpayment set at 3 to 5 percent of the purchase price. The tighter restrictions, designed to reduce the problem of defaults, have limited program activity: in the two years since the reinstatement of the program, subsidy commitments were made for only about 23,000 homes.

The principal effects of the Section 235 program have been on the level of residential construction and the incidence of homeownership among lower-income households. During the years in which the original Section 235 program was active, units built under the program represented as much as 6 percent of the annual number of single-family housing starts.

Section 236 Rental Assistance and Rent Supplements

The Section 236 program, authorized in 1968, provides mortgage interest subsidies to developers of rental projects in which a portion of the housing units are made available to lower-income persons at reduced rates. The interest subsidy alone is sufficient to reduce tenant rental payments to an average of about 30 percent of family income. Additional subsidies are provided on behalf of the occupants of some of the units through rent supplement payments, Section 8 assistance, or "deep subsidy" payments specifically authorized for use in conjunction with Section 236. This piggybacking of those subsidies, which are paid to the project owner, permits tenants' rents for some units to be reduced to 25 percent of their income without jeopardizing the financial viability of the projects. Despite these multiple subsidies, Section 236 has been plagued by the defaults that characterized the original Section 235 program. More than 14 percent of the approximately 4,000 Section 236 mortgages written through 1976, had been assigned to HUD by the mortgagee or foreclosed by the end of that year. A small number of new subsidy commitments are still being made under the program, utilizing spending authority released by the Congress before the 1973 housing moratorium.

The rent supplement program was authorized in 1965 to provide payments to the owners of private rental housing on behalf of lower-income tenants, but it has been used primarily to reduce rental charges in Section 236 and other mortgage subsidy projects. As of the end of fiscal year 1977, there were active rent supplement commitments for approximately 180,000 units.

Section 202 Housing for the Elderly and Handicapped

The Section 202 program provides direct federal loans to nonprofit organizations developing rental housing for the elderly and the handicapped. Under the original Section 202 program authorized in 1959, loans were written at a 3 percent rate of interest and the program primarily benefited persons with incomes too high to qualify for public housing. The program in that form was suspended in 1970, but it was reinstituted in 1974 with the interest charge raised to slightly above the yield on all outstanding Treasury obligations — an interest rate more nearly approximating that of conventional financing. Projects developed under the revised Section 202 program also carry a Section 8 subsidy, which enables the rents of lower-income families and individuals to be reduced to a maximum of 25 percent of their income. To date, the Section 202 program has been used primarily to build housing for the elderly. In recent years, an interest in developing a portion of all Section 202 projects for the exclusive use of the handicapped has been expressed. Through the end of fiscal year 1977, subsidy commitments under the revised Section 202/8 program had been made for about 55,000 units.

Comments: This official report gives a sense of the import of the enormous amount that has been written that is critical of the way these federal housing subsidy programs have worked. Economists have looked at costs, benefits, efficiency, and equity questions. Sociologists and other behavioral scientists have looked at the life lived in these projects. Politicians and policy analysts have examined impacts and interests served. Journalists have written reams of copy. Ideologues have taken positions and argued them at length. No facet of housing has received more attention than subsidies and the way they have worked.

Perhaps it all ties back to something as simple as the number of permutations between the dimensions of need and the dimensions of subsidy policy. Whatever its roots this plethora of written material would be impossible to fit in this text even in the most abstracted form. The following note simply suggests the contours of some of the discussion about experience with existing programs, the critique of them, and possible improvements from future policy changes.

A NOTE ON FEDERAL HOUSING SUBSIDY EXPERIENCE AND THE HOUSING ALLOWANCE ALTERNATIVE

A series of program difficulties have plagued the major federal housing subsidy programs. The initial public housing program worked well until after World War

II, when the tenant mix changed and public housing projects came to be occupied in large measure by welfare families and other tenants "trapped" in poverty. These tenants were unable to meet the rising costs of operation that marked the 1960s. When the St. Louis public housing authority imposed a rent increase in an attempt to meet rising costs, a rent strike followed that helped trigger major changes in the public housing legislation beginning in 1969. Rents were pegged at 25 percent of tenant income and subsidies provided that met operating deficits in part.

There were other major problems with public housing. Financial stringencies in the local public housing authorities led to lack of maintenance, and many projects, often high-rise buildings with minimum amenities, rapidly deteriorated. The ill-fated Pruitt-Igoe complex in St. Louis, now demolished, became the national symbol of this program. (See Chapter 4 supra p. 156 for a comment on life in Pruitt-Igoe.) Public housing became highly segregated as minority groups occupied the projects in great numbers. It was not until after the Supreme Court school integration case in 1954 that integration in public housing became constitutionally mandatory. But this decision had little real effect and if anything, public housing became increasingly ghettoized with each passing year. (See the discussion in Chapter 10 infra p. 355.)

While the high-rise, rundown and vandalized public housing project has become the symbol of program failure in the housing subsidy system, no subsidy program has been subject to more innovative change. A modernization program has been put into effect, tenants have been introduced into management, and procedural guarantees have been afforded to tenants faced with eviction or rent increases. High rise buildings now are generally prohibited. Public housing projects remain racially segregated in many cities but not for want of a series of initiatives to bring about more integration. Federal policies have also required the dispersal of new projects to avoid the overconcentration of projects in areas of the city where minority groups are located. These policies are discussed in Chapters 10 and 11.

Public housing nevertheless remains a stepchild in housing subsidy programs, a fate considered unwarranted by one observer:

> Given the strength of the opposition in American society, congressional agreement to public ownership of housing was a tribute to the power of the critique launched against the performance of the economic system. Until 1965, public housing in the United States meant *publicly owned* housing. The program was one of the few large-scale experiments in public ownership in an area traditionally regarded as part of the private sector. In the early days of the New Deal, ownership was vested in the federal government, and operations were controlled by a centralized bureaucracy. An adverse court ruling in 1935 that prevented the use of eminent domain to obtain land for public housing sites coupled with popular distrust of "big government" forced a change in the rules; the Housing Act of 1937 gave title to local housing authorities (LHAs), which were agencies of local government, created within a framework of state enabling legislation. In the circumstances, if public housing has been a dismal failure, as is often charged, the program is strong evidence against further experimentation along the same lines or in parallel areas. In fact, that is a gross misconception. What failed was a particular form of public housing, foreseeably programmed for failure no matter how earnest, willing, or competent the administration. The attack on "public housing" is perhaps the most arrant example of condemnation without trial in the annals of our society.

. . . .

Meehan, The Rise and Fall of Public Housing: Condemnation Without Trial in A Decent Home and Environment 3, 7 (D. Phares ed. 1977).

In Meehan's view, public housing was "programmed for failure" for several reasons. The quality of construction was poor and the projects deteriorated because funds for maintenance were inadequate and vandalism was not controlled. Tenants were required to shoulder increasingly higher maintenance and operating costs which grew excessively, due to rapid inflation. Not enough housing units were produced to satisfy need, and government policy reacted to this scarcity by excluding the very lower income people the program was intended to serve.

Partly in response to the experience with and criticism of public housing, the federal government developed new subsidy initiatives in the 1960s. (See Chapter 6 supra p. 205.) These programs shifted subsidized housing development and management to the private sector by means of subsidized, below market interest rate mortgages, hence the generic name BMIR programs. Chief among these were the 221(d)3 and 236 rental programs, and the 235 program for owner occupants.

The last reading through an official government publication gave a fair insight into many of the problems associated with BMIR subsidies. Difficulties plagued the Section 236 privately built and managed rental housing program. Many were poorly built, and located on undesirable and impacted sites not well located with respect to demand. Many were in faltering urban renewal areas. Management problems have been epidemic while rising operating costs created financial difficulties. These costs could not easily be met by raising rents because the subsidy afforded in this program limited occupancy to a narrowly defined group of moderate income tenants. An operating subsidy was finally provided by Congress, but not before a large number of these projects had gone into default.

Scandals were endemic in the Section 235 home ownership subsidy program. New construction was often shoddy, partly due to cost limitations built into the statute, while existing homes brought into this program were often patched up with cosmetic repairs only to fall apart soon after their subsidized occupants took possession. Purchasers of these homes simply walked away from their investment, in many cases, with little personal loss since the downpayment required for purchase was minimal. Congress eventually authorized payments to remedy defects in Section 235 housing, but the coverage of this program has not been universal. Racial segregation has also been a problem. Studies by the U.S. Commission on Civil Rights indicated that Section 235 housing tended to concentrate in racially segregated or transitional areas. (See Harvey supra p. 282.)

High-rise public housing ghettos, defaulted 236 projects, and the venal exploitation by unscrupulous real estate professionals in the 235 scandals created a climate that welcomed, in fact required, critical analysis and redesign of the subsidy system. In one of those right people, in the right place, at the right time phenomena, a number of policy analysts in the late 1960s had turned to an examination of housing subsidies. These professionals were trained largely in microeconomics and from it they draw their analytical tools. They share as well the general perspective on public policy that Marcuse (supra p. 223) has called "The myth of the benevolent state." This means they accepted the manifest purposes of subsidies to help poor people in an equitable and efficient way. They did not critically examine such other purposes as serving the interests of elites or sectors of the economy such as construction and financing. Henry Aaron and

Arthur Solomon, from whom the remainder of this note is drawn, are perhaps the ablest of this breed.

In recent years, policy analysts have leveled a compelling critique against conventional housing subsidy programs in which a subsidy is provided on the supply side of the market to support construction of new dwelling units which are then offered directly for rent to eligible applicants. Both public housing and the BMIR program are examples of this kind of subsidy. The dwelling unit is offered on an all-or-nothing basis. In doing so the programs may provide a subsidy greater than the applicant would be willing to pay if left to obtain housing in the private market with a subsidy paid directly to the tenant in cash. As Henry Aaron has pointed out, programs of this kind may confer benefits worth less than their cost. Note well the undercurrent of class-oriented bias in using a gold-plated cigarette lighter to stand for public housing in Aaron's extended metaphor.

> Suppose, for example, a friend gives you a new gold-plated cigarette lighter costing $50. Moreover, he has had your initials engraved on the lighter, so that you cannot exchange it for anything else. How much is the gift worth to you? The answer depends both on your need and on your preferences. If forced to choose between cash and the lighter, you could probably settle on some amount, say $20, that would make you indifferent. In economic terms the cigarette lighter would have brought a benefit of $20 for you; the remaining $30 is "deadweight" loss, a cost incurred that generated no benefits for you. ... In short, gifts that lead the recipient to consume more of a product than he would have consumed if the gift were cash provide him benefits worth less than cost; gifts that do not distort his pattern of consumption bring the recipient benefits equal to cost.
>
> H. Aaron, Shelter and Subsidies 45 (1972).

Programs providing production subsidies for new housing have also been subject to criticism on equity grounds:

> If the intended beneficiaries of a given federal program are assumed to be in some sense "equal," housing assistance under that program may be considered horizontally inequitable to the extent that it provides some members of the target group with more assistance than others. Similarly, a housing program is judged vertically inequitable if a substantial proportion of its benefits are diverted to individuals outside the target population.
>
> A. Solomon, Housing the Urban Poor: A Critical Evaluation of Federal Housing Policy 78 (1974).

Solomon then proceeds to determine whether production-oriented subsidy programs meet the tests of horizontal and vertical equity. He is concerned that subsidies are in fact distributed in proportion to need. He concludes that they are not, "that persons in essentially the same circumstances receive widely varying treatment." He notes that subsidy programs benefit but 2 million of the potentially eligible 25 million they could serve. Some people at the very bottom of the income scale receive no help at all because their incomes are below the level that could pay even the subsidized rents. Others just marginally above the high limit receive nothing while those marginally below may receive substantial aid. Benefit levels among these programs also differ substantially.

Solomon measures vertical equity in housing subsidy programs by assessing the extent to which housing subsidies have been diverted to those who are not poor. This diversion occurs partly because of the costs associated with capital formation and administration. Capital for public housing projects is raised through the sale of tax-exempt bonds to high-income investors. Funds for administration are retained by local public housing authorities charged with administering public housing projects. For privately built and federally subsidized housing, diversion occurs through the tax advantages offered by tax shelters to investors in this housing. These tax shelters are advantageous only to high-income groups.

Solomon recommends making housing assistance directly available to low-income groups. He asserts six compelling reasons for shifting federal housing subsidy policy from the supply side of the market to the demand side, from a production-oriented to a consumer-oriented strategy.

1. Twice as many families can be moved into decent standard housing for any given federal dollar commitment.

2. Short of bulldozing and rebuilding (which [has] already proved itself politically, morally, and financially unacceptable), it is the only strategy designed to stabilize and modestly upgrade declining inner-city neighborhoods.

3. Tying the subsidy to the family rather than the dwelling permits a flexible response to changing local market conditions and programmatic needs.

4. Direct subsidies to consumers offer the most practical means for dispersing low-income households outside impacted, blighted areas.

5. Using the existing supply of older housing minimizes vertical and horizontal inequities.

6. The choice of housing type, structure, and location is placed in the hands of the tenants themselves rather than the government.
Id. at 182-83.

Solomon's assertions that the direct housing allowance is a preferred housing subsidy strategy are drawn deductively from micro-economic arguments and require empirical testing.

An important step toward direct housing assistance was taken in the Section 8 housing assistance program initiated by the federal Housing and Community Development Act of 1974. As described in the preceeding section, the Section 8 existing housing program provides a rental subsidy to eligible participants that reduces the rent payable on an existing housing unit to between 15 and 25 per cent of income. Eligible tenants are given a participation certificate, and are authorized to "shop" for existing housing units which will be brought into the program if the landlord agrees to participate. To be eligible, dwelling units must meet standards of adequacy set by HUD, which also places a ceiling on the rents that can be charged. Results suggest that search and movings costs to participants are high, and that for these and other reasons dispersion effects are not great. A surprising number of Section 8 certificate recipients remain in the same unit occupied before receiving their subsidy. This finding demonstrates that the program functions very simply to reduce housing expenses for eligible households.

An even more explicit step toward a national program of direct housing assistance was taken when Congress authorized the Department of Housing and Urban Development to undertake an experimental housing allowance program in several cities. This experiment has been under way for several years and some of its findings are available. These are described in the following selection drawn from an official report. This remarkable experiment is by far the largest such endeavor ever undertaken by the United States government. It represents the pinnacle of achievement by the rational, microeconomics based policy analysts represented by Solomon, and their most positive contribution to American Housing policy.

U.S. DEPARTMENT OF HOUSING AND URBAN DEVELOPMENT, A SUMMARY REPORT OF CURRENT FINDINGS FROM THE EXPERIMENTAL HOUSING ALLOWANCE PROGRAM 11-23 (1978)

III. Major Findings

A. Participation

To understand how an assistance program operates, we must deal with the issue of participation. Not until we clarify the issues of participation can we answer such questions as: What portion of the eligible population is served? What groups benefit? What are the costs of a program? How are the program funds distributed?

. . .Offers of housing assistance payments [to renter households], households averaging about $70 a month, were made to approximately 1000 eligible households in the Demand Experiment sites of Pittsburgh and Phoenix. Of these eligible households in Pittsburgh, 82 percent became enrollees, and in the course of one year, 41 percent became recipients by satisfying the housing requirements. In Phoenix 86 percent became enrollees and 44 percent recipients. It is possible that the recipient rate could increase during the second year.

After about three years of extensive efforts to inform the eligible population about the opportunity to participate in the Supply Experiment's housing assistance program, 51 percent of the eligible renter households have become recipients in Brown County, Wisconsin, and 39 percent in St. Joseph County, Indiana. For the first two years these rates were changing rapidly; now there are some indications that these rates are stabilizing. Additional analyses are necessary before a more certain statement can be made. We believe the enrollment rates in the Demand sites are higher than in the Supply sites because in the Demand Experiment the households were individually contacted and invited to enroll.

Homeowner participation rates are also available from the Supply Experiment. Again after about three years of program operation, 31 percent of the eligible population have enrolled in Brown County and 29 percent are recipients. In St. Joseph County 32 percent have enrolled and 28 percent are recipients.

Compare these percentages above with the households offered unconstrained assistance: in Phoenix, 92 percent of the households became recipients, in Pittsburgh 84 percent. The earmarking of assistance for housing drastically reduces the number of recipients.

Factors Affecting Participation of Renters

Two primary characteristics distinguish recipients from enrollees who do not attain recipient status: the quality of their housing at the time of enrollment and their propensity to move. Roughly half of the recipients were living in units which met the housing requirements before they enrolled. Most of the other recipients (about one third) moved to housing that met the requirements. And about one out of 8 recipients upgraded the housing they occupied to the standards. It appears that households that live in lower quality housing become recipients less frequently than others.

With other household characteristics being the same, the probability of becoming a recipient increases with higher household income. This comes about primarily because households with higher incomes are more likely to live in units which already meet the housing requirements.

There are variations in the rates at which minorities become recipients. In some localities minorities enroll at rates higher than other groups; in other localities minorities enroll at lower rates. In general it appears that once enrolled they are less likely to become recipients, primarily because their pre-enrollment housing was less likely to meet the requirements.

Older households appear likely to become recipients than younger households, other things being equal. In some cases this difference is traced to their pre-enrollment housing, which is less likely to meet requirements, and in others their apparent reluctance to move. Given these two factors, older households are less likely to become recipients once enrolled.

When payment levels are increased for a given income level and household size, the participation rates increase. This is as might be expected, but large increases in the payment level produce only modest increases in participation. For example, when payment levels were approximately doubled, recipient participation rates increased about 17 percentage points.

B. Mobility

Obviously, many factors ultimately determine whether or not a household moves. But, the process of moving has two basic steps: first searching for another housing unit, then moving. . . .

About 50 percent of the households in the control, housing, and unconstrained assistance groups in Pittsburgh searched for another housing unit. Such variations as exist between the three groups are small. In Phoenix about 62 percent of the households in each group searched, with nearly no variation between groups.

Again with some variation between the groups, in Pittsburgh about one fourth of the households actually moved; with nearly no variation in Phoenix, a little under 50 percent moved.

. . . [T]he housing assistance group [is separated] into those who met housing requirements at enrollment and those who did not. Of those who did, 49 percent in Pittsburgh and 52 percent in Phoenix searched for another housing unit. Since they were receiving payments — that is to say, since their present housing met the standards required — it would appear their search for another unit was not necessarily induced by the assistance program. Households which would receive payments if they met the housing quality requirements searched at slightly higher rates: 53 percent in Pittsburgh and 66 percent in Phoenix. Thus some enrollees may have been induced to search by the promise of payments. However, whatever inducements the payments provided were largely offset by a smaller percentage of the searchers who actually moved. The moving rate differences between those who met and those who did not meet the housing requirements at enrollment were not large: 28 versus 24 percent in Pittsburgh, and 42 versus 50 percent in Phoenix. A statistically controlled comparison yields no significant difference on the basis of these first year data.

It would seem that households with the most incentive to move are those that would receive payments if they moved to housing meeting the housing requirements. Yet in Pittsburgh only 24 percent of those with the most incentive actually did move. That percentage can only be understood in relation to the control group: 23 percent of them moved too. The same comparison in Phoenix shows 50 percent versus 47 percent. In both sites the incentive of payments did not cause households to move significantly more often than control households.

There is another surprising finding . . . . Of those who would receive payments if they moved, 47 percent in Pittsburgh, and 34 percent in Phoenix, did not even search for another place to live.

So far we have found that housing assistance and control households move at about the same rates. But how do the neighborhoods they move to compare?

Again, their behavior appears similar. In both cases they moved to neighborhoods with reduced concentrations of low-income households and which rank more favorably in subjective assessment of less crime, less litter, more public services, better access to public transportation, etc. And when they moved, their choice of neighborhoods (according to racial mixture or whether inner city or suburb) was similar.

C. Use of Payments

To answer the question of how assistance payments are used, we depend on data obtained from the control, unconstrained, and housing assisted households groups of the Demand Experiment. The findings are expressed in terms of increases in expenditures used for housing induced by the housing assistance payments. Since housing expenditures tend to increase over time, with or without assistance, data from the control households are crucial to these findings. By using them to "adjust" the expenditure increases of the assisted households, we can determine what changes of expenditure are the result of the program itself.

Using rents as the measure of change, we can say that housing assistance payments do cause renter households to spend more for housing. But the payments in the first year primarily served to reduce out-of-pocket expenses for housing, in most cases from over 40 percent of a household's income to about 25 percent.

Households that already met the housing requirements at enrollment generally showed a smaller program-induced increase in expenditure than households that did not meet the requirements until after enrollment. For both types of households combined, the program-induced increases averaged about 29 percent of the housing assistance payments. For the households receiving unconstrained assistance, the program-induced increases were only 10 percent of the assistance payment, a third of that of the housing assistance households . . . .

To the extent that all households eventually move, households that moved during their first year in the experiment are particularly interesting because they may foreshadow the eventual response of other households. [H]ouseholds who moved generally spent about 40 percent of their housing assistance payments on program-induced housing expenditures. Unconstrained households used only 10 percent of their assistance payments for program-induced increases.

D. Improvements in Housing

To determine the improvements in housing experienced by households, we require some measure of housing quality. . . .

. . . [I]n this report rent expenditure is used as proxy for housing quality. The findings are based on the Demand Experiments' data from the first year. Experiences of the control households are used to adjust the data for those changes that would have occurred without the program.

As might be expected, modest increases in rent expenditure were made by those households which, at the time of enrollment, already lived in units that met the housing requirements. Those whose units did not meet housing requirements until after enrollment increased their rental expenditures by about 37 percent. Some of this increase would have occurred even without the program because of general inflation and the rent adjustments that often accompany a change of units. After adjusting for this normal change, we estimate that the program induces a 19 percent increase in rent expenditure. These are the combined results from the two sites. . . .

E. Housing Market Effects

The Supply Experiments, which were primarily designed to address the issues of market responses, involve a ten-year long program open to all eligible renters and homeowner households in each of two metropolitan areas, chosen for strong contrasts in their housing markets, Brown County, Wisconsin (whose central city is Green Bay), and St. Joseph County, Indiana (whose central city is South Bend).

The sites were selected from among all metropolitan areas whose populations in 1970 were under 250,000, the size limit reflecting resource constraints. In the one case, Brown County is a "tight" housing market undivided by racial segregation; in the other case, St. Joseph County is a "loose" housing market with a segregated minority population.

As of the end of September 1977 the program had been operating for about 39 months in Brown County and 30 months in St. Joseph County. There were 3,148 households receiving payments in Brown County (about 7% of all households) and 4,913 in St. Joseph County (about 8% of all households). Payments averaged about $900 per year for each household.

The response of a market to the increased demand for housing created by an allowance program might show up in the form of higher prices or increased housing production, or both. The evidence gathered from both sites indicates that as of now, the additional demand for acceptable housing has had virtually no effect on either rents or home prices. Nor is there evidence that the program has been responsible for any new construction.

In fact, in both sites rents have increased somewhat less than the national or regional averages. Moreover, virtually the entire increase is attributable to higher fuel and utility bills.

The Supply Experiment's finding that the increased demand for housing created by assistance payments has had no effect on prices is consistent with the other. . .[housing allowance experiment] results. . . . [T]he additional demand on the housing market is small. It comes from less than 5 percent of the total household population using about 40 percent of the assistance received (roughly $40 per month) for additional housing.

Although the program has not caused any price or quantity effects in the housing markets, it has been directly responsible for modest improvements to the recipient's home, whether rented or owned. Through September 1977, over 2,406 units in Brown County and 4,000 units in St. Joseph County were repaired by or at the request of enrollees seeking to qualify for payments. Another 900 and 1,200 units, respectively, were repaired following annual reinspections of the recipient's housing. Because many of the defects — especially the health and safety hazards — were easily remedied and because homeowners, landlords, tenants and their friends provided most of the labor, cash outlays were usually modest.

Comments: 1. Perhaps the most important finding from the Experimental Housing Allowance Program is the low income elasticity of demand among the experimental populations. In contrast to most conventional wisdom and prior research (see Note supra p. 146 and deLeeuw supra p. 142) elasticities were very low, only about 0.2 overall. This finding means that only twenty cents of each additional housing allowance dollar went to housing. As a device for improving peoples housing quality by increasing their expenditure level, EHAP seems to show housing allowances would be inefficient indeed.

Related to this finding is the low participation rate. This too can be taken as evidence that other aspects of the family budget have a higher priority than housing. More detailed study of the results suggests that part of the low participation problem may lie in a substantial underestimation by policy makers of search and moving costs. Reluctance to participate in the program and to move to upgrade housing quality may be rational and appropriate behavior given the costs of relocation.

2. People with a stake in housing subsidy programs designed to improve housing quality have been confounded by the EHAP results. Attacks on the experimental design have resulted. For instance, a report critical of the experiment has been issued by the Comptroller General of the United States, An Assessment of the Department of Housing and Urban Development's Experimental Housing Allowance Program (1978). In addition to criticizing the research design and the selection of the experimental sites, the report draws negative conclusions on the effectiveness of the program.

> For most recipients the allowance payment increased their disposable income because they already lived in housing that met program standards but housing expenses exceeded 25 percent of their adjusted gross income. Thus, the housing allowances have enabled participants . . . to increase expenditures for goods and services other than housing.
> Id. at 26.

Even more controversial has been the surprising finding that EHAP had minimal price effects. Conventional microeconomic analysis held that a widespread housing allowance would cause price and rent inflation because there would be no expansion of the housing supply to meet augmented demand. RAND, the research contractor on the supply experiment and HUD report, reported that no inflation occurred. The Comptroller General report disputes this finding:

Some important reasons for the noninflationary effect on housing prices in Green Bay are:

> —Rand has been unable to attract the number of participants expected, thus reducing the economic stimulus that might have caused inflation.
> —Rand's results show that, generally, participants have not increased their housing expenditures, moved or substantially repaired their units. The allowance has supplemented income.
> Id. at 24.

At the present time a contradiction remains between the puzzling EHAP results and conventional supply and demand theory. No generally accepted reconciliation appears likely soon.

3. Some more fundamental criticisms of the housing allowance concept have survived untouched by the findings of EHAP. While traditional economists would argue that the low income elasticities and other experimental evidence suggest poor people put little value on improved quality housing, others disagree. Among the more effective of those holding the latter position is housing expert-activist Chester Hartman. His commentary concludes this chapter.

C. HARTMAN, HOUSING AND SOCIAL POLICY 155-59 (1975)

Housing Allowances: The Grand Delusion

The problem with the housing allowance approach as it is presently conceived is that making the poor "free-market" consumers leaves unchanged the numerous defects of that market, which will severely hamper, if not totally undermine, efforts on the part of recipients to find and keep decent housing. The elaborate social science experiments that are being undertaken will, to be sure, produce much important information about the mechanics and results of the housing allowance approach. But we already know from experience a great deal about what the poor and near-poor get for their housing dollars, how much their housing costs, how landlords behave, and how well housing codes are enforced; and we know enough about the housing market to explain the results we see.

The housing allowance approach assumes that the sole cause of housing problems is inadequate incomes. It pays insufficient attention to the vast shortage of decent, moderate-rent housing in most urban and suburban areas, particularly for groups the market now serves poorly, such as large families. Only in those few areas where there is a high vacancy rate for such housing will allowances be successful (the Kansas City experiment that HUD touted so widely was undertaken in an area with a 6.2 percent metropolitan vacancy rate, 8.7 percent in the county where most of the participants found housing). While allowances by law will be available only for standard housing, few doubt that the introduction of housing allowances into a static supply of housing will lead to rent inflation (on a short-term basis at least), not only for recipients but also for other low-and moderate-income households competing for the same units. Rents are spiralling across the country even without an allowance program, and as a result many cities have introduced or plan to introduce rent control. . . . Yet the design of the housing allowance experiments does not call for any form of rent control, and it is highly improbable that an administration-introduced program will include regulation of rents to be charged in the private sector. Without such measures, housing allowances will benefit landlords far more than they will benefit low-income families.

The housing allowance approach also ignores pervasive housing discrimination with respect to acceptance of tenants, eviction, and rents charged — on the basis of race, welfare status, number of children, family composition, age, and life style, which are all grounds for systematic discrimination on the part of landlords and others who control the allocation of private housing. Extensive racial discrimination was reported in the Kansas City housing allowance pilot project. The mere ability to pay the rent by no means guarantees that the housing consumer will get what he or she wants. Landlords may charge to housing allowance recipients a covert premium for the privilege of being accepted as tenants. Nor will lending institutions and insurance companies cease to "redline" areas occupied by nonwhites and the poor. A sellers' market prevails, and just as housing code enforcement has been a failure, so strict attempts to police a quality standard requirement will also be ineffective. Allowances may induce some owners to upgrade their units, but wherever possible landlords will attempt to capture the additional consumers' income made available through allowances without doing renovation, or by making minimal, nondurable repairs.

. . . .

Finally, the state of most landlord-tenant legal relationships throughout the country will severely limit the ability of housing allowance recipients to get a fair shake in the housing market. . . . Without good lease protections, warranty of habitability rights, rent withholding provisions, and protection against retaliatory evictions and other forms of intimidation, the low-income tenant is at the mercy of the landlord. If a federal model lease that incorporated most or all of these protections were made a mandatory part of the housing allowance program, this would be a substantial step toward creating a set of balanced legal relationships between landlord and tenant — and toward reform of landlord-tenant law nationwide — but there is virtually no likelihood of this, in light of the program's announced emphasis on the "free market" and minimal government intervention.

These, then, are the characteristics of the housing market in which housing allowance recipients will be permitted to exercise their "free choice." If the nature of the market does not raise severe doubts about the fate of housing allowance recipients, the results of two very similar programs — public welfare and the [Section 8] public housing leasing program — should. While families receive a lump sum under the public welfare program, a specified portion of this amount, based on standard budgets, is earmarked for housing. As Martin Rein notes, "If the federal government were seriously to consider developing a housing allowance to low-income households, the experience of those on welfare could serve as a useful guide in anticipating some of the strains and difficulties that such a program might encounter." Those strains and difficulties are [:] ... just about the worst housing conditions of any group in the society, inadequate government supervision and intervention, and widespread discrimination and maltreatment by landlords. Leased public housing is also similar to housing allowances, the principal difference (other than administrative arrangements for handling the subsidy) being that the housing authority instead of the family itself locates the unit. In some communities the local housing authority permits or encourages eligible tenants to find units on their own and bring them to the housing authority, which virtually obliterates the distinction between the two programs. According to an Urban Institute study, "because the leasing program uses the private real estate market to a much greater degree than other housing programs, it can be viewed as a test of what the market can deliver in the way of decent but not luxurious housing services when the effective demand is increased." ... Studies by HUD's Office of Audit and other independent researchers found widespread incidence of substandard housing and inflated rents. (The Urban Institute study was based on interviews with local housing authorities; while it put forth more positive conclusions about the leasing program than those of the independent studies, this may have stemmed from the desire of housing authorities to furnish overly roseate reports about their own work.) The presence of a public agency as intermediary should, if anything, produce results more beneficial to the low-income tenant than the proposed housing allowance system, which would leave the poor and powerless tenant to bargain directly with the landlord.

The housing allowance is only part of a good idea. It fosters the principle of individual choice in the housing market, which is a critical component of housing satisfaction, but it takes no steps to ensure that market conditions will be such that the low-income consumer can truly have free choice or satisfaction. With the present realities of housing conditions and the housing market, freedom of choice can only be enhanced by more government intervention, not less. As Miles Mahoney, former Commissioner of Community Affairs of Massachusetts, noted, "unless the government is, in fact, willing to intervene forcefully in the workings of the private market, the housing allowance program will prove to be no more than yet another subsidy program for the private sphere — the poor will benefit only marginally and the near poor will likely be harmed." Housing allowances are a backward step, as they are being developed, for they will not improve the housing conditions of the poor and will postpone the basic changes that are needed in the housing system if all Americians are to be decently housed.

BIBLIOGRAPHY

H. Aaron, Shelter and Subsidies (1972)
    Reviews federal housing programs and assesses economic impact of subsidies.

A. Downs, Federal Housing Subsidies: How Are They Working? (1973)
A comprehensive review of federal housing policy undertaken following the suspension of federal subsidies by President Nixon in 1973.

L. Friedman, Government and Slum Housing (1968)
Excellent review of the history of housing subsidies and the public housing program.

D. Mandelker, Housing Subsidies in the United States and England (1973)
Contains chapters analyzing American public housing subsidies and history of the congressional Brooke Amendment setting limits to tenant rents in public housing projects.

E. Meehan, Public Housing Policy: Myth Versus Reality (1975)
Concentrates on the experience with the ill-fated Pruitt-Igoe project in St. Louis.

E. Meehan, The Rise and Fall of Public Housing: Condemnation Without Trial in a Decent Home and Environment (D. Phares ed. 1977)
Evaluates the origins, difficulties and reforms in the public housing program.

L. Rainwater, Behind Ghetto Walls: Black Family Life in a Federal Slum (1970)
Classic sociological study of the Pruitt-Igoe project.

A. Solomon, Housing the Urban Poor: A Critical Evaluation of Federal Housing Policy (1974)
Evaluates housing subsidy programs and makes a case for housing allowances as an alternative.

G. Steiner, The State of Welfare (1971)
Contains chapters on public housing.

Chapter 9

NEIGHBORHOOD REVITALIZATION

Neighborhood revitalization and the accompanying preservation of the existing housing stock have emerged as the glamour issues of the late 1970s and early 1980s. Beginning with a spotlight on redlining, or the refusal of financial institutions to loan money for housing in certain inner city neighborhoods, the seventies have seen a meteoric rise in public concern with neighborhood housing issues. Since then neighborhood organizations, bootstrap neighborhood development, various public-private betterment partnerships, and urban pioneering by adventurous relatively high income buyers, renters and rehabilitators signaled the emergence of neighborhood revitalization as an issue whose time has come.

The dynamics of neighborhood change were explored in Chapter 5. As a beginning, the concept of filtering provides the main idea. As the comments on Smith's presentation of the filtering model (supra p. 172) pointed out, whole neighborhoods filter as units locked together by similarities in the neighborhood housing stock in age, house type, urban services and the like, and by similarities among households who tend to be relatively homogeneous in terms of race, social class, and demographic variables. Chapter 5 elaborated on this concept and concluded with Leven's careful presentation of the arbitrage model for neighborhood change (supra p. 192) and its extensions in terms of filtering.

Leven made the distinction between passive and active filtering. In the former case people stayed put but their neighborhoods changed and with that the quality of their housing. In active filtering people moved, changing neighborhoods and houses to ones of poorer or better quality. Note that in both cases qualitative changes can be for the better or for the worse. In neighborhood revitalization both active and passive filtering may be involved although the archetypal idea is the stimulation of passive upward filtering. Almost always, however, this change is combined with some active filtering, particularly by upper status, higher income urban pioneers interested initially in taking an active role by entering a low status area which they can help passively filter upward. To do this generally they must replace former occupants. This latter process is the displacement or gentrification issue so much in the forefront of inner city housing issues today.

The passive-active filtering dichotomy emphasizes another aspect of neighborhood change: the fact that it combines social, economic, and physical processes. Economically, houses change in quality and market value; socially, households and their housing preferences change. Both of these kinds of change are clear in Leven's arbitrage process and in the more primitive stage concepts of neighborhood change. Physical change is usually conceived as tightly tied to the age of housing. (See the note on condition-aging in the comments on the Smith filtering model, supra p. 172). The normal process of neighborhood decline is associated with physical aging and obsolescence. This process in turn emphasizes the importance of physical improvement of housing units within the overall neighborhood revitalization process.

Here we return to the list of issues which have evolved into present day concern with revitalization. Housing finance is a resource critical to physical improvement, hence the importance of redlining and its abatement. This policy issue keys into another — changing neighborhoods as distinctive submarkets. Deteriorated areas stand out as a special type of housing submarket characterized by distinctive classes of people on the demand side, often people who must rent rather than own; a distinctive group of owners, particularly among those who hold the rental stock (see Sternlieb supra p. 88 and Goetze supra p. 92 in Chapter 3); diminished capital values of the stock, and reduced levels of public service.

The readings in this chapter follow the general pattern of policy response to neighborhood decline and revitalization. In broad terms this pattern began with attention to health and safety issues in which the power of government was directed at the social welfare problems associated with bad housing. Whether this movement toward the enforcement of safety, sanitary, and housing codes stemmed from a benevolent concern for the ill-housed or whether it was undertaken on behalf of threatened elites as Marcuse suggested in Chapter 6 (supra p. 223) is perhaps pointless to debate here. In any case, the housing code campaign discussed by Fishman in the first reading addresses the housing conditions of people in poor quality units and the externalities that both threatened the better housed and accelerated the cycle of neighborhood decline. (In relation to the externalities issue, remember the prisoner's dilemma model set forth in Chapter 5, supra p. 188.)

Explicitly or implicitly, the policy concept behind housing code enforcement does not take filtering to be a completely determinist process. Instead, it depends upon the idea that housing quality is largely a function of physical condition, and that it is subject to change or modification either upwards or downwards. Not so with another major neighborhood revitalization policy, slum clearance. This idea takes downward filtering as an inexorable process, and directs policy toward hastening its conclusionary stages: abandonment and redevelopment. The various branches of slum clearance policy are reviewed below in a short historical note following the Fishman reading.

A much more positive program aimed at genuine neighborhood revitalization has largely supplanted slum clearance and has burgeoned in recent years. The next two readings treat the Neighborhood Housing Services program, which is the most widely recognized of these new generation revitalization packages. While in part it evolved from dissatisfaction with previous policies it also drew on a quite different body of theory taken from the social welfare and self-help economic improvement fields. Called community development, the central idea in this theory asserts that every community has untapped resources. These can be brought to bear on problems, according to the theory, by social mobilization efforts including community organization, citizen participation, establishment of new institutions, and various kinds of partnership activities that concert and coordinate these untapped resources.

Compelling as is the community development idea, its limitations clearly prevent blanket application. This conclusion leads to questions on how to ration resources. After a short selection dealing with this question, the chapter turns to some of the structural problems that inhibit community development and revitalization. Readings follow dealing with two of these, tax perversities and discriminatory lending practices by financial institutions.

In conclusion the chapter turns to the negative side of revitalization. As neighborhoods improve prices rise, higher income people compete to enter, and lower income people, even long term residents, may be displaced. This brings the treatment of revitalization up to date for the late 70s and 80s, when the crunch between rising housing costs and rising demand seems destined not only to insure that revitalization occurs frequently, but that when it occurs it will often have sharply negative outcomes. In this it has an ironic and contradictory quality that seems to mark all neighborhood revitalization efforts, even simple housing codes to which the legal scholar Fishman addresses the first reading.

R. FISHMAN, ED., HOUSING CODES, IN HOUSING FOR ALL UNDER LAW 553-57 Report of the American Bar Association's Advisory Commission on Housing and Urban Growth (1977)

Housing codes are like building codes in that they apply to structures; they have no direct effect on new construction, however, because they apply only to existing dwellings. Whereas building codes regulate the minimum conditions for development housing codes regulate the minimum conditions for occupancy. They are applied retroactively to remove substandard nonconformities created by changes in minimum housing requirements. They establish minimum standards for such things as sanitation, light, ventilation, space heating, and cooking equipment. They also regulate maintenance and safety; fix the responsibilities of owners, operators, and occupants of all buildings; and provide for administration, enforcement, and penalties.

While the four model codes currently in use contain similar statements of purpose, the place of such codes in a larger housing policy is a matter of controversy. The National Commission on Urban Problems has observed that at "almost all levels of government there are conflicting policies as to what housing codes are and confusion as to what they should do, how they can be enforced, and what role if any, they should play in helping to provide an abundance of decent housing for American people." To most nineteenth-century reformers, improved housing was essential to any program that could hope to wipe out the pattern of social evils represented by slum life. The proponents of the New York Tenement House Law of 1867, which many regard as the first housing code, blamed the slumlord not only for the appalling physical conditions in which urban slum dwellers had to live, but also for the social pathology typical of slum life. For the reform movement, the purpose of housing codes was to eliminate the social pathology of poverty.

Most people today are skeptical of single-factor explanations for eliminating poverty. Social scientists prefer to speak more modestly about "correlations among various factors" than about "causes" of such things as poverty. This tendency is salutary insofar as it deflates overblown expectations about the likely result of public policies. Yet in spite of what may be a growing sophistication about poverty, many still assert that the housing code is an important tool that can improve neighborhoods or prevent their decline. Is this true? What role should these codes have in an equitable housing policy?

How Housing Codes Work

. . . .

The first step in code enforcement is a visit by an inspector from the municipal department charged with the supervision of existing housing. Such an inspection may be part of a regular system or it may come in response to a particular complaint. In either case, if the housing code provides for criminal penalties the inspector must have either the consent of the occupant or a search warrant in order to enter. The occupant, owner, or other appropriate party is then informed of any violations that may exist, and requested or ordered to remove the violations and "bring the dwelling up to code." The responsible party who fails to comply is subject to coercive administrative, judicial, and private remedies.

In New York, for example, the Commissioner of Real Estate can be appointed by the court as a receiver to collect rents and use the money to make repairs. And where a New York tenant's rent is paid by welfare agencies, payment may be withheld as long as the unit remains in noncompliance with the housing code. In some jurisdictions any tenant has a right to withhold rent for code violations.

Most municipalities are authorized to prosecute violations of housing codes and other ordinances as misdemeanors. Jail terms are often authorized, and civil penalties may be available. For the most part, however, criminal sanctions tend to be used only after administrative persuasion has failed to produce voluntary compliance. In a limited number of localities, occupants may institute their own actions, but more typically only the municipality may start the proceeding.

Routine inspections are rare in most slums, and violations are handled only after a private complaint has been received. Even then, code enforcement is insisted on only for conditions that pose immediate threats to health or safety. Not only is it usual for the level of enforcement to be lowest in the worst parts of town, but the applicable standards may also vary (at least in practice) with the neighborhood. In effect, therefore, there is often no uniform standard. The recent trend has fortunately been to consolidate code enforcement in a single agency, though it is still typical for related standards to be enforced by different local agencies or departments. In New York during the 1960s, for example, six separate agencies shared administrative responsibilities for the housing code. The recent rationalization is partly a result of the federal Housing Act of 1964, which authorized federal assistance for some types of local code enforcement activities. Under the Act, only those municipalities with coordinated enforcement could qualify for funds, and this requirement in many instances led to consolidation of code-enforcement responsibilities in a single agency. Both the 1964 Act and the Housing and Urban Development Act of 1965 required a local code-enforcement program as a condition for receiving federal funds, and these enactments resulted in the adoption of housing codes by almost 5,000 municipalities.

Housing codes across the nation have been adopted on the premises that housing could be improved, neighborhoods maintained, and adequate housing provided by requiring that owners of dwellings maintain them to a minimum standard. Now that housing codes have become widely adopted, it is apparent that they are not achieving these goals. The question is, why not? There is almost always an administrative explanation for the failure of a policy such as the cost and difficulty of training an adequate staff to perform inspections, difficulties in gaining entrance to dwellings, and so on. And almost always there are deeper explanations, too. To begin with, housing codes primarily affect the dwellings of persons with lower incomes, who generally live in rental housing. Their effect on more expensive housing (owned-occupied or rental) is rarely as severe. Code violations are a particular problem for tenants who do not have sufficient resources to make repairs, and it is these people whom housing codes are intended primarily to benefit.

Economics has more bearing on modern housing maintenance and improvement than does the law. A landlord thinking about modernizing a kitchen, for example, will calculate whether an increase in rent will exceed the cost of the work over the life of the improvement. If it does, an economically rational landlord will modernize the kitchen, and will make every other improvement whose cost is less than the increase in rent the improvement will generate. When an improvement would support a rental increment that is less than the cost of improvement, the landlord will stop making improvements. In economic terms, the marginal rate of return on investment at this point is zero, and any further investment will actually diminish the return. Unfortunately, the point at which the marginal rate of return is zero (or even worse) is reached sooner rather than later as a housing unit becomes less desirable and the people who live in it have less money to spend on rent. Some landlords may decide to increase their return by deferring maintenance. Even for the conscientious landlord whose tenants are poor, or whose tenants are not respectful of the property, the cost of maintenance and improvements can become uneconomic.

Part of what housing codes attempt to do is to change this situation by fiat; that is, they compel landlords to improve and maintain certain properties at a costlier level than some landlords think they are worth. Such codes typically do not distinguish between the landlord who is milking a property and a landlord who is conscientious but faced with economic losses. The point may come where the landlord's rate of return is less than just comparable to what could be realized if the money were invested elsewhere or simply put in a bank.

Strict housing code enforcement can thus persuade a landlord to go out of business, and if some other or more efficient landlord does not take over that share of the market, the housing code will [be] counterproductive, at least in this case, for instead of improving the quality of rental housing, it will have reduced the supply. The fact that a few marginal landlords of low-quality housing are driven off the market, however, may not in itself be significant. Indeed, this may be a desirable result if the general tendency of the code is to improve low-income housing without having much effect on supply. Therefore, in order to decide whether a housing code is a desirable policy tool, one has to know a great deal about the landlords who supply poor people's housing in a given metropolitan area. The effects of a code's standard will vary from place to place and from time to time.

Comments: 1. Historically, housing codes have not worked well as a technique for compelling housing maintenance and improvement. Institutional and administrative problems such as sporadic and ineffective inspection programs, poorly structured penalties for violations, and even corruption are often cited as impediments to successful code enforcement. While these institutional barriers certainly exist, they are perhaps rather causal forces impeding the upgrading of houses and neighborhoods. The following brief excerpt enlarges on this point:

> ... [T]he root problems of local code enforcement run much deeper than the foregoing catalogue of defects. The futility of most local housing code enforcement programs stems from failure to recognize the realities of the housing market, particularly for low-income families. Where there is a shortage of decent, low-rent housing, where tenants' rent-paying capacities are limited, and where landlords have little cash equity in their buildings, code enforcement is a two-edged sword, difficult to wield and capable of inflicting injury on those it is designed to aid. Since virtually all residential properties are privately owned, the aim of an enforcement program is to cajole or coerce the private owner into bringing his property into compliance. To do this his motivations and economic capabilities must be taken into account. To proceed oblivious of these factors is to risk forcing the owner to abandon the building, a phenomenon that is already occurring on a large scale in many cities without the inducement of code enforcement. Proposals to "put teeth" into the process — through vacate orders, municipal repair, demolition and receivership powers, denying federal income tax depreciation allowances to buildings in violation of the housing code, making the mortgagee party to enforcement actions — all run the risk that landlords will walk away from their properties rather than make the required repairs. Very few city governments are willing to assume direct responsibility for removing code violations and managing or disposing of buildings abandoned by their owners. ... What is "uneconomic" for a private owner is usually equally uneconomic for the government, and a combination of the general financial difficulties of local governments and the limited notion of municipal

responsibility in the housing field have led to a hands-off policy regarding code enforcement in many blighted areas. In Frank Grad's words, "where there are no vacancies, a code enforcement agency has virtually no room to maneuver in, for even the most miserable shelter is better than none."

If the housing code is enforced, the results may be highly damaging to low-income residents. . . . The supply of low-rent housing may be reduced, through demolition or abandonment, or rents may be raised, which necessitates either a move to lower-priced, and probably substandard, quarters, or added costs that the family cannot afford without taking money away from other necessary budget items.

C. Hartman, Housing and Social Policy 67 (1975)

Hartman points to the potential perverse effects of code enforcement, namely abandonment and displacement.

2. It is not enough to legislate improved housing. Good intentions must be backed by sufficient funds to finance them. While there have been a few subsidy programs to fund housing rehabilitation and code enforcement, federal, state and local support in the past simply has not been extensive or stable enough to be effective. This experience suggests that legislation to improve housing must be backed by broad based political support. Political support, as Keith explains in Chapter 6, is a prerèquisite for the financial support necessary for serious housing rehabilitation efforts. Without sufficient resources, such as loans, grants, and subsidies, history tells us that code enforcement can work to destabilize rather than upgrade urban neighborhoods.

3. The following note discusses slum clearance, the other main body of policy behind the present neighborhood revitalization efforts. It is from these policies that public funds were first made available for the necessary reinvestment in old areas.

A NOTE ON THE EVOLUTION OF NEIGHBORHOOD REVITALIZATION POLICY

Contemporary neighborhood revitalization policy is in part the outgrowth of two older streams of housing policy, tenement house reform and slum clearance. Housing codes exemplify in modern form the nature and direction of the first of these. The underlying objective is to achieve housing and the betterment of neighborhoods by mitigating negative externalities or neighborhood effects. The tools used to achieve this objective depended upon influence, laws, informal sanctions, persuasion and example to secure conforming behavior from property owners and others directly responsible for housing quality. Housing codes represent the most highly developed and successful version of the tenement reform idea. The immediately preceding reading and comments have adequately explored the problems and contradictions in this approach.

The other policy stream from which present day revitalization programs derive consists of slum clearance concepts and the multi-faceted urban renewal program to which they gave birth. At root, slum clearance held that old city neighborhoods were hopeless and that the only answer lay in the wholesale clearance of slums and the development of ideal neighborhoods in their place (see Note on Physical Design supra p. 24). Although the concept was completely articulated in the 1920s, not until the Housing Acts of 1937 and 1949 was public policy developed to implement the idea. In the earlier law, enacted during the depression, slum clearance was coupled with public housing. It provided that slum housing had to be destroyed on a one-for-one basis, and new housing laid out according to the Neighborhood Unit Formula built in its place. Given the conditions of the time and the approaching war, only a few fragments of such totally reconstructed neighborhoods were ever realized.

After World War II the 1949 Act provided for slum clearance, but with the critical difference that the private sector was given full responsibility for the redevelopment phase. Behind it lay the notion that, by assembling large, neighborhood-sized parcels and selling them at below cost prices, private investment would be unleashed to construct new ideal neighborhoods. By and large it did not work. In some favored locations private capital did invest in new housing. When they did, of course, it was for upper income households or solvent demand, not the insolvent former slum dwellers. The same old contradiction between unit prices and household incomes remained. That did not exhaust the problems. After a review of the extent of the slums in the mid-1950s and the staggering costs of slum clearance, a major shift in Federal policy occurred. This is in part chronicled in the Chapter 6 HUD report (supra p. 213). From the standpoint of neighborhood revitalization two critical policies came into being. First, FHA mortgage insurance and later federal secondary mortgage market institutions began to actively support, with guarantees, insurance, and subsidies to developers, the risks of rebuilding slum clearance sites. Second, urban redevelopment was converted into urban renewal. This meant that moneys could be allocated to certain aspects of neighborhood rehabilitation. From this change comes most of the federal government's recent experience with neighborhood revitalization.

By the early 1960s it was clear that renewal worked little better than redevelopment. During that decade several major policy modifications emerged. First, favorable programs for investment in housing unit improvement were developed including outright grants to qualified low-income owners. Second, a modest shift was made from the total physical, brick, mortar, and land orientation to a more social one. Social surveys and social planning went into project design. Citizen project area committees were established at the neighborhood level and funded. In the jargon of the time, urban renewal was expanded to become human renewal.

The third modification was one of the boldest federal programs of modern times. In the late 1960s the Model Cities program was added although it did not replace urban renewal. The character of Model Cities programs varied from locality to locality, but everywhere they emphasized coordination of all available federal funds for local programs, social welfare, health, law enforcement, educational, economic and political development. The program provided a whole array of services to targeted areas including educational and nutrition programs, day care, youth employment and an incredible range of others. Generally, Model Cities programs focused on the social and institutional aspects of neighborhood development rather than on physical conservation or renewal. Model Cities is the antecedent of today's community-based activism and in its day fostered in some cities a high degree of local organization.

The Housing and Community Development Act of 1974 signaled a return to the physical approach to community problems. Aside from its emphasis on physical improvements, the block grant program also embodied a relative shift in federal aid from older cities to new areas and suburbs. Another significant aspect of the program is that fund allocation decisions among competing projects are made on the local level in contrast to the preceding programs in which the federal agency allocated funds and signed off as well on all project details. The combination of scarce resources, local control, and physical orientation has led to a new approach to the revitalization of older neighborhoods, one which relies extensively on local organization and local generation of funds to support rehabilitation activities.

Comments: The Neighborhood Housing Services strategy referred to in the introduction and discussed in the two following sections is the latest wrinkle in neighborhood revitalization. Though not without liabilities, its strength lies in a social, physical, and financial or reinvestment approach to the preservation and improvement of neighborhoods. Additionally, and certainly not of lesser importance, the demographic and economic trends of the times provide powerful support for these recent triumphs in neighborhood improvement.

R. CASSIDY, NEIGHBORHOOD HOUSING SERVICES: EVERYBODY'S GETTING SOMETHING OUT OF IT, PLANNING, NOVEMBER, 1975, at 18

Neighborhood Housing Services of Pittsburgh is one of the most innovative, important, and successful housing programs in operation today. It's so successful that cities across the country are scrambling to duplicate what Pittsburgh has done in its Central North Side, the target area for the NHS program. But before I get too detailed, let me describe two cases that underscore the human side of NHS.

A few years ago Mr. Smith (a pseudonym), a Central North Side homeowner, got hurt on his job. He was laid up in the hospital for months, his doctors fearful that he might never walk again. Smith had to sue his employer for damages; meanwhile, he had no income and could not make the payments on his house and a car he had bought before the accident. Through NHS he got a loan to cover his debts and didn't have to pay anything until he settled his claim against his employer two years later.

Mrs. Johnson (a pseudonym), a 71-year-old cancer victim, was living on welfare and social security. By the time she paid her mortgage and other expenses, her food budget was only $12 a month — not enough to buy food stamps. She wrote President Nixon for help; he replied that there was nothing the government could do. Then NHS stepped in, refinanced her home with a no-interest mortgage, paid off the back taxes, and got her mortgage payments down to $35 a month. This left her with $92 a month with which to buy food stamps.

Without Neighborhood Housing Services, neither Mr. Smith nor Mrs. Johnson would have had anyone to turn to for help.

NHS was started in 1968 by a group of Central North Side residents, most of them women, who were fed up with dilapidated houses (90 percent of them built before 1940), rats, rotten treatment by slumlords, and the refusal of banks to make loans and mortgages in the neighborhood. Since then, NHS has been one of the key components in an overall action plan that has "turned around" the Central North Side from an area where the overwhelming majority of the houses had serious code violations to one where most of the houses have been brought up to code. The Federal Home Loan Bank Board, which regulates mortgage lenders, and HUD have been so impressed with Pittsburgh's NHS that they are using it as a prototype for programs in 28 other cities.

NHS is built on a partnership composed of citizens, city officials, and lending institutions. The citizens provide broad public support for the upgrading of the neighborhood and agree to work cooperatively with the city and the lenders. In Pittsburgh, eight of the 15 board members of the NHS's nonprofit corporation (which runs the organization) are local residents, many of them associated with block clubs and other civic groups, assuring a firm grass-roots base for the program. City involvement includes a comprehensive housing inspection program that is "sensitive" to the needs of the individual homeowners; the complete renovation of nearby West Park (at a cost of $1 million); two new schools (the first new schools built in the city in 40 years); new mercury-vapor street lights, repaved streets, and street trees; and the demolition of many dilapidated houses.

Lender involvement means 23 institutions donating some $230,000 (as of last December) to cover the NHS's administrative costs. All of the institutions must be committed to making "bankable" (normal-risk) loans in the neighborhood, although four of the lenders — the ones represented on the NHS board — have been making most of the loans in the Central North Side.

One other group is involved: foundations and corporation, which make grants to the NHS toward a high-risk revolving loan fund, so that NHS can make low-interest (zero to six percent), low-monthly-payment loans to "unbankable" people like Mr. Smith and Mrs. Johnson. The fund has reached the $850,000 level, most of it from the Sarah Mellon Scaife Foundation.

"It all got started because of one block club," said Dorothy Richardson, a community leader with experience in school reform and the Community Action Program, and now NHS president. "We planned to clean up 24 houses in a courtyard near where I live. We got the landlord to agree to the plan, and he gave us the spray and stuff to kill the rats and cockroaches. We got through five houses and ran out of the stuff, and he reneged on his promise.

"A blind lady was living in one house, and all the roaches wound up in there — more roaches than I have ever seen. We called the police, and they called the health department, and they called the media. The landlord retaliated by trying to evict the blind lady." Outraged by the landlord's action, the residents got together to form CASH, Citizens Against Slum Housing.

The problems faced by the CASH members were really part of a much larger set of problems afflicting the Central North Side. A rundown area of equal parts black and white population about two miles from downtown, the Central North Side in the late 1960s was surrounded by massive demolition. "They tore out 5,000 houses in this valley for I-279," said Thomas Jones, NHS executive director, as we drove down the right-of-way for the still-to-be-started highway. Other demolition was going on for a neighborhood development project and for Allegheny Center, an urban renewal project built by the Aluminum Company of America. Altogether, Jones said, some 8,000 housing units were taken off the market in the area surrounding the Central North Side. Within the area, Allegheny Hospital was taking up land and housing for expansion. The result was severe overcrowding and competition for existing housing, with landlords taking advantage of the demand to convert already crowded units to still higher densities. At the same time individual homeowners found that their area had been red-lined by local lending institutions, so that they couldn't borrow money to make home improvements. And, Jones said, "There was a breakdown of public services. It was difficult to get the city to put in services and capital improvements."

CASH took their case to then-Mayor Joseph Barr. "Mayor Barr told us that there was *no* slum housing in Pittsburgh," said Richardson. "So we held six months of public hearings on slum conditions. Before we knew it, we were fighting for more health inspectors, stricter code enforcement, and so on." They also harassed the landlord who wouldn't give them the roach spray, picketing his house until he sold the 24 houses to a nonprofit group, which rehabilitated them.

Richardson and the CASH people knew that money was the key to success. "We wanted to get to the banks. They had the money. They just didn't want to give it to us," said Richardson. "We met with the bankers in the mayor's conference room. We met regularly for a year, until they began to understand our problems and we began to understand theirs." Out of that year of meetings came the basic idea for the NHS program.

Through last December, NHS had made 339 loans and 25 direct grants to homeowners from its high-risk fund, at zero to six percent interest. Often, said Tom Jones, these loans were made on the worst properties on a block, thus stimulating adjacent homeowners to fix up their homes. And NHS has been able to encourage home ownership. "We had a lot of families who had been tenants for years," said Jones. "We got the landlords to sell to us cheap; then we packaged the mortgage with a home improvement loan, and now the tenants are homeowners."

NHS also employs "sensitive code enforcement," or what Jones calls a "housing deficiency analysis," to avoid the bad connotations of code enforcement. The city and Allegheny County inspectors try to be reasonable about what to expect in the way of enforcement. For example, if an elderly widow has been living in her house for 40 years with an outdated electrical system, the inspectors will not make her put in a new system — unless there is an immediate danger to her.

NHS is service oriented, too. They will help the homeowners with budget counseling, assist him with information on his construction needs, refer him to a reputable building company, and inspect the work during and after construction. For the past few years, the Pittsburgh NHS has taken on the role of general contractor for each job. To make sure that the builders do a good job, NHS withholds 10 percent of the total cost in an escrow fund, which is returned one year later — provided there are no reasonable complaints from the homeowner. (Jones said, "The builders didn't like it at first, but now they look at this as a forced savings account.") NHS also has a "lending library" of $6,000 worth of tools that any North Side resident can borrow to fix up his home.

The newest service is the home maintenance program. For $96 a year, NHS will service some 104 items on a home, give one free emergency call a year (on such things as broken water lines), and repaint the exterior trim once every three years. The pilot program is being funded by a $125,000 grant from the Ford Foundation.

With such a success story, it is no wonder that federal officials in Washington looked up Pittsburgh's NHS as a model to be spread around the nation — especially after the Nixon administration cut off all categorical grant housing programs in 1973. The Federal Home Loan Bank Board, which regulates mortgage lenders, first sponsored pilot programs in five cities. All were successful. In 1974, HUD joined up, and the two agencies formed the Urban Reinvestment Task Force. The task force performs two major functions. It provides staff to help get a program on its feet, and it offers a one-time matching grant of $50,000 to $100,000 to kick off the revolving fund for each new NHS.

Cities hoping for an NHS program must meet certain requirements, according to David Elliot, a task force staff member. The target neighborhood must have 1,000 to 2,000 housing units (most of them in buildings with fewer than four units), a high degree (50 percent or more) of home ownership, and strong citizen organizations. The neighborhood can't be so badly deteriorated that it is beyond saving. The city's lenders must agree to make all bankable loans in the neighborhood and must contribute to the operating expenses of the NHS. The city government must improve services and capital improvements. A high-risk revolving loan fund must be set up. "The program is not a panacea, and we're not suggesting it offers all the answers to urban housing problems," said Elliot. His boss, William Whiteside, adds that neighborhood improvement in NHS-type areas "really takes a coordinated strategy. The city has to improve service levels, do a good code enforcement job, and take care of public amenities. Individual homeowners have to believe that the neighborhood can be saved. Banks have to make loans. There's a lot of debate about how 'disinvestment' " — the code word for red-lining — "gets started. But if you're going to reverse it, it takes a massive approach." Besides Pittsburgh, there are 14 cities with NHS programs in operation and another 14 cities that have programs in the pipeline, Whiteside said.

A nationwide study of NHS programs reveals that it is "a helluva good program," according to Roger Ahlbrandt, Jr., research director of ACTION-Housing, Inc., of Pittsburgh, which conducted the study for HUD. Ahlbrandt said there are two key elements to NHS's success: "First you've got everybody involved. Second, the program wouldn't have worked if it had been a HUD or federally run program. The only reason the lending institutions got involved was because it was local, with citizen involvement."

Ahlbrandt also did an evaluation of the Pittsburgh NHS for HUD, along with staff member Paul Brophy. They concluded, "The effects of NHS extend beyond the initial actions of the citizens who spawned the code enforcement program and the direct loans made by the corporation. The presence of NHS in the community provided both financial and psychological support which played a role in the changing attitudes that were observed in the optimism expressed by residents toward the neighborhood." The ACTION-Housing study points out that NHS had its biggest effect in one particular section of the Central North Side where most of the high-risk loans were made. "It also had a definite effect on the bankers who were directly involved," said Ahlbrandt. "There's more awareness and interest on their part."

It should be emphasized, however, that NHS was not the only program serving the Central North Side during this period. The spinoff effects of nearby urban renewal projects — the $100-million Allegheny Center and the $63-million Three Rivers Stadium project — cannot be underestimated. The Pittsburgh History and Landmarks Foundation kicked in $325,000 in grants for the restoration of historic buildings, particularly in one section known as the Mexican War streets (named after battles of the Mexican War). AHRCO, a nonprofit housing corporation, pumped in another $3.4 million for residential rehabilitation on the North Side. Allegheny Hospital went through a major renovation program. A new community college was built in the area, and numerous other capital improvements were made by the city and Allegheny County. "There was a lot of activity occurring at the time," said Ahlbrandt. "It's very difficult to say which program was the most influential in making the changes that occurred." He added, "In the areas where NHS concentrated its activity, there is evidence that it did contribute to improvement."

Some of the original euphoria about the program may be wearing off, however. The Pittsburgh NHS is having trouble getting money for its high-risk fund. "The foundations tell us, 'You're the best program we've ever funded, but now it's up to someone else to get involved,' " said NHS Director Jones. Dorothy Richardson is not overly concerned, though, pointing out that the fund is already up to $850,000, close to the $1 million target, and is "revolving" some $100,000 a year in repayments.

They're also having trouble "selling" the home maintenance plan. Only 75 families have signed up, Jones said, and he needs a thousand to make it economically feasible. And rehabilitation costs on recent projects have doubled, from about $3,000 a house in 1969 to $6,000 a house today, both because of inflation and "because we're in tougher areas," Jones said.

The program also has been criticized because of defaults in its high-risk loans. NHS has had to write off about $35,000 as uncollectable (out of more than $800,000 loaned). Fifteen percent of the borrowers are also late in their payments. "I really don't get too concerned about that," said Dorothy Richardson. "I would expect that it will go down. The bankers had no idea what kind of delinquency rate to expect when we started out." NHS has hired a staff person to enforce collections, and they are no longer making debt-consolidation loans — the ones where most of the defaults were occurring. "We feel deep responsibility about getting our money back. It's not a giveaway program," said Richardson.

But somebody up there likes NHS. Recently, the city of Pittsburgh decided to devote $4.3 million of its $16 million in community development funds to a housing rehabilitation program similar to NHS's. NHS will administer the program in two of three target areas. Half the money will be used to make direct high-risk loans in target neighborhoods. The other half will be used to subsidize the interest on short-term loans (less than eight years' term). It works this way: The bank will make the loan at, say, 12 percent. The fund will subsidize the interest rate down to three percent. In this way, the money can be spread around to make more loans — what the money boys call "leveraging."

Perhaps the biggest thing in NHS's favor is the psychological boost it has given everybody. Tom Jones says that "there's a change of attitude. When we first started, people wanted to move out. Now we have people who want to move in." A similar effect is being reported in other cities with NHS programs. Jeanne Davis, assistant director of the Cincinnati NHS, says, "We're particularly pleased that the program is having a ripple effect in the neighborhood. It's sort of like a happy disease. Ladders go up on one building, and then they go up on another building across the street." Syd Kennedy, an NHS board member in Dallas, reports that "we've reversed the deterioration, and now we're on the upswing."

"What's nice about NHS is that everybody feels it's their program," says Jones. "Everybody's getting something out of it."

———

Comments: The success of Pittsburgh NHS program has attracted much attention. Federal government policy makers have been impressed, and have attempted to replicate it in several cities across the country. The piece that follows set forth the official program guidelines that translate the basic features of Neighborhood Housing Services into a kind of recipe for neighborhood revitalization. (The Task Force has now been incorporated by Congress.)

NEIGHBORHOOD HOUSING SERVICES PROGRAMS, 42 FEDERAL REGISTER 6665 (1977)

Neighborhood Housing Services (NHS) programs, as developed by the Urban Reinvestment Task Force, are demonstration projects based on tested experience. Essential features of a typical NHS program include the following.

1. A neighborhood with distinct boundaries characterized by (a) basically sound housing structures showing signs of lack of maintenance and deterioration; (b) difficulty in obtaining mortgages and home improvement loans; (c) a substantial number of owner-occupied structures (usually greater than 50%); (d) an area of from 1000 to 2000 structures in larger cities (fewer structures in

smaller cities) which are predominantly single family dwellings; (e) a median family income in the neighborhood no less than 80% of the city-wide median; and (f) structures where typical repair costs are in the range of $6,000 per unit.

2. A neighborhood of residents who want to preserve their community and improve their homes and who will participate in the program and help create a positive improvement climate.

3. Strong local government involvement in developing and implementing the program. This should take the form of increased capital improvements and city service levels where needed, active participation on boards and committees, and establishment of a sensitive and systematic housing inspection program.

4. A group of financial institution executives who agree to reinvest in the neighborhood by making loans at market rates to all homeowners who meet normal underwriting criteria. Financial institution involvement usually takes the form, in addition, of contributions to the NHS to meet operating costs and active participation during development of the program as well as during operation by service on the board and committees.

5. A revolving loan fund designed to meet the needs of NHS clients who cannot meet commercial credit requirements. The fund is set up as a self-help tool for the neighborhood and is a source of loans, not grants, with repayment terms to fit the ability of the borrower. Loans are secured by the property, usually a second deed of trust or mortgage, and NHS counsels with clients to solve payment difficulties. Funds are normally contributed by foundations, local corporate sources and increasingly by local government from community development block grant funds. The Urban Reinvestment Task Force may provide a seed grant to stimulate capitalization of the revolving loan fund.

6. Establishment of an operating program with the following characteristics and providing the following services.

a. A private, state-chartered corporation with . . . [federal] tax exempt status;

b. The corporation is governed by a local board of directors made up of neighborhood residents, at-large community members as appropriate, financial industry representatives, and city government representation or liaison as appropriate. No partner controls, but neighborhood residents constitute a numerical majority on the board;

c. NHS board and committees carry out the on-going responsibility to keep the basic resources in place to operate the NHS program. These include loan fund and administrative funding, code inspection services, public improvements, bankable lending, an adequate level of organized resident support, designated target areas and adequate staffing.

d. From an office in the neighborhood, a small but skilled and committed staff (usually a director, assistant director and secretary or administrative assistant) carry out administrative responsibilities and provide the following NHS services:

Rehabilitation counseling — an analysis of home repair needs, work write-ups, cost estimates and home repair counseling;

Construction monitoring services — on-site inspections and communication links between contractors and residents;

Financial services — financial counseling with regard to client financial alternatives, helping assess and solve real estate related problems or other blocks to property improvement, and making referrals to lenders or other non-NHS resources as appropriate.

Comments: Lurking in the Urban Reinvestment Task Force release is a description of a specific neighborhood type. These neighborhoods are comprised primarily of single family owner occupied homes, resident incomes are not terribly high but not precariously low, and deterioration is not too severe. This innocent prescription for successful housing improvement actually masks a fundamental problem: there are never enough dollars to support neighborhood revitalization in all of the neighborhoods where it is needed. Thus, implicit in the NHS program and similar schemes is an allocation scheme for spending the few dollars which are available.

The following article presents the uncomfortable dilemma of resource rationing in older urban areas. In it William Baer, a housing and planning professor, discusses the allocation formula known as triage.

BAER, ON THE DEATH OF CITIES, PUBLIC INTEREST, No. 45, at 3, 15-17 (1976)

. . . [T]here is the issue of triage. The term means a "sifting," and refers to the unpleasant but inevitable assigning of priorities for treatment among casualties from battle or natural catastrophe so as to put available aid to best use. Typically, triage takes the form of a tripartite division of the victims: those who will survive only if provided with immediate aid; those who will most likely die in any event; and those who will most likely live in any event. The first group receives the bulk of the assistance, the other two receive only enough help to alleviate their worst suffering. Thus there is always a race in time between the exhaustion of resources and the expiration of the wounded, some of whom might have been saved if efforts had not been mistakenly applied to those beyond hope and those not in need of help.

The direct application of triage to sectors of the city has been best articulated by Anthony Downs. He suggests that neighborhoods in need of attention be separated into three groups. The healthiest would receive only token aid — tree plantings, for instance, which are highly visible but do not cost much. The worst would receive a sizeable portion of community funds, but much of this would be devoted to burial services — e.g., demolition of abandoned housing, elimination of public health menaces, etc. The largest portion of community funds under Downs' scheme would be devoted to those neighborhoods just beginning to show the signs of decline. Here assistance would achieve the greatest effect, being neither wasted on neighborhoods too far gone to be helped, nor devoted to neighborhoods that can in part look to their own resources for sustenance.

Local officials in many cities are sympathetic to the triage-like approach. Twenty years of chasing slums around the city have demonstrated to urban renewal specialists the futility of devoting all of its resources to its most blighted areas. In the past, either large investments were sunk into a deteriorated area with scarcely any lasting effects, or its former function was entirely destroyed in the effort to "save" the area. This dilemma has resulted in the pragmatic reconsideration, expressed *sotto voce:* "Don't treat the worst first!" The ramifications of the policy (What happens to those untreated areas? Which areas do you treat instead? In what order?) are not carefully spelled out, no doubt, for political reasons.

The allocation of resources in our society is a political act, and triage is a very deliberate policy of allocating resources. Purposely to withhold resources from some groups clearly in need of help, while providing for others who are clearly in less need, quickly stirs political conflict. No matter what a long-term, objective rationality might suggest for sick and dying neighborhoods, the immediate political reality tends to rule out overt acts of triage as a heartless policy. Triage is simply not a strategy that can be openly espoused in a political setting.

While the connotation of triage is politically unacceptable, this does not mean that the issue simply goes away. Acts of triage are already taking place. Financial ill health has forced cities across the United States to rid themselves of their least essential functions and cut back severely on more basic services so that the civic corpus might be saved. Decisions are thus being made that treat certain public functions as expendable, others not. The focus of triage in these cases is on paring away the least efficient services — they may be healthy (so long as funds are provided) but their continuance is not healthy for the community because of their inefficient use of scarce funds.

Sifting and sorting of neighborhoods also goes on when there is insufficient aid to treat all. A triage-like allocation occurs when some vocal neighborhood groups demand and receive aid while less well-organized areas in similar straits receive none. This is politically acceptable because the underlying premise of the allocation has shifted. Long-term objective calculations — made by policy analysts — of marginal rates of return on investments in different neighborhoods are replaced by short-term political calculations by elected officials showing visible compassion. The ultimate result may be similar to an "inefficient" practice of triage. Resources are devoted to neighborhoods at all three levels: the worst neighborhoods, where aid will do little long-term good but will act as a palliative; those neighborhoods that need aid but have it within their own resources to provide it; and those neighborhoods that both need public assistance and can put it to good use. This may not be the optimum use of aid in a technical sense, but it is a strategy at least superior to that of single-mindedly assisting the worst first. Furthermore, "inefficient" triage may even accomplish neighborhood euthanasia, at least in some instances. I do not mean "mercy killing," but rather what is literally meant by the term: a painless death.

Comments: 1. People do remain in those dead end neighborhoods where just a few dollars will not help. Short term political considerations and the knowledge that we can not write off people as easily as buildings mean that we will tamper with the harsh logic of triage. Triage, like filtering is not a statement about how the world ought to work. Instead, it is an empirical model and pragmatic calculation based upon current political and economic alignments and the limitations they impose.

The triage theory deals with neighborhoods as almost autonomous entities which, by virtue of their internal order, are capable or incapable of improvement. However, Stegman, in Chapter 5 (supra p. 161), provides a neat example of the way in which "exogenous" forces operating at the metropolitan level, such as overproduction by the home building industry, have profound effects upon inner city neighborhoods. Gibson and Harvey in Chapter 7 show the linkages between macro scale political and economic developments and local housing economies. These analyses suggest that structural and institutional forces are awfully powerful at the local level and that they dominate their small economies.

A triage-like allocation plan, or the withdrawal of support from older urban neighborhoods, was practiced by the private sector long before it was discovered by public policy. This suggests that the practices of private sector and government institutions are linked together systematically, and work together in the shaping of urban futures. The consistent over-taxation of older urban properties and the widespread withholding of loan funds in older urban areas represent two detailed examples of the confluence of policies affecting the vitality of neighborhood housing markets. These issues are discussed in the following two readings.

2. The perverse taxation of older urban properties is a widespread phenomenon in this country. Though not intended by theories of property taxation, the owners of older apartments and older homes in declining areas tend to pay higher effective tax rates given the depressed market value of their properties. In a study of New York City analysts Drennan and Tobier noted that, "effective tax rates tend to vary inversely with income and positively with the proportion of poverty households and building size. Market values, on the other hand, tend to vary inversely with poverty households and building age, and positively with income and building size." Other similar studies have produced similar answers. Simply put, this finding means that inner city households pay a disproportionate amount in property taxes relative to wealthier households and to the community services they receive.

When an older neighborhood is rehabilitated, property tax assessments may increase as a result of the increase in property value occasioned by rehabilitation. These tax increases may reinforce the dislocation effect of rehabilitation since lower income residents remaining in an area are unable to meet the increased tax burden. As a consequence, it is generally held that the property tax serves as a disincentive to rehabilitation because by rehabilitating property owners simply price themselves out of their local market. The following article reviews the impact of property taxes on low income housing and evaluates the disincentive theory.

PETERSON, THE PROPERTY TAX AND LOW-INCOME HOUSING MARKETS, IN PROPERTY TAX REFORM 107, 112-21 (G. Peterson ed. 1973)

The Disincentive to Rehabilitation

Perhaps the most frequently alleged harmful effect of the property tax is the discouragement it provides to improvement or rehabilitation of the existing housing stock in low-income neighborhoods. Coupled with this evaluation of the current, detrimental effect of property taxation is the claim that a skillful use of property tax abatements, or a sizable shifting of the tax burden from structures to land, would make it possible to improve the quality of the housing stock dramatically in low-income markets.

The theory behind the property tax's disincentive effect is clear. According to the legal discription of each city's tax system, residential property is supposed to be taxed at a uniform proportion of its true value. If an improvement to a property augments its market value, this increment to value ought to be taxed at the overall property tax rate, just as if the value were attributable to the original portion of the property. Now a tax on the market value of an improvement represents an additional cost which the investor must take into account when deciding whether or not to upgrade his parcel. For an investor who requires a 10 percent rate of return on invested capital, the imposition of a 4 percent effective tax rate on a parcel's market value will effectively discourage all improvements whose original pre-tax rate of return lies between 10 percent and 14 percent, unless market conditions allow the investor to pass on the tax burden to his tenants.

Whether the property tax actually discourages housing investment in this way will depend on whether improvements to the housing stock in fact result in reassessment, or at least are perceived to do so. In a study of property taxation in ten cities, several colleagues and I followed the case histories of some 420 central city parcels. As Table 12 shows, of all the improvements which cost less than $10,000 per unit to carry out, only 10 percent were reassessed within the four years following completion of the improvement, and these had their assessments raised by only a fraction of the cost of improvement. Of the 152 properties in the sample which had undergone private market rehabilitation or upgrading only 19 were reassessed within the four-year period. While it is likely that some of the other improvements eventually will be reflected in assessed valuation — it is common practice for instance, to reassess properties following a sale and the sale price indirectly incorporates the market value of improvements which the previous owner has made — the disincentive which the property tax provides to housing improvements may well have been exaggerated, for the simple reason that reassessment only infrequently occurs as a result of upgrading, and then with great lag.

More immediately to the point, this study found *no* instance where improvement to a property in a blighted neighborhood resulted in reassessment. As was pointed out earlier, residential properties in blighted neighborhoods typically are overassessed, so that even a significant improvement to a building is unlikely to do more than bring the market value of the parcel into line with its assessed valuation. Assessors seem to recognize this fact, and refrain from penalizing improvements in blighted neighborhoods. (See Table 13.)

Table 12. Reassessment as a result of private market rehabilitation

Value of Rehab Per Unit	Number Properties Rehabilitated	Number Properties Reassessed as a Result of Rehab	Percent Reassessed
Less than $500	53	1	1.9%
$ 500 to $2,999	62	10	16.1
$ 3,000 to $9,999	30	4	13.3
$10,000 and over	7	4	57.1
ALL PROPERTIES	152	19	12.5

SOURCE: Peterson et al., *Property Taxes, Housing, and the Cities.*

Table 13. Reassessment of private market rehabilitation by neighborhood

	Less than $300 Per Unit			More than $300 Per Unit		
	Number of Properties Rehabilitated	Number of Properties Reassessed	Percentage Reassessed	Number of Properties Rehabilitated	Number of Properties Reassessed	Percentage Reassessed
Blighted	32	0	0.0	3	0	0.0
Transitional downward	30	5	16.7	3	0	0.0
Rest of City	53	6	11.0	31	8	26.0
ALL NEIGH-BORHOODS	115	11	9.6	37	8	21.6

SOURCE: Peterson et al., *Property Taxes, Housing, and the Cities.*

Investors' reports tend to confirm that fear of reassessment plays a small role in the decision whether or not to make improvements in blighted neighborhoods. As part of the above study, investors were asked to identify what they regarded as the principal obstacles to upgrading their parcels. . . . [O]nly one owner in a blighted neighborhood designated fear of reassessment as a "major obstacle" to upgrading. On the demand side, neighborhood deterioration and inability to raise rents were cited as the most important obstacles. On the supply side, investors assigned most importance to the lack of financing. Outside the blighted neighborhoods, fear of reassessment played a somewhat more important part in investors' calculations, but in low-income areas the prospect of increased property tax liability was the least important obstacle cited by those who thought their properties could benefit from upgrading.

. . . .

The Property Tax and Housing Abandonment

. . . .

At least one link between property taxation and housing abandonment has been firmly established. Almost without exception, several years of property tax delinquency have been found to precede abandonment of a housing parcel. In a typical scenario, the housing investor, once he sees that operating costs have risen to the level of rental receipts or soon will do so enters into an end-game strategy, leading to the ultimate abandonment of his structure. With abandonment in mind, he squeezes the last rental income out of his units, while skimping on maintenance expenditures and defaulting on property tax payments. How long the landlord can operate his structure without making property tax payments depends on the delay involved in the *in rem* proceedings by which a city acquires title to delinquent parcels. Usually, however, these proceedings drag on for many years. In New York City, for example, more than six years elapse between the initiation of sustained property tax default and city takeover of property. During this time a landlord may continue to extract a positive cash flow from his property, even though he does not meet the legal obligations of ownership.

Now if property assessments were fairly and efficiently carried out, most of this linkage between tax delinquency and abandonment would not arise. Insofar as the abandonment of housing is a rational process, it occurs at the moment when the discounted net income that is generated by a property turns negative, with no substantial prospect for recovery. At this time the market value of the property also should become zero. If the assessed valuation accurately reflected market value, ownership of the structure then would carry no property tax liability at all since the property would have no value. In this case avoidance of property tax liability could never be the cause of abandoning a structure.

In the real world, of course, the stickiness of assessments makes for quite a different picture. In their studies of St. Louis and Chicago, the firm of Linton, Mields, and Coston showed that not only did vacant structures go on accumulating tax liabilities, even after abandonment; but often, prior to abandonment, while the market value of these parcels was declining drastically, property tax bills actually were increasing. George Sternlieb's analysis of abandonments in Newark reveals the same pattern of collapsing market values, accompanied by constant or increasing tax liabilities. In both of these studies, the authors imply that the property tax is a major cause of housing abandonment, since it is one of the principal costs that a landlord must face. Without property tax payments the operating statement of a landlord often would show a profit whereas, after tax payments, it shows a sizable loss. The owner, it is claimed, is forced to walk away from his property because of the tax burden.

. . . .

Let us suppose, however, that a significant fraction of the total property tax burden is borne by landlords. Even so, a further look at the process of abandonment casts doubt on the conclusion that property tax liability importantly affects the abandonment decision. Housing abandonment, above all, is a neighborhood phenomenon. In urban areas where rates of abandonment are high, bad neighborhood conditions — as evidenced by crime rates, poor quality public services, and dilapidated housing — typically place a ceiling on the rents a landlord can charge. If tenants are going to pay more than this amount for housing, they prefer to acquire neighborhood amenities that are available only by moving to another part of the city. Against this rent ceiling imposed by neighborhood conditions must be set the landlord's increasing operating costs — the higher costs of labor and maintenance, increasing utility charges, and increasing expenses due to vandalism that he must absorb, as well as possibly increasing property taxes. The property tax may well make the difference as to whether a building is *presently* profitable or not; but given the across-the-board nature of the landlord's cost squeeze in low-quality neighborhoods, once a building turns unprofitable net of property tax payments, it is generally only a matter of a few years until it turns unprofitable to operate, even without property taxes. In this case, the most the property tax does is advance the date of abandonment.

Given the delay with which cities acquire title to tax-delinquent parcels, however, the property tax may not affect even the date of abandonment. If an investor succeeds in estimating the date at which his net cash flow excluding property tax payment will hit zero, and can time his property tax defaults so that the city does not foreclose on his property while it still has income potential for him, the investor can simply cease paying his property taxes in advance and then abandon the parcel at the moment it is privately advantageous to him. In effect, the property tax obligation becomes irrelevant, since long before abandonment occurs the landlord has stopped paying his taxes. The empirical data show that very few properties are abandoned by their owners while still generating a positive cash flow, exclusive of tax liability, as would have to be the case if the property tax were a decisive influence on the timing of abandonment decisions.

Here again, the theoretical effect of the property tax is neutralized by the realities of its administration. Just as cities typically refrain from assessing private market rehabilitation in low-income areas, so they prove loath to take over properties which are laggard in their tax payments. The result is that at the margin, property tax considerations may scarcely enter into the owner's decision to upgrade or abandon a parcel.

It is true, though, that the accumulation of back property taxes on parcels can make it immensely more difficult to turn a *neighborhood* around through public policy. Once a landlord begins to default on property tax payments, even though he may continue to operate his parcel for some time, he in effect has made his abandonment decision. The necessity of paying off the back tax liability makes it much less likely that a change in public policy can convince an owner that it makes economic sense to restore his parcel to good operating condition. For this reason, any plan for neighborhood revitalization in areas where tax delinquency is high ought to include some provision for forgiveness of back tax liability, perhaps upon transfer of title to a new owner or adequate evidence of upgrading by the present owner.

Comments: 1. While Peterson does not believe that property tax reassessment acts as a disincentive to reinvestment and rehabilitation, he does believe that the excessive tax burdens usually imposed upon the owners of older, less valuable urban properties contribute substantially to disinvestment. Landlords faced with declining income, rising operating costs, and excessive tax burdens are likely to respond by cutting back on services to tenants and by defaulting on property tax payments. Transfer of ownership from absentee owner to owner occupants or tenants is often seen as a useful strategy to encourage rehabilitation and maintenance. But the potential of this strategy is limited because a transfer would impose large capital losses including the payment of accumulated back taxes. A one-time equalization of property tax liability across neighborhoods would increase the market value of inner city homes and apartments and could provide adequate incentive to transfer ownership to owners willing to improve their dwellings.

2. Many states have adopted programs that provide relief for homeowners hard hit by property taxes. Tax abatement is one form of relief. Either rehabilitated property is completely exempt from a tax increase that would result from added value to the structure or the property tax is fixed at a certain level and reassessment is deferred for a number of years. States offering complete exemption usually allow municipalities to collect a service charge in lieu of taxes set according to previous tax liability and collected as a proportion of the gross rent.

The basic barrier to widespread use of tax abatement programs is that cities relying heavily on property tax revenues lose a substantial amount of income unless state or federal subsidies are available to replace the loss. Some states, Connecticut for example, do provide compensatory financial assistance to cities that offer abatement programs.

A second form of property tax relief, called the circuit breaker, is designed to protect a family's income from "tax overload." A maximum amount of tax is computed based on household income and if the tax exceeds this maximum the taxpayer is entitled to receive either a state income tax credit equal to the overload, a cash rebate equal to the overload, or to deduct this amount from the property tax due. Those eligible for circuit breaker relief differ from state to state but generally include the elderly and families below a certain income level. Circuit breakers have two major advantages. They are financed by the state so that the local tax base remains stable and they can be targeted to those people most in need. Circuit breaker programs have now been adopted in a majority of the states.

3. Withholding of mortgage and home improvement loans from older neighborhoods constitutes an external structural or contextual factor of widespread incidence. This disinvestment by financial intermediaries, or redlining as it is commonly known, is often attributed to factors internal to the neighborhood such as neighborhood effects on future value and marketability of property, the old prisoner's dilemma. Yet, external forces such as the poor marketability of such mortgages on secondary markets, or the desire to stimulate newer, more profitable investment opportunities elsewhere are involved in this process, though usually not acknowledged by financial institutions. The following article discusses the relationship between the availability of credit and housing market dynamics at the local level.

BAPTISTE, ATTACKING THE URBAN REDLINING PROBLEM, 56 BOSTON UNIVERSITY LAW REVIEW 989-98 (1976)

Redlining appears in a variety of forms. The most common of these is the outright denial of loans within a particular locale. More subtle, although frequently as effective, is the granting of a mortgage with substantially less favorable terms than might be available in a more desirable location. Thus, the lender might demand shorter repayment periods or higher interest rates, thereby requiring inflated monthly debt service payments. In other instances, the institution might offer a loan at a low loan to value ratio and thereby force the urban purchaser either to shoulder a greater downpayment or to negotiate a costly second mortgage elsewhere. Similarly, a lender might underappraise the value of the property, thus forcing the buyer to make up the difference between the deflated appraised value and the true selling price. Finally, the institution might actually relocate itself outside of the urban neighborhood, generally by establishing a branch office in a more desirable area and subsequently phasing out the original facility. Whatever form redlining takes, its effect is always the same — to dissuade buyers from investing in disfavored neighborhoods and to encourage them to look elsewhere.

Redlining can have a considerable impact upon an urban community. Neighborhood vitality bears a direct relationship to the adequate availability of mortgage credit. Because of the enormous costs involved, very few individuals can afford to buy or even repair a home with their savings alone. Thus, to a large extent, institutional lenders determine the futures of individual urban neighborhoods. Those neighborhoods that receive adequate funding will remain viable while those that do not are likely to decay. As a result, redlining can often be a self-fulfilling prophecy; frequently, a lender's fear that an area is on the decline ultimately causes that decline to occur.

Lenders do not necessarily reserve redlining treatment for slum areas alone. Disfavored areas may be well-maintained blue collar or middle income neighborhoods characterized by aging but well-built housing stock. Frequently, these areas consist of racially integrated, white ethnic, or black populations and border upon poorer communities. Such neighborhoods have been referred to as the "building blocks of American cities." As such, their preservation is essential to the continuing vitality of entire urban centers, particularly "at a time when an energy shortage, [an] increase in housing costs, and a shift in values [are leading many Americans to reconsider [these] older, established communities as attractive places to live." Moreover, America's present housing shortage and projected population growth suggest that these neighborhoods are necessary for the adequate housing of the American people.

. . . .

Institutional Justifications for Redlining

Lending institutions are influenced by several constraining factors when considering loan applications. As corporate officers, bankers must exercise prudence and sound judgment in investing depositors' money. In addition, the federal and state agencies that oversee banking operations prohibit lenders from making unsound loans. Finally, professional considerations influence a lender's decision in granting a loan. Because bankers' careers depend upon favorable lending records, individual loan officers tend to make only the safest investments.

Lenders determine the safety of a particular mortgage loan by evaluating both the risk of default and the risk that in the event of a default the proferred collateral will prove insufficient to satisfy the outstanding obligation. If either poses an undesirable though nonetheless acceptable risk, lenders may alter the terms of the mortgage to compensate. However, if the risk involved is totally unacceptable, the loan must be denied.

In assessing these risks, lenders consider many factors. Clearly, they must examine the ability of the individual to repay the loan. In addition, the loan officer must appraise the value of the collateral, a process which requires examination of the structural soundness, the degree of obsolescence and depreciation and the extent of wear and tear of the house in question. Appraisal of the value of the proffered collateral must also include an evaluation of the quality of the neighborhood in which the home is situated. Because mortgage loans generally provide for repayment terms of between twenty and thirty years, evaluation of the collateral's present value cannot suffice. If a lender is to be adequately protected, it must anticipate the probable course of values for that collateral over the next several decades.

In some situations, the lender's evaluation of the neighborhood in which the collateral is located determines either its willingness to lend or its willingness to lend on favorable terms. Banks have frequently allowed area considerations to control both their evaluation of the resale value of collateral and their determination of the likelihood that the loan will be repaid. Urban redlining focuses upon the relationship between mortgage risk and the location of the collateral. When a lender redlines a neighborhood, it determines that the characteristics of the neighborhood render default unacceptably probable and that the subsequent sale of the property will not yield a price at least equal to the loan's outstanding balance. Lenders rely on this determination regardless of the credit standing of the potential borrower or the condition of the building offered as collateral.

The relationship between a property's location and the price it will command in foreclosure is obvious. More subtle is the relationship between the location of the property and the inclination to default. A borrower who can well afford a mortgage would not be expected to default merely because of the condition of the neighborhood. In so doing, he would forfeit valuable equity and incur substantial loss. A more reasonable alternative for such a borrower would be to sell the house, repay the loan and move elsewhere. Yet, this is not always the economically sound course to take. When a neighborhood deteriorates, individual property values decline regardless of their condition. If the value of a borrower's property has decreased to the extent that the proceeds of a sale would fail to equal even the balance of the loan, default would be in the borrower's economic best interests. This incentive to default is especially strong when the neighborhood has declined so greatly that no potential buyers exist. Because the borrower receives no additional funds with which to pay off the loan, unless he has substantial monetary reserves, he has little choice but to forfeit that equity through abandonment. Neighborhood deterioration and declining property values therefore are directly related to the increased possibility of mortgage default.

Neighborhood deterioration results from a variety of interrelated factors. The combination of lower per capita incomes and older homes in a neighborhood often contributes to that neighborhood's decline. Older homes frequently suffer from obsolescence and deterioration and therefore require a high level of expenditure for maintenance and repair. When lower income homeowners fail to make these expenditures, houses begin to falter. Isolated instances of such neglect can often result in the decline of entire communities.

This combination of factors has been shown to bear a close relationship to default risk. A recent study conducted at the University of Pittsburgh found that a high rate of unemployment and a correspondingly low per capita income in an area significantly increases the possibility of default on a mortgage granted in that area. The study also found a direct relationship between the likelihood of default and the age of the mortgaged building. Understandably, owners of older homes frequently suffer a reduction in the amount of money available for mortgage payments because of the increased costs necessary to maintain their residences.

A high rate of foreclosure in a community presents an additional factor contributing to neighborhood deterioration. A large number of foreclosures can have two destructive effects. First, it can serve to lower property values in an area by creating an inordinate excess in the supply of housing. Second, it can cause further decay. A family that resides in a building in the process of foreclosure has little incentive to spend additional funds on upkeep. That building is therefore likely to deteriorate. However, deterioration will also result if the family moves out. In such a case, the building will remain unoccupied until sold by the bank. If the bank cannot find a buyer, the building will be boarded up and left abandoned. This may lead to the deterioration of the entire area. Because of improper sealing and upkeep, vacant buildings decay rapidly. Frequently, such buildings become meeting places for drunks, vagrants and drug addicts. The influx of such undesirables invariably causes an increase in crime, which contributes further to the undesirability of the neighborhood. This course of events demonstrates the dynamic relationship between foreclosure and neighborhood deterioration. The decline of a community leads to a high rate of foreclosure which, in turn, results in further decay. The result is a self-perpetuating cycle.

Many of the factors contributing to neighborhood decline and high levels of foreclosure are more prevalent in urban neighborhoods than elsewhere. . . . A recent study provided empirical support for this practice, finding that urban loans result in forty-seven percent more delinquencies than nonurban loans.

Lenders also perceive a relationship between mortgage risk and neighborhood racial transition. They reason that whites will not live with blacks or other minorities and fear that once blacks move into an area whites will abandon it en masse. As a result, a great many homes will be placed on the market at one time, thereby creating a dramatic excess of supply over demand. This causes a decline in property values and thus jeopardizes the loan's safety. The Pittsburgh study demonstrated that there is a greater likelihood of default on mortgages in communities with racially mixed populations. The study, however, focused on the correlation between racial composition and unemployment rates rather than on the effect of minority influx on property values. Because blacks generally suffer from higher [un]employment rates and lower incomes, they often seek shelter in older, lower priced communities. These factors all contribute independently to higher rates of default. Therefore, whether or not minority influx causes lower property values, a greater proportion of minorities in an area is indicative of increased mortgage risk.

In view of the above considerations, many of the justifications for redlining practices are credible. Urban neighborhoods that both contain elements of decay and demonstrate a trend toward future deterioration empirically present lenders with an enhanced risk of loss. Insecurities about the potential for default on loans secured by urban properties and about the ability to sell those properties if necessary to recover losses suffered through default provide a serious incentive to avoid lending to current and potential homeowners in these neighborhoods. However, the interest of mortgage lenders in avoiding loans to disfavored areas cannot end the inquiry. Instead, the impact of the practice upon residents of the communities, upon people seeking housing in the communities and upon the communities themselves must also receive considerations.

The Impact of Redlining upon Urban Neighborhoods

. . . .

The major effect of institutional redlining practices is to severely limit the availability of adequate mortgage credit in a community. In most instances, the neighborhoods being starved for credit are the very same neighborhoods from which the financial institutions that utilize the practice draw their deposits. Thus, local residents cannot draw upon their collective funds. Instead, these funds frequently provide the financing necessary for the development of distant suburban communities, areas that pose little risk and thereby provide desirable lending forums to the institutional lenders. This removal of capital from areas of collection to different areas for investment is technically known as "disinvestment."

In addition to its economic effect, the decreased availability of institutional credit in a community has devastating psychological and sociological effects. Current homeowners, recognizing both the lower demand for housing in their neighborhood and its resultant effect on property values, realize that the sale of their homes will no longer yield a return equivalent to their investments. Owners of multi-family homes no longer feel capable of refinancing their properties in order to retrieve capital for further investment purposes. Thus, the homes in the area become nothing more than costly burdens to their owners. Any further expenditures seem both unwarranted and wasteful. As a result, homeowners keep maintenance and repair costs at a minimum, and the neighborhood deteriorates.

. . . .

Because of the unavailability of other buyers and the resulting low property values, disinvested neighborhoods are prime targets for real estate speculators. Speculators view such areas as bright prospects for quick profits. Their goal is to buy cheaply, perhaps perform some inexpensive, cosmetic rehabilitation and then sell as quickly as possible at a sizeable profit. Frequently, speculators acquire properties inexpensively through blockbusting. Rumors of impending racial transition and even greater drops in property values are intentionally started. Fearful of losing their equities, homeowners sell their homes at severely depressed prices to speculators who then resell at greatly inflated prices. Most often, these homes are purchased by black families who are unable to find housing elsewhere. Frequently, the speculators themselves provide the necessary financing for these purchases.

Even when blockbusting is not involved, homeowners in disinvested neighborhoods often have little choice but to sell to speculators. Speculators can often obtain financing when ordinary homebuyers cannot. In addition, speculators are infrequently deterred by high debt-service payments. Because they generally seek quick sales, they regard these payments as only temporary inconveniences. When resale is not attractive, speculators often retain these properties, drastically reduce maintenance and repair costs and generate rental incomes through subdividing existing apartments.

Once speculators are the predominate homeowners in a community, the levels of maintenance and rehabilitation plummet dramatically. Because they rarely live in either their buildings or the neighborhoods in which these buildings are situated, little incentive exists for the speculator to invest funds in upkeep. As a result, the individual homes fall into disrepair and the general level of deterioration in the community accelerates. Consequently, more and more homeowners seek to leave. If unable to find buyers, they have little choice but to abandon their properties. As the abandonment phenomenon grows, the neighborhood becomes more unlivable and a greater prospect for urban renewal. Once leveled, its premature demise is complete. A recently stable community with sound housing stock therefore becomes a series of vacant lots. Ironically, this process operates at a time of national housing shortage.

Comments: 1. Efforts to prevent the withdrawal of capital from inner city neighborhoods have taken several forms. Federal law requires that financial institutions make public annually their lending and borrowing activities disaggregated by geographical area. Disclosure is intended primarily to threaten banks and savings and loans (S&Ls) with adverse publicity, if in fact they have withdrawn from the markets they are expected to serve. Exporting deposits made by inner city residents to invest in suburban housing markets is in some few cases subject to outright prohibition. A more widespread method of encouraging inner city institutions to serve the credit needs of depositers is to refuse to allow banks to open branches in new locations unless they can demonstrate they are meeting the demands in their current market areas.

Banks and S&Ls can also attempt to avoid lending in certain neighborhoods by discouraging people from applying for loans by imposing restrictive and unfavorable terms. To counter these practices, neighborhood activists have encouraged legislation to prohibit banks from offering loans on discriminatory terms to redlined areas.

2. Community groups have led the campaign to regulate the activities of financial intermediaries in inner city housing markets. From time to time in some neighborhoods they have been quite successful. Where reinvestment has occurred, it has created new, relatively low risk opportunities for mortgage lending that provide banks and S&Ls with lending opportunities comparable to the suburbs. These neighborhoods, described in the introduction as gentrifying neighborhoods, have experienced dramatic social as well as physical changes. The following article focuses on the social aspects of neighborhood revival in a neighborhood in our nation's capital which was recently viewed as a prime candidate for urban renewal.

S. LEWIS, ADAMS MORGAN: SPIFFED UP AND SPECULATED UPON, PLANNING, Vol. 42; No. 3, at 25

Lavinia Harvey remembers how angry she was. In 1972 she and her husband and 10 of their children had been evicted from the small house they rented on Seaton Place in the Adams Morgan section of Washington, D.C. They wanted to stay in the neighborhood, but the only house large enough to buy was owned by a realtor who said he didn't want to sell to a black family. This was too much. So Lavinia Harvey brought the realtor to court — federal district court, in a courtroom next to where the Watergate trial was taking place — and, when she finished telling her story, the realtor was found guilty of discrimination and fined $850. A year later, Mrs. Harvey and her family moved into a six-bedroom house on U Street, a block south of their previous house. "He had this big house in a black community where people needed housing so badly," Mrs. Harvey recalls. "I couldn't figure out why he'd hold out for white, middle-income people."

Four years later, the reason is obvious. The realtor who balked at selling to Mrs. Harvey was not alone in his plans for her neighborhood — he was just a bit ahead of his time. For Adams Morgan — Washington's model of an integrated, multiracial neighborhood, where millionaires live next door to welfare recipients — is changing. Part of Adams Morgan has always been white and upper middle class. Now more of it is becoming that way. Even in the poorest sections of the neighborhood, in Mrs. Harvey's area, for example, where families could buy houses for $7,000 a few years ago, the asking price is now between $15,000 and $25,000. People in Adams Morgan call that kind of price hike, and the quick buying and reselling of previously low-cost housing, speculation. In fact, there's a new verb Adams Morgan people use to describe what happened to the Harveys and other low-income families throughout Adams Morgan and other parts of the city. Forced out by landlords who want to renovate and sell at inflated prices, people say they are being "speculated" out of their houses.

No one knows exactly how many low-income families — usually black and Latino — are being evicted from their homes and forced to leave Adams Morgan because they can no longer afford housing there, but neighborhood people point to apartment houses and say, "Thirty Latino families used to live there, now it's all condominiums and the Latinos are gone." Or, "That empty site used to hold a big, gorgeous house that was used as a halfway house for mental patients. Now townhouses are going in there." Twenty houses on Seaton Place have been sold in the past three years, and many are boarded up, awaiting renovation. On Willard Street, two blocks south of Seaton, 13 houses have changed hands in the same period, sometimes at a profit of more than 200 percent. The realtors involved have offices elsewhere in the city or in Maryland or Virginia. George Dravillas, who has owned a real estate office in Adams Morgan for 23 years, says that in the last three years he has sold 100 houses in Adams Morgan to young white couples and that prices have doubled on the nineteenth-century rowhouses in the predominantly white section of the neighborhood.

Alfredo Niera, who works with Latino families at Housing Counseling Services in Adams Morgan, says that, although Latinos want to stay in Adams Morgan because it contains the largest number of Spanish-speaking people in the city, many Latinos are leaving for suburbs such as Silver Spring, Alexandria, and Arlington. Black families who leave Adams Morgan stay within the city limits but move north of Adams Morgan, which is about a mile north of downtown Washington. In Washington, as in other cities, poor families are being pushed out of solid, inner-city houses to the outskirts of the city, while middle-class, suburban families, with money to renovate and visions of an urban life style, are moving back in. Some people say that middle-class people are moving back into the District because a sewer moratorium in surrounding suburban counties has limited new construction there and because the energy crisis convinced suburbanites to move closer to downtown.

The reasons these newcomers are attracted to Adams Morgan has something to do with available housing, but more to do with the unusual qualities of the neighborhood. It is a small, residential area, and people there are proud of its diversity. Packed into an area of less than one square mile are 30,000 people — black, white, and Latino. There are welfare families and working-class families, government officials, counterculture types, political activists, and millionaires. Six U.S. Presidents have lived in Adams Morgan; and, neighborhood people say, so did Al Jolson and Carl Bernstein. In its heyday before World War II, Adams Morgan housed many embassies and was a rich man's enclave, with the best furrier and best caterer in town. Vestiges of that past remain, especially in the northwest wedge of the neighborhood bordering Rock Creek Park, where solid brick houses cost more than $100,000.

Just east of this wedge, serving as a buffer between the rich and poor sections of Adams Morgan, run Columbia Road and Eighteenth Street, the main commercial streets in Adams Morgan. Here, tucked into modest storefronts, which cheap apartments above, are the usual signs of a hip community: leather and antique stores, natural food stores, a nonprofit grocery called Fields of Plenty. But the two streets are also lined with Spanish restaurants and groceries and numerous service agencies. At Eighteenth and Columbia you can buy the *New York Times* and eat a flan, then gab about the latest rent strikes. On one corner of Eighteenth and Columbia stands an empty lot with a big, bold graffito painted on the adjacent building: "Our people want no gas station." This is the ghost of an old fight, in which the community successfully opposed a zoning variation and kept the gas station out. Catercorner across the road flies the community flag, a multicolored affair now weatherworn and gray, that reads, "Unity in Diversity."

Several blocks downhill from this corner, on either side of Eighteenth Street, is the black section of Adams Morgan, where Lavinia Harvey lives. Houses here are modest; some are dilapidated. Many houses flood during heavy rains, as does the basement of Morgan Elementary School, located just east of Eighteenth and half a block from the gingerbread, two-story house where Fanny Hill lives. Miss Fanny, as the people of Adams Morgan call her — godmother to 40 Adams Morgan children and resident of the neighborhood for 30 years — is a neighborhood institution, the dispenser of Band Aids, cookies, and good advice. She doesn't like what's happening in Adams Morgan one bit. "It's frightening," she says of the whitening and middle-classifying of Adams Morgan. "I feel very sad about it. People are moving out who have worked to get this community where it is."

One obvious sign of that change looms right over Miss Fanny and the 400 black children in Morgan School. Just one block uphill from them sits an empty, six-acre lot that once held the home of a Washington grande dame and later became the property of Katherine Graham's family. (Graham is publisher of the *Washington Post.*) The latest owner, a realtor, expects to build 213 townhouses on the site and sell them for between $45,000 and $80,000 each. Once that happens, the houses in black Adams Morgan may get very expensive indeed.

Adams Morgan has turned around in the last five years. In the late 1960s, when property values were depressed and Adams Morgan was mostly black, the neighborhood became the home of Rennie Davis and other political radicals. Leslie Bacon, an antiwar activist, was arrested on a roof on Lanier Place, in the heart of Adams Morgan. Lanier Place, once the focus of much counterculture activity, has recently become one of the most renovated blocks in Adams Morgan. Hippies and New Left types, says Marie Nahikian, were the block busters in Adams Morgan, the pied pipers for the middle-class.

Nahikian, a member of the city's rent control commission, has lived in Adams Morgan for seven years. She served as the first executive director of the Adams Morgan Organization, a community group with several hundred members that have been trying to keep low-income people in Adams Morgan and speculators out. AMO also has organized tenant unions and community cleanup days and tried to save vacant land for parks. In short, it has spruced up the neighborhood, ironically making it more attractive to newcomers, Nahikian says. Five years ago, when the housing crunch and AMO were just beginning, the neighborhood was "a little seedier, a little less restored, and a lot less speculated upon," Nahikian recalls. "Maybe we should never have swept the streets or created a community government, because the people who worked so hard for that won't be able to live here."

That kind of frustration spilled out more graphically in Adams Morgan two years ago. One April day, an executive council member of AMO, Walter Pierce, with a little help from friends, painted a sign on a wall at Eighteenth and California. "Beware, whitey," it said. "Blacks left Southwest, Georgetown, and Capitol Hill. It's your turn now. Blacks are here to stay." Later Pierce explained he had painted the sign because black families had been displaced from other neighborhoods and he didn't want it to happen again in Adams Morgan. AMO did raise the flag at the corner of Eighteenth and Columbia and prevented the gas station from being built across the street. AMO helped Lavinia Harvey win her discrimination suit. AMO members, too, have visited Congress with a videotape of people in a neighborhood park. AMO wants to persuade Congress to keep the $2 million allotted in the city budget for purchase of the property. And most important in this changing neighborhood, AMO, along with groups from other neighborhoods, has pushed the city council to pass laws that would keep a lid on the price of housing. As a result, the city council has passed a rent control law and placed a moratorium on conversions of apartment buildings into condominiums and cooperatives. The council is also considering imposing a tax on high real estate profits to discourage speculation. "The principle behind AMO," explains Marie Nahikian, "is that you are responsible not only for yourself but for the people around you, your neighborhood."

AMO was not the first community-wide organization in Adams Morgan, but it emerged at a critical time. With foundation money and the help of American University, Adams Morgan residents in the late 1950s had formed block-by-block planning groups to chart the future of the neighborhood and get federal money for its upgrading. The neighborhood was divided, however, over the question of whether it should become an urban renewal area. After bitter fights, that proposal was defeated in Congress in 1964.

. . . .

People in Adams Morgan agree that the major issue facing the neighborhood is the housing crunch. Until now, AMO has had no housing program and no formal way of getting mortgages for low-income people. Instead, the group has pushed for citywide rent control and a speculation tax to keep the lid on the housing market and to buy time until AMO can set up a housing program. In January, AMO decided to establish a separate corporation in the form of a housing cooperative to help low-income people become homeowners. The group also has been negotiating to take over the mortgages on three properties in the community and has been contacting individuals and foundations to find the money to do it.

Even so, some people think that Adams Morgan is doomed as a diverse community and that low-income people will have left within five years. "I'm optimistic about keeping a few moderate-income blacks and a handful of poor people, but they won't be strong enough to control the politics of the area," says Frank Smith, chairman of AMO's executive council. He adds, however, "Adams Morgan will become a Georgetown unless there's a speculation tax." (Along with "getting speculated," people in Adams Morgan speak of "getting Georgetowned," which means getting renovated, spiffed up, expensive, and racially homogeneous. Georgetown, like Adams Morgan, once housed lower-income blacks.)

. . . .

[For discussion of the District of Columbia speculation tax see Chapter 12 infra. — Eds.]

People in Adams Morgan are looking for an answer. Some hope the neighborhood will be able to influence city policy through its new advisory neighborhood commission. In early February, a majority of seats on the commission in the Adams Morgan area were won by AMO members. One AMO member notes that since the city is just now devising a comprehensive plan, the neighborhood commission could write its own plan for Adams Morgan. Others think the neighborhood commission will remain toothless but add that AMO could be effective as a watchdog group. . . .

Many AMO members hope the group's new housing program will stablize the neighborhood by keeping low-income people there. But even optimists like Marie Nahikian can't ignore the encroaching signs of Georgetown. One night, over a beer at Columbia Station, Adams Morgan's newest bar — a wood-panelled affair with a dart board and Coca-Cola signs all over the walls — she looked around and said, "Adams Morgan has really changed in the last two years. Now I walk out my door and see people walking their Afghans. What are they doing here? That's not what this neighborhood is all about." But both Afghans and Columbia Station are, in part, what Adams Morgan is becoming. As Lavinia Harvey notes, watching other black families leaving Adams Morgan, "The situation here can't get better. We were one of the fortunate ones."

Comments: The problems posed by gentrification and renovation for the maintenance of a sufficient supply of reasonably priced and reasonably maintained housing often seem to defy resolution. Market processes which allocate housing quality by ability to pay almost require that low income tenants will be displaced when their residences become attractive and marketable to in-migrants with higher incomes. Part of the reverse side of this calculus is that low income homeowners and tenants in particular cannot command support for renovations and improvements unless such improvements are economically viable. Without substantial subsidies to ameliorate deficiencies and to support the ongoing operation and maintenance of older urban housing, lower income households will be "assigned" to neighborhoods in which the quality of housing will be less than desirable. Given the effects of price inflation on middle income housing demand, the extension of deep subsidies to low income households seems remote. Instead public policy is likely to focus on the housing problems of the middle class. The upfiltering of older dwellings fueled by inflation seems likely to continue, most notably in cities where price effects are greatest. When combined with neighborhood preservation programs and anti-redlining efforts, reinvestment in some inner city neighborhoods may work wonders, but at considerable cost. It will generate conflicts among housing classes, particularly between low income and upper middle class households as they compete in the same housing market.

BIBLIOGRAPHY

R. Ahlbrandt & P. Brophy, Neighborhood Revitalization: Theory and Practice (1975)
  Reviews National Housing Services Program with an emphasis on Pittsburgh.

J. Black, A. Borut & R. Dubinsky, Private-Market Housing Renovation in Older Urban Areas (Urban Land Institute Research Report No. 26, 1977)
  National overview and review of private rehabilitation in several cities.

A. Clark & Z. Rivin, Homesteading in Urban U.S.A. (1977)
  Reviews homesteading programs.

R. Goetze, Building Neighborhood Confidence (1976)
  An approach to revitalization that synthesizes several sets of ideas about how neighborhoods change.

J. Huges & K. Bleakly, Urban Homesteading (1975)
  Reviews early program experience in several cities.

R. McNulty & S. Kliment, eds., Neighborhood Conservation: A Handbook of Methods and Techniques (1976)
  City-by-city thumbnail sketches of rehab in action.

P. Myers & G. Binder, Neighborhood Conservation: Lessons from Three Cities (Conservation Foundation, 1977)
  Reviews neighborhood renovation programs in Cincinnati, Seattle and Annapolis.

G. Peterson, A. Solomon, H. Madjid & W. Apgar, Property Taxes, Housing and the Cities (1973)
  Selection of conference papers.

Chapter 10

PROBLEMS OF RACE AND LOCATION

Racial discrimination is pervasive throughout American housing markets. Discrimination not only severely restricts the residential choices of minority households, but affects access to schools and other public services, jobs, and many other elements which are tied to the bundle of services we call housing. It is because housing and its location are strongly linked to so many aspects of life that housing policy has been the focus of efforts to deal with this seemingly intractable social problem.

Housing markets as explained by Grigsby in Chapter 2 (supra p. 47) are in fact a collection of submarkets. Variations in both physical and social dimensions define submarkets. Race is a major basis for dividing the market into submarkets. The existence of distinct submarkets identified by the race of occupants certainly implies that people of different races are supplied housing on a differential basis. The black-white distinction is the dominant one here, and the resulting market subdivision is often termed the dual market. This is not to say that the supply of housing available to whites and non-whites is static over time, but that supply tends to shift from one submarket to another in ways that reinforce existing patterns of residential segregation. The microeconomist's understanding of this process is presented by Leven et al. in Chapter 5 (supra p. 192).

The most difficult question about racially defined submarkets is why such divisions exist. The analysis of the political, social and economic history of racial discrimination in this country required to do justice to this question is well beyond the scope of this book. The question which can be answered in this context is how racially defined submarkets are maintained. One view of discrimination in housing which will be discussed later in this chapter sees persisting segregation as the result of autonomous individual preferences. Microeconomists usually takes this view. Another perspective suggests that discrimination is embedded in the system and institutions of housing production, allocation, and consumption. Both views reflect back to the notion of housing class presented in Chapter 4. Edward Banfield presents a case for viewing discrimination as the result of internalized individual preferences in his well known book, *The Unheavenly City*. In it he asserts that racism is not related to skin color, but to class antagonism, or more specifically to a middle class aversion to the habits of the lower class. A more structural analysis of discrimination sees it rooted in the political economy, reinforced and perpetuated by the social, economic, and political power of the white American majority. The salience of racism in American housing politics at the national level was discussed by Keith in Chapter 6. In the same chapter, Mollenkopf looks at racism in politics at the local level.

This chapter discusses discrimination as it affects the spatial allocation of housing opportunities in both public and private housing in city and in suburb. Policies aimed at eliminating or at least inhibiting the most blatant of discriminatory practices of actors and institutions are explored as well. The chapter opens with an article by a sociologist who has specialized in this area. He discusses the extent of segregation in American housing markets over time and the role of institutions in its perpetuation.

355

K. TAEUBER, RACIAL SEGREGATION: THE PERSISTING DILEMMA, 442 ANNALS OF THE AMERICAN ACADEMY OF POLITICAL AND SOCIAL SCIENCE 87 (1975)

The National Advisory Commission on Civil Disorders, appointed by President Johnson in response to the ghetto riots of the mid-1960s, reported in early 1968 its basic conclusion: "Our nation is moving toward two societies, one black, one white — separate and unequal." The image of "two societies" took root in people's minds in a way that the commission's recommendations for action never could. Translated into geographic terms, this image now dominates the nation's perception of central city and suburbs: a black core surrounded by a white noose.

For decades scholars and the public have used battlefield imagery to describe residential patterns of blacks and whites. Early in this century, as black populations grew in the cities, the so-called colored were said to be threatening and invading white neighborhoods. During my childhood in World War II, a "block-buster" was a bomb of awesome destructive power; in college in the 1950s I learned that a "block-buster" was an unscrupulous character who dared to sell or rent to Negroes in white areas. In the years since the Kerner Commission report, the imagery has become that of defeat and panic, of white flight to the suburbs in fear of blackening central cities.

This racial battlefield imagery of cities and suburbs is, like the other city-suburban imagery, a gross exaggeration that nevertheless blinds the national perception to reality. Racial conflict is a prominent aspect of the American metropolitan scene, but the two-society image is too narrow a perspective. A survey of certain census data on population distribution and migration can broaden the perspective and provide a glimpse of both the uniformities of racial residential patterns throughout the nation and of the diversities in scale and character of the problems posed by these patterns in individual metropolitan areas.

The Blackening of Central Cities

What did the 1970 census reveal about the so-called blackening of central cities? In the 243 metropolitan areas, blacks composed a majority of the population in only three central cities. These three cities — Washington, Newark and Atlanta — are each severely under-bounded with respect to the spread of urbanization around them. (Washington had 26 percent of the metropolitan area's population; Newark, 21 percent; and Atlanta, 36 percent.) In the total metropolitan population of these three places, blacks were outnumbered three or four to one.

In only 12 other metropolitan areas did blacks in 1970 compose between 40 and 50 percent of the central city population. Four of these 12 were Southern cities in which the black percentage either declined or increased only slightly during the 1960s: Birmingham, Alabama; Charleston, South Carolina; Pine Bluff, Arkansas; and Richmond, Virginia. The other eight cities experienced rapid increases in percentage of blacks during the 1960s, and most will probably have black majorities by the time of the 1980 census. These eight, in declining order of city size, are Detroit, Baltimore, St. Louis and New Orleans, among the nation's large cities, and Savannah, Wilmington, Augusta and Atlantic City among the medium-size cities.

A few central cities other than these eight may experience such rapid white out-movement and black increase during the 1970s that they, too, will have black majorities by 1980. But in 211 of the 243 central cities, whites outnumbered blacks more than two to one in 1970. Many of the 32 cities in which blacks composed more than one-third of the 1970 population were medium-size Southern cities from which blacks were fleeing as fast as whites in the 1960s. In other medium-size cities whites were moving in, not out, and at a faster rate than blacks.

About one of every eight persons in the United States is Negro (according to census classification). A minority group, outnumbered seven to one, cannot "take over" all of the nation's central cities. Indeed, more than half of the nation's black population already lives in central cities of metropolitan areas. Black urbanization in the future cannot continue at the former pace. There are not enough blacks left in the rural South to provide a continuing large flow into the cities.

Although 198 of the 243 metropolitan areas experienced an increase during the 1960s in the percentage of blacks in the central city, there is no typical metropolitan area. Black population in New York City increased by more than half a million. In Provo-Orem, Utah, the black central city population increased from 18 to 28 persons. There are prevailing patterns of racial population change, but the specific pattern in each metropolitan area takes on a unique size and shape.

. . . .

Economics or Discrimination?

The residential segregation of blacks from whites within central cities and the exclusion of blacks from suburbs are often assumed to be a reflection of the relatively poorer economic circumstances of blacks. In fact, although metropolitan areas have both wealthier and poorer neighborhoods, most residential neighborhoods throughout the metropolis have housing that rents or sells for a wide range of prices. Thus, the first premise of the poverty interpretation of racial residential patterns is only a half-truth. The residential distribution of persons among neighborhoods in the metropolis is only in small part a function of housing costs, family income or other economic factors.

The second premise of the poverty interpretation of housing segregation is that blacks are poorer than whites. This is again only a partial truth. If the entire distribution of families by income is considered, rather than just average incomes, a considerable overlap is seen among races. Many wealthy and middle income black families have greater economic resources than do millions of poor white families. The conclusion from the two premises of the poverty interpretation of residential segregation is that the residential locations of blacks and whites differ because of economic differences. The reality, alas, is not so simple. Sociologists and economists have devised various statistical techniques for assessing the influence of economic factors on the differential residential location of black and white households, but they have not reached any consensus beyond agreement that other factors are important. I have contributed to the esoteric literature on this topic, but I am more impressed by the results of common sense and simple statistics. Common sense and open eyes reveal that rich blacks do not live interspersed with rich whites. Poor whites do not live interspersed with poor blacks. Racial residential segregation exists to far too high a degree in all American cities for economic factors to be the primary cause. Simple statistics offer surprising confirmation. In Chicago in 1960, the average rent paid by white tenants was $88 a month; the average rent paid by black tenants was $88 a month. Black renters were highly segregated from white renters despite their obvious ability to pay as much.

But suburbanization is different, is it not? Granted that patterns of housing segregation in the central city are not primarily economic in origin, is it not true that economic factors play a more important role in suburban locations? Consider data for 29 of the nation's largest metropolitan areas. Among white families with incomes of $5,000 to $6,999 (not a very good income even by 1969 standards), the proportion who lived in the suburbs was greater in every case than the suburban proportion among black families with incomes of $15,000 to $24,900. Consider also a specific metropolis. In Detroit in 1970, more than half of the white families in each income level, from very poor to very rich, lived in the suburbs. Among blacks, only one-tenth of the families at each income level (including very rich) lived in the suburbs.

I have concluded from my own research and a review of the work of others that the prime cause of residential segregation by race has been discrimination, both public and private. Racial discrimination was influential in developing the racially segregated pattern of American cities. In recent years, despite court rulings and legislation clearly outlawing virtually all types of racial discrimination in housing, past patterns persist, and every investigation uncovers evidence that old impediments to free choice of residence by blacks continue. I refer specifically to practices such as:

1. racially motivated site selection and tenant assignment policies in public housing;
2. racially motivated site selection, financing, sales, and rental policies of other types of government subsidized housing, such as Federal Housing Administration and Veterans Administration insurance programs;
3. racially motivated site selection, relocation policies and practices, and redevelopment policies in urban renewal programs;
4. zoning and annexation policies that foster racial segregation;
5. restrictive covenants attached to housing deeds;
6. policies of financial institutions that discourage prospective developers of racially integrated private housing;
7. policies of financial institutions that allocate mortgage funds and rehabilitation loans to blacks only if they live in predominantly black areas;
8. practices of the real estate industry such as (a) limiting the access of black brokers to realty associations and multiple listing services; (b) refusals by white realtors to cobroke on transactions that would foster racial integration; (c) block-busting, panic selling, and racial steering; (d) racially identifying vacancies, either overtly or by nominally benign codes (advertising housing according to racially identifiable schools or other neighborhood identifiers); (e) refusing to show houses or apartments or refusing to encourage blacks to consider housing in white neighborhoods; (f) reprimanding or penalizing brokers and salesmen who act to facilitate racial integration; and
9. racially discriminatory practices by individual homeowners and landlords.

Mass Migration to Metropolis

A century ago the black population in the United States was predominantly a rural agricultural one because the South of which blacks were a part was itself a rural agricultural region. As the South slowly urbanized, blacks participated. Southern cities, together with their outlying suburbs, grew with a pattern of separate housing for blacks. A slow northward movement of black population that had been occurring in the first half-century after the emancipation of slaves accelerated during the 1910-20 decade. Continuing for the next half-century and a few years beyond, the flow of blacks to Northern cities was truly a mass migration. Between 1920 and 1930 in Georgia and between 1940 and 1950 in Mississippi, nearly half of the young black males reaching adulthood left their states. In 1920, 1930 and 1950, in Michigan, Illinois and New York, from one-third to more than one-half of the young adult blacks enumerated in the census had moved to those states within the preceding 10 years.

The mass migration northward drew blacks from all over the South, from cities as well as villages and tenant farms. The Northern destinations, by contrast, were few in number. Of all Northern blacks in 1970, two-thirds lived in seven metropolitan areas containing more than 300,000 blacks each (New York, Chicago, Philadelphia, Detroit, St. Louis, Newark and Cleveland). In the West, two-thirds of the blacks lived in Los Angeles or San Francisco. In the South, only five metropolitan areas contained more than 300,000 blacks each, and the 16 containing more than 100,000 blacks included only one-third of the region's total black population.

End of an Era?

Any mass migration carries within itself the seeds of its own destruction. As youth move from one region to another, they transfer future natural increase from the place of origin to the place of destination. This demographic fact of life ensures that new generations will be born and raised in the destination places and that the supply of future migrants from the place of origin will be depleted. In addition, any mass migration is cause and effect of massive social and economic transformations at origin destination.

During the half-century of massive black migration, the character of the migration was continually changing. By the time national attention was focused on the so-called urban crisis following the Watts riots of 1965, Northern black populations were increasingly Northern-born and Northern-raised. Northern blacks who migrated from the South were increasingly from the urban South. For blacks, as for whites, long distance migration was a feature of a metropolitan industrial economy in which those persons with greater education and marketable skills moved for economic benefit and for a better life. The poor and poorly educated rural blacks who were still being displaced from agriculture were far more likely to move a few miles to a Southern town or city than to take off directly for a Northern metropolis.

The steady aggregation of Americans, white and black, into metropolitan areas is a mass migration that must come to an end sometime. This migration has ebbed and flowed with economic circumstances — as in the slowdown during the depression of the 1930s — but at least until 1970 it was a continuing feature of American demographic history. No one foresaw the sudden cessation of this steady population concentration, but cessation is what appears to have happened since 1970. From 1970 to 1974, metropolitan areas lost migrants to nonmetropolitan territories. Analysts first thought that the results might simply reflect a spilling over of metropolitan expansion beyond the current boundaries of metropolitan areas. Further investigation revealed, however, that the population in counties adjacent to metropolitan areas was growing less rapidly than the population in nonmetropolitan counties not adjacent to any metropolitan area.

The national shift away from an ever-greater piling up of population in metropolitan areas has been matched by an extraordinarily sharp decline in black metropolitan movement. During the early 1970s there was still a slow rate of net in-movement of blacks to metropolitan areas, but it hardly compared to the rapid pace of the 1950s and 1960s. It is the nation's largest metropolitan areas that have experienced the sharpest shift in total migration rates, and it is these areas that in the past were most attractive to black migrants. As the black population has become increasingly urban, and as young blacks have become increasingly well educated, the character of black migration has increasingly resembled that of white migration. During recent decades white migration to central cities declined and then reversed, first in the largest cities and more recently in many of the medium-size centers. Already in the 1960s, blacks displayed a net out-movement from some central cities, and it should not have surprised us so much that this trend would gain momentum in the 1970s.

Persisting Segregation

Recent information on population redistribution of both whites and blacks during the 1970s has surprised demographers and other social scientists. The sharp changes in fundamental long term trends were not anticipated and have not yet been investigated. It is difficult to change long-accustomed perceptions, and many observers suspect (or hope) that the latest demographic shifts are a temporary response to the unusual economic circumstances of the early 1970s. Taking cognizance of the fact that no trend continues forever, I am much less skeptical of the new information. We may well be entering a new era in American population distribution.

The identification of eras is an analytical distinction imposed on a continuous reality. The trends of population concentration in metropolitan places and dispersal within metropolitan areas have not suddenly been obliterated; rather, the magnitude of the former has declined, and we do not yet know how the pace of suburbanization has been and will be affected. Thus it is extraordinarily difficult to assess the future of black suburbanization.

In the early decades of the twentieth century, as the so-called Great Migration of blacks to Northern cities accelerated, the black newcomers to the cities behaved much like other newcomers of those times. Negro migrants repeated the behavior of Italian and Polish migrants and other ethnic groups in settling initially in certain downtown areas of inexpensive housing accessible to public transportation. As numbers grew, ethnic colonies spread. With time, increasing numbers of the group became familiar with the ways of the city, with how to get along economically, and with other residential choices that might be more pleasant than crowded central neighborhoods. From the beginning of mass concentration of each successive European ethnic group in New York, Chicago, Detroit and other great cities, some members of the group were moving elsewhere in the city, sometimes establishing secondary colonies, sometimes settling into ethnically heterogeneous neighborhoods. Many of the children and grandchildren, natives of America and of the city, exercised even wider ranges of choice of residence. Statistical measures of the degree of segregation of each major European ethnic group document declining segregation as time passed.

For blacks, however, residential patterns took a different twist. The mechanisms of racial discrimination identified above were deliberately devised and elaborated to control the dispersal of blacks and to produce a more "orderly" channeling of rapidly growing black populations. Statistical measures document increasing segregation of blacks. The residential segregation between blacks and whites increased well beyond the levels characteristic of turn-of-the-century ethnic group segregation in Northern cities. Some Southern cities that grew to prominence after the Civil War also experienced their first large influx of black population during this period, and their residential patterns developed similarly to those in the North. In some older Southern cities, where a large black population was present ever since the days of slavery, a more dispersed racial residential pattern survived for many decades. But even in those cities, such as Charleston, South Carolina, with its traditional pattern of backyard and alley dwellings for blacks, the modern national style of separate residential areas eventually took over. Urban renewal in the 1950s largely completed the task of racially modernizing these cities.

During the 1950s in the North, and during the 1960s in both Northern and Southern cities, the intensity of residential segregation of blacks and whites diminished somewhat from its peak levels. These declines were too small to reflect or presage a new liberalism in race relations. Rather they arose, I believe, from the large scale of the white out-movement from central cities and from the simultaneous rapid increase in the numbers of black families (native Americans all and many second or third generation urbanites) who did not like the ghettos and who pursued as best they could — within the confines of a discriminatory housing market — the standard American dream of a decent home and a decent neighborhood in which to raise one's children.

The slight diminution in the degree of racial residential segregation within the central cities occurred during a period of rapid increase in white suburban populations. The 1970 census was the first to provide data for individual city blocks throughout the urbanized area, and hence for 1970 it is possible to calculate area-wide segregation indexes of the same sort described above for central cities. Among 40 of 44 Northern metropolitan areas, the segregation index for the total urbanized area is greater than that for the central city alone. Among Southern metropolitan areas, with their historical pattern of suburban black enclaves, the area index is higher in 27 of 44 cases.

These statistical data document the severity of the two-society pattern of increasingly black central cities and white suburbs. Until there is a much more even distribution of blacks and whites among central cities and suburbs, segregation indexes for metropolitan areas cannot fall. The evidence presented above indicates that black suburbanization to date, while numerically greater than ever before, remains a minor pattern in black population redistribution. Suburbia shows no signs of quickly becoming for blacks, as for whites, the primary destination of migrants. The evidence further shows that the suburbanization to date has occurred with the same racially discriminatory channeling of black residents into selected localities that characterizes central cities.

The lowered birth rate in the United States and the lowered rate at which whites and blacks are moving into metropolitan areas should sharply reduce population pressure on urban and suburban housing. Older and less desirable housing seems increasingly likely to be abandoned, as happened in the 1950s and 1960s even with growing populations. Reduction of central city densities should occur, and a potential exists for greatly increased black suburbanization. With black populations growing more slowly, and with blacks interested in the full spectrum of metropolitan residential neighborhoods, there could be rapid residential desegregation without the population pressures that in the past led so often to immediate resegregation. This pattern could develop, but there is no evidence yet that it will. Racial segregation persists in suburban housing because racial discrimination persists in suburbia.

Whether these patterns change depends not only on whether we develop the will and devise the means to enforce existing nationwide laws against all types of housing discrimination; change in the racial patterns of housing also depends on what happens to segregation in schooling and employment. It has become somewhat fashionable to recognize these linkages only to use them as an excuse. Segregated schools are said to depend on segregated housing, which depends on black poverty, which depends on occupational discrimination, which depends on earlier discrimination in Southern schooling, which depends on antebellum social institutions. This kind of logic rests on a specious reading of social science evidence. There is indeed a certain "unity of the Negro problem," as Gunnar

Myrdal noted more than 30 years ago, but that unity may be expressed in the present tense, not only as a historical residue of slavery:

Behind the barrier of common discrimination, there is unity and close interrelation between the Negro's political power; his civil rights; his employment opportunities; his standards of housing, nutrition and clothing; his health, manners, and law observance; his ideals and ideologies. The unity is largely the result of cumulative causation binding them all together in a system and tying them to white discrimination.

Comments: 1. Taeuber's view that the "prime cause of residential segregation by race has been discrimination, both public and private," is the subject of considerable controversy. Microeconomists trying to analyze the phenomena underlying segregation in housing markets have advanced several theories. The disequilibrium theory which supports Taeuber's thinking states that there are institutional mechanisms which produce segregation independent of people's preferences or incomes. In this view, there are structural or institutional obstacles to expanding the supply of housing quality at the quality levels desired by black and other minority households. These obstacles include the discriminatory practices of real estate brokers and mortgage lenders, and exclusionary land regulations which are discussed in detail later in this chapter. The disequilibrium in the housing market created by restricting the supply available to blacks independent of demand means that blacks pay more for less than whites. The term disequilibrium derives from the use of that term by microeconomists to denote a situation in which nonmarket factors prevent achieving a market price equilibrium between supply and demand. In the absence of discrimination, or attenuation as Grigsby calls it, minority households would be free to seek better housing in other submarkets at competitive prices. This view thus emphasizes the role of powerful individuals and institutions in obstructing black entry into white submarkets.

In contrast to the disequilibrium theory, the equilibrium theory posits that segregation results from individual preferences. This theory holds that racial clustering occurs on a voluntary basis and that some groups will pay a premium to either locate in the vicinity of similar groups or to locate away from groups that are dissimilar. If neither the minority nor white population at racial boundaries is growing so that the distribution of population is in equilibrium, the price of housing at the boundary will be the same regardless of race.

If, however, the market is in disequilibrium because the black population is growing, the price offered by blacks for homes on or near the racial boundary will increase. This is known as the Bailey boundary effect, discussed in Chapter 5 (supra p. 193). It implies that whites are willing to pay more to live with other whites, while blacks appear to prefer integration for its own sake, or, more likely, to obtain the improved services that are available in predominantly white areas. The equilibrium theorists' notions of the preferences of minority households seem to ignore the fact that if demand is increased in any housing market without a corresponding increase in supply, prices will rise. Despite the paucity of theory at this point, the fact remains that when black demand outstrips supply, blacks will outbid whites, and the conversion from white to black occupancy will become profitable. It is at this point that blockbusters, real estate agents who negotiate changes in racial occupancy, can take advantage of the price differential. The equilibrium theory thus predicts that growth of one racial neighborhood will change the available supply of housing in such a fashion that normal equilibrium will be re-established. This process is called arbitrage and is described in detail in Chapter 5.

A new phenomena has become visible in recent years involving the conversion of black neighborhoods into white ones under current inflationary conditions. The demand for affordable housing units is quite high on the part of white households. Because whites tend to have higher incomes and face less discrimination on the part of lenders, if they can overcome their preferences, they can outbid blacks for housing. Brokers can facilitate this process by fixing up older homes and marketing them to higher income (white) households. This process is another face of the gentrification process discussed at several points in this book, particularly in the last reading in the preceding chapter.

2. Taeuber also pioneered a residential segregation index that provides one basis for measuring residential racial segregation in cities. The index value indicates the extent to which minority presence in a given census tract differs from a pro rata proportional distribution of minorities for the total jurisdiction or metropolitan area. When the indices are summed an overall index value of 0 indicates a proportional number of blacks and whites in all tracts, while an index value of 100 indicates that no census tract contains both blacks and whites. The table that follows updates the Taeuber index and compares residential segregation in a group of major cities and metropolitan areas from 1960 to 1970. (A few smaller southern cities have been added for comparison.) As the table indicates, values of residential segregation have been high at each census and have not been improving overall.

Residential segregation in selected standard metropolitan statistical areas and central cities: 1970 and 1960

	SMSAs		Central Cities	
	1970	1960	1970	1960
Atlanta	81.7	77.1	83.4	83.1
Baltimore	81.0	82.4	84.3	83.0
Boston	79.3	80.8	81.2	83.9
Buffalo	85.7	86.8	83.4	84.5
Charleston	62.8	62.8	80.3	72.2
Chicago	91.2	91.2	91.0	91.8
Cleveland	90.2	89.6	86.7	85.6
Dallas	86.9	81.2	91.7	88.8
Denver	84.7	84.6	84.6	83.4
Indianapolis	83.8	78.7	80.3	76.0
Jackson, Miss.	80.9	80.2	67.1	65.0
Los Angeles	88.5	89.2	88.6	85.4
Miami	85.7	89.5	84.3	90.7
Milwaukee	89.5	90.4	87.0	88.4
Minneapolis	79.9	83.3	74.6	75.8
New Orleans	74.2	65.0	70.9	67.7
New York	73.8	74.4	71.6	75.2
Philadelphia	78.0	77.1	76.8	79.0
Pittsburgh	74.5	74.4	79.2	81.1
Salt Lake City	70.1	71.6	57.9	67.9
San Diego	76.2	79.5	76.1	80.2
San Francisco	77.3	79.4	67.8	71.1
Seattle	78.1	83.3	76.7	82.2
Washington	81.1	77.7	72.3	66.4

SOURCE: Van Valey, Roof & Wilcox, Trends in Residential Segregation: 1960-1970, 82 American Journal of Sociology 826 (1977).

NOTE: Indices for 1960 are based on whites and non-whites; those for 1970 are based on whites and blacks.

3. Taeuber, in the preceding article, lists a series of nine practices which affect the racial composition of housing markets. His first three examples indicate the salience of discrimination in the formulation of public policy at the national and local levels. Until the 1950s federal insuring agencies not only sanctioned segregation, they encouraged it. At the same time federal public housing programs implemented site and tenant selection policies that support segregation in local projects. In the former case, racially biased underwriting policies are an example of the institutionalization of racism by the real estate industry. In the case of public housing, local class conflicts dictated that if public housing was to exist, it would indeed be segregated or blocked by political opponents.

The following article describes site selection policies for public housing in Baltimore,

Maryland, and how they contributed to patterns of residential segregation in the housing market. In so doing, the author also describes the relationship between housing location and access to services, employment, and amenities contributing to the disenfranchisement of minorities economically and politically.

C. GOTTLIEB, THE EFFECT OF SITE SELECTION POLICIES ON THE SUCCESS AND FAILURE OF THE FEDERAL PUBLIC HOUSING PROGRAM: THE CASE OF BALTIMORE 41-52 (1975) (M.A. Thesis, Johns Hopkins University, 1975)

The population of Baltimore in the early thirties was a little over 800,000. Unlike many American cities, Baltimore was not characterized by large tenement projects, and 50 percent of the households owned their homes. Nevertheless, Baltimore was not without its share of blight. A 1933 report from the Public Works Administration's Housing Division in Washington noted that the centre of the city was surrounded by a belt of residential property which unless rehabilitated would become an increasing menace to all properties inside and outside this belt. . . . In 1937 the Housing Authority of Baltimore City (now a part of the Baltimore Department of Housing and Community Development (HCD)) was chartered by the state of Maryland to attack the problems of blight in the inner-city and housing for the poor. Its policies were established by a five-member commission appointed by the Mayor. . . . In 1968 a Resident Advisory Board, composed of two elected delegates from each project, was established to serve as liaison between the LHA and the public housing tenants; the chairman of the Board now usually serves as a member of the commission.

The first five public housing projects opened in the early forties — Edgar Allen Poe Homes, Latrobe Homes, McCulloh Homes, Douglass Homes and Perkins Homes — were located in predominantly residential neighborhoods surrounding the central business district. . . . These projects usually consisted of low-rise blocks of about six attached units, each with a small sitting yard or a clothes-drying yard out front; they were generally laid out in a simple grid pattern, and public open space was minimal. A lack of imaginative planning characterized many of the early public housing projects, particularly those built on limited downtown sites. Of the remaining seven projects established in the forties, five were built for war workers, and four of these — Fairfield Homes, Brooklyn Homes, Westport Homes and O'Donnell Heights — were located on vacant land outside the inner-city in areas of heavy industry. . . . After World War II they were turned over to the Housing Authority of Baltimore City. Though in some cases the units were intended for temporary shelter only, they continued to serve as homes for low-income families long after the war; at Brooklyn Homes, for example, one thousand temporary wooden units, constituting two-thirds of the project's housing stock, were not demolished until 1962.

In 1950 the Baltimore City Housing Authority published a report . . . declaring most of the inner-city blighted . . .; this marked the beginning of the urban renewal movement, though it did not become an official program in Baltimore for another few years. As in many American cities, the enthusiasm generated over urban renewal took its toll on public housing; only five new projects (3030 units) and three extensions to existing projects (1229 units) were opened between 1950 and 1969, whereas twelve projects (5421 units) had been opened in half those years during the forties. Claremont, the first of the fifties projects, was built outside the inner-city in a White neighbourhood and for White tenants; the remaining four projects were located in the inner-city. . . . It was believed at the time that inner-city sites were "intrinsically the best in the metropolitan area. They have that rarest of all modern residential advantages — a convenient location. In addition, they have community facilities worth millions of dollars in the form of street improvements, utilities and neighbourhood recreational, social and shopping facilities." . . . Furthermore, studies showed that the inner-city Black population was in the greatest need of public housing. Where less than 10 per cent of the White households in Baltimore lived in substandard or deteriorating dwelling units in 1960, one-third of the non-white households lived in such conditions, even though 55 per cent of the low-income population was White. . . . In 1960 the Regional Planning Council studied thirty-nine census tracts to determine whether or not a "rent deficit" — that is, the excess of actual rent payments over the rent that a family with a particular income could be expected to pay, where the expected rent was derived by means of linear regression analysis — was being paid and by whom. It was found that "almost without exception, the rent deficit tracts were low-income tracts, as well as predominantly Negro tracts," and that the general concentration of deficits was in the inner-city with a "peaking of intensity . . . predominantly in Negro areas near the central business district." . . . Since the population with the greatest need for public housing lived in the inner-city, the LHA felt justified in selecting over-whelmingly inner-city sites. Except for George B. Murphy Homes (opened in 1963) which was part of a larger urban renewal program, all inner-city projects opened in the fifties and early sixties were characterized by high-rise apartment buildings, the first being built for Lafayette Courts in 1955.

The latter half of the sixties introduced a number of new aspects to public housing in Baltimore. Federal aid became available for the rehabilitation of existing units for low-income occupancy and the leasing of existing units for public housing tenants. In 1969 the first major rehabilitated public housing project opened in Baltimore at Mount Winans, next to Westport Homes (an old war workers project of the forties). The first Turnkey project in Baltimore (Oswego Mall) also opened in 1969 outside the inner-city but in an area of Black concentration. . . . [A turnkey project is built by a private builder, who "turns the key" over to the local housing authority when the project is completed. — Eds.]

Although some of the early Turnkey projects presented problems in that they did not conform to HUD standards and required rehabilitation by the HCD subsequent to completion, the majority of projects presently under construction and recently completed have been Turnkey projects. The late sixties also saw an increase in housing specifically for the elderly; more than half the units completed in 1970 through 1973 have been for elderly tenants, and more are under construction. This sudden enthusiasm for elderly projects resulted, not only from the need for such housing, but also from the new federal emphasis on desegregation requiring that an effort be made to locate public housing outside the inner-city. The ease with which such sites could be acquired depended to a great extent upon the household composition of the proposed tenant body, and projects for the elderly were more readily accepted by local communities than family projects. Furthermore, since private Turnkey developers, who already owned sites generally outside the inner-city, were handling the majority of projects, they could not afford to incite community opposition with a controversial tenantry. Other attempts which were made to lessen community opposition to public housing and to reduce the concentration of subsidized units included the introduction of scattered sites . . . and the possibility of public housing tenants becoming self-sufficient property owners, their rent being a down payment on their dwelling units (Oswego Mall).

The Application of Site Selection Criteria

The first thirty years of public housing in Baltimore were, for the most part, associated with a general city plan to reduce the amount of blight in the inner-city. Because of this long-term association, most public housing projects were located in a ring around the central business district.... Except for the war workers projects and those outlying projects opened since 1969, only Cherry Hill Homes and Claremont were built outside the inner-city. In interviews with public housing managers, all those associated with inner-city projects, except for one, believed that their projects had been well-located since all were within walking distance of elementary schools, and either within walking distance or a short bus trip from a city library and downtown shopping. Recreational facilities were provided by the projects and the schools, and some were located near city parks. Some managers complained that the food market facilities were inadequate.... The managers of inner-city projects considered access to public transportation to various parts of the city excellent, and felt that their tenants had adequate job opportunities. Most work in the downtown shops, the university hospitals, and the school system, requiring at the most a half hour bus trip. Only a few work in outlying employment centers, such as Social Security Mall and Bethlehem Steel, to which bus travel is very time consuming. Only one inner-city housing manager volunteered the opinion that the inner-city location, though desirable at the time when his project was established (1942), had since lost its attractiveness in all respects....

The outlying projects, and particularly those built for war workers, were located near centres of heavy industry which have continued to grow. Most of the employed tenants work in the local industries, and a direct bus route is available for those who work downtown. Fairfield Homes is the only exception in an otherwise good accessibility record for the outlying projects. Access from Fairfield to downtown employment and shopping is poor, and, unlike the other projects, it is not located close to large community shopping centres and recreational facilities.

. . . .

Until 1964 the only racial consideration governing the location of public housing in Baltimore, as in any other American city, was the early USHA requirement that the LHA preserve, rather than disrupt, community social structures.... Since most of the public housing projects presently existing in Baltimore were built or planned prior to 1964, it is not surprising to find that their locations generally support existing racial residential patterns. Most projects intended for Black occupancy were located in the inner-city, while most White projects were located in White neighbourhoods. In 1965 Baltimore officially integrated its public housing program. Those projects which were significantly affected were the few all-White projects, such as Brooklyn Homes, O'Donnell Heights and Claremont. Much planning went into the integration process to prepare both the tenants and the surrounding community. At Brooklyn and Claremont the process was executed relatively smoothly; at O'Donnell the period of adjustment was longer as there was strong opposition, particularly by the surrounding White community, and the new Black tenants found few shops and recreational facilities where they were welcome. Similar problems associated with the integration process . . . [occurred in] Flag House Courts, an inner-city project which changed from White to predominantly Black as the result of a racially changing neighourhood rather than the new integration policy. When it was built in 1955, the surrounding neighourhood was White with Little Italy on one side and a Jewish community, which has since moved to the suburbs, on the other. The project manager expressed the feelings that, while the original location was good from the point of view of White public housing tenants in a White neighbourhood, the new tenants were being exploited by the White shopkeepers and would be better off in an all-Black neighourhood rather than in an integrated one. Whether this would indeed be so is questionable. In any case, the new integration policy had little influence in changing the racial make-up of existing public housing projects; most of the projects continued to exhibit the same racial characteristics as the immediate surrounding community.

The Baltimore experience demonstrates the ineffectiveness of public housing in its present form to reduce racial concentration and its adverse economic effects. In spite of its good national record, Baltimore's public housing program has failed to introduce a significant number of Black families to the residential amenities, educational advantages, and new job opportunities of suburban communities. The fault lies not with the Baltimore program, but with the federal restrictions on public housing. The federal requirement that public housing can be constructed only where a Local Housing Authority exists has confined Baltimore projects to within the city limits plus a ten mile radius — the extent of the HCD's authority. [This extraterritorial authority is unusual. Most local housing authorities are confined to their city limits. — Eds.] The ten mile radius does not include incorporated towns where the HCD is required to obtain the special permission of the local council to execute a project; beyond the ten mile limit Baltimore County is opposed to public housing and does not have a Local Housing Authority, thus excluding many of the desirable suburban locations. The federal requirement that the city council must approve all sites selected by the LHA has resulted in the rejection of a number of sites proposed by the HCD, because a particular constituency objected to the location of public housing projects in its area. A recent example involved the scattered sites project. . . . One site was rejected after much time and money had been expended on the plans; and the development on another site was slowed down while local citizens attempted to halt the construction already in progress.

Thus it is doubtful whether public housing can successfully fulfill the new federal fair-housing objectives, if some of the old requirements are not modified. The Baltimore program is considered to be as good as, and better than, many of the programs in the country, yet few of its projects, old or new, offer public housing families the advantages associated with suburban locations. Most of the existing projects are located in the inner-city, and so long as they continue to hold up structurally, they will continue to serve as public housing. Family projects (as opposed to those built for the elderly) recently completed or presently under construction do not change the picture appreciably. . . . The Gay Street project is located downtown among a number of existing projects; the scattered sites project, though not downtown, is located in a high-density-close-to-inner-city Black neighbourhood. Only one non-elderly project, Rosedale Farms, is presently being developed on a site significantly distant from the inner-city. Hence it does not appear that even a good local public housing program, such as in Baltimore, is about to make rapid headway into modifying existing racial residential patterns and accessibility to improved commercial and cultural ciated amenities and to new employment and educational opportunities.

Comments: 1. The Baltimore experience in the location of public housing projects has been repeated in cities across the country, sometimes accompanied by an explicit municipal intent to manipulate the location of public housing projects to foster segregation. While the federally-financed urban renewal slum clearance program was in operation, public housing locations inducing residential segregation were also supported by slum clearance projects aimed at strengthening segregation lines by eliminating black neighborhoods contiguous to white areas. These efforts were aimed at staving off white flight to the suburbs, the erosion of municipal tax bases, and in some cases, outright urban apartheid.

Even without an explicit discriminatory intent, decisions locating public housing in minority areas affect work and living patterns and the character of city service. The preceding article on Baltimore attempts to capture the relationship between housing opportunities and access to jobs, stores, and other services. It sets the stage for the following comment which discusses attempts to provide public housing in diverse neighborhoods.

2. Chicago was the stage for one of the more dramatic and pitiful controversies about segregation in public housing. Local housing politics in Chicago, as in many other metropolitan areas, prevented the provision of public housing in white neighborhoods (see Meyerson and Banfield in Bibliography, infra p. 382). The Chicago experience led to the *Gautreaux* litigation, which attempted to force integration of public housing in the city. A lower Federal court first ruled that additional public housing units could not be built in neighborhoods where the black population exceeded 30% of the total population until after a substantial number of units were built in white neighborhoods. While the court's ruling might have improved the locational choices of public housing tenants had units been constructed in specified neighborhoods, the fact is that additional family units were not built anywhere and the housing opportunities of low income households have not been increased. The city has now negotiated an agreement with its housing authority to build public housing at locations consistent with the court order.

Frustrated by the failure of the city to respond to the judicial order, proponents of the *Gautreaux* litigation next sought to mandate the construction of public housing across the Chicago metropolitan area. This strategy was possible because the Chicago housing authority has jurisdiction beyond the city limits, an unusual power held by very few such authorities. The United States Supreme Court ultimately heard the case and authorized the provision of public housing on an integrated basis throughout the metropolitan area. Some subsidized housing has been provided in suburban areas under the terms of a settlement negotiated following the Supreme Court decision.

While the *Gautreaux* approach to integrating public housing may represent a major breakthrough in constitutional principle, in reality it has not resulted in the greater provision of housing opportunities for public housing tenants regardless of location. The dilemma posed by *Gautreaux* is that it attempted to promote integration and to provide shelter for low income households in an institutional setting which impeded the realization of either goal. The two goals, however, are not necessarily mutually exclusive, and the fact that it is so difficult to begin to improve the spatial allocation of housing opportunities for all social groups is indicative of problems deep within the existing social order. The failure of the *Gautreaux* litigation to affect more than the law is also indicative of the significance of local politics, and the ability of local officials to thwart the realization of significant reforms desired at the federal level. These dilemmas also speak to the general powerlessness of low income people to assure that their needs will be met within the local political arena.

Whether court decrees which attempt to promote the provision of low cost housing on an integrated basis can be implemented presents serious questions for integration strategists. In Chicago, the impact of the *Gautreaux* decisions was frustrated by the refusal of the city to build housing under the conditions specified in court. Because the court's decision does not cover privately developed housing receiving public assistance and does not override local zoning ordinances, the impact on the improvement of housing opportunities for minority households, even if pursued vigorously by the housing authority, would be very small indeed. The fact that the private market supplies the great majority of all housing narrows the potential impact of the *Gautreaux* strategy even further.

In May, 1979, the *Gautreaux* case was finally settled by court order when the Chicago Public Housing Authority agreed to construct and rehabilitate over 2000 units of public housing. Eight hundred of these units will be for low income families, equally split between white and minority neighborhoods.

3. Civil rights litigation in housing and other programs has sparked an intensive debate over the judicial role in achieving the major changes in social policy that an extensive program of racial integration requires. In a comment applied to the open suburbs movement, see Chapter 11, but equally applicable to long-running litigation such as *Gautreaux,* one critic has urged that the permanence of judicial victories is often fragile. It depends on factors such as the degree of change in social institutions that is required and the complexity and visibility of the changes that are mandated. Racial integration victories in court require both painful social change and complex judicial intrusion into public affairs. The author adds:

> A group that seeks legalist victories in the latter situation must, therefore, be acutely aware that the litigation is only part of a political process. To the degree that the factors guaranteeing permanence are not present, the group must couple litigation with efforts to change the political context. This will mean that it must accompany its legalistic efforts with measures that are designed to secure broad political support for the measure being sought. Without such efforts legal victories will be pyrrhic ones.

Trubek, Law and the Politics of Justice in National Committee Against Discrimination in Housing, Exclusionary Land Use Litigation 108, 141.

4. Taeuber, earlier in this chapter, also discussed the fact that white migration to the suburbs was not paralleled by minority households. The following article describes trends in black suburbanization.

P. MULLER, THE OUTER CITY: GEOGRAPHICAL CONSEQUENCES OF THE URBANIZATION OF THE SUBURBS 18-23 (1976)

Black Suburbanization Trends

Twentieth-century black suburbanization trends (Figure 8) reveal that such popular suburban epithets as "lily white" and "white noose" have some factual basis. It would certainly not be an overstatement to claim that blacks largely have been denied entrance to the suburbs. Prewar patterns are insignificant since comparatively few blacks lived in the North, but postwar trends clearly show a rapidly widening divergence of whites and blacks in the suburbs. Both graphs in Figure 8 indicate a stable black suburban population over recent decades. A large proportion of this population still inhabits tiny, widely dispersed, and highly segregated traditionally black areas with settlement histories of five decades or more. In some instances, large enclaves of similar age are present in satellite towns adjacent to large central cities, i.e., Evanston, Illinois; Pasadena, California; and Mount Vernon, New York. Together, these black suburbs have accounted for a stable three percent of the total population in the outer rings of non-Southern SMSAs since the 1920s. . . . The modest postwar growth of black suburbs has intensified residential densities within these older pockets. Very recently, however, black population increases have also resulted from selective expansion of central city ghettos into contiguous inner suburbs — a potentially significant trend for future suburban social geography.

An overview of the latest census data indicates that America's suburbs remain all but closed to blacks. During the 1960s the percentage of blacks in the suburban population of SMSAs (as defined in 1970) increased imperceptibly from 4.78 to 4.82. Although 800,000 blacks did enter suburbia in the sixties, their gains were all but obliterated by the more than 15.5 million whites who constituted 95 percent of the decade's new suburban migrants.

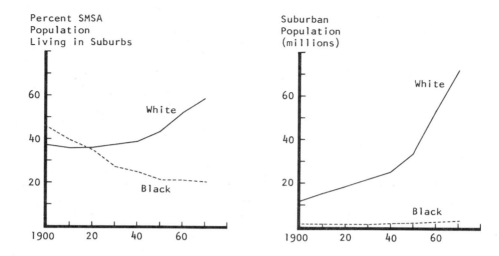

Figure 8 (a and b) Black suburbanization trends, 1900-1970 (Redrawn from Muller)

Viewed from the slightly different perspective of the total black population itself, census findings are similar. From 1960 to 1970 the percentage of this group residing in the suburbs increased only from 15.1 to 16.2 percent, compared to the 35.4 to 40.4 percent rise for whites; in terms of percentage increases whites (+14 percent) again led blacks (+7.2 percent) by a wide margin. . . . On the other hand, black concentration in central cities during the sixties increased notably (52.8 to 58.0 percent) at a time when the corresponding white population declined (from 31.5 to 27.8 percent).

Because of the much smaller absolute number of suburban blacks in the 1960 base data — 2.8 million to 56.3 million whites — suburbanization rates during the 1960s are deceptive (29 percent growth for blacks, 28 percent for whites). Nevertheless every region recorded modest black gains except the South, where overall black suburban population declined from 12.6 to 10.3 percent. This trend must be balanced against the conclusive findings of a study undertaken by the Federal Reserve Bank of Boston indicating that black suburbanization in the sixties did not result in any meaningful progress toward racial integration. Specifically, this study concluded that: (1) there was very little change in the distribution of blacks both between and within central cities and suburbs during the 1960s; (2) new suburban black migrants were moving overwhelmingly into widely scattered already-black neighborhoods with almost no penetration of white residential areas; and (3) despite small absolute and proportionate nonwhite suburban SMSA increases from 1960 to 1970, intermunicipal segregation in the decade actually increased by an average of 15 percent in 14 large SMSAs surveyed.

Thus, in the 1970s suburbia remains largely off-limits to nonwhites. And for those blacks who do manage to enter the few relatively undesirable suburban neighborhoods abandoned to them by whites, "it has meant little more than exchanging one hand-me-down neighborhood for another," as improvement in the quality of life over the inner city ghetto is usually negligible. . . . Before treating this restricted suburban access of higher income nonwhites, we will discuss the two varieties of black suburbs which have emerged.

Black Suburban Settlement Types

Spatial patterns of black suburban settlement are intricately tied to the urban ghettoization process which concentrates blacks in a limited number of residential areas (to the extent that they dominate neighborhoods in excess of fifty percent of the total population). These are sealed off, surrounded by powerful social barriers maintained through constant external pressures. Rose has classified these outlying racial concentrations into two district spatial forms: *colonized* and *ghettoized* black suburban enclaves (Figure 9).

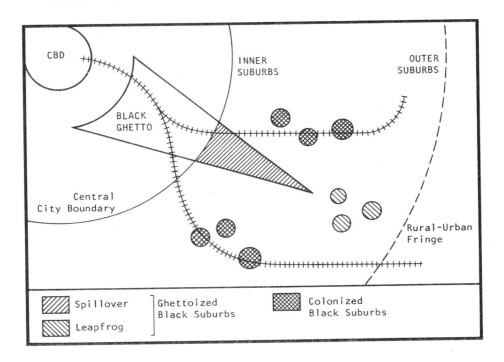

Figure 9 Spatial forms of black suburbanization (Redrawn from Muller)

Colonized black communities tend to be small stable pockets which have persisted for several decades originating as "shacktowns" on the then rural-urban fringe. In the Northeast these congregations are commonly attached to old rail corridors, such as suburban Philadelphia's Main Line, and are direct descendants of the nineteenth-century servants' quarters, usually relegated to undesirable trackside locations, which housed the domestic employees of wealthy landowners of the period. Always segregated, these low income black colonies have become completely isolated by the social barriers erected as modern suburban development engulfed them. . . .

Since World War Two *ghettoized* black suburbanization commonly has been of the spillover type. This results from a sectoral expansion of the central city ghetto across city lines into adjacent suburban territory (Figure 9). As poorest blacks are forced to abandon unlivable dwellings at the inner edge of the ghetto, they move outward to the nearest available housing. This housing in turn has been abandoned by less poor blacks seeking better housing in outer ghetto neighborhoods. The more favorable residential environment of the inner suburban margins of the advancing black community has attracted a middle-class population of better-educated, young black families. This spillover process is well-advanced in many cities, such as Cleveland, St. Louis, Washington, D.C., Chicago, Atlanta, Miami, Los Angeles, and parts of the New York metropolis. . . .

The other form of ghettoized suburb is the *leapfrog* type, most often an exclave located beyond the spillover ghetto (Figure 9). This is a newly emerging phenomenon. . . . These black pockets are relatively undesirable residential areas and almost always consist of deteriorating, cheaply constructed early postwar tract housing which whites have abandoned. . . .

Mechanisms Perpetuating Suburban Racial Segregation

Thus suburban blacks live in residential areas which are quite different from those occupied by whites. Even when blacks are able to find suburban housing outside of their colonized and ghettoized enclaves, they tend to be tightly segregated at the block level. . . .

The Suburban Dual Housing Market and Its Impact

. . . .

White Resistance to Suburban Integration

White resistance to the suburbanization of blacks is universal. Skin color is a "master status-determining trait," and white suburbanites at every income level perceive blacks as a threat to their own social status. . . . In order to protect their status, whites must avoid sharing residential space with blacks and must preserve geographical separation of the races.

Low and moderate income suburban working-class neighborhoods are especially blunt in their hostility toward nonwhites. The lack of upward mobility aspirations found in these communities reinforces neighborhood attachment and the desire to maintain an image of respectability, thus eliciting a passionate defense of the neighborhood. Vandalism and even full-scale rioting often accompany attempts by pioneering black families to penetrate these white communities whose unity is often accentuated by tight ethnic clannishness. Upper income residential suburbs handle similar conflicts in a more refined but just as effective manner, usually through adroit maneuvering by sellers and realtors. Consider the response of the affluent Main Line district west of Philadelphia to a recent Pennsylvania fair housing law designed to curb excesses in the state's real estate industry: in the first year following implementation of this legislation nearly two thirds of local house turnovers were transacted privately without any official involvement of a realtor, and the social *status quo* of this wealthy area remained unaffected. . . . There is also intense resistance to black entry into acutely class-conscious, upwardly mobile middle-class suburbs, particularly since social status is almost always derived from the externally perceived image of one's neighborhood. Only in a very few middle income suburbs is there even reluctant acceptance of a limited number of black households, which results in "salt-and-pepper" integration — insignificant sprinklings of blacks here and there — frequently characterized by the "Ralph Bunche syndrome" of welcoming one respectable black family to the street but not two or more. . . .

Some proponents of suburban integration are seizing upon this entree into certain "liberal" middle income suburban communities by attempting to devise programs for the orderly influx of more blacks while preventing the flight of white residents common in situations of rapid neighborhood racial change. The belief underlying these schemes is that whites might well wish to remain in a community if firm assurances can be given that the entry of blacks will be controlled so as to guarantee a large local white majority. At issue is the size of the critical mass of black immigrants or the *tipping point,* purported to be in the 20 to 30 percent range, beyond which whites pull out and the entire neighborhood rapidly turns all black. The inner middle-class Chicago suburb of Oak Park recently has been attempting to draw up this kind of "social compact" ordinance whereby a maximum of 30 percent black population would be mandated. . . . Prior to 1974 only two percent of Oak Park's residents were nonwhite. Local fear of an imminent spillover from the adjacent Austin neighborhood — the leading edge of Chicago's expanding West Side ghetto — and the subsequent likelihood of black "flooding" followed by white abandonment, has prompted Oak Park to explore the controversial black quota solution. Although it is too soon to tell if such a scheme can work to integrate a large suburban community, the initial results have not been productive. So far, blacks have been segregated within Oak Park and are heavily concentrated in neighborhoods bordering the city line which directly face the Austin ghetto; the community remains "redlined". Nonacceptance of the social compact idea has been widespread, especially in black quarters where several community leaders have been particularly outspoken in their opposition to the quota concept. As a result the quota has been tabled, and a policy of selective discrimination prevails. . . .

Rising Black Frustration

The immovability of suburban racial barriers is now resulting in such rising black frustration that nonwhite pressures to enter suburbia are declining in many metropolitan areas. Endless obstacles thrown up by dual housing market mechanisms have greatly increased black cynicism in the 1970s. Nonwhite realtors and those sympathetic to minorities are almost always kept from membership on suburban real estate boards and therefore from access to better house listings. Black home-seekers are constantly reminded of racial discrimination in newspaper advertisements containing such wording as "exclusive," "secluded and private," and "country club," which are interpreted as cues that minorities are unwelcome. . . . Nonwhite buyers are seldom given a chance to negotiate or "sleep" on a price without having a house suddenly disappear from the market. When they are able to enter a newly opened suburban area, middle-class blacks are often forced to share residential space with socially dissimilar lower income blacks, thus considerably reducing perceived levels of neighborhood quality. . . . Despite ongoing attempts to modify these conditions, little change is taking place because

> . . . by preventing the minority person from being able to shop for housing in the way that is normal for his white peers, a permanent barrier to residential desegregation has been created which may be beyond the power of positive law to reach. . . .

With heightened black suburban disillusionment in the 1970s has come an intensified aversion to "pioneering" formerly all white areas, always a distressing practice involving exposure to white hostility and frequently physical violence. In a mid-sixties study of suburbs outside Seattle, Norwood and Barth. . . concluded optimistically that initial opposition to blacks might subside over time. They even proposed a multi-stage assimilation model (pre-entry, entry, accommodation) leading toward residential integration. However, a newer analysis of the Philadelphia suburbs by Cottingham. . . paints a more accurate picture of the contemporary metropolitan reality. She finds an increasing reluctance among central city blacks — regardless of income level — to move beyond their established neighborhoods.

———————

Comments: Muller's article notes substantial white resistance to residential integration. This conclusion is supported by a 1977 study of discriminatory practices in the real estate industry by the National Committee Against Discrimination in Housing under contract with HUD. The information was obtained by 300 teams of testers. Each team consisted of one black and one white who answered newspaper advertisements and visited real estate sales and rental offices to see if they encountered differential treatment because of race. These surveys were conducted in 40 metropolitan areas with a population of at least 100,000 and a black population of at least eleven percent.

The major conclusion from a preliminary analysis of this survey was that blacks attempting to rent housing from a single rental agent are likely to encounter discrimination 29 percent of the time while if four rental projects are contacted the probablity of discrimination is 75 percent. In the sales market, blacks are likely to encounter discrimination 21 percent of the time if they look at a single home for sale and 62 percent of the time if four homes are visited. These conclusions are only preliminary but indicate that actors and institutions in the housing market have considerable influence in the allocation of housing by race. Subsequent findings may show increased levels of discrimination when an analysis of racial steering is carried out. Blacks are "steered" when real estate agents covertly refuse to show them housing in white neighborhoods.

Other preliminary findings were that real estate agents more frequently inquired about the financial status of blacks, and that rental agents volunteered information more frequently to whites. No substantial differences were found in the terms and conditions on which apartments were made available for rent.

The following article discusses attempts to prohibit the discriminatory practices described by Muller in the preceeding article. It describes the evolution of civil rights legislation in housing.

TWENTY YEARS AFTER BROWN: EQUAL OPPORTUNITY IN HOUSING 33-39 (A Report of the U.S. Commission on Civil Rights, 1975)

Legislation to Assure Equal Housing Opportunities

Since the latter part of the 19th century, Federal law has been in existence that requires equality of housing opportunity for all American citizens. Until 1962, however, the Federal housing agencies and the majority of State governments either openly endorsed or ignored discriminatory practices of private housing interests which acted in direct opposition to these laws. As the Nation entered the decade of the 1960's, the impetus of the burgeoning civil rights movement brought the issue of discrimination in housing to the forefront. Indeed, within the short period of 12 years, the long tradition of restricting the access of minorities and women to housing was denied all legal and administrative support by the Federal Government and most State governments.

Executive Order 11063

In attempting to shed the legacy of discrimination in housing and prevent its perpetuation, the Federal Government first took a piecemeal approach to the revival of the guarantees of the 14th amendment and the Civil Rights Act of 1866 by banning discrimination in some types of housing but not others.

Under Executive Order 11063, issued in November 1962, a broad intent was stated to prevent discrimination because of race, color, creed, or national origin in all housing financed through Federal assistance. In the preamble to the Executive order, President Kennedy pointed to the problem of discrimination and the effect it had in denying to "many Americans" the benefit of federally-assisted housing, thus confining them to substandard, unsafe, unsanitary, and overcrowded housing. Citing the goal established by Congress in the 1949 Housing Act, the President alluded to the impossibility of achieving a "decent home in a suitable living environment for every American family" as long as discrimination persists.

Although the order was couched in broad terms, it was, in fact, limited in scope. It covered only housing provided through mortgage insurance by FHA or loan guarantees by VA and federally-assisted public housing. Conventionally-financed housing (non-FHA or VA) financed by mortgage lending institutions, representing the great bulk of the Nation's housing supply, was excluded from coverage. Furthermore, the principal content of the order related almost entirely to housing provided through Federal aid agreements executed after November 20, 1962.

Builders and owners of housing could be subject to disbarment from further participation in Federal programs, if found to discriminate. With respect to owners of existing housing that previously had received Federal assistance or that was still receiving such assistance, the order provided only for the exercise of "good offices" by Federal administrative personnel, who were to attempt to bring violators into compliance with the order.

Title VI of the Civil Rights Act of 1964

Overall, Executive Order 11063 had only minor impact in assuring equal opportunity in housing provided through FHA, VA, and public housing programs. In 1964, therefore, Congress took a second step to redress racial discrimination in federally-assisted housing and other Government programs, spurred into action by the growing protests of the civil rights movement and by such events as the massive March on Washington in August 1963. With enactment of Title VI of the Civil Rights Act of 1964, discrimination was prohibited on the basis of race, color, or national origin against persons who were eligible to participate in and receive the benefits of any program receiving Federal financial assistance.

Title VI filled in some of the gaps in coverage of federally-assisted housing left open by Executive Order 11063. For example, all housing in urban renewal areas was made subject to the provisions of Title VI, as well as all public housing, regardless of the date of contract for assistance, as long as Federal financial contributions were still being received for the operation of a public housing program. However, housing provided through FHA mortgage insurance and VA loan guarantee programs outside urban renewal areas, as well as the Farmers Home Administration housing, was exempted from coverage, a mark of the considerable power exercised by private housing interests on Capitol Hill. Likewise, conventionally-financed housing was not affected unless it was located in urban renewal areas.

Title VIII of the Civil Rights Act of 1968

In the same year as the passage of the landmark Housing and Urban Development Act of 1968, which established specific goals for the production and rehabilitation of housing, Congress once again focused on the need to expand Federal law to prevent discrimination in housing. In Title VIII of the Civil Rights Act of 1968, Congress made its intentions clear by declaring that "[i]t is the policy of the United States to provide, within constitutional limitations, for fair housing

throughout the United States." Two months after passage of Title VIII, the
Supreme Court brought its weight to bear in support of this policy through the
majority opinion in *Jones v. Alfred H. Mayer Co.* [This case upheld the
constitutionality of a post-civil war civil rights act that also prohibits
discrimination in the sale of rental of housing. — Eds.]

Title VIII prohibits discrimination in the sale or rental of all housing,
federally-assisted and nonassisted, except:

1) single family homes sold or rented without use of a broker and without
publication, posting or mailing of any advertisement "that indicates any
preference, limitation, or discrimination based on race, color, religion, or
national origin, or an intention to make any such preference, limitation, or
discrimination."

2) dwellings providing units or rooms for up to four families living
independently of each other, and in one unit of which the owner resides.

Title VIII became fully effective on January 1, 1970, at which time more than
80 percent of all housing came under its coverage. The following specific
discriminatory acts are prohibited:

1) To refuse, after a bonafide offer is made, to negotiate on a sale or rent, or to
otherwise deny a dwelling to any person because of race, color, religion, or
national origin.

2) To discriminate in the terms, conditions or privileges of a sale or lease or in
providing services or facilities in connection with a sale or lease.

3) To make, print, or publish (or cause to be made, printed, or published) any
notice, statement or advertisement that indicates preferences or limitations based
on race, etc.

4) To represent to any person because of race, etc., that a dwelling is not
available, when in fact it is.

5) To induce or attempt to induce any person to sell or rent any dwelling by
telling them that persons of a particular race, etc., are moving into the
neighborhood.

6) To deny because of race, etc. a loan or other financial assistance to any person
applying for such assistance for the purpose of purchasing, constructing,
improving, repairing or maintaining a dwelling.

7) To deny any person because of race, etc., access to or membership or
participation in multi-listing services, real estate organizations or other services
relating to the business of selling or renting dwellings.

The Housing and Community Development Act of 1974 amends Title VIII by
prohibiting discrimination in the sale or rental of housing on the basis of sex. In
addition, the 1974 act provides that federally-related mortgage loans or Federal
insurance, guarantees, or other assistance cannot be denied to any person on
account of sex and that the combined income of both husband and wife must be
considered for the purpose of extending mortgage credit in the form of a
federally-related mortgage loan to a married couple or either member thereof.

Persons who believe they have been the victims of discrimination in housing
may file a complaint with HUD, which is the agency responsible for
administration of Title VIII, or, after having exhausted HUD's complaint

procedure, they may file a civil action in the proper Federal district court or State or local courts of general jurisdiction.

In the enforcement of Title VIII, HUD's powers are limited to the receipt, investigation, and conciliation of complaints. If HUD is unable to resolve a complaint, HUD may refer the matter to the Department of Justice for further action. HUD is not empowered to request a temporary or permanent injunction or restraining order against the person or persons accused of discriminatory action.

Title VIII authorizes the Attorney General to bring a civil action in a Federal district court against any person or group of persons who are believed to be engaged in a pattern or practice of resistance to the rights granted by Title VIII, or if any group of persons are believed to have been denied these rights and the denial raises an issue of general public importance. The Attorney General may apply for a permanent or temporary injunction, restraining order, or other order against those responsible for such pattern or practice or denial of rights.

In vesting responsibility for the administration of Title VIII with the Secretary of HUD, Congress provided for an additional Assistant Secretary in HUD, to whom the Secretary could delegate Title VIII enforcement functions. In addition, the Secretary of HUD as well as *all* executive departments and agencies were required to "administer their programs and activities relating to housing and urban development in a manner affirmatively to further the policies" of Title VIII.

Comments: 1. Critics object to the litigation approach to integrating subsidized housing because the complexities of racial segregation are not amenable to easy correction by court order. Comparable difficulties face legislation, like Title VIII of the federal Civil Rights Act, which controls racial segregation through a one-dimensional prohibition against racially discriminatory practices in the sale and rental of housing. Problems in the enforcement of Title VIII highlight the limitations of this type of legislative approach, and the administrative procedures under which it is implemented.

Problems in the enforcement of housing discrimination laws serve as a disincentive for complainants who might otherwise seek assistance. Delays in processing the complaints that are received and the ineffective monitoring of settlements discourage people who have encountered unlawful discrimination from using the law to improve their housing opportunities. Recently, amendments to fair housing legislation have been introduced to improve enforcement by HUD, but the fate of these administrative changes remained in doubt at the close of the 1978 congressional session. Whether or not these procedures are improved, the fact remains that the law can only work to serve those who make formal complaints. It is doubtful that the many people who encounter discrimination as they seek housing have the time or the willingness to invoke the enforcement of fair housing legislation on their behalf.

2. Discriminatory practices in the distribution of housing are highly institutionalized in the housing market, and appear in forms more subtle than outright discrimination in the sale or rental of housing. Real estate brokers are often viewed as transmitters of residential segregation, and Risa Palm in Chapter 2 calls them the "social engineers of the urban landscape." Taeuber, in his article appearing earlier in this chapter, noted an example of discriminatory practices in the activities of real estate brokers who accelerate the rate of turnover in racially transitional neighborhoods by blockbusting or hastening sales to blacks:

Blockbusting is a drama enacted on the block or in the neighborhood, and the synopsis varies little from community to community. The blockbuster, the principal actor, induces panic in white homeowners by means of harassment meant to induce a rapid racial turnover of residences at greatly distressed prices. In its mild form, blockbusting may consist merely of excessive solicitation of sales, which may engender panic. More severely, blockbusting can be an intensive campaign to disseminate the rumor, based on half truths, that blacks have purchased or will purchase a residence and that, as a result, the neighborhood will become inundated by blacks with an accompanying decline in property values and quality of housing. To substantiate his propaganda and to heighten fear, the blockbuster may hire black welfare mothers to parade up and down the block or vandals to throw bricks through windows in order to foster the impression of a black invasion.

The blockbusting saga typically opens in a white neighborhood lying in the path of an expanding black ghetto. On the whole, local realtors abstain from disrupting the homogeneity of a white neighborhood by the introduction of the first black family, so the racial integrity of the neighborhood is generally preserved and neighborhood turnover stagnated until several blacks enter as purchasers through outside realtors not subject to community pressures. The blockbuster comes on the scene with prophecies of neighborhood doom, communicated to homeowners by repeated telephone calls, post cards, and door-to-door visits. In these communications he preys upon latent fears of white homeowners, falsely representing that many neighbors have already sold to blacks or are contemplating doing so — evidenced by "sold" and "for sale" signs placed throughout the neighborhood by the blockbuster without the owners' consent or he may claim that property values are plummeting, and that the property owner should sell quickly before it is "too late."

In the earlier years of blockbusting, the blockbuster reaped substantial gain, especially if he took a house for resale rather than as a mere listing. The ready cash offered by the blockbuster induced many desperate homeowners to sell, even at greatly depressed prices, in order to avoid further loss. Yet, in resales to blacks who were eager to escape the ghetto, the blockbuster received amounts exceeding the fair market value of the residences. Moreover, sales were frequently made to poor blacks, who accumulated funds for housing payments by subdividing residences into units leased on a room basis, clearly in violation of local zoning laws, and contributing to the decline of the neighborhood. Inevitably, no funds would remain for maintenance purposes, thus leading to further deterioration of buildings.

Current blockbusting practice relies less on flagrant harassment and speculation and more on subtler tactics, predominantly representations regarding the "changing neighborhood," often without reference to race. To insure the turnover of the neighborhood, the blockbuster also discourages potential white purchasers, showing available listings only to blacks. Although the profits are not as great as on resales, the high turnover rate assures substantial earnings in the form of commissions. Each sale accelerates the turnover rate by giving credence to a prophecy which has become self-fulfilling. The blockbusting campaign ends with the annexation of the neighborhood to the ghetto, continued segregation, the involuntary relocation of former white residents, and the infusion of new life into stereotypes and prejudices about racial minorities.

Glassberg, *Legal Control of Blockbusting,* 1972 Urban Law Annual 145-49.

3. Blockbusting, like other forms of discrimination in housing, is illegal. Enforcement is difficult because offenses are difficult to prove and because formal legal action is required in each and every case to be effective. Clearly it is difficult to control the micro-motives of individuals using legal sanctions alone. Blockbusters base their operations on the existence of a dual housing market and white fears of declining housing values. Edel, in Chapter 5, suggests that brokers profiteer on a macro scale phenomenon, namely the filtering process which imposes capital losses on the owner of older homes. By blaming minority newcomers for declining values, brokers are able to capitalize on intergroup tensions rather than having to rely on the economics of property markets as a whole.

Steering is another discriminatory practice that limits the supply of housing available to minorities and reinforces residential segregation. Steering occurs when a real estate agent fails to show homes for sale in a white neighborhood to blacks and vice versa. It perpetuates the dual market. In addition to steering, dual housing markets are maintained through control of listings — the right to sell property, either exclusively or in cooperation with other real estate brokers. The existence of the dual market is in itself a segregation-enforcing institution. There is evidence of substantial pressure within the real estate community to maintain the dual market system. It is considered more profitable than an integrated market, so that this discriminatory practice is based in part on economic motivation. As one St. Louis real estate agent explained, "Selling to blacks is bad business for us, we have to consider our reputation."

4. Another form of discrimination can be found in the racially biased lending practices of some lending institutions. This discrimination may parallel or be part of the redlining process discussed in Chapter 9 (supra p. 325). Discrimination in lending occurs in a variety of ways. A very high interest rate may be quoted to discourage the applicant, the loan applicant may be told that the dwelling is "too old" to qualify, higher downpayments may be requested, and appraisals of the dwelling may be manipulated. Racial bias in lending may take even more subtle forms, as this report indicates:

> The subjective latitude exercised by a loan officer in judging the merits of individual applications is reflected in the case of a black couple who were rejected because they had "a lot of debts." The couple's combined income was $18,700, which normally would have qualified them to purchase the $32,000 house of their choice. They had on hand the 20 percent downpayment required. Yet because of a long term debt of $3,000, their application was refused by a white loan officer who argued that the debt was too much for them to handle in addition to the mortgage payments. The same loan officer counsels all minority families to save $15,000 before attempting to purchase a house. The couple subsequently obtained a mortgage at another institution.
>
> U.S. Commission on Civil Rights, Mortgage Money: Who Gets It? A Case Study in Mortgage Lending Discrimination in Hartford, Connecticut 22 (1974).

Racial bias in lending has gradually been made subject to control by the federal agencies regulating lending institutions. Like the prohibition against racially discriminatory practices in the sale and rental of housing, the prohibition against discrimination in lending is also enforceable on a complaint basis and can be expected to raise similar problems. Moreover, discrimination in lending is only one of a larger set of lending practices, such as redlining, that have negative effects on neighborhoods. In this context, legislation prohibiting discrimination in lending is equally narrow in focus, and cannot reach the complex problems posed by the role of lending institutions in the housing market.

5. Quotas for housing integration are another remedy that has been proposed for housing segregation. The use of a quota in an Illinois community and the tipping point concept that underlies its adoption are discussed in the Muller article. Such quotas have been called benign quotas because they have the benign purpose of achieving and maintaining a stable interracial community. The following article discusses the attempt to regulate the racial composition of neighborhoods by means of benign quotas. It focuses on public housing, but is equally applicable to neighborhoods generally.

GRAHAM, THE BENIGN QUOTA: A LEGITIMATE WEAPON TO FIGHT WHITE FLIGHT AND RESULTING SEGREGATED COMMUNITIES?, 42 FORDHAM LAW REVIEW 891, 898-900 (1974)

The argument for a benevolent quota in housing is based on the often recurring pattern of white flight when blacks begin to move into a housing project or community in significant numbers. As the influx of minorities to the area increases, the remaining whites grow more conscious of the change-over process. Eventually, as the white flight continues, the community will cross the tipping point, i.e. "the theoretical maximum minority group proportion which whites will tolerate in any given area." Thereafter, the change-over process is irreversible; a wholesale flight of whites is set off, leaving a predominantly black neighborhood.

The purpose of the benign quota is to utilize affirmative tenant assignment in such a manner as to bring about a gradual reduction of the psychological barrier of whites to integrated living. The housing authority interjects a restriction on the normal entrance of an "invading" minority group-at the maximum possible level of stability in order to assure the dominant white majority that they will not be inundated by an overwhelming influx of minorities. Once assured of a stably integrated habitat, the two groups will gradually develop a certain degree of neighborly contacts. As these contacts erode the whites' fear and as both races become further accustomed to integrated living, the quota — an expedient measure to be used in the transitional stage — will itself become increasingly more flexible until eventually it becomes expendable.

The expected benefits of the minority group from use of benign quotas are substantial. Initially there are immediate material advantages as the blacks and other disadvantaged minorities — whose housing is "generally far more expensive, more crowded and less adequate than comparable housing for whites" — are able to procure better housing and community services at a lower cost. In addition, there are psychological advantages in that the feeling of rejection caused by segregation becomes less substantial. Finally, successful implementation of racial quotas in public housing demonstrates the feasibility of racially mixed housing in the private sector.

There are, of course, substantial criticisms. On a practical level, generally it will prove much more difficult for a black to acquire suitable private housing than a corresponding white. Therefore, if a black is refused available public housing because he is not within the quota, the burden of finding housing elsewhere is much greater. Another detrimental factor may be the additional hostility aroused in whites at being forced to accept blacks as neighbors or, possibly, having their applications refused because of their majority status. Psychologically, the classification according to race, despite the benevolent objective, is not a particularly attractive concept. Although the majority member feels no racial stigma because of his color, the use of the benign quota implies to both black and white that the former is racially inferior and needs special state protection.

Perhaps the primary criticism is found in the nature of the tipping point itself. In reality, it is merely an estimate of white racism and reaction to the black encroachment. As a result, it is subject to a wide range of fluctuation in response to many subjective factors such as the geographic location, the intensity of community prejudice, the availability of low cost private housing and abuse by those officials, including judges, charged with implementing the quota. Indeed, the quota could become a strait jacket which would inhibit rather than advance the cause of racial integration. To prevent such abuses would necessitate constant legal supervision by an already overburdened judiciary.

Comments: 1. Benign quotas may also violate the provision of the federal constitution prohibiting racial discrimination because the housing quota makes the availability of housing dependent on an individual's race. A classification based on race is subject to very strict review in the federal courts, and unless a compelling reason for the classification can be shown it will be held unconstitutional. One federal court has implicitly upheld the use of quotas in the selection of public housing tenants, but the United States Supreme Court has indicated in the *Bakke* decision that the constitutionality of quotas is by no means settled and may well raise substantial constitutional questions. (The *Bakke* case tested the use of a quota policy for admission to a state medical school.)

There is also an equity problem in imposing a quota on the number of minorities that may live in a residential area. When the quota has been exhausted, housing will be denied to any additional minorities who seek housing in the area subject to the quota. While the objective of integrated housing may be met, discrimination arguably occurs if a minority group member is denied housing because the minority housing quota is exhausted.

2. The efforts of voluntary neighborhood organizations to stabilize racial occupancy and prevent "white flight" in neighborhoods undergoing racial transition are another important component in the open housing effort. These organizations have adopted a variety of neighborhood strategies to achieve this objective. Blockbusting tactics by real estate brokers are opposed and attempts made to secure open housing ordinances and statutes if they have not been adopted. Neighborhood housing standards are enforced through pressure directed to homeowners and city enforcement agencies. Neighborhood morale and cohesion are stressed to emphasize neighborhood pride.

Neighborhood organizations may seek to stabilize occupancy patterns by actively promoting sales of housing to incoming whites. In some cases they have opened real estate offices and assumed the broker's role in bringing buyers and sellers together. Neighborhood organizations may also seek to discourage the entry of "too many" blacks, although they would not like to describe their efforts in this language. Although some have attempted openly to prevent racial tipping, a more indirect approach is to encourage the movement of blacks into the suburbs and any remaining white city neighborhoods. These efforts have found support in the open suburbs movement, which is discussed in the next chapter. Opposition has arisen in the black community when the emphasis shifts from the right to live in an area to the value or need for racial mixture. For a description of voluntary neighborhood organization strategies to maintain racial balance see Wolf & Lebeaux, *Class and Race in the Changing City: Searching for New Approaches to Old Problems* in Urban Research and Policy Planning 99 (L Schnore & H. Fagin eds. 1967).

3. Even broader attempts at voluntary housing integration have been put forward by concerned real estate agents and others who argue for the establishment of unitary housing markets. A unitary market could be achieved by the creation of a common source of information on housing availability, both sale and rental. The unitary market could be made self-sustaining from brokers license fees and fees charged to brokers and individuals using the market facilities. A monitoring system would be necessary to audit landlords and agents circumventing the system by not listing all vacancies, by steering, and by other discriminatory practices. Auditing could be accomplished by testers and random checks. For a detailed proposal for a unitary market plan see L. Rosser, Ending the Dual Market in Real Estate: A Proposal to Create a Metropolitan-Wide Unitary Real Estate Marketing System for Sales and Rentals (National Committee Against Discrimination in Housing Information Series No. 5, 1975).

A NOTE ON THE CASE AGAINST RACIAL INTEGRATION

In all of this chapter the benefits of desegregation have implicitly been assumed, but a case can be made that a conflict exists between the aims of the racial integration movement and the provision of needed housing for minority groups. This issue arose when the public housing provisions of the federal Housing Act of 1949 were debated. A southern and conservative amendment to this legislation would have required racial integration in public housing but was defeated by liberal Senators who saw it as a covert attempt to kill the public housing program. This conflict surfaced pointedly in the *Gautreaux* litigation.

The anti-desegregation argument was forcefully put in a major article by Piven & Cloward, *The Case Against Urban Desegregation,* 12 Social Work 12 (1967). They argued that efforts to desegregate housing have been and will be futile. Whites oppose the location of desegregated housing in their neighborhoods, and integration in public housing is near to impossible because whites desert projects in which blacks appear in any number. They also noted that the massive shifts required to secure any kind of racial integration in cities frustrates any widespread integration policy. See the Table, *supra* p. 363. Piven and Cloward viewed the "moral imperative" of racial integration as self-defeating and urged a policy of more intensive subsidies for minority housing at the expense of racial integration efforts.

Piven and Cloward concluded:

For integration must be understood, not as the mingling of bodies in school and neighborhood, but as participation in and shared control over the major institutional spheres of American life. And that is a question of developing communal associations that can be bases for power — not of dispersing a community that is powerless.

Id. at 21.

BIBLIOGRAPHY

R. Helper, Racial Policies and Practices of Real Estate Brokers (1969)
    An interview study of the attitudes of brokers toward discrimination.

M. Meyerson & E. Banfield, Politics, Housing, and the Public Interest
    Excellent case study of racial problems in Chicago public housing.

M. Milgram, Good Neighborhoods: The Challenge of Open Housing (1977)
    An evaluation of integrated housing projects.

National Academy of Sciences, Segregation in Residential Areas: Papers on Racial and Socioeconomic Factors in Choice of Housing (1973)
    Series of papers on factors affecting residential discrimination.

H. Rose, Black Suburbanization: Access to Improved Quality of Life or Maintenance of the Status Quo? (1976)
    The author evaluates the black movement to the suburbs and concludes that the process is not a reversal of the ghettoization process, but a continuation.

A. Schnare, Residential Segregation in Race in U.S. Metropolitan Areas: An Analysis Across Cities and Over Time (Urban Institute, 1977)
    An analysis of the forces that work to generate and maintain a segregated housing market based on the experience of the 1960s and the formulation of a statistical measure to assess current needs in cities today.

G. Von Furstenburg, B. Harrison & A. Horowitz, eds., Patterns of Discrimination, Vol. 1: Housing (1974)
    A compilation of essays examining racial discrimination in housing and the interaction between discrimination in housing and employment.

United States Commission on Civil Rights, The Federal Fair Housing Enforcement Effort (1979)
    Details fair housing enforcement efforts in HUD and other federal agencies.

Chapter 11

OPENING UP THE SUBURBS

Suburbanization denotes a process that concentrates new urban growth on the fringes of presently urbanized areas. It tends to occur at lower densities (see Note on the Physical Design of Housing supra p. 24) than earlier urban growth, and often it leapfrogs over open tracts. In most American metropolitan areas a rough correspondence exists between political geography and the relative locations of older areas and newer ones. This pattern results in a widespread pattern of central city and suburb as separate entities. As Chapter 6 made clear, this separate existence is reflected in political struggles.

However, both the struggles and the underlying issues involve a more basic cumulative and circular interacting process composed of several interacting factors:

1. New housing is built on open land to house new urban population growth on the fringes of older growth areas.

2. New infrastructure and services, both public and private, ranging from freeways to parks to shopping centers and medical complexes, are built on the fringe to serve actual and anticipated new growth.

3. New employment especially in the service sector, and older employment relocated from central areas because of technical or class considerations, also locates on the fringe.

4. More new housing locates on a new fringe, and so on with each factor cumulatively and circularly reinforcing the others.

This process is sufficiently ubiquitous and widely recognized not to need further description here. Nor is this the place to explore various theoretical and empirical explanations for suburbanization.

What requires emphasis here are the results of suburbanization. Perhaps most important among these, suburbia holds the newest and often the best of the services and facilities that are outside the structure itself but included in the housing bundle. If one wants good schools, the best selection of shoppers' goods and medical care, and attractive outdoor recreation, one needs to live in the suburbs in most metropolitan areas. There is no mystery in this statement. Practically every American knows and believes it to be true. What is important for this text is to emphasize the meaning of this phenomenon for housing.

The locational distribution of services and facilities does not end the discussion. Perhaps the most important consequence of suburbanization comes to another dimension, in the skewed geographic distribution of employment opportunities. As central cities have declined while suburbs continue to grow this trend accelerates.

Jobs shift away from metropolitan areas have been especially rapid in manufacturing and especially severe in declining regions. Much expansion of the Nation's manufacturing is not located along major interstate highways outside metropolitan areas. Morever, this outlying growth is not limited to manufacturing. "A new metropolitan economy has emerged, based initially on manufacturing, but now expanding with employment in trade, services, recreation, retirement."

. . . .

Many central cities lost large numbers of jobs and people between 1960 and 1970. . . . Further, most central cities fared badly with respect to manufacturing employment. . . . Between 1963-72, manufacturing jobs declined, but only by a small amount — less than 1 percent per year. More recently, however, manufacturing jobs dropped by nearly 4 percent per year. And central cities in the northeast and north central regions, areas of extensive job loss, faced substantially larger rate declines than central cities in other regions. Clearly, manufacturing is no longer the driving force of urban development. In 1950, one worker in three was in the manufacturing sector: now it is less than one in four. In 1950, most manufacturing jobs were in central cities in the north. Now there is not one major city which has as great a share of its labor force in manufacturing as its suburban ring, and the north now counts for barely half of all manufacturing.

U.S. Department of Housing and Urban Development, Urban and Regional Policy Group Report 8, 10 (1978)

No signs that this trend will soon shift seem visible.

Given these trends the question becomes: who benefits from suburbanization? Are all sectors equally represented? Of course not! The Muller article in the last Chapter (supra p. 369) showed how few blacks benefit from suburban services, facilities, and jobs. The same can be said for the opportunities of other racial minorities. So too it holds for many poor people. In this lies the essence of the inequality attending the American system of suburbanization. Poor people by virtue of their exclusion from new housing are prevented from having access to many of the best schools, shops, recreational opportunities, medical services, living environments and economic opportunities.

All of this is compounded by the simultaneous decline of central cities. The USDHUD publication quoted above puts it like this.

Today's widespread population loss in the Nation's central cities is unprecedented. While some cities have lost population for many years, most have not until recently. In the 70's, for the first time, the total population of our major central cities as a group began to decline. On the whole, population growth within metropolitan areas is now occurring in the suburbs.

One observer notes that "the image of the 'declining' central city has become so firmly embedded in discussion of problems that it may be forgotten how recent a development actual population loss is. Of the 60 cities that had a population of 200,000 or more in 1960, only 38 percent declined in size between 1950 and 1960. In the 60's, the proportion of such cities losing population rose to 45 percent, by 1970-73, it had reached 73 percent."

The loss of population from the central cities is most noticeable in the older cities of the northeast and north central regions. But even in growing regions of the country, many central cities — including some in economically healthy metropolitan areas — are losing population. Suburbs, on the other hand, are gaining population in every region.

As with migration from the older regions of the country, the people leaving central cities tend to be among the more affluent.

Id. at 3, 5.

Central city decline as the negative opposite of suburbanization obviously further intensifies suburban-central city inequalities.

One final question remains before turning to the question of opening the suburbs to all. Is suburbanization and its skewed benefit structure a "natural" phenomenon? The answer is both yes and no. The microeconomists say yes. In their view the result is inevitable or natural given the economic man rationale and an unequal distribution of income. But there is another side. The institutionalists and political-economists claim that in part at least suburbanization is a result of non-market factors. Institutions and social structures promote and maintain suburban exclusion. It is this view that underlies much of the analysis and policy design to be covered in this chapter.

The pages that follow contain discussions of several of the institutional practices and arrangements that maintain suburbs closed to the poor. The first of these is exclusionary zoning. The discussion of this long-established practice is followed by treatment of newer arrangements which have similar exclusionary outcomes. This chapter concludes by turning to the ideas and initiatives that have been embodied in policies designed to open the suburbs to those now excluded.

Exclusionary zoning was the subject of a landmark case in 1975 before the New Jersey Supreme Court, popularly known as the *Mt. Laurel* decision. The court's findings in that case have become the classical statement of the issue. They are reproduced next. Note that the decision describes the process of exclusionary zoning in considerable detail, explores the reasons for its occurrence, and argues the moral and legal case against it. This classic deserves a careful reading.

SOUTHERN BURLINGTON TOWNSHIP NAACP v. TOWNSHIP OF MT. LAUREL

New Jersey Supreme Court*

I

The misuse of the municipal zoning power at issue in this case, generically described as "exclusionary zoning," involves two distinct but interrelated practices: (1) the use of the zoning power by municipalities to take advantage of the benefits of regional development without having to bear the burdens of such development; and (2) the use of the zoning power by municipalities to maintain themselves as enclaves of affluence or of social homogeneity.

Both of these practices are improper and to be strongly condemned. They are violative of the requirement, found both in the Constitution of 1947, and the zoning enabling statute itself, that municipal zoning ordinances further the general welfare. They are inconsistent with the fundamental premise of the New Jersey zoning legislation that zoning is concerned with the physical condition of the municipality not its social condition. In a deeper sense, they are repugnant to the ideals of the pluralistic democracy which America has become.

The motivations for exclusionary zoning practices are deeply embedded in the nature of suburban development. In part, these practices are motivated by fear of the fiscal consequences of opening the community to all social and economic classes. Residents of the municipality anticipate that higher density development will require the construction of additional roads, sewers, and water systems, the provision of additional municipal services, and the increase of school expenditures, all of which must be financed through local property taxes. Often, although not universally, this is a reasonable concern, and, as long as these costs are primarily financed through local property taxes, will continue to impel suburban communities to use the zoning laws to encourage commercial development and discourage settlement of less affluent families. Insofar as this

---

* The case was appealed to the United States Supreme Court but was dismissed. The New Jersey Supreme Court's opinion can be found in volume 336 of the Atlantic Second Reporter at page 736. Citations in the opinion have been omitted but these and other omissions have not been indicated.

fiscal situation prevails, suburban communities will find the temptation of exclusionary zoning alluring.

In addition, exclusionary zoning practices are also often motivated by fear of and prejudices against other social, economic, and racial groups. Thus, in a recent survey of suburban municipal leaders, 42.6% identified social and racial conflict as being the chief impact of low and moderate cost subsidized housing on the municipality, while only 21.3% identified fiscal problems as the chief impact. A large proportion felt that even State assumption of the additional municipal costs of a balanced housing policy would not make a great impact on the general unacceptability of low or moderate income housing. Nor are these attitudes, however disappointing we may find them at this late date, wholly surprising. Many people who settle in suburban areas do so with the specific intention of living in affluent, socially homogeneous communities and of escaping what they perceive to be the problems of the cities. They do not wish their insular communities to be disturbed by the introduction of diverse social, racial, and economic groups. The experience of the nation over the past 20 years must serve as a caution that, however much we might wish it, we cannot expect rapid, voluntary reversal of such attitudes.

Exclusionary zoning may assume a wide variety of forms. Ultimately, the existence of such practices must be measured by exclusionary intent and actual or potential exclusionary effect. Some zoning devices, however, which are inherently exclusionary in effect or which lend themselves especially readily to abuse have come into widespread use and are a revealing gauge of the extent of exclusionary zoning in New Jersey:

1) *Minimum house size requirements*

As of 1970, 92% of the land in the [New Jersey] Department of Community Affairs study area zoned for single family housing was covered by some minimum house size requirement. More than 65% was zoned for houses with 1,000 square feet or more of floor space, and 38.9% for houses of 1,200 square feet or more. By contrast, the controversial [New Jersey] case of Lionshead Lake v. Wayne Tp., upheld a minimum of 768 square feet in all districts. There is wide variation from county to county and within the various counties. In the so-called "outer-ring" counties in northern New Jersey — Morris, Somerset, Middlesex, and Monmouth — houses of less than 1,000 square feet may be built on only about 10% of the land zoned for single family dwellings. On 77% of the land zoned for single family dwellings, houses must have 1,200 square feet or more of floor space. In the South Jersey outer-ring counties, Burlington, Camden, and Gloucester, the figures are 31.9% and 43.5% respectively.

The effect on the cost of housing of such requirements is obvious. If one assumes construction costs of $20 per square foot of floor space, a 1,000 square foot minimum imposes a corresponding minimum figure of $20,000 upon the portion of the cost of a new house attributable to construction. A recent study of housing costs indicates that floor space is the single most important factor contributing to differences in prices for new housing, even more important than the socio-economic status of the municipality.

2) *Minimum lot size and minimum frontage requirements*

On two-thirds of the land in the Department of Community Affairs study area zoned in 1970 for single family dwellings, houses could not be built on lots of less than an acre. Upon only 5.1% could houses be built on 10,000 square feet or less. Approximately 10% of such land in the outer-ring counties in South Jersey was zoned for 10,000 square foot lots or less; 45.9% was zoned for an acre or more. In the North Jersey outer-ring counties only 1.2% of the land zoned for single family dwellings was available for use as lots of 10,000 square feet or less; 77% was zoned for one acre or larger lots. Here, too, there are wide variations among counties. In Camden, 24.5% of the land was zoned for lots of 10,000 square feet or less, and less than 34% for lots of an acre or more. In Somerset County, only .2% of the land was zoned for lots of 10,000 square feet or less; 85.3% was zoned for lots of an acre or more, and 24.6% was zoned for three acres or more. By way of comparison, the American Public Health Association, a vigorous advocate of high minimum standards, recommends 6,000 square feet as a suitable minimum lot size based upon health considerations.

Minimum frontage requirements frequently, although not invariably, are found together with minimum lot size requirements. Only 13.5% of the land zoned in 1970 for single family housing in the Department of Community Affairs study area was zoned for 100 foot minimum frontage or less. In that area, 54.3% was zoned for 150 feet or more. This device was widely used in the northern outer-ring counties, where only 5% of the land is zoned for less than 100 foot frontage and 68.4% is zoned for more than 150 feet, but somewhat less widely used in the southern outer-ring counties, where 22.7% of the land was zoned for less than 100 foot frontage and 42.5% was zoned for more than 150 feet.

Analysis of the exclusionary impact of the widespread use of minimum lot size and minimum frontage requirements is a more complex task than that of analyzing minimum building requirements. There is a significant correlation between lot size and price of housing in areas without sewage service and between frontage and price in areas with sewage service. At the very least, it can be said with certainty that extensive mapping for large lots or large lot widths drives up the costs of smaller lots and thereby significantly raises the overall price of housing.

3) *Prohibition of multifamily housing*

Realistically, much of the housing needs of persons with low or moderate incomes will have to be met through various forms of multifamily housing. Hence, restrictions upon the construction of such housing have a highly exclusionary effect. In the Department of Community Affairs study area, construction of multifamily housing was permitted on only 6.2% of the land zoned for residential uses. If six aberrant rural municipalities are disregarded, the percentage falls to 1.1%. In the South Jersey outer-ring counties, 2.7% of such land is zoned for multifamily housing; in the northern outer-ring counties, only ½ of 1% is so zoned. There is no land zoned for multifamily housing in Somerset County and only .006% is so zoned in Monmouth County.

5) *Prohibition of mobile homes*

Mobile homes offer an alternate, less expensive form of housing. They have long since ceased to be mere "house trailers" but have become an important form of mass produced semi-permanent housing. Indeed, for many persons they may be the only form of new housing available. However, only .1% of the land zoned for residential use in the Department of Community Affairs study area was zoned for use by mobile homes. In the South Jersey outer-ring counties, .3% of the residential land was so zoned, the bulk of it being in Gloucester County, which had twice as much land zoned for mobile homes as the rest of the study area combined. None was zoned for this purpose in Camden County. No land was zoned for mobile homes in the northern outer-ring counties.

6) *Overzoning for nonresidential uses*

Zoning a great proportion of the developable land in a municipality noncumulatively for nonresidential uses may have the effect of forcing the price of land zoned for residential purposes up beyond the reach of persons with low or moderate incomes. Neither statewide nor county wide figures provide unambiguous evidence of the use of such practice at present in New Jersey. At the municipal level, the use of such practices is more evident in some areas. Thus, in Mt. Laurel itself, 29.2% of the land in the township, totaling 4,121 acres, is zoned for industrial uses, although only 100 acres within the township has actually been developed for such use in the past 10 years, and there is no reasonable prospect for industrial uses expanding to such proportions.

If anything, these figures underestimate the extent of exclusionary zoning in this State. A wide variety of other techniques may be used to achieve an exclusionary effect. In addition, a municipality need not use all of these techniques to achieve exclusionary ends. Municipalities which have large lot-size and frontage requirements may not have high building-size requirements and vice versa. Thus, only 18% of the land in the Department of Community Affairs study area zoned for single family residences permitted houses with less than 1,200 square feet of floor space to be constructed on a ¼ acre or less site with 100 foot or less frontage.

Forceful judicial intervention is necessitated not only by the already widespread use of exclusionary zoning practices and by the fact that the motivations for such are deeply ingrained in the suburban zoning and planning process, but also by certain extrinsic factors of which the Court may take notice.

First, the United States suffers from an acute national housing shortage. It has been estimated that over 10 million dwelling units would be needed to provide each family in the country with adequate housing. In New Jersey, it has been estimated that there is an immediate need for over 400,000 dwelling units. New Jersey, already the second most densely populated state in the country, is experiencing continuing population growth — it is estimated that by 1985 the total population will have increased from its 1970 figure of 7,200,000 to about 10,000,000. Housing, particularly in urban areas, is deteriorating. The percentage of substandard units throughout the State increased from 14.8% in 1960 to 17.4% in 1969. In Hudson County, the increase was from 22.3% to 31.3%. Some of these units dropped out of the housing market altogether. It has been estimated that simply to keep up with population growth and to replace units which drop out of the housing market, 100,000 new units would have to be constructed in the State each year.

The brunt of this shortage is, of course, borne by persons with low or moderate incomes. As of 1970, it was estimated that not only were half of all low income families in the State obliged to live in inadequate housing, but so were approximately 125,000 families with moderate incomes. Analyses by both the federal and state governments indicate that the majority of families can afford to neither rent nor buy new housing at current prices. Other authorities estimate that such housing may be beyond the financial capacity of as much as ¾ of all the families in the State and as much as 90% of those families in which the head of the household is below the age of 35. In theory, low and moderate income families should benefit even from construction of new housing which they themselves cannot afford because such housing creates vacancies which "filter down." In reality, however, most of these vacancies are absorbed by the enormous lag between population growth and new housing construction. The housing which does "filter down" to persons with low or moderate incomes is often badly dilapidated and in deteriorating neighborhoods.

Second, the growing movement of commerce and industry to the suburbs is imposing a heavy burden upon employees who are unable to obtain housing in these suburban areas. The trend, which began after World War II and has continued unabated, arises from a variety of causes — need for additional land for expansion, automated methods of handling goods which make single-floor layout of manufacturing plants economically desirable, increased access provided by superhighways, desire for aesthetic surroundings, lower suburban property taxes, etc. Retail establishments have also relocated in the suburbs, taking advantage of the shift in the affluent population, the access provided by suburban highways, and the more attractive surroundings. The result has been a shift of blue-collar jobs from the cities to the suburbs. This is, of course, the natural and foreseeable consequence of "fiscal zoning" that encourages the development within a municipality of commercial establishments, which are net tax-providers, and discourages the development of housing for persons who would work in such establishments, on the grounds that they are net revenue-absorbers.

This trend is one that imposes unfair burdens on the worker who is locked out of suburban residential areas. For blue-collar workers, commutation from the cities to suburban job locations is both time-consuming and prohibitively expensive. There is often no access at all by public mass transit and even when such transportation is available in theory it is frequently impractical in fact.

Third, even as we write, development proceeds apace. Once an area is developed, it becomes much more difficult to alter its social and economic character. There is a hazard that prolonged judicial inaction will permit exclusionary practices to continue to operate and will allow presently developing communities to acquire permanent exclusionary characteristics. The concern is not that New Jersey will soon be without developable land, but that large areas now in the process of development will have already acquired irrevocably exclusionary characteristics before the courts effectively intervene.

Comments: Recent years have witnessed the emergence of two new policy thrusts, growth management and environmental protection, both of which further limit suburban housing opportunities and thus compound the impact of exclusionary zoning. Localities may use growth management techniques, including development quotas and staged development requirements, to regulate the rate and absolute amount of population growth within the controlled jurisdiction. These may work directly as is the case with the widely known Petaluma, California ordinance that limits building permits to 500 per year. Or growth control may work indirectly as in the equally well known Montgomery County, Maryland example where the local sewer board limited the number and location of sewer hook-ups, ostensibly to coordinate service demand with new facility construction.

Environmental protection legislation, often enacted at the state or federal rather than local level, has the objective of protecting valued resources from destruction by urban or suburban development processes. For example: flood plains and coastal zones may be protected by outright prohibitions against development; restrictions may require development impacts on air or water quality to be held below threshhold levels; and blanket regulations may require exhaustive study and review of environmental impacts.

Growth control efforts have been referred to as the no-growth movement, and environmental protection as a central element in the environmental movement. Whatever names are used, the effects on the housing economy are the familiar effects of exclusionary zoning. The conflicts explored in *Mt. Laurel* only become more intense under the impetus of no-growth and environmental controls. Further analysis of these conflicts and efforts at their solution will constitute a major housing policy arena in the years to come.

The next two readings explore some of the impacts of growth control and environmental protection. The first article concentrates on price effects and analyzes these measures in rather conventional microeconomic terms with respect to the new home builders' production function or calculus of product costs.

CASE, THE IMPACT OF LAND USE AND ENVIRONMENTAL CONTROLS ON HOUSING COSTS, from The Cost of Housing, Proceedings of the Third Annual Conference 141-65 (Federal Home Loan Bank of San Francisco, 1977)

Introduction

There is agreement that land use and environmental controls have increased housing costs, but the arguments over how much they have increased costs, and whether the controls are necessary, have set in motion an interminable battle of rival virtues. A resolution of the conflict will not be achieved soon because of the poorly defined qualitative and shakily developed quantitative evaluations on which sides are chosen. In the meantime, many kinds of benefits that might accrue because of controls tend to be minimized or forgotten. Much of the discussion currently is similar to a situation in which an investor establishes what the purchase price should be for a property on the basis of the accumulated initial purchase costs.

All too often, those who favor controls defend their actions on the basis of somewhat nebulous goals of "clean air and water," "freedom from pollution and congestion," "open space preservation," or protection of the "quality of living." On the other hand, those who attack controls tend to lean heavily on the vaguely stated egalitarian principle that all American families have a "right" to own, or at least rent, affordable, safe, sanitary, quality family housing. Unfortunately, both groups have yet to support their positions with the same certainty with which they advance their preferences.

. . . .

Housing Prices, Costs, and Family Income

. . . .

[Case then details the inflationary trends that have led to a substantial increase in the cost of home ownership. — Eds.]

Simultaneously with efforts to encourage and support widespread homeownership, population booms and inflation began to have important impacts on housing markets. As important natural resources became scarce and demands for housing, neighborhood, and living quality accelerated, citizen participation in shaping urban environments emerged as a dominant force influencing home construction. Increases in costs were inevitable. Building codes were used to require improved materials and equipment that would make homes and residential neighborhoods safer and "better" places in which to live. Zoning was expanded to require wider spacing of homes, compatibility of uses, and favorable living environments. But for many years, the costs of these "improvements" were balanced by increased abilities of families to buy homes, not only because family incomes were actually rising faster than costs, but also because home financing became more liberal and widely available.

Unfortunately, as affluence spread, shortages developed among those natural resources necessary to provide adequate family housing; these shortages began to threaten the quality of living for existing homeowners. Environmental controls were proposed spurred by the national air quality legislation and programs. Communities faced with greater strains on public facilities and natural resources introduced stiffer conditions on new-home construction and even began to slow or prohibit growth. Out of this began to emerge greater recognition of social costs.

Environmental Control Costs

In short, in a period of only about five years, the limitations of the physical environment were becoming increasingly apparent. The inability of the marketplace to produce the kinds of adjustments that would protect the resources and still permit quality in homeownership and living became evident, and the need for some changes in housing markets seemed urgent. It is this urgency that leads to an abundance of laws, rules, regulations, and controls and an inevitable increase in housing costs. In general, the costs were increased by the following factors:

  1. New and higher fees and licensing costs;
  2. More complicated and extended review processes and reports;
  3. Requirements for front-end and absorption of the costs of public facilities such as parks, open space, sewers, water, electricity, and schools; and
  4. Reduced intensities in developments.

Each of these costs was legitimatized by reference to public health, welfare, or safety. Each was usually imposed incrementally, so that any particular cost did not seem too extravagant, given the purposes for which the costs were imposed. Numerous individual studies reported on the particular kinds of control costs imposed on individual projects, but only minor attention was being paid to their totals or cumulative effects. The accumulative impact of these costs became acutely apparent only after 1975, when a combination of inflation, housing shortages, and the costs of the new controls combined to shatter any previous assumptions about what housing should cost and what families should or could pay for it.

. . . .

Controls and Their Associated Problems

The identification of the impact of land use and environmental controls on housing costs is extremely difficult, and only tenuous conclusions can be drawn, not only because the controls are numerous and complex, but also because they are changed constantly as a result of court orders or interpretations and operational improvements.

Controls are possible because they are imposed as a means of protecting public health, safety, and general welfare. They add to costs not only because of many direct charges, but also because they add delays to the construction process, require more labor and materials, and affect the costs of using the home.

Front-End Costs

Controls begin as soon as raw land is purchased for housing construction. If environmental or growth controls exist, the builder will have to conduct a market survey to establish that his proposed development is needed and will conform to the local use and density standards. Next, there are the costs of engineering, geological, and other reviews to determine where and what types of homes can be supported on the land. In the process, the builder may have to hire the services of land planners, civil engineers, soil and geology experts, architects, landscape architects, zoologists, biologists, traffic engineers, and other special consultants.

Before construction begins, a host of governmental reviews, permits, and processing must be dealt with . . . . For example, approvals are needed for the master land use plan, environmental impact and review reports, subdivision plans, grading permits, building permits, plumbing permits, electrical permits, and provision for or payment of fees for water, electricity, gas, sewer, flood control, fire protection, schools, parks, open space, access roads, drainage, landscaping, traffic signals, and signs.

Environmental Impact Considerations

If the land is located in an area subject to additional environmental constraints because of the existence of a coastal commission or other special land use control body, the processes become even more complex and costly. A single example from the files of the California Coastal Commission exemplifies this problem. The act implementing the work of the Commission requires that the Commission assure "access to publicly owned or used beaches, recreation areas, and natural resources. . . ." In most localities, such beaches are under the control of local and city governments as well as the Coastal Commission, so that at least three governmental units must approve the project. Local builders are required to plan for access when constructing homes near the beach. If the builder decides to shift to another market because of the restriction, inputs are denied to local business and employment markets. If the builder stays and improved access is provided, then the increased use could destroy the fragile nature of the local beach environment. Improved access might also mean additional costs for providing roads and public transportation to the area.

If all additional construction is denied and the access remains relatively limited, then this could mean that only local residents would be able to or want to use the beach. If homes were provided, their number would be limited and prices, as well as the costs of operating the homes, probably would be higher.

. . . .

Zoning, Codes, and Growth Controls

There is almost universal agreement that zoning and growth controls do add to the costs of housing. From the evidence available, an added annual cost equal to approximately 2 percent of the sales price seems reasonable. However, environmental concerns and desires to halt or slow growth have caused these traditional controls to be used in new ways that are introducing added, and sometimes new, kinds of costs.

. . . .

In Orange County, California, one of the most rapidly growing counties in the state, a study in 1975 indicated that the selling price of a new single-family home was rising 1.9 times faster than average family income, which meant that 44 percent of all Orange County families could not afford to purchase such a home. The extra costs of governmental control in Orange County were identified as fees for tentative tract map review, engineering and grading requirements, Environmental Impact Reports, sewers, park fees in lieu of dedicating land, building permits, plan check, plumbing and electrical inspections, and flood and drainage controls. For a 50-unit, single-family detached residential project, in which the homes would cost $30,000 and contain 1,300 square feet, the total fee costs were estimated at $1,125 — 4 percent of total costs — in city areas and $1,195 — 4 percent of total costs — in the unincorporated areas. For $40,000 houses, the fees ranged between $1,203 and $1,270; and for a $50,000 homes, between $1,294 and $1,365. Fees related to governmental controls were estimated to average 3 percent of the sales price; however, these estimates did not include the costs associated with waiting for approvals. Generally, a 28-month approval period was involved, which represented a 22-month increase from 1965. For a $40,000 house, these carrying costs could amount to as much as 1 percent a month of the final sales price. . . .

A recheck of construction costs in Orange County in 1977 indicated that the direct costs associated with governmental controls were still nominal, accounting for 2 percent of the total subdivision costs. The real costs were associated with the delays in receiving the approvals, because these were estimated to be adding to total project costs at the rate of 1.5 percent a month.

An Evaluation of Public Review Processes

The mayor of Los Angeles appointed an ad hoc committee in 1976 to review the construction processes in the city. The committee found that the process took 36 months — as compared with 12 months in San Diego, 12 to 18 months in Los Angeles County, and 12 to 20 months in San Francisco — and added at least 10 to 20 percent to the cost of a $40,000 home. The committee recommended 45 changes in the construction process reviews that would affect the operations of the four major city departments involved in construction review processes.

Among the items adding to both the construction review process times and overall costs that the committee found were the following:
1. Rereviews;
2. Inconsistent interpretation of applicable codes;
3. Changes required by field inspectors that were not required in the approved plans;
4. Duplicate processing of required reports;
5. Significant variations in estimating the costs of plan checks and other fees;
6. Lack of key information needed to comply with codes;
7. Temporary interpretations that become permanent without adequate review; and
8. Lengthy and costly new materials checking, even though other responsible agencies had reviewed and approved the materials.

One builder, frustrated by the entire process, addressed the Los Angeles City Planning Commission directly and asked for immediate improvement of the review process after the rereview of one of his residential developments required the following:
1. The park fee be refigured;
2. A crosstown trip to secure sewer approvals that could not be made at the office reviewing his project;
3. Referrals to three different offices to get his grading standards approved; and
4. Inordinate time to get street plans approved, even though they met all standard design criteria.
. . . .

Controls and Market Conditions

Reasonably clear evidence of the extent to which market conditions can change the impact of controls and affect housing costs is provided in two studies completed for the Urban Land Institute in San Jose, California, and Jacksonville, Florida. In general, the studies reflect the same findings that were inherent in an analysis of the various California Coastal Commissions' actions. Growth controls tend to restrict the amount of construction while adding to costs. If, as in the case of San Jose, the market demand is strong, the costs can be passed on and higher profits earned. If, as was true in Jacksonville, the controls increase prices but the market is not strong, then not all costs can be passed on and the builder has to accept a lower profit.

The case studies compared costs for builders in 1967 and 1976. In San Jose, the price of the homes built by one builder increased by 80.2 percent and for the other builder, 121.3 percent. Local growth management policies were identified as being responsible for 20 to 40 percent of the price increases. In Jacksonville, governmental controls added $1,000 to $1,500 to the costs of a house but market resistance prevented builders from passing on these added costs.

Conclusions about the two area studies follow classical economic reasoning. In the case of San Jose, restricted housing supplies produced by the controls in the face of strong demand pressures permitted builders to pass on extra costs and to protect their profit margins. In Jacksonville, the controls did not restrict the supplies of new land for housing; demand was not strong, so builders had to accept lower profits.

The details provided in the two studies provide other valuable insights into the relationships between controls and housing prices. They found that direct costs were rather easily measured and reflected the same kinds of cost impacts that other similar kinds of studies had found. Jacksonville, Florida, increased water main sizes and the frequency of fire hydrants that added $280 directly to the cost of developing a new lot in the city.

Jacksonville, Florida

Jacksonville is a growing city "without strong growth controls but with fairly stringent environmental and subdivisions design regulations in a state which has implemented a number of land use control programs." Direct costs, adjusted for inflation and related to improved water supply, added $450 to each lot ($280 over 1970); roads added $1,475 ($830 over 1970). Connection fees increased by $185, and increased building code requirements added $150. The overall impact on housing sales prices was less than might be expected. In 1976, selling prices had increased on an average for a 1,500 square foot house by 36.7 percent. However, raw land costs were up 87.5 percent, site improvement costs by 70.6 percent, and overhead interest and profit by 23.7 percent, thus increasing lot costs by 52.4 percent. For housing construction, the costs increased by 38.1 percent and the overhead profit by 17.7 percent. The major conclusion was that the Jacksonville market was such that housing demand was price-elastic, and many of the increased costs could not be passed along to buyers of lots or homes. Among the causes identified as explanatory of what had happened, a major one was that difficulty in forming new utility districts and sewage treatment plants shifted attention to areas where lots were already developed and could be serviced.

San Jose, California

In San Jose, the experiences of two builders were compared. Builder A was able to complete and sell his homes faster than Builder B, so that his holding costs, including those related to public policy, were lower. Taxes and fees for both builders increased substantially, even though policies of growth restriction reduced the amount of vacant land that could be used for residential construction.

Both builders were able to charge prices that included the increased costs, so that both were able to increase their profit margins over 1967. Builder A sold his homes for prices 80.2 percent more than the equivalent home sold in 1967 but increased his profit and marketing returns by 231.1 percent. The total public policy-related costs, on the other hand, had increased by only 118.9 percent. Builder B increased the sales prices by 121.3 percent and profit and marketing costs by 158.3 percent and suffered a 195.3 percent increase in public policy-related costs. When the costs were adjusted to 1976 dollars, policy-related costs were responsible for all of the increase in the costs for Builder A and for 65.8 percent of Builder B's increases.

A very important conclusion in the study was that generalizations could not be made from the two case studies, since each city had differing market conditions and the builders had different problems. In the case of San Jose, public policy in conjunction with local market conditions permitted builders to pass on costs; in the case of Jacksonville, they did not. Although the study does not contain the finding, another conclusion is that extra regulation means extra cost — to investors, builders, and homebuyers. However, both the investors and the builders leave the market once the products they own are sold. The homeowner is saddled with the added costs of ownership that are related directly to the added public costs.

Comments: 1. Evidence and analysis continues to pile up in support of the argument Case makes. For instance, MIT housing professor Frieden has portrayed the impact of environmental controls on land use and housing in a series of fascinating case studies. In one of these cases, a developer proposed to build a development of 2200 housing units in the foothills near Oakland, California, an attractive site overlooking San Francisco Bay. In response to opposition and the threat of a lawsuit, the developer substantially modified its plan, eliminating proposed open space to lower the density and multi-family units which made up half of the original development. Frieden questions this result:

What had the opponents achieved? They prevented grading and earth moving from spoiling their view. They preserved open space, but only to look at not to use. The city park was eliminated, and community open space was no longer provided. The 480 acres of open space originally proposed had been converted into larger lots for the people who would buy or build houses. An analysis of the compromises the developer made and the resulting price changes is revealing. The 1972 plan called for 2,200 units, with the single-family attached houses to be sold for about $33,000, and the apartments for about $24,000. The 1976 plan offered 100 lots for estate homes. The lots alone will cost more than the houses themselves would have originally — from $35,000 to $75,000. In all probability, families paying that much for a lot will put on it a house worth at least $100,000. What housing remained in the plan consisted of 150-200 single-family houses, ranging in price from $40,000 to $60,000. The ultimate result was a deep cut in the number of units — to about one-tenth the original housing — combined with an increase to three times the original price on the average. What started as middle-income housing emerged as luxury homes.

Frieden, "Environmental" Politics, Urban Land, Vol. 36, No. 3, at 3, 4 (1976).

2. The price effects studied by Case and Frieden only scratch the surface of the debate. In one view the growth and environmental movements involve a fundamental critique of the American system of private land ownership. A colleague of Frieden at MIT has put this succinctly:

The Land Market and Public Regulation

In the United States the free play of the private market traditionally has determined the price and allocation of land. Aside from the relatively well-defined system of private property rights, this has been possible because Americans view land primarily in commercial terms, as a capital resource. Thus, the price of land has been determined through the competitive interaction of supply and demand. And individual land parcels have been allocated to different uses according to their private rate of return. Decisions about the amount, time, and location of development have been left primarily to private owners and land developers so that our land resources would be used in the most economically efficient manner.

As the prestigious Rockefeller Commission report on the use of land indicates, however, there is a new mood in the United States which challenges not only the narrowness of our traditional concept of land as a commercial resource, but also our unquestioned reliance on the workings of the private land market. The primary cause of this new mood is a rapidly growing dissatisfaction with market outcomes. There is a new awareness that our traditional land use system does not adequately control the quality, pace, or distributional effects of land development. Critics of that system argue that exclusive, or even primary, reliance on the private market exacerbates a number of social problems. First, market outcomes are not neutral. They favor those who enter the market place with more money; this leads to the exclusion of the poor and minorities from most suburbs, resulting in a society increasingly separated along economic and racial lines. Second, the allocation of land use according to the test of profitability tends to neglect broader societal objectives such as the preservation of flood plains, watersheds, and other natural resources. Because there are no dollar values placed on so-called spillover effects, the private land market produces too much air and water pollution, while paying too little attention to the depletion of natural resources. But in recent years, protection of our air, water, and other environmental surroundings has been deemed by some to be as important as the development of an industrial park, or a new residential and office complex. Finally, current patterns of sprawl and leapfrog growth are costly in terms of the demands they make for the provision of access roads, water lines, and sewage disposal, as well as energy and fuel consumption. In essence, the market approach tends to slight environmental, natural and humanistic values.

Solomon, The Effects of Land Use and Environmental Controls on Housing in Resources for Housing, Proceedings of the First Annual Conference 178-79 (Federal Home Loan Bank of San Francisco, 1975)

The argument Solomon describes suggests that these movements represent a basic attack on the established economic order. Others argue a diametrically opposed case. They see the same fiscal, property wealth, housing class, and racial issues as in exclusionary zoning, and discount the apparent attack on private property rights that some see in growth control and environmental protection. Policy analyst White spells out this other view and gives particular attention to the fiscal and property wealth issues.

M. WHITE, SELF-INTEREST IN THE SUBURBS: THE TREND TOWARD NO-GROWTH ZONING, 4 POLICY ANALYSIS 185-94, 196, 198-200, 203 (1978)

Suburbanites seem to be closing the gates behind them. Communities that once permitted the construction of only large, expensive, single-family houses are now signaling that they would prefer no new housing at all or as little as possible. In other words, the rich used to be welcome in suburbia; now even they are not welcome anymore. This new trend in exclusionary zoning has been dubbed the "no-growth movement."

This movement is important for a variety of reasons. First, as business and industry suburbanize at a rapid rate, interference with the ability to acquire suburban residences must doom central-city dwellers to long, inefficient, out-commuting trips if they are to compete for suburban jobs. Or worse: center-city dwellers may choose not to take suburban jobs at all if they cannot move to nearby suburban housing. But the pool of available jobs in central cities has been declining in recent years. Thus we can expect rising unemployment rates in central cities if the cities' residents cannot take suburban jobs. Second, the "closing" of the suburbs denies the housing needs of the poor. A defense of new housing construction in the suburbs — even of large, single-family houses — has been the "trickle-down theory." New housing is built for the rich, whose vacated housing is then occupied by the middle class. Formerly middle-class housing is then occupied by the poor, whose needs are thus met indirectly. But if no new housing is provided in the suburbs (little new construction occurs in the central cities), the housing needs of the poor and the lower middle class will not be provided for at all. Third, by presenting itself as a movement to preserve the environment, no-growth zoning has gained a degree of respectability that simply exclusionary zoning never had. As a result, the no-growth movement has survived several initial court challenges and appears to be much less legally vulnerable than simple exclusionary zoning. Yet, as I argue below, although the "new" zoning appears to be a different policy, it has the same basically exclusionary goal as the old — to make suburbanites better-off at the expense of everyone else.

"No Growth" and the Courts

Recent court cases illustrate the threat posed by the no-growth zoning movement. The most important are the Petaluma, Ramapo, and Eastlake cases. In 1972 the town of Petaluma, California, adopted a zoning ordinance that allowed a maximum of 500 building permits to be issued per year, thus reducing the previous rate of population growth. The town set up an auction system to choose which builders would get permits. Plans submitted by builders were assigned points for such factors as "excellence of design," access to existing sewage and drainage, and provision of open space, public facilities, and low-to-moderate-cost housing. Plans accumulating the most points received permits. A challenge to the ordinance by builders succeeded in Federal District Court but was reversed by the Ninth Circuit Court of Appeals. The U.S. Supreme Court has refused to hear the case, thus allowing the ordinance to stand.

A 1969 zoning ordinance to Ramapo, New York, specified a twelve-year plan for capital improvements by the town. Housing development could proceed only if builders' proposed plans accumulated fifteen points on a sliding scale that assigned points for access to existing public facilities — sewers, drainage, parks, schools, roads, and firehouses. In effect the ordinance required that the building of houses await the building of schools and other public facilities, rather than the reverse. The ordinance did not specifically set an upper limit on new construction, but the town accomplished this by spacing the development of public facilities over time. The New York State Court of Appeals upheld this ordinance. . . .

[White next notes a 1976 U.S. Supreme Court decision upholding an Eastlake, Ohio, ordinance requiring all zoning amendments to be placed on a ballot and approved by a 55 percent majority. The Eastlake ordinance restricts any housing development, such as multi-family housing, that requires an amendment to the zoning ordinance. The voter approval requirement will delay the developer and approval may not be forthcoming. The Supreme Court decision did not consider exclusionary zoning issues but will nevertheless encourage municipalities to adopt ordinances of the Eastlake variety. Mandatory voter approval of all zoning amendments is unwieldy, however, and some municipalities may hesitate to imitate Eastlake. Some state courts have also prohibited zoning referenda. — Eds.]

These no-growth policies, whether carried out as zoning ordinances or by other means, appear to be quite different in intent and emphasis from traditional exclusionary zoning. In the latter, communities normally place no overall limitation on the amount of development that may occur or on its timing, but they control the type of development that occurs by banning multifamily housing and mobile homes or by requiring that all houses be single-family, detached dwellings or that they meet certain quality standards. Such zoning ordinances are often attacked in the courts on the ground that they fail to consider regional housing needs; they provide for housing for well-off families who wish to live in an area, but not for poor families making the same demand. These ordinances presumably reflect a desire on the part of the community to keep out poor people (and perhaps blacks), but not to restrict the access of potential residents who are desirable because they can pay their own way. In other words, the rich are welcome, the poor are not. In contrast, the no-growth zoning cases cited above seem to reflect a different intent. In these cases, the primary goal is to restrict growth of any sort. A community may prefer the rich to the poor, but no newcomers at all is its strongest preference. In short, both the rich and the poor have become unwelcome.

"Old-Style" Exclusionary Zoning

Communities' incentives with respect to new development can be better understood if we set out some of the basic demographic-fiscal "facts" under which local governments operate. These are not without exception, but they are generally true for suburban communities likely to engage in restrictive zoning.

1. Communities can use their zoning power to determine the basic types of housing constructed within their borders, i.e., detached, single-family houses; cluster housing (townhouses); low-rise or high-rise apartments....

2. Communities finance local spending predominantly from property taxes levied on both residential and nonresidential property.

3. School services, which absorb the bulk of local government expenditures in suburban areas, mainly benefit residents, not businesses. Property taxes paid by businesses generally exceed the use of community services by those businesses. Hence, businesses subsidize residents' consumption of education.

4. For any single community, business moves are mostly unaffected by new residential development. To the extent that business moves are sensitive to the local property-tax rate, new residential development that raises or lowers the tax rate discourages or encourages businesses to locate in the community. But since business moves depend on a variety of factors, such as access to transportation and utility connections and the location of similar businesses, this effect is probably small. Thus the subsidy of education by business is essentially a fixed amount. The existence of business ratables already in place thus discourages communities from allowing new housing to be built, since new housing causes this fixed fund to be spread more thinly over more public school pupils.

5. Within a community, all public school pupils receive educational services of generally equal quality. Thus households with several school-age children require much greater expenditure in public services than do childless households. Other local services, however, such as police and fire protection, require generally equal expenditures per household.

With these "facts" as background, we can examine a community's incentives for new housing development. Suppose a community's residents attempt to use local zoning power to prevent new development that would make them financially worse-off. This might be considered a minimum fiscal goal. Going further, local residents might try to use zoning to ensure that new development actually makes them financially better-off. Such a strategy would suggest that the community encourage whatever type of housing will generate more in new property-tax revenues than it will cost in added local service expenditures. If a new housing development generates revenues in excess of costs, the new residents subsidize the older residents of the community. The latter can then enjoy more public services at no extra cost or can continue current service levels with lower property taxes. If they sell their houses, the subsidy is capitalized as an increase in housing value. Thus if a proposed housing development will generate a positive subsidy, the community should allow it to be built, particularly if no alternative proposed development will generate an even greater positive subsidy. If a proposed development will generate a negative subsidy, the community should reject it.

The "facts" outlined above suggest that a community encourage high-value housing. On the revenue side, high-value housing generates higher property-tax receipts. On the cost side, high-value housing generates either higher or lower expenditures than low-value housing, depending primarily on the number of public school children per household. But communities can only choose among types of housing, not among types of households. Therefore, if large families are as likely to move into high-value as into low-value houses, high-value houses are more likely to generate a fiscal surplus.

This zoning strategy implies that communities generally should not allow housing to be built unless the new houses are of higher value than the existing houses in the community. If costs are constant per household, new houses of exactly the same value as the community's existing houses would generate a zero net transfer to the community at large. Only new houses of a value higher than the old can generate a positive subsidy. Thus communities will tend continuously to "upgrade" their zoning as new housing is built. Residents of the new higher-value houses in effect bribe the older community residents to swallow a loss of environmental values and to accept new housing.

What implications does this "fiscal-transfer" zoning strategy have for community growth? Clearly growth qua growth is by no means discouraged. The rich, i.e., those who can afford high-value houses, are encouraged to move into a community. The poor and those of status equal to that of existing residents are excluded, however, because property-tax payments on their housing would not cover costs. Obviously growth does not proceed rapidly under a fiscal-transfer zoning strategy. As a community upgrades its zoning, the percentage of households able to afford the housing that the community allows to be guilt becomes progressively smaller. Insiders profit from zoning via the fiscal transfer itself and via the zoning-induced scarcity of housing in the community, which raises the value of houses already built. Outsiders lose as a result of fiscal-transfer zoning because they cannot afford housing in the suburbs, because their mobility is restricted, and because there is greater competition for housing in the few remaining unzoned areas, i.e., the central cities.

An example of fiscal-transfer zoning in operation: a survey of new single-family housing built in 1970-71 in the New Jersey portions of the New York and Philadelphia metropolitan areas showed that the average value of new houses was $51,000, compared to an average value of $23,400 for existing single-family houses in the same area in 1970. Mortgage lenders generally limit potential buyers to houses worth approximately two and one-half times their annual income. This means that only purchasers with an annual income in 1970 of $20,400 or more could qualify for new houses in areas covered by the survey, which represents the upper 15 percent of the income distribution of New Jersey. Another route to the suburbs is also blocked for lower-income families, since, as part of the same general strategy, most suburban communities either ban outright or tightly restrict the availability of apartments.

The Trend Toward No-Growth Zoning

Thus fiscal-transfer zoning — a zoning strategy in which the rich are acceptable as newcomers, the poor are not, and only a certain kind of growth is desirable

— would seem to be a rational response to the fiscal facts of suburban life. This sort of zoning has been widely employed by suburban communities since the early 1960s. The recent trend toward no-growth zoning clearly suggests that something is different today, however. One possibility is that the values of community leaders have changed; they may now be interested in something other than maximizing the fiscal well-being of a community's existing residents. Alternatively, goals may have remained the same while fiscal "facts" have changed. In that case communities would pursue the old goals with a new set of zoning requirements. We discuss both of these possibilities separately.

Environmental Values

The most obvious candidate for a changed value in suburbia that affects zoning is the increased environmental consciousness of suburban residents. Under this rubric would come preferences for a small-town atmosphere, the desire to avoid pollution and congestion, an esthetic preference for open space over additional housing, and a desire to maintain local control by "oldtimers." Environmental motives have not remained constant over time. In the 1950s and 1960s, growth was itself an environmental ideology; in the 1970s attitudes have shifted, and protection of open space is highly valued.

For our purposes, the shift in environmental attitudes suggests that communities may be weighting fiscal gains and environmental goals differently than they used to. Previously, growth that generated fiscal gains was generally welcomed, with little regard for its environmental consequences. Now even growth that generates fiscal gains may be rejected because local residents are willing to give up dollar benefits in return for a higher-quality environment. To some extent this change in values may reflect the fact that many postwar suburban communities are filling up and their residents feel that further growth will cause congestion. This change in attitudes is certainly not surprising when we recall that incomes have risen over the years and that demand for a pollution- or congestion-free environment is highly income-elastic.

. . . .

Fiscal Realities

Alternatively, all the fuss over preserving the environment simply may be a cover allowing communities to continue pursuing the fiscal self-interest of their residents. A change in the fiscal "facts" for local governments, rather than a change in values, may have occurred. Governments then have to pursue the same goals with different zoning strategies. We explore two sets of "fact" changes that have occurred recently — the sharp increase in municipal-bond interest rates and the changes in the demographic characteristics of households buying new suburban housing.

Municipal-Bond Interest Rates — Suburban housing development usually requires the construction of new public facilities, such as schools, parks, and libraries. These are financed by floating municipal bonds backed by property-tax revenues. As an example, suppose a community contains 1000 houses and a single school. A developer proposes building another 1000 houses, which would necessitate an additional school. Ignoring zoning considerations for the moment, suppose the new and the old houses are identical, as would be the new and the old school. The existing school was financed with thirty-year 2½ percent bonds that still have ten years to run. To build a new school would require another bond issue at the current interest rate of, say, 6 percent. All interest and amortization payments are financed from several property-tax revenues. Thus if the new school were built, all residents of the community would share liability for both sets of bond issues. This sharing of liability would hurt the older residents, since they would have to contribute toward payments on the new bonds but would receive no offsetting increase in the quality of their own local services. New residents, on the other hand, would benefit, since they would pay less in taxes than the cost of payments on the 6 percent bonds that financed their new school.

. . . .

Demographic Characteristics — The demographic characteristics of households occupying suburban housing have changed, making high-value, single-family houses less desirable fiscally than they once were. In particular the average number of persons per household in rental housing of all types fell by 4.3 percent from 1960 to 1970. The average number of people in owner-occupied housing also fell, but by only 3.1 percent over the same period. For large owner-occupied houses, however, average household size actually rose by 5 percent. Larger household size presumably implies more school-age children, and vice versa. On the one hand, these changes reflect the tendency of families with children to move from rental apartments to their own houses at an earlier age, as income rose during the 1960-70 period. On the other hand, the enormous increase in the number of single-person households that occurred during the period is probably responsible for the decrease in the number of children in rental units and in lower-value, owner-occupied houses. Clearly these changes make less attractive from a fiscal standpoint the traditional zoning strategy of banning apartments but welcoming expensive single-family houses.

. . . .

We can conclude that communities' incentives to admit new residential developments have decreased substantially since the suburban building boom of the 1950s and 1960s. Ironically, now only the poorer suburban communities, those with high tax rates and little nonresidential tax base, will find new development strongly attractive. All communities, however, will find apartments and townhouses relatively more attractive than they used to be. But zoning plans that encourage only high-rise luxury condominiums and high-value townhouse developments, say, but exclude other types of housing are unlikely to become common because they are not likely to survive a court challenge. The traditional fiscal-transfer zoning plan that excluded apartments but encouraged detached houses could sometimes make a precarious journey past court scrutiny by invoking the "police power" argument that a community can regulate land use so as to promote general health and welfare. It could be argued that apartments were detrimental to a community because of their greater tendency to burn down, attract undesirables, lower property values, and so forth. Often blatantly discriminatory zoning plans chiefly intended to exclude the poor could successfully invoke such an argument when challenged by disgruntled developers. However, the same argument is much less likely to hold when it is in fact high-density apartments that are to be encouraged and single-family houses that are to be blocked. In addition, apartments have never been particularly welcome in suburbia, either for their looks or for their traditional association with low-income, "problem" families. Many communities, facing the set of choices described here, are likely to opt for a no-growth strategy.

. . . .

Implications for Public Policy

Is Petaluma the blueprint for the future? We have examined several reasons why communities' incentives have changed, causing them now to favor a no-growth zoning strategy over the former strategy of encouraging the construction of luxury, single-family houses. Increased environmental consciousness is partly responsible for the change, as well as the rising cost of financing public facilities for newcomers and a shift in the relative profitability of single-family houses versus apartments.

Thus the Petaluma zoning plan is not inconsistent with the community's fiscal self-interest. Primarily the community is attempting to cut down its rate of population growth. Secondarily it is attempting to maintain control over the type of new development built within its borders. Petaluma's auction procedure for allocating the 500 yearly building permits to developers allows the community to scrutinize proposed developments and to select those that make its residents as well-off as possible. Even the procedure that encourages developers to submit plans for low- and moderate-income housing is not illogical. Planners in favor of no-growth have sometimes referred to such provisions as "environmental blackmail," i.e., in return for support of no-growth zoning for environmental reasons, citizens' groups demand that what residential development does occur be reserved for low- and moderate-income families. Such provisions are also useful in themselves, however. No-growth zoning plans may have a greater chance of passing a court test if, while generally restricting population growth, they do not particularly discriminate against the poor.

Perhaps the most worrisome feature of the Petaluma, Ramapo, and Eastlake plans is the fact that they have survived court challenges. At a time when advocates of economic and racial integration have not yet won a definite victory against even clearly exclusionary fiscal-transfer zoning, they are faced with a new fight against no-growth zoning, and they have lost some crucial battles in the courts. This suggests that they will need to seek statutory, rather than judicial, relief. [Several state courts have now struck down exclusionary local zoning of the fiscal-transfer variety. The *Mt. Laurel* decision, supra p. 385, is one example. — Eds.]

Taking a broad perspective, it is clear that no-growth zoning is a strategy that benefits the local community at the expense of the region at large. It is tempting to assume that, with overall population growth approaching the zero-population-growth (ZPG) level, little new housing is needed, and that no-growth zoning is a movement consistent with public interest. ZPG does not necessarily imply a society without movement, however. In the United States in the 1970s, middle-income families are continuing to migrate from central cities to the suburbs, although at a rate slower than in the previous decade. And more important, the movement of business and industry into the suburbs may be just starting rather than almost ending. If the poor in the central cities are to retain access to jobs, it is increasingly important that they be able to find housing near the growing job opportunities in the suburbs. Otherwise, the poor will be faced with the ever-worse option of finding employment in the declining pool of central-city jobs, taking jobs in the suburbs for wages that hardly justify long commuting journeys, or remaining unemployed.

The following are several possible public-policy measures that would increase the access of low-income workers to suburban housing.
[White proposes a variety of state actions to increase lower income housing opportunity, including state review of local zoning. One state, Oregon, requires mandatory local planning and requires local planning to be consistent with state land use goals. One of these goals requires localities to make provision for lower income housing. White does not mention an important proposal of the American Law Institute put forward in its 1975 Model Land Development Code. That Code is intended as a model for state planning and land use control legislation. It

authorizes state review of local decisions disapproving development providing housing opportunities. Only Florida has adopted this provision of the Code. — Eds.]

The no-growth movement should be seen for what it is — a new and modernized form of exclusionary zoning that plays on the environmental consciousness of the 1970s. It is still primarily a zoning game, and its goal is still to use a community's exclusionary powers to make existing residents better-off at the expense of outsiders. The new twist is that almost all new residential development — not merely apartments and low-income housing — has become fiscally unprofitable. Thus communities prefer no growth over growth, but "no growth" is defined to exclude people only, not fiscally profitable business and industry. Access to suburban housing remains as crucial for the poor as it ever was, however, and public-policy actions to restrict local zoning power are crucially needed. The no-growth movement has strengthened local communities' monopoly power over land use within their borders, but it has not weakened the argument that control over local land use must be directed to benefit not merely the locality but the entire interdependent region.

Comments: 1. White reiterates a main theme of the *Mt. Laurel* decision in asserting the primacy of fiscal motives in exclusionary suburban practices. Given the deep division between the institutional-structural orientation and the traditional economic view which starts with individual preferences and motives, disagreement on first principles is inevitable. The following brief excerpt suggests the nature of the debate.

For all the diversity of respondents and respondent communities, a series of consistent threads runs through the interviews, which can be seen as a representative pattern of suburban attitudes on the subject of multifamily housing development. Suburban officials are ambivalent about multifamily housing in their communities, perceiving potentially valuable fiscal benefits to be obtained despite the potential dangers to the social or visual character of the community. At the same time, they feel constrained by what they perceive as the hostility of their constituents, who are felt to be less aware of the fiscal benefits, and more concerned about real or imaginary social dangers. Given that the dominant theme in suburban politics has been moving from that of growth, or the traditional ideal of 'progress', to one of environmental protection and opposition to growth, the tightrope on which the local official must walk would appear to be getting progressively more slippery.

In the realm of low and moderate income housing the picture is less ambiguous — the officials, civic leaders, and (one can assume) the citizens, of those towns that fit the classic suburban image want nothing to do with subsidized housing. This opposition, however, is based not on a rational calculus but instead on a combination of limited or inaccurate information from the experience of other communities and a preconceived notion of the inappropriateness of low and moderate income housing in their town. In contrast, most towns in which some subsidized housing already exists appear much more ready to accept additional housing that the others are willing to take the initial plunge. Similarly, fiscal considerations do not appear to be prominent in the minds of those excluding subsidized housing; policies likely to change the cost-revenue balance of such housing developments do not strike them as being significant, or likely to change the perspective they presently hold.

The degree of opposition felt toward multifamily development, however, may not, in the end, determine the number or type of multifamily housing that will be built. Many officials, and still more civic and community leaders, see a difference between what they would like to happen and what they expect to happen. Growth, urbanization, and its concommitant, greater density and greater development of multifamily housing, are seen by most leaders as an inevitable process. The local officials, in fact, are in a triple bind: they must respond to socially-based community pressures against growth and multifamily development; they must respond to a wider series of pressures demanding more development, particularly apartments; and, at the same time, confront a network of municipal services and facilities that is, as often as not, inadequate to serve even the existing population.

New Jersey County and Municipal Government Study Commission, Housing and Suburbs 99-100 (Ninth Report, 1974).

Another view put forth by some legal commentators ties exclusionary practices to the multiplicity of jurisdictions created by the typically fragmented political structure of suburbia. While the correlation doubtless exists, the relationship derives from the single class structure of the typical small suburban municipalities, hence the ease with which they can adopt exclusionary practices. This correlation is independent of the reason for such practices, attitudinal or fiscal.

2. Note that White argues a fiscal basis for exclusion, Solomon suggests it may be in an environmentalism powerful enough to challenge the institution of private property, the New Jersey survey suggests more diffuse attitudinal causes, Case by-passes causality and discusses effects on house prices, and the court in *Mt. Laurel* identified both fiscal and attitudinal causes. This is the same dichotomy of first principles that has emerged again and again in this book, the contradiction between the microeconomists' psychological starting point and the political-economists' social-structural and institutional beginning.

The concept of housing class helps reconcile these conflicting interpretations. Recall the words of John Rex (supra p. 146), who speaks of "groups differently placed with respect to the means of housing." As applied to the idea of suburban exclusion, different placement means differences in access to jobs, services, and amenities at fiscally advantageous costs. Rex then goes on to say that such housing classes or differently placed groups may engage in struggles "as acute as the class struggle in industry." This comment suggests likening the defense of suburban turf to the conflicts between labor and management in industry. Since housing bundles together in a single indivisible package the attributes that establish the consumption and opportunity structures accessible to household members, exclusionary practices become more understandable. They represent a broad defense of economic and social status and opportunity, not merely a narrow fiscal self-interest or abstracted, Banfieldian antipathy toward lower class neighbors.

3. The Massachusetts Anti-Snob Zoning Law is another state remedy for exclusionary local zoning that deserves mention. It allows a developer or sponsor of multifamily or assisted housing to appeal to the state if refused necessary zoning changes by a community. If the town in question has not met the fair share criteria spelled out in the law, the state can override the local zoning provisions prohibiting the development. If the state, after hearing both sides of the question, decides to override local zoning it will also issue all of the necessary permits and approvals requisite for building. The all-in-one permit procedure is necessary to inhibit localities from blocking the development with design reviews and other time-consuming procedures. Although the anti-snob zoning process in Massachusetts was initially plagued with administrative boondoggles, it has recently proved to be more successful.

4. Given the local importance of the central city-suburban split in terms of basic political and economic interests, and the still considerable political clout of central cities, it should be predictable that the most energetic responses to suburban exclusion would come at the local level, not at the state level as White recommends. Locally the conflict has shown up most sharply in regional planning agencies that embody representation from all metropolitan area jurisdictions including both central cities and suburbs. At the regional planning level the conflict is inescapable. In some propitious cases the conflict is squarely addressed by public policy. One such policy that shows some promise of providing lower-income housing, especially subsidized lower-income housing, is the so-called fair share housing plan adopted in several metropolitan areas and encouraged by the U.S. Department of Housing and Urban Development. Regional fair share plans are explained in the following article:

R. FISHMAN, ED., HOUSING ALLOCATION PLANS in HOUSING FOR ALL UNDER LAW 468-77 (Report of the American Bar Association Advisory Commission on Housing and Urban Growth, 1977) Housing Planning at the Regional Level

Two types of regional agencies are involved in housing planning: (1) councils of government, which are voluntary organizations of public officials and local governments created by interlocal agreement or state enabling legislation; and (2) regional planning commissions, which are multijurisdictional agencies created by state legislatures to carry out comprehensive areawide planning. Much attention has been given to the need for planning that crosses municipal boundaries. . . . However, few metropolitan units of government have a sufficient legal-political base to implement these efforts.

. . . . The housing planning effort most commonly associated with regional agencies is the fair-share, or allocation, plan. Housing allocation plans have played a key role in defining housing planning not only for planning agencies but for counties and states as well. The housing allocation plan has been described as:

> an attempt to distribute future housing units throughout a jurisdiction in such a way as to balance overconcentration of such units in some areas with available resources in other areas for receiving them. The plan is generally applied to low- and moderate-income units and/or publicly subsidized units to be distributed in a manner that promotes equal opportunities for low- and moderate-income households in making locational choices.

Surveys of housing need, housing market analyses, studies of housing location or site-election standards, and even studies of jobs/housing balance, are important components of a housing allocation plan.

The first housing allocation model was developed by the Miami Valley Regional Planning Commission (Ohio) as a part of its housing element. It was accepted and promoted by HUD as a means of satisfying the housing element requirement of the 701 program. It is important to realize that the allocation plan was only a part of a much more comprehensive planning effort on the part of Miami Valley. In its housing plan summary the Miami Valley Regional Planning Commission states well its broader planning aims:

> It is important to understand . . . that expanding the lower-income housing supply is just one part of the comprehensive Regional Housing Program. The provision of physical shelter alone is recognized as an incomplete approach to solving housing problems, a fact that has been demonstrated many times in recent decades. For this reason, it is the responsibility of the MVRPC and its staff to carry out a comprehensive effort that addresses the many concerns related to housing itself. During the four and one half years of the program, a substantial number of components have been incorporated that broaden and strengthen it.

Because of its special treatment by HUD in the allotment housing subsidies, the Miami Valley plan met some measure of success. Subsequent efforts by other regional agencies have fallen short, some because of the lack of housing subsidies, others due to the inherent weaknesses of the agencies themselves. This has not been the case for the Twin Cities Metropolitan Council in Minnesota which, as a legislative-created agency with actual power and a tax base, produced a regional housing plan that resulted in the allocation of low- and moderate-income units. Yet its efforts, too, were impeded by the moratorium on federal subsidies.

Had there not been a moratorium on federal subsidies in January 1973, it is possible that many of the regional allocation plans would have produced more significant results. One study has analyzed three allocation plans adopted before the 1973 moratorium. It found that suburban participation in low- and moderate-income housing development had begun to increase, that more such housing was being produced, and that it was distributed on a wider geographical basis than before. When viewed against the total supply of low- and moderate-income housing, the impact was negligible; most public and subsidized housing was still concentrated in central cities. Nevertheless, the plans are generally regarded as the singular most successful effort to date to increase housing opportunities for lower income households throughout a metropolitan region.

. . . .

Allocation plans have concentrated on distributing either shares of available federal subsidies or portions of the regional housing need. Very often the need has been defined as a portion of new housing construction possible within a designated time period. The plans to date have concentrated on housing for low- and moderate-income groups. It is possible, however, to develop an allocation for any portion of housing need. It requires only the quantification of some housing goals and the distribution of that number throughout a housing market area or region.

Formulating a Housing Allocation Plan

The Underlying Concept
The purpose of an allocation plan is to expand housing choices and opportunities throughout a geographic region. It is a conscious effort to quantify housing goals and distribute them in a region or housing market. The assumption underlying an allocation plan is that every jurisdiction within a region has a responsibility to assume a fair share of housing required to meet the needs of the region. It is an attempt to equalize (or to move toward equalizing) the provision of housing throughout a region. The distribution considers the capacity and responsibility of political subdivisions within a region to absorb housing.

Without quantification of goals, it is unlikely that governments will work to accomplish housing objectives. Without the cooperation of all units of government in a metropolitan area, the likelihood of satisfying housing needs is seriously curtailed. In essence these plans seek three objectives: (1) to expand available housing supply; (2) to increase geographical dispersal of housing opportunities; and (3) to promote cooperation in meeting these needs by local units of government.

Housing allocation plans do not produce housing, they do not identify specific sites for housing, and they provide no assurance that funds will be forthcoming. So they are not self-implementing. Since the adoption of the first of these plans in 1970, many have been produced, and shelved, with little effort and perhaps no intent to use them even as guidelines for future low- and moderate-income housing. Political commitment, involvement and cooperation is absolutely essential for allocation plans to be implemented.

. . . .

The steps in an allocation model are not always explicit, but there are generally eight steps involved:

1. Defining the structure of government in the area.
2. Defining the housing market area (or areas) to be considered.
3. Defining needs and goals.
4. Establishing the distribution process.

5. Establishing the criteria for distribution.
6. Finding adequate measures of the criteria.
7. Deriving the formula for utilizing the criteria and measures.
8. Implementing the allocation developed.

Example of an Allocation

It is easier to understand the process of housing allocation when illustrated by an example. It also becomes apparent that there are infinite combinations of criteria, measures, and applications that can be utilized. The example here is a simple one: it assumes that the allocation is done by a regional agency, either independently or as part of an overall state approach.

The region given as an example is comprised of four counties, each of which contains several municipalities. The region contains a total of 500,000 households. The four-county region defines itself as the housing market area. After surveying housing needs, the regional agency sets a goal of attaining 10,000 units of low- and moderate-income housing within the next four years. This would be an annual addition for low- and moderate-income households of 0.5 percent per year — relatively modest, but considerable in view of the current housing situation. It determined that such housing can be provided by Section 8 contracts, shares of community development block grants, and mobile homes, depending upon the desires of the individual communities.

The agency establishes a two step distribution process, first to counties, and then within counties to the municipalities or unincorporated areas. The first allocation to the counties is done with the assumption that every county should have an amount of low- and moderate-income housing in proportion to its share of the regional or housing market area households. . . . Each county is given a share of the 10,000 unit goal in proportion to its share of households. . . .

From the county to the governmental subdivisions within the county, the agency selects a more complex allocation procedure (although it could reasonably repeat the same process). Within each county it further allocates units to the political subdivisions on the basis of four measures: (1) the number of poverty households; (2) the fiscal capacity of the units of government; (3) the households in each area; and (4) the areas' current amount of assisted housing. These reflect the criteria outlined previously, with the first measuring need; the second, capacity; the third, size of community; and the fourth, previous housing effort. Other criteria could easily be substituted for those illustrated here. By adding more complex variables and components, the allocation formula can become more sophisticated. Alternatively, fewer criteria could be used, resulting in a more simplified, but nonetheless adequate, system.

. . . .

In this instance, the way in which the area meets its allocation is determined by the unit of government itself. As pointed out earlier these can be met by Section 8 housing, a share of block grants, or accommodations for mobile homes. A community might develop some other strategy for meeting its goal, as long as it resulted in additional housing for low- and moderate-income households.

Comments: 1. The fair share plan in the Twin Cities (Minneapolis-St. Paul), Minnesota, area has been one of the more successful examples. The following short account of that plan illustrates the application of the planning concepts explained in the previous selection:

The council's first allocation plan, adopted in 1971, identified only general priority areas for subsidized housing. The plan established priorities to achieve two basic objectives: first, to locate subsidized housing in areas that were well serviced and close to metropolitan services and facilities; and, second, to locate subsidized housing in areas that were providing limited low- and moderate-income housing.

Priority areas were basically urban and appropriate for subsidized housing. The land outside the urban area was considered inappropriate for subsidized housing because it was too rural and lacked adequate services to support such housing. The more developed and better serviced suburban communities received highest priority for subsidized housing. The developing suburban communities that were farther away from employment, shopping, and service concentrations received lower priority.

The 1971 plan, however, contained no numerical goals. In 1973, the council adopted a revised allocation plan that contained numerical goals by subsector, but goals were still not assigned at the municipal level except in Minneapolis and St. Paul. The concept of priority designation by community within subsectors was retained.

The plan adopted in 1976 has numerical goals at the municipal level. This change was required to give communities a better basis for their local planning and is particularly needed to enable the council to review local housing assistance plans required by the federal government.

The numerical goals are determined by applying a five-part formula that compares each community to the total area with regard to total households, anticipated growth in the number of households to 1990, the number of jobs, anticipated employment growth in 1990, and the number of low- and moderate-income households from which the existing supply of subsidized housing is subtracted.

The formula provides a numerical goal that relates to the general growth and development of the area, the community's need for low- and moderate-income households, and its supply of existing subsidized housing. Under the plan, Minneapolis and St. Paul would receive about 30 per cent of the subsidized housing, with the remainder designated for suburban communities. The plan indicates the share of the subsidized units that each community can realistically expect, given the anticipated amount of federal funds. It also indicates each community's share of the necessary subsidized housing in the next 10 years if identified needs are fully met. Inclusion of the 10-year goal should stimulate communities to be aware of the long-term need for lower income housing.

The plan continues the original concept of priority designation, although the method of identifying the levels of services and facilities has grown more technically sophisticated. Even with the addition of numerical goals, the priority classifications are still useful when considering competing housing proposals and in directing developers to priority locations.

McFall, *Fair Share Housing: The Twin Cities Story,* Planning, August, 1977, at 22, 23.

The fair share housing plan is reinforced in the Twin Cities area by a housing policy that assigns priority for state and federal program funding based on a community's performance in providing low and moderate income housing.

2. Several urban counties or large central cities which to some extent combine the interests of central place and suburb have sought to remedy exclusionary zoning by enacting ordinances that require all new housing developments to include a minimum number of units for sale or rent to low and moderate income families. Fairfax County, Virginia, Montgomery County, Maryland, and the City of Los Angeles, California are among the communities that have taken this approach, although the Fairfax County ordinance was subsequently invalidated by the Virginia Supreme Court. While the three ordinances vary greatly in detail, they have certain essential elements in common.

Each ordinance applies to residential development over a minimum number of units. The minimum is 50 units in the two suburban ordinances and five units for Los Angeles. Approximately 15 per cent of the new dwelling units in a development must be sold or rented to low and moderate income families. In two of the ordinances, six per cent of the units are reserved for low income families within public housing income limits, and an additional nine per cent are reserved for moderate income families.

These ordinances seek to make mandatory low income housing economically feasible through two methods: federal housing subsidies to support the lower and moderate income units and density bonuses. The Fairfax County and Los Angeles ordinances excuse the developer from compliance if federal subsidies are not available. Density bonuses are offered in Montgomery County, which allows one additional market rent unit for every two low and moderate income units, up to a 20 per cent density increase. Density bonuses are intended to lower the land costs for low and moderate income units, so that they may be sold or rented at a reasonable profit. The price and rent level of these units is controlled for five years, and they may be built with or without federal subsidies. The Los Angeles ordinance does not offer a density bonus. It requires all low and moderate income units to be rented at fair market value, in theory making certain that the developer will not suffer any losses. Any losses the developer does suffer will have to be made up on units in the development not set aside for low and moderate income families. These families are then subsidized by the more affluent families living in the development. Is this an equitable solution to the problem of providing lower income housing?

3. Another alternative to the state level remedies advocated by White appears in a series of federal housing strategies designed to reinforce local and regional efforts for the dispersion of housing to the suburbs. These strategies have been undertaken in the federal block grant Community Development program that funds housing rehabilitation and other local development activities. One important component of this strategy is the Housing Assistance Plan (HAP) which must be prepared by every municipality and county receiving community development funds. It estimates local lower income housing needs for those residing or "expected to reside" in the community and indicates the general locations for federally assisted housing projects. Housing needs identified in the HAP may be based on an areawide fair share housing plan. An important provision in the statute contains a clear direction to communities to use the HAP as a basis for the dispersal of lower income housing.

Fair share housing plans, called Areawide Housing Opportunity Plans (AHOP) in the HUD terminology, also provide the basis for distributing federal subsidies in areas covered by plans approved by HUD. All HAPs subject to an areawide plan are to be generally consistent with the plan and provide a more detailed assessment of lower income housing needs and location consistent with AHOP policies. Obstacles to the dispersal of lower income housing, such as exclusionary zoning, are to be identified. Additional federal housing subsidies are available to areas whose areawide plans adopt specially designated additional measures to implement the dispersal of lower income housing.

HUD has also adopted regulations governing the selection of sites for federally subsidized housing, in response to a 1970 federal court decision invalidating federal funding of a subsidized project in a racially concentrated neighborhood in Philadelphia. These regulations have generally favored the location of federally subsidized housing projects in suburban locations to the disadvantage of the inner city. They raise once more the conflict between housing integration and subsidies for inner city housing needs as the basis of federal housing policy. Amendments have been proposed to these regulations that would moderate the preference for suburban areas.

Exclusionary local zoning has also been attacked under the fair housing title of the federal Civil Rights Act of 1968. A few federal courts have invalidated suburban zoning exclusions on the basis of broad language appearing in the statute that may or may not be applicable to these practices. Pending amendments to the Act would clarify this ambiguity and invalidate local land use controls excluding lower income housing because it is funded by governmental assistance or because of the race or income of its occupants.

A NOTE ON THE FUTURE PROSPECTS OF THE OPEN SUBURBS MOVEMENT

This review of the open suburbs movement should not end without a note of caution. Restrictive suburban land management practices, like racial discrimination in housing, are deeply embedded in the governmental and institutional framework. Court decisions and federal initiatives are unlikely to achieve major changes in these practices in the near future.

There are several reasons for this conclusion. Judicial authority to bring about changes in exclusionary suburban zoning practices, like judicial authority to alter racial discrimination in housing, is quite limited. Court cases review the exclusionary practices of suburban communities one at a time. It is doubtful that state courts would entertain litigation challenging exclusionary suburban practices over an entire metropolitan area, and one state court has already rejected this strategy. While some state courts have demanded the wholesale revision of exclusionary local zoning, obtaining this kind of judicial relief is expensive and time-consuming. Local resistance will also frustrate judicial intervention. In New Jersey, for example, the sweeping opinion of the supreme court in the *Mt. Laurel* case has so far been frustrated by a stubborn local judge who has refused exemplary judicial relief.

Federal initiatives face comparable obstacles. They are tied to the availability of federal housing subsidies, which are often limited and cannot provide more than token opportunities for lower income groups. Neither has experience with Housing Assistance Plans been encouraging. Suburban communities have underestimated lower income housing needs and have been slow to implement housing goals specified by these plans, often with federal tolerance. Areawide fair share plans are voluntary, not mandatory, under federal regulations. The incentives offered by these plans have so far not stimulated their widespread adoption. While Congress appears committed to the housing dispersal objectives of the federal community development legislation, this commitment may weaken in a changing and less favorable political climate. The suburban dispersal thrust of this federal legislation is also countered by the strong push for inner city housing rehabilitation which is also embedded in federal community development programs.

The question to consider is whether the open suburbs movement is more symbol than substance. There does not seem to be the rigorous consideration of viable housing dispersal strategies that an effective open suburbs movement requires. Isolated court decisions and voluntary federal strategies may symbolize a moral commitment to a more diversified suburban housing market rather than an effective program to make that market a reality.

The ultimate consequences of efforts to knock down the exclusionary wall are difficult to predict. Such efforts depend upon the extent to which they are supported and promoted politically. Political commitments must also be backed by financial commitments to produce housing in suburban locations at affordable prices. To use scientific terminology, reforming exclusionary land use regulations is a necessary but not sufficient condition for expanding housing opportunities throughout metropolitan areas. For the producers of housing to respond, the demand for suburban locations must be solvent, or subsidized when non-solvent.

Looking at the demographics of the day, suburban jurisdictions may well have their way in terms of attracting low cost populations and repelling those with high fiscal and social costs. The rate of household formation is high, but these new households are smaller. Given the increasing housing cost crunch facing the middle class, it is likely that governmental support will be directed to the non-poor. The very low income households, and perhaps minorities as well, may not receive the federal support necessary to change their housing opportunities.

BIBLIOGRAPHY

M. Danielson, The Politics of Exclusion (1976)
    A thorough review of all aspects of the exclusionary zoning problem. Reviews

the tactics of the open suburbs movement and early HUD strategies for housing dispersal.

A. Downs, Opening Up the Suburbs: An Urban Strategy for America (1973)
An influential book supporting the open suburbs movement.

R. Fishman, ed., Housing for All Under Law (1977)
The report of the American Bar Association's Advisory Commission on Housing and Urban Growth surveying exclusionary zoning problems, housing planning, and other issues related to the provision of lower income housing.

H. Franklin, D. Falk & A. Levin, In-Zoning: A Guide for Policy-Makers on Inclusionary Land Use Program (1974)
A review of techniques available to remedy exclusionary zoning practices.

B. Frieden, The Environmental Protection Hustle (1979)
A series of case studies from California that indicate the negative effect of environmentalism on house price inflation and new construction.

D. Listokin, Fair Share Housing Allocation (1976)
An extensive analysis of the origins and characteristics of fair share housing plans.

L. Masotti & J. Hadden, The Urbanization of the Suburbs (1973)
A collection of papers on social, political, economic and policy issues in suburbanization.

D. Moskowitz, Exclusionary Zoning Litigation (1976)
Reviews the major exclusionary zoning cases.

J. Rose & R. Rothman, eds., After Mount Laurel: The New Suburban Zoning (1977)
A collection of papers exploring the implications of the Mount Laurel decision.

S. Seidel, Housing Costs and Government Regulations: Confronting the Regulatory Maze (1978)
A survey of the effect of environmental, growth management, zoning and other regulations on housing costs.

Chapter 12

RESTRUCTURING THE MARKET

In this country, the vast majority of all housing is provided in the private market, either in the form of owner-occupied houses or as rental units made available to tenants by private property owners. Historically this market has been unregulated, as near a free market in the textbook sense as that in any major sector of the national economy. No impediments have limited the transfer of property for profit, except capital gains taxation, and this tax is usually avoided in the case of owner-occupied units by prompt reinvestment in a comparable dwelling. The price mechanism has worked to facilitate transactions between the proverbial willing sellers and willing buyers. In general, the institutions of American society have facilitated the operation of our housing market. Reciprocally, our market has responded with the broadly satisfactory performance that in turn supports the other institutions of the society.

Some dimensions of this satisfactory performance were summarized earlier in this book in a Note on the Performance of the Housing Economy at the end of Chapter 2 (supra p. 70). As the discussions in that chapter emphasized, the institutional context of the market plays an essential role in its functioning. This chapter will address currently critical aspects of the relationship between the market and its institutional context, especially the legal context and the institution of private property ownership. The American private housing economy has benefited greatly from a set of legal principles and institutions well adapted to its needs. In turn these legal institutions and guiding ideas have been confirmed and supported by that market's effective performance. This mutually supporting relationship has engendered further layers of support in the social and political structures of American society. In fact, few institutions have weathered recent history as well as the nation's housing economy. Only during the worst depressions, notably that of the 1930s, has the private market failed for long to work in a way that gave the vast majority of Americans confidence in the prospect of ever improving housing.

Recently evidence has surfaced that critical, long term changes may be in the wind. The great majority of people are faced with sharply spiralling house prices relative to income at the same time they choose to live in smaller households, each in a separate unit, and choose to relocate in less developed locations away from central cities and the bulk of older housing. Growing numbers of people have housing problems. Predominantly these afflicted people are mainstream, middle Americans, who until recently could count on their pale skins and solid income prospects to assure themselves of ever better housing. But no longer are housing problems something only poor people and the non-whites must confront. Practically everyone has housing problems now.

Housing policy is changing too, from a social welfare policy aimed at the poor and minorities to a broad economic and political concern with maintaining the solvent demand of the middle class. No longer are housing problems seen as mere market imperfections impinging on but a few unfortunate folk and soluble by minor tinkering, modifications, and aids to market operations. Now these issues are seen by many as structural problems soluble only by non-market processes, socialization of management and ownership, and new forms of voluntary social organizations such as tenant unions and cooperative ownership groups.

The ever greater role of federal, state, and local governments in capital formation as detailed in Chapter 7 actually may be conceived as representing a major thrust in this new direction. Policies such as secondary mortgage markets and state and local housing finance bond issues may be viewed as either modifications designed to circumvent imperfections in the market, or as structural changes designed to supplement or even supplant market processes. The structural view of capital formation policy is possible because the whole housing economy is somewhat restructured by responding to the housing needs of the broad masses rather than those of minorities of poor or non-white households. This sets capital formation apart from the other issues treated in Part II of this book. Housing subsidies, declining neighborhoods, racial discrimination, and suburban exclusion usually have been treated as market imperfections, problematic only to a small fraction of all households. Policy need only impinge peripherally on the housing economy. Now that has changed. We see tax policy as the chief form of subsidy and it serves all homeowners, the well-to-do better than the poor. Its pervasiveness and the size of the debt it generates constitutes a structural change. We sense neighborhood revitalization as a broad, middle class interest. Even suburban exclusion cuts more broadly as its price effects and other symptoms wall out young, middle class households. Both of these issues may engender basic shifts in the economy. Only racial issues remain as a market imperfection affecting only a minority, rather than an integral structural problem of the private housing market which negatively affects important majority interests.

While consciousness of these changes has only just begun to be widely felt, or at least felt more keenly than at any time since the early 1930s, policy responses and resulting structural changes in the housing economy can only be guessed at. Little other than modest reforms directed at modifying the legal environment of private property rights and the private housing market have surfaced to date. A more fundamental series of independently conceived reforms has sought to alter the traditional legal rights and freedoms accorded to owners in the private housing market. Foremost among these are court decisions and legislative changes that restructure the landlord-tenant relationship to improve the lot of the urban tenant. A second of these independent reforms derives from the continuing rent inflation in tight rental housing markets. It has led to a revival of interest in rent control, especially on the east and west coasts. An even newer and fledgling reform seeks the recapture of speculative gains from housing sales. This reform is in part a reaction to the speculative gains from housing sales in the suburbs, and in part a reaction to the speculation that drives up housing prices in inner city areas undergoing gentrification. Each of these reforms is treated in the readings that follow.

Reforms in the landlord-tenant relationship need to be understood against the historic legal background that formed this relationship and that left the tenant with little if any recourse against landlords, even when rental housing was substandard. Landlord-tenant relations have been governed by centuries-old, court-made doctrine that favors the owner over the tenant and was formulated for a rural rather than an urban society. These rules seriously disadvantage the urban tenant, who may be evicted without cause and who has no recourse against rent increases beyond the protection offered by the dwelling lease.

The article that follows offers an overview of the traditional landlord-tenant relationship that has placed the urban tenant at a serious disadvantage in finding and keeping rental housing of adequate quality. It was written by a judge and former law professor. It proposes a series of reforms in that relationship, many of which have gained increasing acceptance and have been adopted in a growing number of states. General interest in these reforms was spurred by the consumerism movement of the middle 1960s, which included greater protection of urban tenants as a major reform effort.

Some basic understanding of the nature of the landlord-tenant relationship is necessary to an understanding of the critique contained in this article. In the eyes of the law, a tenancy was not a contract that could be enforced on both sides. Instead, a tenancy was treated as an interest in property. The landlord's obligation was to deliver possession to the tenant and not to interfere with that possession. The tenant's obligation was to pay rent. If the tenant failed to pay rent, the landlord could recover possession without giving any reason for doing so. Because the law treated the tenancy as a property interest, the rules of "conveyancing" applied, and at first there were no mutual obligations on both sides during the tenancy. As the article demonstrates, this rigid doctrine was gradually changed, but not in a manner that could be helpful to urban tenants living in lower quality housing.

GARRITY, REDESIGNING LANDLORD-TENANT LAW FOR AN URBAN SOCIETY, 46 JOURNAL OF URBAN LAW 695 (1969)

Economic and Historical Impediments to Change

It is debatable whether economics or history has determined the condition and the status of the modern urban tenant. The economic impotency of the ghetto resident is underscored by statistics which are readily available to indicate that a very large percentage of low-income housing alternatively available to these urban tenants is appallingly deficient. If food, clothing, or other necessities were in similarly short supply, government would be compelled to institute rationing or massively intervene with other appropriately severe controls. Urbanologists pathetically decry the disparate bargaining power between the urban landlord and his tenant as if this condition were a recent phenomenon. However, even assuming an ample supply of suitable low-income housing, it could be argued that the "take it or leave it" attitude of most urban landlords would continue unchanged unless current landlord-tenant law is revised.

. . . Courts occasionally reflect on the causes and conditions of urban slums and even less frequently do they display an appreciation of the significance and scope of the broader issues involved. Moreover, where courts react favorably to tenant requests for relief, inappropriate after-the-fact remedies are compelled by juridical inability to fashion solutions constructively. A court may excuse a tenant from paying rent for premises which were untenantable at the time of the letting, but this prevailing tenant most likely will relocate to or is already occupying premises only somewhat more suitable but still in violation of the local housing code.

The typical urban low-income tenant rarely appreciates or considers the unsuitability of the premises he occupies unless a crisis in habitability occurs or he is contacted by an organizer. Either he has been evicted from or he has abandoned a prior uninhabitable apartment, and he must house his family as quickly as possible. Once in possession of new premises, the low income tenant is subject to continued oppression by his landlord. Either the tenant has executed a standard lease both reinforcing protectionist legal principles favoring the landlord and waiving what few benefits that he may have, or he occupies his apartment at the will of the landlord for a mutually renewable or cancelable term.

While the attitude of the landlord at the letting is "take it or leave it," his attitude now is "if you don't like it, move." If the tenant becomes militant or overly demanding in the landlord's judgment, he will be forced to vacate and to incur the expense and social dislocation of removing his family to a questionably improved or equally substandard apartment.

Numerous historical factors have combined to contribute to the unfortunate modern legal status of the urban tenant. The earliest tenants were either serfs or small farmers renting land for agricultural purposes with little thought given to housing which may have been included within the terms of the tenancy or negotiated separately. If a lease was executed between the parties . . . [the land] rather than housing was the basis of the transaction. The terms and conditions of these early tenancies were recognized and reinforced by the common law of conveyancing and were designed and structured for a rural society by landlord-oriented lawyers and courts. Typical premedieval and medieval tenants were without a lease and occupied premises, which between the parties were viewed as consisting of land for tillage, made available entirely at the will of the landlord. Remedies that developed, such as ejectment and actions for waste, focused on land, rather than dwellings, which constituted the basis of the landlord-tenant relationship.

As commerce and business developed, theories and practices were revised, and certain contract principles became intertwined with the conveyancing-based law of landlord and tenant in response to the demands of an increasingly mercantile society. The subject of negotiations between the landlord and the merchant-tenant was a business or commercial property or both. However, these parties also had to contend with the rigid rules and concepts that had been carried over from earlier periods, and provisions were developed concerning assignment, repairs, insurance, and the like, which, although intended for use solely in commercial transactions, in turn became inflexible and grafted onto the common law of landlord and tenant. Medieval conveyancing doctrines were not sufficiently modified, however, to incorporate into landlord-tenant theory such contract principles as mutuality of covenants and mitigation of damages.

As society became predominantly urban, the theory that a lease or tenancy was a conveyance and in some respects an express contract with certain implied covenants did not become further altered to adapt to the reality that the non-commercial urban landlord-tenant relationship involved a hiring of premises suitable for dwelling purposes. The "take it or leave it" and "if you don't like it, move" responses imputed to the urban landlord have been fostered by almost a millennium of legal theory protective of his interests and are quite inappropriate when contrasted with contemporary needs and realities.

The Trend of the Law

Early Legislative Efforts at Reform

. . . .

[The author discusses the adoption and enforcement of housing codes, and notes that they have not generally been effective. See *supra* p. —. The remedy of constructive eviction, which is discussed next, was an early judicial innovation that relieved the plight of the tenant to some extent. Since the tenant is entitled to title and possession, the obligation to pay rent terminates if the tenant is actually evicted by the landlord. Cases then arose that recognized a constructive eviction. If the dwelling unit became uninhabitable, the tenant could leave and justifiably refuse to pay rent.—Eds.]

Early Litigation Aimed at Reform

Decisional law focusing on mitigating certain harsh aspects of landlord and tenant law developed some impetus at the time housing codes became widely adopted. The remedy of constructive eviction was fashioned to relieve a tenant of liability for rent for premises which deteriorated during the tenancy to an extent precluding use or occupancy, assuming the untenantable conditions were not caused by the act or omission of the tenant. This theory gained wide acceptance and was rationalized variously on contract principles. Most reported decisions, however, have involved commercially leased premises. Courts, moreover, manifested certain misgivings in departing from venerable precedent by emasculating or seriously restricting the scope of this remedy. In most jurisdictions, a precondition to its utilization has involved relinquishment of the premises by the tenant. Procedural technicalities and intricate problems of proof of facts have also militated against the use by low income tenants of this essentially negative remedy. Such tenants usually have unsuccessfully asserted a defense of constructive eviction, after abandoning substandard premises, in answer to a slumlord's claim for rent due for the unexpired remainder of a term.

Recent Litigation

... The thrust of most of the cases decided has revolved around problems of unsuitability for occupancy existing either at the original letting of the premises or arising during the course of occupancy. A plethora of imaginative theories based on current and emerging contract, tort, equity, and consumer doctrines have been advanced and argued with disappointing success.

At common law, there was no implied condition or covenant of suitability for occupancy at the commencement of the tenancy in the absence of statute. The rule then, as now, in most jurisdictions was simply *caveat emptor*. Additionally, landlords had no duty to repair premises deteriorating during the course of tenancy. These rules may have had an arguable rationale in an agrarian milieu where a tenant-farmer's expectations were limited to four walls and a roof or between the landlord and a merchant-tenant at least theoretically engaged in some negotiating process. However, these concepts are absurd when applied to immigrants or migrants arriving in the North during winter months to occupy barely livable and inadequately heated apartments.

. . . .

[Court decisions and state legislation have increasingly recognized an implied warranty of habitability that gives the tenant a remedy against the landlord when the dwelling unit is not fit for habitation. The implied warranty of habitability modifies the traditional property interest enjoyed by the tenant by providing a contract remedy that may relieve the tenant from paying rent when the dwelling is uninhabitable. Garrity continues by noting that these remedies may be inadequate.—Eds.]

These imaginative proposals to provide additional tenant remedies are essentially unresponsive to the needs of most urban low income tenants. Applying consumer principles is intriguing since the tenant is certainly a consumer of housing, but the tactic required in this instance is legislation and not litigation. The contract and consumer remedies convincingly argued are unfortunately defensive and come into play either just prior to or subsequent to eviction from or abandonment of the substandard premises. . . .

Recent Legislation

Evolutionary legislation attempting to render code enforcement more viable by the creation of affirmative tenant remedies has been widely adopted and has taken the form of rent withholding, rent escrow, and rent receivership. In addition to a recognition that housing codes standing alone are conceptually and practically inadequate, other rationales exist for this spate of legislation authorizing economic retaliation by tenants. Absent statutory approval, the individual rent strike to compel code compliance has often led to a judicially sanctioned eviction for nonpayment of rent. Moreover, while organized tenants acting in concert may lead to an equalization of bargaining power, the slumlord of marginally profitable housing may well decide to abandon the premises.

Under the usual rent withholding statute, the tenant withholds his rent if the premises are in violation of the local sanitary code, and he may subsequently assert this fact as a defense to eviction for nonpayment of rent. Such statutes variously require notification by the tenant of an intent to withhold, a prior certification of code violations, and perhaps payment of back rent when the complained of conditions are corrected. Rent escrow statutes require paying of rent due to a court or local administrative agency and may or may not allow use of the rent collected to correct the violations complained of. Under statutory rent receivership, courts are granted broad equitable powers to provide for the suspension of the incidents of ownership to a building to enable an appointed receiver to collect rent and to apply it to needed repairs. A revolving fund may be authorized and may possibly be appropriated to facilitate early and speedy rehabilitation. Unfortunately, all of these remedies are quite complicated, require initiation by well-counseled tenants, and often become a trap for the unwary. Moreover, they have seldom been availed of by low income residents absent time-consuming efforts by organizers attempting to unify and to infuse militancy into the life style of the urban poor.

Summary
Assuming an attainment of competitive parity between urban landlords and tenants in the renting of premises for dwelling purposes, the public interest demands that government ensure such premises be in conformance with housing codes. To achieve this end, litigation is too time-consuming and its impact is not sufficiently broad to upgrade low-income housing generally. Considering the magnitude of the problem, the case-by-case approach is almost irrelevant. Most legislative proposals also develop after-the-fact remedies, *e.g.,* the unfortunate tenant or tenants' council is either attempting to have upgraded a particularly dilapidated apartment or is asserting a defense to an action for rent after being forced to vacate substandard and perhaps unsafe premises. The private counsel to poor clients and the legal services program attorney rarely have the opportunity to engage in preventive law practice as do their downtown colleagues and, aside from mostly ineffective community education projects, this dilemma is highlighted by the results obtained in representing ghetto tenants.

Modernizing the Landlord-Tenant Relationship

A thorough revamping of landlord-tenant legal concepts is imperative to respond to the peculiar problems created by the urbanization of modern America. The nature of existing landlord-tenant relationships is characterized by the law's failure to recognize adequately or to protect sufficiently a tenant's status and interest in the dwelling-property which he rents. Statutory schemes which have been created and precedents which have been established have been inappropriate to alleviate the chronic shortage of low-income housing and to secure safe and decent housing. Noninvolvement in regulating terms and conditions of occupancy by courts and legislatures has led to unconscionable and oppressive results. The indigent urban tenant's situation is exacerbated by virtue of his poverty. I have selected four areas which are especially demanding of reform in which to recommend proposals for the restructuring of landlord-tenant relationships. The ultimate and perhaps only appropriate solution is a complete revamping of landlord-tenant law and perhaps a Model Code or Uniform Act. [Since this article was written a Uniform Residential Landlord-Tenant Act (URLTA) has been drafted and adopted by the National Conference of Commissioners on Uniform State Laws, a prestigious national organization which has adopted model legislation in a variety of areas. URLTA has been adopted in several states and is discussed in the comments that follow.—Eds.]

The Anachronism of Discretionary Termination of Tenancies

One of the more repugnant aspects of landlord-tenant law, irrespective of the affluence of the tenant, is the long-established doctrine, statutorily authorized, of allowing the landlord to terminate a tenancy unilaterally and permitting him to institute process to expel his tenant without requiring an assignment of any reason for this action. The tenant who rents premises for a term without the dubious benefit of a lease, and alternatively described as a "periodic tenant" or a "tenant at will," occupies the premises by the grace of the landlord. The unchallenged rationale underpinning this rule is that the owner of property should be free to use it as he sees fit. In all jurisdictions requiring a legal process, a court merely rubber stamps and approves a landlord's application for eviction assuming notice provisions are complied with. In such cases, unless the tenant can prove that the termination and eviction are motivated by racial or other discrimination or in retaliation for informing public officials of housing code violations, or the tenant's attorney can ferret out a procedural flaw in the dispossess proceedings, the tenant must vacate. Some jurisdictions allow the dispossessed tenant time to secure new dwelling premises. In most cases, this allowance of time for voluntary, unaided relocation rests with the discretion of the court, and, while such a remedy may be theoretically appropriate, it falsely assumes that alternative housing is readily available to the indigent tenant or to the tenant with a large family. This rule authorizing a landlord unfettered discretion to evict operates with equal harshness on the tenant for years whose lease has expired at the end of the stated term. Such tenants are rarely allowed a grace period to secure alternative premises since it is again erroneously assumed that such housing is available and also that this tenant has made advance arrangements to occupy a mythical apartment. In some jurisdictions, the tenant with a lease can be summarily evicted by the terms of his lease without notice or court process.

[In an important case decided subsequent to this article, the United States Supreme Court upheld as constitutional an Oregon tenant eviction statute that did not allow the state court to consider the condition of the dwelling unit as a defense to the eviction action. Although the Supreme Court did strike down a provision of the statute requiring the tenant to post a heavy bond as a condition to an appeal, the case means that reforms in landlord-tenant law must be made legislatively or by state courts willing to reinterpret landlord-tenant doctrine.—Eds.]

The nonavailability of suitable, alternative low income housing requires the modification or suspension if not the abolition of the rule sanctioning untrammeled discretion in the landlord to terminate tenancies. Aside from intrafamily rentals, the urban landlord constantly stresses to his critics and proponents of government regulation that he is an entrepreneur engaged in the business of furnishing premises for occupancy at a profit. It logically follows that he should have no objection to allowing the continuation of occupancy by orderly and nondestructive tenants who pay their rent. A landlord should certainly have the right to control the use of his premises by evicting undesirable tenants. If a new rule creating a tenant vested-interest in continuing occupancy is adopted, the landlord should not be allowed to resort to subterfuge by dispossessing tenants through arbitrary and excessive rent increase. The adoption of appropriate safeguards may require the imposition of a regulatory scheme controlling unreasonable spiraling of rentals for the duration of the low income housing crisis.

A less stringent proposal modifying the classical rule of absolute discretion to evict might be to require landlords who terminate a tenancy without cause to assume the responsibility of finding alternative housing and to bear the expense of relocating the dispossessed tenant. This could be accomplished in partnership with the local urban renewal agency supposedly expert in such matters. Such a program should not be available to the tenant evicted for cause or who has voluntarily relinquished his premises, although many critics of urban renewal relocation efforts have pointed out that tenants fearing eviction often voluntarily move prior to becoming eligible for relocation assistance and benefits. This rule would in part suitably counterbalance the protectionist legal principles allowing landlords to accelerate term rentals when a tenant fails to pay rent on time or abandons the premises as well as the failure of most courts to adopt the contract rule of mitigation of damages in such cases. There can be no rebutting the fact that when the landlord unilaterally decided upon eviction, his intentional action results in monetary and social harm to the unfortunate tenant which should be compensated and redressed.

. . . .

Statutory Terms and Conditions of Occupancy

Among low-income tenants, the impetus to execute a lease usually comes from the landlord. Where local law is ambiguous or extends a tenant's common law rights as to significant terms and conditions of occupancy, it is clearly to the landlord's advantage to propose to the prospective tenant a lease favoring the landlord's interests and usually on a "take it or leave it" basis. It is conjectural whether in fact any bargaining takes place at the original execution of a lease for low income premises. Where statutes and decisional law reinforce the disparate status between landlord and tenant, the landlord may either propose a lease or let the premises under an oral tenancy depending on local practice and circumstances. In such cases, any lease that is entered into is for a relatively short term or contains an escalation of rent clause to enable the landlord to increase rentals at the expiration of the brief terms or at his option.

. . . .

The most repugnant features of such private landlord-tenant leases are the waiver and exculpatory clauses which they contain and which have been judicially upheld unless contrary public policy considerations prevail. Waivers have been incorporated into leases where the tenant has relinquished a statutory notice to vacate, a judicially supervised civil process of eviction, or the right to notify enforcement agencies of housing code violations. Exculpatory lease provisions have been drafted which relieve the landlord of his responsibility to repair untenantable premises, which do not hold him responsible for a failure to provide necessary utilities such as heat and water, and which absolve him of liability caused by his negligence or culpable nonfeasance.

Most objectionable lease provisions other than waiver or exculpatory clauses center around terms imposing on the tenant the duty to repair irrespective of fault, allowing the landlord unrestrained apartment inspection privileges, including automatic lease renewals providing for rental increases at the option of the landlord, and such procedural matters as acceleration of the term rent in event of nonpayment of a portion thereof and reimbursement by the tenant of court costs and attorney's fees. The dimensions of the problem are such that when tenants' councils have become sufficiently organized to achieve a semblance of bargaining power, the initial manifestation of their militancy is usually an insistence to commence negotiations for a lease treating equitably both the landlord and his tenants.

Terms and conditions of occupancy based on local statutes and case law not incorporated in most form leases or underlying the creation and duration of oral tenancies are in some cases more repugnant than standard landlord leases. At common law as now in most jurisdictions the landlord has no duty to repair deteriorated or deteriorating premises absent an effective housing code or similar remedies. The landlord is usually under no duty to mitigate damages when a tenant abandons the premises, and there exist no realistic tenant remedies when he is summarily ejected from an apartment without notice or process.

Many commentators have applied contract and consumer law principles recommending theories of unconscionability and adhesion to relieve the low income tenant from onerous lease provisions. However, courts have been slow to react in this moribund area of landlord-tenant law. Moreover, such theories suffer from defects similar to the inherent drawbacks of the code inspection and rent withholding spectrum of remedies. These theories presuppose tenant initiation, they ignore preventive law considerations, and they are not applied to a class of landlords for truly effective results. Additionally, many equally unconscionable common law concepts of landlord and tenant, either standing alone, included in a lease, or incorporated in a statute, are not susceptible to change by application of these inadequate theories. What is needed is a broad legislative revision and recodification of the terms and conditions of occupancy affecting low income tenants with strict provision for nonwaiverability.

An alternative to this method of reform would be mandatory administrative approval required prior to signing by the parties of all noncommercial dwelling leases. Unfortunately, this approach has been unsuccessful in preventing the adoption of one-sided leases and would not affect those tenants occupying premises under oral tenancies. A third possible resolution of the problem also presupposes legislative intervention and would involve the enactment of a model lease, with negotiable minor provisions, to be executed by all landlords and tenants of dwelling premises. This solution borrows from retail installment sales acts which have been uniformly adopted and minutely regulate an area as subject to abuse as low income housing. The consumer analysis is most appropriate and effective when considered in this frame of reference.

Situations Especially Oppressive to Low-income Tenants

. . . .

Certain aspects of landlord-tenant legal theory and practice are especially repugnant to and oppressive of low income tenants. Many low-income tenants are recipients of inadequate public assistance and social security benefits or are underemployed. Their indigency is compounded by unregulated security deposit practices, by rental of premises where local law is unclear as to whether the landlord or tenant is obligated to provide for utilities and essential appliances, by summary evictions for late or nonpayment of rent where the tenant has not been responsible for the delinquency, and by the conditioning of appellate review in dispossessory proceedings on the filing of appeal bonds.

The security deposit of one or two months' rental payment or a fixed sum in advance theoretically is designed to reimburse the landlord for tenant-caused damages to the premises or to assure financial protection in the case of the tenant who cannot be traced after abandoning his apartment when the landlord is unable to relet it immediately. Where the required security deposit amounts to a few hundred dollars in this era of inflated rentals, the nonwelfare low-income tenant is often effectively precluded from occupancy. Moreover, it may be somewhat unrealistic to expect the low income tenant to bring suit for an unreturned security deposit and then overcome the defense of unexplained injury to the premises when this tenant neglected to obtain a list of defects at the commencement of his tenancy. Landlords complaining of abandoning tenants who supposedly financially balance matters by unilaterally applying the security deposit to a final month's rent usually have no difficulty in locating these tenants and commencing suit for damages to the premises or for rent due in the amount of an unexpired term. Merchants of commodities in plentiful supply usually exact no deposit for goods sold and delivered even to low income consumers. However, utility companies, of a somewhat analogous situation to landlords of low income housing because of a comparable market situation, exact security deposits from customers and especially discriminate both in frequency and in amounts against low income residential areas. Because of these facts there has been increasing governmental interest in and regulation of deposits by utilities. Such an approach would not be uncalled-for in the area of low income housing, and one solution might require justification by landlords before such deposits are levied with the paying in of deposits to an escrow fund maintained by the municipal housing agency which would adjudicate conflicts as to its payment on the termination of a tenancy.

In the absence of a lease provision, there is usually some doubt under local law as to whether the landlord or the tenant is responsible for furnishing essential utilities such as electricity and natural gas. There is often some question as to who provides the heat and also the heating facility. Although some statutes and municipal ordinances require that such necessary appliances as a stove and a refrigerator be supplied by the landlord, the law is usually silent, and provision of these items depends on a landlord's practice which in turn hinges on the tenant's bargaining power which is clearly nonexistent for low income tenants. It would seem that in the case of low-income tenants that a tenantable apartment should include these utilities and appliances as integral to the premises. In middle-income and luxury-class buildings, such utilities and appliances are usually included with the rental.

An unchallenged tenet of landlord-tenant theory is the absolute right of a landlord to summarily evict with or perhaps without court process a tenant who is late in tendering or neglects to pay rent due. Again, the shortage of low-income housing generally results in intransigent landlord rejection of valid reasons for lateness or for nonpayment combined with promises and even offers of payment. A landlord should probably be permitted, however, to evict a tenant for nonpayment unless government intervenes to subsidize the defaulted rent. But what of the recipient of public assistance or social security benefits whose periodic allotment has been delayed, or of the underemployed parent who has been temporarily laid off or fired and who is unable to secure immediate reemployment, and whose welfare department is slow to begin assistance?

Landlords, irrespective of the fault of the tenant, should not be allowed to dispossess summarily without some court proceedings. To permit a landlord to change locks and literally force the tenant to the sidewalk is unconscionable in terms of basic justice. In a summary dispossessory proceeding for nonpayment of rent, perhaps a valid defense would be nonpayment caused by some intervening factor precluding payment because of absence of funds. Continuation in occupancy conditioned on repayments of rent due by either the tenant himself or a welfare agency might be an appropriate result.

Comments: 1. In the decade since this article was written, many state courts and legislatures have adopted the after-the-fact remedies discussed by Garrity. One of the most important of these is the implied warranty of habitability mentioned in the article, which has been adopted by statute or court decision in a majority of the states. As Garrity notes, the implied warranty is based on contract rather than property law, and allows the tenant to sue for damages or to withhold rent without being subject to eviction when the dwelling is substandard.

The warrant of habitability is the issue which the Dallas, Texas poor peoples organization, the Bois de Arc Patriots, used to enlist broad middle class support for their housing struggles, as the case study in Chapter 6 recounted (supra p. 240). This is a perfect example of the process noted in the introduction of this chapter. An issue that had seemed a relatively minor market imperfection became, in Dallas in 1973, a broad-based issue the resolution of which led to a modest but significant change in the legal structure within which the market operates.

Another and possibly more effective remedy for the tenant living in substandard premises allows the tenant to make necessary repairs and deduct the cost of the repair from the rent. This remedy is presently available in about half the states. Repair and deduct remedies are nevertheless limited in effectiveness because rents may not be sufficient to cover needed repairs. Some statutes also limit the size of the deduction and the frequency with which the remedy can be used.

Other reforms have afforded fairer treatment to the urban tenant. Tenants complaining about housing code violations or attempting to organize tenant action are protected against retaliatory eviction in half the states by judicial decisions or statutes. Statutes authorizing the landlord to lock the tenant out or to seize the tenant's property for payment of rent without notice have also been held unconstitutional in a number of states. Other reforms regulate the terms of the tenancy in a fairer manner. For example, some legislation limits the amount that can be deposited as security and requires the return of security deposits within a reasonable time after the tenancy has terminated.

These and other reforms have now been codified in the Uniform Residential Landlord-Tenant Act (URLTA), which was noted earlier and which has been adopted in several states. URLTA goes beyond the reform measures mentioned earlier and modifies many of the features of the landlord-tenant lease noted by Garrity as objectionable. Changes in the landlord-tenant relationship legislated by URLTA are described in the following excerpt:

> The URLTA was drafted in response to the sporadic reform of landlord and tenant law in most states, and in recognition of the value of comprehensive and uniform change. The value of uniformity was considered particularly important in view of the facts that a metropolitan housing market frequently transcends state boundaries (for instance, the Philadelphia housing market includes Pennsylvania, Delaware and New Jersey), and that housing finance is increasingly arranged in a national market. The goals of the commissioners in drafting the URLTA were to equalize the bargaining position of landlords and tenants; to force landlords to meet minimum standards for providing safe and habitable housing; to spell out the responsibilities of tenants for maintaining the quality of their housing units; and to insure tenants the right to occupy a dwelling as long as they fulfill their responsibilities.

In the decent housing category the URLTA includes warranty of habitability, repair and deduct, and rent abatement. In the fair treatment category, it covers protection against retaliatory action, prohibition of distress and distraint, security deposit regulation, and prohibition of utility shut-off. The URLTA has the additional virtue of expanding the fair treatment area to include a number of other basic reform measures, which include prohibitions against abuse of access, unfair landlord rules and regulations, and unconscionable lease provisions. Only a few non-URLTA states have adopted one or more of these additional protections.

Counterbalancing the obligations of the landlord are those imposed upon the tenant. The URLTA requires the tenant to keep the premises clean and sanitary, to dispose of garbage and rubbish, to keep plumbing fixtures clean and sanitary, to use plumbing and electrical fixtures properly, to refrain from the willful or negligent destruction of property, to permit reasonable access to the lessor, not to disturb neighbors' peaceful enjoyment of the premises, and to comply with local codes. Breach of any of these warranties creates an actionable violation of the tenant's obligation to his or her landlord. These obligations promote proper management of the premises.

The landlord also has specific remedies. One is the "repair and add" remedy, which is the converse of the repair and deduct remedy of the tenant. If the tenant breaches any of these obligations, and the breach materially affects health and safety and can be remedied by repair, the landlord can have it done and charge the tenant. In addition, if the rental agreement requires notice of absence for an extended period, and the tenant does not give it, there are actual damages available to the landlord. There are also specific remedies for a holdover tenancy or for unreasonably withholding access.

R. Fishman, ed., Housing for All Under Law 603-04 (1977).

2. Judicial and legislative reforms of the landlord-tenant relationship will be effective only if the new rights and remedies conferred on tenants are used. As yet there have been only limited studies of the use of these new remedies in practice, but those few studies have been discouraging. For example, a study of the Landlord-Tenant Court in Detroit concluded:

> One inescapable conclusion from the study results is that . . . the [landlord-tenant] reform legislation passed in Michigan was not meeting the goals that had been set for it. . . . The new statutory defenses and warranties affected Detroit tenants, and thus landlords, very little. . . . The court continued to serve the landlords as before, and the new defenses were only slightly utilized.

Moiser & Soble, Modern Legislation, Metropolitan Court, Miniscule Results: A Study of Detroit's Landlord-Tenant Court, 9 University of Michigan Journal of Law Reform 9, 61 (1973).

The authors concluded that the statutory reforms had little impact because tenants often were not represented by lawyers, because the judges were biased against tenants and the reform legislation, and because tenants were largely reluctant to use the new remedies. The authors were particularly dismayed at the continued large percentage of default judgments against tenants — cases in which landlords prevailed because tenants did not attempt a defense.

This experience, if typical, again raises questions about the effectiveness of legal remedies in changing prevailing practices affecting the availability of housing in urban housing markets. Are the prevailing norms affecting landlord-tenant relationships so pervasive that more than legal surgery is required to bring about a change? Or does the Detroit experience simply confirm Garrity's conclusions that after-the-fact tenant remedies will be largely ineffective because tenants will be unwilling or unable to use them? Consider again the critique of legal remedies for exclusionary zoning, supra p. 385.

3. In some communities, tenants have attempted to improve their bargaining power by organizing tenant unions. Some tenant unions have been permanent and have assumed the role of negotiator in disputes with landlords, but tenant union organizing usually has a crisis orientation. See E. Achtenberg & M. Stone, Tenants First! (Urban Planning Aid, 1974). This orientation has often been their undoing. As one commentary pointed out:

[T]he tenant unions approach is very difficult. It requires the patience of a saint and a certain measure of masochism, for the likelihood of failure in an individual situation is very high. Although tenant organization in any form has been rare, in those instances where it has happened the accomplishments have almost invariably been minimal. Tenants get upset about a particular problem, such as the landlord's failure to provide heat or to get rid of rats. They get together, stage a rent strike or set up a picket line at the landlord's home, and, in some cases, they will "win." What they "win" is the landlord's agreement to accede to *that particular demand*. The tenants do not ask for the right to deal with the landlord collectively on various matters on a regular basis, and therefore they do not get it. The boiler is fixed or the rats are poisoned and everybody goes home. When something else goes wrong, or when the boiler breaks down again next year, the landlord behaves as he always did. Even where the tenants' group does have the foresight to demand a collective bargaining agreement — recognizing the group as the bargaining agent for tenants and granting tenants specific rights — the group usually fades away after this "victory" and the collective bargaining agreement is never really enforced.

National Housing and Development Law Project, Handbook on Housing Law, vol. 2, at 9 (1970).

4. Tenants in public housing projects, while initially in a less protected position than tenants in the private market, have now won substantial legal gains that protect their occupancy status. Evictions may only occur following a procedural hearing, and a series of court cases has ruled that eviction may not be based on reasons unrelated to the management of the public housing project. Fewer safeguards are available to applicants for admission, although the federal public housing statute requires informal notice if admission is denied. Neither may admission be denied for reasons unrelated to the applicant's expected ability to become a satisfactory tenant. A rule denying admission to all applicants receiving welfare assistance would be invalid, for example. One other important protection available to public housing tenants prohibits eviction except for just cause.

Just cause eviction is a step toward the security of possession guaranteed to tenants under the English and other foreign rent control laws and is included in rent control regulation in a few American jurisdictions. Rent control is an example of government intervention in the private housing market which even more completely controls the landlord's freedom of ownership by regulating not only the rent but other aspects of management. Policy issues raised by rent control are examined in the next section.

Except during wartime and periods of rapid inflation when rent controls were imposed by the federal government, rents have been unregulated in this country. Only in New York City has a rent control program been continuously in effect since the Second World War. New York has now been joined by other cities and states, largely on the east and west coasts, in which a "second generation" of rent controls has been adopted. The following article outlines the characteristics of this "second generation" of rent controls and discusses some of the policy issues that rent control creates.

E. ACHTENBERG, THE SOCIAL UTILITY OF RENT CONTROL (1971)

. . . .

While the details of rent control systems in this country have varied, most have followed a standard framework. Rents are "frozen" or "rolled back" to some previous date, with a variety of grounds prescribed for future adjustments upward or downward. Provisions may be made for general rental adjustments, covering all units or selected categories, and for individual adjustments on petition of the landlord or tenant. Rent control laws usually state that the landlord is entitled to earn a "fair return" on his investment and may include statutory standards for defining what a "fair return" should be.

The range of housing covered by rent control is subject to considerable variation. At one extreme, all existing and future construction may be included. Commonly exempt, for both political and economic reasons, are such categories of housing as rental units in small owner-occupied dwellings, new construction, "luxury" housing, and publicly subsidized housing. The scope of controls may also extend beyond rent regulation *per se,* to include controls over eviction and, to some extent, over building conversions and demolition.

. . . .

Clearly, the limited form of rent control practiced in the United States cannot go very far toward alleviating the housing crisis — particularly in the absence of controls over prices in other sectors of the economy which affect housing costs. And most housing policy planners would agree that long-range solutions to the housing crisis must involve a vast expansion of the supply or a vast increase in purchasing power for some sectors of the population or both. Either approach would seem to require a level of government subsidization and control far beyond that which is presently available or contemplated. At the same time, there is a recognized need for some form of public intervention to protect tenants from the exploitation which occurs in a "landlords' market," until a more equitable balance of housing supply and demand can be achieved.

The real issue, then, is whether some form of controls makes sense under present circumstances as part of a broader housing policy. From this perspective, a number of important questions may be asked about the social utility of rent control. How effectively does it accomplish its primary purpose — that of reducing housing costs to levels more commensurate with tenants' ability to pay? How equitably and efficiently are the costs and benefits of rent control distributed? Finally, what is the potential impact of rent control on other housing policy goals, such as the equitable distribution of housing space, the expansion of housing supply, and the improvement of housing quality?

Effectiveness

The effectiveness of rent control in reducing rent, relative to "free market" levels, depends on two major variables: the degree to which rents prior to control are inflated above and beyond the level dictated by costs and reasonable profits, and the nature of rent increase mechanisms built into the rent control system.

It is important to recognize that rent control directly affects only the limited portion of rent which is attributable to the landlord's "cash flow" — the amount he actually "puts in his pocket" after all other expenses have been deducted. Tenants are often surprised to find that this is relatively small in relation to major components of the rent dollar such as taxes and debt service costs — even if the landlord is earning more than a "fair return" on investment. (Generally speaking, the capital gains and "tax shelter" aspects of real estate investment are far more profitable to an owner than the cash flow potential — and neither of these forms of profit is directly reflected in the rent level.)

Any reasonable rent control system will permit rent increases to cover actual operating cost increases — such as a rise in the tax rate or an increase in fuel oil prices. Thus rents will most certainly continue to increase as long as local public services are financed from property tax revenues and prices in other sectors of the economy remain subject to inflationary pressures. Increases in the tax rate have a substantial impact on rent levels, since taxes constitute about 15 percent of rental occupancy costs nationally and considerably more in some areas.

Rent control may have some impact on debt service costs, to the extent that it can discourage owners from choosing more expensive forms of financing. For instance, a "fair return" standard which allows only reasonable financing costs could reduce the extent of second and third mortgage financing at high interest rates, a major source of rent escalation in the uncontrolled market. On the other hand, without provisions for rent increases to cover reasonable increases in financing costs on new or refinanced mortgages, the liquidity of investments in rent controlled buildings will be threatened. Generally speaking, then, rent levels in controlled housing will continue to follow the trend in interest rates over time.

One important consequence of this limited nature of controls is that rents in controlled housing will continue to be higher than what most low and moderate income familes can afford to pay. . . . Obviously, broader solutions to the problem of housing cost are needed than those which merely limit the landlord's cash flow profits.

At the same time, the value to tenants of a control system which succeeds in keeping rents in line with costs should not be underestimated. In New York City, households occupying rent controlled units pay less rent, in proportion to income, than households occupying uncontrolled units, at all income levels. While rent control has not reduced rents to levels that low and moderate income tenants would consider "fair," in terms of ability to pay, it has left them considerably better off than they would have been in an uncontrolled market.

Finally, the benefits of rent control to tenants may increase over time. In the uncontrolled market, the landlord's ability to capitalize excess profits into increased property values results in higher debt service, higher taxes, and once again, higher rents. By reducing and possibly stabilizing cash flow profits, rent control should also have a stabilizing effect on property values insofar as values reflect net income and expectations of future gain. To the extent that rent control succeeds in interrupting this circular process, there should be important secondary impacts on the more substantial components of the rent dollar, with cumulative cost savings to tenants over time.

Equity and Efficiency

In one sense, rent control may be regarded as a means of redistributing the costs and benefits of housing that exist in the uncontrolled market. The redistribution operates not only between landlords and tenants of rent controlled housing but also between owners of controlled and exempt buildings and between protected tenants and other housing consumers. To the extent that the costs and benefits of rent control are arbitrarily distributed among various groups, it may be considered an inequitable and inefficient remedy for the problem of housing cost.

On the cost side, the primary burden rests with owners of controlled housing, who are deprived of some portion of the profits they might have earned in the "free" market. The assignment of these costs to landlords in a profiteering situation is not unreasonable, provided the rent control system allows a "fair return" on investment. To the extent that rent control meets this criterion, the burden imposed on landlords is merely that of a return to the *status quo ante* of reasonable — rather than excessive — profits.

Defining an equitable "fair return" standard is perhaps the most difficult aspect of rent control. Apart from the need to satisfy judicial standards for due process in rate regulation, the rate of return must be sufficiently attractive from an economic standpoint to permit continued investment in the housing market by reasonable investors and landlords. Presumably, a fair rate of return should therefore reflect the rate commanded by alternative investments with comparable risk elements. At the same time, a fair rate of return should reflect what landlords would earn in a "normal" or balanced housing market — a condition more abstract than real in this economy, but which may be approximated by some point in time prior to the onset of rapid rent escalation.

However difficult, the need to arrive at a reasonable "fair return" standard, as well as equitable procedures for enforcing it, is fundamental to the utility of a rent control system. If the standard or its administration unduly penalizes landlords, tenants will pay the price in terms of gradual disinvestment by owners and lenders. If the standard or its administration is overly generous to landlords, tenants will bear the burden of increased rents.

Among landlords as a class, the problem of inequity arises with regard to owners of housing exempt from controls. Owners of sales housing or of rental units not covered by controls would be included in this category. With a disproportionate share of housing demand shifted to their units, owners of uncontrolled housing are potentially able to reap special benefits in the form of increased rents and capital gains beyond what they would have earned in the "free" market. . . .

However, to the extent that owners exempt from rent control are those least likely to translate excess demand into rent increases, this form of inequity may be minimized. Resident owners, for example, may be less interested in maximizing returns than in securing a steady but limited stream of income to help defray amortization expenses. To the extent that such owners operate on the latter philosophy, the excess gains potential of their exempt status will not be realized.

Should substantial price increases occur in the uncontrolled stock, however, arbitrary inequities may also arise between tenants in controlled housing and other housing consumers. But if most families in need of special protection — e.g., the elderly, low income tenants, and others unable to keep pace with the general rise in living costs — live in controlled housing, the inequities should be minimized. For instance, even prior to the extension of controls to recently constructed housing in New York City, more than 90 percent of all households earning less than $4,000 lived in rent controlled units. At the same time, rent control also benefited 43 percent of all households earning more than $15,000, whose relative need for protection was considerably less.

. . . .

[Achtenberg notes that potential inequities in rent control are also compounded if new entrants in the community cannot secure housing in the rent-controlled sector. Rent control may also deflect housing demand to other communities or to the uncontrolled portions of the municipality's housing stock. Alternatively, opportunities may arise from "black market" side payments by tenants to owners of controlled housing units. — Eds.]

The basic shortcoming of rent control as a redistributive measure lies in its application to categories of housing, rather than to categories of housing occupants. A more equitable system of controls — for tenants — would key rents to tenants' ability to pay, as in federally subsidized public housing. However, this system of rent regulation would undoubtedly deprive landlords of a "fair return" when renting to low and moderate income tenants, in the absence of public subsidies. Alternatively, maximum income limits could be established for controlled units that would correspond to the rents being charged, at a reasonable rent-income ratio. Since only tenants within the prescribed income limits would be eligible to occupy a given unit, however, this would constitute an equally threatening limitation on the landlord's freedom of tenant selection.

. . . .

Space Utilization

A related concern, with regard to equity and efficiency, is the distribution of housing space effected by a rent control system. Critics charge that the increased demand for controlled units will generate pressures for overcrowding in the controlled stock. At the same time, rent control is said to induce underutilization of housing space, particularly as small families remain in large units after children have moved away.

In response to these claims, it is argued that rent control should decrease overcrowding by alleviating pressures which give rise to doubling up in order to meet "free market" housing costs. Additionally, if the rent control system allows a reasonable rate of return and contains increase provisions to cover rising costs, the gap between rents in the controlled and uncontrolled markets should not be so large as to inhibit upward mobility substantially.

. . . .

In this context, a more radical form of controls would establish minimum and maximum household size standards for rent controlled apartments. This would considerably enhance the efficiency and equity of controls as a space distribution mechanism — at the expense, once again, of the landlord's freedom of tenant selection.

New Construction

Perhaps the most substantive criticisms of rent control are concerned with the impact of controls on the climate of housing investment. Critics of rent control argue, first, that by reducing incentives for new housing construction, rent control intensifies the very housing shortage it was designed to alleviate. Even where new housing is exempt from control — as it has been generally in the United States — a substantial gap between rents in the controlled stock and the rents required for new housing may weaken the demand for new construction. Consequently, both owners and mortgage lenders may be induced to seek more profitable outlets for their investments.

But by the same token, a reasonable system of controls that allows rents to keep pace with cost increases and provides returns competitive with those from investments of comparable risk should not seriously inhibit construction activity on the part of reasonable investors. At worst, the gap between controlled and uncontrolled rents should be no greater than under "normal" supply and demand conditions. Additionally, it is arguable that the reduced turnover rate in the controlled portion of the housing stock will increase, rather than decrease, the demand for new housing.

Past experience offers little evidence that control of the existing stock has substantially deterred new housing construction. The volume of housing construction generally in the postwar period, and specifically in New York City during the past 25 years, has not been out of line with available resources. In fact, New York City experienced a period of substantial overbuilding during the early 1960s, in reaction to builders' anticipations of a more restrictive zoning ordinance. In general, it appears that broader economic factors — such as the availability and cost of land and mortgage money — are far more critical than rent control in determining the volume of new housing construction.

At the same time, the type of new housing built may be influenced by the existence of controls on older housing. . . . However, other factors — such as the availability of FHA insurance for sales housing and the tax benefits of ownership available to housing consumers — undoubtedly provided more significant incentives.

Finally, it should be noted that an increased volume of new private construction would not substantially benefit the primary victims of the housing shortage — i.e., low and moderate income families. Without subsidies, new housing costs are far beyond what these groups can afford, and in periods of excess demand such housing is more likely to filter "up" than "down" the income scale. Rent control should have no effect on the rate of subsidized housing construction for low and moderate income families, since this type of construction is already subject to controls by public agencies. The only effect of rent control in this regard might be to indirectly increase the number of sites available for such purposes.

Housing Quality

In addition to its impact on new construction, rent control may affect the scope and pattern of investment in existing buildings, by both owners and lenders. Critics charge that rent control inhibits the level of investment required for proper maintenance and improvement, thereby leading to deterioration and in the long run to abandonment.

On the one hand, it should be apparent that a system of controls which denies landlords reasonable profits may well have this effect. Under these conditions, any economically rational owner will be inclined to reduce discretionary expenditures on maintenance and housing improvement, particularly as lenders respond by tightening up credit terms. On the other hand, a system designed to reduce excess profits to a reasonable level should not result in a decline in housing services by reasonable landlords. Under these conditions reasonable lenders should continue to supply credit, thus preserving the liquidity of the owner's investment.

Moreover, while the job of enforcing housing quality standards properly belongs to the code enforcement agency, rent control may provide additional tools to encourage code compliance. Rent reductions for substantial housing may help to ensure that profits earned in excess of a reasonable rate are channeled into upkeep, rather than into the owner's pocket. This tactic is likely to be effective so long as the long-term costs of noncompliance to the owner — i.e., the loss of a significant portion of his income stream and capital gains potential — outweigh the costs of making the necessary repairs. By the same token, if the owner is not sanguine about the future profitability of his building or lacks the necessary resources for compliance, this form of punitive action may lead to further disinvestment.

. . . .

Finally, some forms of incentive may be appropriate in encouraging continued investment in rent controlled buildings. For instance, owners of well-maintained structures might be allowed a higher rate of return than owners of poorly maintained buildings. An owner might be allowed to increase his profit level in return for making certain kinds of capital improvements. Of course, in the absence of subsidies, the goal of housing improvement soon comes into conflict with the goal of rent reduction, and the task of striking a proper balance between the two is one of the more difficult aspects of designing and administering a rent control system.

In short, a rent control system containing a creative balance of economic rewards and penalties can facilitate the optimal level of maintenance and improvement that can be achieved, given other constraints. Beyond this, tighter controls over the level of discretion landlords have in maintaining their properties could be incorporated into the rent control system. For instance, it has been suggested that a special account should be established for rental properties, with each landlord obligated to pay a fixed percentage of rents annually — in the amount of his depreciation allowance — into a state fund. This would establish a continually enlarging reserve fund for housing rehabilitation and replacement, and would ensure that amounts now theoretically set aside for this purpose are appropriately channeled.

Comments: 1. The special characteristics of the New York City housing market make it a less than satisfactory test of rent control. Major demographic changes, a deterioration of median income as compared with the national average, and the complex rent control legislation have made it difficult to determine the extent to which rent control has affected the city's rental housing supply. It is also notable that demolition and abandonment, as well as administrative and statutory decontrol, shrunk the controlled rental sector by one-half from 1965 to 1975.

At the same time, substantial increases in controlled rents to reflect increased operation costs have increased the controlled rent burden while not in some views providing any substantial relief to New York City landlords. Operating cost increases cancelled out rent increases. Kristof, an experienced New York housing professional, offers a critical view of rent control. Noting that rent control had provided a 20 billion income transfer from controlled apartment owners to tenants, he writes:

Since the recipients of this income transfer at its inception constituted 80 percent of the city's families, irrespective of income status, few of the recipients were particularly concerned about the source of this beneficence. In fact, the indiscriminate distribution of the benefits of rent control, regardless of the need in terms of the ability to pay for housing, represents the essence of its political strength over the years — and its fundamental inequity.

Kristof, Rent Control Within the Rental Housing Parameters of 1975, Areuea Journal, Winter, 1975, at 47, 53.

Among the costs of rent control Kristof lists an elimination or reduction of operating profit, a destruction of capital values, a reduction of tenant services, inadequate maintenance, and a loss in city taxes. The view Kristof espouses is shared by most housing policy analysts.

Against this view an alternative reading of this experience suggests that the New York City real estate industry in the absence of rent control continuously escalates housing costs in a drive to produce high capital gain and leverage profits. These are produced by continuous buying, refinancing, raising rents, and selling apartment buildings. The squeeze this creates was well illustrated in Chapter 3 in the Boston case discussed in the Goetze article (supra p. 92). Some tenant-oriented interest groups in New York, such as the Metropolitan Council on Housing, take the view that supplier profit-seeking and not operating costs is the causal factor behind decline and abandonment.

The result in practical policy terms is much the same whether costs or profits are the culprit. The extent to which rent control will encourage undermaintenance and force abandonment depends in large part upon the provisions of individual ordinances. Landlords must be permitted to pass through cost increases. Ordinances which do not allow landlords to adjust rents to meet rising operating and maintenance costs are likely to encourage landlords to cut down on services to maintain their profits. Sternlieb suggests that rent control may accelerate the rate of tax delinquency for similar reasons:

Why do landlords permit their structures to become tax delinquent? . . . [T]here remain two basic rationales: (1) the immediate cash flow from the parcel in question simply cannot support the tax burden; and (2) the landlord's anticipation of the future return is so negative as to occasion his "milking" of the parcel — minimizing inputs, not paying taxes, and accepting ultimate [tax] foreclosure as an end to the process.

The role of rent control clearly is very central to both of these. If tenants have additional rent paying capacity which would be obtainable if not for rent control, then an increase in rent levels might allow landlords to repay arrearages and become current in their tax backlog. . . . The control mechanisms may very well directly result in the initial tax delinquency and then abandonment of the structure. . . .

G. Sternlieb and J. Hughes, Housing and Economic Revitalization: New York City 1976, at 232-33 (1976)

Most recent rent control ordinances such as those in California do provide for rent increases to reflect increasing costs. Ironically, it was just this issue in reverse that led to the recent spate of California rent control ordinances. The nearly universal failure of landlords to pass through the huge property tax savings enacted by Proposition 13 fueled the drive for rent control. (Proposition 13 was an amendment to the State Constitution passed by referendum. It mandated a ceiling on property taxes well below then current rates.)

Even in the absence of rent control, the operating cost rent squeeze occasioned by inflation and rising non-solvent demand may ultimately change the character of the rental housing market. The destabilizing effect of these pressures may lead to a gradual abandonment of the rental housing market by private owners and investors. If this happens it would parallel European experience. This potential future situation is treated more extensively in the note that concludes this chapter.

2. Though much of the public debate tends to center on how rent control will affect landlord and investor behavior in the future, rent control adoption reflects citizen dissatisfaction with current market-determined housing prices. When rental units are in short supply relative to demand, landlords have the opportunity to increase their profits monumentally, especially through the turnover-refinancing-capital gains route. The traditional microeconomic argument posits that increased profits will lure additional housing providers into the market. They will supply additional units until demand and supply reach equilibrium and prices return to their normal levels. The following brief passage debates these traditional assumptions as seen in the Spring of 1979:

Half of California's rental units are due to face some form of rent control or regulation this month. . . .

California's landlords label the rent control movement a "disaster" and claim it will aggravate already acute shortages of rental units throughout the state. Tenants claim the measures are "fair" and needed by families whose incomes are not keeping up with inflation.

Gerson Bakar, President of the California Housing Council and a member of Governor Brown's Housing Task Force, does not see rent control as the answer to the problem of supplying enough affordable rental units. "What we have to keep reminding ourselves of," he says, "is that we don't do tenants (particularly poor tenants) a service if we pass laws and regulations that result in less rental housing. Our housing problems will continue to get worse, whatever the regulations, until we are able to bring supply and demand into balance. Rent control is a very dangerous drug for cities to experiment with. With no state guidelines, political pressures at the local level will turn laws that start out as workable into destructive traps."

On the opposite side of the controversy, Richard Blumberg, Associate Director of the National Housing Law Project, sees short term rent controls as a means of maintaining a supply of affordable rentals until California builders are able to produce enough units to drive rents down through the natural competitive market process. "It takes three to five years to produce houses today. All of the rent controls enacted or proposed in California are interim in nature. They would address the problem for no more than that three to five year period," he said.

According to Blumberg, the argument that rent control stops new construction is false "because all local rent control measures in the state exempt new construction." He said, "the decision to build is based more on the cost of labor, material, financing, and availability of land than any short term local rent regulation."

Blumberg concluded, "The bottom line of the rent control argument is that, as inflation skyrockets and rents increase, tenants have a right — if not a responsibility — to take a stand."

California Department of Housing and Community Development, California Communities, May 22, 1979, at 1-2.

From the tenants' perspective, the housing shortages which allow landlords the opportunity to increase their rents and profits do not insure continued investment in construction of affordable new housing. Instead, in the unfettered market, tenants may find themselves paying increasingly higher rents without experiencing any change at all in the quality or quantity of housing services they receive. For the tenant, rent control serves to replace market-determined prices with prices that are set politically and administratively. Instead of allowing landlords to assert their market power, rent control attempts to regulate rents in a manner somewhat analogous to that used in public utility regulation. Rents are tied to changes in operating costs.

Rent control ordinances usually do not affect new construction. This feature exists because municipalities do not want to mandate continuing housing shortages. However, new construction is most closely correlated with monetary conditions and other such forces exogenous to rent control. Given the way in which changes in housing costs have outstripped changes in household income in recent years, it is questionable whether new multifamily rental properties can be built to meet the economic rent-paying ability of any but the highest income households. Thus in back of solvent demand lies the same problem that caused the shortage and that determines the market absorption rate of new construction.

3. There are yet other issues analysts have raised in considering the pros and cons of rent control. One prominent concern is how housing units should be rationed if not by market-determined rents. Rent control, by holding down rents below levels which would ordinarily be determined by the interaction of supply and demand, can encourage some households to over-consume housing. Overconsumption, the argument goes, will mean a misallocation of housing satisfactions among households. The stereotypical New York case is the elderly widow of reasonable means who holds onto a huge, rent controlled unit for years after her family has left. Current second generation laws claim to avoid widespread problems of this sort by the short term nature of the control period.

4. Often tied to local struggles over rent control is a similar conflict over the conversion of rental units to condominium ownership. Landlords and investors may escape the crunch between higher costs and profit needs and increased resistence to higher rents by "converting" their holdings. They subdivide multifamily structures into separate, legally described properties each available for sale to an individual owner or household. In so doing the original investors and owners get out from under the crunch and at the same time realize substantial, often spectacular, capital gains and leverage profits.

The new owners of individual apartment units ordinarily may qualify for all of the income tax and other benefits of home ownership. The opportunity for ownership, often below the price of available single homes, may help first-time buyers begin the equity accumulation so necessary now to maintaining solvent demand. Though debt service on the increased capital values after conversion coupled with operating charges may average twice the pre-conversion rents, owners may in the end feel they benefit after taking tax treatment and equity accumulation into account.

5. People who cannot qualify for mortgages or who lack the wealth to buy outright are often severely disadvantaged by condominium conversions. Vigorous local political struggles have resulted, struggles on the same order as those over tenants rights, rent control and neighborhood preservation. Several readings in this book have dealt with these struggles. The political action and resulting policy decisions are making major changes in local markets. Expanded tenants rights, rent control, prohibitions or limitations on condominium conversions, and active neighborhood improvement programs have become more and more common features of local housing economies, particularly in older, more central cities.

6. No reform comparable to rent control has called for price regulation in the sales market for existing, used housing. Presumably, this market is sufficiently competitive, and supply and demand in sufficient balance, to produce a price structure not subject to monopolistic pressure. Recently, however, speculative activity has appeared in city neighborhoods subject to the conversion process known as "gentrification." Existing and

often lower income residents are displaced in this process by new, higher income entrants who buy deteriorated housing and restore it through substantial rehabilitation that brings a corresponding increase in property values. See supra p. 169. The gentrification process is often abetted by speculators who buy older properties in these neighborhoods and hold them long enough to reap substantial profits through resale. Because these speculative activities are thought to hasten the conversion process and contribute to the escalation in housing prices, they have been the object of anti-speculation legislation that has been proposed and enacted in some cities.

Anti-speculation legislation may take the form of a tax on gains from speculation in housing, and is based on the assumption that it is short-term rather than long-term speculation that is injurious to the market. The tax eventually disappears as the period of time during which the land or dwelling is held increases. It is levied in addition to the federal and state capital gains taxes also collected on gains in values when housing is sold.

Anti-speculation taxes are intended to have a regulatory effect in addition to their potential for raising revenue:

> The incidental effects of anti-speculator taxes can be divided into two categories:
> Those that result when some individuals end up paying anti-speculation levies, and those that are due to the regulatory nature of these taxes, that is, the rates are so high that individuals will modify their behavior to avoid incurring liability. The tax acts very much like a regulation prohibiting rapid turnover. . . .
> D. Hagman & D. Misczynski, Windfalls for Wipeouts: Land Value Capture and Compensation 124 (1978).

An anti-speculation tax on speculators in neighborhoods undergoing rapid improvement in housing has been adopted in Washington, D.C. Particularly troublesome issues are raised by the enactment of an anti-speculation tax in this setting because of the many crosscurrents affecting the rehabilitation of older areas, some of which have racial implications. These issues are explored in the following article, written before the Washington tax was enacted. For more on the Adams-Morgan neighborhood, which is discussed in this article, see supra p. 349.

RICHARDS & ROWE, RESTORING A CITY: WHO PAYS THE PRICE?, 4 WORKING PAPERS FOR A NEW SOCIETY 54 (1977)

Block by block, private developers in Washington D.C. are converting decaying homes into elegant townhouses. Some see this restoration movement as a godsend, for it promises both to upgrade the city's housing stock and to expand the tax base. But there is another, less rosy side to the neighborhood rehabilitation: it has caused rampant speculation in residential property.

Housing prices, already among the nation's highest, have been driven even higher. And the overall effect is to force the city's poor out of neighborhoods they've lived in for years. Government urban renewal programs in the late 1950s and 1960s disrupted poor neighborhoods in much the same way. This time, however, there are no federal funds to relocate the homeless.

In a kind of reverse blockbusting, speculators comb neighborhoods on foot and by telephone just ahead of the restoration movement, making attractive cash offers to owners. If the owners refuse to sell, the more persistent speculators call in building inspectors who order expensive repairs on the old and dilapidated homes. Homes are bought and sold the same month, week, and even day for profits of up to 100 percent and more.

Often the speculators never even take title to the property but instead sell their purchase contract to a third party, a process called "flipping." (The term also is used to describe quick turnovers generally.) Between October 1972 and September 1974, 21 percent of all recorded sales of row and semidetached homes and flats in Washington involved two or more sales of the same property (80 percent within ten months of each other). Sixty-nine percent of these sales were in five neighborhoods. Moreover, many speculative transfers are not recorded.

Aside from the displacement caused by rehabilitation, the spiraling of home prices has its own dislocation effects. Tenants are sometimes evicted because they cannot afford the rent hikes that go hand in hand with the new landlord's high purchase price and increased property taxes. Since property tax assessments are based largely on sale prices of nearby properties, homeowners face tax increases whether or not their own properties have been improved; these higher taxes also are passed on to renters.

Some speculators turn the tax woes to their own advantage. At a city council hearing on property tax assessments, a woman who lived on a street on which seven homes had been sold in two years testified that speculators had knocked on the doors of the remaining homeowners saying, "I understand your property taxes have gone up. Do you want to sell?"

Speculation is not new to the District of Columbia. Original District planner Pierre L'Enfant fought to keep land speculators from disrupting his plan for the orderly development of the city's neighborhoods. He was fired in the process. In this century, speculation and restoration started with Georgetown in the 1930s, went to Capitol Hill in the 1960s, and to Adams-Morgan, Mt. Pleasant, and other neighborhoods in the 1970s. In each case the pattern has been similar. In 1930, half of Georgetown's population was poor and black; now the neighborhood is rich and predominantly white. But it wasn't until the 1970s that community opposition in the District galvanized into resistance, or that the city itself had the power to do anything about speculation.

In 1974 Congress granted the District a measure of home rule, including its first elected government in 100 years. The 13-member elected city council has been faced with the problem of speculation and displacement of its constituents on the one hand, and the District's financial and housing problems on the other hand.

Washington has an acute housing shortage. The city's vacancy rate is less than 2 percent (anything under 5 percent is considered an "emergency" by HUD). In 1975, one estimate put the District's housing need at over 91,000 units. Much of the existing housing is in disrepair, with nearly half of the units over 35 years old. If these houses are not soon restored, they could be lost to the city forever.

When the redevelopment industry comes before the council and says it produced 3,000 units of housing during the preceding year, it is little wonder that many officials look on with approval and hope. And given the shortage of public initiative or funds to support low-income housing, it's hard to refute John O'Neil of the Office and Apartment Building Association when he says, "It's not a choice between houses for poor people and houses for rich people. It's a choice between houses for rich people or no houses at all."

Jobs and economic growth are also at issue. "Rehabilitation in D.C. has been estimated to create $30 million worth of purchases of services and materials each year and to employ in excess of 5,000 persons," says James Banks of the Washington Board of Realtors. If the bulk of these outlays actually went to District — and not suburban — businesses and employees, they would give a considerable boost to the D.C. economy. Then too, the fiscally hard-pressed city will benefit from the increased property tax assessments. Government and industry officials hail the new townhouse owners as "tax providers" (as opposed to the poor people they replace, who are labeled "tax consumers" because of their heavy use of public services).

Taxing Flippers

On April 1, 1975, D.C. city council members David Clarke and Nadine Winter put a speculation bill before the council. Following the example of legislation in Vermont, Ontario, and New Zealand, they sought to curb speculation by taxing the profits of speculators. Their bill was a simple tax on short-term buying and selling of rowhouses with no deductions permitted for rehabilitation or other expenses. It was seen as a one-year stop-gap measure to allow the council time to develop a longer term solution.

Although the District is commonly perceived as merely a bland federal enclave, it is home for about three-quarters of a million people, who live in well-defined neighborhoods and who have a high degree of community consciousness. Clarke, a lawyer in his early thirties, was spurred to action by the speculation in his ward, which includes the Adams-Morgan neighborhood, one of the few racially mixed areas in the city. Cosponsor Winter represents the heavily speculated Capitol Hill.

Because it was a tax bill, the speculation measure was referred to the council's Committee on Finance and Revenue, which is chaired by at-large council member Marion Barry. During the sixties, as head of the D.C. SNCC office and leader of the fleeting but feisty Free D.C. movement, Barry had been a chronic pain to the established powers, leading a boycott of the bus system and disrupting the Cherry Blossom Festival.

Now Barry is a leading D.C. Democrat and one of the home rule council's more influential members. Despite his radical image, the former chemistry instructor moves deliberately, particularly since he has been in the political arena. After careful — and to some, protracted — study, Barry and his staff decided that a more comprehensive approach to the speculation problem was necessary. What began as a six-page tax bill grew to eighty pages. The new measure not only taxed speculation, but required: licensing dealers in residential property; recording all transfers of residential property; registering vacant property; disclosing the seller's purchase price and costs to buyers of residential property. The bill also strengthened the tenant's right of first refusal under the District's rent control law by providing cash damages to tenants when their landlords fail to honor this right.

Barry, who says, "I like the tough ones," soon found himself in a crossfire gritty even by his own standards. On the one side were the District's real estate and financial interests, probably the largest private industry in town and a major supplier of campaign contributions in D.C. elections. On the other side were community organizations from neighborhoods most directly affected by speculation.

The Adams-Morgan Organization (AMO), probably the most militant, had already picketed weekend showings of rehabilitated townhouses, had splattered paint on billboards announcing luxury condominium conversions, and had even prevented the rehabilitation of an entire block. The anti-speculation tax was the rallying point these groups had been waiting for. They were joined by their professional public interest allies such as Ralph Nader's Tax Reform Research Group. Included were some of Barry's early supporters, along with activists who in general feel entitled to a special claim on his loyalties and who have high expectations of his ability to produce change.

These organizations moved quickly to form a community-based speculation task force. The task force put out a pamphlet called "Our Neighborhoods for Sale" for citywide distribution, lobbied all the council members, and produced a draft antispeculation bill. Perhaps the crest of this activity was the council hearings in June 1975 when the coalition put on an impressive display of community support. Ministers, the teachers union, the Association of Black Social

Workers, even the Afro-American Police Officers, all testified in favor of a tax on speculation. And a coalition-produced slide show on speculation upstaged the hearings.

The real estate industry was somewhat slower to react. Most directly affected by a speculation tax would be the "flippers" who buy and sell houses without improving them, and the "redevelopers" who buy old houses and repair them in varying degrees. (Often the same people do both.) The flippers and redevelopers were perhaps the last unorganized segment of the real estate industry. They are clever business operators whose office addresses are often tawdry mail drops in low-rent areas. They take pride in being "self-made" and genuinely feel that they are making a contribution to the city. "We're taking blights off the market," George Panagos, a long-time D.C. speculator and redeveloper, told the *Washington Post.*

In pre-home-rule days, these real estate operators had done as they pleased. Most lived in the suburbs and were little aware of the intensity of community feeling against them. The Clarke-Winter bill took them by surprise. Within a month of the bill's introduction, however, they had formed a $100-a-head Washington Residential Development Coalition (WRDC) and retained as lobbyist Chester Davenport, a politically connècted black lawyer who was President Carter's transition man on housing and transportation and whose firm was the city's bond counsel. (The industry's contingency plan was to switch to a noted white litigator if the issue went to court.)

Choosing Sides

The developing conflict raised issues beyond the immediate question of whether rehab should be encouraged. Political and even moral dilemmas arose as well. Foremost was the issue of race. In the District, "rehabilitation" is code for "black removal." When the *Post* real estate ads tout a neighborhood as "fast moving" and "up and coming," they mean that poor blacks are moving out and better-to-do whites (and some blacks) are moving in.

Questions of justice aside, black removal is politically ominous for the newly elected council members and mayor. The people being uprooted from their homes are their constituents. The young white townhouse owners who move in have different loyalties and little or no local memory. A sign of what may lie ahead appeared in the recent annual elections for the Adams-Morgan Organization executive board: the white owner of a hip new neighborhood bar called Columbia Station, a symbol of "Georgetownification" to many activists, took one of the offices.

It is not just a matter of politicians nervous about their seats, however. Home rule has a highly charged emotional meaning for many D.C. residents and especially for blacks. The 100 years of congressional rule dominated by peevish white Southerners such as former House District Committee chairman John McMillian of South Carolina is to them parallel in kind if not in degree to South Africa's minority regime. Even today when such otherwise respected senators as Lawton Chiles (D-Fla.) and Thomas Eagleton (D-Mo.) drag D.C. officials before their District Committee hearings, the occasions embarrassingly resemble whipping day at the plantation. The measure of home rule granted thus far, partial as it is, still symbolizes the eventual overthrow of a colonial power. Speculation, however, jeopardizes this dream by eroding the dominant black majority.

The predicament is that not all of the District's 80 percent black population is poor. A solid middle class and pockets of affluence also exist. And at least some of the affluence stems from real estate. In the past, blacks had gained a measure of success in derivative activities such as brokering. As the market for homes in the city has heated up, they have begun to buy and rehab properties on their own behalf. As the newest entrants in the field, they are the most vulnerable. An antispeculation tax could knock them out, while merely inconveniencing the established white entrepreneurs whose deeper pockets, larger inventories, and firmer credit lines enable them to maneuver around it.

In addition, although most black renters and homeowners may resent the effects of speculation, at least some of the homeowners feel otherwise. They are delighted at the prospect of selling their home for a pocketful of cash or of having their neighborhoods upgraded while their own property appreciates in value.

As a result, stereotyped class and race roles have been confounded on this crux of self-interest. While poor blacks and their white activist allies come before the council demanding action against the speculators, the black entrepreneurs demand just as righteously to know how a black elected body can even consider taking away the piece of the action they have laboriously, and against great odds, won.

Redeveloper Don Grey, an earnest young black with a large Afro, begins his testimony at council hearings with a reminder that he assisted Barry while the latter was head of SNCC. Beatrice Reed is the forceful president of the Washington Real Estate Brokers Association, an organization established by black brokers about 15 years ago in reaction to discrimination by the white-controlled Washington Board of Realtors. Reed makes speculation sound like black power. "We blacks will never rule this city," she tells a community forum in the auditorium of an old Baptist church near the 14th Street riot corridor, "until we *own* this city. That's what power is all about — *ownership.* What I do is helping my brothers and sisters to own their homes. And until we all do that, the whites will control us."

Long-time black residents in the audience had applauded and nodded in agreement as earlier speakers had torn into speculators. Now they applauded Reed too. Liberation means different things to different people and even to the same people at different times.

Not all the black real estate entrepreneurs are happy about their role in the speculation controversy. Being portrayed — rightly or wrongly — as the antagonists of their own people is only one reason. Even more important is their relation to the white entrepreneurs. Although the newly organized WRDC is overwhelmingly white and suburban, its leaders pushed efforts to include blacks. Blacks have gone along primarily because their livelihoods are at stake. But they are sensitive to being used as showpieces by the white speculators. Finding themselves in that role is just the latest in the endless series of frustrations that have attended their efforts to earn a dollar in a way routinely accessible to whites.

The issue before the council became still more complex when the redevelopers' rebuttals made them appear less the phalanx of evil than they had first been portrayed. The expensively restored townhouses in the inner city neighborhoods had received most of the public attention, but the bread and butter of many D.C. rehabbers — especially the larger operators — were more modest improvements to properties farther from the urban core. A WRDC official testified at council hearings that of 1,500 units sold by its members the previous two years, the average price had been $24,500 and 90 percent of the purchasers had been black D.C. residents. According to the WRDC official, over 70 percent of the properties had been vacant at the time of acquisition. "I've sold two houses over $40,000 in the last two years," says WRDC president Jerry Lustine. "And most of my houses go to blacks."

Also, at least a few realtors and speculators were quietly attempting to help tenants themselves. Nathan Habib, a puckish, cagey man commonly labeled a "slumlord," has been selling off his properties to his tenants and "taking back the paper" (that is financing them himself) without even requiring a down payment. In the Shaw area, a young broker named Richie Jones has been finding alternative housing in the community for tenants displaced by his transactions. He has also been trying to keep speculators out of the area by dealing directly with homebuyers. "We get better rapport in the community by giving the homebuyers the real price" instead of a price jacked up by a speculator, he says.

While a few good apples cannot redeem a whole barrel, such examples tempered the good-guy, bad-guy melodrama that was important to the antispeculation cause. At the same time, the council's own posture was weakened on several counts. For one, it bears the cross of the D.C. government's own land acquisition activities, which have resulted in large-scale evictions and thousands of boarded-up houses concentrated in poor black neighborhoods throughout the city. "There are blocks and blocks of vacant land here and the government keeps buying more," says Joyce Chestnut of the Shaw Project Area Committee. "The speculation bill does nothing about government speculation, and the government is the biggest menace." This is perhaps the only point on which the industry and community groups agree. "It's criminal," says WRDC president Lustine. "The D.C. government should clean up its own house before picking on us."

More squarely laid to the council is the District's rent control problem. A poorly written, poorly administered law has provided steady ammunition to the real estate industry and has given any public intervention in the real estate market a bad name. Council members are wary of getting burned a second time. Furthermore, the District's precarious budget makes this an unfortunate time to propose slowing down a rehabilitation trend that will improve the tax base. (The city's tax base is expected to grow by less than 5 percent a year between now and 1980, while its expenditures will increase by 9 to 12 percent.)

These complications have left their mark on the bill, especially in its treatment of rehab. The original Clarke-Winter bill, by treating both flipping and rehab with equal severity, amounted to a straight-forward one-year moratorium on redevelopment. Faced with heavy industry lobbying, the opposition of the mayor, and the reluctance of his fellow council members, Barry gradually modified this approach. First, he broadened the deductions for rehab expenses. Then he softened the tax rates on rehab. The emphasis shifted from stopping the redevelopment process to restraining excess profits and generating revenues to provide low and moderate-income people with homeownership assistance. Finally, when his fellow Finance Committee members balked at even this modified approach, Barry had to scrap the tax on rehab entirely, along with some other provisions.

Competing Causes

Even stripped down, the Barry bill is significant. His staff has found no other jurisdiction that requires the recording of all transfers of residential property (including contracts flipped to third parties) or that licenses dealers to the degree the bill does. And no urban area in the United States levies a tax on short-term buying and selling (without improvements) of residential property — let alone a tax in which rates go as high as 75 percent. The tenant's right of first refusal, and the disclosure of the seller's purchase and rehab costs to homebuyers are also trend-setting measures. Yet compared to what it sets out to do, the bill is barely half a loaf in the eyes of its original supporters.

Will the bill, if passed, do anything about the displacement of tenants and low and moderate-income homeowners? The best answer now is, "Probably, to a degree." By curtailing flipping, it should deter the drastic price increases that impel the new landlords to raise rents, and that put houses out of reach of tenants and low and moderate-income persons generally. "I could have bought this place myself if they gave me a chance to buy it at the original price," said one black woman on a heavily speculated street on Capitol Hill. "But nobody offered it to me. And I sure can't pay what it's going for now."

In addition, by deterring flipping-induced price increases, the bill should restrain property tax assessment hikes, which will relieve the plights both of tenants who end up paying the tax in their rents, and of homeowners whose budgets are geared to property tax bills at prespeculation levels. A damper on flipping, moreover, should slow down the rehabilitation-displacement process somewhat, since it is the rapid churning over of properties that breaks them loose for redevelopers and creates a momentum that spreads through the neighborhood. It is nevertheless true that a property may be flipped several times without the tenants being evicted. Rehabilitation, however, means eviction. With rehab alive, evictions will continue.

Would a tax on rehab have stopped such displacement? The real estate industry argued that there are enough wealthy people looking for houses in the District to enable rehabbers simply to pass the tax along in higher prices. Alternatively, the larger speculators could hold houses off the market — perhaps keeping them vacant — for three years, after which time they would be clear of the tax. Then, after rehab, they could charge more to compensate themselves for the holding period. Either way, the real estate industry argued, the result would be a reduction in the number of rehabbed houses coming onto the market and a consequent increase in prices, making houses less, not more, available to low and moderate-income persons. Proponents of the tax argued differently, of course, and it is questionable whether the industry would have lobbied so intensely against the rehab tax if all that was at stake was higher prices for rehabbed houses.

The D.C. council was reluctant to tax rehab for a variety of reasons. The lengthy preparation of an ambitious bill gave opponents both time and openings for attack. Also, the council's principled stands on civil and human rights — a majority of council members were civil rights activists and tolerate few encroachments in that area — do not always translate into similarly progressive economic stands. But most important has been the lack of sustained grassroots pressure. The bill simply has not yet become a highly visible political issue.

The community speculation task force was really a committee of organization employees and leaders. Only one of these organizations — the Adams-Morgan Organization — was genuinely constituent based. The others were United-Fund-supported neighborhood houses and the like. Their proxies were in most cases valid, but they never established the ongoing community support that was necessary to turn on the heat.

As the issue dragged on, the task force wore down — a familiar malady, and fatal in this case. When people left, there was no mechanism for replacing them. The diffusion of the racial issue was also a serious blow. In addition, AMO was so offended by one provision in an early draft — an exemption for moderately priced rehabbed houses — that it went off in a corner and sulked, leaving the lobbying to the speculators. By the late fall of 1976, a week-long series on speculation in the *Washington Post* that would have prompted an angry demonstration at the District Building 18 months before provoked hardly a telephone call or letter to the council.

Among the leaders of the task force were several whites. The role of white activists in the black-majority District is uncertain, and especially so on the speculation issue. For one thing, it is difficult for white activists to invoke the same degree of outrage at black profit seekers as they do when the perpetrators are white. Then, too, white activists themselves play an inadvertent role in the speculation process. Many live in racially mixed, inner-city neighborhoods such as Adams-Morgan, where rents are relatively low and where speculation is booming. Their VWs and white faces calm the jitters of prospective home buyers apprehensive of such threatening surroundings, while their countercultural enterprises create an aura that speculators and realtors can exploit as a lure for affluent people on the search for urban chic. It is understandable that some blacks and Latinos perceive their white activist neighbors as accomplices in the very speculation process they are working to stop.

The irony is that if the anti-speculation proposal accomplishes nothing else, it has molded the rehabilitation industry into a political force. A year and a half ago rehabbers were a loose assortment of staunch individualists. Today the WRDC has 250 members, and its tactics on the speculation bill showed a gain in sophistication over the industry's efforts in its first council battle — the rent control bill.

The positions of the two sides at this point compel a question. Should the antispeculation forces have started with a proposal more modest than a tax, which they could have won before their momentum waned? Some think Barry may have erred in expanding the original Clarke-Winter bill. "It would have been wise in retrospect to pass it" as originally introduced, Clarke said recently of his measure.

The industry has not been the only obstacle to the speculation bill. D.C. mayor Walter Washington, a cautious former housing administrator, has been cool to it from the beginning. "But what's wrong with speculation?" the mayor's city administrator Julian Dugas asked Barry with genuine bewilderment.

. . . .

Then there is Congress, which has kept veto power over all District legislation. Most of the speculators are suburbanites, who get a sympathetic ear from their representatives. Dabbling in real estate, moreover, is common sport among amply paid Congressional staffers, as it is among their bosses. On the 1400 block of Corcoran Street, just off the riot corridor, $20,000 rowhouses are being restored and sold for close to $70,000. The investor is Representative Stewart McKinney (R-Conn.), a liberal House District Committee member and, on most issues, one of the District's best friends on the Hill. McKinney is just one of innumerable examples.

. . . .

[A] few lessons have emerged. The first concerns the limits of a progressive elected body. The D.C. council is probably as receptive to the idea of a speculation tax as any legislative body in the United States, but without solid constituent support it has hesitated to move. Also, the council members have felt intellectually insecure with the tax. It has not been made clear to them how the tax would remedy the displacement problem, nor what it would do to the real estate market generally, nor — and this is most important — what if anything would arise to take the place of the private speculative market. All sides agree that a tough speculation tax on rehab could doom the city to stagnation if positive housing programs were not wheeled quickly into place. Aside from some vague talk about cooperatives, these programs are nowhere in sight.

Comments: 1. The District of Columbia anti-speculation tax was finally passed in watered-down form. As enacted, it applies to dealers who transfer three or more residential properties within three years and to "contract flippers" who buy and sell contracts for gain. Exemptions include any house carrying a warranty on major appliances and against defects, apparently an attempt to encourage rehabilitation. Property held for three years is not subject to the tax. Rates of tax range from zero percent for small gains below ten percent of value on purchase to 97 percent on gains over 300 percent. Tax rates escalate rapidly after reaching what the City Council views as a fair rate of return on investment, considered to be 20 per cent per annum.

2. Note the effects the District of Columbia anti-speculation tax is intended to have. It is expected to deter price, and thus tax assessment increases, and to slow down the rehabilitation-displacement process. This last objective has been downplayed by city staff who drafted the legislation and who contend that it is directed at speculation in "empty shell" structures. Attention can thus be focused on its apparent principal objective — to hold down the price of housing.

An evaluation of this objective requires an analysis of the role of speculation in land and housing markets. A distinction must first be made between the market effects of speculation by small-scale and large-scale speculators. Only the latter may be expected to influence prices by acquiring a monopoly position through their holdings. Most speculators in the District of Columbia appear to be small in scale, and securing a monopoly position in housing in a rapidly improving neighborhood would be difficult in any event. The following commentary examines the effects of speculation when it can be expected to be influential:

Economic theorists have been fairly unified in judging that the small actors cannot permanently increase the price of a commodity. In the end, the price will be determined by user demand and by the nonspeculative supply. In fact, speculation is often hailed as a good thing, because it increases the liquidity of the commodity (that is, an owner can more quickly sell his property because there are more buyers). In addition, it may cause the market to adjust more rapidly to its true equilibrium price, hence giving more accurate price signals to resource users and improving the efficiency with which resources are allocated. These notions, however, have developed largely from studies of speculation in other than real estate markets, notably foreign exchange markets, agricultural product futures markets, and stock exchanges. Price adjustments in these markets tend to be fairly quick, turnover is substantial, and there is considerable short-term trading. These factors cause adjustments to new equilibrium price levels to occur fairly rapidly. Real estate markets, on the other hand, adjust more slowly, are marked by substantially imperfect information, and prices are influenced by expectations into a far longer future than is common with these other commodities. Quite likely, because of these factors, speculation has a less stabilizing effect in real estate markets and speculative cycles may, indeed, cause property prices to deviate from "equilibrium" values for extended periods of time. On the other hand, "speculators" may simply be scapegoats for land price increases that are principally due to other factors.

Hagman & Misczynski, supra p. 434, at 124.

2. Whether or not a tax on short-term speculation in housing will lead to a price decline depends on how the demand for and supply of housing reacts to the tax. If it is assumed that the tax will fully or partially discourage speculative activity there will be a fall in demand if speculators are not replaced with other purchasers. Prices will fall if the supply of housing for sale is not affected or is not affected as severely. This tax effect may actually hasten the gentrification process by lowering prices and easing the entry of more affluent newcomers, but price declines will be offset if the withdrawal of speculators from the market leads to a decline in the amount of housing offered for sale.

This explanation of the effects of the anti-speculation tax offers a static analysis, a comparison of the before and after effects of the tax on a market assumed to be in equilibrium and reaching a new equilibrium after the tax is imposed. It does not take account of market dynamics in reaction to the tax, including the reaction of speculators who attempt to manage their buying and selling activities to minimize tax effects. For an analysis of this type see Hagman & Misczynski, supra, at 119-22.

3. Another approach to speculation in the housing market has been adopted in Davis, California. Like the anti-speculation tax, it is directed at the rising inflation in the cost of housing that has characterized the Davis and California housing markets in recent years. The key section of the local anti-speculation ordinance provides:

It shall be unlawful for any person to purchase an individual residential ownership unit [a single family dwelling located in designated residential zones — Eds.] unless a qualified purchaser intends to occupy such unit as his or her principle [sic] residence for a minimum of twelve (12) consecutive months and that such occupancy is intended to commence within six (6) months following completion of purchase.

Unlike the anti-speculation tax, the Davis ordinance is a direct regulatory measure intended to put a stop entirely to the practices of "flippers" who buy homes solely to realize capital gains. In view of the analysis presented earlier, what likely effects will the Davis ordinance have on the local housing market?

A CONCLUDING NOTE

What is the overall thrust of the reform efforts discussed in this chapter? Do they really constitute part of a major restructuring of the market? How do they tie into the long term secular shifts in the housing economy? What will the future bring for housing in America?

For the short run some answers seem possible. For instance, despite the price problem and possibly depressing efforts at stabilization through antispeculation laws, home ownership seems destined to prosper. The shift to smaller households has if anything been accompanied by greater not lesser interest in dwelling ownership. Doubtless in an inflationary market, multiple earner households give a high priority to investment and inflation-hedge considerations. In any case, the former correspondence between larger household size and home ownership seems to be eroding. Everyone wants a house, and its tax advantaged, inflation-proof equity value.

This preference dovetails with the rapid spread of condominium ownership of apartment-type units. In those localities where conversions are uncontrolled a substantial share of the former rental supply may be converted to condominium ownership. Assuming the existence of a requisite effective demand, this change further tilts the market toward owner occupancy of even the smallest types of units. Somewhat parallel but by no means as vigorous is the rebirth of interest in cooperative housing. Coops do not receive as much market attention because of their more complicated institutional arrangements and because capital gain opportunities are limited. However, interest groups concerned with social issues and with minimizing speculative ownership continue to advocate the development of new coops and the conversion of older buildings, and win local successes.

Perhaps the most potent force associated with home ownership when viewed from a policy perspective is the emerging crisis in maintaining solvent demand. Much of this book has directly and indirectly addressed this issue. In all likelihood the main direction of future policy, at least in the next five or eight years, will combine a continuation of present policies that assure an ever increasing supply of mortgage loan funds with the continuation of middle-mass oriented demand subsidies such as the favorable tax treatment of home ownership financing costs. It seems probable that the use of tax exempt public bonds to provide subsidized interest rates to the next lower income category of demand will also expand, unless restricted by Congress.

If a major crisis in owner-occupied housing is possible in the next decade or less it will probably grow out of the problems of maintaining effective middle-mass homeowner demand. Either the subsidy needs will outstrip politically acceptable funding sources or the weight of debt will become destabilizing to the national economy. So far, neither of these dire futures seem likely. The housing economy has met the inflation-income crunch with remarkable resilience.

A crisis in the rental sector appears more likely. In fact, it may have arrived. Recapitulating material presented in this chapter and earlier in the book, a three-way conflict among contradictory forces is hard upon American rental housing. Need remains high, but falling incomes relative to market rents produce a powerful force to translate need into effective demand through political and government action rather than higher rents. Operating cost increases outstrip tenant incomes and produce continuous pressure for higher rents. Considering alternative investment opportunities, the profit needs of owners and investors require pass-through of higher costs including higher profits and continuing opportunities for capital gains through trading. In this situation, if rents remain stable in terms of tenant incomes, necessary maintenance is put aside, taxes are not paid, owners unload and abandon properties, and investors take their money elsewhere. If operating costs are passed through to tenants, rents climb too steeply in relation to incomes, tenants strike and turn to politics to enact rent control. If needed new private capital is to be attracted and old investments maintained, profitability has to be supported through cost reductions and rent increases. These are the broad outlines of the emergent crisis.

The increasing militance of tenants and their demands for restructuring property rights are an early symptom of this crisis. Rent control is a much more significant response to the situation. As noted earlier in this chapter, rent control reflects dissatisfaction with the market price system. Chapter 8 noted the recent expansion of public subsidy programs to cover operating expenses. This is another restructuring trend. Until recently, these subsidies have been provided only to low income households in public housing and distressed BMIR projects. However, substantial operating cost increases in Coop City, a tremendous middle income private housing development in New York, provoked a very effective rent strike (actually a strike against paying debt service) against the management and long term financing institutions. In order to avert foreclosure, the city was forced to take over the project to keep rents within affordable limits. Given the contradictions between income and housing costs, considerable public subsidy may be required to produce the socially desirable opportunities for rental housing services, particularly to special submarkets such as the elderly for whom conventional home ownership seems inappropriate. Such seems to have been the case in Coop City.

That a crisis sufficiently strong to require structural change can emerge from the present situation lies in the joint effects of actions by both owner-investors and tenants. Though in a sense diametrically opposed to each other, owner-investor and tenant forces can converge toward the same end. As owners and investors withdraw from the market a vacuum occurs. As tenants become more militant, and enlist political power on their behalf, the urgency builds for replacing the market with new institutions. The situation can be likened somewhat to what occurred in urban transit. Where once traction company investment produced generous profits to private owners, later contradictions emerged among consumer demand, cost escalation, and profit requirements. The resulting withdrawal of capital coupled with consumer political pressure led first to universal regulation of transit as a public utility, then finally to outright socialization or municipalization. A number of crystal ball gazers in housing predict a similar future for their field.

Experience outside the United States suggests that major structural changes in the ownership and management of rental housing ultimately become generally necessary in advanced industrial societies. This has been a clear cut consequence of long standing rent controls and demand-expense-profit contradictions in Great Britain. Some British critics, for example, have urged full municipalization of the rental housing stock, which means that local governments would own and operate that housing. Other Western European countries have faced similar crises. The general direction of policy has seen considerable socialization of the rental stock in all but the highest rent submarkets. Portents of comparable changes are already present on the American scene.

New York City, dogged by its continuing housing crisis, has proved fertile ground for proposals to restructure the rental sector. Among them, one of particular interest in the current discussion has come from the Metropolitan Housing Council. As articulated by Peter Hawley (see Bibliography supra p.   ), it proposes the gradual transfer of the City's low- and moderate-income rental housing supply to tenant management under a system of permanent public ownership. Based on enacting a quick take process for public acquisition of tax delinquent buildings, the Council plan proposes a very decentralized system of management and responsibility along with a multi-sided program of long term rehabilitation financing from public sources rather than private market financial institutions. The proposal is based on several years' experience with the "in rem" program under which some tax delinquent properties seized by the city have been successfully rehabilitated and managed by tenants and nonprofit community organizations.

As this book goes to press a team from the Institute of Policy Studies, a Washington, D.C. left-liberal think tank (see Raskin in Bibliography infra p.   ) has put forth a proposal for the nationwide elimination of private rental housing through public acquisition at the federal level. At this point, any such radical solution seems totally beyond the realm of possibility even if it were workable and just. Yet, the fact that such a proposal can be seriously put forth in 1978 suggests how deep a crisis afflicts American rental housing.

BIBLIOGRAPHY

J. Bremer & H. Franklin, Rent Control in North America and Four European Countries (Potomac Institute, 1977)
  A comparative review of rent control experience.

Blumberg & Robbins, *Beyond URLTA: A Program for Achieving Real Tenant Goals,* 11 Harvard Civil Rights-Civil Liberties Law Review 1 (1976)
  A review of statutory innovations in the reform of landlord-tenant relationships.

M. Friedman & G. Stigler, Rent Control: A Popular Paradox (1975)
  A conservative view of rent control.

D. Hagman & D. Misczynski, Windfalls for Wipeouts: Land Value Capture and Compensation (1978)
  Chapters in this book review the arguments for and against taxation of speculative gains in real estate and the economic incidence of this taxation. A review of anti-speculation tax programs is also included.

P. Hawley, Housing in the Public Domain (1978)
  Analyses the financial aspects of New York City's low- and moderate-rent housing stock and proposes municipalization.

M. Lett, Rent Control: Concepts, Realities, and Mechanisms (1976)
  An analysis of rent control concepts and a review of experience in several eastern communities.

M. Raskin, ed., The Federal Budget and Social Reconstruction (1978)
  A chapter in this Institute for Policy Studies volume proposes federal socialization of the rental housing stock. The proposal is the work of C. Hartman and M. Stone.

H. Selesnick, Rent Control (1976)
  A review of recent rent control programs.

G. Sternlieb, The Urban Housing Dilemma: The Dynamics of New York City's Rent Controlled Housing (1976)
  A review of the New York City's experience.